AA

CAMPING AND CARAVANNING IN EUROPE

1991

Produced by the Publishing Division of The Automobile Association

Gazetteer compiled by the AA's Information Research Unit, Information Control

Maps prepared by the Cartographic Department of The Automobile Association

Cover design: Paul Hampson Partnership

Head of Advertisement Sales: Christopher Heard
Tel 0256 20123
Advertisement Production: Karen Weeks
Tel 0256 20123

Phototypeset by Tradespools, Frome, Somerset
Colour Supplement produced by J. B. Shears, Basingstoke
Printed and bound in Great Britain by William Clowes Limited, Beccles and London

A CIP catalogue record for this book is available from the British Library

Published by the Automobile Association, Fanum House, Basingstoke, Hampshire RG21 2EA

ISBN 0 7495 0208 8

CONTENTS

HOLIDAY BEACHES
FLYING THE FLAG

Beautiful stretches of sun-kissed sand, lapped by an azure blue sea are the ideal which many holidaymakers seek when they decide on a continental destination. But how many times have you been lured by a distant view of a fine stretch of sand, only to be disappointed, or even horrified at what greets you as you stroll onto the beach? Thoughts of relaxing sunbathing or a swim rapidly diminish at the sight of overflowing litter bins or empty cans and bottles strewn across the beach, dogs running freely, noise from ghetto-blasters reverberating across the sand, the sight of sewage effluent or oil lapping in the shallows and the prospect of no toilet facilities for the rest of the day!

Experiences such as these have been all too familiar in recent years as pollution levels have risen, but the increase of tourism, and the realisation in individual countries of the importance of the tourism business, have led to a greater demand for better management of beaches and greater control over health and safety issues.

The Blue Flag Campaign, set up in 1987 during the European Year of the Environment, has been a major influence on improving the standards of European beaches, its main objective being the protection of the marine and coastal environment — which, of course, includes the beaches.

Two of Portugal's best beaches
Below: *Armacao*
Opposite: *Alvor*

Millions of people spend their holidays each year on foreign shores and this campaign has united many countries with a common aim to provide clean, safe beaches everywhere and for everyone.

Education on environmental matters is a major consideration in the basic aims of the Blue Flag organisation and has resulted in an increase in public awareness by means of public information material and appropriate teaching aids. Eventually it is hoped that the people who use the beaches will be encouraged to take an active part in the protection of the environment.

The Blue Flag is not simply a name but has also become the symbol of the clean beach. The right to fly a Blue Flag is awarded on an annual basis to resort beaches and ports which have submitted to rigorous national and international judging. The criteria are strict and are rigidly enforced, so that Blue Flags can be withdrawn at any time if the beach or port falls below the required standard.

Not surprisingly these days, there is an EC Bathing Water Directive — a minimum water quality standard that has to be respected in bathing areas — and this is the prime requirement for a Blue Flag to be awarded. Secondly, the beach must be used by a large number of holidaymakers and be actively managed by the owners, whether a local authority of private, as a tourist resort. Lastly, the beach must provide safe bathing under all normal weather conditions.

Spain – a popular destination
***Left:** Benidorm*
***Above:** Sitges*

REQUIREMENTS FOR THE AWARD OF A BLUE FLAG

1. Water and coastal quality

There should be no industrial or sewage discharges and no visible oil pollution or evidence of algal materials growing or decaying around the area of the beach. Bathing water must be subject to reliable and frequent monitoring and emergency plans available to cope with oil or other pollution incidents.

2. Environmental education and information

Each beach must provide the public with adequate information around the beach area, stipulating the laws covering beach use and highlighting protected sites and/or rare and protected species, either in tourist information leaflets or public displays.

Other important considerations are the provision of information on water quality and the beach sampling points, with monthly updates displayed publicly or in the local media. There must also be the provision of educational courses and activities or public lectures on the natural environment of the beach area or on health and safety.

3. Beach area management and safety

The way that the beach area is managed is a major factor and encompasses a number of obligatory requirements. Beaches must be cleaned daily during the bathing season, with litterbins provided in adequate numbers and regularly emptied. Domestic animals must be strictly controlled in the beach area and unauthorised dumping is prohibited. Also of paramount importance are the provision of clean toilet facilities with controlled sewage disposal, easy and safe access to the beach for all, including the disabled, the presence of beach guards during the season, and a first aid post or alternative safety provisions, including lifesaving equipment. Other important considerations include a supply of drinking water, working public telephones and possibly the zoning areas for recreational purposes such as windsurfing.

These criteria represent the minimum which must be respected everywhere. In some countries Blue Flags are awarded to individual beaches, while other countries impose even stricter standards, requiring all the beaches under authority control to meet the criteria.

Since its inception in 1987, the Blue Flag Campaign has made considerable progress and as the campaign becomes better known, more local authorities realise the need to participate. In 1990 Blue Flags were awarded to nearly 700 beaches in Europe and to 160 leisure ports and marinas — a huge increase on the figures for 1989. This growing awareness of the scheme will inevitably lead to an increased demand for accommodation in those areas where holiday-makers are assured of a clean, safe beach, particularly with regard to campsites.

Eight of the countries covered by this guide are involved to some degree in the Blue Flag Campaign, with the most popular camping countries — France and Spain — being particularly active.

On the French Riviera
Right: *St Maxime near St Tropez*
Below: *The fashionable St Raphael*

In France both the number of Blue Flag Beaches and the nearby sites we list are too numerous to mention here, but they are concentrated mainly on the Cote d'Azur, in the Montpelier area, around Nantes, along the Atlantic coast from Biarritz to Bordeaux and the area north of Bordeaux.

Spain's two main regions which can offer both campsites and Blue Flag beaches are the popular Costa Brava area and the coast between Valencia and Benidorm. However, the spread of Blue Flag beaches is very good all around the coast.

In The Netherlands the number of Blue Flag beaches has risen from 7 to 21, with 5 between Vlissingen and Domburg in the south and another little cluster around the western end of Schouwen island, both areas having sites listed in this guide. Moving northwards there are sites and Blue Flag beaches at Hoek van Holland, Noordwijk, Schoorl, Petten and St Maartenzee, and on the northern islands of Terschelling and Ameland.

In Denmark the majority of campsites listed are coastal and with nearly 128 Blue Flag beaches spread along the coast, campers here will never be far from a good beach.

Below: *Blankenberg beach, Belgium*
Opposite: *Zaandvort, Netherlands*

Blue Flag beaches in Belgium
Above: *Knokke beach*
Below: *De Haan*

Holiday Beaches Flying the Flag

The Blue Flag Campaign, with its ultimate goal of 'clean, safe beaches everywhere for everyone' cannot fail to grow in importance as we all become more aware of, and concerned for our environment. More authorities will doubtless come to realise the importance of the demand for better standards and holiday-makers, too, will begin to feel a greater responsibility for leaving Europe's beaches as we would wish to find them.

LAGO D'ISEO

Camping ★★★★

Del Sole

CAMPING DEL SOLE, ISEO, ITALY
I-25049 ISEO (BS)
TEL: 030/980288
FAX: 030/982172

"Camping del Sole" covering an area of 65,000 sq. m. is set in the heart of the countryside and bordered by the shore of the lake. It has over 400 pitches, a variety of entertainment facilities plus well maintained and well equipped washing facilities with hot water. The large car park is located so that it does not disturb the guests.

The Camping del Sole offers wide ranging and lively entertainment for adults and young people. Easy access to the tent site from the Milan/ Venice motorway (Palazzolo or Rotvato exit) or via the Milan/Bergamo/ Brescia trunk road.

Open: 27/04-30/09/91

Guests who can prove that they chose us from this new camping guide will receive the following discounts:

5% during the holiday season for a minimum stay of 14 days.

20% outside the main seasons for a minimum stay of 1 week.

Group discounts (more than 20 guests); 20%, 2 accompanying adults free for a minimum stay of 1 week, in every season.

All guests who stayed with us for more than 10 days receive a bottle of wine on their departure day.

New: water skiing club

New bungalows. 4-6 beds with kitchen and bath.

LES TOURNELS ★★★
Camping Caravanning

Provençale charm and Mediterranean sun on the deep blue backgro of the Gulf of St. Tropez

In the middle of a pine forest and vineyard, no more than 1,000 metres from the sea, in the enchanti Provençale countryside, the peaceful Les Tournels camping park offers you its 3-star facilities on sh marked pitches. Sanitary facilities heated in the cooler seasons. **On site:** a shopping centre, restaur newspapers, children's, playground, tennis, caravans for hire. **New:** heated SWIMMING POOL. **Nearby:** yachting, surfing, water skiing, under water fishing, St. Tropez. Ideal touring base.
Route de Camarat, 83350 Ramatuelle, te. 94.79.80.54

CAMPING
CARAVANING
FONTAINE VIEILLE

4 Boulevard du Colonel Wurtz.
Tel. 56.82.01.67
33510 ANDERNOS LES BAINS

RELAX AND ENJOY PEACE AND TRANQUILITY ON THE BAY OF ARCACHON
COUNTLESS DELIGHTS FOR THE ACTIVE FAMILY

Facilities include supermarket, restaurant, bar, ready cooked meals, newspapers, tobacco, cinema, television, exchange.
You can hire: bungalows, washing machine, bicycles and surf boards.
Sports: tennis, volleyball, table tennis, trampoline, swimming pool, on-site sailing, golf, horse riding and canoeing close to the site.Other activities: sightseeing in the region.

Open from mid May to mid September. For enquiries and reservations please write as from January.

Parco Camping
Large pitches on grassy ground under pine and poplar trees.

Parco Caravan
Well equipped pitches for caravans and motor caravans. – Also caravans and maxi-caravans are available for hire.

Parco Bungalow
Simple adequately furnished bungalows with 2 or 4 beds for a holiday in direct touch with nature.

Park Hotel UNION LIDO
3 Star Hotel with 80 comfortable rooms. Holiday package "VENEZIA SPECIALE" for hotel as well as for caravans and maxi-caravans for hire.

Parco Acquatico
A splendid experience: slow flowing river, "lagoon" with slides, swimming pool and whirlpool.

Parco Giochi
For amusement: playground with many kinds of games and recreational activities organized by trained attendants.

Parco Sport
For the active: tennis courts with tennis coach, riding school, archery and football ground.

IL PARCO DELLE VACANZE

The engaging holiday park offering quality, class and atmosphere in a friendly environment – directly onto the Venetian coast of Cavallino.

Parco Fitness
For well-being: spacious natural park with play and keep fit apparatus. Our own health and fitness programme with qualified staff. Table tennis, minigolf, volleyball, swimming tuition and windsurfing school.

I-30013 Cavallino Venezia
Tel. Camping (041) 968080
Tel. Hotel (041) 968043
Telefax (041) 5370355
Telex 410407 UNILID I

TICINO

Svizzera meridionale
Suisse méridionale
Südschweiz
Zuid Zwitserland
Southern Switzerland

le Camping

TENERO· LOCARNO

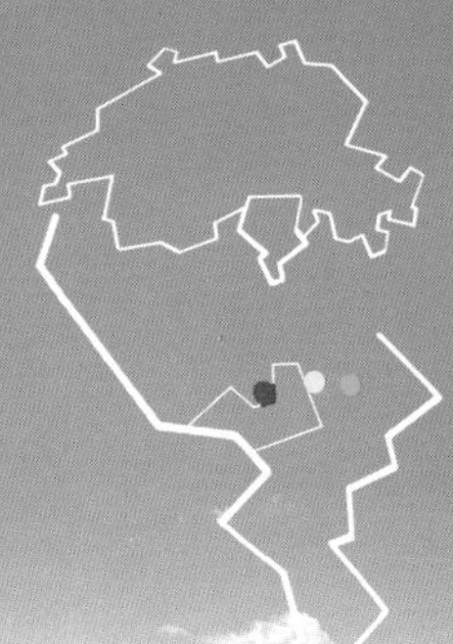

TENERO
- LIDO MAPPO
- TAMARO
- MIRALAGO
- RIVABELLA
- VERBANO
- LAGO MAGGIORE
- CAMPOFELICE

LOCARNO
- DELTA

CUGNASCO
- RIARENA

TOURIST OFFICES
TENERO E VALLE VERZASCA
6598 TENERO
Tel. 093 / 67 16 61 · Fax 093 / 67 42 30
LOCARNO E VALLI
6600 LOCARNO
Tel. 093 / 31 86 33 · Fax 093 / 31 90 70

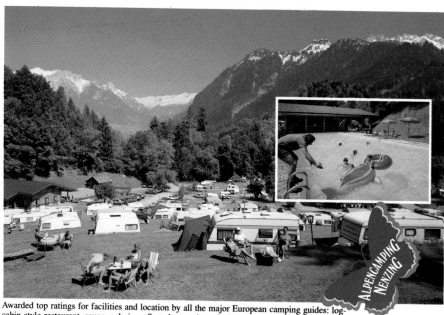

La Rive

Situated on a 40 acre estate, by the shore of Lake Cazaux. Private beach where you can swim and surf.

40600 BICAROSSE TEL: 58.78.12.33

Naturissimo Héliomonde. Discover the attractions of Paris while staying in beautiful countryside. Well-equipped holiday accommodation and extensive leisure facilities, including an enormous swimming pool, are set in a magnificent forest park.

Enjoy the best of both worlds: the pleasures of nature and of busy city life, for Paris is only half an hour away by Tube.

MEDICIS

Naturissimo

For a free of charge brochure, simply write us : Naturissimo
SOCNAT HE/AA 91 - 16, rue Drouot - 75009 PARIS - FRANCE

Le Vallon Rouge ***NN CAMPING * CARAVANING * MOTEL

A 3 hectares park in a delightful riverside setting
In the heart of the Côte d'Azur between Nice and St-Paul-de-Vence (10 min. from the beach)
– PEACE AND TRANQUILITY ON MARKED PITCHES
Bungalows and caravans for hire.

Bar, restaurant, food shop, cooked meals, SWIMMING POOL, video room, fishing, kayak-canoeing, French bowls, children's games, table tennis, volleyball… Tennis and horse riding nearby.
New and very comfortable sanitary installations.
Considerable off-season discount.
Enquiries and reservations: 93.32.86.12
LE VALLON ROUGE 06480 La Colle s/Loup

LUC-SUR-MER (Calvados)
CAMPING CARAVANNING DE LA CAPRICIEUSE

★★★★ (awaiting recognition 4-star grade)

Completely renewed site, 100m from the beach. Good shopping facilities close by. Touring and seasonal pitches (232) to let. Motor caravan area. Bungalows for hire. Tennis. Games for children. Volleyball, French boules. Games room.
Within easy reach: Sailing club – Rambling and horse riding routes – swimming pool, tennis, volleyball, mini golf, French boules – Casino, discotheques, games room. Leisure activities on the beach. Thalassotherapy Centre. Cinema – library.
Open: 1/4-30/9 Tel: 31.97.34.43

Tonic nudity !

Naturissimo CHM de Montalivet. In the Landes region, next to the Atlantic ocean, a long sandy beach lined with pine trees, creates the perfect natural environment in which to enjoy all kinds of outdoor pursuits, including special activities for children.
Nearby you can discover the famous Medoc (Bordeaux) vineyards, and you don't even have to leave the centre to visit gourmet restaurants Enjoy the refreshing climate and the deliciou scent of the pine forest, any time between Apri and October. You can pitch your tent or stay i one of our comfortable bungalows, for peaceful and relaxing holiday.

For a free of charge brochure, simply write us:
Naturissimo SOCNAT CHM/AA 91 - 16, rue Drouot -
75009 PARIS - FRANCE

Naturissimo

Tonic nudity !

Naturissimo La Genèse. A gentle river winds through a magnificent gorge, and delicious perfumes emanate from the wild, green Provençale landscape. Within the woods and by the river, here are many types of accommodation, all arranged to blend in with the wonderful scenery.
All the family can enjoy a wide variety of outdoor activities in country so unspoilt and beautiful, it will take your breath away!

MEDICIS

Naturissimo

For a free of charge brochure, simply write us : Naturissimo SOCNAT GE/AA 91 - 16, rue Drouot - 75009 PARIS - FRANCE

AA
Discover
FRANCE

A colourful gazetteer of more than 600 attractive towns and villages, with information on local customs and specialities. Interesting features on travelling, accommodation and eating out, plus a road atlas and a detailed street plan of Paris and the surrounding area.

Available at good
bookshops and
AA Centres
We're all you need to know.

An exclusive holiday site in beautiful surroundings, in midst woods, with terraced sites on slope of mountain and on flat ground.

It's our guests who promote us.

We offer you, among other services:
- — Panorama-swimming pool (70 × 40 metres, the largest in the Costa Brava).
- — 2 Children's pools.
- — Another 20 × 20m swimming pool.
- — 2 bars. Pub. Sound-proof, underground disco with air-conditioning. Restaurant with air-conditioning. Piano-Bar with air-conditioning. 2 take-aways Barbecue.
- — 2000 square metres of panorama terraces. 600 sq.m. free-covered terraces. 10,000 sq.m. of grass covered solarium.
- — Folklore and shows daily.
- — Minigolf, tennis, football, table tennis, trampoline. Children's castle. Children's playground. Free water slide.
- — Supermarket. Souvenirs gift shop. Newspapers.
- — Excursions. Money exchange. Car rental.
- — Public Relations office.
- — Daily doctor's visit.
- — Car wash. Washing machines. Ironing room.
- — Free hot water. Modern ablution blocks.
- — 200,000 sq.m. tree covered square.
- — Dogs only on lead.
- — TV and Video Jumbo Screen. (4 × 3m)

Just come and see us. We are sure you will want to stay.

Open: 4.5-20.10

SITE FEE REDUCTION:

4.5 till 8.6 & 7.9 till 20.10 **60%**

8.6 till 29.6 & 25.8 till 7.9 **40%**

Road Torroella-Estartit, km 4,7.
Tel. (34-72) 75 86 30
Fax. (34-72) 75 99 06

***NEW:* ARTIFICIAL SWIMMING-LAKE WITH WATER-FALL**

Special prices in low season.

Free bottle of Spanish champagne per family on showing this advertisement.

SALIDA 5 SALIDA 4 SALIDA 3
Barcelona A-17 Francia
Orriols Figueras
N-II
Verges
Torroella M
ESTARTIT
Vilademat
CASTELL MONTGRI

Costa Brava, E-17470 Sant Pere Pescador
Tel. (34-72) 520302, Autopista A-17 salida 5

DISCOUNT on pitch fee

15/5-23/6 & 21/8-15/9	**50%**
16/9-20/10	**55%**
15/5-20/10 old age pens. **another**	**10%**

- Beach frontage along the whole camp
- Quiet, friendly atmosphere
- Installations for children & handicapped
- Modern facilities. English spoken

Barcelona, Costa Dorada Km. 12,5 autovía a Castelldefels
08840 Viladecans (Barcelona), Tel. (34-3) 658 05 04

Off season (15/5-20/6 & 25/8-30/9) attractive fees!

- Beach frontage along the whole camp
- Pine-tree wood throughout the campsite
- All installations and service of a modern holiday camp categorie 1. English spoken.

CARAVANING CAMPING

el delfin verde

E-17257 TORROELLA DE MONTGRÍ - GIRONA -
COSTA BRAVA ESPAÑA

Tel. (34-72) 75 84 50
Fax (34-72) 76 00 70

the most beautiful camping and caravanning sites of the Costa Brava.
tranquil surroundings, by a magnificent, wide and mile-long sand beach,
largest fresh-water swimming pool of the Costa Brava and generously
ed pitches and sites. Many green areas and pine-trees groups.
ercial centre. Gastronomy. (3 bars, 2 snackbars, 2 restaurants, 2 grills,
rias).
se sports area (handball, basket ball, volley, badminton, football), 5 tennis
minigolf (3000 sq. m, 18 holes).
sation of fiestas, excursions, dancing, sports competition.
st modern ablution blocks. Hot water everywhere.
exchange, safe, medical service, telephone, bungalows, apartments for
Ve speak English.

DISCOUNT on pitch fee 11.5-23.6 and 27.8-24.9
from 11.5-24.9

França
Castello d'Empuries
Roses
SORTIDA 3
Figueres
SORTIDA 5
Sant Pere Pescador

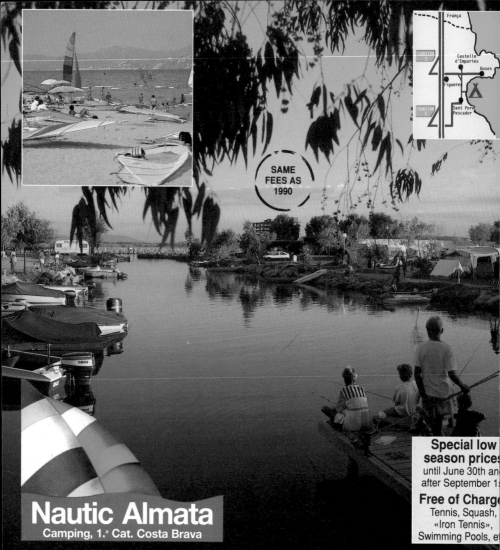

SAME FEES AS 1990

Special low season prices
until June 30th and after September 1st

Free of Charge
Tennis, Squash, «Iron Tennis», Swimming Pools, etc.

Nautic Almata

Camping, 1.ª Cat. Costa Brava

Nautic Almata is no ordinary camp site as it not only provides all the amenities characteristic of modern camp sites, but also enjoys an excellent situation in the National Park of «Els Aiguamolls» in the Emporda region, a unique area with an almost exclusive beach, considered the best part of the Mediterranean for windsurfing activities. In addition to this, the whole area is linked by canals that reach the sea, and is thus suitable for every type of sailing vessel. The camp site has bungalows, three bars, a disco bar, restaurant, supermarket, boutique, etc. and offers the possibility of practising any type of sport with three tennis courts, a riding school, two swimming pools, one multi-sport installation, pelota court, squash, sailing school, kayac and windsurfing, games room, fishing, water ski, hiking etc. There are also organized social events. A laundry service is available. All washrooms and showers have hot water.

Open: 15th May – End September

Camping address
Carretera de Castelló d'Empúries
a St. Pere Pescador. Km. 11.6
17486 Castelló d'Empúries. Girona.
Tel. (9) 72 25 04 77

Winter address
Travessera de Gràcia, 18-20
08021 BARCELONA
Tel. (93) 209 21 77

CLUB CLASS

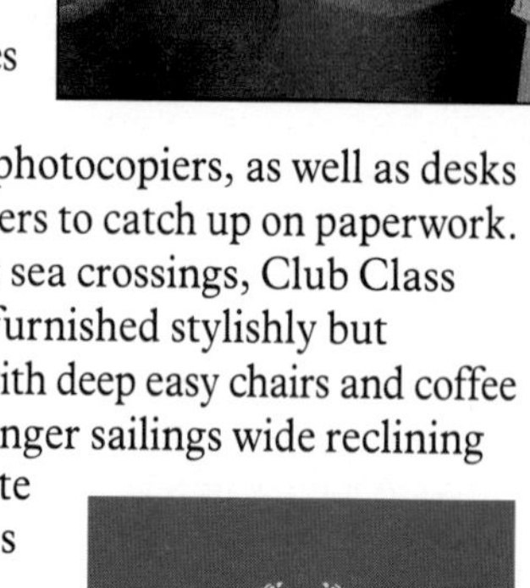

Latest of the innovations with passenger comfort in mind is the introduction of exclusive Club Class services on the Dover and Portsmouth-based fleets.

Catering for discerning travellers, Club Class means traditional cruise-style comfort in peaceful and stylish surroundings.

For a small supplement to the standard fare, Club Class offers a haven away from the crowds even during the busiest holiday periods with a guaranteed seat in luxurious lounges and the exclusive touch of stewards serving complimentary tea, coffee and daily newspapers.

And for a little extra, Executive Club Class makes business trips easy with the provision of office facilities such as fax, phones and photocopiers, as well as desks in quiet corners to catch up on paperwork. On the short sea crossings, Club Class lounges are furnished stylishly but informally, with deep easy chairs and coffee tables. On longer sailings wide reclining seats complete with footrests allow Club Class passengers to catch up on sleep – and generally relax to the full.

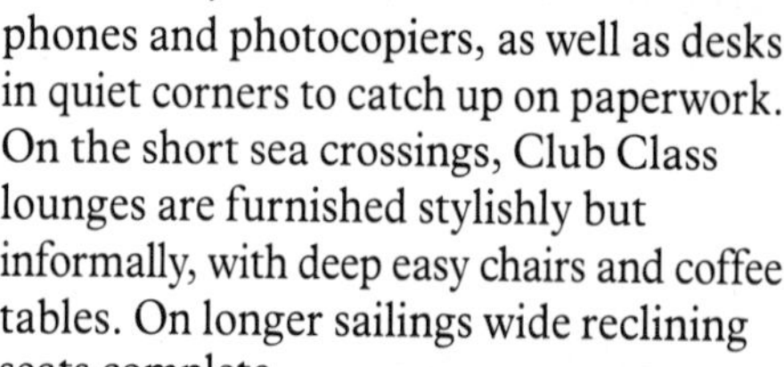

FACILITIES

Facilities have also been widely upgraded elsewhere on board.

Department-store style shopping has been introduced on the two superferries – Pride of Dover and Pride of Calais – which operate the 75 minute Dover to Calais service.

Spacious new duty-free shopping areas boast an enormous range of wine, spirits, tobaccos and perfumes along with gifts and confectionery too.

Cruise-style tax free gift shops also set new standards for shopping at sea with designer label clothing and fashion accessories as well as a greater selection of jewellery, watches and photographic and audio goods.

Also enjoying 'superferry' status by the summer of 1991 will be the Pride of Kent, the third ship operating on the Dover-Calais route. A massive investment to enlarge the ship and increase amenities for passengers not only reflects a policy of continuous improvement but guarantees 'superferry' style on every sailing.

Travelling on ships in the P&O European Ferries fleet is really just like visiting a floating premier class hotel. Behind scenes, officers and crew ensure that everything runs smoothly and efficiently so that passengers can enjoy the same level of service as they would expect at an international hotel.

On the superferries, for example more than 2,000 people can be catered for during the short crossing from Dover to Calais – whether they are enjoying a four-course meal in the à la carte restaurant, a snack in the self-service cafeteria or simply a drink at one of the bars. Most passengers also want to change money and shop in the duty-free supermarket – all in the space of 75 minutes!

On all sailings, passengers can enjoy

excellent food at value-for-money prices in self-service, smart waiter-service or carvery restaurants.

On longer sailings from Felixstowe and Portsmouth there are a range of cabins for both day and night sailings. And on the Portsmouth routes, passengers can enjoy live entertainment on some sailings or relax in first-run movie cinemas showing up-to-the-minute films.

There are currency exchange bureaux on every ship plus, of course, comfortable bars and lounges, and sun decks for soaking up the bracing sea air.

CHILDREN

To give parents the opportunity to relax whilst on board and to make every crossing fun for children, P&O European Ferries has installed colourful play areas on most routes where the under 6's can let off steam in safety.

Older children can browse through their own on-board magazine, Shipmate, or watch cartoons and films in the video lounges on most ships. In addition there are special menus at lower prices in both waiter-service and self-service restaurants.

P&O European Ferries also looks after mothers and babies by providing nursing and changing facilities on board.

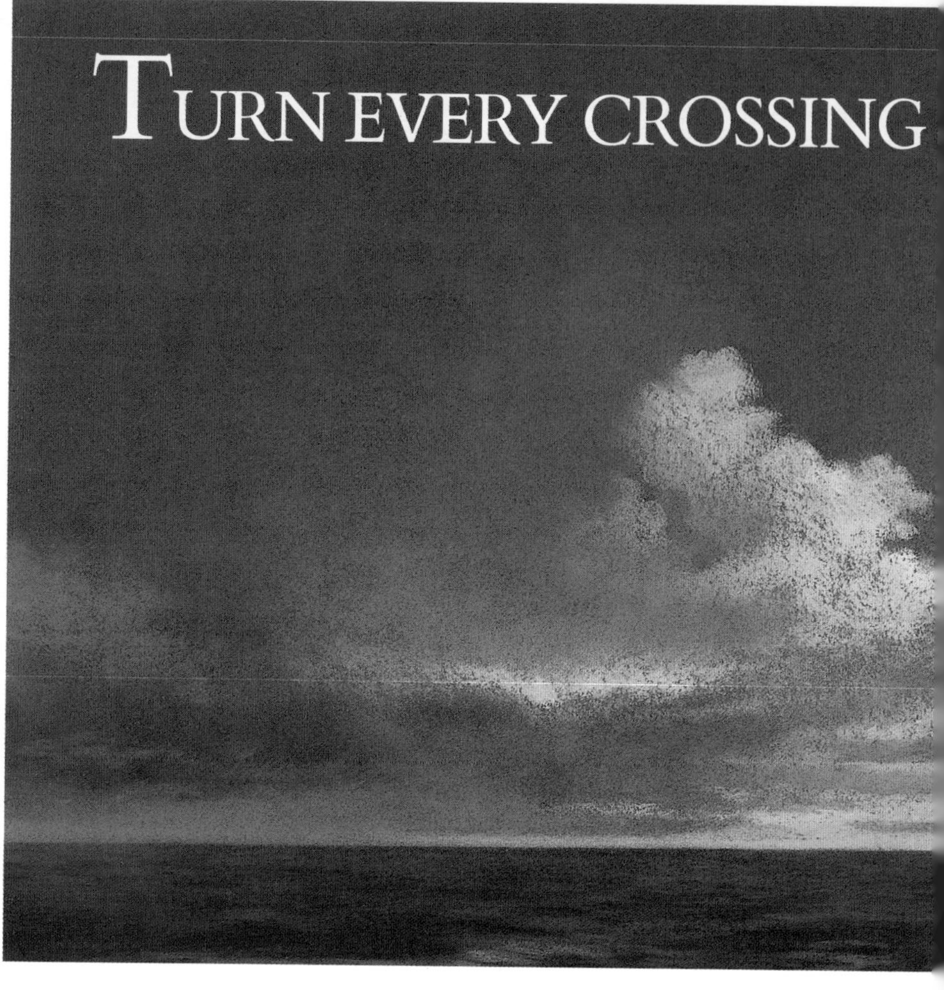

Cruise across to the Continent with P&O European Ferries. That way, your holiday will start as soon as you step aboard.

On our 2 superferries from Dover to Calais, even the time passes quicker as you browse around the new supershop and duty free store.

On selected routes, you'll be able to stretch your legs in Club Class as our stewards serve you. Or, snooze across in one of our luxury cabins on longer crossings.

You can set your own course in the carvery, waiter service or self-service restaurants.

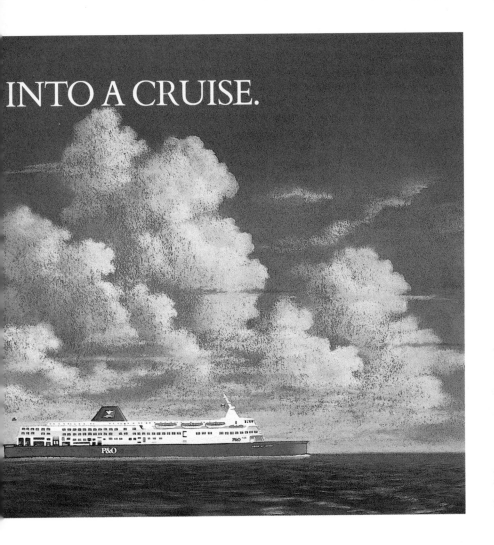

FOR THE DISABLED

An equally warm welcome is extended to disabled passengers with P&O European Ferries.

Facilities such as lifts and wheelchair accessible toilets and cabins are provided on most ships to make sure disabled passengers are not excluded from enjoying a crossing to the full.

With a minimum of 48-hours notice, P&O European Ferries can advise disabled passengers on the most convenient sailings to choose and will arrange for cars to be parked close to lifts to allow easy access to passenger decks.

ROUTES

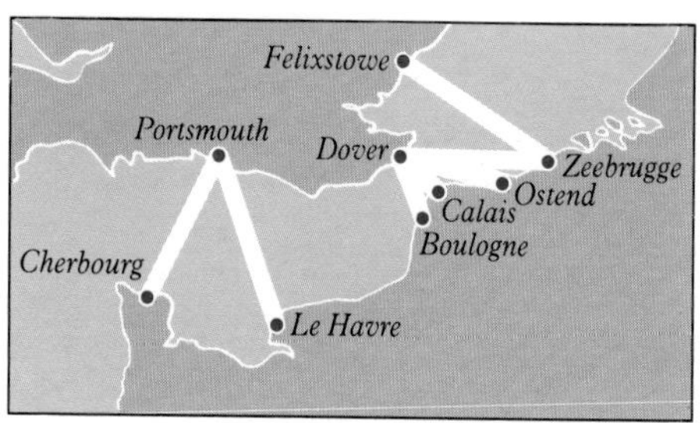

As the leading car ferry operator, P&O European Ferries has more routes and more sailings to the Continent than anyone else, which allows for total flexibility in planning for any holiday destination.

From Dover there is a choice of four routes to France and Belgium. On it's Blue Riband route – at just 75 minutes, the fastest way by ship across the Channel – the two revolutionary 26,000 ton superferries offer a choice of up to fifteen sailings a day throughout the year.

Sailings to Calais or its close neighbour Boulogne are ideal for trips to Northern France or by excellent motorway links, down to hotter holiday spots or for city-centre destinations.

The two Belgian routes from Dover – to Ostend and Zeebrugge – are perfectly placed for trips to the Benelux countries, Germany or beyond.

Sailings to Ostend are operated by P&O European Ferries Belgian partner RMT, which also provides a one hour 40 minute jetfoil service for foot passengers to the Belgian port linking up with rail connections both sides of the Channel.

Two sailings a day to Zeebrugge from Felixstowe on the east coast complete the picture as far as routes to Belgium are concerned. Overnight sailings are a particular favourite as they allow for a refreshing night's sleep in a comfortable cabin, an early arrival in Belgium and a full day ahead for a leisurely drive to a holiday destination.

Day and night sailings from Portsmouth to Le Havre and Cherbourg are especially popular with sun lovers heading to Normandy, Brittany, Central France, or further south.

ROUTE PLANNING

Before booking, it's well worth taking the trouble to plan and cost-out a holiday route. Weigh up the implications of a short or longer crossing by considering timings, driving distances and petrol costs on both sides of the Channel as well as motorway tolls, and hotel and meal expenses en route.

It may perhaps be less costly overall to choose a more expensive overnight's sailing on a longer crossing. Depending on your final destination, it could save on petrol and motorway tolls and by sleeping in a comfortable cabin while you sail, cut out the need for additional nights' stopover costs.

SHORT BREAKS

In addition to the competitive fares for longer stays away, a wide range of special short break fares are offered for those taking off to Europe for a few days.

Discounted fares are available for trips of five days (and 10 days via Portsmouth) and for weekends away, 60-hour return rates at half price apply. Campers and caravanners can now also take advantage of fare savings for short breaks.

As a special offer for readers of AA Guides, P&O European Ferries is offering £10 off the cost of short break trips. To take advantage of this offer and sample a short break saver, see the £10 off voucher (below) for details. (Only one voucher per purchase.)

P&O also operates its own range of short-break and full scale holiday self-drive packages, which combine the freedom of exploring by car, with the security of pre-booked accommodation. These include châteaux, self-catering and simpler chambres d'hôtes stays in France as well as city-centre stays in Paris, Brussels or Amsterdam.

Themed 'Breakaway' trips are also available from Dover, Felixstowe or Portsmouth and range from champagne tasting in Reims to a gastronomic weekend in Ostend – or for the really adventurous, Treasure Hunts Continental-style!

MOTOR POINTS

Single, standard return fares, short breaks and motoring inclusive holidays qualify towards the ferry operator's MOTORPOINTS club – another innovation for passengers which brings rewards, particularly for those who travel regularly.

MOTORPOINTS membership is free on completion of an application form and works by allocating points for every cross-Channel trip with a car. Points can be exchanged for gifts from the MOTOR-POINTS catalogue or for free or discounted travel with P&O European Ferries.

BE SURE

P&O European Ferries enjoys a long association with the Automobile Association and with first-timers in mind, the two organisations have teamed up to produce a practical video on continental motoring. Presented by Pamela Armstrong, it is full of useful information on planning, the law, insurance requirements, breakdowns and so on.

AA 5 Star-Service is also available to those booking with P&O European Ferries as is the exclusive Green Card Plus scheme, providing comprehensive vehicle and legal expenses cover together with no claims bonus protection.

Further information on P&O European Ferries services, or copies of its brochures are available from AA Travel Shops or the company direct at: Channel House, Channel View Road, Dover, Kent CT17 9TJ, telephone 0304 203388.

AA SHOP TELEPHONE NUMBERS

Aberdeen 0224 647677.
Barnsley 0226 731848.
Basildon 0268 293181.
Basingstoke Fanum House 0256 492004.
Basingstoke Copenhagen Court 0256 493760.
Bedford 0234 218155.
Belfast 0232 328924.
Birmingham 021 643 3373.
Bournemouth 0202 293241.
Bracknell 0344 861515.
Bradford 0274 308355.
Brighton 0273 220692.
Bristol 0272 290991.
Bromley 081 466 6672.
Cambridge 0223 65613.
Cardiff 0222 397616.
Cheadle 061 485 8551.
Chelmsford 0245 284681.
Chester 0244 351111.
Colchester 0206 575091.
Coventry 0203 222529.
Croydon 081 680 1772.
Derby 0332 365561.
Dundee 0382 29531.
Edinburgh 031 225 3301.
Exeter 0392 434236.
Gateshead Metro City 091 493 2321.
Glasgow 041 204 0911.
Guildford 0483 32023.
Halesowen 021 550 7646.
Hounslow 081 572 8878.
Hull 0482 23496.
Ipswich 0473 259573.
Jersey 0534 23344.
Leeds 0532 439090.
Leicester 0533 625948.
Lincoln 0522 510115.
Liverpool 051 708 7337.
London: City 071 623 4152;
Ealing 081 567 1266;
Hammersmith 081 748 0555;
Haymarket 071 930 9559;
Merton 081 542 1511;
Wood Green 081 881 7673.
Luton 0582 417207.
Maidstone 0622 675321.
Manchester 061 832 6014.
Middlesbrough 0642 248361.
Newcastle 091 261 0864.
Norwich 0603 612661.
Northampton 0604 37187.
Nottingham 0602 789326.
Oxford 0865 725040.
Plymouth 0752 229651.
Preston 0772 28861.
Reading 0734 580334.
Romford 0708 750020.
Salisbury 0722 413266.
Sheffield 0742 730226.
Slough 0753 822166.
Southampton 0703 636836.
Staines 0784 466833.
Stanmore 081 954 6177.
Stirling 0786 51470.
Stockport 061 480 5633.
Stoke-on-Trent 0782 280385.
Swansea 0792 463013.
Swindon 0793 485207.
Truro 0872 76458.
Twickenham 081 891 1287.
Welwyn Garden City 0707 371699.
Wolverhampton 0902 26861.
York 0904 652921.

Specimen letters for booking sites

Please use block letters and enclose an *International reply coupon*, obtainable from the post office. Be sure to include your own name and address.

ENGLISH
Dear Sir,
I intend to stay at your site for..........days
arriving on..........and departing on..........
We are a party of..........adults and..........children (aged..........)
and shall require a site for..........tent(s) and/or parking space for our car/caravan/caravan trailer.
We wish to hire a tent/caravan/bungalow.
Please quote full charges when replying and advise on the deposit required, which will be forwarded without delay.

FRENCH
Monsieur,
Je me propose de séjourner â votre terraine de camping pour..........jours
depuis le..........jusqu'au..........
Nous sommes..........personnes en tout, y compris..........adultes et..........
enfants (âgés de..........) et nous aurons besoin d'un emplacement pour..........tente(s) ainsi quel ou pour notre voiture/caravane/un bungalow.
Veuillez me donner dans votre réponse une idée de votre tarif de prix, m'indiquant en même temps le montant que vous demandez comme arrhes, ce qui vous sera ensuite envoyé aussitôt.

GERMAN
Sehr geehrter Herr!
Ich beabsichtige, mich auf Ihrem Campingplatz..........Tage aufzuhaulten und zwar vom-..........bis zum..........
Wir sind im ganzen..........Personen..........Erwachsene und..........
Kinder (im Alter von..........) und benötigen Platz für..........
Zelt(e) und/oder unseren Wagen/Wohnwagen/wohnwagenanhänger.
Wir möchten ein Zelt/Wohnwagen/Bungalow mieten.
Bitte geben Sie mir in Ihrem Antwortschreiben die vollen Preise bekannt und ebenso die Höhe der von mir zu leistenden Anzahlung, die Ihnen alsdann unverzüglich überwiesen wird.

ITALIAN
Egregio Signore,
Ho intenzione di rimanere presso di voi per..........giorni
arrivero il..........e partiro il..........
Siamo un gruppo di..........adultie..........bambini (de età..........e)
vorremmo un posto per..........tenda(e) e/o spazio per parcheggiare la nostra vetture/carovana/roulette.
Desideriamo affittare una tenda/carovana/bungalow.
Vi preghiamo die quotare i prezzi completi quandro ci risponderete ed darci informazioni sul deposito richiesto che vi sarà rimesso senza ritardo.

SPANISH
Muy señor mio,
Desearia me reservara espacio por..........dias
a partir del..........hasta el..........
Nuestro grupo se compane de..........adultos y..........niños
(de..........años de edad).
Necesitarimos un espacio por..........tienda(s) y/o espacio para aparcar nuestro choche/caravana/remolque.
Deseariamos alquilar una tienda de campaña/caravana/bungalow.
Le ruego nos comunique los precios y nois informe sobre el depósito que debemos remitirle.

THINGS YOU NEED TO KNOW

Before setting off on your European holiday, there are certain preparations you should make and some regulations you should know about. Experienced campers and caravanners will, of course, be familiar with most of this, but we hope it will be a useful chapter for newcomers.

PREPARING YOUR CARAVAN

The caravan should, of course, be regularly serviced, but the following tips should prove useful, particularly for its first trip out after winter storage.

Just before your trip give the caravan a good airing and if you have a water pump fitted, check the flow and flush with clean water to get rid of any staleness. Make sure that there are no leaks and replace any doubtful washers. Examine all potential leak spots especially around window rubbers, rear light clusters and roof lights, applying sealing compound as necessary. Test all window, cupboard and locker catches to make sure that they shut firmly. Outside clean rain gutters and make sure down-spouts and window channel drain-pipes are clear.

Brakes

Check that the caravan braking mechanism is correctly adjusted. If it has a breakaway safety mechanism, the cable between the car and caravan must be firmly anchored so that the trailer brakes are pulled on immediately if the two part company.

Lights

Make sure that all the lights are working; rear lights, stop lights, number-plate lights and flashers (check that the flasher rate is correct: 60–120 times a minute) and also rear fog guard lamps, where fitted.

Tyres

Both tyres on the caravan should be of the same size and type and it is advisable that they are the same type as those on the rear wheels of the car. Make sure that the tread depth is well above the legal minimum (see under the European ABC) and that there is no uneven wear. Look also for cuts and for cracks that might have developed during the winter.

If the caravan tyres are not going to be used for a long period, they should be properly inflated and have the weight taken off them by jacking the axle on to wood blocks. Leave in an airy place where they would not be exposed to the sun, and cover if possible.

PREPARING YOUR TENT

A tent needs surprisingly little care considering the rugged service it is expected to give. Naturally, much depends on design, quality, and the amount of camping you do, but a good tent is very tough indeed. Of course, you can't ignore maintenance altogether.

Some weeks before your holiday, choosing a fine day, spread the tent on the lawn or some other open space so that you can make a close inspection of all potential stress points – where guylines attach, where the groundsheet meets tent walls and where the frame poles come into contact with fabric. The fabric of the tent can be damaged by branches or sharp objects and by mildew if it has not been stored correctly. Additionally it can lose its proofing through long exposure to the weather, as a result of fat splattering on the fabric or splashing by washing-up water containing detergent. If the tent is damaged in this way it is advisable to consult a good specialist camping supplier. Patch kits of a suitable colour and material are available, as are proofing preparations and sprays.

PREPARING YOUR CAMPING EQUIPMENT

Camp furniture, kitchens, utensils and other hardware generally take care of themselves much as do household items. However, stoves, airbeds, lanterns and sleeping-bags should always be checked-over before departure.

This camping equipment check list may be a useful guide when planning what to take

- ☐ Air mattress and pump, or camp beds
- ☐ All-purpose knife
- ☐ Bucket
- ☐ Camp stove and fuel
- ☐ Clothes-line and pegs
- ☐ Cutlery, including cooking utensils
- ☐ Dish-cloths, scouring pad, and tea towels
- ☐ First-aid kit
- ☐ Folding chairs or stools
- ☐ Folding table
- ☐ Food containers
- ☐ Groundsheet
- ☐ Icebox (portable)
- ☐ Kettle
- ☐ Mallet
- ☐ Matches
- ☐ Plastic bags or bags for litter

- ☐ Plates, cups and saucers, or mugs
- ☐ Rope
- ☐ Saucepans, frying pan
- ☐ Sleeping bags
- ☐ Small brush (useful when camping on sand)
- ☐ Teapot
- ☐ Tent, poles, tent pegs (spares), sand pegs and discs
- ☐ Tent-tidy (for scissors, string, needles, thread, etc)
- ☐ Tin-opener, bottle opener, and corkscrew
- ☐ Torch and batteries
- ☐ Washing powder
- ☐ Washing-up bowl and washing-up liquid
- ☐ Water and milk containers
- ☐ Water-purifying tablets
- ☐ Windshield

HOW TO ENSURE GOOD ROAD HANDLING

Before you load all your luggage and equipment into the caravan it is important to check on the **weight restrictions** that apply to it and to the towing vehicle. The laden weight of the caravan should always be less than, and ideally no more than 85% of the kerbside weight of the towing vehicle.

This kerbside weight is defined as: the weight of the vehicle, inclusive of any towing bracket with which it is normally equipped, a supply of fuel and of other liquids incidental to its propulsion (eg water, oil, brake fluid etc) when it carries no person and no load other than the loose tools and equipment with which it is normally equipped.

The weight of the caravan is normally detailed in the literature that you get with the purchase and usually refers to 'ex works' or 'delivered'. This can be misleading because it is normally based on the standard model and may not take into account any extras fitted. One way to be certain is to take the unladen caravan to your local public weighbridge. Once you have the accurate unladen weight, subtract that from the manufacturer's recommended gross weight and the figure you arrive at will be the amount of personal belongings and equipment you can safely load into the caravan for your holiday. But remember that this weight should not exceed 85% of the kerbside weight of your car, which you should find detailed in the manufacturers handbook.

Loading is very important and can greatly affect the stability of the car/caravan combination on the road. Keep as much weight as possible near the trailer axle and store heavy equipment on or near to the caravan floor. You should never store heavy items at the rear of the caravan in an attempt to counterblanace an excessive weight – this practice causes instability and can be very dangerous. It is also preferable to keep the roof lockers of the caravan free of luggage if possible, to make sure the lockers, drawers and cupboards are securely closed and to make sure that there are no loose items loaded that could roll about or spill their contents during the journey.

Once the loading is done you must check that the caravan, when coupled to the car, is **level** to the ground, or slightly nose down. If the nose is up, this can be corrected by a hitch height adjuster, available in various heights from the caravan manufacturer or dealer. An adaptor plate can be used to lower the tow-ball mounting, but it does put extra pressure on the bracket.

Now check that the **nose weight** of the trailer complies with the car manufacturer's recommendations. As a general guide, the nose weight should be heavier than the rear by about 40–50kg (approximately 90–110lbs). Check the nose weight when the caravan is laden using bathroom scales and blocks of wood or a spring balance. A twin-axle trailer must be weighed when the coupling is at the exact towing height.

Ensuring the ideal weight and weight distribution of the car/trailer combination goes a long way to preventing **pitching** and **snaking**, which reduce stability and control. Pitching can also be prevented by stiffening the towing car's rear suspension – either fit a supplementary rubber or air spring unit to the rear springs, or use heavier duty shock absorbers. The latter is the more expensive option, but before any alterations are carried out, make sure that the car's front and rear shock absorbers are in good condition.

Excessive pitching and/or bad weight distribution can lead to snaking as the vertical movement starts to sway the caravan sideways. This can be particularly dangerous as the first instinct of the driver is to steer against the movement, but this only makes matters worse. The best course is to steer straight and gently decelerate. Stabilisers are available, but it is far better to cure the cause than to rely on prevention.

When choosing a car with which you intend to tow a caravan or trailer, remember that the amount of **overhang** – the distance between the car's rear axle and the towing ball – has an effect on the handling. The greater the overhang the more difficult handling will be.

A FEW FINAL CHECKS

Once you have done all the necessary loading and weighing detailed above you are almost ready to go but before you do, check that:

- ☐ the corner steadies are fully wound up and that the brace is in a handy place for when you arrive on site
- ☐ all windows, ventilators and doors are firmly shut
- ☐ any fires or flames are extinguished and the tap on the gas cylinder is turned off
- ☐ the coupling is firmly in position
- ☐ the over-run brake is working correctly
- ☐ the two wing mirrors on your car give you good visibility down both sides of the caravan
- ☐ all the car and caravan lights are working
- ☐ the safety catch on the hitch is on
- ☐ the jockey wheel is raised and secured and the handbrake is released
- ☐ the fire extinguishers are operational and close at hand

Now all you need to remember is that both the car and the driver will have to contend with the extra strain of towing this considerable weight. Much of the art of towing comes with experience, but many of the problems can be eliminated by being aware of them before you start.

1. Know your car and how to drive it well *before* attempting to tow.
2. Stop before you get tired.
3. Remember the threes Cs: **Care**, **Courtesy** and **Consideration.**
4. Plan the journey in advance, checking that the roads are suitable for towing.
5. Have the appropriate mirrors and use them.
6. Keep well to the nearside of the road so the faster vehicles can overtake. If traffic builds up behind you, pull up in a safe place and let it pass.
7. Keep a safe stopping distance between you and the vehicle in front.
8. **See and be seen** – switch on lights whenever visibility gets poor.
9. Keep to the speed limit and make good use of the gears, especially when descending hills.
10. Allow plenty of time when overtaking or pulling across a main road.
11. Never stop on narrow roads, bends, crests of hills, or anywhere that could be dangerous to yourself and other road users.
12. In case of breakdown or accident, use hazard flashers and advance warning triangle(s).

Off-road handling

When you arrive on site you may encounter difficult ground which requires careful driving. Avoid low sites liable to be waterlogged; sand that will not take the force of a driving wheel; and stone and shingle that may take the weight but not provide any grip.

If you have to drive over difficult ground, keep moving slowly with a very light throttle. If you stop, do not accelerate hard or the wheels will spin and dig in. Move gently backwards and forwards to get out of a dip. If the driving wheels do dig in, put brushwood or sacks in front of and behind the wheels. To move the trailer manually, pull side-ways on the drawbar and work it forwards by chocking alternate wheels.

CAMPING FUELS

Gas in cylinders or bottles, as used in caravans, is mainly of two types, *butane* and *propane*. Both are kept in form liquid under pressure and become a combustible gas once the pressure is released. They are available in Europe, but as they respond differently to weather conditions, propane is more widely distributed in countries where temperatures are likely to be very low in the winter. Propane has a higher pressure than butane. The branded gases and the manufacturers are listed on page 37 and 38.

Carriage of gas by car ferries

Vehicles carrying unsealed cylinders of liquefied petroleum gas (LPG) must report at both United Kingdom and European ports for a leakage test 30 minutes before the published reporting time. A maximum of three Home Office approved cylinders, not exceeding 35lb net weight each, or up to 12 small expendable cartridges, sealed and packed in an outer container, are allowed for each caravan. Cylinders should be securely fixed in, or on, the caravan in the manner and position intended by the caravan manufacturer.

Virtually all campers and caravanners use LPG. New users particularly should follow safety instructions and experienced people sometimes need reminding of the safety rules which say in effect:

–change cylinders with care
–provide fresh air for safe combustion
–don't improvise or tamper with equipment
–carry out regular maintenance

Gas safety rules

1. Always use the right type and length of hose for connecting a container to an appliance. If it is not supplied, or instructions are not given, ask the dealer's advice.
2. Replace any worn or faulty hose. Do not try to repair it.
3. When fitting the hose, where applicable use worm-drive clips and ensure they are tight.
4. Always use a spanner when fitting connections – finger tightness is not enough. Before fitting a regulator or other screwed connection to a butane cylinder, always ensure that the seal-

ing washer is present and in good condition. When fitting to switch-on or clip-on type valves, refer to the manufacturer's/supplier's instructions.

5 Check for leaks by applying soapy water. Any leaks will be shown by bubbles.

6 **Never** check for leaks with a naked flame.

7 Always keep containers away from excessive heat or naked flames.

8 When starting up, open the container valve slowly.

9 If the container is not to be used for some time, close the valve, remove the pressure regulator and replace the valve cover if fitted.

10 When changing a cartridge or container, keep away from any naked light or flame, or any source of ignition. Ensure good ventilation and preferably change cylinders in the open air. With cartridge appliances, check that the sealing washer, usually housed in the appliance inlet connection, is in position and in good condition. Make sure that the valve on the container, where fitted, and the tap on the regulator are fully closed. **Never try to change a pierceable cartridge** (such as the *Camping Gaz type*) **until you are sure all the gas has been expended.** You can usually hear any gas remaining by gently shaking the equipment.

11 Once the pressure regulators are set they should not be tampered with. Any adjustments or repairs should be left to the dealer.

12 Containers must always stand upright, valves uppermost, whether in use or not. They should also be carried upright, but not by the valve.

13 Whether full or empty, never store the containers below ground or near drains, as all these gases are heavier than air and will collect at the lowest point in the event of a leak.

14 **Make sure there is good ventilation where gas burning appliances are used.** Unflued appliances must not be installed in sleeping accommodation. Only room-sealed appliances should be installed in bath or shower rooms.

15 When moving, turn off all appliances and cylinder valves.

16 Do not sleep in a room where gas cylinders are in use.

17 Permanent storage should always be out of doors.

18 When fitting cylinders, always check that the cylinder valve is fully closed in a clockwise direction before removing the valve-sealing cap or plug.

Branded gases

Shell Gas Butane This product is marketed in 5.5kg, 7kg, 13kg and 15kg cylinders, with a variety of connecting systems, by eight local subsidiary companies operating in England and Wales. Details of these companies, who in turn can advise on the location of stockists, can be obtained by ringing Freephone Shell Gas. However, because of differing official standards and regulations to which cylinders must conform, *Butane* cylinders cannot be exchanged for European ones. Neither can they be refilled abroad. Foreign cylinders must not be brought back to the United Kingdom, nor British cylinders left in Europe. For these reasons it is recommended that, if conditions permit, you take sufficient gas to last throughout the holiday.

A list of main agents from whom cylinders are available can be obtained from Shell Gas, 7 Oxford Road, Manchester M60 7HH ✆ 061-277 2000. The main agents will be able to supply you with the names and addresses of local sub-agents.

Butane is, however, marketed by *Shell* in France, the Netherlands, Switzerland, Belgium, Portugal and Luxembourg, usually cylinders of 13kg capacity (approximately 29lb). British butane regulators will not connect direcly with cylinders obtained in these countries because of differing connections. A regulator must be obtained on loan. Deposits on cylinders are payable at the time of purchase and it is essential that you get a receipt for this from the sub-agent so that you have no difficulty in getting the deposit refunded. If your burner is specifically designed for use with butane, it is inadvisable to use it with any other gas such as propane or a propane/butane mixture.

Shell Gas (propane): Marketed by *Shell Gas* in 3.9kg, 11kg, 18.5kg and 46kg cylinders in England, Scotland and Wales.

Calor Gas (butane): Marketed by *Calor Gas Ltd.*, Appleton Park, Datchet, Slough, Berks SL3 9JG ✆ (0753) 40000. Although Calor Gas refills are not available abroad, it is possible to take sufficient with you to last for a short holiday. The following are suggested:

Camping: Single-burner picnic set or double-burner camping stove with 4.5kg cylinder;

Motor Caravan: Two-burner hotplate or two-burner hotplate grill with 4.5kg cylinder;

Trailer: Two-burner hotplate or small cooker, with 4.5kg cylinder with screw-on connections or 15kg cylinder which will accept the *switch-on* regulator.

If you follow the simple instructions on economical use, a 4.5kg cylinder will last a month on either the single or double-burner units. If you are travelling by car or motorcycle combination, one 4.5kg cylinder will be sufficient, especially if you are eating out occasionally.

If you cannot take enough Calor Gas cylinders in your outfit, you are advised to buy a *Camping Gaz* connecting tap before leaving this country. This enables a Calor Gas regulator or flow-control valve (or just the Calor Gas connecting nut in the base of appliances not using regulating equipment) to be connected to a Camping Gaz 904 or 907 cylinder (the exception to this is the quick-boiling ring or single burner, which fits directly to the 4.5kg cylinder shroud). The connecting tap is available from all Calor Gas sales and service centres, and other stockists.

Calor Gas (propane): Marketed by *Calor Gas Ltd.*, in 3.9kg, 13kg and 47kg cylinders. This is suitable for those wishing to undertake all year round camping and caravanning.

Primus (propane): Primus cylinders are available in three sizes – **2000** (0.34kg). **2005** (0.8kg) and **2012** (1.98kg) – to complement the company's extensive range of leisure, DIY and industrial appliances. Cylinders are filled and distributed in this country by *Calor Gas Ltd.*, and are available from most Calor Dealer or Calor-Primus stockists.

Primus (butane): Cartridges nos. **2201** (200g), **2202** (420g) and the new **2207** (220g) low profile, are widely available in this country and in Europe (with the exception of Spain and Eastern Europe). Due to recent legislation in France you are strongly advised to carry sufficient cartridges for passage through this country.

Camping Gaz International (butane): Marketed in the United Kingdom by *Camping Gaz (GB) Ltd.*, 9 Albert Street, Slough, Berks SL1 2BH ✆ (0753) 691707. This product is widely marketed throughout Europe (see below) but prices can vary considerably in different countries. A list of general agents can be obtained from the company. Cartridges and cylinders are available in the following sizes:

Cartridge 'GT106' (3oz gas approx)
Cartridge 206 (7oz gas approx)
901 cylinder (0.45kg)
904 cylinder (1.81kg)
907 cylinder (2.72kg)

The cartridges are expendable but cylinders are fully interchangeable for use with cooking, lighting and heater units. A special connecting tap unit is available to fit Shell Gas or Calor Gas regulators to Camping Gaz 904 or 907 cylinders. Also, the Camping Gaz regulator with hexagon nut enables Calor Gas cylinders to be connected to Camping Gaz low pressure stoves via the flexible hose supplied with these stoves.

Safety

- Always make sure you have the right size and type of gas cartridge for the appliance.
- Never put a cartridge in a cartridge holder unless the upper part of the appliance has been unscrewed and completely removed.
- A cartridge with gas in it must never be removed from an appliance nor must the upper part of the appliance be unscrewed.

The following shows the present availability in Europe: Andorra, Austria, Belgium, France, Italy, Luxembourg, Netherlands, Portugal, Spain including Majorca and Ibiza (cartridge 206 and 901 and 907 only), Switzerland and the United Kingdom.

Paraffin

Paraffin (*pétrole* or *kerosene*) is not easily obtainable in country districts in Europe and you are advised to get supplies on arrival in large towns. Methylated spirit (*alcoöl à brûler*) is easier to get.

EUROPEAN ABC

MOTORING AND GENERAL INFORMATION

The ABC provides a wide background of motoring regulations and general information, and is designed to be read in conjunction with the relevant country section(s).

Motoring laws in Europe are just as wide-ranging and complex as those in the UK, but they should cause little difficulty to the average British motorist. Drivers should, however, take more care and extend greater courtesy than they would normally do at home, and bear in mind the essentials of good motoring – avoiding any behaviour likely to obstruct traffic, endanger persons or cause damage to property. It is also important to remember that tourists are subject to the laws of the country in which they travel.

Road signs are mainly international and should be familiar, but in every country there are a few exceptions. One should particularly watch for signs indicating crossings and speed limits. Probably the most unusual aspect of motoring abroad to the British motorist is the rule giving priority to traffic coming from the right, and unless this priority is varied by signs, it must be strictly observed.

As well as a current passport a tourist temporarily importing a motor vehicle should always carry a full valid national driving licence (even when an International Driving Permit is held), the registration document of the car and evidence of insurance. The proper international distinguishing sign should be affixed to the rear of the vehicle and caravan or trailer if you are towing one. The appropriate papers must be carried at all times, and secured against loss. The practice of spot checks on foreign cars is widespread and, to avoid inconvenience or a *police fine*, ensure that your papers are in order and that the international distinguishing sign is of the approved standard design.

Make sure that you have clear all-round vision. See that your seat belts are securely mounted and not damaged, and remember that in most European countries their use is compulsory. If you are carrying skis, remember that their tips should point to the rear. You must be sure that your vehicle complies with the regulations concerning dimensions for all the countries you intend to pass through (see *ABC* and relevant *Country sections*). This is particularly necessary if you are towing a trailer of any sort.

Mechanical repairs and replacement parts can be very expensive abroad. While not all breakdowns are avoidable, a vast number occur because the vehicle has not been properly prepared before the journey. A holiday abroad involves many miles of hard driving over unfamiliar roads, perhaps without the facilities you are accustomed to. Therefore, you should give serious consideration to preparing your vehicle for a holiday abroad.

We recommend that your car undergoes a major service by a franchised dealer shortly before you holiday or tour abroad. In addition, it is advisable to carry out your own general check for any audible or visible defects.

It is not practicable to provide a complete list of points to look for, but the *ABC* contains information under the following headings:

Automatic gearboxes
Automatic transmission fluid
Brakes
Cold-weather touring
Direction indicators
Electrical
Engine and mechanical
Lights
Spares
Tyres
Warm-climate touring

These, if used in conjunction with the manufacturer's handbook, should ensure that no obvious faults are missed.

If AA members would like a thorough check of their car made by one of the AA's experienced engineers, any AA Shop can arrange this at a few days' notice. Our engineer will then submit a written report complete with a list of repairs required. There is a fee for this service. For more information please ask for our leaflet *Tech 8*.

Accidents *(See also Country sections)*

The country sections give individual country regulations, and information on summoning the fire, police and ambulance services. The international regulations are similar to those in the UK; the following action is usually required or advisable:-

If you are involved in an accident you *must* stop. A warning triangle should be placed on the road at a suitable distance to warn following traffic of the obstruction. The use of hazard warning lights in no way affects the regulations governing the use of warning triangles. Medical assistance should be obtained for persons injured in the accident. If the accident necessitates calling the police, leave the vehicle in the position in which it came to rest; should it seriously obstruct other traffic, mark the position of the vehicle on the road and get the details confirmed by independent witnesses before moving it.

The accident must be reported to the police: if it is required by law, if the accident has caused death or bodily injury, or if an unoccupied vehicle or property has been damaged and there is no one present to represent the interests of the party suffering damage. Notify your insurance company (by letter if possible), within 24 hours of the accident; see the conditions of your policy. If a third party is injured, the insurance company or bureau, whose address is given on the back of your Green Card or frontier insurance certificate, should be notified; the company or bureau will deal with any claim for compensation to the injured party.

Make sure that all essential particulars are noted, especially details concerning third parties, and co-operate with police, or other officials taking on-the-spot notes by supplying your name, address or other personal details as required. It is also a good idea to take photographs of the scene; try to get good shots of other vehicles involved, their registration plates and any background which might help later enquiries. This record may be useful when completing the insurance company's accident form. If you are not involved in the accident but feel your assistance as a witness or in any other useful capacity would be helpful then stop and park your car carefully, well away from the scene. If all the help necessary is at the scene, then do not stop out of curiosity or park your car at the site.

Automatic gearboxes

The fluid in an automatic gearbox does more work when it has to cope with the extra weight of a caravan. It becomes hotter and thinner, so there is more slip and more heat generated in the gearbox. Many manufacturers recommend the fitting of a gearbox oil cooler. Check with the manufacturer as to what is suitable for your car.

Automatic transmission fluid

Automatic transmission fluid is not always readily available, especially in some of the more remote areas of Western Europe, and tourists are advised to carry an emergency supply.

BBC World Service

BBC World Service transmissions in English can be heard in many European countries. A full programme including current affairs, sport and music is available, with world news at approximately every hour. Most car radios operate on medium and long wave, so BBC World Service programmes may normally be obtained in north-western Europe by tuning to the following frequencies between the times mentioned.

kHz	Metres	Summer broadcasting times – GMT
1296	231	03.00–03.30, 06.00–06.30, 17.00–19.00, 22.00–23.15.
648*	463	02.30–03.15, 05.00–5.30, 06.00–10.30, 11.00–15.15, 16.00–16.15, 19.00–02.15.
198	1515	23.45–04.50.

*BBC 648 is Europe's first trilingual radio station. It carries World Service programmes in English for most of the day, but includes French and German sequences, news for Europe and 'BBC English' at certain times.

In some Western European countries, it may be possible to receive BBC national services with the exception of Radio 3. For more comprehensive information on BBC transmissions throughout Europe, write to BBC World Information Centre and Shop, Bush House, Strand, London WC2B 4PH.

Boats

All boats taken abroad by road should be registered in the UK, except for very small craft to be used close inshore in France*. You must take the original Certificate of Registry with you, not a photocopy. Registration may be carried out through the Royal Yachting Association at a current fee of £10.00. A Helmsman's Overseas Certificate of Competence is required for Germany, Italy (in some parts), Netherlands (if using a speedboat), Portugal, and Spain. All applications to the Royal Yachting Association, RYA House, Romsey Road, Eastleigh, Hampshire

SO7 4YA ✆ (0703) 629962. See also *Carnet de Passages* under *Customs regulations for European countries,* page 42 and *Insurance,* page 47.

**In France very small craft are exempt from registration and the dividing line falls approximately between a Laser dinghy (which should be registered) and a Topper (which need not). The precise details are available from the RYA.*

Brakes

Car brakes must always be in peak condition. Check both the level in the brake fluid reservoir and the thickness of the brake lining/pad material. The brake fluid should be completely changed in accordance with the manufacturer's instructions or at intervals of not more than 18 months or 18,000 miles. However, it is always advisable to change the brake fluid before starting a Continental holiday, particularly if the journey includes travelling through a hilly or mountainous area.

Breakdown

If your car breaks down, try to move it to the side of the road, or to a position where it will obstruct the traffic flow as little as possible. Place a warning triangle at the appropriate distance on the road behind the obstruction. Bear in mind road conditions and, if near or on a bend, the triangle should be placed where it is clearly visible to following traffic. If the car is fitted with hazard warning lights these may be switched on but remember that they will only be effective on straight roads, and will have no effect at bends or rises in the road. If the fault is electrical, the lights may not operate, and it is for these reasons that they cannot take the place of a triangle.

Motorists are advised to take out ***AA 5-Star Service***, the overseas motoring emergency service which includes breakdown and accident benefits, and personal travel insurance. It offers total security and peace of mind, and is available to all motorists travelling in Europe, although non-AA members pay a small additional premium. The AA and/or the Insurer may also ask for an indemnity or guarantee if the proposer is under 18 or not permanently resident within the British Isles. Details and brochures are available from AA Shops or telephone 021-550 7648.

Note: Members who have not purchased ***AA 5-Star Service*** prior to departure, and who subsequently require assistance, may request spare parts or vehicle recovery, but the AA will require a deposit to cover estimated costs and a service fee prior to providing the service. All expenses must be reimbursed to the AA in addition to the service fee.

British Embassies/Consulates *(See also Country sections)*

In most European countries there is usually more than one British Consulate, and degrees of status vary. The functions and office hours of Vice-Consulates and Honorary Consuls are naturally more restricted. Generally, Consulates (and consular sections, of the Embassy) stand ready to help British travellers overseas, but there are limits to what they can do. A Consulate cannot pay your hotel, medical or any other bills, nor will they do the work of travel agents, information bureaux or police. Any loss or theft of property should be reported to the local police not the Consulate, and a statement obtained confirming the loss or theft. If you still need help, such as the issue of an emergency passport or guidance on how to transfer funds, contact the Consulate. See respective *Country sections* for addresses/locations of British Embassies/Consulates.

Caravan and luggage trailers

Take a list of contents, especially if any valuable or unusual equipment is being carried, as this may be required at a frontier. A towed vehicle should be readily identifiable by a plate in an accessible position showing the name of the maker of the vehicle and the production or serial number. See *Identification plate* page 46. See also *Principal mountain passes* page 61.

Claims against third parties

The law and levels of damages in foreign countries are generally different to our own. It is important to remember this when considering making a claim against another motorist arising out of an accident abroad. Certain types of claims invariably present difficulties, the most common probably relating to the recovery of car-hiring charges. Rarely are they fully recoverable, and in some countries they may be drastically reduced or not recoverable at all. General damages for pain and suffering are not recoverable in certain countries but even in those countries where they are, the level of damages is usually lower than our own.

The negotiation of claims against foreign insurers is extremely protracted, and translation of all documents slows down the process. A delay of three months between sending a letter and receiving a reply is not uncommon.

If you have taken out the ***AA 5-Star Service***

cover, this includes a discretionary service in respect of certain matters arising abroad requiring legal assistance, including the pursuit of uninsured loss claims against third parties arising out of a road accident. In this event, AA members should seek guidance and/or assistance from the AA.

Cold-weather touring

If you are planning a winter tour, fit a high-temperature (winter) thermostat and make sure that the strength of your antifreeze mixture is correct for the low temperatures likely to be encountered.

If travelling through snow-bound regions, it is important to remember that for many resorts and passes the authorities insist on wheel chains or spiked or studded tyres. However, as wheel chains and spiked or studded tyres can damage bare road surfaces, there are limited periods when these may be used, and in certain countries the use of spiked or studded tyres is illegal. Signposts usually indicate if wheel chains or spiked or studded tyres are compulsory.

In fair weather, wheel chains or spiked or studded tyres are only necessary on the higher passes, but (as a rough guide) in severe weather you will probably need them at altitudes exceeding 2,000ft.

If you think you will need wheel chains, it is better to take them with you from home. They may be hired from the AA, and further details are available from your nearest AA Shop.

Wheel chains fit over the driven wheels to enable them to grip on snow or icy surfaces. They are sometimes called *snow chains* or *anti-skid chains*. Full-length chains which fit tight around a tyre are the most satisfactory, but they must be fitted correctly. Check that the chains do not foul your vehicle bodywork; if your vehicle has front-wheel-drive put the steering on full lock while checking. If your vehicle has radial tyres it is essential that you contact the manufacturers of your vehicle and tyres for their recommendations, in order to avoid damage to your tyres. Chains should only be used when compulsory or necessary, as prolonged use on hard surface will damage the tyres.

Spiked or studded tyres are sometimes called *snow tyres*. They are tyres with rugged treads on to which spikes or studs have been fitted. For the best grip they should be fitted to all wheels. The correct type of spiked or studded winter tyres will generally be more effective than chains.

Note: The above guidelines do not apply where extreme winter conditions prevail. For extreme conditions it is doubtful whether the cost of preparing a car, normally used in the UK, would in this instance be justified for a short period. However, the AA's Technical Services Department can advise on specific enquiries.

Compulsory equipment

All countries have differing regulations as to how vehicles circulating on their roads should be equipped, but generally domestic laws are not enforced on visiting foreigners. However, where a country considers aspects of safety or other factors are involved they will impose some regulations on visitors and these will be mentioned in the *Country sections.*

Crash, or safety, helmets

All countries in this guide require visiting motorcyclists and their passengers to wear crash, or safety, helmets (except Belgium where they are strongly recommended).

Credit/charge cards

Credit/charge cards may be used abroad but their use is subject to 'conditions of use' set out by the issuing company who, on request, will provide full information. Establishments display the symbols of cards they accept.

Currency *(See also Country sections)*

There is no limit to the amount of sterling notes you may take abroad. However, it is best to carry only enough currency for immediate expenses. As many countries have regulations controlling the import and export of currency, you are advised to consult your bank for full information before making final arrangements.

Customs regulations for European countries (other than the UK)

Bona fide visitors to the countries listed in this Guide may assume as a general rule that they may temporarily import personal articles duty free, providing the following conditions are met:

- **a** that the articles are for personal use, and are not to be sold or otherwise disposed of;
- **b** that they may be considered as being in use, and in keeping with the personal status of the importer;
- **c** that they are taken out when the importer leaves the country;
- **d** that the goods stay for no more than 6 months in any 12 months period, whichever is the earlier.

All dutiable articles must be declared when you enter a country, otherwise you will be liable to penalties. Should you be taking a large number of personal effects with you, it would be a wise measure to prepare in advance an inventory to present to the Customs authorities on entry. Customs officers may withhold concessions at any time, and ask the traveller to deposit enough money to cover possible duty, especially on portable items of apparent high value such as television sets, radios, cassette recorders, pocket calculators, musical instruments, etc, all of which must be declared. Any deposit paid (for which a receipt must be obtained) is likely to be high; it is recoverable on leaving the country and exporting the item but only at the entry point at which it was paid. Alternatively the Customs may enter the item in the traveller's passport and in these circumstances, it is important to remember to get the entry cancelled when the item is exported. Duty and tax free allowances may not apply (except for EC countries), if travellers enter the country more than once a month, or are under 17 years of age (an alternative age may apply in some countries). Residents of the Channel Islands and the Isle of Man do not benefit from EC allowances due to their fiscal regimes.

A temporarily imported motor vehicle, boat, caravan, or any other type of trailer is subject to strict control on entering a country, attracting Customs duty and a variety of taxes; much depends upon the circumstances and the period of the import, and also upon the status of the importer. People entering a country in which they have no residence, with a private vehicle for holiday or recreational purposes and intending to export the vehicle within a short period, enjoy special privileges, and the normal formalities are reduced to an absolute minimum in the interests of tourism. However, a *Customs Carnet de Passages en Douane* is required to temporarily import: **a)** all trailers not accompanied by the towing vehicle into *Belgium* and **b)** all boats into *Luxembourg* unless entering and leaving by water.

The *Carnet*, for which a charge is made, is a valuable document issued by the AA to its members, or as part of the ***AA 5-Star Service*** – further information may be obtained from most AA Shops. If you are issued with a *Carnet* you must ensure that it is returned to the AA correctly discharged in order to avoid inconvenience and expense, possibly including payment of customs charges, at a later date. A temporarily imported vehicle, etc, should not:

- **a** be left in the country after the importer has left;
- **b** be put at the disposal of a resident of the country;
- **c** be retained in the country longer than the permitted period;
- **d** be lent, sold, hired, given away, exchanged or otherwise disposed of.

Generally, people entering a country with a motor vehicle for a period of more than six months (see also *Visa* page 54), or to take up residence, employment, any commercial activity or with the intention of disposing of the vehicle should seek advice concerning their position well in advance of their departure. Most AA Shops will be pleased to help.

Customs regulations for the United Kingdom

If, when leaving Britain, you take any items which look very new, for example, watches, items of jewellery, cameras etc, particularly of foreign manufacture, which you bought in the UK, it is a good idea to carry the retailer's receipts with you. In the absence of such receipts, you may be asked to make a written declaration of where the goods were obtained.

There are prohibitions or restrictions on taking certain goods out of the UK. These include controlled drugs, most animals, birds and some plants; firearms and ammunition; strategic and technological equipment (including computers); and items manufactured more than 50 years before the date of exportation.

When you enter the United Kingdom, you will pass through Customs. You must declare everything in excess of the duty and tax free allowances (see below) which you have obtained outside the United Kingdom, or on the journey, and everything previously obtained free of duty or tax in the United Kingdom. You may not mix allowances between duty-free and non-duty-free sources within each heading, except for alcohol, which allows, for example, 1 litre of duty and tax-free spirits in addition to 5 litres of duty and tax-paid still wine. Currently, as a concession only, travellers may use their entitlement of alcoholic drinks not over 22% vol to import table wine, in addition to the set table wine allowance. You must also declare any prohibited or restricted goods, and goods for commercial purposes. **Do not** be tempted to hide anything or to mislead the Customs! The penalties are severe and articles which are not properly declared may be forfeit. If articles are hidden in a vehicle, that too becomes liable to forfeiture. Customs officers are legally entitled to examine your luggage. Please cooperate with them if they ask to examine it. You are responsible for opening, unpacking and repacking your luggage.

There are also prohibitions and restrictions on bringing certain goods into the UK. These include: controlled drugs such as opium, morphine, heroin, cocaine, cannabis, amphetamines, barbiturates and LSD (lysergide); counterfeit currency; firearms (including gas pistols, electric shock batons and similar weapons), ammunition, explosives (including fireworks) and flick knives, swordsticks, butterfly knives and certain other offensive weapons; horror comics, indecent or obscene books, magazines, films, video tapes and other articles; animals* and birds, whether alive or dead (including stuffed); certain articles derived from endangered species, including fur-skins, ivory, reptile leather and goods made from them; meat and poultry and their products including ham, bacon, sausage, pâté, eggs, milk and cream (but 1kg per passenger of fully cooked meat or poultry products in hermetically sealed containers, which include cans, glass jars and flexible pouches is allowed. The fully cooked products must have been heat treated in the hermetically sealed containers and be capable of being stored at room temperature), plants, parts thereof and plant produce, including trees and shrubs, potatoes and certain other vegetables, fruit, bulbs and seeds; wood with bark attached; certain fish and fish eggs, whether alive or dead; bees; radio transmitters (*eg* citizens' band radios, walkie-talkies, cordless phones etc) not approved for use in the United Kingdom.

***Note:** Cats, dogs and other mammals must not be landed unless a British import licence (rabies) has previously been issued.

Customers Notice No. 1 is available to all travellers at the point of entry, or on the boat, and contains useful information of which returning tourists should be aware. Details for drivers going through the red and green channels are enclosed in *Notice No. 1*, copies of which can be obtained from HM Customs and Excise, CDE, Room 201, Dorset House, Stamford Street, London SE1 9PS.

Goods obtained duty and tax-free in the EC, or duty and tax-free on a ship or aircraft, or goods obtained outside the EC	Duty and tax-free allowances	Goods obtained duty and tax-paid in the EC
	Tobacco products	
200	Cigarettes	300
	or	
100	Cigarillos	150
	or	
50	Cigars	75
	or	
250g	Tobacco	400g
	Alcoholic drinks	
2 Litres	Still table wine	5 litres
1 litre	Over 22% vol (*eg* spirits and strong liqueurs)	$1^1/_2$ litres
	or	
2 litres	Not over 22% vol (*eg* low strength liqueurs or fortified wines or sparkling wines)	3 litres
	or	
2 litres	Still table wine	3 litres
	Perfume	
50g/60cc		75g/90cc
	Toilet water	
250cc		375cc
	Other goods	
£32	but no more than: 50 litres of beer 25 mechanical lighters	£265

Note
Persons under 17 are not entitled to tobacco and drinks allowances.

Dimensions and weight restrictions

For an ordinary private car, a height limit of 4 metres and a width limit of 2.50 metres are generally imposed. However, see *Country sections* for full details. Apart from a laden weight limit imposed on commercial vehicles, every vehicle has an individual weight limit. See *Overloading* page 50. See also *Major road and rail tunnels* page 58, as some dimensions are restricted by the shape of the tunnels. If you have any doubts, consult the AA.

Direction indicators

All direction indicators should be working at between 60 and 120 flashes per minute. Most standard car-flasher units will be overloaded by the extra lamps of a caravan or trailer, and a special heavy duty unit, or a relay device should be fitted.

Drinking and driving

There is only one safe rule – **if you drink, don't drive.** The laws are strict and the penalties severe.

Driving licence and International Driving Permit

You should carry your national driving licence with you when motoring abroad. If an International Driving Permit (IDP) is necessary (see *IDP* below), it is strongly recommended that you still carry your national driving licence. In most of the countries covered by this guide, a visitor may use a temporarily imported car or motorcycle without formality for up to three months with a valid full licence (not provisional) issued in the United Kingdom or Republic of Ireland, subject to the minimum age requirements of the country concerned (see Country sections). If you should wish to drive a hired or borrowed car in the country you are visiting, make local enquiries.

If your licence is due to expire before your anticipated return, it should be renewed in good time prior to your departure. The Driver and Vehicle Licensing Agency (in Northern Ireland – the Licensing Authority) will accept an application two months before the expiry of your old licence. In the Republic of Ireland, licensing authorities will accept an application one month before the expiry of your old licence.

An **International Driving Permit (IDP)** is an internationally recognised document which enables the holder to drive for a limited period in countries where their national licences are not recognised (see Austrian and Spanish Country sections under *Driving licence*). The permit, for which a statutory charge is made, is issued by the AA to an applicant who holds a valid full British driving licence and who is over 18 years old. It has a validity of 12 months and cannot be renewed. Application forms are available from any AA Shop. The permit cannot be issued to the holder of a foreign licence, who must apply to the appropriate authority in the country where the driving licence was issued.

Note: Residents of the Republic of Ireland, Channel Islands and the Isle of Man should apply to their local AA Shop for the relevant application form.

'E' card

This card may be displayed in the windscreen of your vehicle to assist the traffic flow across certain frontiers within the European Community. Full conditions of use are given on the card which may be obtained from AA Shops.

Electrical

General: The public electricity supply in Europe is predominantly 220 volts (50 cycles) AC (alternating current), but can be as low as 110 volts. In some isolated areas, low voltage DC (direct current) is provided. European circular two-pin plugs and screw-type bulbs are usually the rule.

Electrical adaptors (not voltage transformers) which can be used in European power sockets, shaver points and light bulb sockets are available in the United Kingdom, usually from the larger electrical retailers.

Vehicle: Check that all the connections are sound, and that the wiring is in good condition. If problems arise with the charging system, it is essential to obtain the services of a qualified auto-electrician.

Emergency messages to tourists

In cases of emergency, the AA will assist in the passing on of messages to tourists in Austria, Belgium, France, Italy, Luxembourg, Netherlands, Portugal, Spain, and Switzerland.

The AA can arrange for messages to be published in overseas editions of the *Daily Mail,* and in extreme emergency (death or serious illness concerning next-of-kin) can arrange to have personal messages broadcast on overseas radio networks. Anyone wishing to use this service should contact their nearest AA Shop.

Before you leave home, make sure your relatives understand the procedures to follow should an emergency occur.

If you have reason to expect a message from home*, you will be wise to contact the tourist office or the motoring club of the country you are staying in. They will be able to tell you to which frequency you should tune your radio and at what time such messages are normally broadcast.

No guarantee can be given, either by the AA or by the *Daily Mail,* to trace the person concerned, and no responsibility can be accepted for the authenticity of messages.

*Emergency 'SOS' messages concerning the dangerous illness of a close relative may be broadcast on BBC Radio 4's Long Wave transmitters on 1515m/198kHz at 06.59 and 17.59 hrs BST (see *BBC World Service* page **40**). Such messages should be arranged through the local police or hospital authorities.

Engine and mechanical

Consult your vehicle handbook for servicing intervals. Unless the engine oil has been changed recently, drain and refill with fresh oil and fit a new filter. Deal with any significant leaks by tightening up loose nuts and bolts and renewing faulty joints and seals.

Brands and grades of engine oil familiar to the British motorist are usually available in Western Europe, but may be difficult to find in remote country areas. When available, they will be much more expensive than in the UK and generally packed in 2-litre cans ($3^1/_2$ pints). Motorists can usually assess the normal consumption of their car, and are strongly advised to carry what oil is likely to be required for the trip.

If you suspect that there is anything wrong with the engine, however insignificant it may seem it should be dealt with straight away. Even if everything seems in order, do not neglect such commonsense precautions as checking valve clearances, sparking plugs, and contact breaker points where fitted, and make sure that the distributor cap is sound. The fan belt should be checked for fraying and slackness. If any of these items are showing signs of wear you should replace them.

Any obvious mechanical defects should be attended to at once. Look particularly for play in steering connections and wheel bearings and, where applicable, ensure that they are adequately greased. A car that has covered many miles will have absorbed a certain amount of dirt into the fuel system, and as breakdowns are often caused by dirt, it is essential that all filters (fuel and air) should be cleaned or renewed.

The cooling system should be checked for leaks, and the correct proportion of anti-freeze and any perished hoses or suspect parts, replaced.

Owners should seriously reconsider towing a caravan with a car that has already given appreciable service. Hard driving on motorways and in mountainous country puts an extra strain on ageing parts and items such as a burnt-out clutch can be very expensive.

Ferry crossings

From Britain, the shortest sea crossing from a southern port to the Continent would be the obvious but not always the best choice, bearing in mind how it places you on landing for main roads to your destination. Your starting point is important, because, if you have a long journey to a southern port, then a service from an eastern port might be more convenient. Perhaps a *Motorail* service to the south might save time and possibly an overnight stop? In some circumstances, the south-western ports may offer a convenient service and before making bookings it may be worth seeking advice so that your journey is as economic and as comfortable as possible.

The AA can make your motorail reservation and book your sea crossing (ferry, hovercraft or seacat). Instant confirmation can usually be obtained by ringing the appropriate number listed below (Mon–Fri, 09.00–17.00 hrs). Ring these numbers too if you want information and booking on Continental car-sleeper and ferry services.

UK ✆ 021-550 7648
Republic of Ireland ✆ Dublin (0001) 833656

Fire extinguisher

It is a wise precaution to equip your vehicle with a fire extinguisher when motoring abroad. A fire extinguisher may be purchased from AA Shops.

First-aid kit

It is a wise precaution (compulsory in Austria) to equip your vehicle with a first-aid kit when motoring abroad. A first-aid kit may be purchased from AA Shops.

Foodstuffs *(See also Country sections)*

What you take with you is largely a question of the space available and personal choice. Countries do have regulations governing the types and quantities of foodstuffs which may be imported, but generally they are not strictly applied. However, visitors should be aware of the existence of these regulations and only take reasonable quantities of foodstuffs with them. Where specific regulations exist for a country, they are listed under the general section of the country heading.

Convenience foods offer great variety, are ideally suited to camping, and come in many forms; the three main types are tinned, dehydrated and, if you possess a cool box, frozen. Nevertheless, resist the temptation to take too much as this only means a large number of tins making a long round trip.

It is far better to take only as much as you need until you can shop locally. Best value for money will be found in supermarkets or in the open markets in towns. However, the golden rule is to shop where you see locals shopping – a sure sign of good quality and the best prices.

Horn

In built-up areas, the general rule is not to use the horn unless safety demands it; in many large towns and resorts, as well as in areas indicated by the international sign (a horn inside a red circle, crossed through), the use of the horn is totally prohibited.

Identification plate

If a boat, caravan or trailer is taken abroad, it must have a unique chassis number for identification purposes. If your boat, caravan or trailer does not have a number, an identification plate may be purchased from the AA. Boats registered on the Small Ships Register (see *Boats* page **40**) are issued with a unique number which must be permanently displayed.

Insurance, including caravan insurance

Motor insurance is compulsory by law in all the countries covered in this Guide, and you must make sure you are adequately covered for all countries in which you will travel. Temporary policies are available at all frontiers, but this is a very expensive way of effecting cover. It is best to seek the advice of your insurer regarding the extent of cover and full terms of your existing policy. Some insurers may not be willing to offer cover in the countries that you intend to visit and it may be necessary to seek a new, special policy for the trip from another insurer. If you have any difficulty, *AA Insurance Services* will be pleased to help you. *Note:* extra insurance is recommended when visiting Spain (see *Bail Bond*). Third party insurance is compulsory for boats with engines of more than 3hp in Italian waters and for craft used on the Swiss lakes (see also *Boats* page 40); it is recommended elsewhere for all boats used abroad. It is compulsory for trailers temporarily imported into Austria and must be a separate policy from that covering the towing vehicle.

An international motor insurance certificate or ***Green Card*** is recognised in most countries as evidence that you are covered to the minimum extent demanded by law. Compulsory in Andorra, the AA strongly advises its use elsewhere. It will be issued by your own insurer upon payment of an additional premium, although some insurers now provide one free of charge to existing policyholders. A Green Card extends your UK policy cover to apply in those countries you intend visiting. The document should be signed on receipt as it will not be accepted without the signature of the insured. Green Cards are internationally recognised by police and other authorities, and may save a great deal of inconvenience in the event of an accident. If you are towing a caravan or trailer, it will need separate insurance, and mention on your Green Card. Remember, the cover on a caravan or trailer associated with a Green Card is normally limited to third-party towing risks, so a separate policy (see *AA Caravan Plus* below) is available to cover accidental damage, fire or theft.

In accordance with a Common Market Directive, the production and inspection of Green Cards at the frontiers of Common Market countries are no longer legal requirements, and this principle has been accepted by other European countries who are not members of the EC. However, the fact that Green Cards will not be inspected does not remove the necessity of having insurance cover as required by law in the countries concerned.

Motorists can obtain expert advice through *AA Insurance Services* for all types of insurance. Several special schemes have been arranged with leading insurers to enable motorists to obtain wide insurance cover at economic premiums. One of these schemes, ***AA Caravan Plus,*** includes damage cover for caravans, and their contents, including personal effects. Protection against your legal liability to other persons arising out of the use of the caravan while it is detached from the towing vehicle is also provided. Cover is extended to most European countries for up to 60 days without extra charge. *AA Caravan Plus* also provides cover for camping equipment. Full details of *AA Caravan Plus* may be obtained from any **AA Shop** or direct from AA Insurance Services Ltd, PO Box 2AA, Newcastle upon Tyne NE99 2AA.

Finally, make sure that you are covered against damage in transit (*eg* on the ferry or motorail). Most comprehensive motor insurance policies provide adequate cover for transit between ports in the UK, but need to be extended to give this cover if travelling outside the UK. You are advised to check this aspect with your insurer before setting off on your journey.

International Camping Carnet

An *International Camping Carnet* may be purchased by anyone over 18 who is a member of an organisation such as the AA, affiliated to one of the three major camping federations *ie* AIT, FIA or FICC. Recognised at most campsites in Europe, the *carnet* is essential in some cases and you will not be allowed to camp without it. At certain campsites a reduction to the advertised charge may be allowed on presentation of the *carnet.* An application form may be obtained from any AA Shop. **However, no more than 12 persons may be covered by any one *carnet*.**

From 1991 the *carnet* will be in the form of a plastic card valid for the calendar year of purchase. Details of the *Camper's Code,* together with conditions governing the issue of the *carnet* and a summary of the third-party insurance cover will be provided with every *carnet* issued.

On arrival at the campsite, report to the campsite manager who will tell you where you may pitch your tent or caravan. You may be asked to pay in advance, or alternatively, to give into charge the *carnet* for the length of your stay. Some campsite managers may also insist upon the retention of all passports.

International distinguishing sign

An international distinguishing sign of the approved pattern, oval with black letters on a white background, and size (GB at least 6.9in by 4.5in), must be displayed on a vertical surface at the rear of your vehicle (and caravan or trailer if you are towing one). These distinguishing signs indicate the country of registration of the vehicle. On the Continent, checks are made to ensure that a vehicle's nationality plate is in order. Fines are imposed for failing to display a nationality plate, or for not displaying the correct nationality plate, see *Police fines* page **51**.

Level crossings

Practically all level crossings are indicated by international signs. Most guarded ones are the lifting barrier type, sometimes with bells or flashing lights to give warning of an approaching train.

Lights *(See also Country sections)*

For driving abroad headlights should be altered so that the dipped beam does not dazzle oncoming drivers. The alteration can be made by fitting headlamp converters (PVC mask sheets) or beam deflectors (clip-on lenses), on sale at AA Shops. It is important to remember to remove the headlamp converters or beam deflectors as soon as you return to the UK.

Dipped headlights should also be used in conditions of fog, snowfall, heavy rain and when passing through a tunnel, irrespective of its length and lighting. In some countries, police will wait at the end of a tunnel to check this requirement.

Headlight flashing is used only as a warning of approach or as a passing signal at night. In other circumstances, it is accepted as a sign of irritation, and should be used with caution lest it is misunderstood.

It is a wise precaution (compulsory in Spain and recommended in France and Italy) to equip your vehicle with a set of replacement bulbs when motoring abroad. An AA Emergency Auto Bulb Kit, suitable for most makes of car, can be purchased from AA Shops. Alternatively an Emergency Repair Incident Kit, which can include the bulbs, may be hired from the AA.

Note: Remember to have the lamps set to compensate for the load being carried.

Medical treatment

Travellers who normally take certain medicines should ensure they have a sufficient supply to last for their trip, since they may be very difficult to get abroad.

Those with certain medical conditions (diabetes or coronary artery diseases, for example) should get a letter from their doctor giving treatment details. Some Continental doctors will understand a letter written in English, but it is better to have it translated into the language of the country you intend to visit. The AA cannot make such a translation.

Travellers who, for legitimate health reasons, carry drugs or appliances (*eg* a hypodermic syringe), may have difficulty with Customs or other authorities. They should carry translations which describe their special condition and appropriate treatment in the language of the country they intend to visit in order to facilitate their passage through Customs. Similarly, people with special dietary requirements may have difficulty in making them understood to hotel and restaurant staff. Translations would also be invaluable in those circumstances.

The National Health Service is available in the UK only, and medical expenses incurred overseas cannot generally be reimbursed by the UK Government. There are reciprocal health agreements with most of the countries covered by this Guide, but you should not rely exclusively on these arrangements, as the cover provided under the respective national schemes is not always comprehensive. (For instance, the cost of bringing a person back to the UK in the event of illness or death is never covered). The full costs of medical care must be paid in Andorra and Switzerland. Therefore, as facilities and financial cover can vary considerably, you are strongly advised to take out comprehensive and adequate insurance cover before leaving the UK such as that offered under the ***AA's 5-Star Service***, personal insurance section.

Urgent medical treatment in the event of an accident or unforeseen illness can be obtained for most visitors, free of charge or at reduced costs, from the health care schemes of those countries with whom the UK has health-care arrangements. Details are in the Department of Health leaflet *T1 'The Travellers'*

Guide to Health. Free copies are available from post offices, by ringing 0800 555 777 or from Health Publications Unit, No 2 Site, Manchester Road, Heywood, Lancs OL10 2PZ. In some of these countries, visitors can obtain urgently needed treatment by showing their UK passport, but in some a NHS medical card must be produced, and in most European Community countries a certificate of entitlement (E111) is necessary. The E111 can be obtained over the counter of the post office. Residents of the Republic of Ireland must apply to their Regional Health Board for an E111. The Department of Health leaflet T1 also gives advice about health precautions and international vaccination requirements.

Minibus

A minibus constructed and equipped to carry 10 or more persons (including the driver) and used outside the UK is subject to the regulations governing international bus and coach journeys. This will generally mean that the vehicle must be fitted with a tachograph, and certain documentation obtained *ie* driver's certificate, model control document and waybill. For vehicles registered in Great Britain (England, Scotland and Wales), contact the authorities as follows:

a for driver's certificate (not required by holders of new style part pink/part green licences) and details of approved tachograph installers, apply to the local Traffic Area Office of the Department of Transport;

b for model control document and waybill, apply to the Bus and Coach Council, Sardinia House, 52 Lincoln's Inn Fields, London WC2A 3LZ ✆071-831 7546.

For vehicles registered in Northern Ireland, contact the Department of the Environment for Northern Ireland, Road Transport Department, Upper Galwally, Belfast BT8 4FY ✆ (0232) 649044.

For vehicles registered in the Republic of Ireland, contact the Department of Labour, Mespil Road, Dublin 4 for details about tachographs, and the Government Publications Sales Office, Molesworth Street, Dublin 2 for information about documentation.

A minibus driver must be at least 21 years of age and hold a full UK driving licence valid as follows:

i Group A (or if automatic transmission group B) if an all green or all pink licence. Existing drivers who have held licence before 1 June 1990 may drive a vehicle with **more** than 16 passenger seats in addition to the driver's seat up to 31 December 1991.

ii Category D1 if new style part pink/part green licence. Drivers whose licence came into force on or after 1 June 1990 may only drive a minibus with **up to** 16 passenger seats.

Note: All the above minibus references are subject to the vehicle not being used for hire or reward.

Mirrors

When driving abroad, on the right, it is essential, as when driving on the left in the UK and Republic of Ireland, to have clear all-round vision. Ideally, external rear-view mirrors should be fitted to both sides of your vehicle, but certainly on the left, to allow for driving on the right.

When towing a caravan it is essential to fit mirror accessories for better rear vision. The accessories available include: extensions that clip on existing wing mirrors; arms to extend wing mirrors; long-arm wing or door mirrors; and periscopes which are fitted on the car roof and reflect the rear view through the caravan window. A periscope and wing mirrors used together should eliminate all blind spots. The longer the mirror arm is, the more rigid its mounting has to be. Some mirrors have supporting legs or extra brackets to minimise vibration. A mirror mounted on the door pillar gives a wide field of vision because it is close to the driver. However, it has the disadvantage that it is at a greater angle to the forward line of sight. Convex mirrors give an even wider field of vision, but practice is needed before distances can be judged accurately due to the diminished image. Mirrors should be fitted to both sides of the towing vehicle.

Motoring Clubs in Europe

The *Alliance Internationale de Tourisme (AIT)* is the largest confederation of touring associations in the world, and it is through this body that the AA is able to offer its members the widest possible touring information service. Its membership consists not of individuals, but of associations or groups of associations having an interest in touring. The Alliance was formed in 1919 – the AA was a founder member, and is represented on its Administrative Council and Management Committee. The General Secretariat of the **AIT** is in Geneva.

Tourists visiting a country where there is an **AIT** club may avail themselves of its touring advisory services upon furnishing proof of membership of their home **AIT** club. AA members making overseas trips should, whenever possible, seek the advice of the AA before setting out and should only approach the overseas **AIT** clubs when necessary.

Off-site camping

Apart from observing local regulations, you are strongly advised not to camp by the roadside and in isolated areas.

Overloading

This can create risks, and in most countries commiting such an offence can involve on-the-spot fines (see *Police fines* page **51**). You would also be made to reduce the load to an acceptable level before being allowed to continue your journey.

The maximum loaded weight, and its distribution between front and rear axles, is decided by the vehicle manufacturer, and if your owner's handbook does not give these facts you should contact the manufacturer direct. There is a public weighbridge in all districts, and when the car is fully loaded (not forgetting the passengers, of course) use this to check that the vehicle is within the limits.

Load your vehicle carefully so that no lights, reflectors, or number plates are masked, and the driver's view is not impaired. All luggage loaded on a roof rack must be tightly secured, and should not upset the stability of the vehicle. Any projections beyond the front, rear, or sides of a vehicle, that might not be noticed by other drivers, must be clearly marked.

Overtaking

When overtaking on roads with two lanes or more in each direction, always signal your intention in good time, and after the manoeuvre, signal and return to the inside lane. Do NOT remain in any other lane. Failure to comply with this regulation, particularly in France, will incur an on-the-spot fine (immediate deposit in France) – see *Police fines*, page **51**.

Always overtake on the left and use your horn to warn the driver of the vehicle being overtaken (except in areas where the use of a horn is prohibited). Do not overtake whilst being overtaken or when a vehicle behind is preparing to overtake. Do not overtake at level crossings, at intersections, the crest of a hill or at pedestrian crossings. When being overtaken, keep well to the right and reduce speed if necessary – *never increase speed.*

P

Parking

Parking is a problem everywhere in Europe, and the police are extremely strict with offenders. Heavy fines are inflicted, and unaccompanied offending cars can be towed away. Besides being inconvenient, heavy charges are imposed for the recovery of impounded vehicles. Find out about local parking regulations and make sure you understand all relative signs. As a rule, always park on the right-hand side of the road or at an authorised place. As far as possible, park off the main carriageway, but not in cycle or bus lanes.

Passengers *(See also Country sections)*

It is an offence in all countries to carry more passengers in a car than the vehicle is constructed to seat, and some have regulations as to how the passengers should be seated. Where such regulations are applied to visiting foreigners it will be mentioned in the *Country sections.*

For passenger-carrying vehicles constructed and equipped to carry more than 10 passengers, including the driver, there are special regulations (see *Minibus* page **49**).

Passports

Each person must hold, or be named on, an up-to-date passport valid for all the countries through which it is intended to travel.

Passports should be carried at all times when travelling outside the UK or Irish Republic and, as an extra precaution, a separate note kept of the number, date and place of issue. There are various types of British passport, including the standard or regular passport and the limited British Visitor's Passport. Standard UK passports are issued to British Nationals, *ie* British Citizens, British Dependent Territories Citizens, British Overseas Citizens, British Nationals (Overseas), British Subjects, and British Protected Persons. Normally issued for a period of 10 years, a standard UK passport is valid for travel to all countries in the world. A related passport may cover the holder and children under 16. Children under 16 may be issued with a separate passport valid for 5 years, and renewable for a further 5 years on application. Full information and application forms in respect of the standard UK passport may be obtained from a main Post Office or from one of the Passport Offices in Belfast, Douglas (Isle of Man), Glasgow, Liverpool, London, Newport (Gwent), Peterborough, St Helier (Jersey) and in St Peter Port (Guernsey). Application for a standard passport should be made to the Passport Office appropriate for the area concerned, allowing at least one month, or between February and August (when most people apply for passports) – three months, and should be accompanied by the requisite documents and fees.

British Visitor's Passports are issued to British Citizens, British Dependent Territories Citizens or British Overseas Citizens over the age of 8 resident in the UK, Isle of Man or Channel Islands. Valid for one year only and acceptable for travel in Western Europe. A British Visitor's Passport issued to cover the holder, spouse and children under 16 may only be used by the first person named on the passport to travel alone. Children under 8 cannot have their own Visitor's Passport. Full information and application forms may be obtained from main Post Offices in Great Britain (England, Scotland and Wales) or Passport Offices in the Channel Islands, Isle of Man and Northern Ireland. However, Visitor's Passports or application forms for Visitor's Passports are NOT obtainable from Passport Offices in Great Britain. All applications for a Visitor's Passport must be submitted *in person* to a main Post Office or Passport Office as appropriate. Provided the documents are in order the passport is issued immediately.

Irish citizens resident in the Dublin Metropolitan area or in Northern Ireland should apply to the Passport Office, Dublin; if resident elsewhere in the Irish Republic, they should apply through the nearest Garda station. Irish citizens resident in Britain should apply to the Irish Embassy in London.

Petrol

You will find comparable grades of petrol in all of the countries in this guide, with familiar brands available along the main routes. You will normally have to buy a minimum of 5 litres (just over a gallon) but it is wise to keep the tank topped up, particularly in more remote areas. Remember, when calculating mileage per gallon, that the extra weight of a caravan or roof rack increases petrol consumption. We would advise the use of a locking filler cap. Some garages may close between 12 noon and 3pm, but petrol is generally available, with 24 hour service on motorways.

Fuel grades. In Europe both unleaded and leaded petrol is graded as 'Normal' and 'Super' but if you are not sure how that compares to the grade you normally, use, look for the Octane rating. In the UK unleaded Premium grade is 95 octane and Super is 98 octane; for leaded petrol 2 star is 90 octane, 3 star is 93 octane and 4 star is 97 octane. Be careful to use the recommended type of fuel for your car, particularly if it is fitted with a catalytic converter, and use an octane which is the same or higher. If your car can only use leaded petrol and you accidentally fill up with unleaded – don't panic. It won't do any harm, but make sure you get it right next time.

If you are in any doubt about the kind of fuel to use ask the manufacturer or appointed agent.

Prices for petrol on motorways will normally be higher than elsewhere; self service pumps will be slightly cheaper. The current position on petrol prices can be checked with the AA. Concessions in the form of petrol coupons are available for Italy and the AA can provide information.

Importing petrol. The fuel in a vehicle tank is not liable for duty. Whilst it is usually a good idea to carry a reserve supply of fuel in a can, remember that on sea and air ferries and on European car-sleeper trains, spare cans *must* be empty. In Italy motorists are forbidden to carry petrol in cans in the vehicle.

Police fines

Some countries impose on-the-spot fines for minor traffic offences, which vary in amount according to the offence committed and the country concerned. Other countries, *eg* France, impose an immediate deposit, and subsequently levy a fine which may be the same as, or greater or lesser than, this sum. Fines are either paid in cash to the police, or at a local post office against a ticket issued by the police. They must usually be paid in the currency of the country concerned, and can vary in amount from £3–£690 (approximately). The reason for the fines is to penalise and, at the same time, keep minor motoring offences out of the courts. Disputing the fine usually leads to a court appearance, delays and additional expense. If the fine is not paid, legal proceedings will usually follow. Some countries immobilise vehicles until a fine is paid, and may sell it to pay the penalty imposed.

Once paid, a fine cannot be recovered, but a receipt should always be obtained as proof of payment. AA members who need assistance in any motoring matter involving local police should apply to the legal department of the revelant national motoring organisation.

Pollution

Tourists should be aware that pollution of the seawater at European coastal resorts, including the Mediterranean, may still represent a severe health hazard, although the general situation has improved in recent years. A number of countries publish detailed information on the quality of their bathing beaches, including maps, which are available from national authorities. Furthermore, in many, though not all, popular resorts where the water quality may present dangers, signs (generally small) are erected, which forbid bathing. These signs are as follows:

French

No bathing	Défense de se baigner
Bathing prohibited	Il est défendu de se baigner

Italian

No bathing	Vietato bagnàrsi
Bathing prohibited	Èvietato bagnàrsi

Spanish

No bathing	Prohibido bañarse
Bathing prohibited	Se prohibe bañarse

Poste restante

If you are uncertain of having a precise address, you can be contacted through the local *poste restante.* Before leaving the United Kingdom, notify your friends of your approximate whereabouts abroad at given times. If you expect mail, call with your passport at the main post office of the town where you are staying. To ensure that the arrival of correspondence will coincide with your stay, your correspondent should check with the Post Office before posting, as delivery times differ throughout Europe, and appropriate allowances must be made. It is important that the recipient's name be written in full: *eg* Mr. Richard Jarvis, Poste Restante, Sintra, Portugal. Do not use *Esq.*

Italy: Correspondence can be addressed, 'c/o post office' by adding *Fermo in Posta* to the name of the locality. It will be handed over at the local central post office upon identification of the addressee by passport.

Spain: Letters should be addressed as follows: names of addressee, *Lista de Correos,* name of town or village, name of province in brackets, if necessary. Letters can be collected from the main post office in the town concerned upon identification of the addressee by passport.

For all other countries letters should be addressed as in the above example.

Priority including roundabouts *(See also Country sections)*

The general rule is to ***give way to traffic entering a junction from the right***, but this is sometimes varied at roundabouts (see below). This is one aspect of European driving which may cause British drivers the most confusion, because their whole training and experience makes it unnatural. Road signs indicate priority or loss of priority, and tourists must be sure that they understand such signs.

Great care should be taken at intersections, and tourists should never rely on receiving the right of way, particularly in small towns and villages where local traffic, often slow moving, such as farm tractors, etc, will assume right of way regardless of oncoming traffic. Always give way to public services and military vehicles. Blind or disabled people, funerals and marching columns must always be allowed right of way. Vehicles such as buses and coaches carrying large numbers of passengers will expect, and should be allowed, priority.

Generally, priority at roundabouts is given to vehicles *entering* the roundabout unless signposted to the contrary (see *France*). This is a complete reversal of the United Kingdom and Republic of Ireland rule and particular care should be exercised when manoeuvring whilst circulating in an anti-clockwise direction on a roundabout. It is advisable to keep to the outside lane on a roundabout, if possible, to make your exit easier.

Radio telephone/Citizens' band radios and transmitters in tourist cars abroad

Many countries exercise controls on the temporary importation and subsequent use of radio transmitters and radio telephones. Therefore, if your vehicle contains such equipment, whether fitted or portable, you should contact the AA for guidance.

Registration document

You must carry the original vehicle registration document with you. If you do not have your registration document apply to a Vehicle Registration Office (in Northern Ireland a Local Vehicle Licensing Office) for a temporary *certificate of registration (V379)* to cover the period away. The address of your nearest Vehicle Registration Office can be obtained from a post office. You should apply well in advance of your journey as there could be delays of up to 2 weeks in issuing the certificate if you are not already recorded as the vehicle keeper. Proof of identity (*eg* driving licence) and proof of ownership (*eg* bill of sale), should be produced for the Vehicle Registration Office.

If you plan to use a borrowed, hired or leased vehicle, you should be aware that:

a for a borrowed vehicle, the registration document must be accompanied by a letter of authority to use the vehicle from the registered keeper

b for a UK registered hired or leased vehicle, the registration document will normally be retained by the hiring company. Under these circumstances, a *Hired/Leased Vehicle Certificate (VE103A)*, which may be purchased from the AA, should be used in its place (for Portugal, the certificate should be accompanied by an officially authenticated photocopy of the registration document).

Road signs

Most road signs throughout Europe are internationally agreed, and most will be familiar. Watch for road markings – do not cross a solid white or yellow line marked on the road centre. In *Belgium* there are two official languages, and signs will be in Flemish or French, see *Country Introduction* for further information. In the Basque and Catalonian areas of *Spain* local and national place names appear on signposts, see *Country Introduction* for further information.

Rule of the road

In all countries in this guide, drive on the right and overtake on the left.

Seat belts

All countries in this guide require wearing of seat belts.

Spares

The problem of what spares to carry is a difficult one; it depends on the vehicle and how long you are likely to be away. However, you should consider hiring an AA Emergency Repair Incident Kit; full information about this service is available from any AA Shop. AA Emergency Windscreens are also available for hire or purchase. In addition to the items contained in the Emergency Repair Incident Kit, the following are useful:

- ☐ a pair of windscreen wiper blades;
- ☐ a length of electrical cable;
- ☐ a roll of insulating or adhesive tape;
- ☐ a torch;
- ☐ a replacement fan belt.

Remember that when ordering spare parts for dispatch abroad, you must be able to identify them as clearly as possible, and by the manufacturer's part numbers if known. When ordering spares, always quote the engine and chassis numbers of your car. See also *Lights* page **48**.

Speed limits

It is important to observe speed limits at all times. Offenders may be fined, and driving licences confiscated on the spot, causing great inconvenience and possible expense. The standard legal limits are given in the appropriate Country sections for private cars and for car/caravan/trailer combinations, but these may be varied by road signs and where such signs are displayed the lower limit should be accepted. At certain times, limits may also be temporarily varied, and information should be available at the frontier. It can be an offence to travel at so slow a speed as to obstruct traffic flow without good reason.

Tolls

Tolls are payable on most motorways in France, Italy, Portugal, Spain and on sections in Austria. Charges on the French autoroutes are particularly expensive especially over long distances. For example, a single journey from Calais to Nice costs about £36 for a car and about £54 for a car with a caravan. Always have some currency of the country in which you are travelling ready to pay the tolls: as traveller's cheques etc, are ***not*** acceptable at toll booths.

Note: In Switzerland the authorities charge an annual motorway tax. See under *Motorway tax* in the Country Introduction for further information.

Tourist information *(See also Country sections)*

National Tourist Offices are especially equipped to deal with enquiries relating to their countries. They are particularly useful for information on current events, tourist attractions, car hire, equipment hire and specific activities such as skin-diving, gliding, horse-riding, etc. The offices in London (see Country sections for addresses) are most helpful, but the local offices overseas merit a visit when you arrive at your destination because they have information not available elsewhere.

Traffic lights

In principal cities and towns, traffic lights operate in a way similar to those in the United Kingdom, although they are sometimes suspended over the roadway. The density of the light may be so poor that lights could be missed – especially those overhead. There is usually only one set on the right-hand side of the road some distance before the road junction, and if you stop too close to the corner the lights will not be visible. Look out for 'filter' lights enabling you to turn right at a junction against the main lights. If you wish to go straight ahead, do not enter a lane leading to 'filter' lights or you may obstruct traffic wishing to turn right.

Trams

Trams take priority over other vehicles. Always give way to passengers boarding and alighting. Never position a vehicle so that it impedes the free passage of a tram. Trams must be overtaken on the ***right***, except in one-way streets.

Traveller's cheques

We recommend that you take Traveller's Cheques. You can use them like cash, or change them for currency in just about any country in the world.

Tyres

Inspect your tyres carefully; if you think they are likely to be more than three-quarters worn before you get back, it is better to replace them before you leave. If you notice uneven wear, scuffed treads, or damaged walls, expert advice should be sought on whether the tyres are suitable for further use. In some European countries, drivers can be fined if tyres are badly worn. The regulations in the UK governing tyres call for a minimum tread depth of 1mm over 75 per cent of the width of the tyre all around the circumference, with the original tread pattern clearly visible on the remainder. European regulations are stricter: a minimum tread depth of 1mm or 1.6mm over the whole width of the tyre around the circumference.

If you are towing a caravan, find out the recommended tyre pressures suitable for the extra load from the manufacturer. They will vary according to type, size and ply-rating of the tyres. If a lot of high speed driving is anticipated, check that the ply-rating is adequate. The rear tyre pressures, for example, may have to be increased by 2–3lb per square inch. Pressures can only be checked accurately when the tyres are cold. Do not forget the spare tyre.

V

Vehicle excise licence

When taking a vehicle out of the UK for a temporary visit (*eg* holiday or business trip) you must remember that the vehicle excise licence (tax disc) needs to be valid on your return. Therefore, if your tax disc is due to expire whilst you are abroad, you may apply by post to the Post Office* for a tax disc before you leave up to 42 days in advance of the expiry date of your present disc. You should explain why you want the tax disc in advance, and ask for it to be posted to you before you leave, or to an address you will be staying at abroad. However, your application form must always be completed with your UK address.

To find out which Post Office in your area offers this service, you should contact the Post Office Customer Service Unit on the number listed in your local telephone directory.

*Residents of Northern Ireland must apply to the Vehicle Licensing Central Office, County Hall, Coleraine BT51 3HS.

Visa

A visa is not normally required by United Kingdom and Republic of Ireland passport holders when visiting Western European countries for periods of three months or less. However, if you hold a passport of any other nationality, a UK passport not issued in this country, or are in any doubt at all about your position you should check with the Embassies or Consulates of the countries you intend to visit.

Visitors' registration

All visitors to a country must register with the local police. This formality is usually satisfied by the completion of a card or certificate when booking into a hotel, campsite or places offering accommodation. If staying with friends or relatives it is usually the responsibility of the host to seek advice from the police within 24 hours of the arrival of guests.

For short holiday visits, the formalities are very simple, but most countries place a time limit on the period that tourists may stay, after which a firmer type of registration is imposed. If you intend staying in any one country for longer than three months (*Portugal,* 60 days*) you should make the appropriate enquiries before departure from the UK.

*Visitors wishing to stay in Portugal for more than 60 days must apply in person for an extension to the

Serviço de Estrangeiros (Foreigners' Registration Service), 1200 Lisboa, Av Antonio Augusto de Aguiar 20 ✆ 7141027/7141179. Applications must be made before expiry of the authorised period of stay. The cost is *Esc* 1,500.

Warm-climate touring

In hot weather, and at high altitudes excessive heat in the engine compartment can cause carburation problems. It is advisable, if you are towing a caravan, to consult the manufacturers of your towing vehicle about the limitations of the cooling system, and the operating temperature of the gearbox fluid if automatic transmission is fitted (see *Automatic gearboxes* page **40**).

Warning triangles/Hazard warning lights *(See also Country sections)*

The use of a warning triangle is compulsory in most European countries, and is always a wise precaution. It should be placed on the road behind a stopped vehicle to warn traffic approaching from the rear of an obstruction ahead. The triangle should be used when a vehicle has stopped for any reason – not just breakdowns. It should be placed in such a position as to be clearly visible up to 100m (110yds) by day and night, about 2ft from the edge of the road, but not in such a position as to present a danger to on-coming traffic. It should be set up about 30m (33yds) behind the obstruction, but this distance should be increased to 100m (110yds) on motorways. A warning triangle is not required for two-wheeled vehicles.

An AA Warning Triangle, which complies with the latest international and European standards, can be purchased from the AA. Alternatively, a warning triangle can form part of the Emergency Repair Incident Kit which may be hired from the AA.

Although four flashing indicators are allowed in the countries covered by this Guide, they in no way affect the regulations governing the use of warning triangles. Generally, hazard warning lights should not be used in place of a triangle, although they may complement it. See the Country Introductions to France, Netherlands and Switzerland. See also *Breakdown* page **41**.

Weather information, including winter conditions

UK regional weather reports (followed by a 2-day forecast) and European forecasts are provided by the **AA Weatherwatch** recorded information service. The **AA Roadwatch** service also provides UK weather reports with its traffic and roadworks information. **Continental Roadwatch** provides ferry news, road conditions to and from the ferry ports and details of any adverse Continental weather. See page **56** for numbers and charges.

The **Met. Office Weather Centres** listed below can also provide local, national and Continental forecasts, but **not** direct information about road conditions. These are busy offices and their numbers are often engaged – particularly when the weather is bad. A charge may be made for answering complex or lengthy enquiries. The *Advisory Service* of the Met. Office, London Road, Bracknell, Berks RG12 2SZ can provide worldwide climatic information, but will make a charge for answering lengthy or complex enquiries.

Aberdeen
Seaforth Centre, Lime Street
✆ (0224) 210574

Belfast *(telephone calls only)* ✆ (08494) 22339

Bristol
The Gaunts House, Denmark Street
✆ (0272) 279298

Birmingham
✆ 021-782 4747

Cardiff
Southgate House, Wood Street
✆ (0222) 397020

Glasgow
33 Bothwell Street
✆ 041-248 3451

Leeds
Oak House, Park Lane
✆ (0532) 451990

London
284–286 High Holborn
✆ 071-836 4311

Manchester
Exchange Street, Stockport
✆ 061-477 1060

Newcastle upon Tyne
7th Floor, Newgate House, Newgate Street
✆ 091-232 6453

Norwich
Rouen House, Rouen Road
✆ (0603) 660779

Nottingham
Main Road, Watnall
✆ (0602) 384092

Plymouth *(telephone calls only)*
✆ (0752) 402534

Southampton
160 High Street-below-bar
✆ (0703) 228844

Full details of the Met. Office Weather Centre being established in Birmingham are not yet available.

If you require information about climate when abroad and are an AA member contact the nearest office of the appropriate national motoring club for weather details (see *Country sections*). It is advisable to check on conditions ahead as you go along, and campsites and garages are often helpful in this respect.

Winter conditions: Motoring in Europe during the winter months is restricted because of the vast mountain ranges – the Alps sweeping in an arc from the French Riviera, through Switzerland, Northern Italy and Austria to the borders of Yugoslavia; the Pyrénées which divide France and Spain, as well as extensive areas of Spain and France. However, matters have been eased with improved communications and modern snow-clearing apparatus.

Reports on the accessibility of mountain passes in Austria, France, Italy and Switzerland are received by the AA from the *European Road Information Centre* in Geneva. Additionally, during the winter months, and also under certain weather conditions, the AA in France collect information regarding the state of approach roads to the Continental Channel ports. AA members can obtain information during office hours by ringing ✆ (0345) 500 600 or enquiring at the **AA Port Shop** before embarking.

Details of road and rail tunnels which can be used to pass under the mountains are given on pages **58–60** and the periods when the most important mountain passes are usually closed are detailed on pages **61–70**. If you want a conventional seaside holiday between October and March, you will probably have to travel at least as far south as Lisbon, Valencia, or Naples to be reasonably certain of fine weather. Further information on this subject is given in the leaflet entitled *Continental Weather and Motoring in Winter* which is available from the AA.

ROUTE PLANNING

EUROPEAN ROUTES SERVICE

Individually Prepared Routes to Your Own Requirements

The AA's Overseas Routes Unit has a comprehensive and unique database of road and route information built into the very latest computerised equipment. The database holds all the relevant information needed for an enjoyable trouble-free route, including distances in miles and kilometres for estimating journey times. A prepared route gives route numbers, road signs to follow, motorway services, landmarks, road and town descriptions, frontier opening times, etc.

Overseas Routes can supply you with any route you may require: scenic routes – direct routes – by-way routes – fast routes – coach routes – caravan routes – motorway routes – non-motorway routes – touring routes – special interest routes – and more.

You may believe you know the best route – we can confirm if you are correct or tell you if we believe you are wrong, and probably save you time and money.

Can we help you further?

If we can please contact any AA Shop for a European Route Application form. Telephone Overseas Routes for credit card requests on (0272) 308242/3, or complete the application form below, and we will send you full details of the European Routes Service and the prices charged.

Send the form below to:
Overseas Routes, The Automobile Association, Fanum House, Basingstoke RG21 2EA.

Application form for details of the European Routes Services

Complete in BLOCK CAPITALS

Mr/Mrs/Ms/Miss/Title: ______________ Initials: ______________ Surname: ______________

Address: ____

____

____

______________________________ Postcode: ______________________

Membership number (or 5-Star number): ______________________________

Date of request: ______________________________

(If you are not a Member of the AA an additional fee is payable unless you have paid the 5-Star non-member's service fee.)

Countries/places to be visited: ______________________________

____

Date of departure: ______________________________

MAJOR ROAD AND RAIL TUNNELS

See *Lights* page 48. There are also minimum and maximum speed limits in operation in the tunnels. **All charges listed below should be used as a guide only.**

Bielsa *(France – Spain)*

The trans-Pyrénéan tunnel is 3km (2 miles) long, and runs nearly 6,000ft above sea level between Aragnouet and Bielsa. The tunnel is usually closed from October to Easter.

Cadí *(Spain)*

The tunnel is 5km (3 miles) long and runs at about 4,000ft above sea level under the Sierra del Cadí mountain range between the villages of Bellver de Cerdanya and Bagá, and to the west of the Toses (Tosas) Pass.

Charges *(in Pesetas)*

	Single
Cars (with or without caravan)	**661**

Fréjus *France – Italy*

This tunnel is over 4,000ft above sea level and runs between Modane and Bardonecchia. The tunnel is 12.8km (8 miles) long, 4.5m (14ft 9in) high, and the single carriageway is 9m (29ft 6in) wide. The minimum speed is 60kph (37mph) and the maximum 80kph (49mph).

Charges (in French francs)
The tolls are calculated on the wheelbase:

Motorcycles		**73**
Cars	wheelbase less than 2.30m (7ft 6½in)	**73**
	wheelbase from 2.30m but less than 2.63m (7ft 6½in to 8ft 7½in)	**110**
	wheelbase from 2.63m to a maximum of 3.30m (8ft 7½in to 10ft 10in)	**144**
	caravans	**144**
	wheelbase over 3.30m (10ft 10in)	**360**
Vehicles	with three axles	**548**
	with four or more axles	**730**

Mont Blanc *Chamonix (France) – Courmayeur (Italy)*

The tunnel is over 4,000ft above sea level and is 11.6km (7 miles) long. Customs and passport control are at the Italian end. The permitted maximum dimensions of vehicles are: height 4.20m (13ft 9in); length 19m (62ft 4in); width 2.60m (8ft 5in). Total weight: 35 metric tons (34 tons 9cwt); axle weight 13 metric tons (12 tons 16cwt). The minimum speed is 50kph (31 mph) and the maximum 70kph (43mph). Do not stop, overtake, sound your horn or make U-turns. Use only side/rear lights not headlights and keep 100m (110yds) distance between vehicles.

Make sure you have sufficient petrol for the journey, 30km (19 miles). There are breakdown bays with telephones. From November to March, wheel chains may occasionally be required on the approaches to the tunnel.

Charges *(in French francs)*
The tolls are calculated according to the wheelbase:

		Single
Motorcycles		**75**
Cars	wheelbase less than 2.30m (7ft 6½in)	**75**
	wheelbase from 2.30m but less than 2.63m (7ft 6½in to 8ft 7½in)	**110**
	wheelbase from 2.63m to a maximum of 3.30m (8ft 7½in to 10ft 10in)	**145**
Caravans		**145**
	wheelbase over 3.30m (10ft 10in)	**365**
Vehicles	with three axles	**530**
	with four, or more axles	**730**

Grand St Bernard *Switzerland – Italy*

The tunnel is over 6,000ft above sea level; although there are covered approaches, wheel chains may be needed to reach it in winter. The Customs, passport control and toll offices are at the entrance. The tunnel is 5.9km (3½ miles) long. The permitted maximum dimensions of vehicles are: height 4m (13ft 1in), width 2.5m (8ft 2½in). The minimum speed is 40kph (24mph) and the maximum 80kph (49mph). Do not stop or overtake. There are breakdown bays with telephones on either side.

Charges *(in Swiss francs)*
The tolls are calculated according to the wheelbase:

		Single
Motorcycles		**16**
Cars	wheelbase less than 2.30m (7ft 6½in)	**16**
	wheelbase from 2.30m but less than 2.63m (7ft 6½in to 8ft 7½in)	**23.50**
	wheelbase from 2.63m to a maximum of 3.30m (8ft 7½in to 10ft 10in)	**32**
	caravans	**32**
	wheelbase over 3.30m (10ft 10in)	**61**
Vehicles	with three axles	**80.50**
	with four, or more axles	**120**

St Gotthard *Switzerland*

The world's longest road tunnel at 16.3km (10 miles) is about 3,800ft above sea level; it runs under the St Gotthard Pass from Göschenen, on the northern side of the Alps, to Airolo in the Ticino. The tunnel is 4.5m (14ft 9in) high, and the single carriageway is 7.5m (25ft) wide. The maximum speed is 80kph (49mph). Forming part of the Swiss national motorway network, the tunnel is subject to the annual motorway tax, and the tax disc must be displayed (see *Switzerland – Motorway tax*).

From December to February, wheel chains may occasionally be required on the approaches to the tunnel, but they are **NOT** allowed to be used in the tunnel. (Laybys are available for the removal and refitting of wheel chains.)

San Bernardino *Switzerland*

This tunnel is over 5,000ft above sea level. It is 6.6km (4 miles) long, 4.8m (15ft 9in) high, and the carriageway is 7m (23ft) wide. Do not stop or overtake in the tunnel. Keep 100m (110yds) between vehicles. There are breakdown bays with telephones. Forming part of the Swiss national motorways network, the tunnel is subject to the annual motorway tax, and the tax disc must be displayed (see *Switzerland – Motorway tax*).

From November to March, wheel chains may occasionally be required on the approaches to the tunnel.

Arlberg *Austria*

This tunnel is 14km (8¾ miles) long and runs at about 4,000ft above sea level, to the south of and parallel to the Arlberg Pass.

Charges
The toll charges for cars (with or without caravans) are **150** *Austrian schillings*; motorcycles **100** *Austrian schillings.*

Bosruck *Austria*

This tunnel is 2,434ft above sea level. It is 5.5km (3½ miles) long and runs between Spital am Pyhrn and Selzthal, to the east of the Pyhrn Pass. With the Gleinalm Tunnel (see below) it forms an important part of the A9 Pyhrn Autobahn between Linz and Graz, now being built in stages.

Charges *(in Austrian schillings)*

	Single
Cars	**70**
Motorcycles	**60**

Felbertauern *Austria*

This tunnel is over 5,000ft above sea level; it runs between Mittersill and Matrei, west of and parallel to the Grossglockner Pass.

The tunnel is 5.3km (3¼ miles) long, 4.5m (14ft 9in) high, and the two-lane carriageway is 7m (23ft) wide. From November to April, wheel chains may be needed on the approach to the tunnel.

Charges *(in Austrian schillings)*

		Single
Cars	summer rate (May–Oct)	**180**
	winter rate (Nov–Apr)	**110**
Motorcycles		**100**
Caravans		**40**

Gleinalm *Austria*

This tunnel is 2,680ft above sea level; it is 8.3km (5 miles) long and runs between St Michael and Friesach, near Graz. The tunnel forms part of the A9 Pyhrn Autobahn which will, in due course, run from Linz, via Graz, to Yugoslavia.

Charges *(in Austrian schillings)*

	Single
Cars	**130**
Motorcycles	**100**
Caravans	**40**

Tauern Autobahn (*Katschberg* and *Radstädter*) *Austria*

Two tunnels, the Katschberg and the Radstädter Tauern, form the key elements of this toll motorway between Salzburg and Carinthia.

The **Katschberg** tunnel is 3,642ft above sea level. It is 5.4km (3½ miles) long, 4.5m (14ft 9in) high, and the two-lane carriageway is 7.5m (25ft) wide.

The **Radstädter Tauern** tunnel is 4,396ft above sea level and runs to the east of and parallel to the Tauern railway tunnel (see page 60). The tunnel is 6.4km (4 miles) long, 4.5m (14ft 9in) high and the two-lane carriageway is 7.5m (25ft) wide.

On both sections a second tunnel is being built to allow for dual-carriageway throughout. This should be completed by 1993.

Charges *(in Austrian schillings) for the whole toll section between Flachau and Rennweg:*

		Single
Cars	summer rate (May–Oct)	**190**
	winter rate (Nov–Apr)	**120**
Motorcycles		**100**
Caravans		**40**

Switzerland and Switzerland – Italy

Vehicles are conveyed throughout the year through the **Simplon** Tunnel (Brig–Iselle) and the **Lötschberg** tunnel (Kandersteg–Goppenstein). It is also possible to travel all the way from Kandesteg to Iselle by rail via both Tunnels, total journey time is about 1–1½ hours. Services are frequent with no advance booking necessary; the actual transit time is 15/20 minutes for each tunnel but loading and unloading formalities can take some time.

A full timetable and tariff list which is available from the *Swiss National Tourist Office* (see *Switzerland – Tourist information* for address) or at most Swiss frontier crossings.

Albula Tunnel *Switzerland*

Thussis (2,372ft)–**Samedan** (5,650ft)
The railway tunnel is 5.9km (3½ miles) long. Motor vehicles can be conveyed through the tunnel, but you are recommended to give notice. **Thusis** ✆ (081) 811113 and **Samedan** ✆ (082) 65404. Journey duration 90 minutes.

Services
9 trains daily going *south*; 6 trains daily going *north*.

Charges
Given in *Swiss francs* and likely to increase

Cars (including driver)	77
Additional passengers	12
Car and caravan	154

Furka Tunnel *Switzerland*

Oberwald (4,482ft)–**Realp** (5,046ft)
The railway tunnel is 15.3km (9½ miles) long. Journey duration 20 minutes.

Services
Hourly from 06.50–21.00hrs

Charges
These are in *Swiss Francs*

Cars (including passengers)	20
Car and caravan	36

Oberalp Railway *Switzerland*

Andermatt (4,737ft)–**Sedrun** (4,728ft). Journey duration 50 minutes.

Booking
Advance booking is necessary **Andermatt** ✆ (044) 67220 and **Sedrun** ✆ (086) 91137.

Services
2–4 trains daily, winter only (October–April).

Charges
These are in *Swiss francs*

Cars (including driver)	56
Additional passengers	9
Car and caravan	112

Tauern Tunnel *Austria*

Böckstein (3,711ft) (near Badgastein)–**Mallnitz**, 8.5km (5½ miles) long.

Maximum dimensions for caravans and trailers: height 8ft 10½in, width 8ft 2½in.

Booking
Advance booking is unnecessary (except for request trains), but motorists must report at least 30 minutes before the train is due to depart. Drivers must drive their vehicles on and off the wagon.

Services
At summer weekends, trains run approximately every half-hour in both directions. 06.30–22.30hrs; and every half-hour during the night. During the rest of the year, there is an hourly service from 06.30–22.30hrs (23.30hrs on Friday and Saturday between 7 July–9 September). Journey duration 12 minutes.

Charges
These are given in *Austrian schillings* and are for a single journey.

Cars (including passengers)	160
Motorcycles (with or without sidecar)	70
Caravans	60

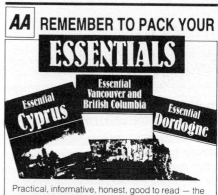

PRINCIPAL MOUNTAIN PASSES

It is best not to attempt to cross mountain passes at night, and daily schedules should make allowances for the comparatively slow speeds inevitable in mountainous areas.

Gravel surfaces (such as dirt and stone chips) vary considerably; they are dusty when dry, slippery when wet. Where known to exist, this type of surface has been noted. Road repairs can be carried out only during the summer, and may interrupt traffic. Precipitous sides are rarely, if ever, totally unguarded; on the older roads, stone pillars are placed at close intervals. Gradient figures take the mean figure on hairpin bends, and may be steeper on the insides of the curves, particularly on the older roads.

Conversion table gradients

All steep hill signs show the grade in percentage terms. The following conversion table may be used as a guide:

30%	1 in 3
25%	1 in 4
20%	1 in 5
16%	1 in 6
14%	1 in 7
12%	1 in 8
11%	1 in 9
10%	1 in 10

Before attempting late evening or early morning journeys across frontier passes, check the times of opening of the Customs offices. A number close at night, *eg* the Timmelsjoch border, closed between 20.00 and 07.00hrs and throughout the winter.

Always engage a low gear before either ascending or descending steep gradients, keep well to the right-hand side of the road and avoid cutting corners. Avoid excessive use of brakes. If the engine overheats, pull off the road, making sure that you do not cause an obstruction, leave the engine idling, and put the heater controls, including the fan, into the maximum heat position. Under no circumstances remove the radiator cap until the engine has cooled down. Do not fill the coolant system of a hot engine with cold water.

Always engage a lower gear before taking a hairpin bend, give priority to vehicles ascending and remember that, as your altitude increases, so your engine power decreases. Priority must always be given to postal coaches travelling in either direction. Their route is usually signposted.

Caravans

Passes suitable for caravans are indicated in the Table (pages **62–90**). Those shown to be negotiable by caravans are best used only by experienced drivers in cars with ample power. The remainder are probably best avoided. A correct power-to-load ratio is always essential.

Conditions in winter

Winter conditions are given in italics in the last column. *UO* means usually open although a severe fall of snow may temporarily obstruct the road for 24–48 hours, and wheel chains are often necessary; *OC* means occasionally closed between the dates stated. Dates for opening and closing the passes are approximate only. Warning notices are usually posted at the foot of a pass if it is closed, or if chains or snow tyres should or must be used.

Wheel chains may be needed early and late in the season, and between short spells (a few hours) of obstruction. At these times, conditions are usually more difficult for caravans.

In fair weather, wheel chains or snow tyres are only necessary on the higher passes, but in severe weather you will probably need to use them (as a rough guide) at altitudes exceeding 2,000ft.

PRINCIPAL MOUNTAINS PASSES

Pass and height	From To	Distances from summit and max gradient		Min width of road	Conditions (see page 61) for key to abbreviations
***Albula** 7,595ft (2315m) Switzerland	Tiefencastel (2,821ft) La Punt (5,546ft)	30km 9km	1 in 10 1 in 10	12ft	*UC Nov–early Jun.* An inferior alternative to the Julier; tar and gravel; fine scenery . Alternative rail tunnel.
Allos 7,328ft (2250m) France	Barcelonnette (3,740ft) Colmars (4,058ft)	20km 24km	1 in 10 1 in 12	13ft	*UC early Nov–early Jun.* Very winding, narrow, mostly unguarded but not difficult otherwise; passing bays on southern slope, poor surface *(maximum width vehicles 5ft 11in).*
Aprica 3,858ft (1176m) Italy	Tresenda (1,220ft) Edolo (2,264ft)	14km 15km	1 in 11 1 in 16	13ft	*UO.* Fine scenery; good surface, well graded; *suitable for caravans*
Aravis 4,915ft (1498m) France	La Clusaz (3,412ft) Flumet (3,008ft)	8km 12km	1 in 11 1 in 11	13ft	*OC Dec–Mar.* Outstanding scenery, and a fairly easy road.
Arlberg 5,912ft (1802m) Austria	Bludenz (1,905ft) Landeck (2,677ft)	35km 35km	1 in 8 1 in $7\frac{1}{2}$	20ft	*OC Dec–Apr.* Modern road; short, steep stretch from west easing towards the summit; heavy traffic; parallel toll road tunnel available. *Suitable for caravans*; using tunnel (see page 59). Pass road closed to vehicles towing *trailers.*
Aubisque 5,610ft (1710m) France	Eaux Bonnes (2,461ft) Argelès-Gazost (1,519ft)	11km 32km	1 in 10 1 in 10	11ft	*UC mid Oct–Jun.* A very winding road; continuous but easy ascent; the descent incorporates the Col de Soulor (4,757ft); 8km of very narrow, rough, unguarded road, with a steep drop.
Ballon d'Alsace 3,865ft (1178m) France	Giromagny (1,830ft) St-Maurice-sur-Moselle (1,800ft)	17km 9km	1 in 9 1 in 9	13ft	*OC Dec–Mar.* A fairly straightforward ascent and descent, but numerous bends; *negotiable by caravans.*
Bayard 4,094ft (1248m) France	Chauffayer (2,988ft) Gap (2,382ft)	18km 8km	1 in 12 1 in 7	20ft	*UO.* Part of the Route Napoléon. Fairly easy, steepest on the southern side with several hairpin bends; *negotiable by caravans* from north to south.
***Bernina** 7,644ft (2330m) Switzerland	Pontresina (5,915ft) Poschiavo (3,317ft)	15.5km 18km	1 in 10 1 in 8	16ft	*OC Dec–Mar.* A good road on both sides; *negotiable by caravans.*
Bonalgua 6,797ft (2072m) Spain	Viella (3,150ft) Esterri d'Aneu (3,140ft)	23km 21km	1 in 12 1 in 12	14ft	*UC Nov–Apr.* A sinuous and narrow road with many hairpin bends and some precipitous drops; the alternative route to Lleida (Lérida) through the Viella tunnel is open in winter.
Bracco 2,011ft (613m) Italy	Riva Trigoso (141ft) Borghetto di Vara (318ft)	15km 18km	1 in 7 1 in 7	16ft	*UO.* A two-lane road with continuous bends; passing usually difficult; *negotiable by caravans;* alternative toll motorway available.
Brenner 4,508ft (1374m) Austria–Italy	Innsbruck (1,883ft) Vipiteno (3,110ft)	38km 15km	1 in 12 1 in 7	20ft	*UO.* Parallel toll motorway open; heavy traffic may delay at Customs; *suitable for caravans using toll motorway.* Pass road closed to vehicles towing *trailers.*
†Brünig 3,340ft (1007m) Switzerland	Brienzwiler Station (1,886ft) Giswil (1,601ft)	6km 13km	1 in 12 1 in 12	20ft	*UO.* An easy but winding road; heavy traffic at weekends; *suitable for caravans.*

*Permitted maximum width of vehicles 7ft 6in

†Permitted maximum width of vehicles 8ft $2\frac{1}{2}$in

Pass and height	From To	Distances from summit and max gradient		Min width of road	Conditions (see page 61) for key to abbreviations
Bussang 2,365ft (721m) France	Thann (1,115ft)	22km	1 in 10	13ft	*UO*. A very easy road over the Vosges; beautiful scenery; *suitable for caravans.*
	St-Maurice-sur-Moselle (1,800ft)	8km	1 in 14		
Cabre 3,871ft (1180m) France	Luc-en-Diois (1,870ft)	22km	1 in 11	18ft	*UO*. An easy pleasant road; *suitable for caravans.*
	Aspres-sur-Buëch (2,497ft)	17km	1 in 14		
Campolongo 6,152ft (1875m) Italy	Corvara in Badia (5,145ft)	6km	1 in 8	16ft	*OC Dec–Mar*. A winding but easy ascent; long level stretch on summit followed by easy descent; good surface; *suitable for caravans.*
	Arabba (5,253ft)	4km	1 in 8		
Cayolle 7,631ft (2326m) France	Barcelonette (3,740ft)	32km	1 in 10	13ft	*UC early Nov–early Jun*. Narrow and winding road with hairpin bends; poor surface and broken edges; steep drops. Long stretches of single-track road with passing places.
	Guillaumes (2,687ft)	33km	1 in 10		
Costalunga (Karer) 5,751ft (1753m) Italy	Cardano (925ft)	24km	1 in 8	16ft	*OC Dec–Apr*. A good well-engineered road but mostly winding; *caravans prohibited.*
	Pozza (4,232ft)	10km	1 in 7		
Croix 5,833ft (1778m) Switzerland	Villars-sur-Ollon (4,111ft)	8km	1 in 7½	11ft	*UC Nov–May*. A narrow and winding route but extremely picturesque.
	Les Diablerets (3,789ft)	9km	1 in 11		
Croix-Haute 3,858ft (1176m) France	Monestier-de-Clermont (2,776ft)	36km	1 in 14	18ft	*UO*. Well-engineered; several hairpin bends on the north side; *suitable for caravans.*
	Aspres-sur-Buëch (2,497ft)	28km	1 in 14		
Envallra 7,897ft (2407m) Andorra	Pas de la Casa (6,851ft)	5km	1 in 10	20ft	*OC Nov–Apr*. A good road with wide bends on ascent and descent; fine views; *negotiable by caravans* (max height vehicles 11ft 6in on northern approach near L'Hospitalet).
	Andorra (3,375ft)	29km	1 in 8		
Falzárego 6,945ft (2117m) Italy	Cortina d'Ampezzo (3,983ft)	17km	1 in 12	16ft	*OC Dec–Apr*. Well-engineered bitumen surface; many hairpin bends on both sides; *negotiable by caravans.*
	Andraz (4,622ft)	9km	1 in 12		
Faucille 4,341ft (1323m) France	Gex (1,985ft)	11km	1 in 10	16ft	*UO*. Fairly wide, winding road across the Jura mountains; *negotiable by caravans*, but it is probably better to follow La Cure–St-Cerque–Nyon.
	Morez (2,247ft)	28km	1 in 12		
Fern 3,967ft (1209m) Austria	Nassereith (2,766ft)	9km	1 in 10	20ft	*UO*. An easy pass, but slippery when wet; heavy traffic at summer weekends; *suitable for caravans.*
	Lermoos (3,244ft)	10km	1 in 10		
Flexen 5,853ft (1784m) Austria	Lech (4,747ft)	6.5km	1 in 10	18ft	*UO*. The magnificent 'Flexenstrasse', a well-engineered mountain road with tunnels and galleries. The road from Lech to Warth, north of the pass, is usually closed between November and April due to danger of avalanches.
	Rauzalpe (near Arlberge Pass) (5,341ft)	3.5km	1 in 10		

PRINCIPAL MOUNTAINS PASSES

Pass and height	From To	Distances from summit and max gradient		Min width of road	Conditions (see page 61) for key to abbreviations
***Flüela** 7,818ft (2383m) Switzerland	Davos-Dorf (5,174ft)	13km	1 in 10	16ft	*OC Nov–May.* Easy ascent from Davos; some acute hairpin bends on the eastern side; bitumen surface; *negotiable by caravans.*
	Susch (4,659ft)	13km	1 in 8		
†Forclaz 5,010ft (1527m) Switzerland France	Martigny (1,562ft)	13km	1 in 12	16ft	*UO Forclaz; OC Montets Dec–early Apr.* A good road over the pass and to the frontier; in France, narrow and rough over Col des Montets (4,793ft); *negotiable by caravans.*
	Argentière (4,111ft)	19km	1 in 12		
Foscagno 7,516ft (2291m) Italy	Bormio (4,019ft)	24km	1 in 8	11ft	*OC Nov–Apr.* Narrow and winding through lonely mountains, generally poor surface. Long winding ascent with many blind bends; not always well guarded. The descent includes winding rise and fall over the Passo d'Eira (7,218ft).
	Livigno (5,958ft)	14km	1 in 8		
Fugazze 3,802ft (1159m) Italy	Rovereto (660ft)	27km	1 in 7	10ft	*UO.* Very winding with some narrow sections, particularly on northern side. The many blind bends and several hairpin bends call for extra care.
	Vali del Pasubio (1,148ft)	12km	1 in 7		
***Furka** 7,976ft (2431m) Switzerland	Gietzch (5,777ft)	10km	1 in 10	13ft	*UC Oct–Jun.* A well-graded road, with narrow sections and several sharp hairpin bends on both ascent and descent. Fine views of the Rhône Glacier. Alternative rail tunnel available.
	Realp (5,046ft)	13km	1 in 10		
Galibier 8,678ft (2645m) France	Lautaret Pass (6,752ft)	7km	1 in 14	10ft	*UC Oct–Jun.* Mainly wide, well-surfaced but unguarded. Ten hairpin bends on descent then 5km narrow and rough. Rise over the Col du Télégraphe (5,249ft), then eleven more hairpin bends. (Tunnel under the Galibier summit is closed.)
	St-Michel-de-Maurienne (2,336ft)	34km	1 in 8		
Gardena (Grödner-Joch) 6,959ft (2121m) Italy	Val Gardena (6,109ft)	6km	1 in 8	16ft	*OC Dec–Jun.* A well-engineered road, very winding on descent.
	Corvara in Badia (5,145ft)	10km	1 in 8		
Gavia 8,599ft (2621m) Italy	Bormio (4,019ft)	25km	1 in 5½	10ft	*UC Oct–Jul.* Steep and narrow, but with frequent passing bays; many hairpin bends and a gravel surface; not for the faint-hearted; extra care necessary. *(Maximum width, vehicles 5ft 11in.)*
	Ponte di Legno (4,140ft)	16km	1 in 5½		
Gerlos 5,341ft (1628m) Austria	Zell am Ziller (1,886ft)	29km	1 in 12	14ft	*UO.* Hairpin ascent out of Zell to modern toll road; the old, steep, narrow, and winding route with passing bays and 1-in-7 gradient is not recommended, but is negotiable with care; *caravans prohibited.*
	Wald (2,904ft)	15km	1 in 11		
†Grand St Bernard 8,114ft (2473m) Switzerland–Italy	Martigny (1,562ft)	44km	1 in 9	13ft	*UC Oct–Jun.* Modern road to entrance of road tunnel (usually open; see page **58**) then narrow but bitumen surface over summit to frontier; also good in Italy; *suitable for caravans* using tunnel. Pass road closed to vehicles towing *trailers.*
	Aosta (1913ft)	33km	1 in 9		
***Grimsel** 7,100ft (2164km) Switzerland	Innerkirchen (2,067ft)	25km	1 in 10	16ft	*UC mid Oct–late Jun.* A fairly easy, modern road, but heavy traffic at weekends. A long winding ascent, finally hairpin bends; then a terraced descent with six hairpins into the Rhône valley.
	Gletsch (5,777ft)	6km	1 in 10		
Grossflockner 8,212ft (2503m) Austria	Bruck an der Glocknerstrasse (2,480ft)	33km	1 in 8	16ft	*UC late Oct–early May.* Numerous well-engineered hairpin bends; moderate but very long ascent, toll road; very fine scenery; heavy tourist traffic; *negotiable preferably from south to north, by caravans.*
	Heiligenblut (4,268ft)	15m	1 in 8		

*Permitted maximum width of vehicles 7ft 6in
†Permitted maximum width of vehicles 8ft 2½in

Pass and height	From To	Distances from summit and max gradient		Min width of road	Conditions (see page 61) for key to abbreviations
Hochtannberg 5,509ft (1679m) Austria	Schröcken (4,163ft)	5.5km	1 in 7	13ft	*OC Jan–Mar.* A reconstructed modern road.
	Warth (near Lech) (4,921ft)	4.5km	1 in 11		
Ibañeta (Roncesvalles) 3,468ft (1057m) France–Spain	St-Jean-Pied-de-Port (548ft)	26km	1 in 10	13ft	*UO.* A slow and winding, scenic route; *negotiable by caravans.*
	Pamplona (1,380ft)	52km	1 in 10		
Iseran 9,088ft (2770m) France	Bourg-St-Maurice (2,756ft)	49km	1 in 12	13ft	*UC mid Oct–late Jun.* The second highest pass in the Alps. Well-graded with reasonable bends, average surface; several unlit tunnels on northern approach.
	Lanslebourg (4,587ft)	33km	1 in 9		
Izoard 7,743ft (2360m) France	Guillestre (3,248ft)	32km	1 in 8	16ft	*UC late Oct–mid Jun.* A winding and, at times, narrow road with many hairpin bends. Care required at several unlit tunnels near Guillestre.
	Briançon (4,396ft)	20km	1 in 10		
***Jaun** 4,951ft (1509m) Switzerland	Broc (2,378ft)	25km	1 in 10	13ft	*UO.* A modernised but generally narrow road; some poor sections on ascent, and several hairpin bends on descent; *negotiable by caravans.*
	Reidenbach (2,769ft)	8km	1 in 10		
†Julier 7,493ft (2284m) Switzerland	Tiefencastel (2,821ft)	36km	1 in 10	13ft	*UO.* Well-engineered road, approached from Chur by Lenzerheide Pass (5,098ft); *negotiable by caravans, preferably from north to south.*
	Silvaplana (5,958ft)	7km	1 in 7½		
Katschberg 5,384ft (1641m) Austria	Spittal (1,818ft)	35km	1 in 5	20ft	*UO.* Steep though not particularly difficult, parallel toll motorway, including tunnel available; *negotiable by light caravans*, using tunnel (see page **59**).
	St Michael (5,340ft)	6km	1 in 6		
***Klausen** 6,391ft (1948m) Switzerland	Altdorf (1,512ft)	25km	1 in 11	16ft	*UC late Oct–early Jun.* Narrow and winding in places, but generally easy, in spite of a number of sharp bends; *no through route for caravans as they are prohibited from using the road between Unterschachen and Linthal.*
	Linthal (2,126ft)	23km	1 in 11		
Larche (della Maddalena) 6,542ft (1994m) France–Italy	Condamine (4,291ft)	19km	1 in 12	10ft	*OC Dec–Mar.* An easy, well-graded road; narrow and rough on ascent, wider with better surface on descent; *suitable for caravans.*
	Vinadio (2,986ft)	32km	1 in 12		
Lautaret 6,752ft (2058m) France	Le Bourg-d'Oisans (2,359ft)	38km	1 in 8	14ft	*OC Dec–Mar.* Modern, evenly graded, but winding, and unguarded in places; very fine scenery; *suitable for caravans.*
	Briançon (4,396ft)	28km	1 in 10		
Loibl (Ljubell) 3,500ft (1067m) Austria–Yugoslavia	Unterloibl (1,699ft)	10km	1 in 5½	20ft	*UO.* Steep rise and fall over Little Loibl pass to tunnel (1.6km long) under summit; from south to north *just negotiable by experienced drivers with light caravans.* The old road over the summit is closed to through traffic.
	Kranj (1,263ft)	29km	1 in 8		
***Lukmanier (Lucomagno)** 6,286ft (1916m) Switzerland	Olivone (2,945ft)	18km	1 in 11	16ft	*UC Nov–late May.* Rebuilt, modern road; *no throughroute for caravans* as they are prohibited from using the road between the Lukmanier Pass and Olivone.
	Disentis (3,772ft)	22km	1 in 11		

*Permitted maximum width of vehicles 7ft 6in
†Permitted maximum width of vehicles 8ft 2½in

PRINCIPAL MOUNTAINS PASSES

Pass and height	From To	Distances from summit and max gradient		Min width of road	Conditions (see page 61) for key to abbreviations
†Maloja 5,955ft (1815m) Switzerland	Silvaplana (5,958ft) Chiavenna (1,083ft)	11km 32km	level 1 in 11	13ft	*UO.* Escarpment facing south; fairly easy, but many hairpin bends on descent; *negotiable by caravans*, possibly difficult on ascent.
Mauria 4,285ft (1298m) Italy	Lozzo Cadore (2,470ft) Ampezzo (1,837ft)	14km 31km	1 in 14 1 in 14	16ft	*UO.* A well-designed road with easy, winding ascent and descent; *suitable for caravans.*
Mendola 4,472ft (1363m) Italy	Appiano (Eppan) (1,348ft) Sarnonico (3,208ft)	15km 8km	1 in 8 1 in 10	16ft	*UO.* A fairly straightforward, but winding road; well guarded; *suitable for caravans.*
Mont Cenis 6,834ft (2083m) France–Italy	Lanslebourg (4,587ft) Susa (1,624ft)	11km 28km	1 in 10 1 in 8	16ft	*UC Nov–May.* Approach by industrial valley. An easy broad highway, but with poor surface in places; *suitable for caravans.* Alternative Fréjus road tunnel available (see page **58**).
Monte Groce di Comélico (Kreuzberg) 5,368ft (1636m) Italy	San Candido (3,847ft) Santo Stefano di Cadore (2,978ft)	15km 21km	1 in 12 1 in 12	16ft	*UO.* A winding road with moderate gradients; beautiful scenery; *suitable for caravans.*
Montgenèvre 6,070ft (1850m) France–Italy	Briançon (4,334ft) Cesana Torinese (4,429ft)	12km 8km	1 in 14 1 in 11	16ft	*UO.* An easy, modern road; *suitable for caravans.*
Monte Giovo (Jaufen) 6,870ft (2094m) Italy	Merano (1,063ft) Vipiteno (3,110ft)	40km 19km	1 in 8 1 in 11	13ft	*UC Nov–May.* Many well-engineered hairpin bends; *caravans prohibited.*
Montets (see Forclaz)					
Morgins 4,491ft (1369m) France–Switzerland	Abondance (3,051ft) Monthey (1,391ft)	14km 15km	1 in 11 1 in 7	13ft	*UO.* A lesser used route through pleasant, forested countryside crossing the French/Swiss border.
***Mosses** 4,740ft (1445m) Switzerland	Aigle (1,378ft) Château-d'Oex (3,153ft)	18km 15km	1 in 12 1 in 12	13ft	*UO.* A modern road; *suitable for caravans.*
Nassfeld (Pramollo) 5,020ft (1530m) Austria–Italy	Tröpolach (1,972ft) Pontebba (1,841ft)	10km 10km	1 in 5 1 in 10	13ft	*OC late Nov–Mar.* The winding descent in Italy has been improved.
Nufenen (Novena) 8,130ft (2487m) Switzerland	Ulrichen (4,416ft) Airolo (3,747ft)	13km 24km	1 in 10 1 in 10	13ft	*UC mid Oct–mid Jun.* The approach roads are narrow, with tight bends, but the road over the pass is good; *negotiable by light caravans* (limit 1.5 tons)
***Oberalp** 6,706ft (2044m) Switzerland	Andermatt (4,737ft) Disentis (3,772ft)	10km 22km	1 in 10 1 in 10	16ft	*UC Nov–late May.* A much improved and widened road with a modern surface; many hairpin bends, but long level stretch on summit; *negotiable by caravans.* Alternative rail tunnel during the winter (see page 60).

*Permitted maximum width of vehicles 7ft 6in
†Permitted maximum width of vehicles 8ft $2^1/2$in

Pass and height	From To	Distances from summit and max gradient		Min width of road	Conditions (see page 61) for key to abbreviations
***Ofen (Fuorn)** 7,051ft (2149m) Switzerland	Zerne (4,836ft) Santa Maria im Münstertal (4,547ft)	22km 14km	1 in 10 1 in 8	12ft	*UO*. Good, fairly easy road through the Swiss National Park; *suitable for caravans*.
Petit St Bernard 7,178ft (2188m) France–Italy	Bourg-St-Maurice (2,756ft) Pré St-Didier (3,335ft)	31km 23km	1 in 16 1 in 12	16ft	*UC mid Oct–Jun*. Outstanding scenery; a fairly easy approach, but poor surface and unguarded broken edges near the summit; good on the descent in Italy; *negotiable by light caravans*.
Peyresourde 5,128ft (1563m) France	Arreau (2,310ft) Luchon (2,067ft)	18km 14km	1 in 10 1 in 10	13ft	*UO*. Somewhat narrow with several hairpin bends, though not difficult.
***Pillon** 5,072ft (1546m) Switzerland	Le Sépey (3,212ft) Gsteig (2,911ft)	14km 7km	1 in 11 1 in 11	13ft	*OC Jan–Feb*. A comparatively easy modern road; *suitable for caravans*.
Plöcken (Monte Croce-Carnico) 4,468ft (1362m) Austria–Italy	Kötschach (2,316ft) Paluzza (1,968ft)	14m 17km	1 in 7 1 in 14	16ft	*OC Dec–Apr*. A modern road with long, reconstructed sections; heavy traffic at summer weekends; delay likely at the frontier; *negotiable by caravans*.
Pordoi 7,346ft (2239m) Italy	Arabba (5,523ft) Canazei (4,806ft)	9km 12km	1 in 10 1 in 10	16ft	*OC Dec–Apr*. An excellent modern road with numerous hairpin bends; *negotiable by caravans*.
Port 4,098ft (1249m) France	Tarascon (1,555ft) Massat (2,133ft)	18km 13km	1 in 10 1 in 10	14ft	*OC Nov–Mar*. A fairly easy road, but narrow on some bends; *negotiable by caravans*.
Portel-d'Aspet 3,507ft (1069m) France	Audressein (1,625ft) Fronsac (1,548ft)	18km 29km	1 in 7 1 in 7	11ft	*UO*. Approached from the west by the easy Col des Ares (2,611ft) and Col de Buret (1,975ft); well-engineered road, but calls for particular care on hairpin bends; rather narrow.
Pötschen 3,221ft (982m) Austria	Bad Ischl (1,535ft) Bad Aussee (2,133ft)	19km 10km	1 in 11 1 in 11	23ft	*UO*. A modern road; *suitable for caravans*.
Pourtalet 5,879ft (1792m) France–Spain	Eaux-Chaudes (2,152ft) Biescas (2,821ft)	23km 34km	1 in 10 1 in 10	11ft	*UC late Oct–early Jun*. A fairly easy, unguarded road, but narrow in places.
Puymorens 6,283ft (1915m) France	Ax-les-Thermes (2,362ft) Bourg-Madame (3,707ft)	28km 27km	1 in 10 1 in 10	18ft	*OC Nov–Apr*. A generally easy, modern tarmac road, but narrow, winding and with a poor surface in places; not suitable for night driving; *suitable for caravans* (max height vehicles 11ft 6in). Alternative rail service available between Ax-les-Thermes and Latour-de-Carol.
Quillane 5,623ft (1714m) France	Quillan (955ft) Mont-Louis (5,135ft)	63km 5km	1 in 12 1 in 12	16ft	*OC Nov–Mar*. An easy, straightforward ascent and descent; *suitable for caravans*.

*Permitted maximum width of vehicles 7ft 6in

PRINCIPAL MOUNTAINS PASSES

Pass and height	From To	Distances from summit and max gradient		Min width of road	Conditions (see page 61) for key to abbreviations
Radstädter-Tauern 5,702ft (1739m) Austria	Radstädt 2,808ft) Mauterndorf (3,681ft)	21km 17km	1 in 6 1 in 7	16ft	*OC Jan–Mar.* Northern ascent steep, but not difficult otherwise; parallel toll motorway including tunnel available; *negotiable by light caravans, using tunnel* (see page **59**).
Résia (Reschen) 4,934ft (1504m) Italy–Austria	Spondigna (2,903ft) Pfunds (3,182ft)	29km 20km	1 in 10 1 in 10	20ft	*UO.* A good, straightforward alternative to the Brenner Pass; *suitable for caravans.*
Resterfond (La Bonette) 9,193ft (2802m) France	Jausiers (near Barcelonnette) (3,986ft) St-Etienne-de-Tinée (3,766ft)	23km 27km	1 in 9 1 in 9	10ft	*UC Oct–Jun.* The highest pass in the Alps, completed in 1962. Narrow, rough, unguarded ascent with many blind bends, and nine hairpins. Descent easier, winding with twelve hairpin bends. Not for the faint-hearted; extra care required.
Rolle 6,464ft (1970m) Italy	Predazzo (3,337ft) Mezzano (2,098ft)	21km 25km	1 in 11 1 in 14	16ft	*OC Dec–Mar.* Very beautiful scenery; bitumen surface; a well-engineered road; *negotiable by caravans.*
Rombo (see Timmelsjoch)					
Route des Crêtes 4,210ft (1283m) France	St-Dié (1,125ft) Cernay (902ft)	— —	1 in 8 1 in 8	13ft	*UC Nov–Apr.* A renowned scenic route crossing seven ridges, with the highest point at 'Hôtel du Grand Ballon'.
†St Gotthard (San Gottardo) 6,916ft (2108m) Switzerland	Göschenen (3,629ft) Airolo (3,747ft)	19km 15km	1 in 10 1 in 10	20ft	*UC mid Oct–early Jun.* Modern, fairly easy two- to three-lane road. Heavy traffic; *negotiable by caravans* (max height vehicles 11ft 9in). Alternative road tunnel available (see page **58**).
***San Bernardino** 6,778ft (2066m) Switzerland	Mesocco (2,549ft) Hinterrhein (5,328ft)	22km 9.5km	1 in 10 1 in 10	13ft	*UC Oct–late Jun.* Easy, modern roads on northern and southern approaches to tunnel (see page **58**); narrow and winding over summit, via tunnel *suitable for caravans.*
Schlucht 3,737ft (1139m) France	Gérardmer (2,182ft) Munster (1,250ft)	15km 17km	1 in 14 1 in 14	16ft	*UO.* An extremely picturesque route crossing the Vosges mountains, with easy, wide bends on the descent; *suitable for caravans.*
Seeberg (Jezersko) 3,996ft (1218m) Austria–Yugoslavia	Eisenkappel (1,812ft) Kranj (1,263ft)	14km 33km	1 in 8 1 in 10	16ft	*UO.* An alternative to the steeper Loibl and Wurzen passes; moderate climb with winding, hairpin ascent and descent.
Sella 7,349ft (2240m) Italy	Plan (5,269ft) Canazei (4,806ft)	9km 13km	1 in 9 1 in 9	16ft	*OC Dec–Jun.* A finely engineered, winding road; exceptional views of the Dolomites.
Semmering 3,232ft (985m) Austria	Mürzzschlag im Mürztal (2,205ft) Gloggnitz (1,427ft)	14km 17km	1 in 16 1 in 16	20ft	*UO.* A fine, well-engineered highway; *suitable for caravans.*
Sestriere 6,670ft (2033m) Italy	Cesana Torinese (4,429ft) Pinerolo (1,234ft)	12km 55km	1 in 10 1 in 10	16ft	*UO.* Mostly bitumen surface; *negotiable by caravans.*

*Permitted maximum width of vehicles 7ft 6in
†Permitted maximum width of vehicles 8ft 2½ft

Pass and height	From To	Distances from summit and max gradient		Min width of road	Conditions (see page 61) for key to abbreviations
Silvretta (Bielerhöhe) 6,666ft (2032m) Austria	Partenen (3,448ft) Galtür (5,197ft)	16km 10km	1 in 9 1 in 9	16ft	*UC late Oct–early Jun.* For the most part reconstructed; thirty-two easy hairpin bends on western ascent; eastern side more straightforward. Toll road; *caravans prohibited.*
†Simplon 6,578ft (2005m) Switzerland–Italy	Brig (2,231ft) Domodóssola (919ft)	22km 41km	1 in 9 1 in 11	23ft	*OC Nov–Apr.* An easy, reconstructed modern road, but 13 miles long, continuous ascent to summit; *suitable for caravans.* Alternative rail tunnel (see page **58**).
Somport 5,354ft (1623m) France–Spain	Bedous (1,635ft) Jaca (2,687ft)	31km 30km	1 in 10 1 in 10	12ft	*UO.* A favoured, old-established route; generally easy, but in parts narrow and unguarded; fairly good-surfaced road; *suitable for caravans.*
***Splügen** 6,932ft (2113m) Switzerland–Italy	Splügen (4,780ft) Chiavenna (1,083ft)	9km 30km	1 in 9 1 in 7½	10ft	*UC Nov–Jun.* Mostly narrow and winding, with many hairpin bends, and not well-guarded; care also required at many tunnels and galleries (max height vehicles 9ft 2in).
††Stelvio 9,054ft (2757m) Italy	Bormio (4,019ft) Spondigna (2,903ft)	22km 28km	1 in 8 1 in 8	13ft	*UC Oct–late Jun.* The third highest pass in the Alps; the number of acute hairpin bends, all well-engineered, is exceptional – from forty to fifty on either side; the surface is good, the traffic heavy. Hairpin bends are too acute for long vehicles.
†Susten 7,297ft (2224m) Switzerland	Innertkirchen (2,067ft) Wassen (3,005ft)	28km 19km	1 in 11 1 in 11	20ft	*UC Nov–Jun.* A very scenic and well-guarded mountain road; easy gradients and turns; heavy traffic at weekends; *negotiable by caravans.*
Tenda (Tende) 4,334ft (1321m) Italy–France	Borgo S Dalmazzo (2,103ft) La Giandola (1,010ft)	24km 29km	1 in 11 1 in 11	18ft	*UO.* Well-guarded, modern road with several hairpin bends; road tunnel at summit; *suitable for caravans; but prohibited during the winter.*
†Thurn 4,180ft (1274m) Austria	Kitzbühel (2,500ft) Mittersill (2,588ft)	19km 10km	1 in 12 1 in 16	16ft	*UO.* A good road with narrow stretches; northern approach rebuilt; *suitable for caravans.*
Timmelsjoch (Rombo) 8,232ft (2509m) Austria–Italy	Obergurgl (6,322ft) Moso (3,304ft)	14km 21km	1 in 7 1 in 8	12ft	*UC mid Oct–late Jun.* Roadworks on Italian side still in progress. The pass is open to *private cars (without trailers)* ***only*** *as some tunnels on the Italian side are too narrow for larger vehicles; toll road.*
Tonale 6,178ft (1883m) Italy	Edolo (2,264ft) Dimaro (2,513ft)	30km 27km	1 in 14 1 in 8	16ft	*UO.* A relatively easy road; *suitable for caravans.*
Toses (Tosas) 5,905ft (1800m) Spain	Puigcerdá (3,708ft) Ribes de Freser (3,018ft)	25km 25km	1 in 10 1 in 10	16ft	*UO.* Now a fairly straightforward, but continuously winding, two-lane road with many sharp bends; some unguarded edges; *negotiable by caravans.*
Tourmalet 6,936ft (2114m) France	Luz (2,333ft) Ste-Marie-de-Campan (2,811ft)	19km 17km	1 in 8 1 in 8	14ft	*UC Oct–mid Jun.* The highest of the French Pyrénéan routes; the approaches are good, though winding and exacting over summit; sufficiently guarded.
Tre Croci 5,935ft (1809m) Italy	Cortina d'Ampezzo (3,983ft) Auronzo di Cadore (2,835ft)	7km 26km	1 in 9 1 in 9	16ft	*OC Dec–Mar.* An easy pass; very fine scenery; *suitable for caravans.*

*Permitted maximum width of vehicles 7ft 6in †Permitted maximum width of vehicles 8ft 2½in ††Maximum length of vehicle 30ft

PRINCIPAL MOUNTAINS PASSES

Pass and height	From To	Distances from summit and max gradient		Min width of road	Conditions (see page 61) for key to abbreviations
Turracher Höhe 5,784ft (1763m) Austria	Predlitz (3,024ft)	20km	1 in $5\frac{1}{2}$	13ft	*UO.* Formerly one of the steepest mountain roads in Austria; now much improved; steep, fairly straightforward ascent, followed by a very steep descent; good surface and mainly two-lane width; fine scenery.
	Ebene-Reichenau (3,563ft)	8km	1 in $4\frac{1}{2}$		
***Umbrail** 8,205ft (2501m) Switzerland–Italy	Santa Maria im Münstertal (4,547ft)	13km	1 in 11	14ft	*UC early Nov–early Jun.* Highest of the Swiss passes; narrow; mostly gravel surfaced with thirty-four hairpin bends, but not too difficult.
	Bormio (4,019ft)	19km	1 in 11		
Vars 6,919ft (2109m) France	St-Paul-sur-Ubaye (4,823ft)	8km	1 in 10	16ft	*OC Dec–Mar.* Easy winding ascent with seven hairpin bends; gradual winding descent with another seven hairpin bends; good surface; *negotiable by caravans.*
	Guillestre (3,248ft)	20km	1 in 10		
Wurzen (Koren) 3,502ft (1073m) Austria–Yugoslavia	Riegersdorf (1,775ft)	8km	1 in $5\frac{1}{2}$	13ft	*UO.* A steep two-lane road, which otherwise is not particularly difficult; heavy traffic at summer weekends; delay likely at the frontier; *caravans prohibited.*
	Kranjska Gora (2,657ft)	5km	1 in $5\frac{1}{2}$		
Zirler Berg 3,310ft (1009m) Austria	Seefeld (3,871ft)	7km	1 in 7	20ft	*UO.* An escarpment facing south, part of the route from Garmisch to Innsbruck; a good, modern road, but heavy tourist traffic and a long steep descent, with one hairpin bend, into the Inn Valley. Steepest section from the hairpin bend down to Zirl; *caravans prohibited.*
	Zirl (2,041ft)	5km	1 in 6		

*Permitted maximum width of vehicles 7ft 6in

ABOUT THE BOOK

Each country in the guide has been split into regions, so that all the sites in your chosen holiday area can easily be found. Within the regions place-names are listed in alphabetical order, and details of regional boundaries and site locations can be found on the country maps which are at the back of the book. If you need overnight stops on the way to your destination, the country maps should help you find something in the right place. We would emphasise that the maps are provided for location purposes only and not for finding your way around. We would recommend that you buy the AA Big Road Atlas of Europe for that purpose.

Advance booking

Despite the carefree nature of a camping or caravanning holiday, it is advisable to book well in advance for peak holiday seasons, or for your first and last stop close to a ferry crossing point. Having said that, we do find that some sites will not accept reservations. Although the AA cannot undertake to find sites or make reservations for you, we do include in the guide specimen booking letters in English, French, German, Italian and Spanish. **Please note that, although not common practice, some campsites may regard your deposit as a booking fee not deductable from the final account.**

On arrival

We do advise you to look over the site if possible before you decide to stay. The information for any publication must of necessity be collected some time in advance and it may well be that ownership and standards have changed since that time. Even where standards are of the expected quality, the site may be very crowded and you may prefer to look elsewhere for more space and less noise.

When you look over a site, consider the following:

> Pleasant general situation, clean and tidy with plenty of refuse bins, site fenced and guarded.
>
> Sufficient and clean lavatories, washing facilities and showers with hot water. Well defined roads on site, preferably lit at night.
>
> Pitches should not be cramped.
>
> If you have a tent, make sure the surface is suitable for pegs; if you have a caravan, make sure ground is firm enough.
>
> In hot weather there should be suitable shading and if damp, ground should appear well drained.
>
> A good supply of safe drinking water.
>
> If you need the following, confirm their existence: electric point for razors, Camping Gaz, a well-stocked shop, laundry facilities, restaurant serving reasonably priced food, ice for sale.

Although the majority of the sites in this guide have been selected for the high standards they maintain, we have included, at the request of our members, a number of sites along touring routes and others near the Channel ports which are suitable for overnight stops. These transit sites tend to become crowded at the height of the season, but provide the necessary amenities. If you require information on additional sites, lists may be obtained free from most national tourist offices, and in the country sections we give details of local organisations which either publish a camping guide or provide more detailed information.

Campsite entries In order to update the information provided, we send out questionnaires each year to every campsite. Inevitably a number of the questionnaires are not returned to us in time for publication, and where this is the case the campsite name will appear in *italic* type.

Prices are given in the relevant currencies and are detailed per night, per adult, car, caravan and tent. We do not give charges relating to children as these vary, but generally a 50% reduction is made for children aged 3–14. To determine the cost of one night, simply add up those charges as they apply to your party.

Some campsites do have different ways of structuring their prices. Whatever the permutations may be, all variations will be reflected in the entry, the exceptions being:

pp — Campsite charges per person. The charge for the vehicle and caravan/tent is included in each person's price. For a party of four people, multiply the pp price by four for the total cost per night.

pitch — This is the price per pitch, regardless of whether it is a caravan or a tent. Where the word pitch follows the **'A'** for adult price, you should multiply the **'A'** price by the number of adults in the party, then add the pitch price to obtain the cost per night.

Opening times

Dates shown are inclusive opening dates. If the site is open all year, then 'All year' will appear in the entry. All information was correct at the time of going to press, but we recommend you check with the site before arriving. Changes of date often occur because of demand and/or weather conditions. Sometimes restricted facilities only are available between October and April.

Complaints

Should you have any complaint about a site, the best policy is to inform the site proprietor immediately so that the matter can be dealt with promptly. If the personal approach fails, please inform the AA as soon as possible on return to this country.

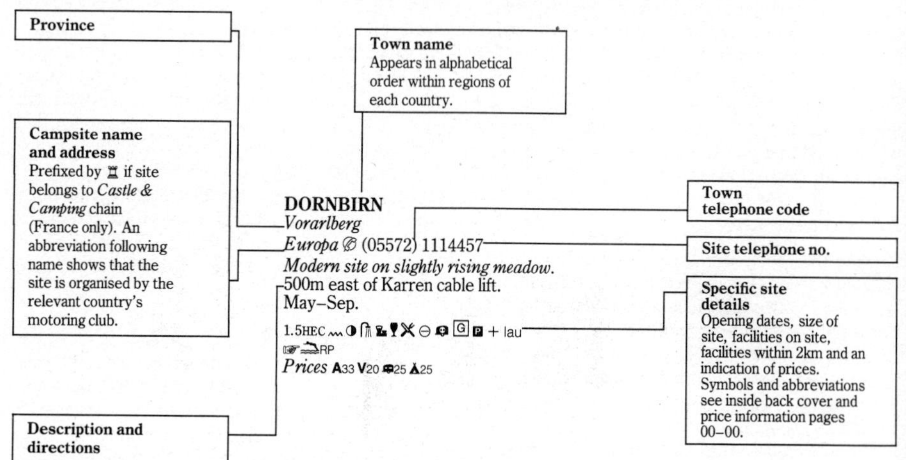

Province
Town name
Appears in alphabetical order within regions of each country.
Campsite name and address
Prefixed by ♖ if site belongs to *Castle & Camping* chain (France only). An abbreviation following name shows that the site is organised by the relevant country's motoring club.
DORNBIRN
Vorarlberg
Europa (05572) 1114457
Modern site on slightly rising meadow.
500m east of Karren cable lift.
May–Sep.
1.5HEC + lau
RP
Prices A33 V20 25 Å25
Town telephone code
Site telephone no.
Specific site details
Opening dates, size of site, facilities on site, facilities within 2km and an indication of prices. Symbols and abbreviations see inside back cover and price information pages 00–00.
Description and directions

Austria is a land of chalet villages and beautiful cities bordered by seven countries: Czechoslovakia, Germany, Hungary, Italy, Liechtenstein, Switzerland and Yugoslavia. The scenery is predominantly Alpine, an enchanting mix of mountains, lakes and pine forests. The splendour of the mountains is seen in the imposing Dachstein region of upper Austria and the massive Tyrolean peaks. The lakes of Burgenland and Salzkammergut, the river Danube, the forests and woods of Styria and the world-famous city of Wien (Vienna) are outstanding features of the landscape.

Most of the country enjoys a moderate climate during the summer, although eastern areas are sometimes very hot. The heaviest rainfall occurs in midsummer. The language of Austria is German, and English is not widely spoken.

Austria offers a variety of outdoor activities to suit everyone and there are numerous campsites throughout the country. Most are open from May to September, although a number remain open all year.

International camping carnet is not compulsory, but recommended. Some campsites will allow a reduction to the advertised charge to the holders of a camping carnet. See the European ABC for further information.

Off-site camping is possible in state forests with permission from the local Bürgermeister, but open fires are generally prohibited in woodland areas. Campers not on an official site, staying in Austria for more than three days should report to the police as soon as possible, and also inform them of subsequent changes of location. Within Wien (Vienna) any form of off-site camping or caravanning is prohibited.

HOW TO GET THERE

The usual Continental Channel ports for this journey are Calais, Oostende (Ostend) or Zeebrugge.
For Salzburg and central Austria drive through Belgium to Aachen then via Köln (Cologne), Frankfurt, Nürnberg and München (Munich).
For Innsbruck and The Tirol as above to Frankfurt, then via Karlsruhe and Stuttgart.

As an alternative, you could cross to Dieppe, Le Havre or Cherbourg and drive through northern France via **Strasbourg** and **Stuttgart**, or via **Basle** and northern Switzerland. But see 'Motorways' in the Switzerland section for details of motorway tax.

Distance

From the Continental Channel ports, Salzburg is about 1130km (700 miles) and Vienna is about 1450km (900 miles), and you would normally need one overnight stop on the way.

Car sleeper trains

Services are available in summer from Brussels in Belgium and 's-Hertogenbosch in the Netherlands to Salzburg and Villach.

GENERAL INFORMATION

The information given here is specific to Austria. It **must** be read in conjunction with the European ABC at the front of the book, which covers those regulations which are common to many countries.

Boats*

Motorboats are not allowed on most of Austria's lakes. It is advisable to check with the Tourist Office before taking a boat into Austria (see *Tourist information* below for address).

British Embassy/Consulates*

The British Embassy is located at 1030 Wien, Jaurèsgasse 12 ✆(0222) 7131575; consular section, Jaurèsgasse 10 ✆(0222) 756117/8. There are British Consulates with Honorary Consuls in Bregenz, Graz, Innsbruck and Salzburg.

Currency, including banking hours*

The unit of currency is the *Austrian schilling* (*ASch*) divided into 100 *groschen*. At the time of going to press £1 = *ASch* 20.93. Denominations of bank notes are *ASch* 20, 50, 100, 500, 1,000; standard coins are *ASch* 1, 5, 10, 20, 25, 50, 100 and 2, 5, 10, 50 *groschen*. There are no restrictions on the amount of foreign or Austrian currency that a *bona fide* tourist may import into the country. No more than *ASch* 100,000 in local currency may be exported, but there is no restriction on the export of foreign currency.

Banks are open Monday to Friday from 08.00–12.30hrs and 13.30–15.00hrs (extended to 17.30hrs on Thursday). The bank counter at the Austrian Motoring Club (ÖAMTC) head office is open during office hours; exchange offices at some main railway stations are open Saturdays, Sundays and public holidays.

Emergency telephone numbers

Fire ✆122, police ✆133, ambulance ✆144

Foodstuffs*

Visitors may import tea, coffee and foodstuffs for their own personal use but raw meat (fresh or frozen) from hooved animals (*eg* beef, pork) and shellfish (*eg* mussels, crab) cannot be imported.

Shopping hours

Generally shops are open from 08.00–18.00hrs Monday to Friday with a one or two hour break for lunch, except in central Wien (Vienna), where shops do not close for lunch. On Saturdays, most shops close at 12.00 or 12.30hrs.

Some shops operate a tax-free service whereby, on leaving the country, visitors are reimbursed for VAT paid. A special form (*U34*) must be obtained, completed and stamped, from the shop and presented to the Austrian customs when crossing the border. Look for shops displaying the blue 'Tax-free Shopping' sign, or go to the local tourist information or ÖAMTC office for address lists.

Tourist information*

The Austrian National Tourist Organisation maintains an information office at 30 St George Street, London W1R 0AL ✆071-629 0461, which will be pleased to assist you with any information regarding tourism. In most towns in Austria there is a local or regional tourist office which will supply detailed local information.

MOTORING

Children in cars

Children under 12 are not permitted to travel in front seats unless they are using a special seat or safety belts suitable for children.

Dimensions and weight restrictions

Private **cars** and towed **trailers** or **caravans** are

***Additional information will be found in the European ABC at the front of the book.**

restricted to the following dimensions – height, 4 metres; width, 2.50 metres; length, 12 metres. The maximum permitted overall length of vehicle/trailer or caravan combination is 18 metres.

Trailers without brakes may weigh up to 750kg and may have a total weight of up to 50% of the towing vehicle.

Driving licence

A valid UK licence is acceptable in Austria and, although language difficulties may give rise to misunderstanding in a few isolated cases, it is legally valid. The minimum age at which a visitor may use a temporarily imported motorcycle (exceeding 50cc) or car is 18 years. The Austrian motoring club (ÖAMTC) will supply a free translation of your licence into German, but it is only available from their head office in Wien (Vienna) and therefore will only be of use if touring in eastern Austria. However, an *International Driving Permit* is required by the holder of a licence issued in the Republic of Ireland – compulsory if a red three-year licence and recommended if a pink EC type licence. See under *Driving licence and International Driving Permit* in the European ABC for further information.

First-aid kit*

In Austria all vehicles (including motorcycles) must be equipped with a first-aid kit by law and visitors are expected to comply. This item will not be checked at the frontier, but motorists can be stopped at the scene of an accident and their first-aid kit demanded; if this is not forthcoming the police may take action.

Motoring club*

The **Österreichischer Automobil-Motorrad- und Touring Club** (ÖAMTC) which has its headquarters at 1010 Wien, Schubertring 1–3 ✆(0222) 71199-0 has offices at the major frontier crossings, and is represented in most towns either direct or through provincial motoring clubs. The offices are usually open between 08.30 and 18.00hrs weekdays, 09.00 to 12.00hrs on Saturdays and are closed on Sundays and public holidays.

Roads

The motorist crossing into Austria from any frontier enters a network of well-engineered roads.

The main traffic artery runs from Bregenz in the west to Wien (Vienna) in the east, via the Arlberg Tunnel (Toll: see *Major Road and Rail Tunnels*), Innsbruck, Salzburg, and Linz. Most of the major alpine roads are excellent, and a comprehensive tour can be made through the Tirol, Salzkammergut and Carinthia without difficulty. Service stations are fairly frequent, even on mountain roads.

In July and August, several roads across the frontier become congested. The main points are on the Lindau-Bregenz road; at the Brenner Pass (possible alternative – the Resia Pass); at Kufstein; on the München (Munich)–Salzburg *Autobahn* and on the Villach–Tarvisio road. For details of mountain passes consult the Contents page.

Speed limits*

Car

Built-up areas	50kph (31mph)
Other roads	100kph (62mph)
Motorways	130kph (80mph)

Car towing caravan not exceeding 750kg (1,650lb)†

Built-up areas	50kph (31mph)
Other roads	100kph (62mph)
Motorways	100kph (62mph)

Car towing caravan exceeding 750kg (1,650lb)†

Built-up areas	50kph (31mph)
Other roads	80kph (49mph)
Motorways	100kph (62mph)

†If weight of the trailer exceeds that of the towing vehicle (or if the total weight of the two vehicles exceeds 3,500kg) then the following speed limits apply:

Built-up areas	50kph (31mph)
Other roads	60kph (37mph)
Motorways	70kph (43mph)

Note when the total weight of the two vehicles exceeds 3,500kg, it is not permissible to tow with a motor-car driving licence.

***Additional information will be found in the European ABC at the front of the book.**

Prices are in Austria Schillings.
Abbreviation: str strasse

Each place name preceded by 'Bad' is listed under the name that follows it.

TIROL

Magnificent lofty peaks, crystal-clear mountain lakes, peaceful forests and tranquil valleys characterise this internationally-famous corner of Austria. The high mountain regions, reaching altitudes of over 10,000ft (4,000 metres), are accessible by mountain road passes and dozens of cable-cars and chair lifts, and for the climbing and walking enthusiast this is a wonderland of opportunity.
The Tirol has a long architectural heritage; even the trim little provincial towns and villages have dignified burgher houses with impressive façades; there are mosaics on public buildings and private houses, and medieval castles and castle ruins command some of the finest settings in the Tirol. The cheerful hospitality of the region is renowned, and folk festivals, dancing and yodelling are colourful local traditions.
Innsbruck, the capital of the region, still boasts its medieval old town, with handsome houses facing narrow, irregular streets. Highlights here include the Golden Roof (Goldenes Dachl), with its gilded copper tiles; the Cathedral (Dom), with its imposing west front and rich interior; and the fascinating and extensive displays in the Museum of Folk Art (Tiroler Volkskunstmuseum).

ACHENKIRCH AM ACHENSEE
Tirol

Achensee ✆(05246) 6239
On N shore of lake, on level grassland with gravel paths.
Opposite Hotel Scholastika. Turn off B181 in Achenkirch.
All year
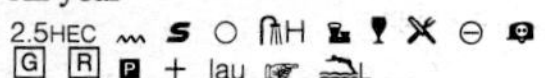
2.5HEC ~ S ○ ⋒H ⊖ G R + lau L

ASCHAU
Tirol

Aufenfeld ✆(05282) 2916
Level meadowland on forest slope.
Signposted.
All year
3HEC ~ ◑ ⋒H ✕ ⊖ G R PR + lau
Prices A55-60 pitch60-80

BRIXEN IM THALE
Tirol

Brixen im Thale ✆(05334) 18113
On partly sloping grassland with some terraces and a fine view over the valley.
Access via Kufstein-Innsbruck motorway (exit Wörgl-Ost). Site lies to the S of town past the level crossing.
All year
2HEC ~ ○ ⋒H ✕ ⊖ G R + lau LP
Prices A35 V30 30 A25

EHRWALD
Tirol

International Dr-Ing E Lauth ✆(05673) 2666
On undulating grassland, surrounded by high conifers, below the Wetterstein mountain range.
To the right of the access road to the Zugspitz funicular.
All year
1HEC ~ ◑ ⋒H ✕ ⊖ G H + lau

Tiroler Zugspitzcamp ✆(05673) 2745 & 2254
Several grassy terraces. Modern sanitary installations with bathrooms.
Near the Zugspitz funicular station.
All year
5HEC ~ ○ ⋒H ✕ ⊖ P +

FÜGEN
Tirol

Zillertal-Hell ✆(05288) 2203
In a meadow surrounding a farm.
1km N of Fügen on the B169.
All year
1.5HEC ~ ◑ ⋒H ✕ ⊖ G R + lau P

GRÄN
Tirol

Tannheimer Tal ✆(05675) 6570
1km N of the village centre on the Pfronten-Tannheimer Tal road.
21 Apr-19 Dec
3HEC ⋒H ✕ ⊖ G H + lau

HAIMING
Tirol

Center Oberland ✆(05266) 294
On a sloping meadow behind the BP garage.
Off B171 at Km485.
15 Apr-Nov
4HEC ~ ◑ ⋒H ✕ ⊖ G R H PR + lau

HÄRING, BAD
Tirol

Kur-und Sportcamping ✆(05332) 74871
All year
1HEC ~ ◑ ⋒H ✕ ⊖ G P + lau
Prices A40 V25 35 A25

HÄSELGEHR
Tirol

Rudi Luxnach 122 ✆(05634) 6425
Camping Carnet Compulsory.
All year
1HEC ~ ◑ ⋒H ⊖ G H PR + lau ✕
Prices A41-44 V24 27-29 A18-26

HEITERWANG
Tirol

Heiterwanger See ✆(05674) 5116
In a quiet situation in a meadow beside lake.
By Hotel Fischer am See.
All year
1HEC ~ ◑ ⋒H ✕ ⊖ G R L + lau
Prices A60 pitch35-55

HOPFGARTEN
Tirol

See also BRIXEN IM THALE

Relterhof Penningberg 90 ✆(05335) 3512
All year
2HEC ~ ◑ ⋒H ✕ ⊖ G R R lau
Prices A38-42 V28-32 30-35 A25-35

Schlossberg-Itter ✆(05335) 2181
In terraced meadowland below Schloss Itter on the Brixental Ache.
2km W on B170.
All year
4HEC ~ ◑ ⋒H ✕ ⊖ G R PR + lau
Prices A45-58 V30-38 30-38 A30-35

HUBEN
Tirol

Huben ✆(05253) 5855
All year
3.5HEC ~ ○ ⋒H ✕ R R + lau
Prices A38-42 V15 22-30 A15-22

IMST
Tirol

Imst-West ✆(05412) 2293
On open meadowland in the Langgasse area.

Off the bypass near the turn for the Pitztal.
All year
1HEC H G R + lau LPR
Prices A40 pitch50

At **OBERSTADT**
Böss Engererweg 5 ✆(05412) 2866
In meadow surrounded by fruit trees.
Access from B197.
May-Sep
7HEC H G R P + lau

KITZBÜHEL
Tirol
Schwarzsee ✆(05356) 2806
In meadowland on the edge of a wood behind a large restaurant.
2km from town on B170 towards Wörgl turn right, 400m after Schwarzsee railway station.
All year
6HEC H G R L + lau
Prices A54-62 pitch52-78

KÖSSEN
Tirol
Wilder Kaiser ✆(05375) 6444
Situated in a lovely position below Unterberg, this level site is adjoined on three sides by woodland.
For access follow road to Unterberg Lift, then turn right and continue for 200m.
All year
4.2HEC H G P + lau
Prices A40-55 pitch45-85

KRAMSACH
Tirol
Tonis Ferien Comfort Seeblick Toni Brantlhof ✆(05337) 3544
Rural site near the Brantlhof above Lake Reintaler.
Camping Carnet Compulsory.
From Inntal Motorway (Rattenberg/Kramsach exit) follow signs 'Zu den Seen' for about 3km, then drive through Seehof site.
All year
2HEC H G R L + lau

KUFSTEIN
Tirol
Kufstein Salurnerstr 36 ✆(05372) 3689
Site has sporting facilities.
1km W of Kufstein between River Inn and B171.
May-Oct
1HEC H G + lau PR
Prices A35 V25 25 24

Tiroler Filegerstuben ✆(05372) 4170

Site situated on level meadowland.
All year
0.5HEC H + lau L

LADIS
See **RIED BEI LANDECK**

LANDECK
Tirol
See also ZAMS
Huber Muhlkanal 1 ✆(05442) 4636
All year
12HEC H G R H PR + lau
Prices A35-40 V18 55-68 25-65

Riffler ✆(05442) 39405
Site on meadowland between residential housing and banks of Sanna.
100m from Camping Landeck-West.
Closed 1-15 May
0.3HEC H + lau G P
Prices A40-45 V15-20 50-65 40-60

LÄNGENFELD
Tirol
Ötztal ✆(05253) 5348
In meadowland with some tall trees on the edge of woodland.
Turn right off E186 at fire station.
All year
3.1HEC H G R H PR + lau
Prices A50 V20 38 38

LERMOOS
Tirol
Hofherr Garmischer Str 21 ✆(05673) 2980
15 Dec-Apr & Jun-Oct
0.7HEC H R + G
Prices A58-65 pitch45-65

Larchenhof Bes Schonger Wilhelm ✆(05673) 2197
20 May-10 Oct & 15 Dec-10 Apr
0.3HEC H G R + P
Prices A35-40 V15-25 20-30 20-30

LEUTASCH
Tirol
Holiday ✆(05214) 6570
A modern site on level grassland screened by trees on the Leutascher Ache.
Turn off B313 (Mittenwald-Scharnitz) towards Leutasch.
25 Apr-10 May & Nov
2.5HEC H G R H P + lau
Prices A66 pitch88-154

MAURACH
Tirol
Karwendel ✆(05243) 6116
In town turn off the B181 and follow the Pertisau road.
All year

1.5HEC H G R L lau P +
Prices A40-50 V25-30 40-60 35

MAURACH-BUCHAU
Tirol
Seecamping Wimmer Buchau 7 ✆(05243) 5217
All year
1HEC H G R + lau L

MAYRHOFEN
Tirol
Laubichl ✆(05285) 2580
On a gently sloping meadow near a farm at N entrance to village.
All year
2HEC H G R + lau
Prices A40 V20 20 20

NATTERS
Tirol
Natter See ✆(0512) 583988
A terraced site beautifully situated amidst woodland and mountains on the shore of Nattersee.
Approach via Brenner Motorway, exit 'Innsbruck Süd', via Natters, onto B182 and follow signs.
15 Dec-Sep
7HEC H G R L + lau
Prices A52-64 pitch65-88

NEUSTIFT
Tirol
Gasthof Weiss ✆(07284) 8104
All year
1HEC H G R + lau
Prices A25 V20 25 25

Hochstubai ✆(05226) 2610
On slightly sloping meadowland.
Near the Geier Alm approximately 5km S of town on the road towards the Gletscher bahn.
All year
2.7HEC H G R + lau P

OBERSTADT
See **IMST**

OETZ
Tirol
Oetz ✆(05252) 6485
In a park-like area with hedges and trees.
Apr-15 Oct
1.5HEC H G R P + lau L

PFUNDS
Tirol
Sonnen ✆(05474) 5232
Site in meadowland with some fruit trees.
On road B315 between SHELL Garage and Gasthof Sonne. ➔

All year
1HEC H G + P
Prices A25 V20 20-40 15-50

PILL
Tirol
Plankenhof (05242) 4195
Site in meadow.
On B171 near Gasthof Plankenhof.
May-Oct
0.6HEC H G R P + lau

PRÄGRATEN
Tirol
Venediger (04877) 5213
On uneven meadow next to a Pension.
500m from Matrei-Hinterbichl road.
All year
0.5HEC H + lau G R
Prices A35 V20 35 35

PRUTZ
Tirol
Prutz (05472) 6825
All year
3HEC H R + G P
Prices A29-30 V25-26 25-26 25-26

REUTTE
Tirol
Reutte (05672) 2809
Well kept site on a meadow on the edge of a forest near the sports centre. Modern swimming pool in town.
Turn right towards Waldrast.
Closed May
2.2HEC H G R H + lau LP
Prices A55-65 V30-35 30-35 30-35

Seespitze (05672) 8121
May-Sep
3HEC H G L + lau
Prices A39 V14 25 14-35

Sennalpe (05672) 8115
In a quiet situation on a grassy mountain slope above the lake.
On Reutte-Oberammergau road 200m from the Hotel Forelle.
15 Dec-15 Oct
4HEC H G L + lau
Prices A39 V14 25 14-35

RIED BEI LANDECK
Tirol
Dreiländereck (05472) 6294
Level site in centre of village.
All year
1.5HEC H G H + lau LP

At **LADIS**(3km N)
Sonnenterrasse (05472) 6607
Situated on gently sloping meadowland between a school and swimming pool. Views of the upper Inn and Burg Laidegg.
In Ried turn off the B315 towards Ladis, and follow a winding road with slight gradients for 4km.
Etr-Oct
2.5HEC H + LP
Prices A37 V13 20 18

RINN
Tirol
Judenstein (05223) 8620
Apr-15 Oct
0.6HEC H G + lau
Prices A25 V20 30-40 20-30

ST JOHANN
Tirol
Michelnhof Weiberndorf 6 (05352) 2584
All year
1.8HEC H G R + lau R
Prices A50 V30 30 30

SCHARNITZ
Tirol
Alm
On level, open grassland. Near B313.
Access from S outskirts.
Nov-16 Dec
0.6HEC H G R + lau
Prices A40-45 pitch30-40

SCHWAZ
Tirol
At **WEER**(6km W)
Alpencamping Mark Maholmhof (05224) 8146
Situated on meadowland by a farm on the edge of a forest.
Off B171.
Apr-30 Oct
2HEC H G H P + lau L
Prices A50 pitch50

SÖLDEN
Tirol
Sölden (05254) 2627
Situated on meadowland on left bank of Ötztaler tributary. Beautiful views of the surrounding mountains.
By Grauer Bär Inn at Km28 on the B186.
Closed May
0.5HEC H G + lau P

STAMS
Tirol
Eichenwald (05263) 6159
Well managed terraced site in oak wood.
Turn off B171 at ESSO filling station in direction of abbey, onto a steep, narrow access road.
15 May-Sep
2HEC H G H + lau

TELFS
Tirol
Schwimmbad (05262) 2849
150m off B171.
All year
0.7HEC H + lau PR

THIERSEE
Tirol
Rueppenhof (05376) 5419
Site made up of several meadows

surrounding a farm that lies on the banks of a lake.
Apr-Oct
1HEC ◑ H ✕ ⊖ L + lau

UNTERPERFUSS
Tirol
Farm ✆(05232) 2209
Modern site on gently sloping meadow.
W end of village near Amberg railway and main road.
All year
3HEC ◑ H ✕ ⊖ [G] [R] PR + lau
Prices A50 pitch60

VOLDERS
Tirol
Schloss ✆(05224) 2333
Grassland site with lovely trees.
Camping Carnet compulsory.
Access from the B171 by ARAL filling station or from motorway exit Schwaz or Wattens.
15 May-15 Oct
2.5HEC H ✕ ⊖ [G] P + lau
See advertisement on page 78

VÖLS
Tirol
Völs ✆(0572) 303533
May-Oct
0.4HEC ● H ✕ ⊖ PR +
Prices A45 V40 40 Å40

WAIDRING
Tirol
Steinplatte Unterwasser 43 ✆(05353) 5345
All year
4HEC ○ H ⊖ [G] [R] L +
Prices A55 pitch40-65

WALCHSEE
Tirol
Seespitz Wassersportzentrum ✆(05374) 5359
Site made up of several plots of land.
Between B172 and bank of lake.
All year
2HEC ○ H ✕ ⊖ [G] [H] L +
Prices A45-50 pitch45-75

Terrassencamping Süd-See Seestr 76 ✆(05374) 5339
Extensively terraced site, the lowest are reserved for tourers.
500m W on B172 turn into 'no through road' and continue for 1500m.
All year
11HEC ◑ H ✕ ⊖ [G] [R] L + lau
Prices A45-50 pitch60-70

WEER
See **SCHWAZ**

WIESING
Tirol
Inntal ✆(05244) 2693
Partially terraced site on sloping grassland.
Access via Wiesing-Zillertal-Achensee exit on A12 in direction of Achensee.
All year
1.7HEC ◑ H ✕ ⊖ [G] [R] [H] P + lau
Prices A38-50 V25-35 30-45 Å25-35

ZAMS
Tirol
See also LANDECK
Zams Magdalenaweg 1 ✆(05442) 3289
3km NE of Landeck on B1.
16 Jun-10 Sep
0.2HEC ◑ H ⊖ LP + ✕
Prices A30-32 V17-19 25-45 Å25-45

ZELL AM ZILLER
Tirol
Hofer Gerlospasstr ✆(05282) 2248
On meadowland with some fruit trees.
Site lies to the end of Zillertal off the road leading to the Gerlos Pass.
All year
1.5HEC ◑ H ✕ ⊖ [G] [R] P + lau S
Prices A45 pitch45

ZIRL
Tirol
Alpenfrieden Eigenhofen 11 ✆(05238) 27204
Near the B171.
14 Apr-15 Oct
2HEC ◑ H ✕ ⊖ [G] P + lau

CARINTHIA

High mountains on all sides tumble down to this sunny, southern, gentle land of soft light and over a thousand warm, clear lakes. The climate is kind to holiday-makers – most of the weather troughs are broken up by the surrounding mountains, so this province gets many more sunny days than the rest of the country. The lakes provide a wealth of water sports in the summer, frequently reaching temperatures of over 75 degrees F (24 degrees C) – ideal for swimmers, wind-surfers and sailers. Anglers can fish for pike, whitefish and carp, and hot springs in the region have been channelled into waterpark complexes with chutes and whirling currents, or health spas offering the 'gift of youth'. But the mild summers are complemented by sharp winters, making Nassfeld and the Nock district popular areas for winter sports.

There is a relaxed Mediterranean atmosphere in this region, and a substantial Slovene minority, dating back to the 6th century, adds its own distinct character and language to southern parts.

The capital of Kärnten is Klagenfurt which, according to legend, was built on a swamp once dominated by a dragon. The centre of the town now is the Dragon Fountain (Lindwurmbrunnen), with its huge grim 16th-century sculpture of the town's heraldic emblem. Now an important junction and commercial centre, Klagenfurt's old quarter has many handsome baroque buildings set in attractive lanes and passageways.

AFRITZ
Kärnten
Bodner Lierzberg 38 ✆(04247) 2579
S of B98
May-Oct
1HEC ○ H ✕ ⊖ [G] L + lau
Prices A35-50 V20-25 20-25 Å20-25

ANNENHEIM
Kärnten
Bad Ossiacher See ✆(04248) 2757
An extensive level site with adjoining meadow.
Situated on B94 Villach-Wien road.
15 May-15 Sep
5.4HEC ◑ H ✕ ⊖ [G] L + lau
Prices A45-60 pitch60-75

BODENSDORF
Kärnten
Glaser ✆(04243) 568
On shore of Lake Ossiach with private ➔

bathing area. Quiet at night despite lying beside railway line. Badly signposted access.
Turn off B94 at BP garage towards lake. Cross railway and continue for 200m.
All year
1.5HEC ◑ H ✕ ⊖ L + lau

DELLACH
Kärnten
Neubauer (04766) 2530
Access from B100, Leinz-Spittal road. The turn-off is well signposted in the village.
15 Apr-15 Oct
1.5HEC ◑ H ✕ ⊖ L lau
Prices A35-50 V15 20-30 20-30

DELLACH IM DRAUTAL
Kärnten
Waldbad (04714) 288
On NE shore of Millstatter See on W outskirts of town.
May-Sep
3HEC ◑ H ✕ ⊖ [G] P + lau R
Prices pitch120-170

DÖBRIACH
Kärnten
Brunner am See Glanzerstr 108 (04246) 7189
Tidily arranged with poplar trees. Private bathing area.
The access road is at the E end of Lake Millstatt.
All year
2.5HEC ◑ H ⊖ [G] [R] [H] L + lau ✕
Prices pitch180-260 (incl 2 persons)

Burgstaller 16 Seefeldstr (04246) 7774
At SE end of lake. From B98 continue towards Lake Millstatt for 1km.
All year
7HEC ◑ H ✕ ⊖ [G] [R] [H] + lau L
Prices A35-70 pitch40-120

Ebner's Seefeldstr 1 (04246) 7315
On either side of the Seefeldstr, beyond Camping Burgstaller, at E end of lake Millstatt.
14 Dec-27 Oct
1.8HEC ◑ H ✕ ⊖ [G] [R] P P + lau L
Prices pitch132-156

Mössler Glanzerstr 24 (04246) 7735
On meadowland, completely divided into pitches.
At SE end of the lake on right of Döbriach-Feistritz road.
20 Dec-Oct
3HEC ◑ H ✕ ⊖ [G] [R] [H] P lau L

Winkler Strandweg 26 (04246) 7187
On level ground, divided into sections.
Approx. 400m E of the lake.
15 Apr-Oct
2HEC ◑ H ✕ ⊖ [G] [R] [H] L + lau P
Prices A55 pitch100

DÖLLACH
Kärnten
Zirknitzer (04825) 451
Beside the River Möu.
Between Km8 and Km9 on the Glocknerstr (B107).
Jun-Sep
0.6HEC ● H ⊖ R + lau ✕ P
Prices A23-27 V15 20 12-18

DROBOLLACH
Kärnten
Mittewald (04242) 27392
In a hollow on slightly rising ground surrounded by trees and divided into pitches. Large children's playground.
Off Villach-Faaker See road. Signposted 'Serai'.
Apr-Oct
2.5HEC ◑ H ✕ ⊖ P + lau [G] [R] R
Prices A45-52 V20-25 40-45 25-45

FAAK AM SEE
See **VILLACH**

GNESAU
Kärnten
Hobitsch Sonnleiten 24 (04278) 368
31 May-Sep
0.6HEC ◑ H ✕ ⊖ P + lau [G]
Prices A35 V18 18 18

HEILIGENBLUT
Kärnten
Grossglockner (04824) 2048
Closed 16 Oct-19 Dec & 11-30 Apr
2.5HEC ○ H ✕ ⊖ [G] [R] R + lau
Prices A45 V30 30

HEILIGEN GESTADE
See **OSSIACH**

HERMAGOR
Kärnten
Pressegger See (04282) 2039
6km E.
May-Sep
7.2HEC ○ H ✕ ⊖ [G] L + lau
Prices A28-38 pitch35-40

Schluga Seecamping (04282) 2760
Approx. 300m N of lake in meadowland with some terraces and fine views.
20 May-15 Sep
7HEC S ◑ ● H ✕ ⊖ [G] [R] [H] + lau L

KEUTSCHACH
Kärnten
Strandcamping Süd (043) 04273
May-Sep
2HEC ◑ H ✕ ⊖ L lau [G] [R]
Prices A40 V20 50 35

KIRSCHENTHEUER
Kärnten
Shell-Camping (04227) 2279
On road to Loibl Pass behind SHELL garage and motel.
May-Oct
1.5HEC ◑ H ✕ ⊖ [R] LP lau

KLAGENFURT
Kärnten
Strandbad (0463) 21169
Large site divided into sections by trees and bushes.
From town centre take B83 towards Velden. Turn left just outside town in direction of bathing area.
May-Sep
4HEC ◑ H ✕ ⊖ [G] L + lau
Prices A50 pitch25

KÖTSCHACH-MAUTHEN
Kärnten
Alpen (04715) 429
In meadowland beside River Gail.
Turn off B110 in the S part of the village on the road to the Plöcken Pass and drive 800m towards Lesachtal.
May-15 Oct
1.2HEC ● H ✕ ⊖ [G] [H] PR + lau L

LAINACH
Kärnten
Bambi (04822) 376
On undulating wooded meadowland.
By Km45.6 on Möutalstr (B106) behind Gasthof Planegger.
May-Sep
0.5HEC ◑ H ✕ ⊖ [G]

MALTA
Kärnten
Malta (04733) 234
On a gently rising alpine meadow.
In Gmünd turn off B99 and drive 5.5km through Malta valley.
Etr-Oct
3HEC ◑ H ✕ ⊖ [G] P + lau
Prices A40-50 pitch48-90

MÖLLBRÜCKE
Kärnten
Rheingold Mölltalstr 65 (04769) 2338
Site on main road from Spittal to Mallnitz, next to swimming pool.
All year
1HEC ◑ H ✕ ⊖ [G] P

OBERVELLACH
Kärnten
Waldcamping (04781) 2727

May-Sep
2HEC ◑ H ⊖ R + lau P
Prices pp38

OSSIACH
Kärnten
Ossiacher See ✆(04243) 436
Divided into pitches with generally well-situated terraces.
Off B94 on E bank of Kale Ossiacher opposite ARAL garage.
May-1 Oct
8.5HEC ◑ H ⊖ G R H L + lau
Prices A62 pitch40-82

Parth ✆(04243) 421
On hilly ground on S shore of the lake. Steep, but there are some terraces.
Off B94 on S bank of Lake Ossiach.
May-Sep
1.5HEC ◑ H ⊖ G R + lau L

At **HEILIGEN GESTADE**(5km SW)
Seecamping Berghof ✆(04242) 41133
Terraced meadowland in attractive setting. 800m long promenade with bathing areas.
E shore of Lake Ossiacher.
20 Apr-15 Oct
8HEC ◑ H ⊖ G R H L +
Prices A45-67 pitch75-100

REAUZ
Kärnten
Reichmann ✆(0463) 281452
May-Oct
12HEC ◑ H ⊖ H L + lau G R P

REISACH GAILTAL
Kärnten
Ferienpark Alpen ✆(04284) 301
Terraced site almost entirely divided into pitches with fine mountain view.
Turn of B111 in town at the war memorial and continue 1.7km on asphalt road with gradients of up to 13%.
15 May-Oct
3HEC ◑ H ⊖ G H P P + lau

ST GEORGEN
Kärnten
Gerli St Georgenerstr 140 ✆(04242) 27402
Level, quiet, isolated site, with heated swimming pool annexed to it which is open to the public.
From Spittal/Drau turn off B100, turn right just before Villach and continue for 2km.
All year
2HEC H ⊖ G R H P + lau

ST STEFAN
Kärnten
Streit ✆(04352) 2273
E off B70 and then 2.7km to site.
May-Sep
0.8HEC ◑ H ⊖ + lau P

ST VEIT
Kärnten
St Veit Kalten Keller Str 26 ✆(04212) 5130
May-Oct
1HEC ◑ H ⊖ P + lau G R
Prices A50-60 pitch25-65

SCHMELZHÜTTE
Kärnten
Raggaschlucht ✆(04785) 213
May-Oct
0.7HEC ◑ H ⊖ G lau P
Prices A35-45 V10 40-50 35

SEEBODEN
Kärnten
Feriendorf Lieseregg ✆(04762) 2723
On large level meadows; some terraces and asphalt drives.
B99 from Spittal north to B98, then left for 1.5km.
15 Apr-15 Oct
4HEC ◑ H ⊖ G R H P + lau L
Prices A45-70 pitch80

Seecamping Penker ✆(04762) 81927 & 81822
Site situated on meadowland and divided into fields on both sides of the lakeside promenade. There are some rows of poplars and the lower part of the site is terraced.
For access turn off opposite ADEG store and continue for 300m.
May-Oct
6.4HEC ○ H ⊖ G LP +

Terrassen Lärchenfeld ✆(04762) 81267
Gently sloping site with terraces.
Access from village, opposite ADEG store, near the church turn uphill, then 300m to site.
May-Sep
1.6HEC ◑ H ⊖ G + lau L

SPITTAL AN DER DRAU
Kärnten
Draufluss ✆(04762) 2466
A long, narrow riverside site, partly surrounded by a hedge.
From town centre follow road to river towards Goldeckbahn.
Apr-Oct
1HEC ◑ H ⊖ PR + lau G
Prices A50-60 V30-40 30-40 30-40

STEINDORF
Kärnten
Nagele ✆(04243) 8314
In the village of Steindorf on the lake shore.
Off B94 at Km31.8 and cross railway.
Jun-Sep
0.8HEC ◑ H ⊖ G L + lau

STEUERBERG
Kärnten
Goggausee ✆(04271) 2107
All year
4HEC H ⊖ lau G R L
Prices A50 V20 40 40

STOCKENBOI
Kärnten
Ronacher ✆(04761) 256
Situated on meadow between forest slopes, gently sloping to the shore of Lake Weissensee.
Approach for caravans via Weissensee.
May-Sep
1.8HEC ◑ H ⊖ G R L + lau

TECHENDORF
Kärnten
Strandcamping Knaller ✆(04713) 2234
May-Sep
1HEC ○ H ⊖ G L lau +
Prices A60-85 V20-40 25 25

TIGRING
Kärnten
Tigring FKK ✆(04272) 83542
May-Oct
10HEC ● H ⊖ G R H L

VILLACH
Kärnten
Gerli St Georgenstr 140 ✆(04242) 289722
All year
2.3HEC ◑ H ⊖ G R H P + lau
Prices A35-40 pitch35-40

At **FAAK AM SEE**(10km SE)
Poglitsch ✆(04254) 2718
15 Mar-Oct
3.5HEC ◑ H ⊖ G R L +
Prices A50-55 pitch70-90

Strandcamping Arneitz ✆(04254) 2137
26 Apr-5 Sep
6HEC ◑ H ⊖ G R L + lau
Prices A71-78 pitch70-100

Strandcamping Florian ✆(04254) 2261
A partially shaded site between the ➔

lakeside and the road.
Access from road by Hotel Fürst.
May-25 Sep
2HEC H G L + lau

WEISSBRIACH
Kärnten
Alpendorf (04286) 346
Access from Hermagor-Ilkmen road B87 5km S of lake, turn by bridge then site is 300m.
May-Oct
1.5HEC H + lau G P
Prices A27-32 pitch30-35

WERTSCHACH
Kärnten
Alpenfreude (04256) 2708
May-Sep
5HEC H G R H P + lau
Prices pitch60-70

STYRIA

Styria is a mosaic; soft hills in the southern wine-growing area, wide forest areas which have given the province the name of the 'green march', and the grand rocky massifs of the upper Styria. Between the high Alps, crossed by dramatic mountain passes, and the lowland regions, is a spectrum of beautiful scenery, with pleasant summer resorts as well as winter sports areas. The region is rich in beautiful gorges and waterfalls, the largest and best known of which is the Gesause, where the River Enns has carved its way through the mountains.
Caves are a feature of Styria – the large Lurgrotten at Peggau is well-equipped for visitors – and some caves have revealed evidence of prehistoric occupation.
Austria's second largest city and Styria's capital, the lively city of Graz is in the south-east corner of the province. A major industrial and university town, Graz boasts many interesting historic buildings, and above the attractive old town, a funicular leads to the 1,552ft (473 metre) Schlossberg which is dominated by the town's distinctive landmark, the 92ft (28 metre) Clock tower (Uhrturm).

ADMONT
Steiermark
At **HALL**(3km N)
Hall (03613) 2839
In level meadow on banks of the River Enns, near a farm.
Camping Carnet compulsory.
15 Jun-Oct
3HEC H lau

AIGEN
Steiermark
Hohenberg (03682) 8130
Lakeside site on terraced hillside with some fruit trees.
Turn right in Wiler Ketten after the Military Airfield and right again after the ARAL petrol station and follow narrow road to site.
Apr-Oct
1.5HEC H G R L + lau
Prices A27 pitch36

GÖBL
Steiermark
Göbl (06152) 8181
May-Sep
1HEC H G R L
Prices A40 V10 10 A5-10

GRAZ
Steiermark
S C Central Martinhofstr 3 (0316) 281831
A site with many lawns separated by asphalt paths and partly divided into pitches.
Turn off the B70 in Strassgang S of Graz and continue for 300m.
Apr-Oct
3HEC H G R H P + lau
Prices A35-45 pitch90-100

At **MANTSCHA**
Wald Riederhof (03122) 284380
A peaceful, terraced site surrounded by woodlands.
From Graz take Reininghalisstr and Steinbergstr towards Mantscha signposted from railway station.
All year
5HEC H G R lau PR

At **ST PETER**(4km SE)
Ost Neue Welthöhe 71 (0316) 45169
On terraced sloping ground.
3km from the town centre off Waltendorfer Hauptstr.
Apr-Oct
0.6HEC H G + P

HALL
See **ADMONT**

HARTBERG
Steiermark
Hartberg (03332) 2250
In quiet situation surrounded by trees and hedges in meadowland next to an open- air pool.
Turn off B54 towards swimming pool and continue 300m.
Apr-Sep
1HEC H lau P

HIRSCHEGG
Steiermark
Hirschegg (03141) 2201
All year
2HEC H G R R + lau

LANGENWANG-MÜRTZAL
Steiermark
Europa (03854) 2950
On level meadow with some trees, surrounded by hedges.
The B306 (E7) by-passes the town, so be careful not to miss the exit 6km S of Mürzzuschlag.

ll year
.6HEC ◑ H ⊖ R + lau
R
rices A33 V33 33 A33

EIBNITZ
teiermark
eibnitz Hauptpl 24 ✆(03452) 2463
May-Sep
HEC ● H ⊖ PR lau
G R L +
rices A25 V15 30 A20

IEBOCH
teiermark
raz-Lieboch ✆(03136) 2797
May-Sep
.3HEC ◑ H ⊖ P
+
rices A40 V35-40 35-40 A35-40

MANTSCHA
ee **GRAZ**

MARIAZELL
teiermark
rlaufsee ✆(03882) 2148
mall, quiet site on the edge of a wood, way from lake.
km N of Mariazell, off the B20. Access hrough a big car park in front of the Herrenhaus Hotel.
May-15 Sep
.5HEC ◑ H ⊖ L
+ P
rices A27 V12 15-25 A5-20

MURAU
teiermark
Olachgut ✆(03532) 2162

All year
10HEC ◑ H ⊖ G R
H LR + lau P
Prices A37 V25 30 A20-30

OBERWÖLZ
Steiermark
Schloss Rothenfels ✆(03581) 208
All year
8HEC ○ ◑ ● H ⊖ R
+ lau G R P
Prices A40 V25 25 A25

RAMSAU
Steiermark
Dachstein Dachstein ✆(03687) 81280
All year
0.3HEC S ○ H ⊖
lau P
See advertisement on page 82

ST GEORGEN
Steiermark
Olachgut ✆(03532) 2162
Camping Carnet Compulsory.
All year
10HEC ◑ H ⊖ G R
H L + lau
Prices A37 V20 30 A10-30

ST PETER
See **GRAZ**

ST SEBASTIAN
Steiermark
Erlaufsee Bundesstr 1 ✆(03882) 2148
May-15 Sep
0.5HEC ◑ H ⊖
LPR
Prices A27 V12 15 A5

SCHLADMING
Steiermark
Zirngast Langegasse 633 ✆(03687) 23195
Site in meadow on left bank of River Enns next to railway.
Turn off B308 towards town as far as the MOBIL filling station.
All year
8HEC ○ H ⊖ G R
H R + lau P
Prices A50 pitch150

STUBENBURG
Steiermark
Steinmann ✆(03176) 390
All year
2.5HEC ○ ◑ H ⊖ R
L P + G
Prices A35-40 pitch30-35

UNGERSDORF BEI FROHNLEITEN
Steiermark
Lanzmalerhof ✆(03126) 2360
Signposted 2km S of Frohnleiten on the Graz road.
Apr-15 Oct
0.5HEC ◑ H ⊖ G
R R + P
Prices A30 V23 23 A12-24

WILDALPEN
Steiermark
Wildalpen ✆(03636) 342
Apr-Oct
0.8HEC S ○ H ⊖ G R
lau LP +
Prices A22-27 V13 17-27 A11-17

LOWER AUSTRIA (NIEDERÖSTERREICH/BURGENLAND)

Lower Austria, by far the largest of the nine provinces, wraps itself around the federal capital of Vienna, itself a separate province. The Danube divides Lower Austria roughly in half, and has been central to the development of the area for centuries: prehistoric and Roman remains have been found, castles and fortified churches testify to the Romanesque and Gothic periods and great monasteries and pilgrimage churches celebrate the Baroque.
North of the river the countryside, flat in the west, becomes hilly towards the Czechoslovak border; south of the river the land rises into wooded hills (including the well-known Vienna Woods – Wienerwald), and climbs to over 6,560ft (2,000 metres) in the Schneeberg and Rax regions – popular holiday areas for the Viennese.
Good communications have promoted industrial development in the Vienna basin and it is now the largest industrial area in the country. But agriculture is also important in the province, and vineyards around Krems and Weinviertel produce excellent wines.
The south of the province, of Burgenland the 'land of castles', has many monuments to a valient past in what was for centuries a frontier area, occupied by the Romans and later vulnerable to attack from the Huns and the Turks. It is now a peaceful landscape of wooded hills, pastures, fruit orchards and vineyards.
In dramatic contrast is the impressive expanse of the 'paszta' plain in the north east, and the vast Neusiedler See – the only steppe lake in central Europe, and well known for unique flora and fauna – providing good opportunities for bathing and yachting.
Eisenstadt, the provincial capital is dominated by the Schloss Esterhazy, where this aristocratic family had its seat in the 17th and 18th centuries. There is an attractive old town, a cathedral, and the Haydnhaus (now a museum) where Haydn lived during the 30 years he was Kapellmeister here.

DONNERSKIRCHEN
Burgenland
Sonnenwaldbad ✆(02683) 8670
Grassy site with wide terraces beside a wood. View of the lake.
May-Sep
10HEC ~ ◑ H ✕ ⊖ G ≈P P + lau ☞

GMÜND
Niederösterreich
Assangteich Albrechtser St 10 ✆(02852) 2558
Whit-Sep
0.5HEC ~ ○ H ✕ ⊖ ≈LP P + ☞ G R
Prices A30 pitch50

HIRTENBERG
Niederösterreich
Hirtenberg Bahngasse 1 ✆(02256) 81111
Jun-15 Sep
0.5HEC ~ ◑ H ⊖ P ☞ ✕ G R ≈LPR +
Prices A30 pitch40

INPRUGG
Niederösterreich
Finsterhof ✆(02772) 2130
All year
2HEC ~ ○ ⊖ G R H P + lau ☞ ✕
Prices A30-33 V20-22 30-33 Å25-27

JENNERSDORF
Burgenland
Jennersdorf ✆(03154) 6133
All year
1HEC ~ ○ H ⊖ ≈P P + lau ☞ ✕
Prices A30 pitch30

KREMS
Niederösterreich
Donau (ÖAMTC) Wiedengasse 7 ✆(02732) 4455
By river opposite SHELL filling station.
May-Sep
1HEC ~ ○ H ✕ ⊖ R ≈R P

LAXENBURG
Niederösterreich
Schlosspark Laxenburg Münchendorfer Str ✆(02236) 71333
On level meadowland with surfaced roads. The site lies in a recreation centre within the grounds of the historic Laxenburg Castle.
Access 600m s on the road leading to the B16.
Apr-Oct
5.9HEC ~ ◑ H ✕ ⊖ G ≈P P + lau
Prices A50 V48 48 Å48

MARBACH
Niederösterreich
Marbach ✆(07413) 466
Apr-Oct
0.5HEC ~ ◑ H ✕ ⊖ ≈R P lau ☞ G ≈P +
Prices A46 pitch42

OBERRETZBACH
Niederösterreich
Hubertus ✆(02942) 3238
Camping Carnet Compulsory.
All year
1HEC ~ ◑ H ✕ ⊖ R P + lau ☞
Prices A40 V5 35 Å20

OGGAU
Burgenland
Oggau ✆(02685) 7271
Apr-Oct
8HEC ~ ◑ H ✕ ⊖ ≈P P +
Prices A22 pitch22

RAPPOLTENKIRCHEN
Niederösterreich
Rappoltenkirchen ✆(02274) 8425
Turn off B1 at Sieghartskirchen and continue S for 3km.
Mar-Dec
2.6HEC ~ ◑ H ⊖ G R H P + lau ☞ ✕ ≈P
Prices A32 V16 40 Å30

ROSSATZ
Niederösterreich
Rossatzbach ✆(02714) 317
Etr-Oct
0.5HEC ~ ◑ H ✕ ⊖ ≈R P lau ☞ G R ≈P +
Prices A15 V20 20-35 Å15-35

RUST
Burgenland
Rust ✆(02685) 595
Situated on level meadowland with young trees.
From Rust follow the lake road.
Apr-Oct
5HEC ~ ◑ H ✕ ⊖ ≈L P + lau ☞ ≈P
Prices A33-45 V28-55 28-55 Å20-35

SCHÖNBÜHEL
Niederösterreich
Schönbühel ✆(02752) 8510
Apr-Oct

HEC G R
+ lau
Prices A36-40 V15 30-50 A30-50

TRAISEN
Niederösterreich
Kulmhof (02762) 2900

All year
1.7HEC H P
+ lau G
Prices A32 pitch32

TÜRNITZ
Niederösterreich
Gravogl (02769) 201

All year
0.9HEC H G
+ lau
Prices A25 pitch30

UPPER AUSTRIA

The province of Salzburg is wonderfully diverse: in the north mighty massifs fall away to rolling uplands and plains, and to the east the hills of the Salzkammergut merge into the Alpine landscape of Upper Austria. Visitors are drawn to the province by the natural landscape; dozens of attractive summer resorts, from smart cosmopolitan spas to picturesque mountain hamlets; and facilities for winter sports in almost every part of the province.

A magnificent setting and a wealth of beautiful buildings and attractive streets have given Salzburg an international reputation as one of the most beautiful cities in the world. It contains a rich heritage of architecture and the arts, and Mozart was born here in 1756. The city is still a major musical centre, and hosts an annual music festival every summer, with performances of the highest quality.

The scenic facets of Upper Austria (Oberösterreich) stretch from the wooded Mühlviertel area north of the Danube to the lake-studded Salzkammergut and the glacier region of the Dachstein – all dotted with lively holiday centres, peaceful villages and idyllic spas and health resorts.

The provincial capital Linz, Austria's third-largest city, spans both banks of the Danube in the Linz basin. The old town's original market square is flanked by impressive buildings, and the city has many attractive streets and arcaded courtyards.

ALTENMARKT
Salzburg
Götschl-Au (06452) 7821
S towards the Zauchensee
All year
0HEC H G
R lau P
Prices A35-40 pitch32-45

BADGASTEIN
Salzburg
Azur-Kurcamping 'Erlengrund'
(06434) 2790
On meadowland below the road leading to the Tauern railway tunnel.
From Hofgastein turn left off B167 and descend for 100m.
All year
.5HEC H G
H P + lau LR
Prices A52-59 pitch52-80

BRUCK AN DER GROSSGLOCKNERSTRASSE
Salzburg
Woferlgut (06545) 303
Access via exit Bruck-Süd on S11.
All year
HEC H G R
H P + lau LR
Prices A45 V40 50 A35-50

BURGAU
Salzburg
Burgau (07663) 266
Mainly level site surrounded by trees between the road and the Attersee at Weissenbach.
On B152 at Km 27.6 opposite Hotel Burgau.
May-Oct
6HEC H G R
LR +
Prices A41-45 V29-32 29-32 A29-32

Eitzinger (07663) 769
Apr-Sep
6HEC S H L
Prices A39 V20 35 A30

ESTERNBERG
Oberösterreich
Pyrawang (07714) 504
Apr-Sep
0.3HEC H +
LR
Prices A30 V20 20 A20

GLEINKERAU
Oberösterreich
Garstnertal 7066
Mar-Oct
1HEC H + lau
G R
Prices A28 V15 38 A18

GOLLING
Salzburg
Torrener Hof (06244) 380
On the outskirts of the village on the B159.
Mar-28 Oct
3HEC H
+ G LPR
Prices A20 V20 40 A20

HALLEIN
Salzburg
Susi (06245) 765584
Situated in well tended grassland on a tributary of the Konigsee.
Access from Salzburg-Villach motorway exit Salzburg Süd or Hallein, then on B159/E14 to turn off by Brückenwirt in Anif Niederalm.
Apr-15 Sep
0.8HEC H R
+
Prices A35 V20 20 A20

HAMMER
Salzburg
Hammerkeller (06472) 7246
All year
0.8HEC H G
R lau LP +

KAPRUN
Salzburg
Mühle (06547) 8254
On long stretch of meadow by the Kapruner Ache. S end of village towards cable lift.
All year
1HEC H G R
P lau

MAISHOFEN
Salzburg
Kammerlander (06542) 8755
On B168.
Apr-Oct
1.3HEC H
L
Prices A23 V20 20 A20

NUSSDORF
Oberösterreich

See Camping Gruber Dortstr 63 ✆(07666) 80450

On fairly long meadow parallel to the promenade.

S of village, access is at Km19.7. Turn off B151 towards the lake (Attersee).

May-Sep

1.8HEC + lau G

Prices A40-45 pitch48-55

Strandcamping Graus ✆(07666) 8008

Site on long meadow with fruit trees, sloping towards lake and bathing area. Access is within the village.

Turn off main road B151 at Km19.5 towards the lake (Attersee).

May-Sep

2.7HEC G R + lau

PERWANG AM GRABENSEE
Oberösterreich

Perwang ✆(06217) 8247

Site beside lake.

May-Oct

1.5HEC + lau

RADSTADT
Salzburg

Forellencamp ✆(06452) 7861

All year

1HEC R +

Prices A35 V20 25 A15-20

ST JOHANN IM PONGAU
Salzburg

Wieshof Rainbach 4 ✆(06412) 519

On gently sloping meadow behind pension and farmhouse. Modern facilities. Big spa house with sauna, massage facilities and health bars, adjacent to site.

Camping Carnet Compulsory.

Off B311 towards Zell am Zee.

All year

1HEC G + lau

Prices A40 V20 20 A20

ST LORENZ
Oberösterreich

Alten Ischler Bahn St Lorenz 88 ✆(06232) 2902

Clean orderly site, easily accessible in the beautiful Mondsee Valley.

All year

1HEC + lau G

Prices A33 pitch42

Austria-Camp ✆(06232) 2927

Level site on grassland bordered by trees and hedges and divided into fields by internal roads. Separate field for young people.

4km from Mondsee, beside the lake.

May-Oct

3HEC G R + lau

Prices A35 V25 37 A23-32

ST MARTIN BEI LOFER
Salzburg

Park Grubhof ✆(06588) 237

Situated in meadowland on the banks of the River Saalach. Separate sections for dog owners, families, teenagers and groups.

1.5km S of Lofer turn left off B311.

May-Sep

10HEC G R H + lau

Prices A47 V22 28-34 A21-26

ST WOLFGANG
Oberösterreich

Appesbach Au 99 ✆(06138) 2206

On sloping meadow facing lake with no shade at upper end.

0.8km E of St Wolfgang between lake and Strobl road.

All year

2HEC G R H + lau

Prices A44-48 pitch35-85

Berau Schwarzenbach 16 ✆(06138) 2543

Site lies between lake and road from Strobl, N of lake.

1.3km E of entrance to St Wolfgang.

All year

2HEC G R + lau

Prices A40 V15 50-60 A40-60

Ried 18 ✆(06138) 2521

15 May-Sep

0.4HEC + lau G

Prices A38 V15 25 A15-25

SALZBURG
Salzburg

Gnigl-Ost Parscherstr 4 ✆(0662) 702743

May-Sep

3HEC + G R

Prices A28 V25 25 A20

Nord Sam Samstr 22A ✆(0662) 660611

Site divided into pitches.

400m from Salzburg Nord Autobahn Exit.
Apr-Oct
2HEC ◑ H ✕ ⊖ G R P + lau
Prices A33-47 pitch55-70

Schloss Aigen ✆(0662) 22079
Site divided into pitches in partial clearing on mountain slope.
From Salzburg-Süd motorway exit through Anif and Glasenbach.
May-Sep
25HEC ◑ H ✕ ⊖ G R + lau P
Prices A32 pitch32-36

Stadtblick Rauchenbichlerstr 21 ✆(0662) 50652
Leave motorway at exit Salzburg-Nord and follow signs.
15 Mar-Oct
0.8HEC S ● H ✕ ⊖ G R H + lau P
Prices A40-50 50-60 A30-40

See advertisement on page 86

SEEKIRCHEN
Salzburg
Strand ✆(06212) 488
Beside the Wallersee in beautiful meadow.
May-Oct
3HEC ◑ H ✕ ⊖ L + lau

Zell am Wallersee ✆(06212) 480
Level meadowland separated from the lake by the Lido.
Access from A1 exit Wallersee then via Seekirchen to Zell.
15 Apr-30 Oct
3HEC ◑ H ✕ ⊖ L + lau
Prices A25 pitch100

STEINBACH
Oberösterreich
Seefeld ✆(07663) 3420
On meadowland sloping gently towards lake, behind Gasthof Föttinger.
Near MOBIL garage on B152 at Km13.6.
May-Oct
1.2HEC ◑ H ✕ ⊖ + lau L

STEYR-MÜNICHOLZ
Oberösterreich
Forelle
15 Apr-15 Oct
4HEC ● H R P + lau
Prices A35 V60 60

TAMSWEG
Salzburg
Tamsweg ✆(06474) 385
Site lies 700m N off main road at north entrance of village.
All year
1.5HEC ◑ H ✕ ⊖ G + lau

TIEFGRABEN
Oberösterreich
Fohlenhof Hof 17 ✆(06232) 2600
Apr-15 Oct
5.8HEC ◑ H ✕ ⊖ G R H P + lau
Prices A29 pitch60

UNTERACH
Oberösterreich
Insel ✆(07665) 8311
Quiet site on shore of Lake Attersee; divided into two sections by River Seeache. Family site.
Entrance below B152 towards Steinbach at Km24.5; about 300m from fork with B151.
15 May-15 Sep
1.8HEC ◑ H ⊖ L + lau ✕
Prices A40 V20 25 A20

WERFEN
Salzburg
Vierthaler Reitsam 8 ✆(06468) 657
15 Apr-Sep
1HEC ◑ H ✕ ⊖ G R R + lau
Prices A20 pitch45

WESENUFER
Oberösterreich
Nibelungen ✆(07718) 589
Apr-Sep
70HEC ◑ H ✕ ⊖ R +
Prices A27 30 A15

ZELL AM SEE
Salzburg
Südufer Seeuferstr 196 ✆(06542) 6228
All year
0.6HEC ◑ ● H ⊖ G ✕ L
Prices A41 V18 45-50 A25-30

ZINKENBACH
Oberösterreich
Terrassencamping Schönblick Gschwendt 33 ✆(06138) 2471
A terraced site with birch trees. Beautifully situated with views of St Wolfgang and the lake.
Turn off B158 between Zinkenbach and Strobl in direction of landing stage.
May-Oct
1.4HEC ◑ H ⊖ G R L + ✕
Prices A40 pitch40

VORARLBERG

Austria's most western province, Vorarlberg is small but very beautiful. The gardens and orchards in the Rhine valley and on the shores of Lake Constance give way to a forested upland region, and finally to the peaks and glaciers of the Silvretta, rising to over 9,800ft (3,000 metres). With its lovely old towns and villages, clear mountain lakes and rivers, quiet bays on Lake Constance, pastures and meadowlands, steep-sided valleys and peaks, Vorarlberg is a province of special charm. Watersports are popular on Lake Constance, but there is good access to the mountainous regions, making them popular in the summer with walkers and climbers, as well as in winter for skiers.

The onion-domed St Martin's tower (Martinstrum), dating back from 1602, distinguishes the skyline of Bregenz, the provincial capital. The newer districts of the town, on the shores of Lake Constance, have modern well-equipped tourist facilities – an open air-pool, lakeside gardens, a floating stage and a Festspielhaus for festivals and conferences.

AU
Vorarlberg
Au ✆(05515) 2331
On B200 (Dornbirn-Wath)
Closed 7 Apr-8 May & 22 Sep-Oct
0.4HEC ○ H ✕ ⊖ G + lau PR

BLUDENZ
Vorarlberg
At **BRAZ**(7km SE)
Traube ✆(05552) 8103
On sloping grassland.
7km SE of Bludenz via E17, S16 (Blundenz-Arlberg-Innsbruck).
Signposted. Near railway. ➤

All year
2HEC H G R P + R
Prices A45 V15 40 20-40

At **NÜZIDERS**(2.5km NW)
Sonnenberg ✆(05552) 64035
Clean site with modern facilities in gently sloping meadowland and splendid mountain scenery.
Access from Bludenz-Nüziders road, at first fork follow up hill.
15 May-Sep
2HEC H G R + lau P

BRAZ
See **BLUDENZ**

BREGENZ
Vorarlberg
See Bodangasse 7 ✆(05574) 31895
Quiet site on level meadow beside lake.
From town centre (Bahnhofsplatz) follow signs towards 'See Bühne'.
15 May-15 Sep
8HEC H G H L + lau P
Prices A42 V42 42 42

DALAAS
Vorarlberg
Eme ✆(05585) 223
All year
1HEC H G R R P +
Prices A60 pitch40-60

DORNBIRN
Vorarlberg
In der Enz ✆(05572) 69119
A municipal site beside a public park, some 100m beyond the Karren cable lift.
May-Sep
10HEC H G PR + lau
Prices A39 V20 pitch35

FELDKIRCH
Vorarlberg
Waldcamping ✆(05522) 24308
On level grassland, surrounded by tall trees.
All year
3.5HEC H G R H + lau P
Prices A35-40 V24-30 24-30 22-24

GANTSCHIER
See **SCHRUNS**

GASCHURN
Vorarlberg
Nova ✆(05558) 8548
A site on two levels. The upper level only is shaded.
Off B188 towards the river.
May-15 Oct
1HEC H + lau

KLÖSTERLE
See **LANGEN**

LANGEN
Vorarlberg
At **KLÖSTERLE**(2km W)
Alpencamping ✆(05582) 269
Well signposted.
All year
1.5HEC H G R P + lau
Prices A46 V23 40 20-30

LINGENAU
Vorarlberg
Feurstein ✆(05513) 6114
All year
0.8HEC H G R H + lau PR
Prices A40 V15 35 25-35

NENZING
Vorarlberg
Alpencamping Nenzing ✆(05525) 2491
Signposted from B190 from Nenzing-2km towards Gurtis.
All year
3HEC H G R H P + lau
Prices A45 pitch75

See advertisement in colour section

NÜZIDERS
See **BLUDENZ**

RAGGAL-PLAZERA
Vorarlberg
Grosswalsertal ✆(05553) 209
Situated in a quiet location on gently sloping terrain, with pleasant views.
All year
0.8HEC H G P lau
Prices A38 V6 20 16

RIEFENSBERG
Vorarlberg
Hochlitten ✆(05513) 8312
Site on terraced meadow next to the Berghof Inn.
All year
1.2HEC H G P +

SCHRUNS
Vorarlberg
At **GANTSCHIER**(2km NW)
Rhätikon ✆(05556) 29402
Site in level meadowland.
Off the Bludenz-Schruns road (B188) near River Ill.
All year
0.7HEC H G lau

TSCHAGGUNS
Vorarlberg
Zelfen ✆(05556) 2326
Partly uneven, grassy site beside River Ill. Some residential housing and electricity switching station nearby.
All year
2HEC H G R R + lau P
Prices A45 V65 65

VIENNA (WIEN)

For hundreds of years Vienna was the heart of a vast empire and cultural focus of central Europe. Today Vienna is very much one of the world's great modern tourist cities with a confident and cosmopolitan atmosphere, but it still keeps a distinctive charm and native flair. The mighty façades of the buildings and palaces of the city bear witness to the tall, grand Baroque buildings that earn it the name 'Vienna gloriosa'. And it retains and builds on its traditions of the finest music; many of the world's great composers livedand worked here, and the Opera House (Staatsoper) plays a prominent part in the social, cultural and political life of the city.
Vienna's cultural district is encircled by the wide boulevard, the Ringstrasse, on which many of the city's main buildings stand: the Opera House, the Burg Theatre, the Hofburg, the Parliament, and the neo-Gothic City Hall (Rathaus), as well as churches, museums and lovely parks, gardens and squares. There is a full programme of events in the city – everything from operas and concerts to sporting events. For more casual entertainment, though, the Viennese cafés are a famous and historic institution – popular meeting places for the Viennese and a delight for the tourists – with tables outside in the summer, newspapers and magazines always available, and of course, the traditional strong, aromatic Viennese coffee.

RODAUN
See **WIEN (VIENNA)**

VIENNA
See**WIEN**

WIEN (VIENNA)
Wien
Donaupark Klosterneuburg An der Au 4 ✆(02243) 85877
All year
1.7HEC H G R + lau P
Prices A50 V40 ▲40

Wien-West 2 Huttelbergstr 80 ✆(0222) 942314
On slightly rising meadow with asphalt paths.
From end of A1/E5 (Lienz-Wien) to Bräuhausbrücke, then turn left and across road to Linz, continue for approx. 1.8km.
All year
2HEC H G + lau
Prices A52 pitch50

At **RODAUN**(4km SW)
Schwimmbad Camping Rodaun An der Au 2 ✆(0222) 884154
Between An der Austr and Leising River dam. Access from Breitenfürter Str N492.
16 Mar-16 Nov
1.2HEC H G P + lau
Prices A50 V12 47-55 ▲47-55

Belgium is a small, densely populated country bordered by France, Germany, Luxembourg and The Netherlands. Despite the fact that it is heavily industrialised, it possesses some beautiful scenery, notably the great forest of the Ardennes. The resorts in the Oostende (Ostend) area offer a selection of wide, safe, sandy beaches and cover about forty miles of coastline.

The climate is temperate and similar to that of Britain: the variation between summer and winter lessened by the effects of the Gulf Stream. French is spoken in the south, Flemish in the north and a German dialect in the eastern part of the province of Liège.

Belgium is a varied, charming country in which to spend a camping holiday – the rivers and gorges of the Ardennes contrasting sharply with the rolling plains which make up the rest of the countryside. There are now over 800 campsites officially authorised by local authorities. They are normally open from April to October, but many are open throughout the year. Coastal sites tend to be very crowded at the height of the season.

International camping carnet is not compulsory but recommended. Some campsites will allow a reduction to the advertised charge to the holders of a camping carnet. See The European ABC for further information.

Off-site camping is prohibited beside public roads for more than 24 consecutive hours; on seashores; within a 100-metre radius of a main water point; or on a site classified for the conservation of monuments. Elsewhere, camping is permitted free of charge, as long as the stay does not exceed 24 hours and the camper has obtained authorisation from the landowner.

HOW TO GET THERE

Many ferries operate services direct to Belgium:
To ***Oostende*** (Ostend) from ***Dover*** takes 3¾–4 hours.
To ***Zeebrugge*** from ***Dover*** takes 4–4½ hours
from ***Felixstowe*** takes 5¼ hours (8–9 hours at night).
from ***Hull*** takes 14 hours.

Alternatively, you could take a shorter crossing by ferry or hovercraft to Calais or Boulogne in France and drive along the coast road to Belgium.

GENERAL INFORMATION

The information given here is specific to Belgium. It **must** be read in conjunction with the European ABC at the front of the book, which covers those regulations which are common to many countries.

British Embassy/Consulates*

The British Embassy is located at 1040 Bruxelles, Britannia House, 28 rue Joseph II ✆(02) 2179000; *consular section* 32 rue Joseph II ✆(02) 2179000. There are British Consulates with Honorary Consuls in Antwerpen (Antwerp) and Liège.

Currency, including banking hours*

The unit of currency is the *Belgian Franc* (*BFr*) divided into 100 *centimes*. At the time of going to press £1 = *BFr* 61 Denominations of bank notes are *BFr* 50, 100, 500, 1,000, 5,000; standard coins are *BFr* 1, 5, 20, 50 and 50 *centimes*. There are no restrictions on the amount of Belgian or foreign currency which may be taken into or out of Belgium.

Banks are open Monday to Friday from 09.00–15.30hrs; some close during the lunch hour and others remain open until 16.00hrs on Friday. Outside banking hours, currency may be changed in Bruxelles (Brussels) at the Gare du Nord and the Gare du Midi, open 07.00–22.00hrs daily and at Zaventem Airport, open 07.30–22.00hrs daily.

Customs regulations

A *Customs Carnet de Passages en Douane* is required for all trailers not accompanied by the towing vehicle. See also *Customs regulations for European countries* in the European ABC for further information.

Emergency telephone numbers

Fire and **ambulance** ✆100; **police** ✆101.

Foodstuffs*

Visitors from EC countries may import duty-free, 1,000g of coffee or 400g of coffee extract and 200g of tea or 80g of tea extract bought duty- and tax-paid; a reduced allowance applies if bought duty-free. Visitors under 15 years of age do not qualify for the duty-free concessions on coffee.

Language

There are *two* official languages in Belgium – Flemish (Dutch) and French – but in practice there are *four* in use. In the area to the north of, and including Brussels, Flemish is spoken. To the south of the capital, French (or 'Walloon') is in everyday use. And in the eastern provinces, German is the predominant language. These divisions, however, are not absolute.

Some of the town names in the gazetteer are shown in both Flemish and French, and that shown first is the one used locally. However, Brussels (Bruxelles-Brussel) is officially bi-lingual.

Shopping hours

All shops are usually open from 09.00–18.00, 19.00 or 20.00hrs from Monday to Saturday; however, *food shops* may close 1 hour later.

Tourist information*

The Belgian Tourist Organisation maintains an office at 2 Gayton Road, Harrow, Middlesex HA1 2XU ✆ 081-861 3300 and they will be pleased to supply information on all aspects of tourism. In Belgium, the National Tourist Organisation is supplemented by the Provisional Tourist Federation, whilst in most towns there are local tourist offices. These organisations will help tourists with information and accommodation.

MOTORING

Accidents

The police must also be called if an unoccupied, stationary vehicle is damaged, or if injuries are caused to persons; in the latter case, the car must not be moved; see recommendations under *Accidents* (also *Warning triangle*) in the European ABC.

Children in cars

Children under 12 are not permitted to travel in front seats unless they have a special seat or if there are no rear seats or if all rear seats are already occupied by children.

***Additional information will be found in the European ABC at the front of the book.**

Dimensions and weight restrictions

Private **cars** and towed **trailers** or **caravans** are restricted to the following dimensions: height, 4 metres; width, 2.50 metres; length (including any coupling device) up to 2,500kg – 8 metres (over 2,500kg – 10 metres). The maximum permitted overall length of vehicle/trailer or caravan combination is 18 metres.

Trailers without brakes may have a total maximum weight of 750kg.

Driving Licence*

A valid UK or Republic of Ireland licence is acceptable in Belgium. The minimum age at which a visitor may use a temporarily imported car or motorcycle is 18 years.

Motoring club*

The **Touring Club Royal de Belgique** (TCB) has its head office at 1040 Bruxelles, 44 rue de la Loi ✆(02) 2332211 and branch offices in most towns. The Bruxelles (Brussels) head office is open weekly 08.30–17.30hrs; Saturday 09.00–12.00hrs. Regional offices are open weekdays 09.00–12.30hrs (Monday from 09.30hrs) and 14.00–18.00hrs; Saturday 09.00–12.00hrs. All offices are closed on Saturday afternoons and Sundays.

Roads

A good road system is available. However, one international route that has given more cause for complaints than any other is, without doubt, that from Calais (France) through Belgium to Köln/Cologne (Germany). The problem is aggravated by the fact that there are two official languages in Belgium; in the Flemish part of Belgium all signs are in Flemish only, while in Wallonia (the French-speaking half of the country), the signs are all in French. Brussels (Bruxelles-Brussel) seems to be the only neutral ground where the signs show the two alternative spellings of placenames (Antwerpen-Anvers; Gent-Gand; Liège-Luik; Mons-Bergen; Namur-Namen; Oostende-Ostende; Tournai-Doornik. From the Flemish part of the country, Dunkirk (Dunkerque) in France is signposted *Duinkerke* and Lille is referred to as *Rijsel,* and even Paris is shown as *Parijs.*

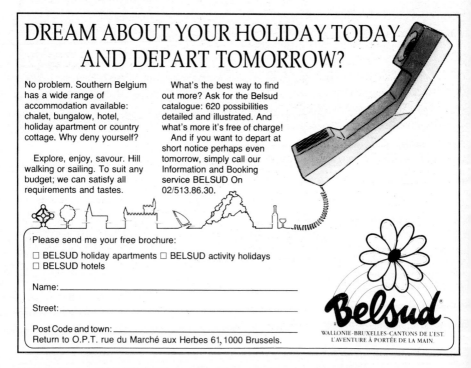

***Additional information will be found in the European ABC at the front of the book.**

Prices are in Belgian Francs
Abbreviations:
av avenue
rte route
r rue
str straat

T C B Touring Club de Belgique
Belgium is divided into the Flemish region in the north and the French-speaking Walloon region in the south. Some of the town names in the gazetteer show both languages, and that shown first is the one used locally. Brussels/Bruxelles/Brussel) is officially bi-lingual.
Each name preceded by 'De' or 'La' is listed under the name that follows it.

SOUTH WEST/COAST

The coastline of Belgium is one of fine sandy beaches backed by dunes, with few openings to the sea. The coast is lined with resorts: De Panne; Niewpoort; Ostende, with its port, is also a fashionable resort; Blankenberge; Zeebrugge; and popular Knokke-Heist. Bruges, once connected to the sea by an inlet, was a great medieval port. When the inlet silted up, the city declined, preserving a city whose architecture and unique atmosphere has survived until today, to the delight of the increasing number of visitors.
Ypres is historically an important textile centre. Reduced to rubble in World War I, the town has been almost completely restored, and now has its lovely Cloth Hall and cathedral. There are hundreds of war cemeteries and memorials near by, recalling the massive war casualties suffered in the area. Tournai is one of the oldest cities in Belgium and an important ecclesiastical centre, evidenced by the remarkable Cathedral of Notre Dame, with its rich interior and wealth of treasures.

BELOEIL
Hainaut
Orangerie r du Major ✆(069) 689190
Etr-Oct
3HEC ◑ H ⊖ R + lau
Prices A60 pitch165

BLANKENBERGE
West-Vlaanderen
Bonanza Zeebruggelaan 137 ✆(0501) 416658
15 Mar-Sep
2HEC ◑ H ⊖ G R P + lau LS
Prices A100-110 V50-60 200-220 ▲100-110

Dallas Rurettelaan 191 ✆(050) 418157
15 Mar-Sep
3HEC ○ H ⊖ G R PS P +
Prices A125 V50 125 ▲80-125

BREDENE
See **OOSTENDE (OSTENDE)**

HAAN, DE
West-Vlaanderen
Holiday Village Bredeweg 115 ✆(059) 234475
Level subdivided grassland site behind a bungalow village.
Off the N72 Blankenberge/Oostende road.
All year
8HEC ○ H ⊖ G R P + lau S
Prices A100-120 V30-60 ▲100-200

Tropical Bredeweg 76A ✆(059) 236341
Apr-Sep
2.6HEC ○ H + lau G PS
Prices A80-110 V40-60 140-170 ▲140-170

KEMMEL
West-Vlaanderen
YPRA Pingelaarstr 2 ✆(057) 444631
Apr-Sep
3HEC ◑ ● H ⊖ G

KNOKKE-HEIST
West-Vlaanderen
Vuurtoren Heistlaan 168 ✆(050) 511782
On level meadow with tarred roads.
Turn S off Knokke-Oostende road 4km from Knokke and follow signposts.
15 Mar-15 Oct
6HEC ◑ H ⊖ + lau PS
Prices A78 V50 90 ▲90

Zilvermeeuw Heistlaan 166 ✆(050) 512726
Mar-15 Nov
7HEC ○ H ⊖ G R H S + lau LP
Prices A75 V25 50 ▲50

At **WESTKAPELLE**(3km S)
Holiday Natienlaan 70-72 ✆(050) 601203
Apr-Sep
1HEC ◑ H ⊖ + P
Prices A90 V48 100 ▲100

LOMBARDSIJDE
West-Vlaanderen
Lombarde Elisabethlaan 4 ✆(0581) 236839
All year
8.5HEC ◑ H ⊖ G P + lau PS
Prices pitch390-485

LOPPEM
West-Vlaanderen
Lac Loppem ✆(050) 822264
All year
9HEC ◑ H ⊖ G R LP P +
Prices A75 V75 75 ▲75

NIEUWPOORT
West-Vlaanderen
Info Burgsesteenweg 49 ✆(058) 236037
A family site. Facilities for watersports.
On N67 between St Joris and Nieuwpoort.
29 Mar-11 Nov
25HEC S ◑ H ⊖ G P +
Prices pitch455-615

OOSTENDE (OSTENDE)
West-Vlaanderen
At **BREDENE**(5km NE)
Duinenpolder-ASTERIX Duinenstr 200 ✆(059) 324202
All year
3HEC S ◑ H ⊖ R H P + lau LPS
Prices A138 V21 84 ▲47

KACB Kon Astridlaan 53 ✆(059) 322475
Only Camping Carnet holders admitted.
Level grassland site on outskirts of village between other sites.
Off the N72 Oostende/Blankenberge road. Signposted.
All year
6.4HEC ◑ H ⊖ S +

WAREGEM
West-Vlaanderen
Gemeentelijk Sportstadion Westerlaan ✆(056) 686289
Camping Carnet compulsory.
Apr-Sep
1HEC ◑ H ⊖ P +
Prices A55 V30 45 ▲45

WESTENDE
West-Vlaanderen
Evergreen Lombardsijdelaan 171 ✆(058) 234804
200m from the Lombardsijde centre.
Apr-1 Oct
1.3HEC

Prices

KACB Duinendorp Bassevillestr 81 ✆(058) 237343
Situated between Westende and Lombardsijde towards the sea.
Camping Carnet Compulsory.
All year
6.5HEC lau
Prices A15-93 pitch265-400

TCB Lombardsijdelaan 153 ✆(058) 233797
All year
6HEC
Prices pitch335-535

WESTKAPELLE
See **KNOKKE-HEIST**

NORTH/CENTRAL

Most of this central region of Belgium is intensely agricultural, vast open plains are covered in crops, with large, compact villages in the valleys. Gent is the capital of the province of East Flanders – one of the most beautiful of Belgian cities with a wonderful medieval heart. Rivers and canals dissect the city, and it buzzes with commerce and industry, lively shopping streets and markets. Imposing buildings are reminders of a colourful past: the view from St Michael's Bridge takes in the towers of St Nicholas' Church (13th to 15th century), the Belfry (13th to 14th century, and the Cathedral of St Bavo (dating from the 10th century). Also in East Flanders, Oodenaarde is historically a textile centre; its tapestries are still renowned, and the town has many beautiful buildings dating from the late Middle Ages. The centre of the south of this region, and capital of Belgium, is Brussels. Although some parts of the old Brussels remain intact, today it is essentially a modern cosmopolitan centre, the cultural and educational capital of Belgium, headquarters of the EEC and NATO and many other international organisations. The city exudes vitality and prosperity, in keeping with its position as an international centre.

GENT (GAND)
Oost-Vlaanderen
Blaarmeersen Zuiderlaan 12 ✆(091) 215399
Mar-15 Oct
4HEC lau
Prices A75 V25 90-95 A90

GERAARDSBERGEN
Oost-Vlaanderen
Gavers Wolvenhoek Onkerzelstr 280 ✆(054) 416324
All year
12HEC lau
Prices pitch300 (incl 4 persons)

GRIMBERGEN
Brabant
Grimbergen Veldkanstr 64 ✆(02) 2692597
Apr-Oct
1.5HEC lau
Prices A70-100 V50-60 100-120 A100-120

HEVERLEE
Brabant
Ter Munck Kampingweg ✆(016) 238668
15 Jun-15 Sep
3HEC lau
Prices A48 pitch70

OUDENAARDE (AUDENARDE)
Oost-Vlaanderen
Vlaamse Ardennen Kortrijkstr 342 ✆(055) 315473
29 Mar-11 Nov
24HEC lau
Prices pitch330-490

STEKENE
Oost-Vlaanderen
Europcamping Baudeloo Heirweg 159 ✆(03) 7796663
All year
3HEC
Prices pitch300 (incl 2 persons)

Reinaert Lunterbergstr 4 ✆(03) 7798525
All year
5HEC lau
Prices A53 V42 42 A42

WACHTEBEKE
Oost-Vlaanderen
Puyenbroeck Puyenburg 1A ✆(091) 557607
Apr-Sep
8HEC lau
Prices pitch135-280

NORTH EAST

The natural entrance to this region is Antwerp. One of the great ports of Europe and a fascinating city to visit, it is dominated by the elegant tower of its cathedral. The cathedral's graceful exterior is complemented by a spacious and rich interior, with some fine Rubens masterpieces. Near the cathedral is the Grote Markt, with an impressive town hall, and several guildhalls with wonderful façades. The extensive old city contains many fine old buildings and some fascinating museums, including the Plantin Moretus Museum, and Rubens' House.

Other interesting towns in this region include Turnhout, a commercial centre with a modern town hall and lovely church in the market place; Mechelen – an ecclesiastical centre with a particularly well preserved old town; Tongeren, known as the oldest town in Belgium and containing many interesting reminders of the past; the quiet picturesque town of Zoutleeuw, with its lovely 13th-century chuch; Lier, with its attractive market place; and the old abbey town of Averbode.

ANTWERPEN (ANVERS)
Antwerpen
Vogelzang Vogelzanglaan ✆(03) 2385717
Apr-Sep
4.2HEC H + lau P
Prices A35 V35 35 A35

BRECHT
Antwerpen
Het Veen Eekhoorlaan 1 ✆(03) 6630165
Sports complex and mini zoo.
Leave Autoroute E10 at exit St Job in't Goor.
Apr-Sep
7HEC H R + lau G R
Prices A70 pitch90

GIERLE
Antwerpen
Lilse Bergen Strandweg 6 ✆(014) 557901
All year
2HEC H G R L P +
Prices pitch370

HOUTHALEN
Limburg
Hengelhoef ✆(011) 382500
Apr-Nov
1.5HEC H G + lau LP
Prices pitch300-600

KASTERLEE
Antwerpen
Houtum Houtum 51 ✆(014) 852365
Apr-Oct
6HEC H R + lau G
Prices A81-89 pitch134-150

LOMMEL
Limburg
Luna Strand Luikersteenweg 313a ✆(011) 643708
On Leopoldsburg road (N446).
Apr-Sep
52HEC H LPR +

OPGLABBEEK
Limburg
Jeugdparadjs Speeltuinstr 4 ✆(011) 854587
Apr-Sep
8HEC H P + lau

OPGRIMBIE
Limburg
Kikmolen ✆(011) 764619
Apr-Oct
35HEC H R H L +
Prices A60 V35 50 A50

REKEM
Limburg
Sonnevijer Heidestr 101 ✆(011) 713048
4km S of Autoroute E39, exit 'Lanaken'.
All year
30HEC H LP + lau

RETIE
Antwerpen
Berkenstrand Brand 78 ✆(014) 377590
3km NE on road to Postel.
Apr-Sep
10HEC H + L

SINT TRUIDEN (ST TROND)
Limburg
Egel Bautershovenstr 97 ✆(011) 687637
Apr-Oct
1.1HEC H +

VORST-LAAKDAL
Antwerpen
Kasteel Meerlaer Verboekt 105 ✆(013) 661420
All year
9HEC H R H L + lau
Prices A51 V51 51 A51

ZONHOVEN
Limburg
Berkenhof Teutseweg 33 ✆(011) 814439
Camping Carnet compulsory.
Apr-Oct
4HEC H G R P + lau
Prices A40 V26 40 A40

Holsteenbron Hengelhoelseweg 7 ✆(011) 813727
All year
6HEC H H P + lau

SOUTH EAST

This region is known as the great garden of the Ardennes – dense forests, hills rising to over 2,000ft, imposing chalk cliffs, deep, wide valleys and serene reservoirs. Small villages, ancient monasteries, high fortress citadels and picturesque towns – with imposing civic buildings and half-timbered dwellings, dot the countryside. The graceful Meuse flows through the north of this area; historically an important north-south artery. Today barges frequent its waters, and the 'castles of Namur' adorn its banks. There are a number of impressive caves in the region – the caves at Han-sur-Lesse are remarkable, streching some miles underground, with fantastic formations.
Towns set on the River Meuse include Dinant, overlooked by the mass of its castle; picturesque Namur, between the banks of the Meuse and the Sambre, also dominated by its castle; and cosmopolitan Leige, a bustling mix of culture and industry. La Roche-en-Ardenne is beautifully set in its deep valley on a loop of the Ourthe, and Spa is a traditional resort with thermal springs.

AISCHE-EN-REFAIL
Namur
Manoir de lá Bas rte de Gembloux 180 ✆(081) 655353
5km W of Eghezée.
Apr-Oct
20HEC ○ H ⊖ P
+
Prices A42 V30 50 50

AMBLÈVE
Liège
Oos Heem Deidenberg 124 ✆(080) 349692
All year
3HEC ◑ H ⊖ [G] [R]
P + lau

AVE-ET-AUFFE
Namur
Roptai Roptai 32 ✆(084) 388319
The site is located in a hilly situation in pretty clearings amidst a large forest about 1km along a dusty track from the village.
All year
10HEC ◑ H ⊖ [G]
[R] [H] P + lau
Prices A54-60 pitch120

BASSE-BODEUX
Liège
Ancienne Barrière ✆(080) 684538
All year
4HEC ● H ⊖ [G] [R] [H]
+
Prices A46 V35 46 46

BASTOGNE
Luxembourg
Renval rte de Marche ✆(061) 212985
All year
7HEC ◑ H ⊖ [G] [R]
+ lau P
Prices pitch398-448 (incl 4 persons)

BERTRIX
Luxembourg
Info ✆(061) 412281
Etr-11 Nov
12HEC ◑ H ⊖ [G]
[R] [H] P + lau

BOIS-DE-VILLERS
Namur
Haute Mariagne r L-Fernand 22 ✆(081) 433533
1km from village. 200m from main road.
Apr-Sep
1HEC ○ H ⊖ + lau
Prices A57 V40 40 40

BONNERT
Luxembourg
Officiel rte de Bastogne 368 ✆(063) 226582
E of E9-N4.
15 Apr-1 Oct
1.4HEC ◑ H ⊖ [G] +
lau
Prices A80 V10 20 12

BÜLLINGEN (BULLANGE)
Liège
Hétraie r en Forêt 264 ✆(080) 647703
This site is situated on a sloping meadow near a fish pond and is surrounded by groups of beautiful beach trees and conifers.
Leave village in direction of Amel then left and continue for 2km.
All year
3HEC ◑ ● H ⊖ [H]
P +

BÜTGENBACH
Liège
Worriken Worriken 1 ✆(080) 446358
Situated on the shores of a lake.
All year
8.5HEC ◑ H ⊖ [G] [R]
LP +

CHASSEPIERRE
Luxembourg
Cabrettes r de la Semois 7 ✆(061) 312994 & 311266
Apr-Sep
2.3HEC ◑ H ⊖ [G] R
+ lau

CHEVETOGNE
Namur
Domaine Provincial ✆(083) 688821
All year
3HEC ◑ H [R]
[H] P +

COO-STAVELOT
Liège
Cascade chemin Faravennes 5 ✆(080) 684312
All year
1.2HEC ◑ H ⊖ [H]
R + [G] P
Prices A53 V53 73 73

EUPEN
Liège
Hertogenwald Oestr 78 ✆(087) 743222
All year
405HEC ◑ H ⊖ [G]
[R] + lau R
Prices A90 V55 110 86

FORRIÈRES
Luxembourg
Pré du Blason r de la Ramée 30 ✆(084) 212867
This well-kept site lies on a meadow surrounded by wooded hills and is completely divided into pitches and crossed by rough gravel drives.
Camping Carnet Compulsory.
Off N49 Masbourg road.
Apr-Sep
3HEC ◑ H ⊖ [G] [R] R
+
Prices A68 V28 39 39

GEDINNE
Namur
Melezes rte Dinant-Bouillon ✆(061) 588560
All year
2HEC ◑ H ⊖ [G] [R]
P + lau
Prices A77 V54 72 68

GEMMENICH
Liège
Kon Tiki Terstraeten 46 ✆(087) 785973
All year

12HEC ○ H G R H PR + lau
Prices pitch300-400 (incl 5 persons)

HABAY-LA-NEUVE
Luxembourg
RACB r du Bon-Bois 3 ✆(063) 422312
Parklike, terraced site on a hill surrounded by woodland.
Camping Carnet Compulsory.
Turn off N48 and follow signs.
All year
4.5HEC ● H ⊖ lau

HAMOIR-SUR-OURTHE
Liège
Dessous Hamoir r de Moulin 31 ✆(086) 388925
All year
1HEC ○ H ⊖ H R +

HOUFFALIZE
Luxembourg
Chasse et Pêche rte de la Roche 2 ✆(062) 288314
All year
1.8HEC ◑ ● H ⊖ G H R + lau

Moulin de Rensiwez Rensiwez 1 ✆(061) 289027
All year
5HEC ◑ H ⊖ G R R P +
Prices A20 pitch420

Viaduc rte de la Roche 53 ✆(061) 289067
All year
4HEC ◑ H ⊖ G R R + lau P
Prices A13 pitch200-400 (incl 2 persons)

JAMOIGNE
Luxembourg
Faing ✆(061) 311687
A municipal camp on a meadow situated behind a sports ground which separates the site from the road.
400m W on N44.
15 Mar-6 Dec

5.5HEC ○ H ⊖ G R H PR + lau

KÜCHELSCHEID
Liège
Küchelschied Ricksheiderweg 6 ✆(080) 446057
Situated in a wooded valley on a long, gently-sloping meadow with some terraces.
0.5km SW of the frontier post Kalterherberg/Küchelscheid.
15 May-Oct
2HEC ◑ ● H ⊖ + lau

LAMORMENIL
Luxembourg
Euro Lamormenil ✆(086) 455350
All year
3HEC ◑ ● H ⊖ H P +

MALONNE
Namur
Trieux r des Trieux 99 ✆(081) 445583
Camping Carnet Compulsory.
Apr-Oct
2HEC ◑ H ⊖ G R H + lau
Prices A72 V40 40 40

MARCHE-EN-FAMENNE
Luxembourg
Euro Camping Paola r du Panorama 10 ✆(084) 311704
A long site on a hill with a beautiful view. The only noise comes from a railway line, which passes right by the site.
Take road towards Hotton, turn right after cemetery and continue 1km.
All year
13HEC ◑ H ⊖ G R + R
Prices A59 V41 41 41

MARTELANGE
Luxembourg
Ranch r de Radelange 49 ✆(063) 600236
Apr-Sep

3HEC ◑ H ⊖ G R H PR + lau
Prices A74 V43 74 74

MESSANCY
Luxembourg
Lac r d'Arlon 52 ✆(063) 377129
All year
13.5HEC ◑ H ⊖ H LR + lau

NEUFCHÂTEAU
Luxembourg
Lac rte de Florenville ✆(061) 277615
All year
2HEC ○ H ⊖ G R H L +
Prices A40 V20 40 40

NOISEUX
Namur
Noiseux r Chasseurs Ardennais ✆(086) 322586
All year
2.1HEC ◑ H ⊖ R P +

OTEPPE
Liège
Hirondelle Château d'Oteppe ✆(085) 711131
Apr-Oct
46HEC ○ H ⊖ G R P + lau
Prices A40 V30 90 90

POLLEUR
Liège
Polleur r de Congrès 90 ✆(087) 541033
Apr-1 Nov
3.5HEC ○ H ⊖ G H PR + lau
Prices A80 V80 80 80

POUPEHAN
Luxembourg
Houlifontaine r des Sneviots ✆(061) 467315
Etr-1 Nov
10HEC ○ H ⊖ R R + lau

PURNODE
Namur
Bocq av de la Vallée ✆(082) 612269
Apr-Sep
2HEC ~ ◑ ⌂H ▾ ✕ ⊖ ⊕ ≈R P + ☞ ⌂
Prices A60 V55 ⊕55 Å55

REMOUCHAMPS
Liège
Eden rte de Trois Ponts 92 ✆(041) 844165
Apr-15 Nov
3.2HEC ~ ● ⌂H ⌂ ⊖ ⊕ G R H ≈R P + ☞ ✕
Prices A48 V58 ⊕78 Å78

Idéal av de la Porallée ✆(041) 844419
On SW outskirts between river, railway and road behind SHELL petrol station.
Apr-Oct
1.5HEC ~ ◑ ⌂H ▾ ✕ ⊖ ⊕ H P + ☞ ⌂ G ≈PR
Prices A50 V50 ⊕100 Å100

ROBERTVILLE
Liège
Plage 33 rte des Bains ✆(080) 446658
All year
1.8HEC ~ ◑ ⌂H ⌂ ✕ ⊖ ⊕ G R P + lau ☞ ▾ ≈L
Prices A54 V47 ⊕47 Å47

ROCHE-EN-ARDENNE, LA
Luxembourg
Benelux r de Harze 14 ✆(084) 411559
Etr-Sep
7HEC ~ ◑ ⌂H ⌂ ⊖ ⊕ G R H ≈R P ☞ ▾ ✕

Floréal rte de Houffalize 18 ✆(084) 412114
15 Mar-Sep
8.5HEC ~ ◑ ⌂H ⌂ ▾ ✕ ⊖ ⊕ P + lau ☞ ≈PR
Prices A66 V48 ⊕59 Å59

Grillon r de Harzé 30 ✆(084) 412062
Apr-Oct
3HEC ~ ◑ ⌂H ⌂ ⊖ ⊕ G R H ≈R P + lau ☞ ▾ ✕ ≈P
Prices A44 V38 ⊕44 Å44

Lohan rte de Houffalize ✆(084) 411545
In a park, on N bank of the River Ourthe.
Mar-15 Oct
6HEC ~ ◑ ⌂H ⌂ ▾ ✕ ⊖ ⊕ G ⌂ ≈R P + ✱
Prices A53 V43 ⊕53 Å53

Ourthe ✆(084) 411459
Well kept site, beside the River Ourthe.
On SW bank of the Ourthe below the N34.
15 Mar-1 Oct
2HEC ~ ● ⌂H ⌂ ▾ ✕ ⊖ ⊕ G R H ≈PR P + lau
Prices A43 V35 ⊕42 Å42

ROCHEHAUT
Luxembourg
Laviot r Laviot 7 ✆(061) 466314
Apr-Oct
6HEC ~ ○ ⌂H ⌂ ▾ ✕ ⊖ ⊕ G ≈R P lau

STE CECILE
Luxembourg
Semois rte de Chassépierre ✆(061) 312187
Apr-15 Oct
3HEC ~ ◑ ⌂H ▾ ⊖ ⊕ ≈R P +

SART-LEZ-SPA
Liège
Touring Club r Stockay 17 ✆(087) 474400
Signposted. The site lies to the E of Spa.
All year
5.5HEC ~ ◑ ⌂H ⌂ ▾ ✕ ⊖ ⊕ G P + lau ☞ ≈P
Prices pitch295-467

SCHÖNBERG
Liège
Waldecho r en Forêt ✆(080) 548222
Spread over two valleys in wooded surroundings.
Turn W off N26 at Km11.1 and continue for 0.5km.
All year
3.5HEC ~ ◑ ⌂H ⌂ ✕ ⊖ ⊕ H ≈P P + lau ☞ G R
Prices A70 V45 ⊕45 Å45

SIPPENAEKEN
Liège
Vieux Moulin ✆(087) 784255
Apr-Sep
8HEC ~ ◑ ⌂H ⌂ ▾ ✕ ⊖ ⊕ G R ⌂ ≈PR P + lau
Prices A60 V60 ⊕70 Å70

SPA
Liège
Parc des Sources av de la Sauvenière 141 ✆(087) 772311
S of town centre on N32.
Apr-Jan
2.5HEC ~ ○ ⌂H ⌂ ⊖ ⊕ G H P + lau ☞ ▾ ✕ ≈LP
Prices A69 V58 ⊕89 Å89

STER
Liège
Francopole ✆(087) 275099
In a secluded position beside the Eau Ronge River.
Off N32 in Francorchamps to Ster and Verviers, then turn right.
All year
10HEC ~ ◑ ● ⌂H ▾ ✕ ⊖ ⊕ R P + lau
Prices A60 V20 ⊕45 Å45

TENNEVILLE
Luxembourg
Pont de Berguème r Berguème 9 ✆(084) 455443
Turn off E40/N4 towards Wyompont then turn right.
All year
3HEC ~ ◑ ⌂H ⌂ ▾ ✕ ⊖ ⊕ G R ⌂ H ≈PR P + lau
Prices A45 V45 ⊕45 Å45

THOMMEN-REULAND
Liège
Hohenbusch Luxemburgstr 44 ✆(080) 227523
All year
5HEC ~ ◑ ⌂H ⌂ ▾ ✕ ⊖ ⊕ G H ≈P P lau

TINTIGNY
Luxembourg
Chênefleur ✆(063) 444078
15 Mar-15 Oct
6HEC ~ ○ ⌂H ▾ ✕ ⊖ ⊕ G R H ≈PR P + lau ☞ ⌂
Prices A60 V53 ⊕53 Å53

VIELSALM
Luxembourg
Casseroles Petites Taulles 2 ✆(080) 418560
All year
4HEC ~ ◑ ⌂H ▾ ✕ ⊖ ⊕ G R H ≈P P + lau
Prices A50 V100 ⊕200 Å100

Salm ✆(080) 216241
All year
2.5HEC ~ ◑ ⌂H ▾ ✕ ⊖ ⊕ G R H ≈R P lau ☞ ⌂ ≈P
Prices A20 V25 ⊕200 Å155

VIRTON
Luxembourg
Vallée de Rabais r du Bonlieu ✆(063) 570144
All year
6HEC ~ ◑ ⌂H ▾ ✕ ⊖ ⊕ ⌂ H P lau ☞ ⌂ G R ≈L +
Prices pitch250-450

WAIMES
Liège
Anderegg Bruyerès 4 ✆(080) 679393
22 Sep-15 Oct
1.8HEC S ◑ ⌂H ⌂ ▾ ✕ ⊖ ⊕ G R P +
Prices A60 V53 ⊕53 Å53

YVOIR
Namur
Repos r du Baly Bauche ✆(082) 611861
Beautiful site on bank of River Bocq.
4km E.
Apr-Sep
0.8HEC ~ ◑ ⌂H ⌂ ✕ ⊖ ⊕ G P

FRANCE

France, rich in history and natural beauty, is bordered by six countries: Belgium, Germany, Italy, Luxembourg, Spain and Switzerland. The country offers a great variety of scenery from the mountain ranges of the Alps and the Pyrénées to the attractive river valleys of the Loire, Rhône and Dordogne. And with some 1,800 miles of coastline, which includes the golden sands of the Côte d'Azur, there is a landscape appealing to everyone's taste.

The climate of France is temperate but varies considerably. The Mediterranean coast enjoys a sub-tropical climate with hot summers, whilst along the coast of Brittany the climate is very similar to that of Devon and Cornwall. The language is, of course, French and this is spoken throughout the country, although there are many local dialects and variations.

France has an enormous number of campsites, over 10,000 of them under the auspices of the *French Federation of Camping and Caravanning.*

There are *castels et camping-caravanning* sites in the grounds of châteaux (castles) and many are included in this Guide. On sites in state forests, *forêts domaniales,* it is necessary to apply to the *garde forestier* for permission to camp and evidence of insurance must be produced (such as the *camping carnet*). Opening periods vary widely and some sites are open all year. Local information offices (see *Tourist information* below) can supply detailed information about sites in their locality.

Camping information can also be obtained from 500 *Total* petrol service stations which have been equipped with information offices. During July and August there is over-demand around the French coasts, particularly on the Mediterranean.

All graded sites must display their official classification, site regulations, capacity and current charges at the site entrance. Some sites have inclusive charges per pitch, others show basic prices per person, vehicle and space, with extra facilities like showers, swimming pools and ironing incurring additional charges. In practice, most campsites charge from midday to midday, with each part day being counted as a full day. Reductions for children are usually allowed up to 7 years of age.

International camping carnet is not compulsory but recommended. However, a camping carnet is advisable when using *castels et camping-caravanning* sites and also the *fôrets domaniales*. See European ABC for further information.

Off-site camping in the South of France is restricted because of the danger of fire; in other parts, camping is possible, provided that permission has been obtained, although camping is seldom allowed near the water's edge, or at a large seaside resort. Casual camping is prohibited in state forests, national parks in the Landes and Gironde *dèpartements* and in the Camargue. Camping in an unauthorised place renders offenders liable to prosecution or confiscation of equipment, or both, especially in the South. However, an overnight stop on parking areas of some motorways is tolerated, but make sure you do not contravene local regulations; overnight stops in a lay-by are not permitted. Camping is not permitted in *Monaco*. Caravans in transit are allowed but it is forbidden to park them.

HOW TO GET THERE

Short ferry crossings
From **Dover** to **Boulogne** takes 1hr 40mins; to **Calais** takes 1¼–1½hrs.
From **Folkestone** to **Boulogne** takes 1hr 50mins.

Longer ferry crossings
From **Ramsgate** to **Dunkerque** (Dunkirk) takes 2¼hrs.
From **Newhaven** to **Dieppe** takes 4hrs.
From **Portsmouth** to **Le Havre** takes 5¾–7hrs; to **Caen** takes 5¾–7hrs; to †**Cherbourg** takes 4¾–6hrs; to **St Malo** takes 9–11hrs.
From †**Poole** to **Cherbourg** takes 4½hrs.
From **Plymouth** to **Roscoff** takes 6–6½hrs.
From †**Weymouth** to **Cherbourg** takes 4–6hrs.
†Summer service only

A car and passenger-carrying **catamaran** service operates from **Portsmouth** to **Cherbourg** (2¾hrs).

Fast hovercraft services
from **Dover** to **Boulogne** takes 40mins; to **Calais** takes 35mins.

Car sleeper trains
Services operate from Boulogne, Calais and Dieppe to the south of the country.

GENERAL INFORMATION

The information given here is specific to France. It **must** be read in conjunction with the European ABC at the front of the book, which covers those regulations which are common to many countries.

British Embassy/Consulates*

The British Embassy is located at 75383 Paris, 35 rue du Faubourg St-Honoré ✆42669142; *consular section* 75008 Paris, 16 rue d'Anjou ✆42669142. There are British Consulates in Bordeaux, Lille, Lyons and Marseilles; there are British Consulates with Honorary Consuls in Biarritz, Boulogne-sur-Mer, Cherbourg, Dunkerque (Dunkirk), Nantes, Nice, St Malo-Dinard and Toulouse.

Currency, including banking hours*

The unit of currency is the *Franc (Fr)* divided into 100 *centimes*. At the time of going to press £1 = *Fr* 9.94. Denominations of bank notes are *Fr*20, 50, 100, 200, 500; standard coins are *Fr*1, 2, 5, 10 and 5, 10, 20, 50 *centimes*.

There are no restrictions on the amount of French or foreign currency that can be taken in or out of France.

Banks In most *large towns* banks are open from Monday to Friday 09.00–12.00hrs and 14.00–16.00hrs and closed on Saturday and Sunday; in the *provinces*, they are open from Tuesday to Saturday as above, and closed on Sunday and Monday. Banks close at midday on the day prior to a national holiday, and all day on Monday if the holiday falls on a Tuesday.

The *Credit Lyonnais* has offices at the Invalides Air terminal in Paris for cashing travellers' cheques, and the *Société Générale* has two offices at Orly Airport, whilst at the Charles de Gaulle Airport, exchange facilities are also available.

Emergency telephone numbers

Fire ✆18 **Police** ✆17. For **ambulance** use the number given in the telephone box or, if no number is given, call the police. On some roads emergency telephones (every 20km) are connected direct to the police. In larger towns emergency help can be obtained from **police secours'** (Emergency Assistance Department).

***Additional information will be found in the European ABC at the front of the book.**

Foodstuffs*

Visitors entering from an EC country may import duty-free, 1,000g of coffee or 400g of coffee extract and 200g of tea or 80g of tea extract bought tax and duty-paid; a reduced allowance applies if bought duty-free. Food for the journey may be imported without formality. However, the quantity of meat is limited to 1kg and any meat or meat products from Africa, Andorra, Portugal and Spain are forbidden.

Shopping hours

Most shops, including department stores, are open Monday to Saturday 09.00–18.30/19.00hrs; *food shops* open earlier at 07.00hrs, and some (*bakers* in particular), open on Sunday mornings. *Hypermarkets* generally remain open until 21.00/22.00hrs. However, outside the larger cities, you will find that many shops close all day, or a half-day, on Mondays. In *small towns,* lunch-time closing can extend from 12.00 to 14.00hrs.

Tourist information*

The French Tourist Office maintains a full information service (Mon–Fri) at 178 Piccadilly, London W1V 0AL and will be pleased to answer any enquiries on touring in France. The telephone number is 071-491 7622 (for general enquiries) and 071-499 6911 (for the 24 hour recorded information service).

Once in France, you should contact the local tourist office, *Syndicat d'Initiative,* which will be found in all larger towns and resorts. They will be pleased to give advice on local events, amenities and excursions, and can also give specific information regarding bus timetables and local religious services (all denominations) not available in the UK.

A further source of information within the country is the *Accueil de France* (Welcome Office), who will also book hotel reservations within their area for the same night, or up to seven days in advance for **personal callers only**. There are fewer of these offices which are mainly located at important stations and airports.

The hours of opening vary considerably, depending upon the district and the time of year. Generally, the offices are open between 09.00–12.00hrs and 14.00–18.00hrs from Monday to Saturday, but in popular resort areas, *Syndicats d'Initiative* are sometimes open later and on Sunday mornings.

MOTORING

Children in cars

Children under 10 are not permitted to travel in front seats when rear seating is available.

Dimensions and weight restrictions

Private **cars** and towed **trailers** or **caravans** are restricted to the following dimensions – height, no restriction, but 4 metres is a recommended maximum; width, 2.50 metres; length, 12 metres (excluding towing device). The maximum permitted overall length of vehicle/trailer or caravan combination is 18 metres.

If the weight of the trailer exceeds that of the towing vehicle, see also *Speed limits* below.

Driving licence*

(see also *Speed limits* below)
A valid UK or Republic of Ireland licence is acceptable in France. The minimum age at which a visitor may use a temporarily imported motorcycle (over 80cc) or car is 18. Visitors may use temporarily imported motorcycles of up to 80cc at 16.

Lights*

It is obligatory to use headlights, as driving on sidelights only is not permitted. In fog, mist or poor visibility during the day, either two fog lamps or two dipped headlights must be switched on in addition to two sidelights. It is also compulsory for motorcyclists riding machines exceeding 125cc to use dipped headlights during the day. Failure to comply with these regulations will lead to an on-the-spot fine (see *Police fines* in the European ABC).

It is recommended that visiting motorists equip their vehicle with a set of replacement bulbs; drivers unable to replace a faulty bulb when requested to do so by the police may be fined. In France, a regulation requires all locally registered vehicles to be equipped with headlights which show a yellow beam and, in the interests of safety and courtesy, visiting motorists are advised to comply. If you are able to use beam deflectors to alter your headlights for driving abroad, you can purchase deflectors with yellow lenses. However, with headlamp converters, it is necessary to coat the outer surface of the headlamp glass with a yellow lacquer which is removable with a solvent. The yellow headlamp lacquer can be purchased from the AA.

Motoring club*

The AA is affiliated to the **Association Française des Automobilistes** (AFA) whose office is at F-75017 Paris, 9 rue Anatole-de-la Forge ✆42278200.

Parking*

In Paris, cars towing caravans are prohibited from

***Additional information will be found in the European ABC at the front of the book.**

the *blue zone* between 14.00 and 20.30hrs. Cars towing trailers with an overall surface of 10sq metres or more may neither circulate nor park in the central *green zone* between 14.00–20.30hrs, except on Sundays and Public holidays. Vehicle combinations with an overall surface exceeding 16sq metres may neither circulate nor park in the *green zone* between 08.00–20.30hrs. Those wishing to cross Paris during these hours with vehicle/trailer combinations, can use the *Boulevard Péripherique*, although the route is heavily congested, except during Public holiday periods. In some parts of the *green zone*, parking is completely forbidden. It is prohibited to park caravans, even for a limited period, not only in the *green zone* but in almost all areas of Paris.

Priority including Roundabouts*

In built-up areas, you must give way to traffic coming from the right – *priorité à droite*. However, at roundabouts with signs bearing the words "*Vous n'avez pas la priorité*" or "*Cédez le passage*" traffic **on** the roundabout has priority; where no such sign exists, traffic **entering** the roundabout has priority. Outside built-up areas, all main roads of any importance have right of way. This is indicated by a red-bordered triangle showing a black cross on a white background with the words "*Passage Protégé*" underneath; or a red-bordered triangle showing a pointed black upright with horizontal bar on a white background; or a yellow square within a white square with points vertical.

Roads

France has a very comprehensive network of roads, and surfaces are generally good; exceptions are usually signposted *Chausée deformée*. The camber is often severe and the edges rough.

During July and August, and especially at weekends, traffic on main roads is likely to be very heavy. Special signs are erected to indicate alternative routes with the least traffic congestion. Wherever they appear, it is usually advantageous to follow them, although you cannot be absolutely sure of gaining time. The alternative routes are quiet, but they are not as wide as the main roads. They are **not** suitable for caravans.

A free road map showing the marked alternative routes, plus information centres and petrol stations open 24 hours, is available from service stations displaying the *Bison Futé* poster (a Red Indian chief in full war bonnet). These maps are also available from *Syndicats d'Initiative* and information offices.

Speed limits*

Built-up areas
60kph (37mph)
Outside built-up areas on normal roads 90kph (56mph); on dual-carriageways separated by a central reservation 110kph (68mph).
On Motorways 130kph (80mph) (**Note** The minimum speed in the fast lane on a level stretch of motorway during good daytime visibility is 80kph (49mph), and drivers travelling below this speed are liable to be fined. The maximum speed on the Paris ring road is 80kph (49mph) and, on other urban stretches of motorway, 110kph (68mph).

In **wet weather** speed limits outside built-up areas are reduced to 80kph (49mph), 100kph (62mph) and 110kph (68mph) on motorways.

These limits also apply to private cars towing a trailer or caravan, if the latter's weight does not exceed that of the car. However, if the weight of the trailer exceeds that of the car by less than 30%, the speed limit is 65kph (39mph), if more than 30% the speed limit is 45kph (28mph). Additionally, these combinations must:
i Display a disc at the rear of the caravan/trailer showing the maximum speed.
ii Not be driven in the fast lane of a 3-lane motorway.

Both French residents and visitors to France, who have held a driving licence for less than one year, must not exceed 90kph (56mph) or any lower sign-posted limit when driving in France.

Warning triangle/Hazard warning lights

The use of a warning triangle or hazard warning lights† is compulsory in the event of accident or breakdown. However, as hazard warning lights may be damaged or inoperative, it is recommended that a warning triangle be carried. The triangle must be placed on the road 30 metres (33yds) behind the vehicle and clearly visible from 100 metres (110yds). For vehicles over 3,500kg warning must be given by at least a warning triangle. See also *Warning triangle/Hazard warning lights* in the European ABC.
†If your vehicle is equipped with hazard warning lights, it is also compulsory to use them if you are forced to drive temporarily at a greatly reduced speed. However, when slow moving traffic is established in an uninterrupted lane or lanes, this only applies to the last vehicle in the lane(s).

***Additional information will be found in the European ABC at the front of the book.**

Prices are in French Francs
Abbreviations:
av avenue
bd boulevard
espl esplanade
fbg faubourg
Gl Général
Ml Maréchal
pl place
Prés President
r rue
rte route
Sgt Sergent
sq square

CM Camping Municipal (local authority site)
Each placename preceded by 'La', 'Le' or 'Les' is listed under the name that follows it.

ALPS/EAST

Within the French Alps is the old Duchy of Savoie, which only became part of France in the middle of the last century, and which still retains a distinctive character. The Alps is a region of clear air, majestic mountain peaks, peaceful valleys and meadows. Good roads link the valleys; steep winding mountain roads lead to delightful villages and spectacular viewpoints, but cable cars offer a unique alternative. A cable car goes up to the 12,000ft Aiguille du Midi, and a funicular railway leads to the spectacular 'Mer de Glace'. Annecy has a delightful, bustling medieval centre, and Lake Annecy, with its backdrop of mountains, provides opportunities for watersports and cruising. There are a number of attractive Alpine resorts – La Clusaz, Morsine, and the sophisticated Camonix, and Savoy's ancient capital, Chambéry, has a fascinating old town and castle. A well-kept secret is the Jura – a land of thickly wooded hills and plateaux and lush meadows grazed by sheep, goats and cattle. The rivers Rhône, Doubs and Ain flow through the region, and the many smaller rivers and lakes make this a fisherman's paradise.

ABRETS, LES
Isère
Coin Tranquille ✆76321348
Completely divided into pitches with attractive flower beds in rural surroundings.
2 km E of village, 500 m off N6.
Apr-Oct
2HEC H G P + lau
Prices A15 V9 13 13

AIX-LES-BAINS
Savoie
Sierroz bd R-Barrier ✆79612143
A wooded site divided into 2 parts each with pitches, separated from the lake by 150m strip of land and the Culoz road. Bathing area nearby on lake.
2.5 km NW.
15 Mar-15 Nov
5HEC H G R P + lau LP
Prices (none)

ALBENS
Savoie
Beauséjour ✆79541520
Signposted
15 Jun-15 Sep
2HEC H G H LPR + lau

Prices A8 V8 8 8

ALBERTVILLE
Savoie
CM Adoubes av des Chasseurs-Alpins ✆79894367
Situated between N525 and River Arly on E side of town.
15 Jun-20 Sep
1.5HEC H G + lau P
Prices A7 V3 3 3

ALLEVARD
Isère
Clair Matin ✆76975519
Gently sloping terraced area divided into pitches.
S of village, 300 m off D525.
15 May-Sep
3.5HEC H G P + lau L

AMPHION-LES-BAINS
See ÉVIAN-LES-BAINS

ANNECY
Haute-Savoie
CM le Belvédère rte du Semnoz ✆50454830
20 Dec-15 Oct
2.7HEC H G + lau LP
Prices A14 V5 22 12

ANTHY
Haute-Savoie
Clos Pallin ✆50703209
Clean and tidy site with attractive flowerbeds on gentle slope.
Signposted from town via D33 and N5.
Apr-Sep
1.1HEC H G H L lau

ARBOIS
Jura
CM Vignes av Gl-Leclerc ✆84661412
Terraced site.
E on D107 Mesnay road at stadium.
Apr-Sep
2.8HEC H G H + lau P
Prices A9 pitch8

ARGENTIÈRE
Haute-Savoie
Glacier d'Argentière ✆50540392
Clean site on sloping meadowland in beautiful quiet situation at the foot of the Mont Blanc Massif.
Access is 1km S of Argentière, turn off N506 towards Cableway Lognan et de Grandes Montets, then a further 200m to site.
15 Jun-25 Sep
1HEC H G + lau P
Prices A15-16 V5 8 6

ARS-SUR-FORMANS
Ain
Bois de la Dame ✆74007723
Camping Carnet Compulsory.
Access from A6, exit Villefranche. Continue E via D904.
May-Sep
1.5HEC H G H + lau
Prices pitch35 (incl 2 persons)

AUTRANS
Isère
Caravaneige du Vercors ✆76953188
0.6km S via D106c towards Méaudre
All year
1HEC H H + lau P
Prices pitch43 (incl 2 persons)

Joyeux Réveil ✆76953344
NE of town via rte de Montaud.
Closed one wk Jun & Sep
1.5HEC H G R P + lau
Prices pitch45 (incl 2 persons)

BALME-LES-GROTTES, LA
Isère
Domaine Beauséjour ✆74906157
Beside the River Rhône.
Jun-Sep
1.3HEC ● H ⊖ P + lau ☞ ✕

BARATIER
Hautes-Alpes
Verger ✆92431587
Terraced site in plantation of fruit trees with fine views of Alps. Divided into pitches. Rest room with TV.
From N94 drive 2.5km S of Embrun, 1.5km E on D40.
All year
2.5HEC ◑ H ⊖ G R H P + lau ☞ ✕ LR

BELLEGARDE-SUR-VALSERINE
Ain
Crêt d'Eau 2 av de Lattre-de-Tassigny ✆50482370
3km N of town, 200m from N84.
Jun-Aug
5.2HEC ◑ H ⊖ P + lau ☞ ✕
Prices A18 pitch19

BONNAL
See **ROUGEMONT**

BOSSONS, LES
See **CHAMONIX-MONT-BLANC**

BOURG-D'OISANS, LE
Isère
Caravaneige le Vernis ✆76800268
Well-kept site with modern sanitary facilities. At foot of mountain in summer ski-ing area.
2.5km of N91, rte de Briançon.
Closed Oct
1.2HEC ◑ H ⊖ G R H + lau ☞ ✕ PR
Prices pitch50 (incl 3 persons)

Cascade ✆76800242
Completely divided into pitches at the foot of a mountain with a waterfall and modern, very well-kept sanitary arrangements. Television lounge with library, open fireplace. Booking essential.
Feb-Sep
2.5HEC ◑ H ⊖ G R H + lau ☞ ✕ PR
Prices pitch83 (incl 3 persons)

Rencontre du Soleil rte de l'Alpe-d'Huez ✆76800033
Charming site in a lovely setting in the Dauphiny Alps at the foot of a mountain. Fine rustic common room with open fireplace. TV, playroom for children.
At the foot of the hairpin road to L'Alp-d'Huez, leave N91 (Grenoble- Briançon road) in the Le Bourge d'Osians.
20 May-10 Sep
1HEC ● H ✕ ⊖ G P + lau ☞ L
Prices pitch67-80 (incl 3 persons)

At **ROCHETAILLÉE**(6km N)
Belledonne ✆76800718
15 Jun-Aug
3.5HEC ◑ H ✕ ⊖ G R P + lau

At **VENOSC**(10km SE on N91 and D530)
Champ de Moulin ✆76800738
All year
1.5HEC ○ H ✕ ⊖ G R H P + lau
Prices pitch71-76 (incl 2 persons)

BOURG-EN-BRESSE
Ain
CM de Challes av de Bad Kreuznach ✆74222779
In football ground near swimming pool.
Well signposted from outskirts of town.
Apr-15 Oct
2.7HEC S ○ H ✕ ⊖ G P + lau ☞ P
Prices A9 pitch14-23

BOURGET-DU-LAC, LE
Savoie
CM Ile aux Cygnes ✆79250176
May-Sep
3.8HEC ◑ H ⊖ G L + lau

BOURG-ST-MAURICE
Savoie
Versoyen rte des Arcs ✆79070345
Two communal sanitary blocks – one heated. Ski-ing facilities. Many secluded pitches in a wood.
On S outskirts of town. Access via N90.
All year
3.5HEC ◑ H ⊖ G R + lau ☞ ✕ P
Prices A13-14 pitch13

BOUT-DU-LAC
Haute-Savoie
CM ✆50443344
Extensive site divided into pitches in attractive surroundings.
150m off N508 at S end of Lac d'Annecy.
May-Sep
6HEC ● H ✕ ⊖ G R lau ☞ LR
Prices A11 pitch14-30

Lac Bleu rte d'Albertville ✆50443018
Modern, well-kept site. Overflow area with own sanitary blocks.
On the southern shores of Lake Annecy via the N508, opposite ANTAR Garage.
Apr-15 Oct
3.3HEC ● H ✕ ⊖ G L + lau ☞
Prices pitch52 (incl 2 persons)

BRIANÇON
Hautes-Alpes
Cinq Vallées St-Blaise ✆92210627
Level site divided into pitches on natural wooded terrain next to River Durance.
2km S on N94 towards St-Blaise.
Jun-15 Sep
4HEC ◑ H ✕ ⊖ G + lau ☞ P
Prices A19 pitch19

CHALLES-LES-EAUX
Savoie
Mont St-Michel chemin St-Vincent ✆79728308
Clean transit site on road to Chambéry and Grenoble. ➤

May-Sep
1.5HEC H + lau L

CHAMONIX-MONT-BLANC
Haute-Savoie
Mer de Glace ✆50530863
2km NE on N506 to Les Praz. On approach to village (from Chamonix) turn right under railway bridge.
May-Sep
2.2HEC H G + lau P
Prices A20 pitch19

Rosières 121 Clos des Rosières ✆50531042
1.2km NE via N506
Closed 10 Nov-15 Dec
1.7HEC H G R H lau P
Prices A17 pitch15

At **BOSSONS, LES**(3km W)
Cimes ✆50535893
In a wooded meadow at the foot of Mont Blanc Massif. Ideal for hiking and mountain tours.
Jun-Sep
1HEC H G + lau

Deux Glaciers 80 rte des Tissières ✆50531584
A glacial stream runs through the site. Pitches shaded by trees, very modern, well-kept sanitary installations. Rustic common room with open fires.
Leave N506 towards road underpass. 250m to site.
15 Dec-15 Nov
1.6HEC H G + lau
Prices pitch48 (incl 2 persons)

CHAMPAGNOLE
Jura
CM Boyse r G-Vallery ✆84520032
Clean and tidy site with asphalt drives and completely divided into pitches. In grounds of municipal swimming pool.
Turn onto D5 just before town and continue 1.3km to site.
12 Jun-10 Sep
7HEC H G R PR + lau
Prices A10 V8 8 A8

CHÂTEAUROUX-LES-ALPES
Hautes-Alpes
Cariamas ✆92432263
On a meadow in an attractive mountain setting beside the River Durance.
1.5km SE.
Jul-Sep
10HEC H H P + lau

CHORGES
Hautes-Alpes
Prévalière ✆92506758 or 92506042
Clean site, on meadowland, partly terraced.
From village follow D3 southwards to Baie des Moulettes, then 500m on.
15 Jun-Aug
2HEC H G + lau
Prices A10-11 pitch11

CLAIRVAUX-LES-LACS
Jura
Grisière et Europe Vacances ✆84258048
Fenced in meadowland with some trees, sloping down to the Grand Lac. The site is guarded during July and August.
From village centre turn off N78, follow D118 towards Châtel-de-Joux for 800m to the site.
May-Sep
11HEC H G L + lau
Prices A10 pitch11

DOLE
Jura
Pasquier ✆84720261
Clean meadow site near River Doubs.
900m SE of town centre.
15 Mar-Oct
2HEC H G H R + lau P
Prices A11 pitch18

DOUSSARD
Haute-Savoie
Serraz ✆50443068
Modern site divided into pitches. Cosy bar in rustic style.
At E end of village 500m from N508 on D181.
15 May-Sep
2.5HEC H G R + lau L
Prices A16 pitch28-43

EGATS, LES
Isère
Belvédère de l'Obiou ✆76304080
Situated in beautiful scenery; modern sanitary installations.
May-Sep
1HEC H G H P + lau
Prices A12 pitch16

EMBRUN
Hautes-Alpes
CM Clapière ✆92430183
Well-managed site with shaded pitches on stony ground, on N shore of lake. Site shop open during summer only.
2.5km SW on N94.
May-Sep
6HEC H H + lau G R LP

ENTRE-DEUX-GUIERS
Isère
Arc en Ciel ✆76660697
On D520 300m from N6.
Mar-Oct
1HEC H G R H R + lau P
Prices A12-13 V6-7 10-11 A10-11

ÉVIAN-LES-BAINS
Haute-Savoie
At **AMPHION-LES-BAINS** (3.5km W on N5)
Plage ✆50700046
NW of town on N5, 150m from lake.
Etr-1 Nov
1.5HEC H L + lau G PR
Prices A14-16 pitch19-24

At **MAXILLY** (2.5km E on N5)
Clos Savoyard ✆50754694/50752584
Very clean and tidy site.
Turn onto D21 in town 1200m after Hôtel de l'Etoile and continue uphill.
Jun-Sep
2HEC H G H + lau P

GAP
Hautes-Alpes
Provence rte de St-Jean ✆92511325
Very clean well-kept site, divided into pitches. On outskirts S of town.
On N85 (rte Napoléon).
27 Apr-15 Oct
1.2HEC H G H + lau LPR
Prices A12 pitch14

GRAY
Haute-Saône
CM Longue Rive rte de la Plage ✆84649044
Camping Carnet Compulsory.
Apr-Sep
4HEC H lau G R PR
Prices A8 pitch8

GRESSE-EN-VERCORS
Isère
4 Saisons ✆76343027
1.3km SW
Jun-15 Sep
2.2HEC H G P + lau R
Prices pitch50 (incl 2 persons)

GUILLESTRE
Hautes-Alpes
CM Rochette ✆92450215
On right bank of River Chagne.
W on D902A.
10 Jun-15 Sep
3HEC H R H P + lau

Villard ✆92450654
2km W via D902A and N4, rte de Gap.
All year
3HEC H G P + lau
Prices pitch54 (incl 2 persons)

HOUCHES, LES
Haute-Savoie
Airhôtel du Bourgeat ✆50544214
1.5 km NE.
Jul-Oct
1HEC
Prices pitch83 (incl 3 persons)

ISLE-SUR-LE-DOUBS, L'
Doubs
CM Lumes ✆81927309
The site lies close to the town. Common room with TV.
Off N83. Entrance near bridge over the Doubs.
15 May-15 Sep
1HEC
Prices A12 pitch16-27

LONS-LE-SAUNIER
Jura
CM Majorie ✆84242694
Clean, tidy site with tent and caravan sections separated by a stream. Caravan pitches (80 sq m) are gravelled and surrounded by hedges. Heated common room with TV, reading area, kitchen. Swimming pool free to campers.
Near swimming stadium on outskirts of town.
Apr-Sep
7.5HEC
Prices A8-10 10-12 9-10

LUGRIN
Haute-Savoie
Myosotis ✆50760759
10 Apr-Sep
1.2HEC
Prices pitch34-40 (incl 2 persons)

Rys ✆50760201
Apr-Oct
1.5HEC
Prices pitch36 (incl 2 persons)

Vieille Église ✆50760195
On rising meadow with good views.
Etr-Oct
1.5HEC
Prices A11-13 V5 8 8

MALBUISSON
Doubs
Fuvettes ✆81693150
Mainly level site with some terraces, gently sloping towards lake.
500m S on D437.
All year
5HEC
Prices pitch55 (incl 2 persons)

MARIGNY
Jura
Pergola ✆84257003
Terraced site.
S of Marigny off D27.
Apr-Sep
10HEC
Prices pitch120-130

MAXILLY
See ÉVIAN-LES-BAINS

MÉAUDRE
Isère
Buissonnets ✆76952104
200m from village centre.
All year
2HEC
Prices pitch43 (incl 2 persons)

MEGÈVE
Haute-Savoie
Ripalle ✆50214724
All year
1HEC

MESSERY
Haute-Savoie
Relais du Léman ✆50947111
1.5km SW via D25
May-Sep
2.5HEC
Prices A20 pitch25

MIRIBEL-LES-ÉCHELLES
Isère
Bourdons ✆76552853
400m from village centre.
All year
2HEC

MONTMAUR
Hautes-Alpes
Mon Repos ✆92580314
Generally well-kept site on wooded terrain with shaded pitches.
1km E on D937 and D994.
May-Oct
10HEC
Prices A11 V7 7 7

MONTREVEL-EN-BRESSE
Ain
Base de Plein Air et de Loisirs ✆74308052
Entrance closed between 22.00 & 07.00 hrs.
0.5km E on D28.
May-Sep
17HEC
Prices A12 pitch30

MOUCHARD
Jura
Halte Jurassienne Bel Air ✆84378392
Camping Carnet Compulsory.
NE, near the service station.
10 Mar-10 Nov
0.5HEC

NANTUA
Ain
Signal ✆74753160
The site is within a sports ground.
SW opposite Nantua railway station.
May-Sep
5HEC

NOVALAISE
Savoie
Charmilles ✆79360467
150m from the lake
25 Jun-5 Sep
2HEC
Prices pitch68 (incl 3 persons)

ORNANS
Doubs
Chanet ✆81622344
1.5km SW on D241. Follow green signs.
Mar-15 Nov
1.5HEC
Prices A12 V2 11 7-9

ORPIERRE
Hautes-Alpes
Princes d'Orange ✆92662253
The site lies on a meadow with terraces.
Apr-15 Nov
20HEC
Prices pitch60-80 (incl 3 persons)

OUNANS
Jura
Plage Blanche ✆84376963
15 Mar-Oct
4HEC
Prices A12 pitch14

PARCEY
Jura
Bords de Loue ✆84710382
A quiet site on the River Loue.
1.5km from the centre of the village via N5. Signposted.
Apr-15 Sep
10HEC
Prices A13 pitch18

PATORNAY
Jura
Moulin ✆84483121
Access is NE via N78, rte de Clairvaux-les-Lacs.
May-15 Sep ➔

5HEC ⩪ ● ⾨H ▙ ▼ ✕ ⊖ ◙ Ⓖ ⩯PR ◘ + lau ☞ ⩯L
Prices pitch78-98 (incl 3 persons)

PLAGNE-MONTCHAVIN
Savoie
CM ✆79078323
All year
1HEC ⩪ ⊟ ○ ⾨H ⊖ ◙ ◘ + lau ☞ ▙ ▼ ✕ ⩯P

PORT-SUR-SAÔNE
Haute-Saône
CM Maladière ✆84915132
S on the D6, between the River Saône and the Canal
15 May-15 Sep
3HEC ⩪ ◑ ⾨H ⊖ ◙ Ⓖ ◘ + lau ☞ ▼ ✕ ⩯R
Prices A7 V4 ◙7 ⛺7

RENAGE
Isère
CM Verdon ✆76914802
5km N of Tullins on D45.
May-Sep
2.5HEC ⩪ ● ⾨H ▼ ✕ ⊖ ◙ Ⓖ ⩯P ◘ + lau ☞ ▙
Prices pitch35 (incl 2 persons)

ROCHETAILLÉE
See **BOURG-D'OISANS, LE**

ROUGEMONT
Doubs
At **BONNAL**(3.5km N on D18)
♖ **Val de Bonnal** ✆81869087
Beside the River Ognon
10 May-15 Sep
15HEC ⩪ ◑ ⾨H ▙ ▼ ✕ ⊖ ◙ Ⓖ ⩯R ◘ + lau ☞ ⩯L
Prices A20 pitch25

ST-CLAUDE
Jura
Martinet ✆84450040
2km SE, beside the river
May-Sep
3HEC ⩪ ◑ ⾨H ▙ ▼ ✕ ⊖ ◙ Ⓖ ⩯P ◘ lau

ST-DISDILLE
Haute-Savoie
St-Disdille ✆50711411
Apr-Sep
12HEC ⩪ ● ⾨H ▙ ▼ ✕ ⊖ ◙ Ⓖ Ⓡ ◘ + lau ☞ ⩯L
Prices A16 pitch12

ST-ÉTIENNE-DU-BOIS
Ain
CM Sevron rte de Bourg-en-Bresse
✆74305065
500m S of village on N83 by river.
Apr-Oct
0.5HEC ⩪ ● ⾨H ⊖ ◙ ◘ + lau ☞ ▙ ▼ ✕

ST-GERVAIS-LES-BAINS
Haute-Savoie
Dômes de Miage Les Bernards
✆50934596
2km S on D902.
May-Oct
2.5HEC ⩪ ◑ ⾨H ▼ ✕ ⊖ ◙ Ⓖ ◘ + lau ☞ ▙ ⩯LPR
Prices pitch65 (incl 3 persons)

ST-INNOCENT-BRISON
Savoie
Rolande ✆79353972
Situated on gently sloping terrain.
Signposted from village centre.
May-Oct
1.5HEC ⩪ ◑ ⾨H ▙ ✕ ⊖ ◙ Ⓖ Ⓗ ◘ + lau ☞ ▼ ⩯L
Prices A11 pitch57

ST-JEAN-DE-COUZ
Savoie
International la Bruyère
✆79657342
2km S via N6, towards Côte-Barrier
15 Apr-15 Oct
1HEC ⩪ ◑ ⾨H ▙ ▼ ✕ ⊖ ◙ Ⓖ ◘ + lau ☞ ⩯R
Prices A10 pitch10

ST-JORIOZ
Haute-Savoie
Europa ✆50685101
1.4km SE
Jun-15 Sep
3HEC ⩪ ⊟ ◑ ⾨H ▙ ▼ ✕ ⊖ ◙ Ⓖ ⩯LP ◘ + lau
Prices pitch72 (incl 2 persons)

International du Lac d'Annecy
✆50686793
1km SE
20 May-5 Sep
2HEC ⩪ ○ ⾨H ▙ ⊖ ◙ Ⓖ ⩯P ◘ + lau ☞ ▼ ✕ ⩯L
Prices pitch72 (incl 3 persons)

ST-PIERRE-DE-CHARTREUSE
Isère
Martinière rte de Grenoble
✆76886036
In pleasant position surrounded by mountains.
Camping Carnet compulsory.
2km SW.
25 May-25 Sep
1.5HEC ⩪ ◑ ⾨H ✕ ⊖ ◙ Ⓖ Ⓡ ◘ + lau ☞ ▼ ⩯PR
Prices A13 V7 ◙14 ⛺14

SALLANCHES
Haute-Savoie
Mont Blanc Village ✆50584367
2km SE off D13.
20 Mar-15 Sep
6.5HEC ⩪ ◑ ⾨H ▙ ▼ ✕ ⊖ ◙ Ⓖ ⌂ ⩯L ◘ + lau ☞ ⩯P
Prices A15 V12 ◙12 ⛺12

SALLE-EN-BEAUMONT, LA
Isère
Champ-Long ✆76304181
15 Jun-Oct
2.2HEC ⩪ ⊟ ◑ ⾨H ▙ ▼ ✕ ⊖ ◙ ⌂ ⩯P ◘ + lau

SAVINES-LE-LAC
Hautes-Alpes
Chaumettes ✆92442016
Shaded terraced site 300m from the lake.
May-Sep
1HEC ⩪ ● ⾨H ▼ ✕ ⊖ ◙ + ⚘ ☞ ▙ Ⓖ Ⓡ ⩯LPR
Prices A16 ◙12 ⛺6-12

SCIEZ
Haute-Savoie
Léman Bonnatrait ✆50727251
On bank of Lake Léman (Lake Geneva).
May-Sep
3.6HEC ⩪ ● ⾨H ⊖ ◙ ⌂ Ⓗ ◘ + lau ☞ ▙ ▼ ✕ ⩯L

SÉEZ
Savoie
Reclus rte de Bourg-St-Maurice
✆79410105
NW on N90.
All year
1.5HEC ⩪ ● ⾨H ⊖ ◙ ◘ + lau ☞ ▙ ▼ ✕ ⩯P
Prices A10 V6 ◙8-10 ⛺8

SERRES
Hautes-Alpes
Barillons ✆92670116
Well-laid out with terraces.
1km SE on N75.
May-Sep
3HEC ⩪ ◑ ⾨H ▼ ⊖ ◙ Ⓖ Ⓗ ⩯L ◘ + lau ☞ ▙ ✕
Prices pitch48 (incl 2 persons)

Domaine des 2 Soleils ✆92670133
Well-kept terraced site in Buëch Valley.
S of town off N75. Signposted.
May-Sep
26HEC ⩪ ◑ ⾨H ▙ ▼ ✕ ⊖ ◙ Ⓖ ⌂ Ⓗ ⛛ ⩯PR ◘ + lau
Prices pitch68-72 (incl 2 persons)

SERVOZ
Haute-Savoie
Plaine St-Jean ✆50472187
E via D13, at the confluence of the Rivers Avre and Diosaz
15 May-15 Sep
5.5HEC ⩪ ● ⾨H ⊖ ◙ Ⓖ Ⓡ ⌂ Ⓗ ⩯R ◘ + lau ☞ ▙ ▼ ✕

SEYSSEL
Ain
International de Seyssel
✆50592847
A quiet site on steep, terraced meadowland, with individual washbasins and clean sanitary installations.
1km SW off Culoz road.
14 Apr-Sep
1HEC ⩪ ● ⾨H ▼ ✕ ⊖ ◙ ⌂ Ⓗ ◘ lau ☞ ▙ Ⓖ ⩯PR

TALLOIRES
Haute-Savoie
Lanfonnet Lac d'Annecy ✆50607212
1.5km SE.
May-Sep
2HEC
+ lau
Prices pitch69

THOISSEY
Ain
CM ✆74040297
Situated between two rivers, the Saône and the Chalaronne.
1km SW on D7.
Apr-Sep
15HEC PR
+ lau
Prices pitch45

THONON-LES-BAINS
Haute-Savoie
Morcy ✆50704487
2.5km W of town.
Etr-15 Sep
1.7HEC +
lau LR
Prices A13 pitch13

TIGNES-LES-BRÉVIÈRES
Savoie
Escapade rte des Ruines ✆79664127
15 Jun-15 Sep
4.5HEC P
+ lau
Prices A12 pitch7

TREPT
Isère
Lac ✆74929206
Etr-Sep
4HEC
L + lau
Prices A20 pitch20

VENOSC
See **BOURG-D'OISANS, LE**

VERNIOZ
Isère
Bontemps ✆74578352
All year
6HEC
PR + lau
Prices A12 V6 16 16

VILLARS-LES-DOMBES
Ain
CM Autières ✆74980021
Clean and tidy park-like site divided into plots and pitches. Part reserved for overnight campers. Clean, modern sanitary installations.
Camping Carnet Compulsory.
SW off N83.
20 Apr-4 Oct
4.5HEC
+ lau P
Prices A10-12 V6-7 12

VOIRON
Isère
CM Porte de la Chartreuse
✆76051420
On level terrain with some trees, divided into pitches. Much traffic noise from nearby N75. Clean and modern sanitary installations.
Access is NW of town next to the ESSO garage.
May-Sep
1.8HEC + lau
LPR

ALSACE/LORRAINE

In its natural border position next to Germany, Alsace enjoys a special identity, neither German nor completely French. And, with Lorraine, it shares some of the most turbulent chapters in French history. They also share the impressive Vosges mountains, with great wooded slopes, gentle pastures, fertile plains, enchanting lakes and famous thermal spas. In the summer this region is ablaze with colour – there are brilliant displays of wild flowers in the Vosges, and in the towns and cities, flowers cascade from every available ledge.
Gerardmer is at the heart of the Vosges, and La Bresse is also popular with visitors.
Nancy, the capital of Lorraine, and Metz, with its lovely old town and fine gothic cathedral, are great centres for the area, but Strasbourg is a delight to discover. The waterways of the 'Petit France' district are charming, and the splendid soaring spine of the cathedral of Notre Dame is unforgettable.
In the countryside, vineyards surround pretty villages with half-timbered houses and cobbled streets, and produce the fine wines of the area, but hops are also grown in the region, and famous beers are brewed in Strasbourg.

BAERENTHAL
Moselle
Ramstein Plage ✆87065073
W via r du Ramstein
Apr-Sep
6HEC
L + lau
Prices A8 pitch5

BERNARDSWILLER
Bas-Rhin
Chataigniers r du Stade ✆88956812
Etr & May-Sep
4HEC
P lau
Prices A12-14 V7-9 16-20 8-11

BRESSE, LA
Vosges
Terrain des Écorces Syndicat d'Initiative, quai des Iranées
✆29254129
In beautiful situation beside River Moselotte.
Off D34.
All year
1.5HEC R +
lau L
Prices A10 V5 7 6

BRUYÈRES
Vosges
At **CHAPELLE-DEVANT-BRUYÈRES, LA** (5km SE via N423)
Pinasses ✆29585110
1.2km NW on D60 towards Bruyères
15 Mar-Oct
3HEC
P + lau
Prices A15 pitch19

CERNAY
Haut-Rhin
CM Acacias r R-Guibert ✆89755697
Clean, quiet site on right bank of the River Thur.
Off N83 between Colmar and Belfort.
May-Sep
4HEC +
lau P
Prices A9 pitch10

CHAPELLE-DEVANT-BRUYÈRES, LA
See **BRUYÈRES**

COLMAR
Haut-Rhin
Intercommunal de l'Ill ✆89411594
On meadow beside the river. Liable to flooding at certain times. Separate sections for campers in transit.
2km E on N415.
Feb-Nov

2.2HEC ⋯ ◑ H ▣ ▼ ✕ ⊖ ▣ G R ▣ + lau
Prices A10 pitch12

CORCIEUX
Vosges
Domaine des Bains pl Notre-Dame ✆29506792
On meadow-land divided into pitches. Restricted facilities out of season.
Camping Carnet Compulsory.
E of village off D8.
All year
15HEC ⋯ S ◑ H ▣ ▼ ✕ ⊖ ▣ G R ⌂ H LP ▣ lau ☞ +
Prices A20 pitch40

EGUISHEIM
Haut-Rhin
CM Aux Trois Châteaux 10 r du Bassin ✆89231939
Camping Carnet Compulsory.
Etr-Sep
1.8HEC ⋯ ◑ H ⊖ ▣ G ▣ lau ☞ ▣ ▼ ✕ R +
Prices A8 ▣9 ▲6

GÉRARDMER
Vosges
Ramberchamp ✆29630382
On S side of Lac de Gérardmer.
May-15 Sep
3HEC ⋯ ◑ H ▼ ✕ ⊖ ▣ G L ▣ + lau

GRANGES-SUR-VOLOGNE
Vosges
Gina-Park ✆29514195
1km SE of town centre.
All year
4.5HEC ⋯ ◑ H ▣ ▼ ✕ ⊖ ▣ G R ⌂ H ▣ + lau ☞ LPR
Prices A10 pitch15

HANAU-PLAGE
Moselle
CM ✆87065155
Site lies beside Hanau lake. Busy at weekends and has many residential campers.
3km NW of Philippsbourg on N62.
Apr-Sep
7HEC ⋯ ◑ H ▣ ▼ ✕ ⊖ ▣ G L ▣ + lau

HEIMSBRUNN
Haut-Rhin
Chaumière ✆89819343 or 89819321
Signposted from village centre.
All year
1HEC ⋯ ◑ H ▣ ⊖ ▣ G ▣ + lau ☞ ▼

HENRIDORFF
Moselle
Plan Incliné ✆87253013
This site lies on a narrow strip of grassland below the railway, beside the canal.
3km W of Lutzelbourg towards Dabo.
Apr-Sep
3.5HEC ⋯ ◑ H ▣ ▼ ✕ ⊖ ▣ G R H P ▣ + lau

HOHWALD, LE
Bas-Rhin
CM ✆88083090
W via D425
All year
2HEC ⋯ ◑ H ⊖ ▣ ▣ + lau ☞ ▣ ▼ ✕
Prices A10 V6 ▣7 ▲7

KAYSERSBERG
Haut-Rhin
CM r des Acacias ✆89471447
Between a sports ground and the River Weiss. Subdivided by low hedges.
200m from N415. Signposted.
Apr-Sep
1.6HEC ⋯ ◑ H ⊖ ▣ ▣ + lau ☞ ▣ ▼ ✕ P

LUTTENBACH
Haut-Rhin
Amis de la Nature ✆89773860
Site on a long strip of land, divided into pitches.
From Munster follow D10 for 1km.
All year
7.5HEC ⋯ ◑ H ▣ ▼ ✕ ⊖ ▣ G ▣ + lau ☞ PR
Prices A8-9 V5 ▲4 pitch5

MANDRES-AUX-QUATRE-TOURS
Meurthe-et-Moselle
CM ✆83231385
1.5km S
Apr-Oct
2HEC ⋯ ◑ H ⊖ ▣ ▣ + ☞ ▣ R
Prices A5 V1 ▣6 ▲2

METZ
Moselle
CM Metz-Plage pl du Pontiffroy ✆87320558
Camping Carnet Compulsory.
Jun-2 Sep
1.2HEC ⋯ ● H ⊖ ▣ G R R ▣ + lau ☞ ▣ ▼ ✕ P
Prices A5 ▣12 ▲7

METZERAL
Haut-Rhin
At **MITTLACH** (3km SW)
CM ✆89776377
Situated in forested area in small village, very quiet.
From Munster follow signs for Metzeral then Mittlach D10vi.
Apr-Sep
3HEC ⋯ ◑ H ⊖ ▣ G R ▣ + lau
Prices A11 V4 ▣4 ▲3

MITTLACH
See **METZERAL**

MOOSCH
Haut-Rhin
Mine d'Argent r de la Mine d'Argent ✆89823066
1.5km SW. Access difficult for large caravans.
May-Sep
2HEC ⋯ ◑ H ⊖ ▣ G ▣ + lau ☞ ▣ ▼ ✕
Prices A9 pitch9

MUNSTER
Haut-Rhin
CM Parc de la Fecht ✆89773108
Almost in town centre within park-like area surrounded by high walls and trees.
Access on D417, 200m after entering Munster town centre by swimming pool.
May-Sep
4HEC ⋯ ○ ◑ H ▣ ▼ ✕ ⊖ ▣ P ▣ + lau
Prices A9 V5 ▣5 ▲5

OBERBRONN
Bas-Rhin
CM Eichelgarten r de Zinswiller ✆88097196
Closed Jan
4HEC ⋯ ◑ H ▣ ⊖ ▣ G ⌂ H P ▣ lau ☞ ▼ ✕ +
Prices A11 V7 ▣6 ▲7

OBERNAI
Bas-Rhin
CM rte d'Ottrott ✆88953848
Partly terraced site, situated in park.
W on D426 towards Ottrott.
Mar-Oct
2.5HEC ⋯ ● H ✕ ⊖ ▣ ▣ + ✱ lau ☞ ▣ P

PHALSBOURG
Moselle
CM Vieux Château r de la Manutention ✆87241372
Site within walls of ancient Castle.
E on rte de Saverne.
Apr-Oct
1.2HEC ⋯ ◑ H ⊖ ▣ ▣ + ☞ ▣ ▼ ✕ P
Prices A8 V7 ▣5 ▲5

RANSPACH-SUR-WESSERLING
Haut-Rhin
Bouleaux ✆89826470
On a long stretch of grassland subdivided by flowerbeds and hedging.
Adjacent to N66 Bâle road between St-Amarin and Wesserling.
Apr-Sep
1.8HEC ⋯ ● H ▼ ✕ ⊖ ▣ G R ⌂ H PR ▣ + lau ☞ ▣

RHINAU
Bas-Rhin
Ferme des Tuileries ✆88746045
Apprpach from Germany via ferry across River Rhine.
Apr-Sep

1HEC ◑ H ⊖ G + lau ⇒P
Prices A9 pitch9

RIQUEWIHR
Haut-Rhin
Inter Communal ✆89479008
Extensive site overlooking vineyards.
Camping Carnet required.
2km E on D16. Turn W off N83 (Colmar-Strasbourg) at Ostheim.
Apr-25 Oct
4HEC ◑ H ⊖ G + lau ⇒P
Prices A13 pitch16

RUAUX
Vosges
CM Fraiteux 81 r du Camping ✆29660071
Etr & May-Sep
0.8HEC ◑ H ⊖ R + lau G
Prices A11 pitch6

ST-MAURICE-SUR-MOSELLE
Vosges
Deux Ballons ✆29251126 / 29251714
1km W on N66.
All year
4HEC ◑ H ⊖ G H ⇒LP + lau
Prices A13 V8 8 A8

SAVERNE
Bas-Rhin
CM ✆88913565
1.3km SW via D171
Apr-Sep
1.6HEC ○ H ⊖ G + lau ⇒P
Prices A11 pitch15

SCHIRMECK
Bas-Rhin
Schirmeck rte de Stasbourg ✆88970161
5km NE. Beside Strasbourg road and railway, on level ground.
All year
3HEC ◑ H ⊖ G ⇒R + lau ⇒P
Prices A10 V6 6 A6

SÉLESTAT
Bas-Rhin
CM Cigognes r de la 1-er DFL ✆88920398
May-15 Oct
0.7HEC ○ H ⊖ G + lau ⇒PR
Prices A6 V5 5 A5

THIONVILLE
Moselle
CM 6 r du Parc ✆82538375
On the edge of River Moselle, adjacent to the Napoléon Park.
Apr-Sep
2HEC ◑ H ⊖ + lau ⇒R
Prices A5 V3 3 A3

THOLY, LE
Vosges
Noir Rupt ✆29618127
2km SE on D417.
Etr-15 Oct
1.2HEC ◑ H ⊖ G ⇒P + lau
Prices A18 pitch73

TONNOY
Meurthe-et-Moselle
Grande Vanné ✆83266236
W via D74, beside the River Moselle
2 Jun-4 Sep
7HEC ◑ H ⊖ G R ⇒R + lau

TURCKHEIM
Haut-Rhin
CM quai de la Gare ✆89270200
Camping Carnet Compulsory.
From Colmar follow N417 to Wintzenheim, then to Turckheim. Before bridge turn left, continue past railway station and stadium.
Mar-Oct
2.5HEC ● H ⊖ G + lau

URBÈS
Haut-Rhin
CM Benelux Bâle ✆89827876
Etr-15 Oct
3HEC ◑ H ⊖ + lau G
Prices A5 pitch6

VERDUN
Meuse
Breuils ✆29861531
Apr-Oct
5.5HEC ● H ⊖ G R H ⇒P + lau

VILLERS-LÈS-NANCY
Meurthe-et-Moselle
C M de Brabois av Paul Muller ✆83271828
Apr-Oct
4.5HEC ● H ⊖ G lau +
Prices A9-10 V5 10-11 A5

WASSELONNE
Bas-Rhin
CM rte de Romanswiller ✆88870008
1km W on D224.
Apr-15 Oct
2.5HEC ◑ H ⊖ G R ⇒P + lau
Prices A11-12 pitch7

WIHR-AU-VAL
Haut-Rhin
Route Verte 13 r de la Gare ✆89711010
15 Apr-15 Oct
0.8HEC ◑ H ⊖ G + lau ⇒R
Prices A8 V6 8 A8

XONRUPT/LONGEMER
Vosges
Eau-Rive ✆29630737
2km SE on D67A next to Lac de Longemer.
All year
1HEC ◑ H ⊖ G R H ⇒R + lau ⇒L
Prices A8 V7 7 A7

Jonquilles ✆29633401
2km SE on D67A beside Lac de Longemer.
Apr-15 Oct
4HEC ◑ H ⊖ G ⇒L + lau ⇒P
Prices pitch36 (incl 2 persons)

BURGUNDY/CHAMPAGNE

The Champagne region is one of the rich greens and huge landscapes of the Ardennes and the wide meadows of the River Marne. Its former capital, Laon, has a rich medieval heritage and a lovely 12th-century cathedral, while, to the south, Troyes boasts wonderful Renaissance treasures. But the jewel of the area is Reims, with its magnificent Gothic cathedral – an important centre for the region and the whole of France for centuries. The local wine of Champagne needs no introduction, and pre-arranged visits and regular tours are available from the famous names – Mercier, Moët, Veuve Cliquot – and there is a Champagne Museum (Musée du Champagne) in Épernay.
The representatives of Burgundy also travel the world – names such as Chablis, Mâcon and Nuits St Georges. A wonderful surprise of the area, though, is the network of hundreds of miles of navigable waterways, accessing a wealth of Romanesque churches, abbeys, castles, and medieval fortress towns, exquisite small villages and quiet rolling expanses of rich pastures and vineyards – the quintessential provincial France. Visitors should include a visit to Beaune, famous for its 14th-century hospice.

ARNAY-LE-DUC
Côte-d'Or
CM de Fouché ✆80900223
0.7km E on D17C.
All year
4HEC H G L P + lau R
Prices A8 pitch5

AUXERRE
Yonne
C M 8 rte de Vaux ✆86521115
SE towards Vaux
Apr-Sep
5HEC H G P + lau R PR
Prices A7-9 pitch4

AUXONNE
Côte-d'Or
CM Arquebuse ✆80373436
Clean, well-equipped site on right bank of River Saône near bathing area.
From Auxonne travel W on N5 for 3km. Then turn northwards on D24 towards Athée and Pontailler-sur-Saône.
May-Sep
2HEC H G H P + lau P

AVALLON
Yonne
CM Sous Roche ✆86341039
2km SE by D944 and D427.
15 May-15 Oct
2HEC H PR P + lau
Prices A8 pitch4

BAR-SUR-AUBE
Aube
Gravière r des Varennes ✆25271294
0.5km E of D13.
Apr-15 Oct
2.8HEC H P + lau P

BEAUNE
Côte-d'Or
CM Cent Vignes 10 r A-Dubois ✆80220391
On outskirts of town. Site divided into pitches, clean, well-looked after sanitary installations. From 20 Jun-31 Aug it is advisable to arrive before 1600 hrs.
On N74 on Savigny-les-Beaune road.
15 Mar-Oct
2HEC H G P + lau P
Prices A10 pitch15

BOURBON-LANCY
Saône-et-Loire
CM de St-Prix ✆85891485
By the swimming pool off the D979a.
15 Apr-15 Oct
2.5HEC H G P + lau P
Prices A9 V5 5 Å5

CM du Plan d'Eau ✆85893427
15 Jun-Oct
1HEC H G P P + lau S
Prices A9 V5 6 Å5

CHAGNY
Saône-et-Loire
CM Pâquier Fané ✆85872142
A clean site 600m W of the church.
Follow the D974 from town centre.
11 May-2 Sep
1.5HEC H G P + lau P
Prices A9 pitch13

CHARLEVILLE-MEZIÈRES
Ardennes
CM Mont Olympe ✆24332360
Level meadowland near the town centre and 100m from municipal indoor swimming pool.
Well signed from town centre.
Etr-15 Oct
2HEC H G R P P + lau

CHARNAY-LÈS-CHALON
Saône-et-Loire
Barrage ✆85491534
May-15 Oct
2HEC H R P + lau
Prices A5 V15

CHAROLLES
Saône-et-Loire
CM ✆85240490
NE of town via D33 towards Viry
15 Mar-15 Oct
1.5HEC H G PR P + lau
Prices A8 V6 5 Å5

CHÂTILLON-SUR-SEINE
Côte-d'Or
CM espl St-Vorles ✆80910305
SE of town off rte de Langres (D928).
Apr-15 Oct
0.8HEC H G P + lau P
Prices A8 pitch6

CHATONRUPT
Haute-Marne
C M ✆25948182
May-Sep
1.5HEC H R P + lau
Prices A4 V2 4 Å4

COSNE-SUR-LOIRE
Nièvre
Ile de Cosne Ile de Cosne, rte de Bourges ✆86282792
Site borders River Loire.
Follow D955 W towards Sancerre.
Mar-Sep
10HEC H R P + lau P
Prices A14 V8 8 Å8

DAROIS
Côte-d'Or
Orée du Bois r d'Etaules ✆80356312
1km N on D104 towards Etaules
Apr-Sep
2.7HEC S H G R H P P + lau
Prices A10 pitch15

DECIZE
Nièvre
CM Halles La Promenade ✆86251405
Water sports on River Loire and tennis nearby.

NW of town centre.
May-Sep
3.5HEC S ◑ H ⊖ G
R H P + lau ✕ PR

DIGOIN
Saône-et-Loire
CM Chevrette r de la Chevrette
✆85531149
W of village on N79.
Mar-Oct
1.6HEC ◑ H ⊖ P P
+ lau ✕
Prices A9 V6 7 4

DIJON
Côte-d'Or
CM Lac 3 bd Kir ✆80435472
1.5km W on N5.
Apr-Nov
2.5HEC ○ H ✕ ⊖ L P
+ lau PR
Prices A6 V3 3 3

ÉCLARON-BRAUCOURT
Haute-Marne
Presqu'Ile de Champaubert
✆25041320
Situated on lake peninsula.
Apr-15 Oct
3.4HEC ◑ H ✕ ⊖ G
L P + lau
Prices A15 V10 13

ÉPERNAY
Marne
CM ✆26553214
A site with poplar trees beside the River Marne within the Municipal Sports Park.
Camping Carnet Compulsory.
In NW suburbs of the town follow signs for Cumières and Damery.
Apr-Sep
10HEC ◑ H ⊖ R P + lau
✕ P
Prices A10 pitch13

GIGNY-SUR-SAÔNE
Saône-et-Loire
Château de d'Epervière ✆85448323
1km S at L'Epervière.
Etr-15 Oct
10HEC ◑ H ✕ ⊖ G
H P + lau PR
Prices A14 pitch25

GRANDPRÉ
Ardennes
CM ✆24305218
150 m from village centre on D6.
Etr-Sep
1.1HEC ◑ H ✕ ⊖ G
R R P + lau
Prices A5 V3 3 3

MÂCON
Saône-et-Loire
CM 'Les Varennes' Sance ✆85381622
Divided into pitches. Water sports centre and pool nearby.

2km N on N6.
15 Mar-Oct
5HEC ◑ H ✕ ⊖ G P
P + lau

MESNIL-ST PÈRE
Aube
Voie Colette ✆25412715
Grassland, with trees, ornamental shrubs and flower beds. Slightly sloping, with a man-made lake nearby.
About 5km from Mesnil-St-Père; signposted from centre.
Apr-15 Oct
4HEC ○ H ✕ ⊖ G P +
lau L
Prices pitch28 (incl 2 persons)

MEURSAULT
Côte-d'Or
CM Grappe d'Or r de 11 Novembre
✆80212248
Clean terraced site.
700m NE on D11b.
Mar-Oct
4.5HEC ● H ✕ ⊖ G
R P + lau P
Prices A12 V7 13 13

MONTBARD
Côte-d'Or
CM r M-Servet ✆80922160
NW via rte de Laignes.
All year
2.5HEC ◑ H ⊖ R H
P + lau ✕ P
Prices A8 pitch8

MONTHERME
Ardennes
Port Diseur r A-Compain ✆24530121
Situated on the confluence of Rivers Meuse and Semoy.
Apr-Sep
2.5HEC ◑ H ⊖ G R P +
✕

MONTSAUCHE
Nièvre
Mesanges ✆86845577
Camping Carnet Compulsory.
May-14 Sep
5HEC ○ ◑ H ⊖ G L
P + lau

Plage du Midi ✆86845197
Camping Carnet Compulsory.
From Salieu (on N6) follow D977. From town centre follow D193 to Les Sultons, then to site.
Etr-Sep
4HEC ◑ H ✕ ⊖ G L
P + lau
Prices A15 pitch10

NEVERS
Nièvre
CM de la Jonction r de la Jonction
✆86375652
S via N7, beside the River Loire
Mar-Oct

1.5HEC S ◑ H ⊖ G R P
+ lau ✕ P
Prices A7 V6 6 6

PARAY-LE-MONIAL
Saône-et-Loire
Pré Barret bd Dauphin Louis
✆85810505
Well signposted from outskirts of town.
All year
0.7HEC ● H ⊖ P + lau
✕ P

POUGUES-LES-EAUX
Nièvre
CM Chanternes ✆86688618
On N7 approx. 7km N of Nevers.
Etr-Oct
1.4HEC ◑ H ⊖ + lau
✕ P
Prices A7 V5 5 6

PREMEAUX
Côte-d'Or
Saule Guillaume ✆80623078
1.5km E via D109G
16 Jun-2 Sep
1.5HEC ● H ⊖ L P
+ lau ✕ G R
Prices A7 pitch7

REIMS
Marne
Airotel de Champagne av Hoche
✆26854122
Approaching from north, turn off on outskirts of town towards Châlons-sur-Marne. Well signposted.
Etr-Sep
4.5HEC ○ H ✕ ⊖ G
P + lau P
Prices A18 pitch15

ROMILLY-SUR-SEINE
Aube
Cerisiers ✆25249398
E of town, 250m from N19 Troyes road.
15 Jun-5 Sep
1.5HEC ◑ H ⊖ G R H
P + lau ✕ P
Prices pitch30-37 (incl 2 persons)

STE-MENEHOULD
Marne
CM de la Grelette ✆26608021
E of town towards Metz, beside the River Aisne
May-15 Sep
0.5HEC ◑ H ⊖ P P lau
Prices A9 pitch3

ST-HONORÉ
Nièvre
Bains 15 av J-Mermoz, rte de Vandenesse ✆86307344
Apr-Oct
2.5HEC ◑ H ✕ ⊖ G
P P + lau R
Prices A15 pitch16

ST-MARCEL
Saône-et-Loire
Butte r J-Leneven ✆85482686
All year
5HEC ⛆ ◑ 🚿H 🛒 🍷 ✕ ⊖ 🚐 G H ⛵R 🅿 + lau ☞ R
Prices A11 pitch15

ST-PÉREUSE
Nièvre
♖ **Manoir de Bezolle** ✆86844255
Situated in grounds of a manor house. Well-kept site divided by hedges.
Camping Carnet Compulsory.
At 'X' roads of D11 and D978.
12 Nov-14 Dec
7HEC ⛆ ◑ 🚿H 🛒 🍷 ✕ ⊖ 🚐 G R H ⛵P 🅿 + lau
Prices pitch60-74 (incl 2 persons)

SAULIEU
Côte-d'Or
CM Perron ✆80641619
1 km NW on N6.
Etr-Oct
8HEC ⛆ ◑ 🚿H 🍷 ⊖ 🚐 🏠 ⛵P 🅿 + lau ☞ 🛒 ✕ ⛵L
Prices A12 V25 🚐25 ⛺25

SEURRE
Côte-d'Or
Piscine ✆80204922
From town centre follow N73 W for 600m in the direction of Beaune.
Jun-Sep
2.5HEC ⛆ ◑ 🚿H 🍷 ✕ ⊖ 🚐 🅿 + lau ☞ 🛒 ⛵PR
Prices A8 V5 🚐5 ⛺5

SÉZANNE
Marne
CM rte de Launat ✆26805700
1.5km W on D239, rte de Launat.
Etr-Oct
1HEC ⛆ ◑ 🚿H ⊖ 🚐 ⛵P 🅿 + lau ☞ 🛒 🍷 ✕ G
Prices A5 V3 🚐3 ⛺3

TAZILLY
Nièvre
Château de Chigy ✆86301080
Etr-Oct
7HEC ⛆ ◑ 🚿H 🛒 🍷 ✕ ⊖ 🚐 G 🏠 ⛵P 🅿 + lau
Prices A16-20 pitch22-27

UCHIZY
Saône-et-Loire
National 6 ✆85405390
Site surrounded by poplar trees on banks of river.
Turn off N6 towards Saône 6km S of Tournus and continue 0.8km.
Apr-Sep
6HEC ⛆ ● 🚿H 🛒 🍷 ✕ ⊖ 🚐 G R 🏠 H ⛵R 🅿 + lau
Prices A10 pitch16

VANDENESSE-EN-AUXOIS
Côte-d'Or
Lac de Panthier Vandenesse ✆80492194
5km SE from Pouilly-en-Auxois on A6.
May-Sep
1.7HEC ⛆ ◑ 🚿H 🛒 🍷 ✕ ⊖ 🚐 G ⛵L 🅿 + lau
Prices A12 pitch15

VERMENTON
Yonne
Coulemière ✆86815001 &
On the N6 S of Auxerre.
15 Apr-Oct
1HEC ⛆ ● 🚿H ⊖ 🚐 R H ⛵R 🅿 + lau ☞ 🛒 🍷 ✕ G
Prices A8 V4 🚐4

SOUTH WEST/PYRÉNÉES

One of the largest regions of France, Aquitaine stretches from the lower plateaux of the Massif Central, west to the Atlantic and south nearly to the foothills of the Pyrénées. This is a land of sunshine, and the three main rivers – the Lot, the Garonne and the Dordogne – wind through valleys and meander through orchards and vineyards, occasionally flowing between high cliffs with castles perched on rocky ledges. Along the Vézère valley in the Dordogne are the impressive caves and grottos with prehistoric remains – the remarkable Lascaux paintings can be admired in Lascaux II – a full-scale replica of the original. On the coast in the south of the region, holidaymakers are attracted by the sophisticated chic of Biarritz, colourful resorts like St-Jean-de-Luz, and Atlantic rollers offering some of the best surfing in Europe. At the foothills of the Pyrénées is Basque country, with charming white houses and timbered cottages, colourful cascading flowers, and rich heritage of festivals and folklore.
Inland, popular centres include Lourdes, which has attracted pilgrims for centuries, and the fascinating Pyrénées National Park with its wild flora and fauna. The Renaissance city of Toulouse has a wonderful heritage, with some of the finest examples of Romanesque architecture in Europe. The region is internationally famous for wonderful cuisine. Here you can find duck liver paté, 'fois gras', Armagnac, and the succulent Toulouse sausage.

ABJAT
See **NONTRON**

ABZAC
Gironde
Paradis ✆57490510
On meadowland near an artificial lake. Pedal boats and fishing nearby.
Drive W on N89 from the direction of Perigueux. After St-Médard-de-Guizières turn onto D17E and follow signposts.
All year
5HEC ⛆ ◑ 🚿H 🍷 ✕ ⊖ 🚐 G 🏠 H ⛵ ⛵LR 🅿 + lau
Prices A12 V7 🚐15 ⛺15

AIGNAN
Gers
Castex ✆62092513
Camping Carnet Compulsory.
800m from D48.
Jun-Sep
3HEC ⛆ S ◑ 🚿H 🍷 ✕ ⊖ 🚐 G ⛵P 🅿 + lau ☞ 🛒

AIRE-SUR-L'ADOUR
Landes
Ombrages de l'Adour ✆58717510
A clean, tidy site next to a sports stadium beside the river. Clean sanitary installations.
May-Sep
3HEC ⛆ 🚿H ⊖ 🚐 H 🅿 + lau ☞ 🛒 🍷 ✕ ⛵P

ALBI
Tarn
Caussels 78 r E-Marty ✆63603706
The site is owned by the local automobile club. It lies on terraced land in a forest next to municipal swimming pools.
Camping Carnet Compulsory.
From village take N99 towards Millau, then turn left onto D100 and left again into site.
Apr-Oct
1HEC ⛆ ◑ 🚿H ⊖ 🚐 G 🅿 P + lau ☞ 🛒 🍷 ✕ ⛵P

AMBARÈS
Gironde
Clos Chauvet ✆56388108
Surrounded by vineyards.
100 m from A10 via D911.
10 May-15 Oct
0.8HEC H G + lau
Prices A17 pitch12

AMÉLIE-SUR-MER, L'
See **SOULAC-SUR-MER**

ANDERNOS-LES-BAINS
Gironde
Fontaine-Vieille 4 bd du Cl-Wurtz ✆56820167
On level ground in sparse forest.
S of village centre.
12 May-16 Sep
12.6HEC H G R H PS + lau
Prices pitch48-75 (incl 2 persons)

See advertisement in colour section

Pleine Forêt ✆56821718
Situated in a quiet location among pines.
Off D106E or D106 Andernos-les-Bains-Bordeaux road.
All year
6HEC S H R H P + lau G S
Prices A15 pitch30-35

ANGLES
Tarn
Manoir ✆63709606
Site lies in the grounds of an old Manor House.
S of village, on rte de Lacabarède.
Etr-mid Oct
3HEC H H P + lau L
Prices pitch76 (incl 2 persons)

ANGLET
Pyrénées-Atlantiques
Barre de l'Adour 130 av de l'Adour ✆59631616
In a hollow between noisy road and jetty, adjacent to River Adour.
17 Jun-17 Sep
2.5HEC S H G H + lau S

Parme Quartier Brindos ✆55230500
3km SW off N10
Mar-Nov
4HEC H G R H P + lau
Prices A15 25 A18

ARCACHON
Gironde
CM des Abatilles allée de la Galaxie ✆56832415
1.5 km S.
25 Mar-15 Oct
7.5HEC S H P + lau PS
Prices A14-15 pitch29-60

ARCANGUES
See **BIARRITZ**

ARCIZANS-AVANT
Hautes-Pyrénées
Lac ✆62970188
Set in Pyrenean landscape on outskirts of village, with very clean sanitary installations.
S on N21 take D101 through St-Savin.
Jun-Sep
2.5HEC H G + lau R
Prices A15 pitch17

ARÈS
Gironde
Abberts ✆56602680
Camping Carnet Compulsory.
Follow signs from D106.
15 May-Sep
2HEC S H + lau G R LS
Prices A16 V6 20 A20

Canadienne 82 r du Gl-de-Gaulle, rte du Cap-Ferret ✆56602491
Shop available Jun-Aug only.
1 km N off D106.
Jun-6 Sep
2HEC H G P + lau

Cigale ✆56602259
Clean tidy site amongst pine trees. Grassy pitches.
0.5 km N on D106.
Apr-15 Oct
2.5HEC H G + lau LS

CM Goëlands ✆56825564
1.7km SE
Apr-Sep
10HEC S H G + lau LS
Prices A12 pitch34-40

ARGELÈS-GAZOST
Hautes-Pyrénées
At **ARRAS-EN-LAVENDAN** (2km SW on N618)
Relais de l'Aubisque rte du Col de l'Aubisque ✆62970211
Etr-20 Sep
1HEC H G H + lau R
Prices A9 pitch9

ARRAS-EN-LAVENDAN
See **ARGELÈS-GAZOST**

ARREAU
Hautes-Pyrénées
Refuge International rte de Lannemezan ✆62986334
Enclosed terrace site.
Camping Carnet Compulsory.
2km N on D929.
Jun-Sep
5HEC H H + lau R

ASCAIN
Pyrénées-Atlantiques
Nivelle rte de St-Pée-sur-Nivelle ✆59540194
2km N of town on D918 to St-Jean-de-Luz.
15 Jun-15 Sep
3HEC H G R + lau P
Prices A11 pitch17

ASCARAT
Pyrénées-Atlantiques
Euro Camping ✆59371278
May-Oct
1.7HEC ○ H ⊖ [G] P + lau R
Prices A22 pitch30

ATUR
Dordogne
Grand Dague ✆53042101
3km NE towards St-Laurent-sur-Manoire
Etr-Oct
23HEC ◑ H ⊖ [G] [R] [H] P lau
Prices A16 pitch20

AUREILHAN
Landes
CM ✆58091088
Quiet site separated by a small road on the banks of Lake Aureilhan.
15 Jun-15 Sep
8HEC ● H ⊖ [G] L + lau
Prices A10 V3 17 A8

♖ **Domaine de Vacances Eurolac** ✆58090287
Well tended site under deciduous trees providing shade, partially on open meadow.
Turn right at Labouheyre off N10 on D626 to Aureilhan. Follow signs.
15 May-Sep
15HEC ◑ ⊖ [G] L + lau

AZUR
Landes
Paillotte ✆58481212
Site on N shore of lake with strip of ptiches over 200m long between forest and lake. Quiet family site (special toilets and washbasins for children) with own private sandy bathing area.
1.5km SW.
Jun-15 Sep
7HEC S ◑ H ⊖ [G] [H] LP + lau S
Prices pitch83-97 (incl 2 persons)

BAGNÈRES-DE-BIGORRE
Hautes-Pyrénées
Bigourdan rte de Tarbes ✆62951357
2.5km NW at Pouzac
Etr-Sep
0.6HEC ◑ H ⊖ [G] [H] P + lau
Prices A13 pitch14

Tilleuls av Alan-Brooke ✆62952604
May-Sep
2.6HEC ◑ H ⊖ [G] + lau PR
Prices A13 pitch14

At **TRÉBONS**(4km N on D935)
Parc des Oiseaux ✆62953026
Clean, well-kept site with large pitches.
All year
2.8HEC ◑ H ⊖ [G] [R] [H] + lau LPR
Prices A12-13 V4-5 4-5 A4-5

BARÈGES
Hautes-Pyrénées
Ribère ✆62926791
All year
2HEC ◑ H ⊖ [G] [R] [H] + lau
Prices pitch33-37 (incl 2 persons)

BAYONNE
Pyrénées-Atlantiques
Airotel la Chêneraie ✆59550131
On gently sloping field divided by hedges.
4km NE off N117 Pau road.
15 Mar-15 Oct
12HEC ◑ H ⊖ [G] P + lau
Prices A17 pitch30-50

BEAUCENS-LES-BAINS
Hautes-Pyrénées
Viscos ✆62970545
1km N on D13, rte de Lourdes.
Jun-25 Sep
2HEC ◑ H ⊖ [G] + lau R
Prices A11 pitch10

BELVÈS
Dordogne
Moulin de la Pique ✆53290115
A quiet site. Surroundings include an old mill which has been converted into high class apartments.
500m S on D710.
Etr-Oct
12HEC ◑ H ⊖ [G] [R] [H] LP + lau R
Prices A21 pitch28-48

Nauves Bos Rouge ✆53291264
Jun-Sep
40HEC ◑ H ⊖ [G] [H] P lau
Prices A18 pitch26

At **STE-FOY-DE-BELVÈS** (5km SE by D710 & D54)
♖ **Hauts de Ratebout** ✆53290210
An old Périgord farm, set in extensive grounds.
May-23 Sep
10HEC ◑ H ⊖ [G] [H] P + lau
Prices A23-25 pitch34-38

BEYNAC-ET-CAZENAC
Dordogne
Capeyrou ✆53295495
Jun-Sep
2HEC ● H ⊖ [G] R + lau
Prices A14 pitch12

BIARRITZ
Pyrénées-Atlantiques
Biarritz 28 r d'Harcet ✆59230012
Site lies 200m from beach; 2km from town centre on N10, follow signs 'Espagne'.
28 Apr-1 Oct
3HEC ◑ H ⊖ [G] [R] + lau LS
Prices A12 pitch15-22

Splendid 12 r d'Harcet ✆59230129
On gently sloping ground.
3km S.
Apr-Sep

1.6HEC ~ ◑ ⌂H ♜ ♀ ✕ ⊖ ◘ [G] [R] ▣ + lau ☞ ≈S
Prices A12 V5 ⛟22 ⛺15

At **ARCANGUES** (4km S on D254)
Aldabénia ✆59430730
4km from beaches.
Jun-Sep
1HEC ~ ● ⌂H ⊖ ◘ [G] [H] ⛰ ▣ + lau ☞ ♜ ♀
Prices A10 pitch13

At **BIDART** (4km SW)
Berrua rte d'Arbonne ✆59549666
Level meadowland in rural surroundings. 800m to sea.
May-Sep
5HEC ~ ● ⌂H ♜ ♀ ✕ ⊖ ◘ [G] ⌂ [H] ≈P ▣ + lau ☞ ≈RS
Prices A14-15 pitch65-75

Ferme Oyamburua ✆59549161
Level meadow site near farm. Views of the Pyrénées. Simple but pleasant site.
Turn off beyond the church in the direction of Arbonne, via N10, for approx 1km.
Jun-Sep
3.5HEC ~ ◑ ⌂H ♀ ⊖ ◘ [G] [R] ⌂ [H] ≈PS ▣ + lau ☞ ♜ ✕
Prices A14 pitch18

Jean Paris Quartier M-Pierre ✆59265558
400m from beaches.
S of town, cross railway line, site on S side of N10.
Jun-Sep
1HEC ~ ◑ ⌂H ♜ ♀ ✕ ⊖ ◘ [G] [H] ▣ + lau ☞ ≈S
Prices A11-12 V6-7 ⛟10-11

Résidence des Pins rte de Biarritz ✆59230029
Terraced site with numbered pitches, 800m from sea.
2km N on N106 Biarritz road.
Jun-Sep
10HEC ~ ● ⌂H ♜ ♀ ✕ ⊖ ◘ [G] [H] ≈P ▣ + lau ☞ ≈LS
Prices pitch70

♖ **Ruisseau** rte d'Arbonne ✆59419450
2km E on D255.
27 May-September
15HEC ~ ◑ ⌂H ♜ ♀ ✕ ⊖ ◘ [G] [R] ⌂ [H] ≈LP ▣ + lau ☞ ≈S
Prices A18 V5 ⛟26 ⛺26

Ur-Onéa r de la Chapelle ✆59265361
0.6km E
Apr-Sep
2.5HEC ~ ○ ⌂H ♜ ♀ ✕ ⊖ ◘ [G] [H] ≈PS ▣ + lau ☞ [R]
Prices A11 pitch17

BIAS
Landes
CM Tatiou St-Julian-en-Born ✆58090476
2km W towards Lespecier
Apr-Oct
8HEC *S* ● ⌂H ♜ ♀ ✕ ⊖ ◘ [G] [R] ≈PS ▣ P + lau

BIDART
See **BIARRITZ**

BISCARROSSE
Landes
Rive ✆58781233
Level site in tall pine forest on E side of lake.
N of town off D652 Sanguinet road.
Apr-Sep
10HEC ~ ◑ ⌂H ♜ ♀ ✕ ⊖ ◘ [G] ⌂ ▣ + lau ☞ ≈L

See advertisement in colour section

BLAYE
Gironde
At **MAZION** (5.5km NE on N937)
Tilleuls ✆57421813
Camping Carnet Compulsory.
5.5km NE on N937.
May-Nov
0.3HEC ~ ◑ ⌂H ⊖ ◘ ▣ lau ☞ ♜ ♀ ✕
Prices A11 V5 ⛟6 ⛺6

BUGUE, LE
Dordogne
At **LIMEUIL**(5.5km SW by D703 and D31)
Port de Limeuil allées sur Dordogne ✆53220210
Adjacent to the confluence of the Rivers Dordogne and Vezère and facing Limeuil.
Jun-Sep 5
6.4HEC *S* ◑ ⌂H ♜ ♀ ✕ ⊖ ◘ [G] ≈R ▣ + lau
Prices pitch70 (incl 2 persons)

CAHORS
Lot
At **ESCLAUZELS**(18km SE)
Pompit ✆65315340
5km NW of Esclauzels village.
15 Jun-15 Sep
1.5HEC ~ ◑ ⌂H ♜ ♀ ⊖ ◘ [G] [H] ≈P ▣ + lau
Prices A12 pitch10

CALVIAC
Lot
Chênes Verts ✆53592107
May-Sep
8HEC ~ ○ ⌂H ♜ ♀ ✕ ⊖ ◘ [G] ⌂ [H] ≈P ▣ + lau ☞ ≈R
Prices A17 pitch29

Trois Sources ✆65330301
May-Oct
3.5HEC ~ ● ⌂H ♜ ♀ ✕ ⊖ ◘ [G] [H] ⛰ ≈PR ▣ + lau
Prices A20 pitch22

CAPBRETON
Landes
Pointe ✆58721498
2km S towards Labenne on N652.
May-Sep
5HEC ~ *S* ◑ ● ⌂H ♜ ♀ ✕ ⊖ ◘ [G] P + lau ☞ ≈RS

CARSAC-AILLAC
See **SARLAT-LA-CANÉDA**

CASTELJALOUX
Lot-et-Garonne
CM de la Piscine ✆53935468
NW on D933 Marmande road.
Apr-Sep
1HEC ~ ◑ ⌂H ♀ ✕ ⊖ ◘ [G] ≈P ▣ + lau ☞ ♜ ≈L

CM Lac de Clarens ✆53930745
S on D933 Mont-de-Marson road.
Apr-Sep
5HEC *S* ◑ ⌂H ♀ ✕ ⊖ ◘ [G] ▣ + lau ☞ ♜ ≈L
Prices A7-10 pitch6

CAUNEILLE
Landes
Sources ✆58730440
N of town, 200m from N117
May-Sep
1.5HEC ~ ○ ⌂H ♜ ♀ ✕ ⊖ ◘ [R] ⌂ [H] ≈P ▣ + lau ☞ ≈R
Prices A9 V6 ⛟10 ⛺10

CAUTERETS
Hautes-Pyrénées
Mamelon-Vert av du Mamelon-Vert ✆62925156
9 May-Sep
3HEC ~ ○ ⌂H ⊖ ◘ ▣ + lau ☞ ♜ ♀ ✕ [G] [R] ≈PR
Prices A12 pitch11

CHAMPS-ROMAIN
Dordogne
Château le Verdoyer ✆53569464
Etr-Oct
9HEC ~ ◑ ⌂H ♜ ♀ ✕ ⊖ ◘ [G] [R] ⌂ [H] ≈LP ▣ + lau
Prices A21 pitch27

CLAOUEY
Gironde
Airotel les Viviers rte du Cap Ferret, Lege Cap Ferret ✆56607004
Beautiful, widespread site in a forest divided by seawater channels.
On the D106, 1km S of the town.
28 Apr-Sep
33HEC *S* ◑ ⌂H ♜ ♀ ✕ ⊖ ◘ [R] ⌂ [H] ≈PS ▣ + lau
Prices A10-20 pitch83-124

COLAYRAC-ST-CIRQ
Lot-et-Garonne
CM 113 rte de Bordeaux ✆53875373
Bordering river.
200m from N113.
Jun-Sep
40HEC ~ ◑ ⌂H ⊖ ◘ ▣ lau ☞ ♜ ♀ ✕

CONTIS-PLAGE
Landes
Lous Seurrots ✆58428582
In pine forest on outskirts of village between road and stream. Beware of current if bathing in stream.
Etr-Sep ➔

15HEC ◑ S ● H ! ✕ ⊖ G R H RS P + lau

CORDES
Tarn
Moulin de Julien ✆63560142
900m E on D600 and D922.
Apr-Sep
8HEC ◑ H ! ⊖ G H P + lau ✕
Prices pitch60 (incl 2 persons)

COUX-ET-BIGAROQUE
See **SIORAC-EN-PÉRIGORD**

CRAYSSAC
Lot
Reflets du Quercy ✆65309148
1.8 km NW via D23 (rte de Catus), then turn left.
Etr-Sep
7HEC ◑ H ! ✕ ⊖ G R H P + lau

DAGLAN
Dordogne
Moulin de Paulhiac ✆53282088
4km N via D57 beside the Céou
Jun-15 Sep
5HEC ● H ! ✕ ⊖ G PR P + lau
Prices A19 pitch38

DAX
Landes
Chênes Bois-de-Boulogne ✆58900553
W of town beside River Ardour.
Apr-Oct
5HEC ● H ! ✕ ⊖ G H P + lau

DEYME
Haute-Garonne
Violettes ✆61817207
Adjacent to N113.
All year
2.5HEC ● H ! ✕ ⊖ G R H P + lau P

ESCLAUZELS
See **CAHORS**

ESCOT
Pyrénées-Atlantiques
Centre de Loisirs le Mont Bleu ✆59344192
Quiet site in beautiful Pyrénéan landscape.
At railway bridge take D294 for approx 6km.
25 Jun-25 Sep
3.5HEC ◑ H ! ✕ ⊖ H PR P + lau
Prices A11 V4 20 A20

ÉYZIES-DE-TAYAC, LES
Dordogne
At **SIREUIL** (7km E off D47)
Mas ✆53296806
N of D47 (Sarlat-Les Eyzies).
Jun-Sep
5HEC ◑ H ! ✕ ⊖ G R P P + lau
Prices pitch50 (incl 2 persons)

FIGEAC
Lot
Carmes chemin de la Curie ✆65340856
On well-kept meadow with flower beds and gravel drives.
From village centre follow N140 towards Brive, turn right at TOTAL garage.
All year
0.7HEC ◑ H ⊖ G H P + lau ! ✕ PR
Prices A13 pitch15

FOIX
Ariège
CM Lac de Labarre rte de Pamiers ✆61651158
On well-kept meadow.
3km N on N20.
Apr-Oct
3HEC ◑ H ! ✕ ⊖ LR P + lau

FOSSAT, LE
Ariège
Laillères ✆61689965
On D626.
Mar-Oct
0.4HEC ◑ H ⊖ R P lau ! ✕ G R P +
Prices A5 V4 4 A4

FRAYSSINET
Lot
Tirelire ✆65310019
All year
2HEC ◑ H ! ⊖ P lau ✕ P

At **PONT-DE-RHODES** (1km N on N20)
Plage du Relais ✆65310016
15 Jun-5 Sep
2HEC ◑ H ! ✕ ⊖ G P P + lau

GASTES
See **PARENTIS-EN-BORN**

GAUGEAC
Dordogne
Moulin de David ✆53226525
May-Sep
14HEC ◑ H ! ✕ ⊖ G R H P P + lau
Prices A14-20 pitch33

GOURDON
Lot
At **GROLÉJAC** (15km N on D704)
Granges ✆53281115
Beautifully situated terraces on a hill with big pitches. Site beside railway bridge. Facilities for sports and entertainment.
Turn off D704 in village towards Domme.
May-Sep
5HEC ◑ H ! ✕ ⊖ PR P + lau G R L

At **ST-MARTIAL-DE-NABIRAT** (6km W)
Carbonnier ✆53284253
Off the D46.
Etr-Sep
10HEC ◑ H ! ✕ ⊖ G R LP P + lau
Prices A22 pitch31

GOURETTE
Pyrénées-Atlantiques
Ley ✆59051147
Terraced site with gravel and asphalt caravan pitches. TV, common room.
From Laruns drive E to Eaux-Bonnes and drive uphill to Gourette.
20 Dec-20 Apr & 30 June-5 Aug

2HEC ○ H R H
P + lau

GRISOLLES
Tarn-et-Garonne
Aquitaine rte de Montauban
63673322
1.5km N off 'X' roads N20/N113.
15 Apr-Oct
3HEC H G H
P + lau
Prices A15 pitch15

GROLÉJAC
See **GOURDON**

HASPARREN
Pyrénées-Atlantiques
Chapital 59296294
1.1HEC H G H P +
lau P

HENDAYE
Pyrénées-Atlantiques
Acacias 59207876
Camping Carnet Compulsory.
Etr-Sep
5HEC H G H
LPS + lau
Prices pitch50 (incl 2 persons)

Airotel Eskualduna rte de la Corniche 59200464
On gently sloping meadow.
2km from village on N10c.
15 Jun-Sep
8HEC H G H
S + lau R

Alturan r de La Côte 59200455
Situated by the sea.
Jun-Sep
4HEC H G
P + lau S
Prices A14 V6 16 16

Ametza rte de l'Empereur 59200705
1km E
Jun-Sep
5HEC H G
H P + lau S
Prices A13 pitch60

Sascoénéa bd du Gl-Leclerc 59200544
On hill, 1km from sea.
From N10C turn into r d'Elissacilo then into r des Lilas.
Etr-Sep
5HEC H G H +
lau S
Prices A16 V8 16 16

HOSSEGOR
Landes
Rey 58435200
Camping Carnet Compulsory.
Off D652.
16 Jun-2 Sep
9HEC H G LS
+ lau
Prices A13 pitch15

HOURTIN
Gironde
Airotel Mauriflaue rte de Pauillac 56091197
Level meadowland, shaded by pines, in rural setting.
Turn onto D4 at the chemist and continue E towards Pauillac.
May-15 Sep
5.6HEC H G
R H + lau PR

Orée du Bois rte d'Aquitaine 56091588
1500m from town centre beside the lake.
Jun-15 Sep
2HEC H G H
+ lau LS
Prices pitch45 (incl 2 persons)

Ourmes 56091276
On well-kept field. Boating nearby.
Follow D4 towards lake.
1 Apr-30 Sep
7HEC H G H
L + lau
Prices pitch54 (incl 2 persons)

HOURTIN-PLAGE
Gironde
Côte d'Argent 56091025
500m from beach.
15 May-15 Sep
20HEC S H G
R H + lau S

HUME, LA
Gironde
At **TESTE, LA** (3km SW)
Village de Loisirs Domaine de la Forge rte Sanguinet 56660772 ➔

Secluded site in very quiet woodland.
3km S on D652.
15 Jun-Sep
4HEC S ◑ H ! ✕ ⊖ G R H P + lau ☞ L
Prices A16 pitch25

IBARRON
See **ST-PÉE-SUR-NIVELLE**

LABENNE
Landes
Savane ✆59454113
On RN10.
All year
6HEC ◑ H ! ✕ ⊖ G R H + lau ☞ LS
Prices A9-11 pitch6-11

LABENNE-OCÉAN
Landes
Boudigau ✆59454207
Situated in pine forest.
Turn right into site after bridge.
Jun-Sep
5HEC ◑ H ! ✕ ⊖ G H PS + lau
Prices A13 pitch21-51

Côte d'Argent ✆59454202
Very well-managed modern site attached to holiday village.
3km W on D126.
All year
4HEC S ● H ! ✕ ⊖ G H P + lau ☞ RS

Mer ✆59454209
On D126 (rte de la Plage).
Jun-29 Sep
6HEC S ● H ⊖ G H R + lau ☞ S
Prices A10-13 pitch15-19

LACANAU-OCÉAN
Gironde
Airotel de l'Océan r du Répos ✆56032445
On rising ground in pine forest. 800m from beach.
May-Sep
9.5HEC S ● H ! ✕ ⊖ H P P + lau ☞ S
Prices pitch90-100 (incl 3 persons)

Grands Pins ✆56032077
On very hilly terrain in woodland. 400m from the beach, access to which is through dunes.
Apr-Oct
10HEC S ● H ! ✕ ⊖ G R H P P + lau ☞ S
Prices pitch100-120 (incl 3 persons)

At **MEDOC** (8km E)
Talaris rte de l'Océan ✆56030415
Camping Carnet Compulsory.
May-Sep
6HEC ● H ! ⊖ G R P + lau ☞ ✕ L
Prices pitch85-91 (incl 2 persons)

At **MOUTCHIC** (5km E)
Ermitage ✆56202522
Camping Carnet Compulsory.
In village centre 150m from lake.
Jul-Aug
3HEC S ● H ⊖ G R L + lau ☞ ! ✕ S
Prices pitch77 (incl 2 persons)

Lac ✆56030026
On D6 rte de Lacanau, 60m from lake.
Apr-15 Oct
1.5HEC S ● H ! ⊖ G R H + lau ☞ ✕ LS

LACAPELLE-MARIVAL
Lot
CM Bois de Sophie ✆65408259
1km NW via D940
15 May-Sep
2.5HEC ● H ⊖ P lau ☞ ! ✕ P

LANTON
Gironde
Roumingue ✆56829748
Level terrain under a few deciduous trees partially in open meadow on the Bassin d'Arcachon.
1km NW of village towards sea.
Jun-Sep
12HEC S ◑ H ! ✕ ⊖ G H S + lau

LARNAGOL
Lot
Ruisseau de Treil ✆65312339
Camping Carnet Compulsory.
0.6km E via D662
16 Apr-14 Oct
4.6HEC ◑ H ! ⊖ G H P + lau ☞ ✕ R
Prices A15-25 pitch15-25

LARUNS
Pyrénées-Atlantiques
Gaves ✆59053237
On the bank of the Gave d'Ossan. Some pitches reserved for caravans.
1km S.
All year
2HEC ◑ H ! ⊖ R H + lau ☞ ✕ PR
Prices A12 pitch23

LARUSCADE
Gironde
Relais du Chavan ✆57686305
On well-kept meadow edged by a strip of forest. Some traffic noise.
6.5km NW on N10 near Km20.3.
15 May-15 Sep
3HEC ◑ H ⊖ G P + lau ☞ ! ✕
Prices A15 11 A11 pitch11

LECTOURE
Gers
Lac des Trois Vallées ✆62688233
This rural site is part of a large park and lies next to a lake. It has spacious marked pitches.
3km SE on N21.
Etr-Sep
40HEC ○ ◑ ● H ! ✕ ⊖ G R L + lau
Prices pitch85-108 (incl 3 persons)

LÉON
Landes
Lou Puntaou ✆58487430
In oak wood with separate sections for caravans.
Turn off N652 in village and continue towards lake for 1.5km on D142.
Jun-15 Sep
15HEC H ! ⊖ G R H LP + lau ☞ ✕ S

LESCAR
Pyrénées-Atlantiques
Terrier rte du Pont-du-Gare ✆59810182
On meadowland split in two with pitches surrounded by hedges in foreground.
From Pau take N117 towards Bayonne for approx. 6.5km, then turn left onto D501 towards Monein to site towards bridge.
All year
5HEC ◑ H ! ✕ ⊖ G R H P + lau
Prices A13 V21 21

LESPARAT
See **PÉRIGUEUX**

LILIAN
See **SOULAC-SUR-MER**

LIMEUIL
See **BUGUE, LE**

LIT-ET-MIXE
Landes
Univers Camping rte des Lacs ✆58428337
A level site in an old park. Rarely crowded.
On southern outskirts of town towards Léon.
Jun-15 Sep
10HEC ● H ! ✕ ⊖ H P + lau ☞

LIVERS-CAZELLES
Tarn
Rédon ✆63561464
4km SE of Cordes on D600.
15 Mar-30 Nov
1HEC ◑ H ✕ ⊖ G R H P + lau
Prices pitch45-48 (incl 3 persons)

LOURDES
Hautes-Pyrénées
Arrouach Quartier Biscaye ✆62942575
Situated on D940 Soumoulou road.
All year
2.5HEC ● H ⊖ G + lau ☞ ! ✕ LPR
Prices A12 V7 7 A7

Domec rte de Julos ✆62940879
Off N21 Tarbes road N of town centre.
Etr-Oct

2HEC ⁓ ● ⋒H ⊖ G H P +
lau ☞ ! ✕ LP
Prices A8 pitch10

Theil No 23 ✆62943633
Quiet side on several levels. Bathrooms available.
Turn off N640 in village and follow signposts.
All year
1HEC ⁓ ● ⋒H ⊖ LP P +
lau

LUCHON
Haute-Garonne
Beauregard av de Vénasque ✆61793074
On level meadow.
Off N125.
Apr-Nov
2.5HEC ⁓ ◑ ⋒H ✕ ⊖ R P +
lau ☞ ! P

LUZ-ST-SAUVEUR
Hautes-Pyrénées
Bergons ✆62929077
600m E on D618 Barèges road.
All year
1HEC ⁓ ◑ ⋒H ⊖ G P + lau
☞ ! ✕ P
Prices A11 pitch10

Pyrénées International rte de Lourdes ✆62928202
1.3km NW on N21.
Jun-Sep
3HEC ⁓ ◑ ⋒H ! ✕ ⊖ G R
H P P + lau

MARCILLAC-ST-QUENTIN
Dordogne
Tailladis ✆53591095
15 Mar-Oct
25HEC ⁓ S ● ⋒H ! ✕ ⊖ G
R H LP P + lau
Prices A19-23 22-26 Å13-18

MAREUIL
Dordogne
Etang Bleu Vieux Mareuil ✆53609270
Jul-Aug
4HEC ⁓ ◑ ● ⋒H ! ✕ ⊖ G
L P + lau
Prices A16 pitch18-32

MARTRES-TOLOSANE
Haute-Garonne
Moulin ✆61988640
1.5km SE
All year
15HEC ⁓ ○ ◑ ● ⋒H ! ✕ ⊖
H PR P + lau ☞ G
Prices pitch50 (incl 2 persons)

MASSEUBE
Gers
CM ✆62660175
500m E on D27.
6HEC ⁓ ● ⋒H ! ✕ ⊖ P P +
lau

MAULÉON-LICHARRE
Pyrénées-Atlantiques
Saison rte de Tardets ✆59281879 or 59280623
1.5km S on D918 Tardets-Sorholus road.
Jun-Sep
1HEC ⁓ ● ⋒H ! ⊖ G H
P P + lau ☞ ✕ R
Prices A10 V4 9 Å9

MAZION
See **BLAYE**

MEDOC
See **LACANAU-OCÉAN**

MESSANGES
Landes
Moisan rte de la Plage ✆58489206
15 May-Sep
5HEC ⁓ ◑ ⋒H ✕ ⊖ G H P
+ lau ☞ S
Prices pitch46 (incl 2 persons)

Vieux Port ✆58482200
2.5 km SW via D652.
Apr-Sep
40HEC ⁓ ◑ ⋒H ! ✕ ⊖ G
R H P + lau ☞ LRS
Prices pitch94-128 (incl 3 persons)

MÉZOS
Landes
Sen Yan ✆58073082
1km E
Jun-15 Sep
8HEC ⁓ ● ⋒H ! ✕ ⊖ G R
H P P + lau
Prices pitch79 (incl 3 persons)

MIÉLAN
Gers
Lac Centre de Loisirs ✆62675176
On slightly sloping, partially uneven ground adjoining the leisure and water sports centre.
2.5km NE via N21 rte d'Auch.
All year
1.5HEC ⁓ ◑ ⋒H ! ✕ ⊖ G
R L P + lau
Prices pitch47 (incl 3 persons)

MILLAC
Lot
Millac Lieu dit Combe de Lafon ✆53297793
Etr-Sep
3HEC ⁓ ○ ⋒H ! ✕ ⊖ G
R H P P + lau

MIMIZAN
Landes
CM Lac av de Woolsack ✆58090121
Level site with pine trees on west bank of Étang d'Aureilhan.
Access by D87 Mimizan/St-Eulalie road.
Etr-Oct
10HEC ⁓ ● ⋒H ⊖ G R L
P + lau ☞ ! ✕

At **MIMIZAN-PLAGE** (6km E by D626)
Marina ✆58091266
In mixed woodland. 300m from beach.
Take D626 from Mimizan Plage. Well signed from paper mill.
15 May-Sep
9HEC ⁓ ● ⋒H ! ✕ ⊖ G
H P P + lau ☞ S
Prices pitch72-95 (incl 2 persons)

MIMIZAN-PLAGE
See **MIMIZAN**

MIRANDOL
Tarn
Clots ✆63769278
Situated in the Viaur valley.
5.5km N via D905, rte de Rieupeyroux.
Etr-15 Oct
3HEC ⁓ ◑ ⋒H ! ⊖ G H
PR P + lau
Prices A18 V7 11 Å10

MOLIÈRES
Dordogne
Grande Veyière ✆53225421
2.4km SE
Apr-15 Nov
4.5HEC ○ H G R H P + lau
Prices A14-16 pitch18-20

MOLIETS-PLAGE
Landes
Cigales ✆58485118
On undulating ground in pine trees.
300m from beach.
Etr-Sep
25HEC ● H G H + lau LRS
Prices A13 pitch16

St-Martin ✆58485230
Etr-12 Oct
18.5HEC ◑ H G R PS + lau
Prices pitch50-91 (incl 2 persons)

MONCRABEAU
Lot-et-Garonne
CM Mouliat ✆53654328 & 53654211
On D219, 200m from D930.
15 Jun-Sep
1.3HEC ● H H + lau P

MONTAUBAN-DE-LUCHON
Haute-Garonne
Lanette ✆61790038
On gently sloping ground surrounded by pastures.
1.5km E of Luchon. Off D27.
All year
4.3HEC ◑ H G R H + lau PR
Prices pitch57-67 (incl 3 persons)

MONTBARTIER
Tarn-et-Garonne
Fongrave ✆63305273
3km SE on N20
Feb-Oct
3HEC ● H G R H P + lau
Prices A20 pitch17

MONTCABRIER
See **PUY-L'ÉVÊQUE**

MONTESQUIOU
Gers
♖ **Château le Haget** ✆62709580
In grounds of Château.
May-1 Oct
12HEC ◑ H G R H P P + lau
Prices A22 pitch25

MONTIGNAC
Dordogne
Castillanderie ✆53507679
Apr-Oct
15HEC ○ H G R H L + lau

MOUTCHIC
See **LACANAU-OCÉAN**

MUSSIDAN
Dordogne
CM Le Port ✆53812009
15 Jun-Oct
0.5HEC ◑ H G P + lau

NAGES
Tarn
Rieu Montagné Lac du Laouzas ✆63374052
4.5km S via D62
3HEC ○ H G R H LR + lau
Prices pitch100 (incl 4 persons)

NONTRON
Dordogne
At **ABJAT** (15km NE)
Moulin de Masfrolet ✆53568270
2.4km N.
June-15 Sep
12HEC ● H G H P + lau

ONDRES
Landes
Lou Pignada ✆59453065
Turn off the N10 in the village onto rte de la Plage.
Etr-Sep
2HEC S ◑ H G R H LS + lau
Prices A13 29 18

ONESSE-ET-LAHARIE
Landes
CM Bienvenu ✆58073049
500m from village centre on D38.
15 Jun-15 Sep
1.5HEC ◑ H + lau
Prices A10 V7 10 10

OUSSE
Pyrénées-Atlantiques
Sapins ✆59817421
On N117.
All year
0.7HEC ◑ H G + lau
Prices A12 pitch17

PAMIERS
Ariège
Ombrages ✆61671224
NW on D119 beside river.
All year
3.5HEC ● H G H R + lau P

PARENTIS-EN-BORN
Landes
Arbre d'Or rte du Lac ✆58784156
A level site in pine wood on S shore of the Étang de Biscarosse.
Turn off D652 2km S of Gastes.
Jun-15 Sep
4.5HEC S ● H G R H + lau LP

Mouteou rte de l'Étang ✆58784227
2.5km W.
15 Jun-15 Sep
4.5HEC S ● H H + lau LS

At **GASTES** (7.5km SW)
Réserve ✆58097596
3km SW via D652
15 Mar-Oct
27HEC ● H G R H L + lau

PAYRAC
Lot
Panoramic ✆65379845
All year
1.5HEC ● H H + lau G R P
Prices A8 pitch8

Pins rte de Cahors ✆65379632
A well-managed site, partly in forest, partly on meadowland. Sheltered from traffic noise.
S of village off N20.
Apr-Sep
4HEC ◑ ● H G H P + lau
Prices A25 pitch38

PÉRIGUEUX
Dordogne
Barnabe-Plage ✆53534145
Signposted from N89, 2km E of town centre.
All year
1HEC ◑ H + lau G R
Prices A11 V7 11 11

At **LESPARAT** (4km E on N89)
Isle ✆53535775
29 Mar-3 Nov
3HEC ◑ H G PR + lau
Prices A16 V11 11 11

PETIT-PALAIS
Gironde
Pressoir Queyrai Petit-Palais ✆57697325
1.7km NW via D21
May-30 Sep
2.5HEC ○ H H P + lau R
Prices A18 pitch21

PEZULS
Dordogne
Forêt ✆53227169
In extensive grounds on the edge of the forest.
600m off D703. 3km from the village centre.
Etr-Oct
12HEC ◑ H G R H P + lau
Prices A13-17 pitch12-16

PONT-DE-RHODES
See **FRAYSSINET**

PONT-ST MAMET
Dordogne
Lestaubière ✆53829815
On wooded pasture in the grounds of Lestaubière Castle.
Off N21.
15 May-15 Sep
5HEC ◑ H G LP
+ lau
Prices A20 V11 11 A10

PRAT-ET-BONREPAUX
Ariège
CM Pont du Bugot ✆61966162
On D117n.
Jun-Oct
0.4HEC ◑ H + lau
G R R
Prices A9 V4 5 A5

PRAYSSAC
Lot
VVF ✆65224198
2km E on D911, rte de Cahors.
Jun-Sep
3HEC ● H + lau
PR

PROISSANS
See **SARLAT-LA-CANÉDA**

PUYBRUN
Lot
Sole ✆65385237
Apr-Sep
3HEC ● H G R
H P + lau R
Prices A15 pitch16

PUY-L'ÉVÊQUE
Lot
At **MONTCABRIER**(7 km NW)
Moulin de Laborde ✆65246206
15 May-Sep
4HEC ◑ H G
PR + lau
Prices A18 pitch25

PYLA-SUR-MER
Gironde
Dune rte de Biscarosse ✆56227217
A beautifully situated and quiet site partly on terraced sandy fields. Opposite a dune of over 100 m in height, which separates the site from the sea.
Follow the road between Pilat-Plage.
Apr-Oct
10HEC S ● H G
R H P + lau S
Prices pitch63-98 (incl 2 persons)

Panorama rte de Biscarrosse
✆56221044
Partially terraced site amongst dunes, on the edge of the 100m high 'Dune de Rilet'. Views of the sea from some pitches.
On the D218. Signposted.
May-15 Oct
15HEC S ● H G
H PS + lau
Prices A20 V22 37 A27

Petit Nice ✆56227403
Sandy terraced site, mainly suitable for tents; in parts sloping steeply in pine woodland. Paths and standings are strengthened with timber. 220 steps down to the beach.
6 km S on D112.
15 Mar-Oct
5HEC ● H G R
H S + lau
Prices A10-18 pitch19-59

Pyla rte de Biscarrosse ✆56227456
May-Sep
8HEC S ● H G
R P lau S
Prices A19 pitch35-52

RIVES
Lot-et-Garonne
Château de Fonrives ✆53366338
15 Apr-Sep
20HEC ◑ H G
R H LP + lau R
Prices A16-20 pitch26-32

ROCAMADOUR
Lot
Relais du Campeur l'Hospitalet
✆65336328
On D36.
Etr-15 Oct
1.7HEC ◑ H G
+ lau PR
Prices A14 pitch14

ROCHE-CHALAIS, LA
Dordogne
Gerbes ✆53914065
Site on banks of River Dronne.
Off D674 in village centre. Signposted.
All year
3HEC S ● H G R
+ lau P
Prices A6-7 pitch6-8

ROQUE-GAGEAC, LA
Dordogne
Beau Rivage ✆53283205
On banks of River Dordogne.
Camping Carnet Compulsory.
Between D703 and river.
All year
6HEC S H G R
H PR + lau

Butte ✆53283028
In very attractive setting around country estate on steep bank of River Dordogne.
Halfway between Vitrac and Cénac off D703.
Mar-Nov
4HEC ● H G H
PR + lau
Prices pitch68 (incl 2 persons)

ROUFFIGNAC
Dordogne
Cantegrel ✆53054830
1.5km N via D31, rte de Thenon.
15 Apr-15 Oct
50HEC ◑ H G
R H LP + lau
Prices pitch78 (incl 3 persons)

SADIRAC
Gironde
Bel Air ✆56230190
Country site.
Beside D671.
All year
3HEC ◑ H G P
+ lau
Prices A12 pitch14

ST-ANTONIN-NOBLE-VAL
Tarn-et-Garonne
Trois Cantons ✆63319857
Divided into pitches, partly on sloping ground within an oak forest. Separate section for teenagers.
8.5km NW near D926. Signposted.
May-Sep
4HEC ◑ H G
H P + lau
Prices A17-20 pitch19-22

ST-BERTRAND-DE-COMMINGES
Haute-Garonne
Es Pibous ✆61883142
Jun-Sep
2HEC ● H G lau
R +
Prices A9 7

ST-CÉRÉ
Lot
CM de Soulhol quai A-Salesse
✆65381237
Camping Carnet compulsory.
200m SE on D940.
Apr-Sep
3.5HEC ● H R +
lau G R LP
Prices V10 A10

ST-CYBRANET
Dordogne
Bol Ombrage ✆53283414
Quiet holiday site in wooded valley.
Jun-15 Sep
5HEC ◑ H G R H
PR + lau S
Prices A18 pitch34

ST-CYPRIEN
Dordogne
Campagnac Castels ✆53292603
Apr-Oct
0.8HEC ● H lau
G +
Prices A6 pitch24

CM Garrit rte de Berbiguières
✆53292056
1.5km S on D48.
May-Sep ➔

0.8HEC H [G] + lau R
Prices A14 pitch18

STE-EULALIE-EN-BORN
Landes
Bruyères chemin Laffont ✆58097001
2.5km N via D652
Jun-Sep
3HEC H [G] [H] P + lau L
Prices A14 V4 19 19

STE-FOY-DE-BELVÈS
See **BELVÈS**

ST-ÉMILION
Gironde
Barbanne ✆57247580
3km N via D122
Mar-Oct
5HEC H [G] [R] [H] P + lau
Prices A16 pitch20

ST-ÉTIENNE-DE-VILLERÉAL
Lot-et-Garonne
Ormes ✆53366026
0.9km S off D255.
Apr-Sep
10HEC H [G] LP + lau
Prices A14-20 pitch21-30

ST-GENIES
Dordogne
Bouquerie ✆53289822
N of village on D704.
15 May-15 Sep
7HEC H [G] [R] [H] LP + lau
Prices A24 pitch34

ST-GIRONS
Ariège
Parc de Palétès ✆61660679
3km SE on D33.
All year
3HEC H P + lau R

Pont du Nert ✆61665848
Grassy site without any trees. Between road and woodland.
Approx 3km SE at the junction of the D33 and the D3.
Jun-15 Sep
1.5HEC H lau
Prices A8 10 9

ST-JEAN-DE-LUZ
Pyrénées-Atlantiques
CM Chibaou Berria ✆59261194
2km SW of Guèthary. Signposted off N10 towards sea.
Jun-Sep
4HEC H [G] S + lau
Prices A13 pitch19

International d'Erromardie ✆59263426
Site is situated by the sea and consists of several sections divided by roads and low hedges. Take away food.
If approached from N to N10, cross railway bridge and turn immediately right and follow signs.
15 Mar-15 Oct
2HEC H [G] S + lau
Prices A14 pitch52

Iratzia ✆59261489
1km NE off N10.
15 Mar-15 Oct
4HEC H [G] [H] + lau S
Prices A13 V7 16 16

Tamaris Plage Quartier d'Acotz ✆59265590
Site divided into sections by drives and hedges.
Signposted from N10 towards the sea.
Apr-Sep
1HEC H [H] S + lau [G] [R]
Prices pitch58-68 (incl 2 persons)

At **SOCOA** (3km SW)
Juantcho ✆59471197
2km W on D912.
Apr-Oct
9HEC H [H] + lau [G] S
Prices A12 V6 12 12

ST-JULIEN-EN-BORN
Landes
Fleurie Lette rte de Contis ✆58427409
On undulating ground in a pine wood.
Apr-Oct
8.5HEC H [G] + lau R
Prices A11 V4 13 11

ST-LÉON-SUR-VÉZÈRE
Dordogne
At **TURSAC** (7km SW)
Vézère Périgord ✆53069631
0.8km NE on D706.
Etr-Sep
3.5HEC H [G] [H] P + lau R
Prices A16-21 pitch20-27

ST-MARTIAL-DE-NABIRAT
See **GOURDON**

ST-PALAIS
Pyrénées-Atlantiques
CM Ur-Alde ✆59657201
On meadow divided into pitches. Near sports complex.
15 Jun-15 Sep
2HEC H + lau P

ST-PÉE-SUR-NIVELLE
Pyrénées-Atlantiques
Goyetchea ✆59541959
0.8km N on rte d'Ahetze
15 Jun-10 Sep
2.2HEC H [G] P + lau L
Prices A15 pitch20

At **IBARRON** (2km W)
Ibarron ✆59541043
2km W on D918.
25 Jun-1 Sep
2.8HEC H +
Prices A11 pitch18

ST-PIERRE-LAFEUILLE
Lot
Quercy-Vacances ✆65368715
On N20. 12km N of Cahors.
15 May-15 Sep
2.8HEC H [G] [R] P + lau
Prices A18 pitch18

ST-SEURIN-DE-PRATS
Dordogne
Plage ✆53686107
0.7kms on D11 alongside the Dordogne.
15 May-15 Sep
4.5HEC H [G] [R] [H] PR + lau
Prices A15 V10 20 20

SALIGNAC
Dordogne
'Les Peneyrals' Le Poujol, St-Crepin Carlucet ✆53288571
Jun-Sep
8HEC H [G] [R] [H] P + lau
Prices A19 pitch30-41

SALLES
Gironde
Val de l'Eyre ✆56884703
SW on D108, rte de Lugos.
All year
13HEC S H [G] [R] [H] R + lau LP
Prices pitch42-65 (incl 3 persons)

SANGUINET
Landes
CM Lac ✆58786194
1.8km W near Cazaux Lake
Apr-Sep
7HEC S H L + lau [G] [R]

SARE
Pyrénées-Atlantiques
Goyenetche rte des Grottes ✆59542171
3.5km S via D306
May-Sep
1HEC H [G] [R] R + lau LPS
Prices A9 pitch10

SARLAT-LA-CANÉDA
Dordogne
Maillac ✆53592212

7km NE on D47.
Jun-Sep
5HEC G H P + lau
Prices A15 pitch21

Moulin du Roch rte des Eyzies
✆53592027
Camping Carnet compulsory.
10km NW via D704-D6-D47.
May-Sep
7HEC G P + lau
Prices pitch60-85 (incl 2 persons)

Périères ✆53590584
Very well kept terraced site on wooded valley.
1km N of town on D47.
Etr-Sep
11HEC G P + lau R

At **CARSAC-AILLAC** (7km SE via D704a)
Aqua Viva ✆53592109
Site has wooded terraces.
3 Mar-20 Oct
10HEC G H LP + lau
Prices A13-20 pitch16-28

At **PROISSANS** (6km NE)
Val d'Ussel ✆53592873
Off D704 or D56.
30 Apr-Sep
7HEC G H P + lau R

SAUVETERRE-DE-BÉARN
Pyrénées-Atlantiques
CM Gave av de la Gare ✆59385330
Turn left before bridge on St-Palais road.
Jun-Sep
1.6HEC R + lau

SAUVETERRE-LA-LÉMANCE
Lot-et-Garonne
Moulin du Périé ✆53406726
In a wooded valley.
E of town off D710.
Apr-Sept
3HEC G H LP + lau
Prices A22 pitch26

SEIGNOSSE
Landes
Chevreuils ✆58433280
In a pine forest.
Camping Carnet Compulsory.
On D79 rte de Hossegor.
Jun-15 Sep
8HEC G H + lau S
Prices A17 pitch15

CM ✆58433030
Very clean and tidy site.
Jun-Sep
16HEC G H + lau LPS
Prices A15 V5 14 A14

Oyats ✆58433794
Level site, subdivided into fields and surrounded by woodland. Separate section for young people. Children's play area.
Turn off D79 in N outskirts towards Plage des Casernes.
Jun-Sep
15HEC G H S + lau
Prices pitch40-66 (incl 2 persons)

At **SEIGNOSSE-LE-PENON** (5km W)
Forêt ✆58433020
10 Jun-15 Sep
11HEC G R + lau LPS

SEIGNOSSE-LE-PENON
See **SEIGNOSSE**

SEIX
Ariège
Haut Salat ✆61668178
Very clean, well kept site beside stream. Big gravel pitches for caravans. Common room with TV.
0.8km NE on D3.
3 Jan-15 Sep & 15 Oct-22 Dec
2.5HEC G R H R + lau
Prices A13 pitch13

SIORAC-EN-PÉRIGORD
Dordogne
At **COUX-ET-BIGAROQUE** (2.5 km NW by D710/D703)
Clou ✆53316332
Separate section for dog owners.
Access via D703 (Le Bugue-Delve road).
Apr-15 Oct
3HEC G H P + lau
Prices A16-19 pitch22-25

Faval ✆53316044
1km E of village on D703, near junction with D710
Apr-15 Oct
2HEC G H P + lau R
Prices A12-19 pitch22-30

SIREUIL
See **ÉYZIES-DE-TAYAC, LES**

SOCOA
See **ST-JEAN-DE-LUZ**

SOUILLAC
Lot
Domaine de la Paille Basse
✆65378548
6.5km NW off D15 Salignac-Eyvignes road.
15 Jun-15 Sep
80HEC G H P + lau
Prices A25 pitch40-50

SOULAC-SUR-MER
Gironde
Océan ✆56097610
3.5km S.
Jun-15 Sep
8HEC G H + lau S
Prices A10 pitch45

Palace rte de l'Amèlie ✆56098022
Well-kept site on sand dunes. Individual pitches, asphalt drives.
1km S from village centre. Access is via D1 and D101.
Apr-Sep
16HEC G H P + lau S
Prices A19 50 A38

Sables d'Argent r de l'Amèlie
✆56098287
1.5km SW of village.
May-Sep
2.5HEC G R H + lau S
Prices A10 pitch55

At **AMÉLIE-SUR-MER, L'** (4.5km S)
Amélie-Plage ✆56098727
In hilly wooded terrain. Lovely sandy beach.
3km S on the Soulac road.
Apr-30 Oct
10HEC G R H S + lau
Prices pp55

At **LILIAN** (4.5km S)
Pins ✆56098252
S on D101.
Mar-Sep
3HEC G H + lau S
Prices A8 pitch20

SOUSTONS
Landes
CM Airial ✆58411248
2km W on D652.
Etr-15 Oct
12HEC G P + lau
Prices A14 28 A17

TARASCON-SUR-ARIÈGE
Ariège
Sédour ✆61058728
1.8km NW via D618
All year
1.5HEC G R + lau P
Prices A9-11 pitch9-11

TERRASSON-LA-VILLEDIEU
Dordogne
CM ✆53500281
500m E.
Jun-Sep

1HEC ∿ ◑ ⫪H ⊖ ⊕ ▣ lau ☞ ⛟ ! ✕ ≋P

TESTE, LA
See **HUME, LA**

TONNEINS
Lot-et-Garonne

CM Robinson ✆53790300

500m from town centre on N113 Agen road.

Jun-Sep

0.7HEC ∿ ◑ ⫪H ⊖ ⊕ [H] ▣ + lau ☞ ⛟ ! ✕ ≋P

TOUZAC
Lot

Ch'Timi ✆65365236

800m from Touzac, beside the River Lot.

13 May-30 Sep

2.5HEC ∿ ◑ ⫪H ⛟ ! ✕ ⊖ ⊕ [G] [R] [H] ≋PR ▣ + lau

Prices A13-17 pitch17-25

Clos Bouyssac ✆65365221

On the fringe of a wooded hillside by the sandy shore of the River Lot. Good for walking.

Apr-Sep

1.5HEC ∿ ◑ ⫪H ! ✕ ⊖ ⊕ [G] [R] ⌂ [H] ≋PR ▣ + lau ☞ ⛟

Prices A18 pitch18

TRÉBONS
See **BAGNÈRES-DE-BIGORRE**

TURSAC
See **ST-LÉON-SUR-VÉZÈRE**

URRUGNE
Pyrénées-Atlantiques

Larrouleta ✆59473784

Hilly meadow with young trees.

1.5 km N of Urrugne on N1 to Spain.

All year

5HEC ∿ ● ⫪H ⛟ ⊖ ⊕ [G] ≋LR ▣ + lau ☞ ! ✕ [R]

Prices A8 V7 ⊕11 Å11

VARILHES
Ariège

CM Parc du Château av du 8 Mai 45 ✆61607117

N on N20.

All year

8HEC ∿ ● ⫪H ⊖ ⊕ ≋PR ▣ + lau ☞ ⛟ ! ✕ [G]

Prices A6 pitch6

VERDON-SUR-MER, LE
Gironde

Cordouan ✆56097142

Clean, pleasant meadowland with some pines and deciduous trees. 1km to sea.

N of Soulac-sur-Mer via D1.

All year

4.5HEC ∿ ◑ ⫪H ⛟ ! ✕ ⊖ ⊕ [G] [R] [H] + lau ☞ ≋PS

Prices pitch36

Royannais Le Royannais ✆56096112

Level, sandy terrain under high pine and deciduous trees. Near tank depot.

S of Le Verdon-sur-Mer in Le Royannais district on D1.

15 Jun-15 Sep

2HEC S ◑ ⫪H ⛟ ! ⊖ ⊕ [G] [R] [H] ▣ + lau ☞ ≋S

Prices pitch37-52

VIELLE-ST GIRONS
Landes

Col Vert ✆58429406

Quiet site on lakeside in sparse pine woodland. Small natural harbour in the mouth of a stream.

Turn off D652 on N side of village and continue towards lake.

Etr-Sep

24HEC ∿ S ◑ ● ⫪H ⛟ ! ✕ ⊖ ⊕ [G] [R] ⌂ [H] ≋L ▣ + lau

Eurosol ✆58479014

Jun-15 Sep

18HEC S ◑ ⫪H ⛟ ! ⊖ ⊕ [G] [H] ⚠ ≋P ▣ + ☞ ✕ [R] ≋S

Prices pitch69 (incl 2 persons)

VIEUX-BOUCAU-LES-BAINS
Landes

CM des Sablères bld du Marensin ✆58481229

Apr-15 Oct

11HEC ∿ S ◑ ⫪H ⊖ ⊕ ▣ + lau ☞ ⛟ [G] [R] ≋LS

Prices A5-8 pitch27-55

VILLENAVE D'ORNON
Gironde

Gravières chemin du Macau ✆56870036

2km NE

All year

10HEC ∿ ● ⫪H ! ✕ ⊖ ⊕ [G] [R] [H] ▣ + lau

Prices A15 ⊕20 Å13

VILLERÉAL
Lot-et-Garonne

Château de Fonrives Rives ✆53366338

2.2km NW via D207

15 Apr-Sep

20HEC ∿ ◑ ⫪H ⛟ ! ✕ ⊖ ⊕ [G] [R] [H] ≋LP ▣ + lau

Prices A16-20 pitch28-35

VITRAC
Dordogne

Soleil Plage ✆53283333

4km E on D703, turn by 'Camping Clos Bernard'.

Apr-Sep

4HEC ∿ ◑ ⫪H ⛟ ! ✕ ⊖ ⊕ [G] ≋PR ▣ + lau

Prices A23 pitch30

LOIRE/CENTRAL

The undoubted highlight of this area is the Loire, France's longest river, which winds its unhurried way through green valleys, vine-covered hills, meadows, and, of course, past the remarkable châteaux and medieval citadels which are masterpieces spanning the changing architectural style of seven centuries. The western Loire region unites a countryside of soft hills little farms and vineyards, and historic châteaux and abbeys with the sea. North of the river the coastline meets the Atlantic at rocky cliffs; south of the river great sandy beaches are backed by great pine woods. Still farther south, the province of Charente-Maritime boasts sunshine totals to rival the Mediterranean, and 150 miles of coastline with busy ports, family resorts – both on the mainland and off-lying islands, and harbours bustling with colourful life. La Rochelle, with its ancient harbour and fine old houses, is a popular centre. Inland, there are literally hundreds of interesting churches and abbeys, and vineyards whose grapes mature into Cognac. Inland still further, the region of Limousin is a charming backwater of rolling hills, with Limoges a fascinating porcelain centre.

AIGREFEUILLE
Charente-Maritime

Ferme Toucherit ✆46277306

Jun-Sep

0.9HEC ∿ ● ⫪H ! ✕ ⊖ ⊕ ⌂ ▣ lau ☞ [G] [R] ≋R

Prices A7 pitch7

AIGUILLON-SUR-MER, L'
Vendée

Bel Air ✆51564405

A long, level stretch of meadowland in

rural surroundings.
1.5 km NW on D44 then turn left.
15 May-10 Sep
7HEC ◑ H ✕ ⊖ G H P + lau LS

ANDONVILLE
Loiret
Chevel Blanc ✆38395707
2.3 km S rte de Richerelles.
All year
13HEC ◑ H ✕ ⊖ R H P + lau

Domaine de la Joullière ✆38395846
1 km E on road to Richerelles.
All year
14HEC ◑ H ✕ ⊖ G R P P + lau

ANGERS
Maine-et-Loire
Lac de Maine ✆41730503
Bar and restraunt available Jul-Aug only.
Access via A11 (Angers/Nantes) at Lac de Maine exit.
All year
4HEC ○ H ⊖ G + lau ✕ L

ANGOULINS-SUR-MER
Charente-Maritime
Chirats rte de la Platière ✆46569416
Modern site 150m from a large, sandy beach. Booking advised.
Etr-15 Oct
2HEC ○ H ✕ ⊖ H + lau

ANTIGES
See **NEUVIC**

ARGENTAT
Corrèze
Gibanel ✆55281011
Pleasant site situated in grounds of a château next to a lake.
Jun-15 Sep
8HEC ◑ H ✕ ⊖ G H LP + lau
Prices A16 V7 11 11

Saulou ✆55281233
6km S on D116.
May-20 Sep
7HEC ◑ H ⊖ G PR + lau
Prices A16 pitch28

At **MONCEAUX-SUR-DORDOGNE** (3km SW)
Vaurette ✆55280967
On the banks of the River Dordogne.
May-Oct
3.5HEC ● H ✕ ⊖ G R H PR + lau
Prices A16 pitch18

ARGENTON-CHÂTEAU
Deux-Sèvres
CM du Lac d'Hautibus ✆49659508
0.4km S on D748.
15 Jun-Sep
1HEC ◑ H ⊖ P + lau ✕ L
Prices A9 pitch7

ARS-EN-RÉ
See **RÉ, ILE DE**

ASSERAC
Loire-Atlantique
Traverno ✆40017335
Jun-Sep
2HEC ◑ H ⊖ H + lau ✕ G R
Prices A11 pitch7

AUBUSSON
Creuse
CM ✆55661800
1.5km S on D982, rte de Felletin.
June-Sep
3HEC H ⊖ G P + lau ✕ R

AVRILLE
Vendée
Mancelières ✆51903597
1.7km S via D105 towards Longeville
May-Sep
2.5HEC ◑ H ✕ ⊖ G H P + lau
Prices pitch49

AZAY-LE-RIDEAU
Indre-et-Loire
Parc du Sabot r du Stade ✆47454272
Site lies in large meadow on bank of River Indre.
Near château in town centre.
25 Mar-15 Nov
9HEC ◑ H ⊖ R P + lau ✕ G R P
Prices A7 pitch5

BALLAN-MIRÉ
See **TOURS**

BARBÂTRE
See **NOIRMOUTIER, ILE DE**

BARDÉCILLE
Charente-Maritime
Ferme de Chez Filleux ✆46900433
Jun-15 Sep
1.5HEC ◑ H ⊖ G H P P + lau
Prices pitch45 (incl 3 persons)

BARRE-DE-MONTS, LA
Vendée
Corsive ✆51685006
Situated in quiet setting on two large fields.
2km on D38A rte de la Grande-Côte.
Jun-15 Sep
1.2HEC ◑ H ⊖ G + lau ✕ S

BATZ-SUR-MER
Loire-Atlantique
Govelle rte de la Côte Sauvage (D45) ✆40239163
On D45 between Le Pouliguen and Batz.
Apr-Sep
1HEC ○ H ✕ ⊖ G H S + lau
Prices pitch74-112 (incl 3 persons)

BAULE, LA
Loire-Atlantique
Ajoncs d'Or chemin du Rocher ✆40603329
Etr-Oct
4.8HEC ◑ H ✕ ⊖ G R H P + lau S
Prices A22 pitch26

CM av P-Minot, av R-Flandin ✆40601740 or 40601148
Site consists of two sections, one for caravans, one for tents, each with separate entrance. Caravan site (off av R-Flandin) is level and has good sanitary installations. Tent site (off av P-Minto) is in hilly, sandy woodland with only simple installations.
Camping Carnet Compulsory.
30 Mar-Sep
5HEC ◑ ● ⊖ + lau G S

Eden St-Servais ✆40600323
1km NW
Etr-Sep
4.7HEC ● H ✕ ⊖ G R P + lau
Prices A20 pitch26

Roseraie 20 av J-Sohier ✆40604666
Etr-Sep
4.5HEC ◑ H ✕ ⊖ G H PRS + lau
Prices A18-22 pitch45-55

BEAUMONT-SUR-SARTHE
Sarthe
CM du Val de Sarthe rte de Mamers ✆43970193
E on D26 then turn right.
May-Sep
3HEC ◑ H ⊖ lau ✕ P

BESSÉ-SUR-BRAYE
Sarthe
CM Val de Braye ✆43353113
Beside River Braye.
On D303.
15 May-Oct
2HEC ◑ H ✕ ⊖ G P + lau
Prices A5 pitch3

BESSINES-SUR-GARTEMPE
Haute-Vienne
At **MORTEROLLES-SUR-SEMME** (4.5km N on N20)
CM ✆55760928
100m from N20; in town centre. ➔

All year
8HEC H + lau LPR

BEYNAT
Corrèze
Étang de Miel ✆55855066
4km E on N121 Argentat road.
15 Jun-15 Sep
9HEC H H L + lau
Prices A12 pitch60

BLÉRÉ
Indre-et-Loire
CM ✆47579260
Well-kept site beside River Cher. Two entrances.
Camping Carnet Compulsory.
Apr-15 Oct
4HEC H G + lau P
Prices A8 pitch34

BLOIS
Loir-et-Cher
CM Boire rte de St-Dye ✆54742278
1.5km E on D751.
Mar-Nov
10HEC H + lau
Prices A7 V4 A10

BOIS-PLAGE-EN-RÉ, LE
See **RÉ, ILE DE**

BONNAC-LA-CÔTE
Haute-Vienne
Château de Leychoisier ✆55399343
Well-managed site on ground sloping gently towards the woods. Divided into roomy pitches.
1km S off N20.
15 Jun-Oct
2HEC H G L + lau
Prices A18 pitch30

BONNY-SUR-LOIRE
Loiret
Val ✆38316491

15 Mar-15 Oct
0.8HEC H lau
Prices A5 V5 5 A5

BOYARDVILLE
See **OLÉRON, ILE D'**

BRACIEUX
Loir-et-Cher
CM des ChÂteaux rte de Blois ✆54464184
N on left bank of River Beauvron.
Apr-20 Oct
9HEC H P + G R
Prices A9 pitch6

BRAIN-SUR-L'AUTHION
Maine-et-Loire
C M Caroline ✆41804218
All year
3HEC H G R lau R +
Prices A9 V6 7 A6

BRETIGNOLLES-SUR-MER
Vendée
Dunes Plage des Dunes ✆51905532
2km S turn right off D38 and proceed for 1km across the dunes. 150m from beach.
15 Mar-15 Nov
12HEC S H G R H P + lau S
Prices A9-15 pitch59-86

Motine 4 r des Morinières ✆51900442
Pleasant site situated 350m from the town centre and 400m from the beach.
Etr-Sep
1.1HEC H H L + lau G R PRS
Prices A9-14 pitch42-66

Vagues 20 bd du Nord ✆51901948
N on D38 towards St-Gilles-Croix-de-Vie
Jun-Sep
3HEC H G H P + lau S

BRIVE-LA-GAILLARDE
Corrèze
CM des Iles bd Michelet ✆55243477
Beside River Corrèze.
All year
1HEC H + lau P

BROU
Eure-et-Loir
Base de Plein Air et de Loisirs ✆37470217
3km W towards Authan-du-Perche
4HEC H + lau P

CHALONNES-SUR-LOIRE
Maine-et-Loire
CM Candals ✆41780227
On the banks of the River Loire.
15 May-15 Oct
3HEC H H + P

CHÂTEAU-D'OLÉRON, LA
See **OLÉRON, ILE D'**

CHÂTEAUDUN
Eure-et-Loir
CM Moulin-à-Tan ✆37450534
NW via D955 beside the River Lois
15 Mar-15 Oct
1.5HEC H G R + lau P

CHÂTELAILLON-PLAGE
Charente-Maritime
Clos de Rivages av des Boucholeurs ✆1646562609
Level, well-kept site.
15 Jun-10 Sep
3HEC H G + lau PS

Deux Plages ✆46562753
May-Sep
4.5HEC H G R H S + lau P

CHÂTILLON-SUR-CHER
Loir-et-Cher
'Parici' ✆54710221

Apr-Oct
.2HEC H G
H R + lau
Prices A7 pitch8

CHÂTRES-SUR-CHER
Loir-et-Cher
CM des Saules ✆54980455
On N76 near bridge.
12 May-17 Sep
.8HEC H G + lau
P
Prices A5 pitch5

CHENONCEAUX
Indre-et-Loire
Moulin Fort ✆47238622
2km SE
1-15 Apr & May-15 Sep
3HEC H G
PR +
Prices A16 pitch16

CHINON
Indre-et-Loire
CM ✆47930835
On the banks of the river opposite the Château and off D951.
15 Mar-15 Oct
6HEC S H H PR
+ lau S
Prices A7 V8 8 Å8

CHOLET
Maine-et-Loire
Lac de Ribou av du Lac ✆41587474
Well set-out site bordering a lake, with fishing, boating, tennis and volleyball.
3km from town centre.
All year
8HEC H G R
H P + lau
Prices A9-11 V4 pitch16-20

CLOYES-SUR-LE-LOIR
Eure-et-Loir
Parc des Loisirs rte du Montifny ✆37985053
On the bank of the River Loire. Extensive leisure facilities. Separate section for teenagers. Lunchtime siesta 12.00-15.00 hrs.
Access from Châteaudun S on N10 towards Cloyes, then right onto Montigny-le-Gamelon road.
All year
5HEC ◑ H ✕ ⊖ G H PR + lau
Prices A20 V12 12 12

COGNAC
Charente
CM rte de Ste-Sévère ✆45321332
2km N on D24.
Jun-Sep
36HEC ● H ⊖ G R P + lau
Prices A12 V2 2 2 pitch2

CONCHES, LES
See **LONGEVILLE**

CONTRES
Loir-et-Cher
Charmoise ✆54795515
N956.
All year
2HEC ◑ H ⊖ G R + lau ✕ PR
Prices pp9

COTINIÈRE, LA
See **OLÉRON, ILE D'**

COUARDE-SUR-MER, LA
See **RÉ, ILE DE**

COUHÉ-VERAC
Vienne
Peupliers ✆49592116
N of village on N10 Poitiers road.
May-Sep
8HEC ◑ H ✕ ⊖ G PR + lau
Prices A15 pitch20

CROISIC, LE
Loire-Atlantique
Océan ✆40230769
1.5km NW via D45
Apr-Sep
7HEC ◑ H ✕ ⊖ G R H PS + lau
Prices A13-17 V7-9 20-30 20-30

See advertisement on page 129

DOLUS-D'OLÉRON
See **OLÉRON, ILE D'**

DOMINO
See **OLÉRON, ILE D'**

EYMOUTHIERS
Charente
Gorges du Chambon ✆45707170
3km N via D163
15 May-15 Sep
7HEC ◑ H ✕ ⊖ G H PR + lau
Prices A23 pitch33

FAUTE-SUR-MER, LA
Vendée
Fautais ✆51564196
Situated in centre of village. Numbered pitches.
On D46.
Jul-Aug
1HEC ◑ H ⊖ G + lau ✕ LRS
Prices pitch45 (incl 3 persons)

FENOUILLER, LE
Vendée
Domaine le Pas Opton rte de Nantes ✆51551198
2km N beside the River Vie
25 May-10 Sep
4.5HEC ○ H ✕ ⊖ G H PR + lau
Prices pitch85-119 (incl 3 persons)

FLÈCHE, LA
Sarthe
Route d'Or allée de la Providence ✆43945590
Besdie the River Loir
All year
2HEC H ⊖ G H + lau ✕ LP

FLOTTE, LA
See **RÉ, ILE DE**

FRESNAY-SUR-SARTHE
Sarthe
CM Sans Souci ✆43973287
Camping Carnet Compulsory.
1km SE on D310.
Apr-Sep
2HEC ○ H ⊖ G P + lau ✕
Prices A8 V5 6 6

GENNES
Maine-et-Loire
Districal du Bord de l'Eau ✆41518177
N, beside the River Loire
May-Sep
3HEC ● H ⊖ P + lau ✕
Prices A7 pitch9

Européen ✆41579163
May-Sep
10HEC ◑ H ✕ ⊖ G H P + lau
Prices pitch60 (incl 3 persons)

GIEN
Loiret
Touristique de Gien rue des Iris, Poilly-les-Gien ✆38671250
Camping Carnet Compulsory.
Mar-10 Nov
6HEC ● H ✕ ⊖ G H PR + lau
Prices A9-10 pitch16-18

GIVRAND
Vendée
Europa ✆51553268
Apr-Sep
4HEC ◑ H ✕ ⊖ G R P + lau LR
Prices A19 pitch43-60

GUÉMENÉ-PENFAO
Loire-Atlantique
CM Hermitage av du Paradis ✆40792348
Camping Carnet Compulsory.
1.5km E on rte de Châteaubriant.
All year
2.5HEC ● H ⊖ G R P + lau ✕

GUÉRANDE
Loire-Atlantique
CM Bréhadour ✆40249312
2km NE on D51, rte de St-Lyphard.
All year
5HEC ◑ H ✕ ⊖ G + lau S

Pré du Château de Careil ✆40602299
Divided into pitches. Caravans only. Booking recommended for Jul & Aug.
2km N of La Baule on D92.
Apr-Sep
2.5HEC ◑ H ✕ ⊖ P + lau S

Tremondec ✆40600007
Subdivided terraced site with view of La Baule.
Approach road opposite Camping Pré du Château de Careil.
May-Sep
2.5HEC ◑ H ✕ ⊖ G H + lau PS
Prices A17 pitch21

HÉRIC
Loire-Atlantique
Pindière ✆40576541
Camping Carnet Compulsory.
1km from town on D16.
All year
3.2HEC ◑ H ✕ ⊖ G H + lau P
Prices A11 pitch13

HOMMAIZE, L'
Vienne
Vertoux ✆49427595
All year
1HEC ◑ H ✕ ⊖ G H L + lau

HOUMEAU, L'
Charente-Maritime
Trépied au Plomb ✆46509082
NE via D106
20 May-25 Sep

2HEC ◑ H ⊖ P + lau G R S
Prices pitch40 (incl 2 persons)

INGRANDES
Vienne
At **ST-USTRE**(2km NE)
Petit Trianon de St-Ustre ✆49026147
In beautiful park surrounding small castle, part of which is open to the public.
Camping Carnet Compulsory.
Turn off N10 at signpost N of Ingrandes and continue for 1km.
May-25 Sep
4HEC ◑ H ⊖ G H P + lau
Prices A25 V12 12 A12

JARD-SUR-MER
Vendée
Curtys r de la Perpoise ✆51336342
Jun-Sep
4.4HEC ○ H ⊖ G R H P + lau S
Prices pitch70 (incl 2 persons)

Écureuils r des Goffineaux ✆51334274
Quiet woodland terrain mear to the sea.
Signposted.
15 May-15 Sep
4HEC ◑ H ⊖ G H P + lau S
Prices A17 pitch58-70

Océano d'Or ✆51933605
Apr-Oct
6HEC ◑ H ⊖ G R H P + lau S
Prices

JARGEAU
Loiret
Isle aux Moulins ✆38597004
Mar-Nov
7HEC ◑ H ⊖ G H R + lau P
Prices A9 V5 6 A6

JAVRON
Mayenne
CM rte de Bagnoles-de-l'Orne ✆43034067
200m SW of town off N12. Signposted.
May-Sep
1.5HEC ◑ H ⊖ + lau G R LR
Prices A7 V3 3 A3

LAGORD
Charente-Maritime
CM Parc ✆46676154
4 Jun-Sep
5.5HEC ◑ H ⊖ + lau S
Prices pitch17

LIMERAY
Indre-et-Loire
Launay 9 r de la Rivière ✆47301682
6km NE of Amboise on N152.
Apr-Sep
1.5HEC ◑ H ⊖ G R H P + lau

LION D'ANGERS, LE
Maine-et-Loire
CM Frénes ✆41953156
NE on N162.
15 Jun-15 Sep
2HEC ◑ H ⊖ R P + lau P
Prices A6 V3 3 A3

LOCHES
Indre-et-Loire
CM rte de Châteauroux ✆47590591
S on N143. Access from r Quintefol.
Apr-Sep
3HEC ● H ⊖ P + lau
Prices A6 V6 11 A11

LONGEVILLE
Vendée
Jarny Océan ✆51334221
Subdivided well tended meadow, with a holiday complex of the same name where shopping facilities are provided. 800m to sea via forest path.
Turn off D105 about 3km S of Longeville.
Apr-Sep ➔

2HEC ● H ⊖ G S + lau

At **CONCHES, LES** (4km S)

Dunes av de la Plage ✆51333293

Well-kept site amongst sand dunes in pine forest.

6km S of Longeville on D105.

Apr-Sep

1.8HEC S ● H ⊖ G H P + lau S

Prices pitch125 (incl 3 persons)

Fief du Bonaire ✆53333109

Well-kept site with special asphalt drives and children's playground. 600m to sea.

Camping Carnet Compulsory or camper is prepared to take out an Insurance.

From village 700m towards the sea.

29 May-13 Sep

1.6HEC S ● H ⊖ G R P + lau S

LUDE, LE

Sarthe

CM rte du Mans ✆43946770

400m from town centre, direct from N307.

Etr-Sep

4.5HEC ◑ H ⊖ G + lau P

LUSIGNAN

Vienne

CM Vauchiron ✆49433008

500m NE on N11.

15 Apr-15 Oct

4HEC ◑ H ⊖ R + lau

Prices A6 V3 4 4

LUYNES

Indre-et-Loire

CM Granges Les Granges ✆47556085

S via D49

15 May-15 Sep

0.8HEC ◑ H ⊖ G + lau P

Prices A8 pitch8

MAGNAC-BOURG

Haute-Vienne

CM Écureuils rte de Limoges ✆55008028

N on N20.

Etr-Sep

1.3HEC ◑ H ⊖ lau P

MATHES, LES

Charente-Maritime

Joy eux Faune av de la Palmyre (D141) ✆46224229

May-Oct

4.8HEC ◑ H ⊖ G R H P + lau

Prices pitch69 (incl 3 persons)

Pinède La Fouasse ✆46224513

3km NW

Apr-Sep

4HEC S ○ ◑ ● H ⊖ G H P + lau

Prices pitch94 (incl 3 persons)

MEMBROLLE-SUR-CHOISILLE, LA

Indre-et-Loire

CM ✆47412040

On level meadow in sports ground beside River Choisille.

North of village on N138 Le Mans road.

May-Sep

1.3HEC ◑ H ⊖ + lau

Prices A7 pitch6

MESCHERS-SUR-GIRONDE

Charente-Maritime

Côte de Beauté Plage de Suzac ✆46052693

Hilly terrain with mixed woodland between the road and the sea. Broad sandy beach.

On the D25 to Plage de Suzac, halfway between St-Georges and Meschers.

Apr-Sep

4HEC ◑ H ⊖ G S + lau

Prices pitch70 (incl 3 persons)

MESLAND

Loir-et-Cher

Parc du Val de Loire ✆54702718

1.5km W

May-15 Sep

12HEC ◑ H ⊖ G H P + lau

Prices A25 pitch40-70

See advertisement on page 131

MESQUER

Loire-Atlantique

Beaupré rte de Kervarin, Kercabellec ✆40426748

On road between Mesquer and Quimiac. Entrance signposted.

Jun-15 Sep

0.6HEC ◑ H ⊖ H + lau S

Prices A10 pitch10

Château de Petit Bois ✆40426877

Apr-Oct

10HEC ◑ H ⊖ G H P lau R S +

Prices pitch44-55 (incl 2 persons)

Welcome ✆40425085

1.8km NW via D352

Apr-Sep

1.6HEC ◑ H ⊖ G R H + lau S

Prices A12 pitch52

MONCEAUX-SUR-DORDOGNE

See **ARGENTAT**

MONTARGIS

Loiret

CM de la Forêt rte de Paucourt ✆38980020

1.5km NE

All year

5.5HEC H ⊖ + lau G R LPR

Prices A7 V4 7 7

MORTEROLLES-SUR-SEMME

See **BESSINES-SUR-GARTEMPE**

MONTGIVRAY

Indre

CM Solange Sand r du Pont ✆54483783

A pleasant, riverside site in the grounds of a château.

15 Mar-15 Nov

1HEC ◑ H ⊖ + lau

MONTLOUIS-SUR-LOIRE

Indre-et-Loire

CM Peupliers rte de Tours ✆47508190

On level meadow.

1.5km W on N751, next to swimming pool near railway bridge.

Mar-15 Oct

6HEC ◑ H ⊖ G R PR + lau

Prices A7-8 pitch7-8

MONTMORILLON

Vienne

CM Allochon av F-Tribot ✆49910233

SE via D54

All year

0.9HEC ◑ H ⊖ G + lau PR

Prices A5 V3 3 3

MONTSOREAU

Maine-et-Loire

Isle Verte ✆41517660

On D947 between road and river.

May-Sep

2.8HEC ◑ H ⊖ R + lau

Prices A8 V4 4 4

NANTES

Loire-Atlantique

CM Val du Cens bd du Petit Port 21 ✆40744794

On modern well kept park. Separate sections for caravans and tents.

In N part of town near Parc du Petit Port. From town centre follow Rennes road (N137) then signs to camp site.

All year

8HEC ● H ⊖ PR P + lau

Prices A6-8 pitch36-46

NEUVIC

Corrèze

Domaine du Mialaret ✆55958545

All year

7HEC ◑ H ⊖ G H PR + lau

Prices A13 pitch15

At **ANTIGES** (2km N)

Centre Président-Queuille Lac de

la Triouzonne ✆55958118
2km NE off N682.
All year
1.3HEC H G H L + lau
Prices A9 V3 4

NIBELLE
Loiret
Nibelle rte de Boiscommune
✆38322355
Level site in the clearing of an oak woodland.
Access via D921 turning off to Nibelle in an easterly direction. Signposted.
Mar-Nov
6HEC H G H P + lau L
Prices pitch88 (incl 3 persons)

NIORT
Deux-Sèvres
Noron bd S-Allende ✆49790506
All year
2HEC H H R + lau
Prices A10 pitch10

NOIRMOUTIER, ILE DE
Vendée
BARBÂTRE
Onchères ✆51398131
In quiet setting on sand dunes.
Camping Carnet Compulsory.
S of village on D95.
25 Mar-Sep
10HEC S H G R S + lau
Prices A11-14 pitch11-14

NOTRE-DAME-DE-MONTS
Vendée
Beauséjour ✆51588388
2km NW on D38.
Etr-Sep
1.5HEC H G + lau S

Bois Soret ✆51588401
2km N
Etr-Sep
0.4HEC S H G P + lau S

Grand Jardin ✆51588776
0.6km N
May-Sep
2HEC H G H + lau S
Prices pitch61 (incl 3 persons)

Pont-d'Yeu rte de St-Jean-de-Monts
✆51588376
1km S
15 Jun-15 Sep
1.3HEC S H G H + lau S
Prices A12 pitch10

NOUE, LA
See **RÉ, ILE DE**

OLÉRON, ILE D'
Charente-Maritime
BOYARDVILLE
Signol ✆46470122
May-Sep
7HEC S H H P + lau S
Prices pitch60-96 (incl 3 persons)

CHÂTEAU-D'OLÉRON, LA
Airotel Domaine de Montreavail
✆46476182
Leisure centre area.
Signposted from town centre.
May-Oct
4HEC H G H P + lau S

Brande ✆46476237
2.5km NW, 250m from the sea
15 Mar-15 Nov
3HEC H G H PS + lau

COTINIÈRE, LA
Tamaris ✆46471051
About 150m from sea. Level site in pleasant olive grove.
W side of island. N of town.
15 Mar-15 Oct
2.5HEC H + lau G S
Prices pitch72 (incl 3 persons)

See advertisement on page 134

DOLUS-D'OLÉRON
Ostréa r des Huitzes ✆37470165
3.5km NE
Apr-Sep
3.5HEC S H G H S lau
Prices pitch59 (incl 3 persons)

DOMINO
International Rex ✆46765597
Etr-Sep
10HEC H G S + lau
Prices pitch53-76 (incl 2 persons)

Montlabeur ✆46765222
W of town on D734.
15 May-Sep
7HEC H G R H PS + lau
Prices pitch63 (incl 2 persons)

ST-DENIS-D'OLÉRON
Phare Ouest ✆46479000
1km NW
15 May-Sep
3HEC G H S + lau
Prices pitch39 (incl 3 persons)

Soleil Levant ✆46478303
Quiet site beside sea.
1km from village adjacent to D734.
All year
7HEC H G H S + lau
Prices pitch47 (incl 3 persons)

ST-GEORGES-D'OLÉRON
Désirade ✆46765443
25 Jun-4 Sep
3HEC H H + lau G
Prices pitch46-54 (incl 2 persons)

Gros Joncs ✆46765229
Quiet location on undulating land in the midst of lovely pine woodland.
On tourist route from La Cotinière about 5km NW in the direction of Domino 1km SW of St-Georges d'Oléron.
Mar-Oct
4HEC S H G H PS + lau

Suroît ✆46470725
5km SW of town.
Apr-Sep
5HEC H G S + lau
Prices pitch85 (incl 3 persons)

Verébleu La Jousselinière ✆46765770
1.7km SE via D273
15 Apr-11 Nov
4.8HEC H G R H P + lau
Prices pitch79-120 (incl 3 persons)

ST-PIERRE-D'OLÉRON
Pierrière rte de St-Georges
✆46470829
NW towards St-Georges-d'Oléron
Apr-Sep
2.5HEC H H P + lau G R
Prices pitch70 (incl 3 persons)

OLIVET
Loiret
CM Olivet r du Pont Bouchet
✆38635394
Site lies partly on shaded peninsula, partly on open lawns beside river.
2km E. Signposted from village.
Etr-15 Oct
1HEC H R + lau

OLONNE-SUR-MER
Vendée
Loubine rte de la Mer ✆51331292
N via D87/D80.
May-Sep
5HEC H G P + lau S

Moulin de la Salle ✆51959910
2.7km W
15 Apr-1 Oct
3HEC H H P + lau
Prices A20-30 V20 5-10 5-10

Oreé rte des Amis de la Nature
✆51331059
3km N
Apr-Sep
3HEC S H G R H P + lau S
Prices A13-16 pitch24-30

ORLÉANS
Loiret
At **ST-JEAN-DE-LA-RUELLE**
CM Gaston-Marchand r de la Roche
38883939
On 80m wide strip of meadow on bank of Loire.
Camping Carnet Compulsory.
2.5km from town towards Blois.
Apr-Sep
1.5HEC H R + lau P
Prices A7 31 16

OROUET
See **ST-JEAN-DE-MONTS**

PALMYRE, LA
Charente-Maritime
Airotel Parc de la Côte Sauvage
Phare de la Coubre 46224018
Well laid out site; some sections under pine woods. Adjacent to beach. Near lighthouse.
4.5km NE on D25. Site entrance hidden down stone track.
May-15 Sep
12HEC S H G R H PS + lau

Bonne Anse Plage 46224090
An extensive, gently undulating site in a pine wood, 200m from the beach.
Camping Carnet Compulsory.
2km NW on D25 towards the lighthouse. Signposted.
25 May-5 Sep
18HEC H G H + lau S
Prices A23 V6 pitch95 (incl 3 persons)

Charmettes 46225096
6 May-24 Sep
23HEC H G R H P + lau S

Palmyre Loisirs La Grande Ligne
46236766
25 May-15 Sep
10HEC S H G R H P + lau
Prices pitch100 (incl 3 persons)

'La Pinède' 46224513
3km NW at La Fouasse
4HEC S H G H + lau

PEZOU
Loir-et-Cher
CM 54234069
SE via D12, 50m from the River Loir
3 May-3 Sep
1HEC H + lau
Prices pp6

PIRIAC-SUR-MER
Loire-Atlantique
Mon Calme rte de Nororet
40236077
On open meadow.
On D99.
May-Sep
1HEC H G H + lau PS
Prices A15 V9 9 9

Parc du Guibel 40235267
3.5km E via D52
Etr-Sep
10HEC S H G R H P + lau S
Prices A17 V10 11 11

Pouldroit 40235091
A modern site on a large field. Divided into pitches.
500m E on D52.
15 May-15 Sep
15HEC H G PS + lau
Prices A18 V13 14 14

POILLY-LES-GIEN
Loiret
Bois du Bardelet 38674739
Access via D940 SW of Gien.
Mar-Nov
12HEC H G H LP + lau
Prices pitch78 (incl 3 persons)

PONS
Charente-Maritime
Chardon Chardon ✆46940486
Quietly situated on the edge of a small village next to a farm.
From Pons take D732 westwards towards Royan. The site is 2.5km on the left. Alternatively from exit 26 of the Autoroute A10 and turn towards Pons. Site is 800m on right.
15 Apr-15 Nov
1.6HEC ～ ◑ ⌂H ✕ ⊖ Ⓖ Ⓗ Ⓟ + lau ☞ 🍷 ≈P
Prices A9 pitch13

PONTAILLAC
See **ROYAN**

PORNIC
Loire-Atlantique
Patisseau ✆40821039
3km E via D751
May-Sep
4.3HEC ～ ● ⌂H 🍷 ✕ ⊖ Ⓖ Ⓡ ≈P Ⓟ lau ☞ ≈LR +
Prices A17 pitch20-24

PORNICHET
Loire-Atlantique
Bugeau ✆40610202
A well-kept site divided into pitches and set away from the main road.
Jun-Sep
2HEC ～ ○ ⌂H ⊖ Ⓖ Ⓟ + lau ☞ 🍷 ✕ ≈S

Forges ✆40611884
2 Jul-Aug
1.7HEC ～ ● ⌂H ⊖ Ⓖ Ⓡ Ⓟ + lau ☞ ≈S
Prices A10 V8 10 A10

PORT-DE-PILES
Vienne
Bec des Deux Eaux ✆47650271
Apr-Sep
2.5HEC ～ ◑ ⌂H 🍷 ✕ ⊖ Ⓖ Ⓡ Ⓗ ≈PR Ⓟ + lau ☞
Prices pitch40 (incl 2 persons)

PORTEAU, LE
See **TALMONT-ST-HILAIRE**

POUANCÉ
Maine-et-Loire
CM Roche Martin r des Étangs ✆41924397
On the edge of a lake.
12 May-16 Sep
1HEC ～ ● ⌂H ⊖ Ⓖ Ⓡ Ⓟ + lau ☞ 🍷 ✕
Prices A6 V3 3 A3

PRÉ-EN-PAIL
Mayenne
CM Alain Gerbault ✆43030428
Apr-Sep
1.5HEC ～ ◑ ⌂H ⊖ Ⓟ + lau ☞ ≈P
Prices A7-8 V4-5 4-5 A4-5

PRÉFAILLES
Loire-Atlantique
Lambertianas Vallée Mouraud ✆402166105
E of town, 450m from the sea
May-Sep
1.7HEC ～ ◑ ⌂H ⊖ Ⓟ lau ☞ 🍷 ✕ Ⓖ ≈S
Prices pitch10-23

RÉ, ILE DE
Charente-Maritime
ARS-EN-RÉ
Dunes ✆46294141
1.5km NW on N735.
Apr-Oct
2HEC S ◑ ⌂H ✕ ⊖ Ⓖ Ⓡ Ⓗ Ⓟ + lau ☞ 🍷 ≈S
Prices pitch37-47 (incl 3 persons)

Soleil ✆46294062 & 46294174
On level, shaded meadow.
Signposted from the N735 shortly before reaching Ars.
All year
2HEC ～ ● ⌂H 🍷 ✕ ⊖ Ⓖ ≈S Ⓟ + lau
Prices pitch73 (incl 3 persons)

BOIS-PLAGE-EN-RÉ, LE
Antioche ✆46092386
In quiet area among dunes.
2km SE of village towards the beach.
Jun-15 Sep ➔

3HEC H G H S + lau
Prices pitch70-84 (incl 2 persons)

Gros Jonc Plage Gros Jonc ✆46091822
May-Sep
5HEC S H G H + lau S

Interlude rte de Gros Jonc ✆46091822
2.3km SE, 250m from the beach
May-Sep
5HEC S H G H + lau S

COUARDE-SUR-MER, LA
Océan rte d'Ars ✆46298770
3km NW on N735.
Etr-Sep
6HEC H G H + lau S

See advertisement on page 135

FLOTTE, LA
Blanche ✆46095243
Apr-11 Nov
3HEC S H G R P + lau S
Prices pitch73 (incl 2 persons)

Peuplers ✆46096235
1.3km SE
Apr-Sep
4.4HEC S H G R P + lau S
Prices pitch70-78 (incl 3 persons)

NOUE, LA
Grenettes ✆46302247
Site in two sections in pine forest separated by hedging.
1.5km W of village off D201. Approach is via narrow track.
All year
6HEC S H G H PS + lau

ST-CLÉMENT-DES-BALEINES
Plage ✆46294262
Meadow subdivided by hedges, close by lighthouse. Access to sea via sand dunes. Mobile shop during peak season.
NW on D735.
2.4HEC H S

ST-MARTIN-DE-RÉ
CM Ste-Thérèse ✆46092196
At foot of ramparts.
Etr-Sep
2.5HEC H G lau S +
Prices A10 V5 9 3

RONCE-LES-BAINS
Charente-Maritime
Pignade av des Monards ✆46362525
1.5km S
19 May-15 Sep
15HEC S H G R H P + lau S
Prices pitch85 (incl 2 persons)

ROSIERS, LES
Maine-et-Loire
Val de Loire ✆41519433
N via D59
May-Oct
2HEC H + lau P

ROYAN
Charente-Maritime
At **PONTAILLAC**(2km NE on D25)
Clairfontaine allée des Peupliers ✆46390811
300m from beach.
Jun-5 Sep
3.5HEC H G + lau S
Prices pitch95 (incl 3 persons)

ROYÈRE-DE-VASSIVIÈRE
Creuse
Masgrangeas ✆55647165
On shore of Lake Vassivière.
5km S of Royère by D8/D3.
21 May-21 Oct
2HEC H LP + lau
Prices pitch60 (incl 3 persons)

SABLES-D'OLONNE, LES
Vendée
Baie de Cayola rte de la Corniche ✆51220009
4km SW of town centre.
Jun-Sep
4HEC H G H P + lau S
Prices pitch49 (incl 3 persons)

CM Roses r des Roses ✆51951042
400m from the beach
Etr-Oct
2.5HEC H G H P + lau LS
Prices pitch63-79 (incl 2 persons)

Fosses Rouges 8 r des Fosses Rouges ✆51951795
3km SE towards La Pironnière.
All year
3.5HEC H G P + lau LS
Prices pitch60-80 (incl 2 persons)

ST-AIGNAN-SUR-CHER
Loir-et-Cher
CM Cochards ✆54751559
On beautiful meadowland, completely surrounded by hedges.
1km from bridge on D17 towards Selles.
15 Mar-15 Oct
4HEC H G H + lau R

ST-AMAND-MONTROND
Cher
CM Roche ✆48960936
1.5km SW near river and canal.
Apr-Sep
4HEC H G + lau R P
Prices A6 pitch8

ST-AVERTIN
Indre-et-Loire
CM Rives du Cher ✆47272760
N on the left bank of the River Cher
Mar-Nov
3HEC H + G LPR
Prices A8 pitch8

ST-BRÉVIN-LES-PINS
Loire-Atlantique
CM Courance 100/110 av Ml-Foch ✆40272291
Camping Carnet Compulsory.
S off D305, in pine forest, by sea.
All year
5HEC S H G S + lau P
Prices pitch47-60 (incl 2 persons)

Fief 57 Chemin du Fief ✆40272386
All year
7HEC H G R H P + lau S
Prices pitch37-63 (incl 2 persons)

See advertisement in colour section

ST-BRÉVIN-L'OCÉAN
Loire-Atlantique
Village Club des Pierres Couchées L'Ermitage ✆40278564
Extensive, well screened terrain made up of 3 sites, 2 of which are open all year.
500 m from the sea, 2 km on D213 toward Pornic.
All year
14HEC S H G H P + lau R S
Prices pitch58 (incl 2 persons)

ST-CLÉMENT-DES-BALEINES
See **RÉ, ILE DE**

ST-CYR
Vienne
Parc de Loisirs ✆94262127
1.5km NE via D4/D82
Mar-20 Nov
8HEC S H G R H + lau S

ST-DENIS-D'OLÉRON
See **OLÉRON, ILE D'**

STE-CATHERINE-DE-FIERBOIS
Indre-et-Loire
♖ **Parc de Fierbois** ✆47654335
Beside artificial lake; good bathing area.
Follow D101 off N10, 1.5km SE.
10HEC H G H LP + lau

STE-REINE-DE-BRETAGNE
Loire-Atlantique
♖ **Château du Deffay** ✆40016384
Situated in the beautiful Parc de Brière

providing fishing, walking and horse riding. Games and TV rooms.
4.5km W on D33 rte de Pontchâteau.
15 May-15 Sep
4HEC ◑ H ✕ ⊖ H LP + lau
Prices A17 pitch41

SAINTES
Charente-Maritime
Au Fill de l'Eau 6 r de Courbiac ✆46930800
1km on D128.
15 May-Sep
3.7HEC ● H ✕ ⊖ G H PR + lau S
Prices A10 pitch8

ST-FLORENT-LE-VIEIL
Maine-et-Loire
CM ✆40834501
6km SE. N of Lac du Boudon.
15 May-Sep
3HEC ● H ⊖ lau ✕ P

ST-GEORGES-DE-DIDONNE
Charente-Maritime
Bois Soleil 2 av de Suzac ✆46050594
Pitches lie on different levels. Direct access to the beach.
Camping Carnet Compulsory.
2.5km S of town on Meschers road (D25).
Apr-Sep
8.5HEC S ● H ✕ ⊖ G H P + lau S
Prices pitch73-97 (incl 3 persons)

Ideal Camping No 1 ✆46052904
May-15 Sep
8HEC S ◑ H ✕ ⊖ G R + lau S
Prices V5 pitch62 (incl 3 persons)

ST-GEORGES-D'OLÉRON
See **OLÉRON, ILE D'**

ST-GILLES-CROIX-DE-VIE
Vendée
Pas Opton ✆51551198
Well tended garden-like site in rural surroundings.
On D754 Nantes Road.
May-10 Sep
4.5HEC ◑ H ✕ ⊖ G H PS + lau R
Prices A19 pitch91-119 (incl 3 persons)

ST-HILAIRE-DE-RIEZ
Vendée
Biches ✆51543882
2km N
20 May-15 Sep
12HEC S ◑ H ✕ ⊖ G P + lau
Prices pitch115-140 (incl 3 persons)

Bois Tordu 84 av de la Pège ✆51543378
5.3km NW.
20 May-10 Sep
1.5HEC ◑ H ✕ ⊖ G H P + lau S
Prices pitch73-97 (incl 3 persons)

Chouans 108 av de la Faye ✆51543490
2.5 km NW.
Etr-Sep
4HEC ◑ H ✕ ⊖ G H P lau S
Prices pitch72 (incl 3 persons)

Ecureuils 100 av de la Pège ✆51543371
From A11 to Nantes, then via D178 and D753 to St-Hilaire-de-Riez.
15 May-15 Sep
3HEC ◑ H ✕ ⊖ P + lau G S
Prices pitch95 (incl 3 persons)

Padrelle 1 r Prévot ✆51553203
May-15 Sep
0.5HEC ○ H ⊖ + lau ✕ G PS
Prices pitch33-48 (incl 3 persons)

Plage 106 av de la Pège ✆51543393
On a meadow with trees. Access to beach via dunes.
5.7km NW.
Etr-Sep
5HEC ◑ H ⊖ G R H P + lau ✕ S
Prices pitch55-65 (incl 2 persons)

Prairie chemin des Roselières ✆51540856
5.5km NW, 500m from the beach
Jun-Sep
4HEC H G H P + lau S
Prices pitch75-85 (incl 3 persons)

Riez à la Vie ✆51543049
Flat site, divided into pitches.
3km NW.
Jun-15 Sep
3HEC H G H P + lau S
Prices pitch46-85 (incl 3 persons)

Sapinière ✆51544574
2km NE
15 Jun-15 Sep
3.5HEC S H G R H P + lau S

Sol-à-Gogo 61 av de la Pège ✆51542900
4.8km NW, directly on the beach
20 May-16 Sep
3.8HEC H G H PS + lau
Prices pitch140 (incl 3 persons)

ST-HILAIRE-LA-FORÊT
See **TALMONT-ST-HILAIRE**

ST-JEAN-DE-LA-RUELLE
See **ORLÉANS**

ST-JEAN-DE-MONTS
Vendée
Abri des Pins rte de Notre-Dame-de-Monts ✆51588386
Level grassland site subdivided by hedges, bushes and trees.
4km N on D38 Notre-Dame-de-Monts road.
15 May-15 Sep
3HEC H G R H P + lau S

Amiaux ✆51582222
On the edge of a forest.
3.5km NW of D38.
May-Sep
8HEC S H G PS lau
Prices A15 pitch80

Bois Joly 46 rue de Notre Dame de Monts ✆51591163
8HEC H H P lau

Bois Masson 149 r des Sables ✆51586262
2km SE
Etr-Sep
7.5HEC S H G H P + lau S

Clarys Plage ✆51581024
Jun-8 Sep
1.7HEC H H P + lau S
Prices pitch70 (incl 3 persons)

Demoiselles ✆51580131
Camping Carnet compulsory.
500m from the beach
Etr-15 Sep
15HEC S H + lau G R LPS

Forêt chemin de la Rive ✆51588463
5.5km NW
Jun-15 Sep
1HEC H G P + lau S
Prices A18 pitch64

At **OROUET** (6km SE)
Yole chemin des Bosses ✆51586717
May-Sep
5HEC H G H P + lau R S
Prices pitch116-132 (incl 2 persons)

ST-JULIEN-DES-LANDES
Vendée
Fôret ✆51056201
NE on D55, rte de Martinet.
15 May-15 Sep
5HEC H G P + lau

♜ **Garangeoire** ✆51386539 or 51466539
2km N of the village.
15 May-15 Sep
6HEC H G R P + lau
Prices pitch95-117 (incl 3 persons)

ST-LÉONARD-DE-NOBLAT
Haute-Vienne
CM Beaufort ✆55560279
Pleasant surroundings.
Access from the D39.
15 Jun-15 Sep
2HEC H G R lau P

ST-MALÔ-DU-BOIS
Vendée
Plein Air de Poupet ✆51923332
From village take D72 for 1km, then take left fork and follow signs. Site on bank of River Sèvre Nantaise.
May-Sep
2.8HEC H R lau
Prices A6-7 V5 15-16

ST-MARTIN-DE-RÉ
See **RÉ, ILE DE**

ST-MICHEL-CHEF-CHEF
Loire-Atlantique
Thar-Cor 43 av du Cormier, Tharon Plage ✆40278281
Subdivided by trees and flowerbeds. Tent campers accommodated in orchard with no parking facilities. Well equipped children's play area. Lunchtime siesta 12.00-13.00 hrs.
Signposted from D213 (St-Nazaire/Pornic).
All year
3.3HEC H + lau G R S

ST-PALAIS-SUR-MER
Charente-Maritime
Côte-de-Beauté La Grande Côte ✆46222059
Situated facing sea.
N of town on road to La Palmyre (D25).
20 Jun-10 Sep
1HEC H + lau S

Deux Plages 41 av des Acacias ✆46231142
500m from beaches.
Etr-Oct

3HEC H G H
+ lau S

Logis 22 r des Palombes ✆46232023
Situated 300m from the sea.
2.5km NW on D25.
Jun-15 Sep
20HEC S H
G H + lau LS
Prices pitch60 (incl 3 persons)

Ormeaux av de Bernezac ✆46390207
15 May-Sep
2.5HEC H G R
+ lau S
Prices A18 pitch16

Puits de l'Auture La Grande Côte
✆46232031
Situated at the edge of a forest facing the sea.
2km NW on D25 La Palmyre road.
May-Sep
5HEC H G H
PS + lau

ST-PÈRE-SUR-LOIRE
See **SULLY-SUR-LOIRE**

ST-PIERRE-D'OLÉRON
See **OLÉRON, ILE D'**

ST-PRIEST-DE-GIMEL
Corrèze
Étang-de-Ruffaud ✆55212665
On hilly wooded ground beside lake. Common room with TV.
2.5km N on D53.
15 Jun-15 Sep
20HEC H L
+ lau
Prices A9 pitch9

ST-RÉMY-SUR-AVRE
Eure-et-Loir
Pré de l'Église ✆37489310
Follow N12 from town centre.
Apr-Sep
1HEC H G + lau
R P
Prices A11 pitch15

ST-USTRE
See **INGRANDES**

ST-VINCENT-SUR-JARD
Vendée
'Bolée d'Air' ✆51903605
2km E via D21
Apr-Oct
5.7HEC H G
R H P + lau S

SAUJON
Charente-Maritime
Chênes Médis ✆46067246
15 Jun-15 Sep
7HEC H G H
+ lau PS
Prices pitch42-43 (incl 3 persons)

SAUMUR
Maine-et-Loire
Chantepie ✆41679534
May-15 Sep
10HEC H G
H P P + lau
Prices A17 pitch22

See advertisement on page 140

Dampierre-sur-Loire ✆41674500
May-15 Sep
2HEC H R + lau
G
Prices A10 V5 5 5

Ile d'Offard Ile d'Offard ✆41674500
On island in the middle of the Loire near municipal stadium.
All year
3.1HEC H P
+ lau

See advertisement on page 140

SILLÉ-LE-GUILLAUME
Sarthe
Privé du Landereau ✆43201269
1.5km NW via D304
Etr-Oct
2.5HEC H G
H + lau R L
Prices A10 V5 4 3

SILLÉ-LE-PHILIPPE
Sarthe
Château de Chanteloup
✆43275107
Set partly in wooded cleanings and open ground. Good sanitary installations.
17 km NE from Le Mans on D301.
15 Jun-2 Sep
20HEC S H G
R P + lau
Prices A20 pitch40

SUÈVRES
Loir-et-Cher
Château de la Grenouillère
✆54878037
Completely divided into pitches. Castle now hotel with common room for campers. Each pitch 150sq m. Separate area for overnight campers.
3km from village towards Orléans.
15 May-15 Sep
11HEC H PR
+ lau

SULLY-SUR-LOIRE
Loiret
CM ✆38362393
Near Château, adjacent to River Loire.
100m from town.
Apr-Oct
3.4HEC S H + lau
G R R
Prices A9 V4 6 6

At **ST-PÈRE-SUR-LOIRE**
St-Père ✆38363594
W on D60, near the river
Apr-Sep
2.7HEC S H +
lau G R
Prices A10 V5 10 10

TALMONT-ST-HILAIRE
Vendée
At **PORTEAU, LE** (10km W via D949)
Joie de Vivre ✆51220827
200m from the sea.
Etr-Oct
4HEC H G R
H + lau S

At **ST-HILAIRE-LA-FORÊT** (7km SE)
Batardières ✆51333385
W on D70
15 Jun-5 Sep
1.6HEC H R lau

TOURS
Indre-et-Loire
At **BALLAN-MIRÉ** (8.5km W D751)
Mignardière ✆47532649
2.5km NE.
May-Sep
2.5HEC H G P
+ lau
Prices A16-18 pitch21-25

TRANCHE-SUR-MER, LA
Vendée
Bale d'Aunis 10 r du Pertuis
✆51274736
On level land on sea-shore.
300m E on D46.
20 Mar-Sep
2.4HEC S H G
P + lau S
Prices pitch102 (incl 3 persons)

Bel r du Bottereau ✆51304739
400m from town centre.
Apr-Sep
3.5HEC H P
+ lau LS
Prices pitch79 (incl 2 persons)

Cottage Fleuri La Grière-Plage
✆51303457
2.5km E, 500m from the beach
20 Mar-15 Oct
7.5HEC H G R
R + lau S
Prices pitch78 (incl 3 persons)

Moncalm ✆51561601
All year
7.5HEC H P
See advertisement under ANGLES

Rouillères ✆51303178
Extensive site by the sea with level ground and pine and poplar trees. Largely subdivided into pitches.
Follow D46 for 3km in direction of L'Aiguillon.
Etr-Oct
23HEC H G
R PS + lau
Prices pitch70-80 (incl 3 persons)

TURBALLE, LA
Loire-Atlantique
Falaise ✆40233253 →

500m W from village centre on D99 towards Priac-sur-Mer.
25 Mar-Oct
2HEC S H G H L + lau S

♜ **Parc Ste-Brigitte** Domaine de Bréhet ✆40233042
Site in grounds of old Château. Parkland divided into pitches and surrounded by hedges.
Camping Carnet Compulsory.
E of village on D99 Guérande road.
Apr-Sep
10HEC H G R H P + lau
Prices A19 pitch20-40

VALENÇAY
Indre
C M Chènes rte de Loches ✆54000392
1km W on D960
Apr-Sep
5HEC H P + lau G R
Prices A12 pitch12-15

VARENNES-SUR-LOIRE
Maine-et-Loire
♜ **Étang de la Brèche** ✆41512292
4.5km NW via N152.
15 May-15 Sep
8HEC H G H + lau P
Prices pitch70-92 (incl 2 persons)

VEILLON, LE
Vendée
St-Hubert av de la Plage ✆51222230
Apr-Oct
1HEC H G R + lau LPS
Prices pitch56-69 (incl 3 persons)

VELLES
Indre
Grands Pins Les Maisons Neuves ✆54366193
The site has individual pitches and has easy access to the countryside.
7km S of Châteauroux on N20, Les Maisons Neuves.
Etr-15 Oct
5HEC H G R H P + lau

VENDÔME
Loir-et-Cher
Grand Prés r G-Martel ✆54770027
Site lies on a meadow, next to a sports ground.
E of town on right bank of Loire.
All year
3HEC H G + lau P

VINEUIL
Loir-et-Cher
Châteaux ✆54788205
Level site on left bank of River Loire with modern buildings. Boating. Bathing not recommended.
Camping Carnet Compulsory.
From Blois drive towards St-Dye. After modern bridge continue towards 'Lac de Loire' for 1.5km.
Etr-15 Oct
7HEC H G P + lau

BRITTANY/NORMANDY

France's most westerly province, Brittany's 750 miles of splendid coastline juts proudly out into the Atlantic. This is a wild and rugged coastline, with great rollers crashing into magnificent cliffs and headlands, the unique wooded estuaries, "abers", and sheltered harbour coves and picturesque fine-sand beaches in the south to rival the best in Europe. The sea dominates the province, and the popular and chic coastal resorts, as well as the charming fishing ports, abound in friendly family-run restaurants serving a wonderful variety of fresh seafood. Away from the sea, this is a land of gentle hills, narrow, wooded valleys, wild moors of gorse and heather, and sunken lanes linking sleepy villages and quaint farmhouses.
Behind the Normandy coastline of splendid sandy beaches and sheer chalk cliffs is a lush agricultural countryside which makes a rich contribution to the region's distinctive cuisine. Apple orchards – a splendid sight in spring – result in the ciders and strong Calvados, and from the dairy farms come the famous fine dairy produce and excellent cheeses. But the region is also rich in history – the beaches recalling the Allied landings, feudal castles, elegant châteaux; and the great religious buildings – Mont St Michel, and the cathedrals at Bayeux, Coutances, Evreux, Lisieux, and the great Cathedral of Notre Dame at Rouen.

ALENÇON
Orne
Guéramé r de Guéramé ✆33263495
Situated in open country near a stream, 500 m from town centre.
Access via the Boulevard Périphérique in the SW part of town.
Apr-Nov
1.5HEC ⁓ ● ⋒H ⊖ ⊕ ≋R ▣ + lau ☞ ⊾ ▼ ✕ ≋P
Prices A7 V8 ⊕8

Jacques Fould ✆33292329
On N12.
All year
1HEC ⁓ ● ⋒H ⊖ ⊕ ▣ + lau ☞ ⊾ ▼ ✕ Ⓖ Ⓡ ≋P
Prices A5 pitch2-3

ARGENTAN
Orne
At **MAUVAISVILLE** (2.8km SE off N158)
Val de Baize ✆33672711
All year
1HEC ⁓ ● ⋒H ⊖ ⊕ ≋R ▣ + lau ☞ ⊾ ▼ ✕
Prices A8 V5 ⊕7 Å7

ARRADON
Morbihan
Penboch ✆97447129
May-20 Sep
4HEC ⁓ ◑ ⋒H ⊾ ▼ ⊖ ⊕ Ⓖ ⌂ Ⓗ ≋P ▣ + lau ☞ ≋S
Prices A14-16 pitch15-40

ARZANO
Finistère
♖ **Ty Nadan** rte d'Arzano ✆98717547
3km W
Etr-15 Sep
8HEC ⁓ ◑ ⋒H ⊾ ▼ ✕ ⊖ ⊕ Ⓖ Ⓗ ≋P ▣ + lau
Prices A20 pitch150-250

AUMALE
Seine-Maritime
CM Grand Mail ✆62050022
In the town centre
May-15 Sep
0.5HEC ⁓ ◑ ⋒H ⊖ ⊕ ▣ + lau ☞ ⊾ ▼ ✕ ≋PR
Prices A6 V3 ⊕3 Å3

AVRANCHES
Manche
At **GENÊTS** (10km W on D911)
Coques d'Or rte de la Plage ✆33708257
1km from the sea.
Apr-Sep
3HEC ⁓ ⋒H ▼ ✕ ⊖ ⊕ ⌂ ≋P ▣ + lau ☞ ⊾ ≋S
Prices A14 pitch8

BAGUER-PICAN
See **DOL-DE-BRETAGNE**

BARFLEUR
Manche
Tamaris 21 r de Réville ✆33540158
SE on D1.
Apr-11 Sep
1.3HEC ⁓ **S** ○ ⋒H ▼ ✕ ⊖ ⊕ Ⓖ ≋S ▣ + lau

BARNEVILLE-CARTERET
Manche
At **BARNEVILLE-PLAGE**
Pré Normand ✆33538564
On slightly hilly meadow away from traffic noise but exposed to sea winds. Vehicles allowed on beach but beware of tide.
Camping Carnet Compulsory.
Off D166.
Apr-15 Sep
1.4HEC ⁓ ◑ ⋒H ⊾ ▼ ✕ ⊖ ⊕ Ⓖ Ⓡ ⌂ ≋P ▣ P + lau ☞ ≋S
Prices A16 pitch18

At **CARTERET**
CM Bocage ✆33538691
Opposite town hall.
Apr-Sep
3HEC ⁓ ◑ ⋒H ⊖ ⊕ Ⓖ Ⓡ ▣ + lau ☞ ⊾ ▼ ✕ ≋S

BARNEVILLE-PLAGE
See **BARNEVILLE-CARTERET**

BAYEUX
Calvados
CM Calvados bd d'Eindhoven ✆31920843
Very clean and tidy site with tarmac drive and hardstanding for caravans. Adjoins football field.
N side of town on Boulevard Circulaire.
15 Mar-15 Nov
3.5HEC ⁓ ◑ ⋒H ⊾ ⊖ ⊕ Ⓖ ▣ + lau ☞ ▼ ✕ ≋P
Prices A11 pitch13

Château de Martragny ✆31802140
SW of Martragny via N13
28 Apr-15 Sep
8HEC ⁓ ◑ ⋒H ⊾ ▼ ⊖ ⊕ Ⓖ ≋P ▣ + lau
Prices A22 pitch40

BEG-MEIL
Finistère
Roche Percée ✆98949415
Camping Carnet Compulsory.
15 May-Sep
2.5HEC ⁓ ⋒H ⊾ ▼ ⊖ ⊕ Ⓖ ⌂ ≋P ▣ + lau

Vorlen Plage de Kerambigorn ✆98949736
In field, partly surrounded by hedges and divided into pitches near beach. Supervised beach with children's playground.
20 May-20 Sep
10HEC ⁓ ◑ ⋒H ⊾ ✕ ⊖ ⊕ Ⓖ ⌂ Ⓗ ▣ + lau ☞ ▼ ≋PS
Prices A17 V8 ⊕25 Å25

BÉNODET
Finistère
Letty ✆98570469
Site divided into sectors. Good sanitary installations, ironing rooms and games room. Good beach for children.
By the sea 1km SE.
21 Jun-6 Sep ➔

10HEC H G R S + lau
Prices A16 V8 pitch26

Mer Blanche ✆98570075
3.5km E on D44 (Fouesnant road).
All year
6HEC H G R H P + lau S
Prices A14 pitch21

Pointe St-Gilles ✆98570537
Holiday site south of village, on fields by beach. Divided into several sectors; individual pitches. Well-equipped sanitary blocks.
May-Sep
7HEC H G R H PS + lau
Prices A16 V8 26 26

Port de Plaisance Prat Poulou ✆98570238
NE off D34
Etr-Sep
4HEC H G H P + lau RS
Prices A12-14 V5-7 20-22 20-22

BÉNOUVILLE
Calvados
Hautes Coutures rte de Ouistreham ✆31447308
15 Mar-15 Oct
3.3HEC H G P + lau RS

BERNIÈRES-SUR-SEINE
Eure
Château-Gaillard ✆32541820
0.8km SW
Feb-Dec
24HEC H R H P + lau
Prices A23 pitch16-33

BILLIERS
Morbihan
Guérandière rte de Penlan-Billiers ✆97416006
Apr-Oct
2HEC H G H + lau S

BINIC
Côtes-du-Nord
Korrigans No.2 ✆96736234
100m from the beach.
Mar-15 Oct
1HEC H G H P + lau PS

Panoramic rte de St-Brieuc ✆96736043
On a meadow divided into pitches, on a hill above the town.
On S outskirts of village.
20 Mar-1 Oct
2.5HEC H G H PS + lau
Prices A15 V8 12 10

BLAINVILLE-SUR-MER
Manche
Mélette ✆33471484
1km W on D651.
15 Jun-15 Sep
6HEC S H + lau PS
Prices A10 pitch14

BLANGY-LE-CHÂTEAU
Calvados
Brévedent ✆31647288
Camping Carnet Compulsory.
3km SE on D51 beside lake.
15 May-15 Sep
4HEC H G LPR + lau
Prices A25 pitch30

Domaine du Lac rte de Mesnil-sur-Blangy ✆31646200
Mar-Oct
7HEC H G LR + lau
Prices A20 pitch20

BLANGY-SUR-BRESLE
Seine-Maritime
CM r des Étangs ✆35945565
300m on N28.
15 Mar-15 Oct
1HEC H + lau
Prices A10 V6 8 8

BOURG-ACHARD
Eure
Clos Normand 129 rte de Pont-Audemer ✆32563484
Apr-Sep
1.4HEC H G + lau

BRÉHAL
Manche
Vanlée ✆33616380
Site by sea on uneven, sandy meadow behind strip of dunes. Quiet situation. Magnificent beach. Good for children. Not crowded in peak season. Big common room, bar, games room. TV room. Golf and stables nearby.
5km W at St-Martin.
May-Sep
11HEC S H H S + lau

CABOURG
Calvados
Plage Cabourg av C-du-Gaulle ✆31910575
W via D514 towards Hôme
15 Mar-11 Nov
5.2HEC S H G H S + lau R PR
Prices A24 pitch40

Vert Pré rte de Caen ✆31914168
2km SW on D513.
Etr-Sep
5.1HEC H G R P + lau S
Prices A16 pitch50

CALLAC
Côtes-du-Nord
CM Verte Vallée ✆96455850
W via D28 towards Morlaix
15 Jun-15 Sep
1.5HEC H G R + lau L
Prices A7 pitch4

CAMARET-SUR-MER
Finistère
Lambézen ✆98279141 or 98279372
3km NE on rte de Roscanvel (D355).
Apr-Sep
1.8HEC H G H P + lau S
Prices A16-20 pitch28-35

Plage de Trez Rouz Prés de Camaret ✆98279396
Etr-Sep
1HEC H G H S + lau
Prices A17 pitch15

CAMPNEUSEVILLE
Seine-Maritime
Monchy-le-Preux ✆35937703
2km N on D260.
Apr-Oct
2HEC H G + lau
Prices A15 pitch20

CANCALE
Ille-et-Vilaine
Notre Dame du Verger ✆99897284
2km from Pointe-du-Grouin on D201.
Apr-Sep
2.5HEC H G R H + lau PS

CARANTEC
Finistère
Mouettes ✆98670246
Level site divided by low shrubs and trees.
1.5km SW on rte de St-Pol-de-Léon, towards the sea.
May-Sep
5HEC H G H PS + lau

CARENTAN
Manche
CM le Haut Dyck chemin du Grand-Bas Pays ✆33421689
Take village road off N13 towards Le Port.
All year
2.5HEC H G R + lau PR
Prices A8 V5 9 9

CARNAC
Morbihan
Étang ✆97521406
2km N at Kerlann.
Apr-Oct

3HEC ◑ H ✕ ⊖ G R H P + lau S L
Prices A17 pitch24

♖ **Grande Métairie** ✆97522401
Holiday site with modern amenities, completely divided into pitches. Country-style bar, terraced restaurant, TV. Swimming lessons.
2.5km NE on D196.
25 May-14 Sep
15HEC ◑ H ✕ ⊖ G PS + lau
Prices A20 pitch80-90

Moulin de Kermaux ✆97521590
2.5km NE.
Etr-15 Sep
3HEC ◑ H ⊖ G H P + lau ✕ S
Prices A16 pitch45

Ombrages ✆97521652
2.5km N on D119.
15 May-15 Sep
1HEC ◑ H ⊖ G R + lau ✕ L
Prices A13 V6 14 Å14

Rosnual rte d'Auray ✆97521457
1.5km from village, 2.5km from the sea.
Etr-Sep
1HEC ◑ H ✕ ⊖ H P + lau G R S
Prices A18 pitch65

Saules ✆97521498
Grassland site between road and deciduous woodland, subdivided by hedges and shrubs.
2.5km N on D119.
Etr-Oct
2.5HEC ◑ H ⊖ G H P + lau ✕

At **CARNAC-PLAGE**(1km S)
Beaumer ✆97520423
end Mar-20 Sep
1HEC ● H ⊖ + lau ✕

Druides Quartier Beaumer ✆97520818
SE of town centre. Approach via D781 or D119.
Etr-14 Sep
2HEC ◑ H ⊖ + lau ✕ G R S
Prices pitch81 (incl 3 persons)

Menhirs ✆97529467
A quiet site near the beach and shops.
May-Sep
6HEC ○ H ✕ ⊖ G H P + lau S
Prices A22 pitch98

Men Dû Quartier Beaumer ✆97520423
1km from Carnac Plage via D781 and D186.
end Mar-20 Sep
1HEC ◑ ● H ⊖ + lau ✕ S

CARNAC-PLAGE
See **CARNAC**

CARTERET
See **BARNEVILLE-CARTERET**

CAUREL
Côtes-du-Nord
Beau Rivage les Pins ✆96285222
2km SW on D111 by Lake Guerlédan.
May-Sep
0.8HEC ● H ⊖ G R + lau ✕ L

Nautic International rte de Beau Rivage ✆96285794
A terraced site on the edge of Lake Guerlédan.
Apr-15 Oct
2.6HEC ◑ H ⊖ LP + lau ✕
Prices A14-19 pitch17

CHAPELLE-AUX-FILZMÉENS, LA
Ille-et-Vilaine
♖ **Château** ✆99452155
A quiet, pleasant site.
Camping Carnet Compulsory.
20 May-10 Sep
5HEC ◑ H ✕ ⊖ G P + lau
Prices A21 pitch46-59

CLÉDER
Finistère
CM Roguennic ✆98696388
5km N on coast.
Jun-15 Sep
9HEC ○ H ⊖ G R S + lau ✕

CONCARNEAU
Finistère
Prés Verts ✆98970974
1.2km NW.
Etr-Sep
2.5HEC ◑ H ⊖ PS + lau
Prices pitch60 (incl 2 persons)

CROZON
Finistère
Pen ar Menez ✆98271236
On fringe of a pinewood. Water sport facilities 5km away. Cycles for hire.
15 Jun-Sep
2.5HEC ◑ H ⊖ H + ✕ G S
Prices A12-13 pitch17-18

Plage de Goulien Kernavèno ✆98271710
5km W on D308
Jun-Sep
1.8HEC ◑ H ⊖ G H + lau S
Prices A15 pitch15

At **ST-FIACRE** (5km NW)
Pieds dans l'Eau ✆98276243
Site on several meadows divided by trees. In quiet secluded situation reaching as far as a pebbly beach. Bathing is dependent on tides.
15 Jun-15 Sep
1.8HEC ● H ⊖ PS + lau ✕ G R
Prices A13 V5 15 Å15

DEAUVILLE
Calvados
At **ST-ARNOULT** (3km S)
Vallée rte de Beaumont ✆31885817
1km S via D27 and D275
Etr-11 Nov
3HEC ◑ H ✕ ⊖ G H LPR + lau
Prices A21 pitch22

At **TOUQUES** (3km SE)
Haras chemin du Calvaire ✆31884484
N on D62, to Honfleur.
All year
4HEC ◑ H ⊖ G R + lau PS
Prices A23 pitch24

DÉVILLE-LÈS-ROUEN
Seine-Maritime
CM ✆35740759
Closed Feb
1.5HEC S ◑ H ⊖ + lau ✕ G R PR
Prices A16 V5 9 Å5

DIEPPE
Seine-Maritime
At **GRAINCOURT** (8.5km NE via D925)
Bois Clieu Château-de-Derchigny ✆35836219
Very pleasant site in wooded countryside.
All year
3HEC ◑ H ✕ ⊖ G H + lau

At **HAUTOT-SUR-MER** (6km SW)
Source Petit-Appeville ✆35842704
15 Mar-15 Oct
2.5HEC ◑ H ⊖ G R H + lau ✕
Prices A16 V6 20 Å16

DINAN
Côtes-du-Nord
At **TADEN** (3.5km NE)
CM Hallerais ✆96391593
Beautiful clean site with level pitches on gentle slope near a country estate. Asphalt drives. Good sanitary installations. Shop, bar and restaurant are only open in July and August.
SW of Taden off D12.
Mar-Oct
10HEC ◑ H ✕ ⊖ G H + lau
Prices A15 pitch18
See advertisement on page 144

DINARD
Ille-et-Vilaine
Mauny ✆99469473
Off St-Briac road (CD603). ➔

Etr-Oct
4HEC ◑ H ⊖ G R H P + lau S
Prices A16 pitch32

CM Port Blanc r du Sgt-Boulanger ✆99461074
Large site between horse riding field and coast. Numbered pitches. Busy, but sanitary installations very clean.
On western edge of town in Quartier de St-Enogat near D786.
Etr-Sep
6.5HEC ◑ H ⊖ G S + lau
Prices A8-9 V5 8-9

Prieuré 20 av Vicomte ✆99462004
SE via D114
Etr-Oct
1.4HEC ◑ H ⊖ G R H S + lau P
Prices A15 pitch24

DOL-DE-BRETAGNE
Ille-et-Vilaine
See also EPINIAC

CM ✆99481468
On level meadow.
SW on rte de Dinan 400m from town centre.
May-Sep
1.7HEC ◑ H ⊖ lau S
Prices A9 V4 4 A4

At **BAGUER-PICAN** (4km E on N176)
Ferme-Camping du Vieux Chêne ✆99480955
Spacious site in pleasant lakeside situation. Farm produce available.
5km E of Dol-de-Bretagne on N176.
15 Apr-Sep
4HEC ◑ H ⊖ G H P + lau S
Prices A22 pitch32

DOUARNENEZ
Finistère

Kerleyou ✆98740352
Family site situated 1km W on r de Prefet-Collignon towards the sea.
20 May-15 Sep
3.5HEC ◑ H ⊖ G R H + lau S
Prices A11 V5 11 A11

Trézulien r F-le-Guyader, Tréboul ✆98741230
Apr-15 Sep
2.7HEC ◑ H ⊖ G H + lau S
Prices A11 V5 11 A11

At **POULLAN-SUR-MER** (5km W on D765)
Pil Koad ✆98742639
E via D7 towards Douarnenez
May-Sep
4.7HEC ◑ H ⊖ G R H P + lau S
Prices A20 pitch46

EPINIAC
Ille-et-Vilaine

Château des Ormes ✆99481019
Site in grounds of château.
7km S of Dol-de-Bretagne on D795 Rennes road.
20 May-10 Sep
35HEC ◑ H ⊖ G H P + lau
Prices A22 pitch45

ERDEVEN
Morbihan

Kerzrho ✆97556317
Level site divided and surrounded by bushes and trees. Each pitch has water and electricity.
1.5km SE on the D781.
Etr-Sep
5.5HEC ◑ H ⊖ R H P + lau
Prices pitch105 (incl 3 persons)

Sept Saints ✆97555265
2km NW via D781 rte de Plouhinec.
15 May-15 Sep
5HEC ◑ H ⊖ G R P + lau RS

ERQUY
Côtes-du-Nord

Pins rte du Guen ✆96723112
Situated in a pine forest.
1km NE of village.
Etr-Sep
8HEC ◑ H ⊖ G H P + lau S
Prices A14 pitch13

Roches Caroual Village ✆96723290
3km SW
Apr-Sep
2.1HEC ◑ H ⊖ G H S + lau R
Prices A10 pitch8

St-Pabu ✆96722465
On big open meadow with several terraces in beautiful, isolated situation by sea. divided into pitches.
W on D786 then follow signposts from La Coutre.
Etr-Sep
5HEC ○ H ⊖ G R H S + lau
Prices A12 pitch17

Vieux Moulin ✆96723423
Clean tidy site divided into pitches and surrounded by a pine forest. Suitable for children.
On D783.
Apr-25 Sep
2.5HEC ● H ⊖ G H PS + lau
Prices A14 V9 13 A13

ÉTABLES-SUR-MER
Côtes-du-Nord

Abri Côtier ✆96706157
1km N of town centre on D786.
Apr-Sep
2HEC ◑ H ⊖ G R H PS + lau
Prices A12 pitch20

ETRÉHAM
Calvados

Reine Mathilde ✆31217655
1km W via D123
May-Sep
3HEC ◑ H ⊖ G H P + lau S
Prices A18 pitch20

EU
Seine-Maritime
CM r Mozart ✆35503017
About 7km SE of town at Incheville, on the road to Beauchamps.
All year
2HEC H ⊖ G + lau
Prices A8 pitch7

FALAISE
Calvados
CM Château ✆31901655
W of town.
Apr-Sep
9.6HEC H ⊖ + lau P
Prices

FORÊT-FOUESNANT, LA
Finistère
Kérantérec ✆98569811
Well-kept terraced site, divided into sections by hedges and extending to the sea.
3km SE.
Apr-Sep
4.5HEC H ⊖ G H PS + lau

Manoir de Pen Ar Steir ✆98569775
NE off D44.
All year
3HEC H ⊖ G R H + lau S

Plage Plage de Kerleven ✆98569625
2.5km SE on D783.
All year
1.2HEC H ⊖ S + lau G
Prices A12 pitch16

Pontérec ✆98569833
0.5km on D44 towards Bénodet.
Apr-Sep
3HEC H ⊖ G H + lau R
Prices A8 pitch10

St-Laurent rte de Kerleven ✆98569765
On rocky coast. Divided into pitches.
3.5km SE of village.
Apr-15 Sep
5HEC H ⊖ G H P + lau

Stéréden-Vor Plage de Kerleven ✆98569643
2.5km SE.
May-Sep
1HEC H ⊖ S + lau
Prices A9 pitch16

FOUESNANT
Finistère
Atlantique rte de Mousterlin ✆98561444
4.5km S
15 May-15 Sep
4HEC H ⊖ G R P + lau S
Prices A12-20 pitch24-40

Piscine Kerleya ✆98565606
4km NW
Etr-20 Sep
2.8HEC S H ⊖ G H P + lau R S
Prices A12-15 pitch15-20

FOUGÈRES
Ille-et-Vilaine
CM Paron ✆99994081
1.5km E via D17
All year
2.5HEC H ⊖ + lau G PR
Prices A10 V7 12 12

GENÊTS
See **AVRANCHES**

GONNEVILLE-EN-AUGE
Calvados
Clos Tranquille ✆31242136
On D95A.
Etr-Sep
1.3HEC H ⊖ G R H lau
Prices A14 pitch14

GONNEVILLE-SUR-MER
Calvados
Falaises ✆31910966
Has terraces and lawns. Steep access to beach by means of many steps. Section reserved for parties of young British campers.
On steep coast road to Deauville, 2.9km NE from village.
Apr-Nov
10HEC H ⊖ G H PS + lau

GOUVILLE-SUR-MER
Manche
Belle Etoile ✆33478687
All year
2HEC S H ⊖ G R H + lau S
Prices pitch50 (incl 2 persons)

GRAINCOURT
See **DIEPPE**

GROS-THEIL, LE
Eure
Salverte rte de Brionne ✆32355134
2.5km SW on D26.
All year
15HEC H ⊖ G R H P + lau

GUIDEL-PLAGES
Morbihan
Kergal ✆97059818
3km SW
Apr-Sep
5HEC H ⊖ G R H + lau RS
Prices A15 pitch25

GUILVINEC
Finistère
Karreg Skividen ✆98582278
15 Jun-15 Sep
1HEC H ⊖ G H S + lau

Plage rte de Penmarc'h ✆98586190
On level meadow. Divided into pitches. Flat beach suitable for children.
2km W of village on the Corniche towards Penmarc'h.
15 May-15 Sep
14HEC H ⊖ G H PS + lau
Prices A20 V8 35 35 pitch35

HAUTOT-SUR-MER
See **DIEPPE**

HAVRE, LE
Seine-Maritime
CM Forêt de Montgeon ✆35465239
Quiet, well-kept site, with lawns, in forest. Cement stands for caravans.
Signposted from harbour and station.
Apr-Sep
3.8HEC H ⊖ G + lau

HAYE-DU-PUITS, LA
Manche
Etang des Haizes St-Symphorien-le-Valois ✆33460116
Bordering a lake.
15 Apr-15 Oct
2.5HEC H ⊖ G H LP + lau S
Prices A10-15 pitch10-18

HOULGATE
Calvados
Vallée rte de la Vallée ✆31244069
1km S
Apr-Oct
8HEC H ⊖ G H P + lau S
Prices A25 pitch35

ISIGNY-SUR-MER
Calvados
CM le Fanal chemin du Stade ✆31213320
All year
3.5HEC H ⊖ LP lau R
Prices pitch15

JUGON-LES-LACS
Côtes-du-Nord
CM le Bocage ✆96316162
1km SE via D52, near the lake
All year
6HEC H ⊖ H LP + lau G R
Prices A9 V3 9 7

JULLOUVILLE
Manche
Chaussée 1 av de la Libération ✆33618018
On large meadow, completely divided into pitches. Separated from beach and coast road by row of houses.
30 Mar-22 Sep
4HEC G R H + lau S
Prices pitch55 (incl 2 persons)

At **ST-MICHEL-DES-LOUPS** (4km SE)
Chaumière Carolles ✆33488293
4km SE on D21 via Bouillon.
Jul-Aug
4HEC G H L + lau
Prices A11 pitch12

JUMIÈGES
Seine-Maritime
CM r Mainberte ✆35372415
Camping Carnet Compulsory.
Apr-15 Nov
20HEC G R +
Prices A6 V3 3 A3

LANDÉDA
Finistère
Abers aux Dunes de Ste-Marguerite ✆98049335
Very quiet beautiful site among dunes. Ideal for children.
2.5km NW on a peninsula between bays of Aber-Wrac'h and Aber Bernoît.
Jun-15 Sep
5HEC S G R S + lau L
Prices A12 pitch14

LESCONIL
Finistère
Dunes ✆98878178
On slightly sloping recently landscaped ground.
Access via D53, turning S in Plobannalac. Signposted.
Etr-Sep
1.5HEC H + lau S
Prices A13 V5 23 A23

Grande Plage rte du Guilvinée ✆98878364
20 Mar-Sep
1.5HEC G R H + lau S
Prices A14 V6 19 A19

LION-SUR-MER
Calvados
Roches rte de Luc-sur-Mer ✆31972115
NW on D514
Apr-Sep
1.3HEC G R H S + lau
Prices A15 pitch10

LOCQUIREC
Finistère
Bellevue ✆98788080
Terraced site on hill with fine sea view.
4km W on D64.
Jun-Sep
1HEC H S + lau

LOUANNEC
See **PERROS-GUIREC**

LOUARGAT
Côtes-du-Nord
At **ST-ELOI**(5km N)
♖ **Cleuziou** ✆96431490
8HEC G H P + lau
Prices A21 pitch27

LOUVIERS
Eure
Bel Air St-Lubin ✆32401077
Small site near a forest.
Mar-Nov
2.5HEC G P + lau

MARTRAGNY
Calvados
♖ **Château de Martragny** Bretteville l'Orguilleuse ✆31812140
In village turn NE and continue for 0.8km.
May-15 Sep
4HEC G + lau

MAUPERTUS-SUR-MER
Manche
Anse du Brick ✆33543357
Terraced site in dense wood.
200m from beach.
Apr-Sep
7HEC G R H S + lau
Prices A12 pitch13

MAUVAISVILLE
See **ARGENTAN**

MESNIL-VAL
See **TRÉPORT, LE**

MONT-ST-MICHEL, LE
Manche
Gué de Beauvoir ✆33600923
4km S of Abbey on D976 Pontorson road.
Etr-Sep
1HEC G + lau R
Prices A10 V6 9 A8

MORGAT
Finistère
Bouis ✆98270468
Divided into hedge-lined pitches.
15 Jun-15 Sep
2HEC G H + lau S
Prices pp16-18

MOUSTERLIN
Finistère
Grand Large Pointe de Mousterlin ✆98560406
1.5km N on D134.
15 Jun-15 Sep
5.8HEC G R S + lau

Kost-ar-Moor ✆98560416
On meadow divided into pitches.
300m from headland off D134.

Apr-Sep
5.5HEC ◑ H ⊖ G H P + lau S
Prices A13 V7 15 15

MOYAUX
Calvados
Colombier ✆31636308
Well-kept site on grounds of manor house.
Camping Carnet Compulsory.
3km NE on D143.
May-15 Sep
10HEC ◑ H ⊖ G P P + lau
Prices A25 pitch50

MUZILLAC
Morbihan
Guerandière rte de Pen-Lan/Billiers ✆97416006
1km from sea.
S of village on D5 Pointe de Pen-Lan road.
Etr-September
2HEC ● H ⊖ G R P + lau
Relais de l'Océan rte de Damgan ✆97416863
2.5km W via D20.
15 Jun-15 Sep
1.7HEC ◑ H ⊖ H P + lau LR
Prices A13 V7 13 13

NEUFCHÂTEL-EN-BRAY
Seine-Maritime
Ste-Claire ✆35930393
NW via D1
Apr-Oct
2HEC ◑ H ⊖ G P lau P +

NÉVEZ
Finistère
Deux Fontaine ✆98068191
Mainly level site, subdivided into several fields.
700m from Ragunes Beach.
15 May-15 Sep
4.5HEC ◑ H ⊖ G P P + lau S
Prices A16 V7 20 20

NOYAL-MUZILLAC
Morbihan
Moulin de Cadillac ✆97670347
25 Jun-15 Sep
1.3HEC ◑ H ⊖ G R P + lau
Prices A7 V4 6 6

OUISTREHAM
Calvados
Pommiers r de la Haie Breton, Riva-Bella ✆31971266
All year
24HEC ◑ H ⊖ P + lau S
Prairies de la Mer rte de Lion, Riva-Bella ✆31962684
Mar 15-Oct 15
2.5HEC ○ H ⊖ P + lau S

PÉNESTIN-SUR-MER
Morbihan
Airotel-Inly rte de Couarne ✆99903509
2km SE via D201
15 May-15 Sep
30HEC ◑ H ⊖ G R H P P + lau
Cenic ✆99903314
In a forested area 2km from the sea.
Apr-15 Oct
4HEC ◑ H ⊖ G H P P + lau S
Prices A13 pitch15
Iles La Pointe du Bile ✆99903024
The site lies beside the beach. Paddling pool for children.
3km S on D201.
30 Mar-15 Oct
3HEC ◑ H ⊖ G R PS P + lau
Prices A16-17 pitch37-46

PENTREZ-PLAGE
Finistère
Tamaris ✆98265395
Level site divided into pitches.
200m from beach.
May-15 Sep
2HEC ○ H ⊖ G H P + lau R S
Prices A9 V5 8 pitch9

PENVINS
See **SARZEAU**

PERROS-GUIREC
Côtes-du-Nord
Claire Fontaine r du Pont Hélé ✆96230355
1.2km SW of town centre, 800m from Trestraou beach.
15 Jun-15 Sep
3HEC ◑ H ⊖ G P + lau S
At **LOUANNEC** (3km SE)
CM ✆96231178
Well situated site next to the sea. Take away food, games room.
1km W.
15 Jun-15 Sep
4HEC ◑ H ⊖ G P + lau S
Prices A10 V6 9 7
At **PLOUMANACH** (2km NW)
Ranolien ✆96914358
The site is divided into pitches by hedges; separate sections for caravans.
500m from the village.
3 Feb-12 Nov
11HEC ◑ H ⊖ G R PS P + lau
Prices A25 pitch18-39

PIEUX, LES
Manche
Forgette ✆33525195
3.5HEC ● H ⊖ H P + lau G P
Prices A15 pitch15
Grand Large ✆33524075
In unspoilt landscape.
3km from the town centre on D117.
Apr-15 Sep
➔

4HEC S ○ H ⊖ G R H PS + lau
Prices pitch65 (incl 2 persons)

PLOËMEL
Morbihan
Kergo ✆97568066
Camping Carnet Compulsory.
2km SE via D186
15 Jun-15 Sep
2.3HEC ● H ⊖ H lau S
Prices A13 V7 16

PLOËRMEL
Morbihan
Belles Rives rte de Taupont ✆97740122
2km from village centre, beside the lake.
All year
3HEC ● H ⊖ G L + lau PR
Prices A7 pitch12

Vallée du Ninian Le Rochen ✆97935301
Apr-Oct
1HEC ◑ H ⊖ H P + lau

PLOMEUR
Finistère
Torche Pointe de la Torche ✆98586282
3.5km W
Apr-Sep
3.5HEC S ◑ H ✕ ⊖ G R H P lau LS
Prices A16-20 pitch20-25

PLOMODIERN
Finistère
Iroise Plage de Pors-ar-Vag ✆98815272
5km SW, 150m from the beach
Apr-Oct
2.2HEC ○ H ✕ ⊖ G R H S + lau
Prices A13 V6 12 A12

PLONÉVEZ-PORZAY
Finistère
International de Kervel ✆98925154
The best site in the region. Ideal for families. 800m from the sea.
SW of the village on the D107 Douarnenez road for 3km, then towards coast at 'X' roads.
May-Sep
7HEC ◑ H ✕ ⊖ G H PS + lau
Prices A19 pitch33

Tréguer-Plage Ste-Anne-la-Palud ✆98925352
1.3km N
Apr-Oct
6HEC S ○ H ✕ ⊖ G R H S + lau

PLOUÉZEC
Côtes-du-Nord
Cap Horn Port Lazo ✆96206428
2.3km NE via D77 at Port-Lazo
May-10 Sep
3HEC ◑ H ✕ ⊖ G H S lau
Prices A13 pitch20

PLOUEZOCH
Finistère
Baie de Térénez ✆98672680
3.5km NW via D76
Etr-Sep
2.3HEC ◑ H ✕ ⊖ G H P + lau RS
Prices A14-17 pitch22-28

PLOUGASNOU
Finistère
CM Mélin-ar-Mésqueau ✆98673745
3.5km S via D46
Apr-Sep
16HEC ◑ H ⊖ G LR + lau
Prices A9 V3 3 A3

CM de Primel-Trégastel ✆98723706
Etr-Sep
16HEC ○ H ⊖ S ✕ G
Prices A9 pitch3

Trégor ✆98673764
Numbered grassy pitches. Surrounded by hedges.
Jun-Sep
1HEC ◑ H ⊖ G H + lau ✕ PS
Prices A7 pitch7

PLOUHA
Côtes-du-Nord
At **TRINITÉ, LA** (2km NE)
Domaine de Keravel ✆36224913
Etr-15 Sep
5HEC ◑ H ✕ ⊖ G R H P + lau S
Prices A22 pitch35

PLOUHARNEL
Morbihan
Bruyères ✆97523057
Etr-Oct
2HEC ◑ H ⊖ G H + lau ✕ R
Prices A12 pitch22

Étang de Loperhet ✆97523468
4km NW via D781
Apr-Oct
15HEC S ○ H ✕ ⊖ H lau G R S
Prices A17 pitch20

Kersily Ste-Barbe ✆97523965
Etr-Oct
2.5HEC ● H ✕ ⊖ G R H + lau S
Prices A10-12 pitch12-13

Lande ✆97523148
18 Jun-8 Sep
1HEC ◑ H ⊖ G H + lau ✕ S
Prices A10 pitch10

PLOUHINEC
Morbihan
Moténo rte du Magouer ✆97367663
On slightly sloping ground, subdivided into several fields in a rural area.
Etr-15 Oct
4HEC S ◑ ● H ✕ ⊖ G R H + lau S
Prices A13 V7 13 A13

PLOUMANACH
See **PERROS-GUIREC**

PLOZÉVET
Finistère
Corniche rte de la Corniche ✆98913293
S towards the sea
Jun-14 Sep
1.5HEC ◑ H ⊖ H P lau ✕ G R S +
Prices A15 pitch20

POINTE-ST-JACQUES
See **SARZEAU**

PONT-AVEN
Finistère
Spinnaker ✆98060177
The site covers a large area, well wooded. Good leisure facilities.
Signposted from main road.
All year
15HEC ● H ✕ ⊖ G R H P + lau
Prices A20 pitch35

PONT-L'ABBÉ
Finistère
Écureuil ✆98870339
3.5km NE
15 Jun-15 Sep
3HEC ◑ H ✕ ⊖ G R H + lau PRS
Prices A14 V7 16 A16

PONT-RÉAN
See **RENNES**

PORDIC
Côtes-du-Nord
Madières rte de Vau Madec ✆96790248
1500m from village on St-Brieuc road (D786).
Jun-Sep
2HEC ◑ H ✕ ⊖ G H + lau PS
Prices A12 V8 8 A8

PORTBAIL
Manche
Vieux Fort ✆33048199
All year

2HEC S ○ H ⊖ G R + lau S
Prices pitch40 (incl 2 persons)

PORT-MANECH
Finistère
St-Nicolas ✆98068975
Divided into hedge-lined pitches.
May-Sep
3HEC ◑ H ⊖ G R H + lau S
Prices A14-15 V5-6 14-16

POULLAN-SUR-MER
See **DOUARNENEZ**

POURVILLE-SUR-MER
Seine-Maritime
Marqueval rte de la Mer ✆35826646
All year
7.5HEC ◑ H ⊖ G H RS lau
Prices A16 pitch16

QUIMPER
Finistère
Orangerie de Lanniron
✆98906202
2.5km from town centre via D34.
May-15 Sep
5HEC ◑ H ⊖ G R P + lau RS
Prices A20 V10 25 25

RAGUENÈS-PLAGE
Finistère
Raguenès-Plage 19 r des Iles
✆98068069
On field with good views. Asphalt drives 400m from beaches.
2.5km SW of Pont Aven.
Apr-Sep
5HEC ◑ H ⊖ G H S + lau R
Prices A21 pitch34

RENNES
Ille-et-Vilaine
CM Gayeulles r du Prof-M-Audin
✆99369122
NE via N12
Apr-Sep

2HEC ○ H ⊖ + lau P
Prices A10 V4 12 9

At **PONT-RÉAN** (12km SW)
Base Nautique ✆99527260
N via D117
Apr-15 Sep
1HEC ◑ H ⊖ G H + lau R

RICHARDAIS, LA
Ille-et-Vilaine
CM ✆99885080
In village centre beside River Rance and church. Clean, quiet site.
3km from sea.
All year
3HEC ● H ⊖ H +

RIEC-SUR-BÉLON
Finistère
Château de Bélon Port de Bélon
✆98064143
3.5km S
Mar-15 Nov
6HEC ● H ⊖ G H S + lau R
Prices A9 pitch15

ROCHE-BERNARD, LA
Morbihan
CM Patis ✆99906013
On banks of River Vilaine.
100m from village centre.
All year
2.6HEC ○ H ⊖ + lau PS

ST-ARNOULT
See **DEAUVILLE**

ST-AUBIN-SUR-MER
Seine-Maritime
Côte de Nacre r Nouvelle (D7)
✆31971445
24 Mar-11 Nov
6HEC ◑ H ⊖ G R H PS + lau
Prices A20 pitch22

CM Mesnil ✆35830283
2 km W on D68.
end Mar-Oct
2.2HEC ◑ H ⊖ G + lau S
Prices A17 pitch14

ST-CAST-LE-GUILDO
Côtes-du-Nord
Châtelet r des Nouettes ✆96419633
1km W, 250m from the beach
May-20 Sep
0.6HEC ◑ H ⊖ G LP + lau R S
Prices A21 pitch37

CM Mielles ✆96418760
500 m NE on coast.
15 May-15 Sep
2HEC S ◑ H ⊖ + lau PS
Prices A10 V4 5 5

ST-COULOMB
Ille-et-Vilaine
Chevrets La Guimorais ✆99890190
On Lupin Bay near Chevrets beach.
3km NW.
Apr-Sep
10HEC S ○ H ⊖ G H S + lau

ST-ELOI
See **LOUARGAT**

STE-MARIE-DU-MONT
Manche
Utah Beach ✆33715369
6km NE via D913 and D421, 150m from the beach
15 Apr-Sep
3.2HEC S ○ H ⊖ G R H lau S
Prices A10 pitch18

STE-MARINE
Finistère
Hellès ✆98563146
400m from the beach
Jun-Sep
3HEC ◑ H ⊖ G H + lau R RS
Prices A10 pitch11

ST-ÉVARZEC
Finistère
Keromen ✆98562063
Children's playground and fishing facilities on site.
Jul-Aug
2HEC ◑ H ⊖ G R P + lau ☞ ✕ S
Prices A8 pitch8

ST-FIACRE
See **CROZON**

ST-GERMAIN-SUR-AY
Manche
Aux Grands Espaces ✆33071014
On slightly sloping ground among dunes. Children's play area. Lunchtime siesta 12.30-14.30 hrs. 500m from sea.
Leave D650 W of town and follow signs 'Plage' on D306.
May-15 Sep
11HEC ◑ H ⊖ G H PS P + lau ☞ ✕
Prices A13 pitch17

ST-GILDAS-DE-RHUYS
Morbihan
Menhir ✆97452288
3.5km N.
15 May-20 Sep
3HEC ◑ H ⊖ G PS P + lau ☞ ✕
Prices A15 pitch34

ST-GUÉNOLÉ
Finistère
International de la Joie r de la Joie ✆98586324
Apr-Oct
4HEC ◑ H ✕ ⊖ G H P + lau ☞ R S
Prices A11 pitch12

ST-LÉGER-DU-BOURG-DENIS
Seine-Maritime
Aubette 23 r D-Buisson ✆35084769
All year
0.9HEC ◑ H ⊖ P + lau ☞ ✕
Prices A8 pitch9

ST-LUNAIRE
Ille-et-Vilaine
Longchamp rte de St-Briac ✆99463398
Turn off D786 towards St-Briac at end of village, site is on left. 100m from the sea.
15 May-15 Sep
5HEC ○ H ✕ ⊖ G P + lau ☞ S
Prices A16 V8 12 A12

Touesse ✆99466113
2km E via D786, 400m from the beach
Apr-10 Oct
2.2HEC ◑ H ✕ ⊖ G R H P + lau ☞ PS
Prices A15-16 pitch17

ST-MALO
Ille-et-Vilaine
At **ST-SERVAN-SUR-MER** (3km S)
Cité d'Aleth ✆99816091
On peninsula near N137.
All year
8HEC ◑ H ⊖ G R S P + lau ☞ ✕ P
Prices —

ST-MARCAN
Ille-et-Vilaine
Balcon de la Baie ✆99802295
10km NW of Pontorson on D797.
15 Jun-15 Sep
3.8HEC ◑ H ⊖ G H P + lau ☞ ✕
Prices A9 V4 6 A6

ST-MICHEL-DES-LOUPS
See **JULLOUVILLE**

ST-MICHEL-EN-GRÈVE
Côtes-du-Nord
Capucines ✆96357228
On D786 Lannion-Morlaix road.
1 Jun-5 Sep
4HEC ◑ H ✕ ⊖ G H P P + lau
Prices A17-19 pitch23-40

ST-PAIR-SUR-MER
Manche
♖ **Château de Lez-Eaux** ✆33516609
Situated in grounds of an old Château. Bank, TV and reading room. Fishing available.
Camping Carnet compulsory.
7km SE via D973 rte d'Avranches.
Apr-20 Sep
5HEC ◑ H ✕ ⊖ G R LP P + lau

Ecutot ✆33502629
Situated in an orchard 1km from the sea.
Apr-Sep
4HEC ● H ✕ ⊖ H PS P + lau ☞

Mariénée ✆33500571
2km from sea; situated in grounds of old farm.
2km S of town on D21.
Etr-Sep
1.2HEC ◑ H ⊖ P + lau ☞ ✕ G R PS
Prices A9 pitch7

ST-PHILIBERT-SUR-MER
Morbihan
Vieux Logis ✆97550117
Beautiful, well-kept site divided by hedges.
2km W.
Etr-Sep
1.5HEC ◑ H ⊖ G H P + lau ☞ ✕ S
Prices A14 V6 16 A16

ST-PIERRE-QUIBERON
Morbihan
Park-er-Lann ✆97502493
1.5km S on D768.
May-15 Sep
2HEC ◑ H ⊖ G H P + lau ☞ ✕ S
Prices A15 pitch17

ST-QUAY-PORTRIEUX
Côtes-du-Nord
Bellevue 68 bd du Littoral ✆96704184
Site adjacent to the sea.
800m from town centre.
May-15 Sep
3HEC ◑ H ⊖ G P + lau ☞ ✕ S
Prices A12 V6 10 A10

ST-SERVAN-SUR-MER
See **ST-MALO**

ST-THURIAL
Ille-et-Vilaine
Ker-Landes ✆99613995
The site is situated in the middle of pine trees near an old market town.
200m W next to the lake.
All year
2HEC ◑ H ⊖ G H P + lau ☞ ✕ P
Prices A11 V4 9 A9

ST-YVI
Finistère
CM Bois de Pleuven ✆98947047
4km from town on N165.
Etr-Sep
12HEC ◑ H ⊖ G P P + lau ☞ S

SARZEAU
Morbihan
Kersial ✆97417559
3km SW.
May-Sep
17.5HEC ● H ✕ ⊖ G H P lau ☞ S
Prices pitch50 (incl 2 persons)

Treste rte de la Plage du Roaliguen ✆97417960
2.5km S
Jun-25 Sep
2.5HEC ◑ H ⊖ G H S P + lau ☞ ✕
Prices A14 pitch25

At **PENVINS** (7km SE D198)
Madone ✆97673330
Situated 400m from the sea. Extensive sites on edge of village near old country estate. Divided into several sections.
15 May-15 Sep
8HEC S ◑ H ✕ ⊖ G H S P lau

At **POINTE-ST-JACQUES** (5.5km S)
CM St-Jacques ✆97417929
On beach protected by dunes. Well kept site with asphalt drives.
Apr-Sept

9HEC ◑ H ⊖ + lau
✕ S
Prices A10 pitch10

SASSETOT-LE-MAUCONDUIT
Seine-Maritime
Trois Plages ✆35274011
1.3km S near D925
Etr-Sep
4HEC ◑ H ⊖ G R +
lau ✕
Prices A13 pitch17

TADEN
See **DINAN**

TELGRUC-SUR-MER
Finistère
Panoramic rte de Trez Bellec-Plage
✆98277841
Quiet terraced site with numbered pitches. Slipway for boats.
W on D887 and then S on D208.
15 May-15 Sep
4HEC ◑ H ✕ ⊖ G R
H P + lau S

THEIX
Morbihan
Rhuys Atlantheix le Porteau Rouge
✆97541477
3.5km NW via N165
15 Mar-15 Nov
4HEC ◑ H ⊖ H + lau
✕ R
Prices A13 pitch20

THURY-HARCOURT
Calvados
CM Bord de l'Orne r du Val-d'Orne
✆31797078
1km W on D6 and D166 near river.
Etr-15 Oct
5.5HEC ◑ H ⊖ G R +
lau ✕

Vallée du Traspy ✆31796180
Level meadow site near a small reservoir.
Etr-15 Oct
1.3HEC ◑ H ⊖ G + lau
✕ R

TINTÉNIAC
Ille-et-Vilaine
Peupliers ✆99454975
2km SE via N137
All year
4HEC ● H ⊖ G R
P + lau

TOUQUES
See **DEAUVILLE**

TRÉBEURDEN
Côtes-du-Nord
Armor-Loisirs ✆96235231
Modern site with individual pitches surrounded by hedges. Hardstandings for caravans.
500m S of the Kernévez road.
21 May-15 Sep
2.2HEC ◑ H ✕ ⊖ G R
H lau S
Prices A16 V9 13 11

TREGUNC
Finistère
Pendruc ✆98976628
On level grassland subdivided by hedging. Separate section for young campers.
Access via D783 at Pont-Minaouët S in direction of Plage de Penduc.
May-Sep
3.6HEC ◑ H ⊖ G H +
lau ✕ S
Prices A17 V7 17

TRÉPORT, LE
Seine-Maritime
CM les Boucaniers av des Canadiens
✆35863547
Well-kept site on flat meadow on E edge of village. Sports and games nearby.
Etr-Sep
6HEC ○ H ⊖ + lau
✕ PRS
Prices A10 V10 10 10

Parc International du Golf rte de Dieppe ✆35863380
1km W on D940.
Apr-Sep
5HEC ◑ H ✕ ⊖ G
+ lau PS
Prices pitch37-50 (incl 2 persons)

At **MESNIL-VAL**
Parc Val d'Albion 1 r de la Mer
✆35867851
Apr-Sep
3HEC ○ H ⊖ G + lau
✕ PS
Prices pitch40 (incl 3 persons)

TRÉVOU-TRÉGUIGNEC
Côtes-du-Nord
Mât 38 r de Trestel ✆96237152
15 Jun-15 Sep
1.0HEC ◑ H ○ G + lau
S
Prices A12 pitch19

TRINITÉ, LA
See **PLOUHA**

TRINITÉ-SUR-MER, LA
Morbihan
Baie Plage de Kervilen ✆97557342
Several strips of land divided by tall trees.
Signposted in the direction of Kerbihan.
12 May-16 Sep
2.2HEC ◑ H ⊖ G H
PS + lau ✕
Prices A10-20 pitch63-68

Kervilor ✆97557675
Camping Carnet Compulsory.
1.6km N
20 May-15 Sep
4.5HEC ◑ H ⊖ G H
P + lau ✕ S
Prices A612-16 pitch26-34

Plage Plage de Kervilen ✆97557328
Divided into pitches and lying behind sand dunes which shield from the wind.
1km S.
23 May-15 Sep
3HEC ◑ H ⊖ G H P
+ lau ✕ S
Prices A20-25 pitch42-59

VALMONT
Seine-Maritime
Parc de Loisirs de Valmont
✆35274011
Apr-Oct
4HEC ◑ H ⊖ G R P +
lau ✕
Prices A16 21

VILLEDIEU-LES-POÊLES
Manche
CM Pré de la Rose r des Costils
✆33610244
In the centre of the village, beside the River Seine
Etr-Sep
2HEC ◑ H ✕ ⊖ G +
lau S

VILLERS-SUR-MER
Calvados
Ammonites ✆31870606
4km SW on rte de Cabourg and D163 towards Auberville.
May-15 Sep
3HEC ◑ H ✕ ⊖ G P
+ lau S
Prices pitch76 (incl 2 persons)

VILLERVILLE
Calvados
Bruyère ✆31982439
All year
3HEC ◑ H ✕ ⊖ G R
H lau S

PARIS/NORTH

The chalk cliffs and sands of the northern coast give way to the two beautiful regions of Picardy and Nord-Pas-de-Calais. Here quiet country roads meander through green wooded valleys and rolling farmland. The area has a wealth of neolithic sites, cathedrals, castles, abbeys, mansions and museums. Lille is an important centre for northern France, with its commercial and industrial interests, and has a bustling cosmopolitan centre. Amiens is the ancient capital of Picardy, and its remarkable 12th-century Cathedral of Nôtre Dame is one of the finest in France.
The Îsle de France, known as the garden of Paris, is a delightful region of famous palaces, parklands, forests and attractive little towns. Visit Fontainbleau, the town of kings and emperors, with its famous palace, and the dazzling palace and grounds at Versailles.
Paris has a wealth of things to do and see – rivalling any other city in the world. Visitors can choose from the traditional rich treasures of the Louvre or the ultra modern exhibits and setting of the Pompidou Centre, immerse themselves in Parisian life along the banks of the Seine or view it from the giddy heights of Monsieur Eiffel's famous tower, discover the wonderful wide spaces of the Trocadero, the Champ de Mars and the Champs Elysées or the buzzing streets of the city's famous districts – Montmartre and Marais. And night life , too, is for all tastes, with everything from the sophisticated entertainment of the Lido, to a small quiet restaurant on the Left Bank.

ABBEVILLE
Somme
At **PORT-LE-GRAND** (5km NW)
Airotels Château des Tilleuls ✆22240775
On gently sloping meadow surrounding a farm.
1 km SE on D940A.
Mar-Oct
20HEC ⏦ ◑ ⋔H ⛾ ! ✕ ⊖ ◘ G ⌂ H ≋P ▣ + lau
Prices A17 pitch19

ARDRES
Pas-de-Calais
At **AUTINGUES** (2km S)
St-Louis 197 r Leulène ✆21354683
Turn off N43 approx 1km SE of Ardres onto D227 and follow signs.
Apr-1 Oct
1.3HEC ⏦ ◑ ⋔H ⛾ ⊖ ◘ H ▣ + lau ☞ ! ✕ ≋L
Prices A12 pitch13

AUTINGUES
See **ARDRES**

BEAURAINVILLE
Pas-de-Calais
CM de la Source ✆21814071
Camping Carnet Compulsory.
1.5km SE via D130
All year
2.5HEC ⏦ ◑ ⋔H ⊖ ◘ ⌂ H ≋R ▣ + lau ☞ ⛾ ! ✕
Prices A13 ⛟11-13 ▲11-13

BEAUVAIS
Oise
CM chemin de Carmard ✆44020022
S off r Binet.
15 Jun-15 Sep
2HEC ⏦ ○ ⋔H ⛾ ! ✕ ⊖ ◘ ≋P ▣ + lau

BERNY-RIVIÈRE
Aisne
Croix du Vieux Pont ✆23555002
North of N31; cross River Aisne, site is500m E of Vic-sur-Aisne on D91.
All year
15HEC ⏦ ◑ ⋔H ! ✕ ⊖ ◘ ⌂ H ⚠ ≋LPR ▣ + lau ☞ ⛾
Prices pitch85-95 (incl 2 persons)

BERTANGLES
Somme
Château ✆22933773
Site in old orchard of Château.
Signed off Amiens-Doullens road.
May-Aug
0.7HEC ⏦ ◑ ⋔H ⊖ ◘ G ▣ lau ☞ ⛾ !

BEZINGHEM
Pas-de-Calais
Aulnes ✆21909388
1km S via D127E
Mar-Oct
4HEC ⏦ ● ⋔H ! ✕ ⊖ ◘ G ⌂ H ≋LR ▣ + ☞ ⛾

BRAY-DUNES
Nord
Perroquet-Plage ✆28583737
3km NE towards La Parine
Apr-Sep
28HEC ⏦ *S* ◑ ⋔H ⛾ ! ✕ ⊖ ◘ G R ⌂ H ≋S ▣ + lau
Prices A21 V8 ⛟9 ▲8

BRUNÉMONT
Nord
Parc de Plein Air de la Sensée ✆27809128
S on D247.
Apr-Oct
6HEC ⏦ ◑ ⋔H ⊖ ◘ ≋L ▣ + lau ☞ ⛾ ! ✕ G R
Prices A11 pitch11

CALAIS
Pas-de-Calais
Peupliers 394 r du Beau Marais ✆21340356
Apr-Oct
1.5HEC ⏦ ◑ ⋔H ! ✕ ⊖ ◘ H ▣ + lau ☞ ⛾ ≋P
Prices pitch57

CAMIERS
Pas-de-Calais
At **STE-CÉCILE-PLAGE** (3km NW)
Mer ✆21849225
Etr-Oct
1HEC *S* ○ ⋔H ⛾ ! ✕ ⊖ ◘ G R ≋S ▣ + lau
At **ST-GABRIEL-PLAGE** (2.5km W)
Dunes ✆21849177
Isolated site. Very bushy. Next to beach.
Etr-Sep
4HEC *S* ○ ⋔H ⛾ ! ✕ ⊖ G ≋S ▣ + lau

CAYEUX-SUR-MER
Somme
Voyeul rte d'Eu ✆22266084
1.5km S on D140.
All year
1.4HEC ⏦ ◑ ⋔H ⛾ ! ⊖ ◘ G R ▣ + lau ☞ ✕ ≋S
Prices A7 ⛟9 ▲8

CHAMPIGNY-SUR-MARNE
See **PARIS**

CHOISY-LE-ROI
See **PARIS**

CLAIRMARAIS
See **ST-OMER**

DESVRES
Pas-de-Calais
CM ✆21917477
In a sports ground near the forest.
Etr-Oct
1HEC ⏦ ⋔H ⛾ ! ✕ ⊖ ◘ ≋P ▣ + lau

DUNKERQUE (DUNKIRK)
Nord
CM bd de l'Europe ✆28692668
Mar-Nov

10HEC S ◑ ⋔H ⛟ ▼ ✕ ⊖ ⊕ [G] PS P + lau
Prices A9 V4 ⊕8 Å4

ÉPERLECQUES
Pas-de-Calais
Château de Gandspette ✆21934393
11.5km NW on N43 and D207.
Apr-1 Oct
8HEC ∿ ◑ ⋔H ▼ ✕ ⊖ ⊕ [G] P
P + lau ☞ ⛟
Prices pitch55 (incl 2 persons)

FERTÉ-GAUCHER, LA
Seine-et-Marne
Joël Teinturier rte de St-Martin-des-Camps ✆64202040
E via D14
All year
4HEC ∿ ○ ◑ ⋔H ⊖ ⊕ P + lau ☞
⛟ ▼ ✕ [G] P
Prices A11 pitch11

FRÉTHUN
Pas-de-Calais
Village 115 r Parenty ✆21852542
Camping Carnet Compulsory.
1km from village centre via D243.
Apr-Oct

3HEC ∿ ● ⋔H ⊖ ⊕ P + lau ☞ ⛟
▼ ✕ [G] [R]
Prices pitch47 (incl 2 persons)

FRÉVENT
Pas-de-Calais
CM ✆21037879
SE via D339 towards Arras
Apr-Oct
4.5HEC ∿ ◑ ⋔H ⊖ ⊕ R P + lau
☞ P
Prices A12 pitch10

GREZ-SUR-LOING
Seine-et-Marne
CM Près ✆64457275
NE towards Loing
Apr-Dec
6HEC ∿ ● ⋔H ⛟ ⊖ ⊕ [G] [R] R
P + lau
Prices A12 V6 ⊕11 Å6

GUINES
Pas-de-Calais
♖ **Bien Assise** ✆21352077
A nice site in the country near to a large forest and a charming little town.
May-25 Sep
6HEC ∿ ◑ ⋔H ⛟ ▼ ✕ ⊖ ⊕ [G] ⌂
[H] P P + lau
Prices A18 pitch30

GUISE
Aisne
Vallée de l'Oise r du Camping ✆23611486
1km SE on D960.
Apr-Oct
4HEC ∿ ◑ ⋔H ⛟ ▼ ⊖ ⊕ [G] ⌂ [H]
R P + lau ☞ ✕

HONDSCHOOTE
Nord
Beverhouck ✆28683398
Apr-Sep
1HEC ∿ ● ⋔H ⊖ ⊕ [G] P +
Prices A8 V8 ⊕8 Å8

LAON
Aisne
CM r J-P-Timbaud 22 ✆23232907
Apr-Oct
1.3HEC ∿ ◑ ⋔H ⊖ ⊕ P + lau ☞
⛟ ▼ ✕ [G] [R]
Prices A8 V5 ⊕5 Å5

LICQUES
Pas-de-Calais
Canchy r de Canchy ✆21826341
All year
1HEC ∿ ◑ ⋔H ⛟ ▼ ⊖ ⊕ [G] [H]
R P + lau ☞ ✕
Prices A11 pitch11

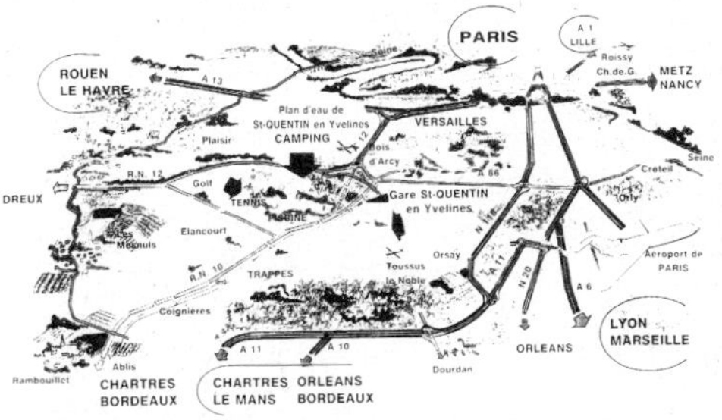

MAMETZ
Pas-de-Calais
Château de Mametz ✆21390631
All year
11HEC ◑ H ⊖ G R + lau LR

MELUN
Seine-et-Marne
Belle Étoile ✆64394812
Pleasant grassy site with two central blocks.
At La Rochette, on left bank of River Seine 1km from the town.
Mar-15 Dec
3.5HEC ◑ H ⊖ G R + lau PR
Prices A14 pitch15

MONCHAUX-LES-QUEND
See **QUEND-PLAGE-LES-PINS**

MONNERVILLE
Essonne
Bois de la Justice ✆64950534
Camping Carnet Compulsory.
Mar-Nov
5.6HEC ◑ H ⊖ G R P + lau
Prices A25 V13 25 13

MONTIGNY-LE-BRETONNEUX
Yvelines
Parc É'tang ✆30585620
All year
12HEC ○ H

See advertisement on page 153

MONTREUIL-SUR-MER
Pas-de-Calais
CM ✆21060728
N of town on N1.
All year
2HEC ● H ⊖ R + lau

NEMOURS
Seine-et-Marne
ACCCF rte nationale 7 ✆64281062
On well-kept meadow. Clean sanitary installations.
200m from N7.
Mar-Oct
4HEC ○ H ⊖ G R R + lau
Prices A11 pitch11

NESLES-LA-VALLÉE
Val-d'Oise
Parc de Séjour de l'Étang ✆34706289
Level site near a small lake.
Take D64 to outskirts of town and continue for 300m.
Apr-Oct
6HEC ◑ H ⊖ + lau G P
Prices A17 pitch17

NEUVILLE, LA
Nord
Leu Pindu ✆20865087
N on D8.
All year
1HEC ● H ⊖ R H + lau

NIELLES-LÈS-BLÉQUIN
Pas-de-Calais
Peupliers ✆21396806
2.5km NE via D202, rte d'Affringues.
Apr-30 Oct
1.5HEC ◑ H ⊖ G + lau PS

NOYELLES-SUR-MER
Somme
Aux Haies de Nolette ✆22232408
1.5km NE via D111
Apr-Oct
7HEC ◑ H ⊖ H + lau R
Prices A17 pitch17

ORVILLERS-SOREL
Oise
Château de Sorel ✆44850274
Divided into pitches. Local tradesmen supply provisions.
Leave route A1 at N17, turn right and continue 400m.
Feb-15 Dec
3HEC ◑ H ⊖ G R H + lau
Prices pitch41 (incl 2 persons)

PARIS
Seine
At **CHAMPIGNY-SUR-MARNE** (12km SE)
Tremblay bd des Allies ✆43974397
Site normally full during peak season. Good transportation into city. Reserved mainly for International Camping Carnet holders. Sanitary installations often overcrowded in morning and evening.
Take N4 and turn left 350m after Joinville bridge.
All year
8HEC ◑ H ⊖ G + lau P

At **CHOISY-LE-ROI** (14km SE)
Paris Sud 125 av de V-St-Georges ✆48909230
Signposted.
Feb-Nov
7.5HEC ◑ H ⊖ G + lau P
Prices A14-15 V6 15 14

POIX-DE-PICARDIE
Somme
Bois des Pêcheurs ✆22901171
W via D919 towards Forges-les-Eaux
Apr-Sep
1.6HEC ◑ H ⊖ G R H + lau P
Prices pitch45 (incl 2 persons)

PORT-LE-GRAND
See **ABBEVILLE**

POTELLE
Nord
Pré Vert ✆27442665
Apr-Sep
2HEC ◑ H ⊖ + lau LR
Prices A10 pitch20

QUEND-PLAGE-LES-PINS
Somme
At **MONCHAUX-LES-QUEND** (3.5km E via D102E)
Roses ✆22277617
Well-kept site with trees and hedges surrounding individual pitches. Only recommended site in area.
Turn off D940 at Quend, site 500m on left of D102.
Mar-Oct
5HEC ● H ⊖ + lau G

RUE
Somme
Garenne de Moncourt ✆22250693
On D85 towards Montreuil-sur-Mer.
All year
3HEC ◑ H ⊖ G H P + lau
Prices A10 pitch10

ST-AMAND-LES-EAUX
Nord
Mont des Bruyères ✆27485687
3.5km SE in the forest of St-Amand
Mar-Nov
4.5HEC S ◑ H ⊖ R + lau P
Prices pitch40 (incl 2 persons)

STE-CÉCILE-PLAGE
See **CAMIERS**

ST-GABRIEL-PLAGE
See **CAMIERS**

ST-GEORGES
Pas-de-Calais
Route Fleurie ✆21419068
Apr-1 Oct
1HEC ◑ H ⊖ R H P + lau

ST-LEU D'ESSERENT
Oise
Campix Chemin vicinal de Thiverny
Due to open spring 1991
8HEC S ◑ H ⊖ G L

ST-OMER
Pas-de-Calais
At **CLAIRMARAIS** (4.5km NE by D928 and D209) ➔

Paris Sud

CAMPING CARAVANNING ★★★ NN
14 KM FROM PARIS
165 pitches on 7,5 ha, bordering a park.
— self service — bar — discotheque — TV — polyvalent room — hot water — phone — electricity etc....
Summer: food supply — meals to take away — snacks.
Access: Direct and frequent communications to PARIS by RER, line "C", crossing the capital on the left bank of the Seine. Stations: Gare d'Austerlitz, St Michel (Notre Dame), Gare d'Orsay (Concorde), Invalides, Tour Eiffel.
INFORMATION: Paris – Sud Camping Caravanning
125 Av, de Villeneuve, St. Georges,
F-94600 CHOISY LE ROI – *Tel (1) 48.90.92.30*
Telex: 260448F

MUNICIPAL CAMPSITE
SECURITY - QUALITY

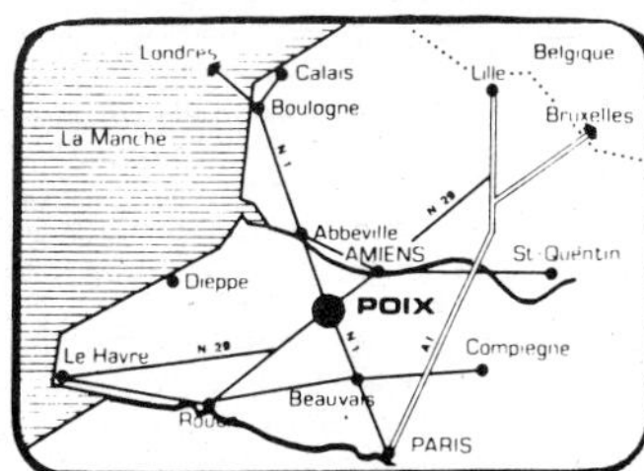

80290 POIX DE PICARDIE
Camping - Caravanning ***

BOIS DE PECHEURS

Quiet situation on the river border.
Sanitary installations of high quality.
All shops and tennis nearby.

Access: Route de Forges-les-Eaux.
D 919

Phone: 22.90.11.71

CAMPING DU MONT DES BRUYERES

Peaceful woodland site situated in a regional natural park.
Dogs admitted.
Reservations possible.

Tel. 27.48.56.87
806, rue Basly St. AMAND LES EAUX

CAMPIX Opening Spring 1991

45 km North of Paris, 4 km from the famous *Château* and forests of CHANTILLY and 15 km from the Asterix Theme Park.
500 metres from excellent swimming facilities, 300 metres from the centre of the historic merchants' borough of SAINT LEU D'ESSERENT (where the train takes you in one hour to Paris).
200 pitches of 3 stars standard in a very special natural and relaxing setting. Reception, clubhouse and a warm welcome in the centrally situated cafeteria.
CAMPIX Chemin vicinal de Thiverny 60340
ST. LEU D'ESSERENT
Off season address: BP 37,60340 St. Leu d'Esserent

Clairmarais ✆21383480
Grassy, rather tough site. Ideal for overnight stays.
Apr-Oct
3HEC ⁓ ◑ ⋔H ⊖ ⊕ [G] [P]

ST-VALÉRY-SUR-SOMME
Somme
♖ **Domaine du Château de Drancourt** ✆22269345
3.5km S via D48
Apr-Sep
5HEC ⁓ ◑ ⋔H ⊕ ▼ ✕ ⊖ ⊕ [G] [R] ⌂ [H] ⛺ ⩦P [P] + lau

SAMOIS-SUR-SEINE
Seine-et-Marne
Petit Barbeau Base de Plein Air ✆64246345
All year
3HEC ◑ ⋔H ⊖ ⊕ [P] + lau ☞ ⊕ ▼ ✕ ⩦LRS

SERQUES
Pas-de-Calais
Frémont rte Nationale 43 ✆21930115
1.5km SW on N43
Apr-Oct
2HEC ⁓ ◑ ⋔H ▼ ⊖ ⊕ [H] [P] + lau
Prices A8 V7 ⊕7

THIEMBRONNE
Pas-de-Calais
Pommiers ✆21395019
NW on D132.
15 Mar-15 Oct
1.8HEC ⁓ ◑ ⋔H ⊖ ⊕ [G] [H] P + lau ☞ ⊕ ▼ ✕
Prices A8 V5 ⊕8

TOLLENT
Pas-de-Calais
Val d'Authie ✆21477427
SE via D119
Apr-Sep
3.3HEC ⁓ ◑ ⋔H ⊕ ▼ ⊖ ⊕ [H] ⩦PR [P] + lau
Prices A10 pitch13

TORCY
Seine-et-Marne
Parc de la Colline rte de Lagny ✆60054232
An ideal base for visiting Paris (30 minutes from the centre by Metro). Separate car park for arrivals after 22.00 hrs.
Access via exit 9 on the A104 and D10E.
All year
8HEC ⁓ ◑ ⋔H ⊖ ⊕ [G] [H] ⛺ [P] + lau ☞ ⊕ ▼ ✕ ⩦LPR
Prices A17 pitch40

VARREDDES
Seine-et-Marne
Ile du Bac rte de Congis ✆64348080
Near the L'Oureq Canal.
Pass through Varreddes and take D121 Congis road for 1km.
All year
6.5HEC ⁓ ◑ ⋔H ⊕ ⊖ ⊕ [P] + lau ☞ ▼ ✕ ⩦P

VILLENNES-SUR-SEINE
Yvelines
Club des Renardières ✆39758897
Site for caravans only, in beautiful hilly park laid out with hedges, lawns and flower beds. Fully divided into completely separated pitches.
Camping Carnet compulsory.
Follow D113 to Maison Blanche turn right and continue 3km.
All year
6HEC ⁓ ● ⋔H ⊖ ⊕ + lau ☞ ⊕ ▼ ✕ ⩦LPR
Prices A13 pitch62

VILLERS-HÉLON
Aisne
Castel des Biches ✆23960499
Attractive site in grounds of old castle.
Camping Carnet Compulsory.
Turn off the N2 onto the D2 between Soissons and Villers-Cotterêts and continue for 7km via Longport.
All year
7HEC ⁓ ● ⋔H ▼ ✕ ⊖ ⊕ [H] [P] + lau ☞ ⊕
Prices pitch49-62 (incl 2 persons)

AUVERGNE

The mountainous Massif Central characterises the Auvergne, giving an atmosphere of grandeur and tranquility to this ancient land. The rivers Dordogne and Allier begin in the region; on the banks of the Allier is the bustling town of Langeac – especially lively on market days. The rivers offer good fishing and recreational opportunities, many of these have been dammed, creating great placid lakes providing wonderful centres for watersports. A unique highlight of the area is the remarkable Parc de Volcans, where 80 extinct volcanos form a majestic line stretching some 20 miles.
South west of the Auvergne, the département of Aveyron is a little-known district with a turbulent past, and ancient abbeys, medieval citadels and fortified towns. Cordes and Villefranche-de-Rourgue are perfect 15th-century garrison towns, and Najac stands in a superb position on its 1,200ft rock. East from Aveyron is Lozère, an arid, rugged landscape. The highlight here is the well-known Gorges du Tarn, where the Tarn slices its way through the land for more than 50 miles, and twisting, narrow roads offer an unforgettable succession of spectacular views.

AGUESSAC
Aveyron
CM ✆65598467
A large level site beside the River Tarn.
Jun-15 Sep
3HEC ⁓ ◑ ⋔H ⊖ ⊕ ⩦R [P] + lau ☞ ⊕ ▼ ✕ [G] [R]
Prices A10 pitch16

ANGLARDS-DE-SALERS
Cantal
CM Fraux ✆71400002
Jul-Aug
0.7HEC ⁓ ● ⋔H ⊖ ⊕ [P] + lau ☞ ⊕ ▼ ✕

ARBRESLE, L'
Rhône
CM ✆74011150
On N7.
Etr-Oct
1.6HEC ⁓ ○ ◑ ⋔H ⊖ ⊕ ⩦P [P] + lau ☞ ⊕ ▼ ✕ [G] [R]
Prices A6 V4 ⊕9

ARNAC
Cantal
CM d'Arnac ✆71629190
On Lake Enchanet.
All year
3HEC ⁓ ◑ ⋔H ⊕ ▼ ✕ ⊖ ⊕ [G] ⌂ [H] ⩦LP + lau
Prices pitch40 (incl 2 persons)

ARPAJON-SUR-CÈRE
Cantal
Sapinière Cros de Ronesque ✆71624844
S via D459.
Jun-1 Oct
0.5HEC ⁓ S ◑ ⋔H ⊕ ▼ ✕ ⊖ ⊕ [R] [P] + lau

BELLERIVE
See **VICHY**

BOURBON-L'ARCHAMBAULT
Allier
CM Parc Bignon ✆70670883
1km SW on N153, rte de Montluçon, turn right.

Mar-Dec
3HEC lau

BRIVES-CHARENSAC
See **PUY, LE**

CANET-DE-SALARS
Aveyron
Caussanel ✆65468519
N of Lac de Pareloup.
Apr-Oct
10HEC LP lau
Prices pitch70-80 (incl 3 persons)

CAPDENAC-GARE
Aveyron
CM bd P-Ramadier ✆65808887
Jun-Sep
1HEC R lau P
Prices A9 V5 12 5

Diège Vallée de la Diège, Sonnac ✆65646125
Level, sub-divided terrain near a 200-year-old farm in a narrow valley of La Diège river, 5km from the prehistoric grottoes of Foissac.
From Figeac on N594 travel in the direction of Capdenac-Gare. Turn sharp right after the bridge and continue on D558 for about 5km in the direction of Naussac.
Apr-Oct
7HEC G H R lau
Prices A13 V5 13 13

CEYRAT
Puy-de-Dôme
CM av J-B-Marrou ✆73613073
On undulating meadow on partly terraced hill. Large common room with games. Supplies only available peak season.
All year
6HEC lau G
Prices A7-10 V5 3-7 3-7

CHÂTELGUYON
Puy-de-Dôme
Clos de Balanède r de la Piscine ✆73860143
15 Apr-14 Oct
4HEC G H P lau R
Prices A15 pitch19

CONDRIEU
Rhône
Belle Rive ✆74595108
Bordering the Rhône.
Apr-Sep
5HEC G LP lau
Prices A9 V8 12 12

CONQUES
Aveyron
Beau Rivage ✆65698223
On D601n.
Apr-Sep
1HEC G R lau
Prices pitch40 (incl 2 persons)

COURNON-D'AUVERGNE
Puy-de-Dôme
C M Plage ✆73848130
Camping Carnet Compulsory.
1.5km E towards Billom
All year
17HEC G R LR lau P
Prices A10 V6 8 8

DALLET
Puy-de-Dôme
Ombrages rte de Pont-du-Château ✆73831097
Beside River Allier.
May-Sep
2.5HEC G R H R lau
Prices A13 V5 12 12

DARDILLY
Rhône
Porte de Lyon ✆78356455
Generously arranged and equipped site divided into pitches. Ideal for overnight stays near motorway.
9km N of Lyon La Garde exit off A6.
All year
6.5HEC R H P lau
Prices A7 pitch31-74

EBREUIL
Allier
Filature rte de Chouvigny ✆70907201
Beside River Sioule.
Etr-Oct
3.5HEC H R lau G
Prices pitch48 (incl 2 persons)

FLEURIE
Rhône
CM la Grappe Fleurie ✆74698007
0.6km SE on D119 E.
20 Mar-15 Oct
1.6HEC lau R LPR
Prices A13 pitch14-23

GOUDET
Haute-Loire
Bord de l'Eau ✆71571682
W via D49, beside the River Loire
Etr-Sep
5HEC S G R H PR lau
Prices A17 pitch13

LANGEAC
Haute-Loire
CM le Prado ✆71770501
15 Apr-Oct
12HEC S PR lau G R +
Prices pitch31 (incl 2 persons)

MALÈNE, LA
Lozère
CM la Malène ✆66485286
Etr-Sep
1.5HEC H R + lau G R
Prices pitch34 (incl 2 persons)

MASSIAC
Cantal
CM Allagnon av de Courcelles ✆71230393
0.8km W on N122.
May-Sep
2.5HEC ● H ⊖ R lau P
Prices A8 V6 8 8

MAURS
Cantal
At **ST-CONSTANT** (4.5km SE via N663)
Moulin de Chaules rte de Calvinet ✆71491102
Camping Carnet Compulsory.
3km E via D28
Etr-20 Oct
2HEC ◑ H ⊖ G H PR +
Prices pitch47 (incl 2 persons)

MENDE
Lozère
Tivoli rte des Gorges-du-Tarn ✆66650038
All year
2HEC ● H ⊖ G PR + lau
Prices A16 V8 8 8 pitch11

MEYRUEIS
Lozère
Ayres rte de la Brèze ✆66456051
0.5km E via D57
Etr-Sep
1.5HEC ◑ H ⊖ G H P + lau R R
Prices A10-12 pitch18-25

MILLAU
Aveyron
Rivages av de l'Aigoual ✆65610107
1.7km E via D991, beside the River Dourbie
May-Sep
7HEC ◑ H ⊖ G R PR + lau
Prices pitch67-85 (incl 2 persons)

MIREMONT
Puy-de-Dôme
Confolant ✆73799276
7km NE via D19 and D19E.
May-1 Oct
2.8HEC ◑ H ⊖ G L + lau
Prices A12 pitch17

MONISTROL-SUR-LOIRE
Haute-Loire
CM Beau Séjour chemin de Chaponas ✆71665390
Adjacent to N88.
Apr-Oct
1.5HEC ◑ H ⊖ + lau R P
Prices A10 V5 9 9

MURAT
Cantal
CM de Stalapos ✆71200183
On hilly meadow in valley. Children may paddle in nearby stream.
Well signposted from village.
Closed Nov & May
4HEC ◑ H ⊖ G + lau

MUR-DE-BARREZ
Aveyron
Trionnac ✆65660691
All year
2HEC S ◑ H ⊖ lau

MUROL
Puy-de-Dôme
Plage ✆73886027
Busy site beside lake. Caravan section divided into pitches, terraced area for tents. Asphalt drive. Cinema.
1.2km from centre of village. turn off into allée de Plage before entering village and follow signposts.
May-30 Sep
7HEC ● H ⊖ G L + lau
Prices A14 pitch18

Pré-Bas Lac Chambon ✆73886304 & 73268555
1 Jun-15 Sep
3HEC ◑ H ⊖ H + lau LR
Prices A13 pitch19

NANT
Aveyron
Val de Cantobre ✆65622548
Large variety of recreational facilities.
4km N of Nant, towards Millau; next to the Dourbie river, and off D591n.
20 Apr-15 Sep
6.8HEC ◑ H ⊖ G H PR + lau
Prices pitch112 (incl 2 persons)

NÉBOUZAT
Puy-de-Dôme
Domes Les Quatre rtes de Nébouzat ✆73871406
15 May-15 Sep
1HEC ● H ⊖ G H P + lau R R
Prices pitch31

NEUVÉGLISE
Cantal
Belvédère du Pont de Lanau ✆71235050
5km S on D921.
27 May-11 Sep
5HEC ◑ H ⊖ G H P + lau LR
Prices pitch90 (incl 2 persons)

OLLIERGUES
Puy-de-Dôme
Chelles ✆73955416
5km from town centre.
15 May-10 Sep
3HEC ◑ H ⊖ G + lau
Prices pitch40 (incl 2 persons)

POLLIONNAY
Rhône
Col de la Luère ✆78458111
All year
4.5HEC ○ ◑ ● H ⊖ G R H + lau

PONT-DE-SALARS
Aveyron
Lac ✆65468486
1.5km N via D523
15 Jun-15 Sep
4.8HEC ● H ⊖ G L + lau
Prices pitch59 (incl 3 persons)

Terrasses du Lac rte du Vibal ✆65468818
4km N via D523
15 Jun-15 Sep
6HEC ○ H ⊖ G R LP + lau
Prices pitch68-77 (incl 3 persons)

PRADEAUX, LES
Puy-de-Dôme
Châteaux la Grange Fort ✆73710593
Parklike area surrounding an old château on the bank of the River Allier.
Turn off D996 at Parentignet and continue S on the D34 for about 3km.
Mar-Dec
22HEC ○ ◑ H ⊖ G H P P + lau R
Prices A13-15 27-29

PUY, LE
Haute-Loire
CM Bouthezard pl de l'Hôtel-de-Ville ✆71095509
From the town centre follow sign for Clermont-Ferrand; at traffic lights by church of St-Laurent, turn right following 'camping' signpost, site is 500m on left of road.
20 Mar-15 Oct
1HEC ● H ⊖ PR
Prices pitch35-45 (incl 4 persons)

At **BRIVES-CHARENSAC** (4.5km E)
Audinet ✆71091018
E on N88.
May-Oct
3HEC ○ H ⊖ G + lau R
Prices A9 V4 6 6

Moulin de Barette ✆71030088
15 Apr-15 Nov
3HEC ○ H ⊖ G PR + lau
Prices A20 pitch15

RIVIÈRE-SUR-TARN
Aveyron
Peyrelade rte des Gorges-du-Tarn ✆65626254
2km E via D907, beside the River Tarn.
Jun-15 Sep
4HEC ◑ H ⊖ [G] [R] [H] PR + lau
Prices A15 V10 ⛟10 ⛺10

RODEZ
Aveyron
CM Layoule ✆65670952
Clean, tidy site in valley below town, completely divided into pitches.
NE of town centre. Well signposted.
All year
3HEC ◑ H ⊖ [G] [R] + lau ☞ R
Prices pitch47-59 (incl 3 persons)

RUYNES-EN-MARGERIDE
Cantal
CM Petit Bois ✆71234226
Camping Carnet Compulsory.
0.5km SW on D13, rte de Garabit. Signposted.
All year
7HEC ● H ⊖ LPR + lau ☞
Prices A8 V7 ⛟7 ⛺7

ST-AMANS-DES-COTS
Aveyron
♖ **Tours** ✆65448810
6km SE via D97/D599, beside the Lake Selves
24 May-Sep
8HEC ◑ H ⊖ [G] [R] LP + lau
Prices pitch96 (incl 3 persons)

ST-CONSTANT
See **MAURS**

ST-GENIEZ-D'OLT
Aveyron
Marmotel ✆65704220
Grassy site on River Lot.
On D19 about 2km NW of St Geniez-d'Olt.
10 Jun-10 Sep
3HEC ◑ H ⊖ [G] PR + lau ☞ L
Prices pitch76 (incl 2 persons)

ST-OURS
Puy-de-Dôme
Bel-Air ✆73887214
1km SW on D941.
Jun-Aug
2HEC ◑ H ⊖ + lau ☞ L
Prices A8 pitch6

ST-PIERRE-COLAMINE
Puy-de-Dôme
Ombrage ✆73967787
300m from D978.
15 Dec-15 Sep
2HEC ◑ H ⊖ [G] [R] [H] + lau ☞ R
Prices A9 V4 ⛟9 ⛺9

ST-RÉMY-SUR-DUROLLE
Puy-de-Dôme
CM Chanterelles ✆73943171
3km NE via D201
May-Sep
3HEC ◑ H ⊖ [G] + lau ☞ LP
Prices A8 V4 ⛟6 ⛺4

ST-SYMPHORIEN-SUR-COISE
Rhône
Intercommunale de Hurongues ✆78484429
3.5km W on Chazelles-sur-Lyon road (D2).
Apr-Oct
3.5HEC S ● H ⊖ [G] P + lau ☞ L
Prices A10 pitch12

SALLES-CURAN
Aveyron
Beau Rivage rte des Vernhes ✆65463332
3.5km N via D993n and D243.
Jun-Sep
2HEC ◑ H ⊖ [G] [R] [H] L + lau
Prices pitch80 (incl 3 persons)

THIZY
Rhône
CM ✆74640529
2km S on D504, rte de Tarare. Access difficult for caravans (gradient of 18%).
15 May-15 Sep
3.2HEC ◑ H ⊖ [G] lau ☞ LP
Prices A18 pitch15

VARENNES-SUR-ALLIER
Allier
♖ **Château de Chazeuil** ✆70450010
On well-kept meadow.
3km NW on N7.
May-Sep
1.5HEC ◑ H ⊖ P + lau ☞
Prices A18 pitch15

Plans d'Eau ✆70450155
3km NW on N7.
15 May-15 Sep
4HEC ◑ H ⊖ P + lau ☞
Prices A18 V5 ⛟8 ⛺8

VICHY
Allier
At **BELLERIVE**(3km W)

Acacias r C-Decloître ✆70323632
Well-managed site, sub-divided into numbered pitches by hedges. Clean sanitary installations. Library, billiard room. Water sports are available nearby on lake.
From Vichy turn left after bridge beside ESSO garage and follow river for 500m.
25 May-25 Oct
2HEC ● H ⊖ [G] [H] P + lau ☞ LR
Prices A15-21 V8-11 ⛟10-15 ⛺10-15

Beau Rivage r C-Decloître ✆70322685
Neat meadowland with marked out pitches. Well kept sanitary installations. TV.
Watch for turning over bridge onto left bank of River Allier.
May-Sep
1.5HEC ● H ⊖ [G] [H] LPR + lau
Prices pitch80 (incl 2 persons)

VIC-SUR-CÈRE
Cantal
CM av des Tilleuls ✆71475104
On level meadow with tarred drives. Large common room with open fireplace.
Apr-Sep
3HEC ◑ H ⊖ + lau ☞ [G] [R] P
Prices A10 V4 ⛟4 ⛺4

Pommeraie ✆71475418
2km SE.
May-15 Sep
3HEC ◑ H ⊖ [G] [R] [H] P + lau
Prices pitch75 (incl 2 persons)

VILLEFRANCHE-DE-PANAT
Aveyron
Cantarelles ✆65464035
On level grassland by Lac de Villefranche-de-Panat.
On the D25 about 3km N of Villefranche-de-Panat.
May-14 Oct
2.5HEC ◑ H ⊖ [G] [R] [H] L + lau ☞
Prices pitch45 (incl 2 persons)

VOREY
Haute-Loire
Pra de Mars ✆71034086
Apr-Sep
5HEC ◑ H ⊖ [G] R + lau ☞ P

YSSINGEAUX
Haute-Loire
CM Choumouroux ✆71590113
800m S of town off the rte de Puy.
15 Jun-15 Sep
0.8HEC ◑ H ⊖ [R] lau ☞ P
Prices A6 V3 ⛟4 ⛺4

SOUTH COAST/RIVIERA

Stretching along the Golfe du Lion between the Pyrénées and Provence for 150 miles, the Languedoc-Rousillon region's vast stretches of beautiful sands are backed by a gentle countryside covered in vineyards and dotted with quiet villages. Inland are attractive Roman and medieval towns – Montpelier, Bézier and the splendid Carcassonne. High on the crags of the Corbières are the remarkable medieval castles of the Cathares.
Although away from the sea, the Rhône Valley region is undoubtedly a Mediterranean land – unparalleled sunshine warms this unspoilt countryside of vineyards, pastel villages and cypressus in the valleys, against dramatic backdrops of the Provençal Alps and Cévennes, with tumbling rivers running through spectacular gorges.
South again towards the coast is Provence – a land of blue clear skies, wonderful wines and superb food. The area's many rivers begin in the Alpine foothills, and these flow south and irrigate the rich plains below, filled with wonderful fruit and herbs.
Popular with visitors since the 18th century, the chic coastal resorts of Nice, Cannes and St Tropez are ablaze with palatial hotels and celebrated restaurants, and, in the summer, swarming with holidaymakers – an acknowledgement of the spectacular coastline where the Alps meet the sea. But there is still a quieter hinterland, with ancient villages perched on high peaks, spectacular deep valleys and canyons, fine lakes, and breathtaking views from high corniche roads.
The principality of Monaco, which is 350 acres in extent, is an independent enclave inside France. It consists of three adjacent towns – Monaco, the capital, la Condamine, along the harbour and Monte-Carlo, along the coast immediately to the north. It is a narrow ribbon of coastline backed by the foothills of the Alps Maritime – a wonderful natural ampitheatre overlooking the sea.

AGAY
Var

Agay Soleil rte de Cannes ✆94820079
A small, sandy site beside a narrow beach. All kinds of watersports nearby.
Between N98 and the sea.
Mar-15 Nov
0.9HEC ~ ● ⋒H ⛟ ❢ ✕ ⊖ ⊕ [G] [R] ⌂ ≋S ▣ + lau
Prices pitch68-110 (incl 2 persons)

♜ **Estérel** ✆94820328
3km from Agay-Plage towards Valescure
Apr-Sep
12.5HEC ~ ◑ ⋒H ⛟ ❢ ✕ ⊖ ⊕ [G] [R] [H] ≋P ▣ + lau
Prices pitch100-105 (incl 2 persons)

Rives de l'Agay av du Gratadis ✆94820274
A level site below a country road.
Turn off N98 at Agay beach and continue for 0.5 km towards Valescure.
15 Feb-4 Nov
1.3HEC ~ ● ⋒H ⛟ ❢ ✕ ⊖ ⊕ [G] ⌂ [H] ≋RS ▣ + lau
Prices A18 pitch22

Vallée du Paradis rte du Gratadis ✆94820146
On a large meadow and a narrow strip of land between the road and the river.
800 m inland from N98.
20 Mar-15 Oct
3HEC ~ ● ⋒H ⛟ ❢ ✕ ⊖ ⊕ [G] [R] ⌂ ▣ + lau ☞ ≋LRS
Prices A20-22 V10-11 ⛟20-22 ▲20-22

AGDE
Hérault

Agde Domaine des 7 Fonts ✆67941462
A park-like site amongst mature pine trees 3 km from sea.
Turn off road between Agde and Sète by a furniture store and the ELF petrol station. Site in 400 m.
15 May-Sep
6HEC ~ ● ⋒H ⛟ ❢ ✕ ⊖ ⊕ [G] [R] ⌂ [H] ⛺ ≋PR ▣ + lau
Prices pitch60 (incl 2 persons)

International de l'Hérault rte de la Tamarissière ✆67941283
A grassy site on W bank of the River Hérault.
Take the exit for 'Agde' off autoroute A9, then continue via D13 and D32E.
Etr-Sep
10HEC ~ ● ⋒H ⛟ ❢ ✕ ⊖ ⊕ [G] [R] ⌂ [H] ≋PRS + lau
Prices pitch84 (incl 2 persons)

See advertisement in colour section

At **ROCHELONGUE-PLAGE** (4km S)

Champs Blancs ✆67942342
Apr-Sep
4HEC ~ ⊟ ● ⋒H ⛟ ❢ ⊖ ⊕ [G] [R] ⌂ [H] ≋P ▣ + lau ☞ ✕ ≋RS
Prices pitch155 (incl 4 persons)

AIGUES MORTES
Gard
Petite Camargue ✆66538477
A grassy site lying amongst vineyards on the D62.3 km from the sea.
Access via autoroute exit Gallargues in direction of La Grande Motte.
27 Apr-21 Sep
10HEC ◑ H ⊖ G R H P + lau
Prices pitch90-105 (incl 2 persons)

AIX-EN-PROVENCE
Bouches-du-Rhône
Arc en Ciel ✆42261428
A pleasant terraced site on both sides of a stream.
Near motorway exit Aix-Est on N7 towards Toulon. 3 km SE near Pont des Trois Sautets.
Mar-Nov
3HEC S ● H ⊖ G R P + lau
Prices A21 pitch20

ALBON
Drôme
♖ **Château de Senaud** ✆75031131
On an elevated meadow.
S of village between N7 and motorway.
Mar-Oct
3HEC ◑ H ⊖ G H PS + lau
Prices A18 pitch26

ALLÈGRE
Gard
♖ **Château de Boisson** Boisson ✆66248221
Camping Carnet Compulsory.
E of village on D37 towards Lussan.
May-Sep
5HEC ◑ H ⊖ G P + lau
Prices A21 pitch43

Domaine des Fumades ✆66248078
On sloping meadow near the river. Extensive leisure facilities. Liable to flooding at certain times.
Turn off D7 (Bourgot-les-Allègre) at TOTAL filling station and follow signs.
May-Sep
15HEC ◑ H ⊖ G R H P + lau
Prices pitch75-95 (incl 2 persons)

AMÉLIE-LES-BAINS-PALALDA
Pyrénées-Orientales
Gaou av Beausoleil ✆68391919
All year
2HEC ● H ⊖ G R H + lau PR

ANDUZE
Gard
Castel Rose rte de St-Jean-du-Gard ✆66618015
1 km NW on D907.
Apr-0ct
6.5HEC ◑ H ⊖ G R H R + lau

At **ATTUECH** (5km SE on D907)
Fief ✆66618171
On level meadow, divided by flowerbeds and shrubs.
Turn off D982 E of Attuech and continue for 400 m on partially rough track.
Etr & Jun-Sep
4.5HEC ◑ ● H ⊖ G H P + lau R
Prices pitch44-58 (incl 2 persons)

Pommeraie rte de Lasalle, Thoiras ✆66852052 & 66514655
May-Sep
7HEC ◑ H ⊖ G R H PR + lau
Prices A13 pitch42

At **CORBÈS** (5km NW on D907)
Cévennes Provence Mas-de-Pont ✆66617310
Near railway station.
Apr-15 Oct
➔

30HEC ~ S ◑ ⋒H ▪ ! ✕ ⊖ ▪ [G] [R] [H] ≈R ▪ + lau
Prices pitch65 (incl 2 persons)

ANTIBES
Alpes-Maritimes
Logis de la Brague 1221 rte de Nice ✆93335472
On a level meadow beside a small river.
On N7.
May-Sep
1.7HEC ~ ◑ ⋒H ▪ ! ✕ ⊖ ▪ [G] ≈R ▪ + lau ☞ ≈S
Prices pitch65 (incl 3 persons)

At **BIOT** (7km N on N7 and A8)
Airotel Parc l'Eden chemin du Val-de-Pome ✆93656370
Site on level meadowland, no tents allowed.
On D4.
15 May-15 Sep
2HEC ~ ● ⋒H ▪ ! ✕ ⊖ ▪ [G] [H] ▪ + lau ☞ ≈S
Prices pitch80 (incl 3 persons)

Prés Quartier la Romaine ✆93656106
2km SE via D4
15 May-25 Sep
11.8HEC ~ ● ⋒H ⊖ ▪ ▪ + lau ☞ ▪ ! ✕ [G] ≈S

At **BRAGUE, LA** (4km N on N7)
Frênes ✆93333652
Opposite Biot railway station.
Jun-Sep
2.5HEC ~ ● ⋒H ▪ ! ✕ ⊖ ▪ [G] ▪ [H] ▪ + lau ☞ ≈S

Pylône av du Pylône ✆93335283
All year
10HEC ~ ● ⋒H ▪ ! ✕ ⊖ ▪ [G] [R] ▪ [H] ▪ ≈P ▪ ▪ lau ☞ ≈S
Prices A25-30 V15 ▪20 Å15

ARCS, LES
Var
Eau Vive Quartier du Pont d'Argens ✆94474066
Camping Carnet Compulsory.
2km S on N7.
Mar-Oct
2.5HEC ~ ● ⋒H ▪ ! ✕ ⊖ ▪ [G] ▪ [H] ≈PR ▪ + lau
Prices A15 pitch25

ARGELÈS-PLAGE
See **ARGELÈS-SUR-MER**

ARGELÈS-SUR-MER
Pyrénées-Orientales
Clos Joli chemin de C-Magnus ✆68810514
800m E on N618.
Jun-Sep
2HEC ~ ◑ ⋒H ▪ ! ⊖ ▪ [G] ▪ [H] ▪ + lau ☞ ✕ ≈PS

Criques de Porteils rte de Collioure ✆68811273
Terraced site with beautiful view of sea.
4km S on N114 turn left through railway underpass and continue for 0.3km.
Apr-Sep
5HEC ~ ◑ ⋒H ▪ ! ✕ ⊖ ▪ [G] ≈S ▪ + lau

Dauphin rte de Taxo d'Avall ✆68811754
On a long stretch of grassland shaded by poplars, 1500m from sea.
3km N of town; at Taxo d'Avall turn right onto unclass road.
Jun-Sep
5.5HEC ~ ◑ ⋒H ▪ ! ✕ ⊖ ▪ [G] [H] ≈PS + lau ☞ ≈R
Prices pitch115 (incl 3 persons)

See advertisement on page 161

Galets rte de Taxo d'Avall ✆68810812
4km N
All year
5HEC ~ ● ⋒H ▪ ! ✕ ⊖ ▪ [R] ▪ ≈P ▪ + lau ☞ [G] ≈RS
Prices pitch51-85 (incl 2 persons)

Marsouins rte de la Plage Nord ✆68811481
2km NE
Apr-Sep
10HEC ~ ● ⋒H ▪ ! ✕ ⊖ ▪ [G] [R] ▪ [H] ▪ + lau ☞ ≈LS
Prices pitch56-75 (incl 2 persons)

Massane ✆68810685
Well laid-out site in shady garden 1km from sea.
Beside D618 near the municipal sports field.
15 Mar-15 Oct
3HEC ⊟ ● ⋒H ▪ ! ⊖ ▪ [G] [H] ≈P ▪ + lau ☞ ✕ ≈S
Prices A12 pitch39

Le Neptune Plage Nord ✆68810298
Separate car park for arrivals after 22.00 hrs.
Camping Carnet Compulsory.
Etr-Sep
3.3HEC ~ ◑ ⋒H ! ✕ ⊖ ▪ [G] [R] ▪ + lau ☞ ▪ ≈PRS
Prices pitch83 (incl 2 persons)

Ombrages ✆68812983
4000HEC ⋒H lau

See advertisement on page 161

Piscines 1 rte de Taxo d'Avall ✆68810638
Off N114, to the right of the Plage Nord/rte d'Avall road.
Jun-15 Sep
3.5HEC ⊟ ● ⋒H ▪ ! ✕ ⊖ ▪ [G] [R] [H] ≈P P + lau

Pujol rte de la Plage Nord ✆68810025
1km NE
Jun-Sep
3.3HEC ~ ● ⋒H ▪ ! ✕ ⊖ ▪ [G] [R] ▪ ≈P ▪ + lau ☞ ≈S
Prices A18 pitch28

Romarin rte de Sorède ✆68810263
2.5km SW on D2.
15 Jun-15 Sep
2HEC ~ ● ⋒H ▪ ! ✕ ⊖ ▪ [G] ▪ P + lau

CM Roussillonnais ✆68811042
On a long stretch of sandy terrain adjoining a fine sandy beach.
In N part of town. Well signposted.
mid Apr-mid Oct
10HEC ~ S ◑ ⋒H ▪ ! ✕ ⊖ ▪ [G] ▪ [H] ≈S ▪ + lau

Sardane ✆68811082
Enclosed pitches under tall trees.
3km E of N114.
Etr-Oct
7HEC ~ ◑ ⋒H ▪ ⊖ ▪ [G] [H] ▪ + lau ☞ ≈S
Prices pitch30-57 (incl 2 persons)

Sirène rte de Taxo d'Avall ✆68810461
4km NE
Etr-Sep
18HEC ⓗ G R H P + lau S

At **ARGELÈS-PLAGE** (2.5km E via D618)
Beauséjour ✆68811448
On a long stretch of grassland on the landward side of D81.
15 May-Sep
15HEC G R H S + lau

Pins av du Tech ✆68811046
On a narrow stretch of grassland with some poplar trees.
Jun-15 Sep
4.5HEC G + lau S
Prices A21 pitch28

Soleil Plage Nord ✆68811448
Peaceful site in wide meadow surrounded by tall trees. Private beach, natural harbour. Best site in region, but pitches must be booked in advance.
Follow rte du Littoral N out of town then 1.5km towards beach.
15 May-Sep
15HEC G R PS + lau
Prices A27 pitch45

ARLES-SUR-TECH
Pyrénées-Orientales
Riuferrer ✆68391106
Quiet holiday site on gently sloping ground in pleasant area. Clean sanitary installations. Separate area reserved for overnight stops. Bar, ice for iceboxes and nearby municipal swimming pool are available in summer only.
Signposted from N115.
All year
4HEC G R R + lau P
Prices A10-13 pitch12-15

Rive ✆68391554
On N115, 200m NE.
May-15 Oct
2.5HEC G R +

ARPAILLARGUES
Gard
Mas de Rey ✆66221827
Etr-25 Oct
2.5HEC G R H P lau +
Prices pitch58 (incl 2 persons)

ATTUECH
See **ANDUZE**

AUBIGNAN
Vaucluse
Intercommunal du Brégoux chemin du Vas ✆90626250
A level site with good views of Mt. Ventoux.
On southern outskirts of town turn off D7 onto D55 and continue towards Caromb for 0.5km.
15 May-Oct
4HEC + lau G R R
Prices A11 V9

AUPS
Var
International ✆94700680
0.5km W via D60 towards Fox-Amphoux
Etr-Sep
4HEC H P + G
Prices A17 pitch12

AVIGNON
Vaucluse
Bagatelle ✆90863039
Pleasant site with tall trees on the Isle of Barthelasse. All pitches are numbered; on hard standing and divided by hedges. Separate section for young people.
Travel alongside the old town wall and the Rhône onto the Rhône bridge (Nîmes road). About halfway along turn right and follow signs.
All year
4HEC G R H + lau P
Prices A11 V5 5 A5

CM Pont St-Bénézet L'Ile de la Barthelasse ✆90826350
On island opposite bridge with fine views of town. Several tiled sanitary blocks with individual wash cabins. Individual pitches. Common room with TV, souvenir shop, car wash. Several playing fields for volleyball and basketball. Definite divisions for tents and caravans.
NW of the town on the right bank of the Rhône, 370m upstream from bridge on right. (N100 leading to Nîmes).
Mar-Oct
9HEC G + lau P
Prices A13 16 A11

AXAT
Aude
Crémade ✆68205064
All year
3HEC G R + lau R

Pont d'Aliés Station des Pyrénéés ✆68205327
1km N on D117.
Apr-Oct
2HEC G R + lau
Prices A12 pitch38-48

AYGUADE-CEINTURON
See **HYÈRES**

BANDOL
Var
Vallongue ✆94294955
Terraced site, parts of which have lovely sea views.
Camping Carnet Compulsory.
Apr-Sep
1.5HEC G + lau

BARCARÈS, LE
Pyrénées-Orientales
Bousigues av des Corbières ✆68861619
Quiet site standing about 1km from the sea.
Apr-Oct
3HEC G R H P + lau S
Prices pitch49-70 (incl 2 persons)

California rte de St-Laurent ✆68861608
1.5km SW via D90
Etr-Sep
5HEC G R H P + lau RS
Prices pitch40-79 (incl 2 persons)

Europe ✆68861536
Via D90 2km SW, 200m from Agly.
All year
6HEC G H P + lau RS

Presqu'île ✆68861280
2km on rte de Leucate, turn right.
15 Mar-15 Nov
3HEC S G R H LP + lau S

Sable d'Or av du Lido la Pinède ✆68861841
Off D627 between Le Barcarès and Port Barcarès.
All year
4HEC G H LPS + lau
Prices pitch75 (incl 2 persons)

BARCELONNETTE
Alpes-de-Haute-Provence
Plan rte du Col d'Allos ✆92810811
Well-managed site divided into pitches.
Turn off D900 in town and head towards Col de la Coyalle.
15 May-Sep
0.5HEC G + lau PR
Prices A13 pitch15

BAR-SUR-LOUP, LE
Alpes-Maritimes
Gorges du Loup 965 chemin des Vergers ✆93424506
Terraced site divided into pitches, in an olive grove. Very steep entrance.
Access from Grasse on D2085 towards Le Pré du Lac (NE), then turn left on to D2210 in the direction of Vence. ➔

Apr-Sep
2HEC 〰 ◑ H ! ✕ ⊖ G H
PR + lau S
Prices A17 V9 45-95 ▲25-95

BEAUCHASTEL
Ardèche
CM Voiliers La Voulte-Rhône
✆75622404
900m S of N86.
All year
1.5HEC 〰 ● H ! ⊖ LP P +
lau ✕
Prices A9 pitch7

BÉDOIN
Vaucluse
Domaine de Belezy ✆90656018
Situated in a fine park with a 'Club House' in a 17th-century mansion. **Part of the site is reserved for naturists.**
20 Mar-16 Oct
30HEC ◑ H ! ✕ ⊖ G
R H P P + lau
Prices A32-45

BELGENTIER
Var
Tomasses Quartier la Tomasses
✆94489270
1.5km SE towards Toulon
Apr-Sep
2.3HEC 〰 ◑ H ! ✕ ⊖ G R
H PR P + lau
Prices A14 pitch16-18

BESSÈGES
Gard
At **PEYREMALE** (3km W)
Drouilhèdes ✆66250480
2km W on D17 rte de Génolhac, and continue 1km on D386.
Mar-15 Oct
2HEC 〰 ● H ✕ ⊖ G
H R P + lau
Prices pitch63 (incl 2 persons)

BEZOUCE
Gard
Cyprés ✆66752430
Slightly sloping meadow; divided into pitches with fruit and poplar trees.
Off N86 N of town centre.
All year
1HEC 〰 ● H ! ✕ ⊖ G R
H P P + lau RS

BIOT
See **ANTIBES**

BOISSERON
Gard
Boisseron Domaine de Gajon
✆66809430
Mar-Oct
3HEC ○ H ! ✕ ⊖ G H
P P + lau R
Prices pitch48 (incl 2 persons)

BOLLÈNE
Vaucluse
Barry ✆90301320
Well-kept site near ruins of Barry.
Signposted from Bollène via D26.
All year
3HEC 〰 ◑ H ! ✕ ⊖ G H
P P + lau
Prices A17 pitch17

BORMES-LES-MIMOSAS
Var
Clau Mar Jo chemin de Benat
✆94715339
Apr-1 Oct
1HEC 〰 ◑ H ⊖ H P + lau
! ✕ G R S
Prices A17 pitch22

Manjastre rte de Dom 98 ✆94710328
5km NW via N98
All year
4HEC 〰 ● H ! ⊖ G H +
lau ✕
Prices A15 V7 11 ▲10

At **FAVIÈRE, LA** (3km S)
Domaine ✆94710312
In a very attractive setting with a long sandy beach and numbered pitches. Food supplies in peak season only. Fine views of sea. Sport facilities.
Camping Carnet Compulsory.
0.5km E of Bormes Cap Bènat road.
Apr-Oct
38HEC 〰 S ● H ! ✕ ⊖
G S P + lau
Prices A19 52 ▲23

BOULOU, LE
Pyrénées-Orientales
Mas Llinas ✆68832546
3km N via N9
All year
3HEC 〰 S ◑ H ! ✕ ⊖ G
R H P + lau
Prices pitch48 (incl 2 persons)

BOULOURIS-SUR-MER
Var
Ile d'Or ✆94955213
Etr-Oct
6HEC 〰 ● H ! ✕ ⊖ G
H P + lau S
Prices pitch79 (incl 2 persons)

Val Fleury ✆94952152
Terraced site with tarred drives.
Off N98 at Km 93.1.
All year
1HEC ● H ! ✕ ⊖ H P +
lau G R S
Prices pitch60-145 (incl 2 persons)

BOURDEAUX
Drôme
At **POËT-CÉLARD, LE** (3km NW)
Couspeau ✆75533014
1.3km SE via D328A
May-Sep

3HEC 〰 ◑ H ! ✕ ⊖ G R
P P + lau R
Prices pitch50-65 (incl 2 persons)

BOURG-DE-PÉAGE
Drôme
CM du Parc des Sports ✆75701280
In football ground near swimming pool.
Camping Carnet Compulsory.
Well signposted from edge of town.
May-Sep
2HEC 〰 ○ H ! ⊖ G P P
+ lau ✕

BOURG-MADAME
Pyrénées-Orientales
Ségre 8 av du Paymorens ✆68046587
100m N on N20.
Closed Oct
1HEC 〰 ● H ⊖ H R
P + lau G R P
Prices A16 pitch15

BOURG-ST-ANDÉOL
Ardèche
Lion ✆75545320
Large well-shaped park in wooded terrain, beside River Rhône.
Etr-15 Sep
8HEC 〰 ● H ! ✕ ⊖ G H
PR P + lau
Prices pitch62 (incl 2 persons)

BRAGUE, LA
See **ANTIBES**

CAGNES-SUR-MER
Alpes-Maritimes
Colombier 35 chemin de Ste-Colombe
✆93731277
15 Mar-Oct
0.6HEC 〰 ● H ! ✕ ⊖
G P P + lau S
Prices pitch51-63 (incl 2 persons)

Country Club Cocagne Camp'otel rte de Vence ✆93209119
A small luxurious family site with numbered pitches divided by hedges. There is a tractor to help vehicles climb the entrance ramp, which is 300m long with a 25% (1 in 4) gradient.
N of Cagnes-sur-Mer on D36.
All year
2HEC ○ H ! ✕ ⊖ P
P + lau
Prices A22-36 pitch46-80

Rivière chemin des Salles ✆93206227
4km N beside River Cagne.
All year
1HEC 〰 ● H ! ✕ ⊖ G R
H P P + lau
Prices pitch57-74 (incl 2 persons)

At **CROS-DE-CAGNES** (2km S)
Panoramer chemin des Gros Buaux
✆93311615
Pleasant terraced site with sea view. Separate sections for tents and caravans
2km N of town.
Etr-Sep

1.4HEC H + lau
Prices pitch120-130 (incl 4 persons)

CAMURAC
Aude
Sapins ✆68203811
Good views.
1.5km from village.
All year
2HEC H H P + lau G R L
Prices A12 pitch12

CANET-PLAGE
Pyrénées-Orientales
Agua Dulce II ✆68804921
5km S of Canet Plage.
All year
1.4HEC H G R H P + lau S
Prices A11-16 pitch17-24

Domino r des Palmiers ✆68802725
Etr-Oct
0.7HEC H G R H + lau S
Mar Estang ✆68803553
28 Apr-7 Oct
10HEC H G R H PS + lau LR
Prices pitch84 (incl 2 persons)

At **CANET-VILLAGE**(2km W)
Brasilia ✆68802382
Near beach. Divided into pitches. Sanitary installations not up to high standard of rest of site.
Turn off main road in village and continue towards beach for 2km.
Apr-15 Oct
15HEC H G H PRS + lau
Prices pitch80 (incl 2 persons)

Ma Prairie ✆68802470
Grassland site in a hollow surrounded by vineyards.
Access from D11 in the direction of Elne of N617 Perpignan-Canet-Plage road.
May-Sep
4HEC H G H P + lau S
Prices pitch72-102 (incl 2 persons)

Peupliers Voie de la Crouste ✆68803587
Quiet site divided into pitches.
Jun-Sep
4HEC H G R H P + lau S
Prices A15-21 pitch23-30

CANET-VILLAGE
See **CANET-PLAGE**

CANNES
Alpes-Maritimes
At **CANNET, LE**
Grand Saule 24 bd de la Frayère ✆93470750

Etr-15 Oct
1HEC H P + lau G S
Prices pitch73-105 (incl 2 persons)

CANNET, LE
See **CANNES**

CAPTE, LA
See **HYÈRES**

CARCASSONNE
Aude
At **PENNAUTIER** (4km NW off N113)
Lavandières N113 ✆68254166
Apr-Oct
1HEC H + lau G R PR
Prices A15 V7 11 11

CARQUEIRANNE
Var
♖ **Beau-Vezé** ✆94576530
2.5km NW via N559 and then D76 between Hyères and Toulon.
Jun-20 Aug
7HEC H G R H P + lau S
Prices A28 29

CARRY-LE-ROUET
Bouches-du-Rhône
Lou Soulei ✆42447575
A terraced site on grassland, some of which is hard and stony. Partly occupied by static vans.
Access via autoroute exit Carry. On D5 between Carry and Sausset.
All year
17HEC H G R H PS + lau

CASTELLANE
Alpes-de-Haute-Provence
International ✆92836667
Signposted.
Apr-Sep
10HEC H G R H P + lau L
Prices pitch70 (incl 2 persons)

Nôtre Dame ✆92836302
In meadowland with deciduous and fruit trees.
200m W on D952.
Etr-Oct
0.6HEC H G H + lau R LPR
Prices pitch42 (incl 2 persons)

♖ **Verdon** Domain de la Salou, rte de Moustiers/Ste-Marie ✆92836129
Well-maintained site on meadowland on banks of River Verdon. Divided into pitches (100-150 sq m). Rooms in rustic style. Reservations recommended Jul-Aug.
Below the D952 towards the Gorges du Verdon.
15 May-15 Sep
14HEC H G R H LPR + lau
Prices pitch73-135 (incl 3 persons)

At **CHASTEUIL** (9km W on D952)
Gorges du Verdon ✆92836364
Situated on bank of the Verdon, surrounded by mountains. Fully divided into pitches split into two by road. Bathing in river not advised due to strong current.
0.5km S of village.
Apr-Sep
7HEC H G PR + lau
Prices pitch41 (incl 2 persons)

At **GARDE-CASTELLANE** (7.5km SE)
Clavet rte de Grasse Napoléon ✆92836896
May-Sep
7HEC H G H P + lau
Prices A24 pitch20

CASTELLET, LE
Var
Domaine de la Bergerie ✆94927120
All year
22HEC H R H P + lau

CAVAILLON
Vaucluse
Durance ✆90711178
2km S.
All year
4HEC H G H P + lau RS
Prices A15 V14 14 5

CAVALAIRE-SUR-MER
Var
Bonporteau ✆94640324
Site divided into pitches and partly terraced, 50m above coast road.
Drive W on N559 on outskirts of town, turn N and continue 0.2km.
20 Mar-15 Oct
3HEC H G R H + lau S
Prices pitch60-84 (incl 3 persons)

Cros de Mouton ✆94641087
Terraced site with individual pitches, separated for caravans and tents. Good view of sea, 1.5km distance.
Turn off N559 in town centre and continue inland for 1.5km.
15 Mar-Oct
4.5HEC H G H + lau S
Prices A20 pitch21

Pinède chemin des Mannes ✆94641114
400m from sea.
8 Mar-Oct
2HEC H G + lau S
Prices A18-19 V18 18 18

CAVALIÈRE
Var
Mimosas rte du Lavandou ✆94058294
➔

Very well-kept and divided into pitches. Specially designed for caravans.
NE of town off N559.
All year
5HEC ∼ ◑ ⋔H ▪ ! ✕ ⊖ ⊙ [G] [R] [P] + lau ☞ ≋S

Parc de Pramousquier ✆94058395
2.5km E on N559, rte de Cavalière to Pramousquier.
May-Sep
3HEC ◑ ⋔H ▪ ! ✕ ⊖ ⊙ [G] [P] + lau ☞ ≋S
Prices A13 pitch19

CHASTEUIL
See **CASTELLANE**

CHÂTEAU-ARNOUX
Alpes-de-Haute-Provence
CM Salettes ✆92640240
1km E beside the lake
All year
4HEC ∼ ◑ ⋔H ▪ ! ✕ ⊖ ⊙ [G] [H] ≋P [P] + lau
Prices A13 pitch13

CHÂTEAUDOUBLE
Drôme
Grand Lierne ✆75598314
Camping Carnet Compulsory.
30 Mar-15 Oct
3.6HEC ∼ ● ⋔H ▪ ! ✕ ⊖ ⊙ [G] [R] ⌂ ⛺ ≋P [P] + ✱ lau
Prices pitch74-88 (incl 2 persons)

CHÂTEAUNEUF-DU-RHÔNE
Drôme
CM ✆75908096
N end of village.
3 Jun-3 Sep
0.5HEC ∼ ◑ ⋔H ⊖ ⊙ [P] + lau ☞ ▪ ! ✕ ≋P
Prices A7 V4 ⊙4 ⛺4

CHAUZON
Ardèche
Digue ✆75396357
1km E, 100m from the River Ardèche
20 Mar-Sep
2HEC ∼ ● ⋔H ▪ ! ⊖ ⊙ [G] [R] ⌂ [H] ≋R [P] + lau ☞ ✕
Prices pitch45-56 (incl 2 persons)

CHAVAGNAC
See **GAGNIÈRES**

CIOTAT, LA
Bouches-du-Rhône
Oliviers rte de Toulon ✆42831504
Terraced site between the N559 and the railway line from Nice.
Turn inland off the N559 at Km34, some 5km E of the centre of the town and drive for 150m.
Mar-Sep
10HEC ∼ ◑ ⋔H ▪ ! ✕ ⊖ ⊙ [G] ⌂ [H] ≋PS [P] + lau
Prices A20 pitch20

St Jean 30 av de St-Jean ✆42831301
Site on the right side of the coast road.
Between N559 and sea behind the motel in NE part of town.
Mar-Oct
1HEC ∼ ● ⋔H ▪ ! ✕ ⊖ ⊙ [G] ⌂ ≋S [P] + lau

Soleil rte de Marseille ✆42715532
Divided into pitches.
Apr-Sep
0.5HEC ∼ ● ⋔H ▪ ! ✕ ⊖ ⊙ [G] [R] ⌂ [P] + lau ☞ ≋PS
Prices pitch68 (incl 3 persons)

COGOLIN
Var
Argentière ✆94545786
Landscaped, partly terraced site.
1500m NW along D48 rte de St-Maur.
Apr-15 Oct
8HEC ∼ ◑ ⋔H ▪ ! ✕ ⊖ ⊙ [G] ⌂ [H] ≋P [P] + lau
Prices pitch55-60 (incl 2 persons)

COLLE-SUR-LOUP, LA
Alpes-Maritimes
Pinèdes rte du Pont de Pierre ✆93329894
Well-kept terraced site on steep slope with woodland providing shade.
Turn right off D6 towards Roquefort.
15 Feb-20 Nov
3.2HEC ∼ ◑ ⋔H ▪ ! ✕ ⊖ ⊙ [G] [R] ⌂ [H] ≋PR [P] + lau ☞ ≋S
Prices A16 V10 ⊙21-32

Vallon Rouge rte Gréolières ✆93328612
Forest-like area, divided into pitches.
3km W of town, 100m to right of D6 towards Gréolières.
Mar-Oct
3HEC ∼ ● ⋔H ▪ ! ✕ ⊖ ⊙ [G] ⌂ [H] ≋PR + lau ☞ ≋S
Prices A15 V10 ⊙30-35 ⛺20-35

See advertisement in colour section

CORBÈS
See **ANDUZE**

CORNILLON-CONFOUX
Bouches-du-Rhône
Pinède ✆90504464
800m N on D70.
All year
1HEC ∼ ● ⋔H ▪ ! ✕ ⊖ ⊙ [G] [R] ⌂ [H] ≋P [P] + lau ☞ ≋LS
Prices A13 pitch13

COURONNE, LA
Bouches-du-Rhône
Cap Martigues ✆42807302
On road leading to the sea. Signposted from village.
All year
2.5HEC ∼ ● ⋔H ▪ ! ✕ ⊖ ⊙ [G] [R] ⌂ [H] ≋S [P] + lau
Prices A17 V10 ⊙18 ⛺18

Mas Plage de Ste-Croix ✆42807034
On sparse, stony grassland on a plateau with a fine view of the bay, and access to a sandy beach.
Access from D49.
Apr-Sep
6HEC ⊟ ● ⋔H ▪ ! ✕ ⊖ ⊙ [G] [R] ⌂ [H] ≋PS [P] + lau
Prices A19 V12 ⊙19 ⛺19

CRAU, LA
Var
Bois de Mont-Redon ✆94667334
3km NE via D29
15 Jun-15 Sep
5HEC ∼ ◑ ⋔H ▪ ! ✕ ⊖ ⊙ [G] ≋P [P] + lau
Prices pitch75 (incl 3 persons)

CRESPIAN
Gard
♖ **Camping Mas de Reilhe** ✆66778212
Individual pitches with hedges and trees dividing them. Recreational facilities.
Camping Carnet Compulsory.
On N110.
20 May-7 Sep
3HEC ∼ ● ⋔H ▪ ! ✕ ⊖ ⊙ [G] ≋P [P] + ✱ lau ☞ ≋R
Prices A17-20 pitch34-40

CREST
Drôme
CM Corinthe quai de Soubeyran ✆75250528
Follow D538 towards Montélimar, cross bridge over River Drôme and continue on embankment to stadium. Site is adjacent to stadium.
Apr-Sep
2.5HEC ∼ ◑ ▪ ⊖ ⊙ [G] ≋R [P] + lau

CROS-DE-CAGNES
See **CAGNES-SUR-MER**

DIE
Drôme
Chamarges ✆75220677 & 75221413
Children's games.
Site lies 1.5km W on D93 road to Crest adjacent to River Drôme. The site is the first on the right from Die.
Etr-15 Oct
3HEC ∼ ◑ ⋔H ⊖ ⊙ [G] ⌂ [H] ≋P [P] + lau ☞ ▪ ! ✕

Pinède Quartier du Pont-Neuf ✆75221777
W via D93 beside the River Drôme
May-15 Sep
8HEC ∼ ● ⋔H ▪ ! ✕ ⊖ ⊙ [G] [H] ⛺ ≋PR [P] + lau

ESPARRON-DE-VERDON
Alpes-de-Haute-Provence
Soleil ✆92771378
Camping Carnet Compulsory.
Etr-Sep
1.5HEC ⊟ ◑ ⋔H ▪ ! ✕ ⊖ ⊙ [G] [H] ≋L P + ✱ lau
Prices A18 ⊙24 ⛺21

FARINETTE-PLAGE
Hérault
Hélios ✆67216366
On level ground divided into pitches.
On D137 S of village signposted 'Farinette'.
26 May-Sep
2.5HEC ⊖ G R H + lau S
Prices pitch45-67 (incl 2 persons)

FAVIÈRE, LA
See **BORMES-LES-MIMOSAS**

FONTAINE-DE-VAUCLUSE
Vaucluse
CM Les Prés ✆90206954
SW on D24.
All year
0.6HEC ⊖ H + lau

FONTES
Hérault
Clairettes Acces par Adissan ✆67250131
Jun-15 Sep
1.3HEC ⊖ G R H P + lau
Prices pitch52 (incl 2 persons)

FONT-ROMEU
Pyrénées-Orientales
CM Menhir rte de Mont-Louis ✆68300932
N on N618.
15 Jun-Oct
7HEC R + lau

FONTVIEILLE
Bouches-du-Rhône
CM Pins ✆90977869
1km from village.
Apr-15 Oct
3.5HEC ⊖ + lau P

FOS-SUR-MER
Bouches-du-Rhône
Estagnon Plage St-Gervais ✆42050119
Level, rather dusty site. Public beach on other side of road.
Camping Carnet Compulsory.
Situated S of an industrial zone-Quartier St-Gervais.
May-Sep
2HEC ⊖ G H S + lau
Prices A17 pitch24

FRÉJUS
Var
Acacias 370 r H-Giraud ✆94532122
On meadowland, divided into several sections. Quiet. Sea views.
NE on N7, then follow D37 towards Valescure.
All year
1HEC ⊖ G S + lau P
Prices pitch46-57 (incl 2 persons)

Bellevue rte de Bozon ✆94520052
2km N.
All year
2.3HEC ⊖ G + lau

Colombier ✆94515601
Widespread site on hill on some individual terraces under pine trees.
Turn N off N7 onto D4 towards Bagnols and continue for 500m.
15 Mar-Sep
10HEC ⊖ G R H P + lau S

Dattier rte de Bagnols-en-Forêt (CD4) ✆94408893
Laid out in terraces with a view of the Esterel mountains.
Access from A8 via RN7, then CD4.
Etr-Sep
4HEC ⊖ G H P + lau R
Prices pitch96 (incl 2 persons)

See advertisement on page 168

Fréjus rte de Bagnols-en-Forêt ✆94408803
Access via N7 and D4.
Apr-Oct
4HEC ⊖ G R H P + lau
Prices A17-20 pitch23-27

Holiday Green rte de Bagnols-en-Forêt ✆94408820
6km N via D4.
Apr-Oct
15HEC ⊖ G R P + lau
Prices A28 84 47

Montourey rte de Bagnols-en-Forêt, chemin du Reyran, St-Jean-les-Cais ✆94522641
2km N.
Etr-Oct
4.3HEC ⊖ G R H P + lau
Prices pitch60-76 (incl 2 persons)

See advertisement on page 168

Pierre Verte 4 rte de Bagnols-en-Forêt ✆94408830
Etr-Oct
14HEC ⊖ G R H P + lau
Prices pitch66 (incl 2 persons)

Pins Parasols rte de Bagnols-en-Forêt ✆94408843
4km N via D4.
Etr-Sep
4HEC ⊖ G P + lau
Prices pitch88 (incl 2 persons)

At **TOUR-DE-MARE** (4km NE)
Europa rte Nationale 7 ✆94532038
Dutch orientated site.
On N7.
Apr-Oct
1HEC ⊖ G H L + lau

FRONTIGNAN
Hérault
Miami 65-6 av d'Ingril ✆67481549
Modern, pleasantly landscaped site next to saltwater lagoon.
NE via D60.
Jun-15 Sep
2.5HEC ⊖ G R H S + lau

See advertisement on page 168

Soleil ✆67481443
Family site bordering the beach.
NE via D60.
May-Sep
3HEC ⊖ S + lau

Tahiti ✆67481243
NE via D60.
May-Sep
2.5HEC ⊖ G R H PS + lau

Tamaris ✆67481691
From N108 take D129 for 6km.
Jun-15 Sep
4.5HEC ⊖ G H S + lau
Prices pitch99-109 (incl 2 persons)

GAGNIÈRES
Gard
At **CHAVAGNAC** (2km N on D430)
Mines d'Or ✆66250667
Well-situated quiet site.
June-15 Sep
1.8HEC ⊖ G R + lau

GALLARGUES-LE-MONTUEUX
Gard
Amandiers ✆66352802
May-15 Sep
3HEC ⊖ G R H P + lau R
Prices pitch55 (incl 2 persons)

GALLICIAN
Gard
Mourgues ✆66733088
Apr-Sep
2.5HEC ⊖ P + lau R
Prices pitch48 (incl 2 persons)

GARDE-CASTELLANE
See **CASTELLANE**

GASSIN
Var
Moulin de Verdagne ✆94797821
All year
8HEC ⊖ G H P + lau
Prices A13-16 28-34 24-30

Parc Montana rte du Bourrian ✆94561249
Park-like site on slopes of a hill.
2.5km E of N559. Access from main road at Km84.5 and 84.9 on D89.

Apr-Sep
40HEC ● H R H P + lau
Prices A15 pitch36

GIENS
Var
Cigales pl de la Badine ✆94582106
A well-kept site with numbered pitches. Special places for caravans.
0.3km E of D97.
Etr-15 Oct
2HEC ● H G H S + lau
Prices A17 V30 30 A30

GILETTE
Alpes-Maritimes
Moulin Noù Pont C-Albert
✆93089240
On the D2209, 1.8km SW of the Pont-Charles-Albert
Etr-Sep
7HEC ● H G R PR + lau
Prices pitch52-111 (incl 2 persons)

GLUIRAS
Ardèche
Ardèchois ✆75666187 & 72021179
Quiet, pleasant meadowland site by River Gluèyre.
Camping Carnet Compulsory.
On D102 from St-Sauveur-de-Montagut in direction of Mezilhac and continue for 1km to site.
Etr-Sep
3.5HEC H G H R + lau
Prices pitch52-70 (incl 2 persons)

GRANDE-MOTTE, LA
Hérault
Garden 46 pl des Tamaris ✆67565009
Completely divided into pitches separated by hedges and surrounded by a wall. 0.3km from beach.
Access from D62. Site by crossroads

towards Palavas/Grand Travers.
Mar-Oct
3.5HEC H G + lau LPS
Prices pitch100-132 (incl 3 persons)

Lous Pibols ✆67565008
Well-organised. Divided into level pitches.
W on D59, 0.4km from sea.
Mar-Oct
3HEC S H G R H S + lau
Prices pitch60-132

Or ✆67565210
Operated by family welfare organisation. Individual pitches separated by hedging each with water and electricity.
May-Sep
5HEC S H +

GRASSE
Alpes-Maritimes
At **OPIO** (8km E via D2085 & D3)
Caravan Inn ✆93773200
Terraced rustic site for caravans only. Occupied largely by static caravans. Steep approach to site (15%) – free towage available.
1.5km S of Opio on D3.
19 Mar-Sep
5HEC H G R P + lau
Prices pitch70-80 (incl 2 persons)

GRAU-DE-VENDRES
Hérault
Foulègues ✆67373365
Camping Carnet Compulsory.
Singposted.
Jun-Sep
4HEC S H G H RS + lau

GRAU-DU-ROI, LE
Gard
Abri de Camargue rte du Phare de l'Espiguette ✆66515483
2.5km from town.
Apr-15 Oct
4HEC H G P + lau S
Prices pitch85-155 (incl 2 persons)

Bon Séjour ✆66514711
Clean, tidy, well-kept site.
3km E of village off road to lighthouse.
Apr-Sep
5HEC H G R H L + lau
Prices A10 pitch32

Eden Port-Camargue ✆66514981
6uiet site on both sides of access road. 300m from beach.
On D626 towards Espiguette.
Apr-4 Oct
5.3HEC H G H PS + lau
Prices pitch141-182 (incl 2 persons)

Elysée Résidence rte de l'Espiguette ✆66519888
26 Mar-15 Oct
3.5HEC S H R + lau PS
Prices pitch76-124 (incl 2 persons)

CM L'Espiguette ✆66514392
Mar-Nov
43HEC H G S + lau
Prices pitch41 (incl 2 persons)

See advertisement on page 170

International La Marine ✆66514622
Camping Carnet Compulsory.
3.5km SW towards lighthouse.
Apr-15 Oct
6HEC H G R H P + lau LS
Prices pitch120-158 (incl 4 persons)

Jardins de Tivoli ✆66518296
15 Mar-15 Oct
7HEC H G H P + lau S
Prices pitch90 (incl 2 persons)

Mouettes rte de Port Camargue ✆66514400
Camping Carnet Compulsory.
1.2km SE.
Etr-Sep
2.4HEC S H G S + lau

Salonique rte de l'Espiguette ✆66515973
May-Sep
3.5HEC H G H P + lau S
Prices pitch50-110 (incl 2 persons)

GRIMAUD
Var
At **PORT-GRIMAUD** (4km E)
Domaine des Naiades ✆94563008
Site on hilly land with terraces divided into pitches and with many modern facilities.
Access via N98 and D244, then turn right and continue uphill.
15 Mar-15 Oct
12HEC H H P + lau

Mûres ✆94563115
The site is divided into two parts by the N98. The land alongside the sea is level and mainly without shade. The other section of the site is on a slope and has some shade.
NE on N98.
15 Mar-Sep
18HEC S H G S + lau

Plage ✆94563115
Wide area of land near Km59.6 on N98 on both sides of road beside sea. Partly terraced and divided into pitches.
15 May-Sep
18HEC S H G S + lau

HYÈRES
Var
At **AYGUADE-CEINTURON** (4km SE)
Ceinturon II ✆94663966
A popular site on level meadowland divided into pitches. some individual washing cubicles.
4km SE of Hyères on D42.
Jun-Aug
5HEC H G S + lau
Prices A15 pitch16-22

Ceinturon III ✆94663265
Well-kept and divided into numbered pitches. Individual washing cubicles.
4km SE of Hyères on D42.
Apr-Sep
2.5HEC S H G S lau +
Prices A16 V17 20 A20

At **CAPTE, LA** (7km S)
CM de la Capte ✆94580020
Mar-Oct
8HEC S H G R + lau S

At **HYÈRES-PLAGE** (4km SE)
Pins Maritimes ✆94576388
Situated in a pine wood close to the beach.
Turn off D42 between Hyères-Plage and L'Ayguade by the water ski lift (Téléskinautique) and continue inland for 0.2km.
16 Jun-15 Sep
12HEC H G H S + lau

HYÈRES-PLAGE
See **HYÈRES**

ISLE-SUR-LA-SORGUE, L'
Vaucluse
CM Sorguette rte d'Apt ✆90380571
Borders the N100 towards Apt.
15 Mar-Oct
2.5HEC H G R H R + lau P
Prices A14 pitch15

LAGORCE
Ardèche
Domaine de Chaussy ✆75939966
Camping Carnet Compulsory.
On D559 near Ruoms.
1 Apr-15 Oct
5.5HEC H G R H P P + lau R
Prices pitch105-110 (incl 2 persons)

LANSARGUES
Hérault
Fou du Roi ✆67867808
1km W via D24
Etr-Sep
2.5HEC H G R H P + lau
Prices pitch56 (incl 2 persons)

LANTOSQUE
Alpes-Maritimes
Deux Rives ✆93030544
Apr-Oct
2HEC H H RS +

LAROQUE-DES-ALBÈRES
Pyrénées-Orientales
Planes rte de Villelongue ✆68892136
15 Jun-Aug
3HEC H G H P + lau R
Prices A16 pitch20

LATTES
Hérault
See also MONTPELLIER
Eden ✆67682968
Camping Carnet Compulsory.
2.7km SW on D986
Jun-Sep
6HEC H G H P + lau S

Lac des Rêves ✆67501546
Individual pitches. Alongside lake.
On the road between Pérols and Lattes.
Etr-15 Oct
33HEC H R H P + lau S

LAURENS
Hérault
Oliveraie ✆67902436
900m from village centre.
All year
4HEC H G R H P + lau LRS
Prices pitch30-80

LEUCATE
Aude
CM Cap Leucate ✆68400137
Beside sea. Divided into pitches. Open air cinema.
All year
4.8HEC H + lau S

LÉZIGNAN-CORBIÈRES
Aude
CM Pinède ✆68270508
Well-kept terraced site with numbered pitches and tarred drives, decorated with bushes and flower beds.
Camping Carnet Compulsory.
Signposted from N113.
Apr-Oct
3.5HEC H G R H P + lau LRS
Prices A11-13 pitch11-13

LONDE-LES-MAURES, LA
Var
Forge ✆94668265
Level meadow with good sanitary facilities.
Camping Carnet Compulsory.
Turn off N98 into village, at traffic lights turn N for 1km to site on outskirts of village.
19 Jun-15 Sep
3HEC H G H + lau S

Moulières ✆94668238
Well tended level meadowland in quiet location. 1km from the sea.
On western outskirts towards the coast.
Jun-15 Sep
3.5HEC H G R + lau S
Prices pitch67 (incl 3 persons)

Pansard ✆94668322
Beautiful, wide piece of land, beside beach and divided into pitches.
Turn off N98.
Apr-Sep
6HEC H G R S + lau
Prices pitch66 (incl 3 persons)

Val Rose ✆94668136
4km NE on N98.
15 Feb-15 Nov
2HEC H G R H P + lau

LUNEL
Hérault
Bon Port ✆67711565
Access via D24.
All year
5HEC H G P + lau
Prices pitch60 (incl 2 persons)

MALAUCÈNE
Vaucluse
Lignol ✆90652278
Well-kept site at edge of village, partly terraced and subdivided.
Well signposted from village.
Apr-14 Sep
2HEC H G + lau

MANDELIEU
Alpes-Maritimes
Cigales bd de la Mer ✆93492353
S on N7.
Mar-Dec
2HEC H G H R + lau P
Prices pitch70-135 (incl 2 persons)

Plateau des Chasses ✆93492593
Terraced land, on hill in a park.
Turn off N7 at KM 4.2 and continue uphill for 1.2km.
Apr-Sep
5HEC H G H + lau
Prices A13 V13 pitch60-130

Roc Fleuri rte de Pégomas ✆93930871
Beautiful well-kept site in orchard. Partly sloping.
N of town on D109.
Apr-20 Sep
2HEC H G + S
Prices pitch68 (incl 2 persons)

MARSEILLAN-PLAGE
Hérault
Charlemagne ✆67219249
250m from the beach
Apr-10 Oct

5HEC ~ 5 ◑ ⛆H ⚑ ⚲ ✕ ⊖ ⊕ G R ⌂ H ≋PS ◘ + lau
Prices pitch81-135 (incl 3 persons)

Grillon des Mers ✆67941683
150m from the beach
Jun-Oct
0.7HEC ~ 5 ◑ ⛆H ⊖ ⊕ ✱ ☞ ⚑ ⚲ ✕ ≋S

Plage 69 chemin du Pairollet
✆67219254
Apr-15 Oct
1.3HEC ~ 5 ● ⛆H ⚲ ✕ ⊖ ⊕ G H ≋S ◘ lau ☞ +
Prices A9-13 pitch20-30

MAUREILLAS
Pyrénées-Orientales
Bruyères rte de Céret ✆68832664
NW off D618 to Céret.
Etr-15 Oct
4HEC ~ ◑ ⛆H ⚑ ⚲ ✕ ⊖ ⊕ G R ⌂ H ≋P ◘ + lau

CM Congo rte de Céret ✆68832321
1km W on N618.
15 May-Sep
0.8HEC ~ ◑ ⛆H ⊖ ⊕ ◘ + lau ☞ ⚑ ⚲ ✕ ≋PR
Prices A6 V4 ⊕6 ▲6

Val Roma Park ✆68831972
2.5km NE on N9.
May-Sep
2HEC ~ ● ⛆H ⚑ ⚲ ✕ ⊖ ⊕ G H ≋PR ◘ + lau
Prices A23 pitch32

MENTON
Alpes-Maritimes
Fleur de Mai 67 Val de Gorbio
✆93572236
Apr-10 Oct
2HEC ~ ◑ ⛆H ⊖ ⊕ P + lau ☞ ⚑ ⚲ ✕ G R ≋PS
Prices pitch52-94 (incl 2 persons)

MÉOUNES-LES-MONTRIEUX
Var
Aux Tonneaux ✆94339834
Site in wooded area, divided into pitches.
200m S of village off N554.
All year
3HEC ~ ◑ ⛆H ⚲ ✕ ⊖ ⊕ G R H ≋P ◘ + lau ☞ ⚑
Prices A10 pitch10

Domaine de Belvoir rte de Signes
✆94908974
Jun-Sep
6HEC ~ ◑ ⛆H ⚑ ⚲ ✕ ⊕ G ⌂ H ≋P P + lau

MONTBLANC
Hérault
Rebau ✆67985078
Divided into pitches and surrounded by vineyards.
From Pézenas follow N113; in La Bégude de Jordy turn off main road and drive 2km on D18 towards Montblanc.
Mar-Oct
2HEC ~ ● ⛆H ⚲ ⊖ ⊕ G ⌂ H ≋P ◘ + lau ☞ ⚑
Prices pitch61 (incl 2 persons)

MONTCLAR
Aude
Au Pin d'Arnauteille ✆68268453
2.2km SE via D43
15 Mar-Sep
4HEC ~ ◑ ⛆H ⚑ ⚲ ✕ ⊖ ⊕ G R ⌂ H ≋PR ◘ + lau
Prices A12 V8 ⊕13 ▲13

MONTÉLIMAR
Drôme
Deux Saisons ✆75018899
From bank of River Roubion.
From town centre follow D540 across Pont de la Libération; then first turning right into chemin des Alexis.
Mar-Nov
1.5HEC ~ ◑ ⛆H ⚲ ✕ ⊖ ⊕ G H ≋R ◘ + lau ☞ ⚑ ≋P
Prices A14 V5 ⊕15 ▲15

MONTPELLIER
Hérault
See also LATTES

Floréal rte de Palavas ✆67929305
On level ground surrounded by vineyards.
500 m off Autoroute A9, exit Montpellier-Sud. From town centre follow road for Palavas (D986).
Apr-Sep
1.5HEC ~ ● ⛆H ⊖ ⊕ ◘ + lau ☞ ⚑ ⚲ ✕ ≋P
Prices pitch45 (incl 2 persons)

MONTPEZAT
Alpes-de-Haute-Provence
Coteau de la Marine ✆92775333
A pleasant wooded site, providing easy access to the Verdon gorges.
15 Mar-15 Nov
10HEC ⊟ ● ⛆H ⚑ ⚲ ✕ ⊖ ⊕ G R ⌂ H ≋LPR ◘ + lau
Prices pitch54-108 (incl 2 persons)

MOURIÈS
Bouches-du-Rhône
Devenson ✆90475201
Terraced site amongst pine and olive trees in Provençal countryside.
Turn off N113 at La Samatane and continue N towards Mouriès. Site is in N part of village.
Etr-15 Sep
3.5HEC ⊟ ● ⛆H ⚑ ⊖ ⊕ G H ≋P ◘ +
Prices A18 pitch25

MOUTONNE, LA
Var
Holiday Giavis ✆94388743
NW of town
Apr-Sep
5HEC ◑ ⛆H ⚑ ⚲ ✕ ⊖ ⊕ G R ⌂ H ≋P ◘ + lau
Prices A27 pitch39

MUS
Gard
International Club ✆66350706
2km N on N113.
All year
0.7HEC ~ ● ⛆H ⚑ ⚲ ✕ ⊖ ⊕ G H ◘ + lau ☞ ≋PS

MUY, LE
Var
Cigales ✆94451208
Hilly terrain with Mediterranean pine trees, many terraces and some large boulders.
Exit 'Draguignan' off A8 onto N7. 0.8km to site. Well signposted.
May-15 Sep
10HEC ~ 5 ● ⛆H ⚑ ⚲ ✕ ⊖ ⊕ G R ≋P ◘ + lau

Sellig rte d'Aix-en-Provence
✆94451171
1.5km W on N7.
All year
1.9HEC ~ ● ⛆H ⚑ ⚲ ✕ ⊖ ⊕ G R ⌂ H ≋P ◘ + lau
Prices A19 pitch18

NANS-LES-PINS
Var
Ste-Baume ✆94789268
0.9km N via D80
Apr-Sep
5HEC ⊟ ● ⛆H ⚑ ⚲ ✕ ⊖ ⊕ G ⌂ H ⚠ ≋P ◘ + lau
Prices pitch60 (incl 2 persons)

NAPOULE, LA
Alpes-Maritimes
Azur-Vacances bd du Bon Puits
✆93499112
Site with many long terraces, on edge of mountain slope in mixed woodland.
Turn inland 200m after fork at railway station and continue 600m.
25 Mar-Sep
10HEC ~ ⊟ ● ⛆H ⚑ ⚲ ✕ ⊖ ⊕ G R ◘ + lau ☞ ≋PRS
Prices pitch68 (incl 2 persons)

NARBONNE
Aude
Languedoc ✆68652465
Situated behind the Montlaur supermarket.
All year
2.7HEC ⊟ ○ ⛆H ⚑ ⚲ ✕ ⊖ ⊕ H ≋P ◘ + lau ☞ ≋S

At **NARBONNE-PLAGE** (15km E D168)
CM de la Côte des Roses rte de Gruissan ✆68498365
3 km SW.
Apr-Sep
17HEC ~ ◑ ⛆H ⚑ ⚲ ✕ ⊖ ⊕ G R ⌂ ≋S + lau
Prices pitch48-60 (incl 2 persons)

CM Falaise ✆68498077
W of Narbonne Plage, 400m from beach.
Apr-Sep
7HEC ◑ ⋔H ✕ ⊖ [G] + lau ⛵S
Prices pitch39-70 (incl 2 persons)

NARBONNE-PLAGE
See **NARBONNE**

NÉBIAS
Aude
Fontaulié-Sud ✆68201762
0.6km S via D117
Etr-Oct
3.5HEC ◑ ⋔H ✕ ⊖ [G] [R] [H] ⛵P lau +
Prices A12 pitch11

NIOZELLES
Alpes-de-Haute-Provence
Moulin de Ventre ✆92786331
2.5km E via N100
Apr-15 Oct
3HEC ◑ ⋔H ✕ ⊖ [G] [H] ⛵L + lau
Prices pitch65 (incl 2 persons)

NYONS
Drôme
CM av de la Digue ✆75262239
Situated on bank of river on level meadow with fruit trees. Sports ground and golf course in town.
All year
1.6HEC S ◑ ⋔H ✕ ⊖ ⛵PR + lau
Prices pitch38 (incl 3 persons)

Sagittaire ✆75276439
Well-kept site divided by hedges.
S of town on D538 road to Vaison-la-Romaine.
15 Mar-Oct
5.6HEC ◑ ⋔H ✕ ⊖ [G] [R] ⛵R + lau

OLLIÈRES-SUR-EYRIEUX, LES
Ardèche
Domaine des Plantas ✆75662153
Games room, discotheque and other leisure activities.
May-Sep
27HEC ◑ ● ⋔H ✕ ⊖ [G] ⛵R + lau

OPIO
See **GRASSE**

ORANGE
Vaucluse
Jonquier r A-Carrel ✆90341983
On the NW outskirts
15 Mar-Oct
5HEC ◑ ⋔H ✕ ⊖ [G] ⛵P + lau [R] ⛵R
Prices A22 pitch25

ORGON
Bouches-du-Rhône
Vallée Heureuse ✆90730278
A quiet transit site in a rocky valley.
1.5km from the village on the N7. Access is past a non-working quarry.
Apr-Sep
6HEC ● ⋔H ✕ ⊖ [G] ⛵LP + lau
Prices A12 V9 11 Å11

PALAVAS-LES-FLOTS
Hérault
Roquilles 267 bis av St-Maurice ✆67680347
An attractive site 50m from the sea.
15 Apr-25 Sep
15HEC S ○ ◑ ⋔H ✕ ⊖ [G] [H] ⛵P + lau ⛵S

PENNAUTIER
See **CARCASSONNE**

PÉROLS
Hérault
Airotel l'Estelle rte de Lattes ✆67500082
800m SE of town on D132.
All year
6HEC ◑ ⋔H ✕ ⊖ [G] [H] + lau ⛵PS

PEYREMALE
See **BESSÈGES**

POËT-CÉLARD, LE
See **BOURDEAUX**

PONT D'HÉRAULT
Gard
Magnanarelles Le Rey ✆67824013
0.3km W via D999, beside the river
All year
2HEC ● ⋔H ✕ ⊖ [G] [R] [H] ⛵PR + lau
Prices A12-14 V5-6 7-8 Å7-8

PONT-DU-GARD
Gard
International Gorges du Gardon rte de Uzès ✆66228181
1 m from aqueduct on D981 Uzès road.
Mar-Oct
3HEC S ● ⋔H ✕ ⊖ [G] [H] + lau ⛵R

Sousta ✆66371280
500m from the aqueduct on D981 Uzès road.
Etr-Oct
12HEC S ● ⋔H ✕ ⊖ [G] [H] ⛵PR + lau
Prices pitch53-64 (incl 2 persons)

Valive ✆66228152
All year
3.1HEC ◑ ⋔H ✕ ⊖ [G] [H] ⛵P + lau ⛵R
Prices pitch44 (incl 2 persons)

PORT-GRIMAUD
See **GRIMAUD**

PORTIRAGNES-PLAGE
Hérault
Mimosas ✆67909292
Leave A9 at exit Béziers Est and continue towards coast via N112 and D37.
24 May-15 Sep
7HEC ◑ ⋔H ✕ ⊖ [G] [R] [H] ⛵PS + lau
Prices pitch70 (incl 2 persons)

Sablons rte de Portiragnes ✆67909055
Large site subdivided into fields by fences. Beside beach. Night club and discothèque.
0.5km N on D37.
Apr-Sep

12HEC S ● H ✕ ⊖ G LPRS P + lau
Prices pitch117-148 (incl 2 persons)

PRADET, LE
Var
Airotel Mauvallon chemin de la Gavaresse ✆94217828
A well-kept site amidst young trees divided into pitches.
Turn off the N559 in Le Pradet and take the D86 for 2.5km towards sea.
Apr-Oct
1HEC ◑ H ✕ ⊖ G H P + lau L

Pin de Galle Quartier San Peyre ✆94212606
All year
1HEC ● H ✕ ⊖ G H P + lau S
Prices A16 pitch22

PRAMOUSQUIER
Var
Pramousquier ✆94058395
2km E via D559
15 May-Sep
3HEC ◑ H ✕ ⊖ G P + lau S
Prices A13 pitch19

PUGET-SUR-ARGENS, LE
Var
Aubrèdes ✆94455146
Situated on undulating meadowland.
Leave autoroute A8 at exit Puget-sur-Argens, then site is 150m. If approaching from Fréjus on N7 turn right before Puget, cross motorway and follow road towards Lagourin.
Apr-Sep
3.8HEC ◑ H ✕ ⊖ G H PS P + lau R
Prices A12-17 pitch11-16

Bastiane ✆94455131
Hilly site divided into numbered pitches in pine and oak wood. Individual washing cubicles. Meals to take away.
Access from N7.
4HEC ◑ H ✕ ⊖ G H P P + lau LR

QUILLAN
Aude
Camping Sapinette ✆68201352
Access W via D79, rte de Ginoles.
All year
5HEC ◑ H ⊖ G P + lau ✕ P
Prices A13 pitch13

RAMATUELLE
Var
Croix du Sud ✆94798084
Terraced site in beautiful pine forest divided into pitches with view of sea. Minimum stay 8 days.
3km NE of town, 80m N of D93.
Apr-Oct

2.5HEC ● H ✕ ⊖ G R H P P + lau S
Prices A16-18 pitch31-34

Tournels rte de Camarat ✆94798054
Lovely views to Pampelonne Bay from part of this site. 1km to beach.
Access from D93 Croix-Valmer/St-Tropez road, follow the signs to 'Cap Camarat'.
All year
20HEC ● H ✕ ⊖ G H P P + lau S

See advertisement in colour section

RÉGUSSE
Var
♖ **Lacs du Verdon** ✆94701795
Stony meadowland with bushes and trees in a quiet secluded location.
2.4km NE of Régusse. Signposted.
May-15 Sep
16HEC ◑ H ✕ ⊖ G R H P P + lau L
Prices A23 pitch29-37

REMOULINS
Gard
Soubeyranne rte de Beaucaire ✆66370321
Camping Carnet Compulsory.
S on D986.
May-15 Sep
5HEC ◑ ● H ✕ ⊖ G H P P + lau R
Prices pitch71-86 (incl 2 persons)

Sousta av du Pont-du-Gard ✆66371280
2km NW
10 Mar-11 Nov
12HEC S ● H ✕ ⊖ G H PR P + lau R
Prices A14-16 pitch26-32

RIA
Pyrénées-Orientales
Bellevue ✆68964896
Beautifully situated terraced site. Very well kept. Beside former vineyard.
2km S on N116, take road to Sirach, turn right and continue 600m up drive which is difficult for caravans.
Apr-Oct
2.2HEC ◑ H ⊖ G P + lau ✕ LPR
Prices A14 pitch15

ROCHELONGUE-PLAGE
See **AGDE**

ROQUEBRUNE-SUR-ARGENS
Var
Blavet ✆94454004
Jun-Sep
2HEC ● H ✕ ⊖ H P P + lau LS
Prices pitch70 (incl 3 persons)

Lei Suves ✆94454395
4km N via D7.
Mar-Nov
7HEC ● H ✕ ⊖ G R H P P + lau LRS
Prices A23 pitch26

Moulin des Iscles ✆94457074
On bank of River Argens.
All year
1.5HEC ◑ H ✕ ⊖ G H R P + lau L
Prices pitch72 (incl 3 persons)

Pêcheurs ✆94457125
0.5km NW via D7, near the lake
May-Sep
3HEC ● H ✕ ⊖ G R H LPR P + lau S
Prices pitch57-96 (incl 2 persons)

ROQUE-D'ANTHÉRON, LA
Bouches-du-Rhône
Domaine les Iscles ✆42504425
1.8km N via D76c.
All year
10HEC ● H ✕ ⊖ G R H LPR P + lau
Prices A19 pitch27

ROQUETTE-SUR-SIAGNE, LA
Alpes-Maritimes
Panoramic Quartier St-Jean ✆93472266
All year
1HEC ● H ✕ ⊖ G R H P + lau S
Prices pitch45-60 (incl 3 persons)

RUOMS
Ardèche
Domaine de Chaussy rte de Lagorce ✆75939966
4km W of Plombières-les-Bains via D20
Apr-Oct
7HEC ○ H ✕ ⊖ G H P P + lau
Prices pitch100-110 (incl 2 persons)

SAILLAGOUSE
Pyrénées-Orientales
Cerdan ✆68047046
On meadow with some terraces. Hot meals served during peak season.
Closed Oct
78.3HEC ◑ H ⊖ G R H P + lau ✕ P
Prices pitch49 (incl 2 persons)

ST-ALBAN-SOUS-SAMPZON
Ardèche
Ranc Davaine ✆753960055
Etr-15 Sep
8HEC S ● H ✕ ⊖ G R H PR P + lau
Prices pitch56-76 (incl 2 persons)

ST-AMBROIX
Gard
Moulinet-Beau-Rivage ✆66241017
3.5km SE, beside the River Cèze
Apr-Sep ➔

3.5HEC ● H ⊖ G R P
+ lau
Prices A13 pitch16

ST-ANDIOL
Bouches-du-Rhône
St-Andiol ✆90950113
Well situated village centre. Divided into pitches.
All year
1HEC ● H ⊖ G
+ lau P
Prices A14 pitch18

ST-AYGULF
Var
Étoile d'Argens ✆94810141
5km NW, beside the River Argers
Etr-Sep
10HEC ○ H ⊖ G
P + lau
Prices pitch133-152 (incl 3 persons)

Paradis des Campeurs ✆94969355
2.5km towards Gaillarde-Plage.
Etr-Sep
1.5HEC ● H ⊖ G
H S lau R
Prices pitch66

St-Aygulf 270 av Salvarelli ✆94812014
Access to beach via underpass.
Inland from N98 at Km881.3 N of town. Entrance on right of av Salvarelli.
1 Jun-15 Sep
25HEC ◑ H ⊖ G H
+ lau R S
Prices A18 pitch20

ST-CYPRIEN-PLAGE
Pyrénées-Orientales
Cala Gogo Les Capellans ✆68210712
4km S towards Les Capellans.
11HEC ○ ◑ H ⊖ G
R H PS + lau
Prices A27 pitch40

STE-ANASTASIE-SUR-ISSOLE
Var
Vidaresse ✆94722175
S on D15
All year
1.8HEC ◑ ● H ⊖ G
H P + lau

STE-MARIE
Pyrénées-Orientales
At **TORREILLES** (4km NW on D11)
Calypso ✆68280947
500m from the sea.
All year
2.5HEC ◑ H ⊖ G S

Dunes de Torreilles ✆68283829
At the sea, with direct access to beach.
All year
16HEC ● H ⊖ R
H PS + lau
Prices pitch63-167

Mar-I-Sol Plage de Torreilles ✆68280407
350m from the beach
All year
9HEC ○ ◑ H ⊖
G R H PS + lau

STES-MARIES-DE-LA-MER
Bouches-du-Rhône
CM Brise r M-Carrière ✆90978467
NE via D85A, near the beach
All year
25HEC ○ H ⊖ S + lau
G
Prices A19 pitch16

Clos-du-Rhône rte d'Aigues-Mortes ✆90978599
2km W via D38, near the beach
Apr-Sep
7HEC ◑ H ⊖ G
PS + lau

ST-JEAN-DU-GARD
Gard
Sources ✆66853803
900m NE on D50, rte de Mialet.
Apr-16 Sep
1.5HEC ◑ H ⊖ G H
P + lau R
Prices A12 V5 11 11

ST-JEAN-PLA-DE-CORTS
Pyrénées-Orientales
Deux Rivières rte de Maureillas ✆68832320
0.5km SE via D13, beside the river Tech
Jun-Sep
8.5HEC ● H ⊖ G R
H PR + lau
Prices A22 pitch18

ST-LAURENT-DU-VAR
Alpes-Maritimes
Lou Pistou av du Zoo ✆93310544
Small site with many terraces. No motor caravans. Advanced booking required.
500m SW, access via N7 and D2209.
Jul-Aug
0.6HEC ◑ H ⊖ G
+ lau LS
Prices pitch60 (incl 2 persons)

Magali 1814 rt de la Baronne ✆93315700
Level meadowland site.
Turn off N7 onto D2209 near the industrial zone.
Feb-Oct
1.2HEC ◑ H ⊖ G R
H P + lau
Prices pitch60-68 (incl 2 persons)

ST-LAURENT-DU-VERDON
Alpes-de-Haute-Provence
Farigoulette ✆92744162
1.5km NE near Verdon
15 May-15 Sep
11HEC ● H ⊖ G
R LP + lau
Prices pitch62 (incl 2 persons)

ST-MARTIN-DE-CRAU
Bouches-du-Rhône
Crau ✆90471709
Etr-15 Oct
3HEC ● H ⊖ G R
H P + lau

ST-MARTIN-DE-LONDRES
Hérault
Pic St-Loup ✆67550053
E via D122
12 Apr-Sep
3HEC ◑ H ⊖ G
H P lau +
Prices pitch45 (incl 2 persons)

ST-PAUL-EN-FORÊT
Var
Parc ✆94761535
Quiet, fairly isolated site surrounded by woodland.
3km N on D4.
All year
0.5HEC ● H ⊖ G
H P P + lau L
Prices A22-23 pitch26

ST-PAUL-LES-ROMANS
Drôme
CM de Romans ✆75723527
27 Apr-2 Oct
1HEC ● H ⊖ H lau
G
Prices A8 pitch10

ST-QUENTIN-LA-POTERIE
See **UZÈS**

ST-RAPHAËL
Var
Beauséjour-les-Tasses ✆94950367
400m from the sea. slightly hilly site in pinewoods. Suitable for small caravans and tents.
2km E of town off N98.
May-Sep
1HEC ● H ⊖ G
+ lau S

Douce Quiétude bd J-Baudino ✆94443000
Meadowland site in quiet location in attractively hilly countryside.
Approach from Agay Plage past Esterel Camping in direction of Valescure.
Apr-Sep
10HEC ◑ H ⊖ G
H P + lau
Prices pitch125-135 (incl 2 persons)

Royal ✆94820020
Level site divided by walls and hedges. Ideal bathing for children. Bar and dance hall next to site.
On N98 towards Cannes.
15 Apr-10 Oct
1HEC ● H ⊖ G
+ lau S

ST-RÉMY-DE-PROVENCE
Bouches-du-Rhône
Pégomas ✆90920121
Well-tended grassland with young trees and bushes. Divided into several fields by high cedars providing shade.
500m E of village. Well signposted.
Mar-Oct
2HEC ● H G R P + lau
Prices pitch64

ST-SAUVEUR-DE-MONTAGUT
Ardèche
Ardechois ✆75666187
8.5km W on D102, beside the River Glueyre
Etr-20 Sep
3.5HEC H G H LR + lau
Prices pitch52-70 (incl 2 persons)

ST-SORLIN-EN-VALLOIRE
Drôme
Château de la Pérouze ✆75317021
2.5km SE via D1.
Apr-15 Sep
14HEC ● H G H P + lau
Prices A19 19 A15-19

ST-THIBÉRY
Hérault
Tane ✆67778429
Jun-Sep
3HEC H H P + lau
Prices pitch50-60 (incl 2 persons)

ST-VALLIER-DE-THIEY
Alpes-Maritimes
Parc des Arboins ✆93426389
Pleasantly situated terraced site on hillside with some oak trees.
Entrance at Km V36 on N85.
All year
4HEC ● H G R H P + lau
Prices pitch42-60 (incl 3 persons)

SALAVAS
Ardèche
Chauvieux ✆75880537
NE off D579.
May-15 Sep
1.8HEC S ● H G + lau R
Prices pitch64

Péquelet ✆75880449
Beside the River Ardèche
Apr-Oct
2HEC ● H G H R lau +
Prices pitch57 (incl 2 persons)

SALINS-D'HYÈRES, LES
Var
Port Pothuau ✆94664117
Completely divided into pitches.
6km E of Hyères on N98 and D12.
Etr-Oct
6HEC ● H G R H P + lau RS

SALON-DE-PROVENCE
Bouches-du-Rhône
Nostradamus rte d'Eyguières ✆90560836
Mar-Oct
3HEC ● H G H PR + lau
Prices A14 pitch14

SAMPZON
Ardèche
Soleil Vivarais ✆75396756
On several levels beside River Ardèche. Good base for canoeing.
From Vallon drive towards Ruoms on D579 for 5km and cross bridge over River Ardèche.
Etr-Sep
8HEC ● H G H PR + lau
Prices pitch58-85 (incl 2 persons)

SANARY-SUR-MER
Var
Girelles chemin de Beaucours ✆94741318
Camping Carnet Compulsory.
3km NW via D539, beside the sea
Etr-Sep
2HEC S ● H G S + lau
Prices A19 pitch24

Mogador ✆94741058
Situated 800m from the sea. The site, divided into pitches by hedges, is well managed and very well kept.
2km NW on N559 turn off at KM 15 and take next left.
Etr-15 Oct
2.7HEC ● H G H P + lau S
Prices A12 pitch36

Pierredon chemin de Pierredon ✆94742502
All year
4HEC H G H P + lau S

SAUVE
Gard
Domaine de Bagard ✆66775599
1.2km SE via D999
Apr-Oct
12HEC ● H G R PR + lau
Prices pitch560-700 (incl 2 persons)

SÉRIGNAN-PLAGE
Hérault
Camargue ✆67321964
Situated in the edge of a wide sandy beach.
Mar-Oct
3HEC H G R H LRS + lau

Clos Virgile ✆67322064
Situated 400m from the beach, the site is level meadowland with big pitches and has two clean, well kept sanitary blocks.
May-Sep
5HEC ● H G R P + lau S
Prices A10-13 pitch64-80

Gabinelle ✆67395087
15 Jun-15 Sep
3HEC H P + lau G R S
Prices pitch68 (incl 3 persons)

Grand Large ✆67396970
Apr-Sep
6HEC ⊖ G R H S + lau
Prices pitch60-84 (incl 2 persons)

SEYNE-SUR-MER, LA
Var
Pins ✆94940689
100m from the sea.
Apr-30 Oct
1HEC ⊖ G H P + lau S
Prices

SIX-FOURS-LES-PLAGES
Var
Héliosports La Font de Fillol ✆94256276
1km W
Apr-Sep
1HEC ⊖ lau G R PS
Prices pitch56 (incl 3 persons)

International St-Jean ✆94875151
Site with pitches, separated by hedges and reeds. Well managed, and lies just below the Fort Six-Fours.
Access from N559 and D63 via chemin de St-Jean.
All year
3HEC ⊖ G R H P + lau
Prices pitch78 (incl 3 persons)

Playes 419 r Grand ✆94255757
Terraced site on north side of town. Trees abound in this excellent location.
Access from N559 and D63 via chemin de St-Jean.
Mar-Nov
1.5HEC ⊖ G R + lau PS
Prices pitch59 (incl 3 persons)

SOSPEL
Alpes-Maritimes
Domaine St-Madeleine rte de Moulinet ✆93041048
4.5km NW via D2566
All year
3HEC ⊖ G H P + lau
Prices A14 V9 13 13

TAIN-L'HERMITAGE
Drôme
CM Lucs 24 av Prés-Roosevelt ✆75083282
Good overnight stopping place but some traffic noise.
S of town near N7. Turn towards River Rhône at ESSO garage.
15 Mar-Oct
2HEC S ⊖ + lau P

TARASCON
Bouches-du-Rhône
St-Gabriel rte de Fontvieille ✆90911983
15 Mar-15 Oct
1HEC ⊖ G H + lau P
Prices A12 pitch15

Tartarin rte de Vallabrèques ✆90910146
Site lies on E bank of River Rhône.
Follow signs for 'Vallabrèques'.
15 Mar-Sep
1HEC ⊖ + lau P
Prices A16 pitch16

TORREILLES
See **STE-MARIE**

TOUR-DE-MARE
See **FRÉJUS**

TOURNON-SUR-RHÔNE
Ardèche
CM ✆75080528
Well laid-out site in town centre beside River Rhône.
NW on N86.
Mar-Nov
1.1HEC ⊖ G + lau PR
Prices A15 V9 9 9

TOURRETTE-SUR-LOUP
Alpes-Maritimes
Camassade 523 rte de Pie Lombard ✆93593154
Quiet site under oak trees and pines with several terraces.
From Vence turn left immediately beyond Tourette. The last 50m is narrow and steep and therefore not suitable for large caravans.
All year
1.7HEC ⊖ G R H P + lau
Prices A15 V11 50-80

UR
Pyrénées-Orientales
Gare d'Ur ✆68048095
May-Sep
1.2HEC ⊖ G H R R
Prices A8 pitch12

UZÈS
Gard
At **ST-QUENTIN-LA-POTERIE** (4km NE)
Moulin Neuf ✆66221721
Quiet site on extensive meadowland within an estate.
4 km NE on D982.
Etr-Sep
5HEC ⊖ G P + lau
Prices pitch65 (incl 2 persons)

VAISON-LA-ROMAINE
Vaucluse
Moulin de César av C-Geoffray ✆90360691
Site divided into pitches by trees and bushes.
800m E of village on D151 towards St-Marcellin and river.
15 Mar-Oct
4.5HEC ⊖ G R H R + lau P

VALENCE
Drôme
CM Centre de l'Epervière ✆75423200
Bordering the Rhône.
Access via exit Valence Sud off A7.
9 Jan-23 Dec
3.5HEC S ⊖ P + lau G R R
Prices A20 pitch35

VALLON-PONT-D'ARC
Ardèche
Ardechois ✆75880663
In a pleasant situation in the Ardèche Gorge. Good access for caravans and plentiful sporting facilities.
From Vallon take D290 towards St-Martin. Signposted.
15 Mar-Oct
5HEC ⊖ G R H + lau PR

Mondial rte des Gorges ✆75880044
Modernised site on the bank of the Ardèche with good sanitary arrangements.
Access from Vallon-Pont-d'Arc D290. 800 m towards Gorge d'Ardèche.
Mar-15 Oct
4HEC ⊖ G R H P + lau R
Prices pitch87 (incl 2 persons)

Plage Fleurie ✆75880115
Holiday site in unspoilt village beside river.
Take D579 towards Ruoms, turn left after 2.5km towards Les Mazes.
Apr-Oct
12HEC ⊖ G R + lau
Prices pitch59 (incl 2 persons)

VALRAS-PLAGE
Hérault
Lou Village ✆93620842
2km SW, 100m from the beach
20 May-10 Sep
10HEC ⊖ G R H L + lau S

Yole BP 23 ✆67373387
Very comfortable site divided into pitches. Good sanitary installations with individual washing cubicles. Hot water tap. Sailing boats for hire. Riding stables in village.
SW of D37E towards Vendres.
12 May-21 Sep
20HEC ⊖ G R H PS + lau
Prices pitch115 (incl 2 persons)

VEDÈNE
Vaucluse
Flory ✆90310051

Well-kept site on hill. Common room with TV.
From motorway, do not head for Vèdene but follow D942 for 800m.
15 Mar-15 Oct
6.5HEC ● ⋔H ⛟ ▼ ✕ ⊖ ⊕ [G] ⌂
[H] ≋P ■ + lau
Prices A11-14 pitch11-14

VENCE
Alpes-Maritimes
♜ **Domaine de la Bergerie** rte de la Sine ✆93580936
Well-kept site on hilly land. Pitches near to a wood.
3km W on D2210.
10 Mar-10 Nov
13HEC ～ ⊟ ● ⋔H ⛟ ▼ ✕ ⊖ ⊕ [G]
[R] ■ + lau ☞ ≋PS
Prices pitch61-86 (incl 3 persons)

VERCHENY
Drôme
Base ✆75217251
Camping Carnet compulsory.
Apr-Sep
3HEC ～ ● ⋔H ⛟ ✕ ⊖ ⊕ [G] [R]
[H] ≋R ■ + lau ☞ ▼
Prices A12-14 pitch14-17

VERCLAUSE
Drôme
Riousset ✆75278022
1km on D94.
Apr-Oct
30HEC ～ ◑ ⋔H ⊖ ⊕ [G] [R] ≋PR
■ + ☞ ⛟ ▼ ✕
Prices pitch85 (incl 2 persons)

VÉREILLES
Hérault
Sieste ✆67237296
Jun-Sep
2HEC ～ ◑ ⋔H ⛟ ▼ ✕ ⊖ ⊕ [G] ⌂
[H] ≋R ■ + lau
Prices pitch45 (incl 2 persons)

VIAS
Hérault
Air Marin ✆67216490 or 67942189
Jun-Sep
7HEC ～ ◑ ⋔H ⛟ ▼ ✕ ⊖ ⊕ [G] [R]
⌂ [H] ≋PS ■ + lau
Prices pitch130 (incl 4 persons)

Bourricot ✆67216427
3km S on D137; at Vias look for Farinette-Plage and in 100m before beach turn right.
22 May-18 Sep
2HEC ～ ● ⋔H ⛟ ▼ ✕ ⊖ ⊕ [G] [R]
≋R ■ + lau ☞ ≋S

Carabasse Farinette Plage ✆67216401
Clean modern well-kept site.
2km S.
19 May-16 Sep
20HEC ～ ● ⋔H ⛟ ▼ ✕ ⊖ ⊕ [G]
[R] ⌂ [H] ⛛ ≋P ■ + lau ☞ ≋RS
Prices pitch107 (incl 2 persons)

Farret ✆67216445
On level meadow beside flat sandy beach, ideal for children.
May-Sep
5HEC ～ S ◑ ⋔H ⛟ ▼ ✕ ⊖ ⊕ [G]
[R] ⌂ [H] ■ + lau ☞ ≋PRS
Prices pitch65-85 (incl 2 persons)

Gai Soleil ✆67216477
On level land near sea. Divided into pitches.
Cross Canal du Midi, S of town, then turn W.
All year
5HEC ～ ● ⋔H ⛟ ▼ ✕ ⊖ ⊕ [G] [R]
⌂ [H] ⛛ ■ + lau ☞ ≋PS

Méditerranée ✆67909907
15 May-Sep
10HEC ～ ○ ◑ ⋔H ⛟ ▼ ✕ ⊖ ⊕ [G]
[R] ⌂ [H] ≋S ■ + lau
Prices pitch72 (incl 2 persons)

Ondines ✆67940153
Etr-15 Sep
3.5HEC ～ S ◑ ⋔H ⛟ ▼ ✕ ⊖ ⊕
[G] ≋PS ■ + ✱

Salisses ✆67216407
Level grassy site, divided into pitches.
2km S and 500m from sea.
Apr-Sep
7HEC ～ ● ⋔H ⛟ ▼ ✕ ⊖ ⊕ [G] ⌂
[H] ⛛ ≋P ■ + lau ☞ ≋S
See advertisement on page 178

VIGAN, LE
Gard
Val de l'Arre rte de Ganges ✆67810277
2.5km E on D999.
Apr-Sep
4HEC ～ ● ⋔H ⛟ ⊖ ⊕ [G] [H] ≋PR
■ + lau
Prices pitch47 (incl 2 persons)

VILLARS-COLMARS
Alpes-de-Haute-Provence
Haut-Verdon ✆92834009
On D908 bordering river.
25 Jun-2 Sep
3.5HEC ～ ● ⋔H ⛟ ▼ ✕ ⊖ ⊕ [G]
⌂ ≋PR ■ + lau
Prices A24 V12 ⛟12 ⛺12

VILLECROZE
Var
Cadenières ✆94706755
A terraced site with games for children.
On the D560.
June-Sep
6HEC ～ ◑ ⋔H ▼ ✕ ⊖ ⊕ [G] [R] ⌂
[H] ≋P ■ + lau ☞ ⛟ ≋LS
Prices A18 pitch17

VILLEMOUSTAUSSOU
Aude
Pinhiers Chemin du Pont Neuf ✆68478190
Mar-Nov
2HEC ～ ◑ ● ⋔H ⛟ ▼ ⊖ ⊕ ⌂ [H]
≋P ■ lau ☞ ✕ [G] [R] +
Prices A13 pitch13

VILLENEUVE-DE-BERG
Ardèche
Pommier ✆75948281
Holiday site in beautiful setting with terraces divided into pitches. Common room. Library.
On winding private road off N102, 2km from village.
Apr-15 Sep
0.6HEC ～ ◑ ⋔H ⛟ ▼ ✕ ⊖ ⊕ [G]
[H] ≋P ■ + lau ☞ [R]

VILLENEUVE-LOUBET-PLAGE
Alpes-Maritimes

Avenc av des Baumettes ✆93732990
NE via N7.
Apr-Sep
1.4HEC ◑ H ⊖ G + lau S

Hippodrôme 2 av des Rives
✆93200200
Divided into two by a busy road. 0.4km from the sea.
Turn right off the N7 at ATLAS furniture store.
All year
0.8HEC ● H ⊖ G + lau S
Prices A15 V7 49-92 A47-92

Panorama ✆93209153
Small terraced site mainly for tents 0.8km from the sea.
About 500km from the Nice-Cannes Autoroute.
All year
1.1HEC ● H ⊖ G H + lau S
Prices A13 V9 50 A30

Parc des Maurettes ✆93209191
Terraced site in a pine forest.
Access from Autoroute exit Antibes (A8 Nice-Toulon) to N7. Continue 4km in direction of Nice. Turn left after Vaugrenier Park and proceed for 1km.
10 Jan-15 Nov
2HEC ● H ⊖ G H P + lau S
Prices A16-20 V5-13 31-70 A16-56

Sourire ✆93209611
2km W on D2085
15 Mar-Oct
8HEC ○ ◑ ● H ⊖ G R H P + lau RS
Prices pitch85-142 (incl 3 persons)

Vieille Ferme bd des Groules
✆93334144
Site lies in Vaugrenier Park. Level meadow, terraced site for tents. Used by package tours. 150m from sea.
All year
2.8HEC ◑ H ⊖ G R P + lau S
Prices pitch68 (incl 2 persons)

VILLEROUGE-LA-CRÉMADE
Aude

Pinada ✆68436193
In pleasant rural surroundings on edge of forest.
600m NW on D106.
Jun-Sep
5HEC ● H ⊖ G R H P + lau
Prices pitch60 (incl 2 persons)

VILLES-SUR-AUZON
Vaucluse

Verguettes rte de Carpentras
✆90618818
W via D942
Jun-Sep
2HEC ◑ H ⊖ P + lau G R L
Prices A20 V10 16 A16

VIOLS-LE-FORT
Hérault

Cantagrils ✆67550188
4.5km S on D127
15 Apr-Sep
4HEC ● H ⊖ P lau
Prices pitch56 (incl 2 persons)

VITROLLES
Bouches-du-Rhône

Europa ✆42870722
3km SW on N113 rte de Salon-de-Provence.
All year
1.8HEC ◑ H ⊖ L + lau

VIVIERS
Ardèche

Centre de Vacances d'Imbours
✆75043950
Apr-Sep
10HEC S ● H ⊖ G P + lau
Prices A13-19 V7-9 6-8 A6-8

Rochecondrie Loisirs ✆75527466
N of town on N86.
Apr-Oct
4HEC ◑ H ⊖ P + lau R
Prices pitch60 (incl 2 persons)

VOGÜÉ
Ardèche

Domaine du Cros d'Auzon
✆75377586
2.5km via D579 bordering the river.
Jun-15 Sep
3HEC ◑ H ⊖ G H R + lau P

VOLONNE
Alpes-de-Haute-Provence

Hippocampe rte Napoléon
✆92690506
Several strips of land, interspersed with trees, and running down the edge of lake. Surrounded by fields and gardens.
On S edge of town. 2km E of N85.
Apr-Sep
5HEC ◑ H ⊖ G H P + lau
Prices pitch50-81 (incl 2 persons)

CORSICA

Corsica is a wonderful blend of green mountains, deep valleys, and spectacular pink granite peaks where rain and melting snow merge into torrents that rush down the hillsides. In the spring the mountains are ablaze with wild flowers and the maquis – the abundance of which gives the island its name 'the scented isle'. This southernmost outpost of France, is some 100 miles south of Toulon in the Mediterranean. Beaches abound, and all kinds of watersports are available in season, but in this relatively undiscovered place it is still possible to find a quiet beach on a summer day.

Corsica's capital is Ajaccio, birthplace of Napoleon, and today a cosmopolitan centre with its busy harbour and broad boulevards with smart shops. From Ajaccio there is a railway to Bastia, in the north. This is a beautiful three-hour trip, and ideal for drivers reluctant to venture onto more tortuous minor roads.

ORSE (CORSICA)

LÉRIA
aute-Corse
arina d'Aléria Plage de Padu-lone
95570142
km E of Cateraggio via N20
ay-Oct
0HEC S H G
RS lau +
rices A22 V9 10 8

BELGODÈRE
aute-Corse
elgodère 95602020
5 May-Sep
HEC H lau
LRS
rices pitch66 (incl 2 persons)

ALVI
aute-Corse
olce Vita Ponte Bambino
95650599
km SW of Calvi between N197 to L'Ile
ousse and the sea.
ay-Sep
HEC H G H
R + lau S
rices A22 V9 11 9

ARGESE
orse-du-Sud
orraccia 95264239
km N on N199.
un-Sep
.4HEC H
+ lau S
rices A22 V8 10 8 pitch8

CENTURI
aute-Corse
sulotta 95356281
tr-15 Oct
HEC H G
+ lau S
rices A15 V8 15 12

LOS-DU-MOUFLON
aute-Corse
ouflon 95650353
Terraced site, divided into pitches. Very steep access via partly asphalted, winding road with gradient of 20%.

Tents and motorised caravans only.
15km from Calvi on D81 on the coastal road, in the direction of Porto.
6 Jun-25 Sep
2.5HEC H G S
+ lau
Prices A23 V11 12 17

CORTE
Haute-Corse
U Sognu rte de la Restonica
95460907
20 Mar-Oct
1.5HEC H H
+ lau PRS
Prices A18 V10 17 11

FARINOLE, MARINE DE
Haute-Corse
A Stella 95301437
On D80 beside the sea
Jun-15 Oct
5HEC H H
S + lau
Prices A16 V9 26 17

GALÉRIA
Haute-Corse
Deux Torrents 95620067
5km E on D51 towards Calenzana.
15 Jun-15 Sep
7HEC H G R
H + lau R
Prices A18-19 V8-9 14-15 8-9

LOZARI
Haute-Corse
Clos des Chênes rte d' Belgodère
95601513
1.5km S via N197 towards Belgodère
Etr-14 Oct
5.5HEC S H
G R H P + lau
LS
Prices A21 V8 11 9

LUMIO
Haute-Corse
Panoramic rte de Belgodère D71
95607313
Very clean and tidy site divided into pitches.
From Calvi, 12km on N197, 200m from main road.
Jun-15 Sep
3HEC H G
H P + lau S
Prices A21 V6 10 10

OLMETO-PLAGE
Corse-du-Sud
Esplanade 93760503
15 May-Sep
4.6HEC H G
H S + lau
Prices A22 V8 13 11

PIANOTTOLI
Corse-du-Sud
Kervano Plage Plage de Kervano
95718322
15 May-Oct
5.7HEC H G
H + lau R S
Prices A20-25 V6-8 16-22 12-16

PISCIATELLO
Corse-du-Sud
Benista 95251930
Apr-Oct
5HEC S H H
R + lau G R S
Prices pitch69 (incl 2 persons)

PORTO-VECCHIO
Corse-du-Sud
Pirellu rte de Palomlaggia 95702344
9km E at Picconagia
15 May-Sep
3HEC H G R
+ lau S
Prices A23 V8 13 8

Vetta La Trinité 95700986
5.5km N
Etr & Jun-Sep
6HEC H G
H P + lau
Prices A22-23 V8 8-9 8-9

PROPRIANO
Corse-du-Sud
Corsica rte d'Ajaccio 95760057
Terraced site.
2.5 km NE by N196.
May-Oct

1.5HEC ● H ⊖ G + lau

Tikiti ✆95760832
1.5km NE via N196 towards Ajaccio
All year
12HEC ◑ H ⊖ G lau S
Prices A28 V10 10 pitch15

ST-FLORENT
Haute-Corse
U Pezzo chemin de la Plage
✆95370165
Pleasant site; partly level, partly terraced under eucalyptus trees. Private access to large beach.
S of town on road to beach.
15 Apr-15 Oct
2HEC ● H ⊖ G S + lau
Prices A13 V6 10 7

SARTÈNE
Corse-du-Sud
Olva les Eucalyptus ✆95771158
4.5km N via D69 towards Loreto
Apr-Sep
8HEC ◑ H ⊖ + lau

TIUCCIA
Corse-du-Sud
U Sommalu rte de Casaglione
✆95522421
Camping Carnet compulsory.
2.5km N via D81 and D25
Jun-Sep
5HEC ◑ H ⊖ G lau RS
Prices A18 V8 12 8

VICO
Corse-du-Sud
Sposata ✆95266155
On partly terraced, partly sloping ground.
1km SW on N195.
Apr-Sept
2.5HEC ● H ⊖ G + lau LRS

ITALY

Italy, with its many beautiful cities and rich architectural heritage, is bordered by four countries: Austria, France, Switzerland and Yugoslavia. The approaches are all dominated by mountains. The lakes of the north present a striking contrast with the sun-parched lands of the south and there is some beautiful countryside in the central Appenines. There are fine, sandy beaches on both the Mediterranean and Adriatic coasts.

The north has a typically Mediterranean climate whilst the south has an almost African climate with extremely hot summers. The language is Italian, a direct development of Latin. There are several dialect forms such as Sicilian and Sardinian, but the accepted standard derives from the vernacular spoken in Florence 700 years ago. German is spoken, to a small extent, near the Austrian frontier.

The International Reservation Centre in Calenzano (near Florence) *Federcampeggio* provides a campsite information and reservation service ✆(055) 882391.

The *Assessorati Regionali per il Turismo* (ART) and the *Ente Provinciale per il Turismo* (EPT) have regional and provincial information offices and can provide details of campsites within their locality. In northern Italy, especially by the lakes and along the Adriatic coast, sites tend to become very crowded and it is advisable to book in advance during the season which extends from May to the end of August.

International camping carnet, although not generally compulsory, is required on certain sites. Some campsites will allow a reduction in the advertised charge to the holder of a camping carnet. See page **47** for further information.

Off-site camping is permitted provided the landowner's permission has been obtained, but is strictly prohibited in State forests and national parks. In built-up areas, if parking is allowed, the towing vehicle must remain connected to the trailer or caravan and the corner steadies must not be used.

HOW TO GET THERE

Although there are several ways of getting to Italy, entry will most probably be by way of France and Switzerland. The major passes, which are closed in winter, are served by road or rail-tunnels.

Distance
From the Channel ports Milano (Milan) is about 1,050–1,130km (650–700 miles), requiring one or two overnight stops. Rome (Roma) is 580km (360 miles) further south.

Car-sleeper services
operate during the summer from Boulogne, Brussels, 's-Hertogenbosch or Paris to Milano; Boulogne to Bologna; and Paris to Rimini.

GENERAL INFORMATION

The information given here is specific to Italy. It **must** be read in conjunction with the European ABC at the front of the book, which covers those regulations which are common to many countries.

British Embassy/Consulates*

The British Embassy together with its consular section is located at 00187 Roma, Via xx Setembre 80A ✆(06) 4755441/4755551. There are British Consulates in Firenze (Florence), Genova (Genoa), Milano (Milan), Napoli (Naples), Turin and Venezia (Venice); there are British Consulates with Honorary Consuls in Cagliari and Trieste.

Currency, including banking hours*

The unit of currency is the *Italian Lira* (*Lit*). At the time of going to press £1 = *Lit*2,170. Denominations of bank notes are *Lit* 1,000, 2,000, 5,000, 10,000, 20,000, 50,000, 100,000; standard coins are *Lit* 5, 10, 20, 50, 100, 200, 500. A visitor may *import* an unlimited amount of Italian and foreign currency and *export* up to the equivalent of Lit 20,000,000 in Italian or foreign currency. However, if you wish to export any amount in excess of this it must have been declared on entry on Form V2 (obtainable at frontier posts) within the preceding 6 months. This form is then shown to the Customs when leaving Italy.

Banks Most banks are open from Monday to Friday 08.30 to 13.00hrs and from 15.30 to 16.30hrs.

Emergency telephone numbers

Fire, police, ambulance (Public emergency service) ✆113.

Fiscal receipt

In Italy, the law provides for a special numbered fiscal receipt (*ricevuta fiscale*) to be issued after paying for a wide range of goods and services including meals and accommodation. This receipt indicates the cost of the various goods and services obtained, and the total charge after adding VAT. Tourists should ensure that this receipt is issued, as spot checks are made by the authorities, and both the proprietor and consumer are liable to an on-the-spot fine if the receipt cannot be produced.

Foodstuffs*

Visitors resident in Europe and entering from an EC country may import, duty-free, 1,000g of coffee or 400g of coffee extract and 200g of tea or 80g of tea extract; a reduced allowance applies for non-residents of Europe or if entering from a non-EC country. A reasonable quantity of foodstuffs may be imported for personal use.

Shopping hours

Generally, *food shops* are open Monday to Saturday 08.00–13.00hrs and 16.00–20.00hrs, but close at 13.00hrs on Thursday. Most *other* shops are open Monday to Saturday 09.00–13.00hrs and 16.00–19.30hrs, but only open at 16.00hrs on Monday.

Tourist information*

The Italian State Tourist Office (ENIT) has an office at 1 Princes Street, London W1R 8AY ✆071-408 1254. It will be pleased to assist you with any information regarding tourism. In Italy, there are three organisations: the *Ente Nationale Italiano per il Turismo* (ENIT), with offices at the frontiers and ports; the *Assessorati Regionali per il Turismo* (ART), and the *Ente Provinciale per il Turismo* (EPT), who will assist tourists through their regional and provincial offices. The *Aziende Autonome di Cura Soggiorno e Turismo* (AACST) have offices in places of recognised tourist interest and concern themselves exclusively with local matters.

MOTORING

Children in cars*

Children under 12 are not permitted to travel in the front or rear seats unless the seat is fitted with a child restraint system or seat belt, which they must wear.

***Additional information will be found in the European ABC at the front of the book.**

Dimensions and weight restrictions

Private **cars** and towed **trailers** or **caravans** are restricted to the following dimensions – **car** height, 4 metres; width, 2.50 metres; length (including tow-bar), with one axle 6 metres, with two or more axles 12 metres. **Trailer/caravan** height, 4 metres; width, 2.30 metres; length with one axle 6 metres, with two axles 7.50 metres. The maximum permitted overall length of vehicle/trailer or caravan combination is 12 metres.

Trailers with an unladen weight of over 750kg or 50% of the weight of the towing vehicle must have service brakes on all wheels.

Driving Licence*

A valid red three-year Republic of Ireland* or green UK* licence is acceptable in Italy if accompanied by an official translation which may be obtained free from the AA. The minimum age at which a visitor may use a temporarily imported car is 18 years. The minimum age for using a temporarily imported motorcycle of up to 125cc, not transporting a passenger, is 16 years; to carry a passenger, or use a motorcycle over 125cc, the minimum age is 18 years.

*The translation is not required by the holder of a UK (all pink or part pink) or Republic of Ireland licence. The respective licensing authorities cannot exchange a licence purely to facilitate continental travel.

Lights*

Full-beam headlights can be used only outside cities and towns. Dipped headlights are compulsory when passing through tunnels, even if they are well-lit.

Motoring clubs*

There are two motoring organisations in Italy. The **Touring Club Italiano** (TCI) which has its head office at 20122 Milano, 10 Corso Italia ✆(02) 85261 and the **Automobile Club d'Italia** (ACI) whose head office is at 00185 Roma 8, Via Marsala ✆(06) 49981. Both clubs have branch offices in most leading cities and towns.

Petrol, including petrol coupons*

At the time of going to press a concessionary package of Italian petrol coupons and motorway toll cards may be purchased from the AA. An additional benefit of the package is a free breakdown and replacement car concession, but see also *Breakdown* in the European ABC for details of the 5-Star Service. The package is available to personal callers only, and a passport and vehicle registration document must be produced at the time of application. Further information may be obtained from any AA Shop. The package **cannot** normally be purchased inside Italy, but may be obtained from ACI offices at main crossing points, and also some ACI offices in port areas, if arriving by ship. However, foreign tourists hiring an Italian registered car on arrival at the intercontinental airports in Rome and Milan may purchase the package from the nearest ACI or ENIT office.

It is **forbidden** to carry petrol in cans in a vehicle.

Roads

Main and secondary roads are generally good, and there are an exceptional number of by-passes. Mountain roads are usually well engineered; for details of mountain passes consult the Contents page.

Speed limits*

The speed limit *in built-up areas* is 50kph (31mph); *outside built-up areas* 90kph (56mph); on *motorways* 130kph (81mph) for vehicles over 1100cc and motorcycles over 350cc. For vehicles up to 1099cc and motorcycles between 150cc and 349cc the speed limit is 110kph (68mph). Motorcycles under 150cc are not allowed on motorways.

For cars towing a caravan or trailer the speed limits are 50kph (31mph), 80kph (49mph) and 100kph (62mph) respectively.

Warning triangle

The use of a warning triangle is compulsory in the event of accident or breakdown. It should be used to give advance warning of any stationary vehicle which is parked on a road in fog, near a bend or on a hill at night when the rear lights have failed. The triangle must be placed on the road not less than 50 metres (55yds) behind the vehicle. Motorists who fail to do this are liable to an administrative fine of between *Lit*25,000 and *Lit*100,000. See also *Warning triangle/Hazard warning lights* in the European ABC.

***Additional information will be found in the European ABC at the front of the book.**

Prices are in Italian Lire
Abbreviation:
pza piazza
Each placename preceded by 'Lido', 'Lido di', 'Marina' or 'Marina di' is listed under the name that follows it.

NORTH WEST/ALPS & LAKES

The Gran Paradiso mountains on the French border, and the Matterhorn and Monte Rosa to the north on the Swiss border, give a dramatic glacier-topped backdrop to the steep-sided valleys and the distinctively Italian Lakes, below where decorated villas and medieval castles border the lakes, and palm trees and magnolias grow. The mountains provide winter skiing, and walking in the summer, and wood and stone chalets contribute to the Alpine landscape. On the lakes, boats take you from harbour to harbour, yet within an hour you can be in Lombardy's capital, Milan. To the west is an elegant town with its Piazza San Carlo and many cafés. Nearby, in the Alba region, the vineyards produce the distinguished Barolo red wine and sparkling Asti Spumante. To the north and eastwards in the Dolomites, roads are good in the summer and the scenery is dramatic with fortresses dominating high peaks. Through wooded countryside is the border town of Bolzano where you will hear German spoken (this was once the South Tyrol) and may be served sausage and sauerkraut and locally produced Reisling wine.

ANFO
Brescia
Palafitte via Calcaterra ✆(0365) 809051
Pleasant site divided into plots, sloping towards the lake where there are some trees.
Camping Carnet Compulsory.
Access as for Pilù, then turn right.
May-19 Sep
1.8HEC H G R H + lau LP
Prices A3200-4750 pitch6700-10000

Pilù via Bersaglio II Lago d'Idro ✆(0365) 809037
Well-maintained, slightly sloping site subdivided by trees and rows of shrubs on pebble beach from which it is separated by narrow public footpath.
On southern outskirts; well signed.
Apr-Sep
2.5HEC H G R LP + lau
Prices A3200-4750 pitch6700-10000

ANGERA
Varese
Città di Angera via Bruschera 99 ✆(0331) 930736
Signposted
Mar-Dec
7HEC H G R LP + lau
Prices A4500-4900 9700 A9700

ARONA
Novara
At **DORMELLETTO** (5km S)
Lago Azzurro via E-Fermi 5 ✆(0322) 497197
Camping Carnet Compulsory.
S of Arona off SS Sempione 33.
All year
2.5HEC H G LP + lau
Prices A4000 V3500 4000 A4000

Lago Maggiore ✆(0322) 497193
Well-maintained site divided into plots, pleasantly landscaped by the lakeside.
Access from SS33, well signposted.
15 Mar-15 Oct
5HEC H G R H LP + lau
Prices A5500-5600 pitch7500-9300

Lido Holiday Inn ✆(0322) 497047
Site on bank of the lake, with some trees.
Turn off the SS33 at Km60/VII and the IP petrol station, then about 250m towards the lake turn off past the Evinrude ship yard.
Apr-Sep
4HEC H G R H LP + lau
Prices A5600 8000-9300

Smeraldo via Cavour 103 ✆(0322) 497031
Well-landscaped site, divided into plots and situated in woodland by lakeside.
Access from SS33.
Mar-Oct
24HEC H G R L + lau
Prices A4700-5600 pitch7500-9300

ARVIER
Aosta
Arvier ✆(0165) 99088
20 Jun-Aug
1HEC H P lau G R
Prices A5500 V3200 4700 A4700

ASTI
Asti
Umberto Cagni strada Valmanera 152 ✆(0141) 271238
Apr-Sep
13HEC H G PR +
Prices A3500 V2000 4000 A4000

BAVENO
Novara
Lido Bruno via Piase 66 ✆(0323) 924775
Etr-Oct
1.5HEC ∼ ◑ H ✕ ⊖ G H L lau ☞ P
Prices A4000-4600 V3500-4000 4000-4600 Ă3500-4000

BOLZANO-BOZEN
Bolzano
Moosbauer ✆(0471) 918492
All year
1HEC ∼ ● H ✕ ⊖ G P lau ☞ +
Prices A6500 V4000 7000

BRÉCCIA
Como
International ✆(031) 521435
On a level meadow near the motorway. Lunchtime siesta 13.00-15.30 hrs.
Off A9 Como-Milan motorway.
15 Apr-15 Oct
2.3HEC ∼ ● H ✕ ⊖ G R H P + lau
Prices A4000 V2600 4000 Ă4000

BRUNICO-BRUNECK
Bolzano
At **RASUN** (10km E)
Corones ✆(0474) 46490
Very quiet site surrounded by trees with woodland.
Turn off SS49 about 10km E of Brunico towards Rasun-Antholz and onwards 1.2km.
Jan-20 Oct
2HEC ○ H ✕ ⊖ G R P + lau

BUISSON
Aosta
Cervino ✆(0166) 48421
All year
6HEC ∼ ◑ H ✕ ⊖ G R R + lau
Prices A5000-7000 V2800-4000 4800-6000 Ă4800-6000

CALCERANICA
Trento
Al Pescatore ✆(0461) 723062
The site consists of several sections of meadowland, inland from the lake shore road to Lago di Caldonazzo. Well maintained with private beach.
Jun-15 Sep
3.8HEC ∼ ◑ H ✕ ⊖ G H + lau ☞ L

Fleiola ✆(0461) 723153
Site is divided into sectors beside lake.
Apr-15 Oct
12HEC ∼ ◑ H ✕ ⊖ G H L + lau
Prices A5250 pitch7500

CALDONAZZO
Trento
Mario via Lungolago 4 ✆(0461) 723341
May-Sep
4HEC ∼ ● H ✕ ⊖ H L P + lau
Prices A5200 pitch8000

CAMPITELLO DI FASSA
Trento
Miravalle ✆(0462) 62002
Camping Carnet Compulsory.
Signposted.
Dec-Apr & Jun-Sep
2HEC ∼ ◑ H ⊖ G R H R + lau ☞ ✕
Prices A5000-6000 pitch8500-9500

CANAZEI
Trento
Marmolada ✆(0462) 61660
Grassland site extending to the river, part of it in spruce woodland.
Located on S outskirts on the right of the road to Alba Penia.
All year
3HEC ∼ ◑ H ✕ ⊖ G R + lau ☞ P

CANNOBIO
Novara
Campagna via Nazionale 22 ✆(0323) 70100
Turn off SS34 to Locarno at Km35/V on N outskirts of village. W of lake on road 21.
15 Mar-15 Oct
1.2HEC ∼ ● H ✕ ⊖ G L + lau
Prices A4700-5100 pitch8200-8900

Gelsi via Casali Darbedo 3 ✆(0323) 71318
Pleasantly landscaped site on meadowland at side of lake.
Access from the SS34 at Km35/V.
Mar-Oct
0.7HEC ∼ ● H ✕ ⊖ G R H L lau ☞ R +
Prices A4700-5100 V4100-4450 4100-4450

International Paradis ✆(0323) 71227
A level site on the bank of a lake.
Access from the SS34 at Km35/V.
Etr-Sep
12.5HEC ∼ ◑ H ✕ ⊖ G H L lau
Prices A4700-5100 V4300 4300 Ă4300

Riviera ✆(0323) 71360
A grassy site with poplar and pine trees. It is divided into pitches next to Camping dei Gelsi.
For access, turn off the SS34 at Km35/11, N of the river bridge and towards the lake.
Apr-Sep
22HEC ∼ ◑ ● H ✕ ⊖ G H L + lau

Valle Romantica ✆(0323) 71249
A pleasant site with trees, shrubs and flowers. Internal roads are asphalted and a mountain stream provides bathing facilities.
1.5km w off road to Malesco.
Apr-Sep
5HEC ∼ ◑ ● H ✕ ⊖ G H PR + lau

CASTELLETTO TICINO
Novara
Italia Lido via Cicognola 88 ✆(0331) 923032
All year ➔

2.5HEC ● H ⊖ G R H L lau
Prices A4000-5000 pitch5500-7000

2000 Residence via del Cantiere 10 ✆(0331) 924092
All year
8HEC ● H ⊖ G R LP lau
Prices A4500 V3000 4900 A3000

CHIUSA-KLAUSEN
Bolzano

Gamp ✆(0472) 47425
The site lies next to the Gasthof Gamp, between the Brenner railway line and the motorway bridge, which passes high above the camp.
Access from the motorway exit and the SS12 is well signposted.
All year
0.8HEC ◑ H ⊖ P lau
Prices A5300 V2800 5500

CHIUSO
Como

Rivabella via Alla Spiaggia 35 ✆(0341) 421143
May-Sep
1.5HEC ● H ⊖ G R L + lau
Prices A3300 pitch7400

COURMAYEUR
Aosta

Tronchey ✆(0165) 89251
15 Jun-15 Sep
2HEC ○ H ⊖ G P + lau

CUNEO
Cuneo

Turistico Communale Bisalta San Rocco Castagnaretta ✆(0171) 491334
All year
4HEC ● H ⊖ P lau

DESENZANO DEL GARDA
Brescia

Vò via Vò 4-9 ✆(030) 9121325
Apr-Sep
1.3HEC ● H ⊖ G R LP +
Prices A4200-6100 pitch9500-13000

DIMARO
Trento

Dolomiti di Brenta ✆(0463) 974332
Turn off SS42, at Km173.5
All year
3HEC ◑ H ⊖ G R PR P + lau
Prices A5000-6200 pitch8000-10000

DOBBIACO-TOBLACH
Bolzano

Olympia ✆(0474) 72147
The extensive site lies next to Hotel Olympia. Part of the camp lies in a wood of tall pine trees.
At Km56/V on the SS49 through the Puster Valley.
All year
4HEC ◑ H ⊖ G H P + lau

DOMASO
Como

Gardenia ✆(0344) 96262
N at Case Sparse
Apr-Sep
2HEC ◑ H ⊖ G R H LR + lau
Prices A3900 pitch8400

DORMELLETTO
See **ARONA**

EDOLO
Brescia

Adamello ✆(0364) 71694
1.5km W of SS39.
All year
1.2HEC ◑ H ⊖ G R H + lau R
Prices A5500 V2500 6000 A4000-6000

FERIOLO
Novara

Orchidea via Repubblica dell'Ossola ✆(0323) 28257
15 Mar-15 Oct
2.5HEC ● H ⊖ G H L + R
Prices A4100-5100 pitch7200-8900

FONDOTOCE
Novara

Continental Lido via'42 Martiri ✆(0323) 496300
10 May-15 Sep
8HEC ◑ H ⊖ G L lau R
Prices A4100-5100 V2950-4000 A2650-3600

Lido Toce ✆(0323) 496087
On E shore of lake.
May-Sep
1.5HEC ◑ H ⊖ LR + lau
Prices A3700-4500 V3000-3600 3300-4200 A3300-4200

Village Isolino via per Feriolo 25 ✆(0323) 496080
23 Mar-22 Sep
12HEC ● H ⊖ G R H L + lau
Prices A4100-5100 V2950-4000 A2650-3600

FUCINE DI OSSANA
Trento

Cevedale ✆(0463) 71630
Closed Dec-Mar
1.5HEC ○ H ⊖ lau G R R +
Prices A4600 pitch5400-8000

GIGNOD
Aosta

Europe Piano Castello 23 ✆(0165) 56195
All year
25HEC ● H ⊖ G R H P
Prices A5500 V2500 5500 A5500

GRESSONEY-LA-TRINITÉ
Aosta

Staffal ✆(0125) 366283
All year
2.2HEC H G P R
Prices A5200 4800 A2800-4800

IDRO
Brescia

AZUR Idro Rio Vantone ✆(0365) 83125
The site lies at the mouth of the river of same name beside Lake Idro. Subdivided into pitches (separate pitches for youths) on grass and woodland at the foot of strange rock formations.
Approach from Idro direction of Vantone, well signed from there.
All year
4HEC ◑ H ⊖ G L + lau

Vantone Pineta ✆(0365) 83347
On eastern shore of lake. Grassland enclosed by rush and willow fencing. Part of site in small woodland on bank of stream.
Camping Carnet Compulsory.
Approach from Idro and follow signs for Camping Idro Rio Vantone.
All year
2HEC ● H ⊖ G H LP + lau

ISEO
Brescia

Quai ✆(030) 981161
15 Apr-25 Sep
1.3HEC ● H ⊖ L + lau G R P
Prices A4000-5000 pitch8000-12000

Sassabanek via Colombera 1 ✆(030) 980300
Apr-Oct
3HEC ● H ⊖ R LP P +
Prices A4500-6100 8000-12300 A2000-3800

Sole via per Rovato 26 ✆(030) 980288
May-20 Oct
6.5HEC ● H ⊖ G LP P + lau

KALTERN
Bolzano

St Josef am See Welnstr 75 ✆(0471) 960170
20 Mar-5 Nov
1.3HEC ◑ H ⊖ G L lau
Prices A4200-4800 V3000-3300 3800-4300 A3500-3800

LAIVES-LEIFERS
Bolzano

Steiner ✆(0471) 950105

The site lies behind the Gasthof Steiner, the AGIP petrol station and a bungalow estate.
Off the SS12 on the northern outskirts of the village.
20 Mar-5 Nov
2.5HEC ⩫ ⊟ ● ⚲H ⛽ ⚲ ✕ ⊖ ⚲ G R ⌂ ⩫P ▣ + lau

LEVICO TERME
Trento
Jolly ✆(0461) 706934 & 234251
The site is divided into plots and lies on the lakeside with its own pool.
15 May-15 Sep
2HEC ⩫ ◑ ⚲H ⛽ ⚲ ✕ ⊖ ⚲ G ⌂ H ⩫P ▣ + lau ☞ R ⩫L
Prices A4100-5150 pitch5650-7100

Levico ✆(0461) 706491
May-Sep
3HEC ⩫ ● ⚲H ⛽ ⚲ ⊖ ⚲ G R ⩫L ▣ + lau ☞ ✕
Prices A5300 pitch8200

LILLAZ
Aosta
Salasses ✆(0165) 74252
Pleasant site surrounded by mountains, grassland and conifers. The site lies at the end of the Val di Cogne.
Entrance to site before Camping al Sole.
May-Sep
1.5HEC ⩫ S ⊟ ○ ◑ ● ⚲H ⛽ ⚲ ✕ ⊖ ⚲ G R H ⩫R ▣ + lau
Prices A4500 V2000 ⚲4000

LIMONE PIEMONTE
Cuneo
Luis Matlas ✆(0171) 927565
This tidy site offers winter facilities and skiing lessons are provided by the owner. Fishing is also available.
It lies to the north of the town, off the Limone-Nice road.
All year
1.5HEC ⩫ ⊟ ○ ⚲H ⚲ ✕ ⊖ ⚲ G R ⩫LP ▣ lau ☞ ⛽

LIMONE SUL GARDA
Brescia
Garda via IV Novembre ✆(0365) 954550
Mar-Nov
2.2HEC ⩫ ● ⚲H ⛽ ⚲ ✕ ⊖ ⚲ R ⌂ H ⩫L ▣ + lau

Nanzel ✆(0365) 954155
Well managed site, with low terraces in olive grove.
Access from Km101.2 (Hotel Giorgiol).
Apr-15 Oct
0.7HEC ⩫ ◑ ⚲H ⛽ ⚲ ✕ ⊖ ⚲ G H ⩫L ▣ + lau
Prices A5000 V3500 ⚲6500 ⛺6500

LINFANO D'ARCO
Trento
Bellavista ✆(0464) 505644
Apr-20 Oct
1HEC ⩫ ● ⚲H ⛽ ⚲ ⊖ ⚲ G ⩫L ▣ + lau ☞ ✕
Prices pp5200

MACCAGNO
Varese
AZUR Park Maccagno ✆(0332) 560203
By the lake.
In village turn off SS394 at Km43/III towards lake and after 500 m turn right.
All year
1.2HEC ⩫ ◑ ⚲H ⛽ ⚲ ✕ ⊖ ⚲ G ⌂ ⩫L ▣ + lau

Lido ✆(0332) 560250
Etr-Sep
8HEC ⩫ ● ⚲H ⛽ ⚲ ⊖ ⚲ ⩫L ▣ ⚓ ☞ G R +
Prices A3400-4800 V1700-2400 ⚲3800-5100 ⛺3800-5100

MAËN
Aosta
Glair Fraz Glair 5 ✆(0166) 92077
All year
2.3HEC ⩫ ○ ⚲H ⊖ ⚲ G R H ⛺ P lau ☞ ⛽ ⚲ ✕ ⩫LR
Prices A3800 V2700 ⚲4800 ⛺3800

MAGGIORE (LAGO)
See **ARONA, BAVENO, CANNOBIO, FONDOTOCE, MACCAGNO**

MANERBA DEL GARDA
Brescia
Rio Ferienglück ✆(0365) 653450
Follow SS572 Desenzano-Salo road, turn off between Km8 and 9, site 4km N.
May-Sep
11HEC ⩫ ● ⚲H ⛽ ⚲ ✕ ⊖ ⚲ G R ⌂ ⛺ ⩫L ▣ + ⚓

Rocca via Cavalle 22 ✆(0365) 551738
Apr-Sep
4.5HEC ⩫ ◑ ⚲H ⛽ ⚲ ✕ ⊖ ⚲ G R ⌂ ⩫LP ▣
Prices A5000 pitch12000-13000

San Biagio via Cavalle 19 ✆(03651) 551046
Apr-Sep
4.5HEC ⩫ ● ⚲H ⛽ ⚲ ✕ ⊖ ⚲ G R ⩫L ▣ + lau ☞ ⩫P
Prices A5000 pitch11000-12000

Zocco ✆(0365) 551605
The site consists of several, terraced sections. The section below the maintenance/supply building lies on a sloping olive grove and is somewhat obstructed by bungalows.
500m S of Gardonicino di Manerba.
20 Apr-Sep
5HEC ⩫ ◑ ⚲H ⛽ ⚲ ✕ ⊖ ⚲ ⌂ ▣ + lau ☞ R ⩫L
Prices A4500-5000 pitch10000-12000

MERANO-MERAN
Bolzano
Camping Merano Piavestr 44 ✆(0473) 31249
The site is stretched over a numbner of fields with little or no shade.
10 Apr-Oct
1.5HEC ⩫ ⊟ ● ⚲H ⚲ ⊖ ⚲ G R ▣ + lau ☞ ⛽ ✕ ⩫P

MOLINA DI LEDRO
Trento
International Camping Al Sole via Raffei ✆(0464) 508486
May-Sep
2HEC ⩫ ⊟ ◑ ⚲H ⛽ ⚲ ✕ ⊖ ⚲ ⩫L ▣ + ☞ G R
Prices A4500 pitch6500

MOLVENO
Trento
Spiaggia-Lago di Molveno ✆(0461) 586978
All year
4HEC ⩫ ◑ ⚲H ⛽ ⚲ ✕ ⊖ ⚲ G ▣ + lau ☞ ⩫LP
Prices A4800-6200 pitch5900-9500

MONIGA DEL GARDA
Brescia
Fontanelle ✆(0365) 502079
Apr-Sep
4HEC ⩫ ◑ ⚲H ⛽ ⚲ ✕ ⊖ ⚲ G ⌂ H ⩫L ▣ + lau
Prices A5900 pitch12000

Rose ✆(0365) 502031
This site lies on gently sloping ground with a few terraces.
Turn off the main road at Km7.5 near Ristorante La Pergola and drive down to lake for 1km.
Mar-Oct
2HEC ⩫ S ● ⚲H ⛽ ⚲ ✕ ⊖ ⚲ G R ⌂ ⩫L ▣ + lau
Prices A4400-5100 pitch9500-10900

San Michele via San Michele 8 ✆(0365) 502026
Apr-Sep
3.2HEC ⩫ ● ⚲H ⛽ ⚲ ✕ ⊖ ⚲ ⌂ ⩫LP ▣ + lau ☞ G R
Prices A4800-5100 pitch12000-13000

Sereno ✆(0365) 502080 & 502220
Well-maintained and appointed site with good lakeside and swimming facilities.
Turn off SS572D-S at Km13/VII or (better for caravans) 13/IV.
Apr-Sep
6HEC ⩫ ◑ ⚲H ⛽ ⚲ ✕ ⊖ ⚲ G ⌂ ⩫LP ▣ + ⚓ lau

NATURNO-NATURNS
Bolzano
Wald ✆(0473) 87298
The site lies on gently rising ground, in a forest of pine and deciduous trees.
For access, turn off the SS38 near the Gasthof Alderwirt in the village, and drive 0.8km S over the railway line.
15 Mar-Oct
1.5HEC ⩫ ⊟ ◑ ● ⚲H ⛽ ⚲ ⊖ ⚲ R ⩫P ▣ + lau ☞ ✕ G ⩫R
Prices A4500-5000 V3000-3500 ⚲4000-4500 ⛺4000-4500

NOVATE MEZZOLA
Sondrio
El Ranchero via Nazionale N3 (0343) 44169
Apr-Sep
1.4HEC H L + G R R
Prices A3000 V2000 3000-5000 3000-5000

ONNO
Como
Jost al Melgone (0341) 581373
May-Oct
1HEC H L P

ORA-AUER
Bolzano
Wasserfall (0471) 810519
Sloping site in front of the Gasthaus Wasserfall, between wooded rocky hills and the River Schwarzbach.
For access turn off Fleimstralstrasse (SS48) E of the bridge over the River Schwarzbach and drive N for 300m.
Apr-5 Nov
1HEC S H G P + lau
Prices A4800-6000 V4800-6000 4800-6000 4800-6000

ORTA SAN GIULIO
Novara
Cusio Lago d'Orta (0322) 90290
Mar-Dec
2HEC H H P lau L
Prices A3500-4500 5000-8000 2500-3000

PADENGHE
Brescia
Cá (030) 9907006
The site lies in a park-like setting on terraced ground.
For access, turn off the road along Lake Garda, 1.5Km N turn for Padenghe, and drive down a very steep road towards the lake.
Mar-20 Oct
2HEC H G R H L + lau
Prices A3000-5500 V3000-5500 3000-5500 3000-5500

Campagnola (030) 9907523 & 9142151
Turn off SS572 at Km17.7.
15 May-Sep
5HEC H G R LP +

Valtenesi (030) 9907023
The site lies in a beautiful, quiet setting on terraces that slope down to the lake.
Turn off road along Lake Garda, 1.5km N of turning for Padenghe, and drive down a steep road to lake and in 150m turn right into site after the AGIP petrol station.
Apr-15 Oct
6HEC H G R LP + lau
Prices A4000-6000 pitch9000-12400

PEIO
Trento
Val di Sole (0463) 73177
The site lies on terraced slopes at the foot of the Ortier mountain range.
400m off SP87.
Dec-Apr & Jun-Sep
2.3HEC H G R + lau P
Prices A3600-4800 pitch5500-6800

PERA DI FASSA
Trento
Soal via Dolomiti 32 (0462) 64519
All year
2HEC S H G R R lau +
Prices A5500-6400 7500-9200 5000-6000

PERGINE
Trento
Punta Indiani Lago di Caldonazzo (0461) 531262
15 May-Sep
1.5HEC H L G R
Prices A5000 pitch6400

PETTENASCO
Novara
Punta di Crabbia via Crabbia 4 (0323) 89117
All year
2HEC H G R L
Prices A5000 V1500 5500 4000-5500

PIETRAMURATA
Trento
Daino (0464) 507131
May-Nov
1.6HEC H G P + lau R R
Prices A5350 pitch8000

PIEVE DI MANERBA
Brescia
Faro via Repubblica 52 0365) 651704
Apr-Sep
1HEC H H P G R L +
Prices A5000 pitch11500

PISOGNE
Brescia
Eden (0364) 8050
The site lies on eastern lake shore with tall trees and a level beach.
Turn off SS510 at Km37/VII, over railway line and towards lake.
15 Mar-15 Oct
2.5HEC H L + lau G

PONTE TRESA
Varese
Trelago via Trelago 20 (0332) 716583
10 Apr-15 Sep
3.5HEC H G R H L + P
Prices A4000 pitch8000

PORLEZZA
Como
Costa Azzurra via Lago 2 (0344) 70024
14 Apr-Sep
1.4HEC H G R L + lau R
Prices A3100 V2700 2700 2700

Paradiso (0344) 61027
The site lies in meadowland on the north eastern lake shore.
S from SS340.
Apr-Sep
5HEC H G LP + lau

POZZA DI FASSA
Trento
Rosengarten via Avisio 15 (0462) 63305
Jun-Oct
3.5HEC H G R + lau
Prices A4800-5800 pitch8400-9400

Vidor via Valle S Nicolo (0462) 63247
All year
1.5HEC H G R + lau
Prices A4000-5200 pitch6000-8000

RASUN
See **BRUNICO-BRUNECK**

RHÊMES ST GEORGES
Aosta
Val di Rhêmes (0165) 95648
Jun-Sep
18HEC H R H R + lau
Prices A5200 V2500 4900 3100-4400

RIVA DEL GARDA
Trento
Bavaria viale Rovereto 100 (0464) 552524
Apr-Oct
0.6HEC S H + lau G L

RIVOLTELLA
Brescia
San Francesco (030) 9110245
This well-kept site is divided into many sections by drives, vineyards and orchards and has a private gravel beach.
At Km268 on SSN11.
Apr-Sep
8.5HEC H G H L + lau

SALLE, LA

Aosta

Mont Blanc ✆(0165) 861183

A grassy site on sloping ground, provided with flat terraces; lovely views of Mont Blanc and Grivola.

Take road towards La Salle from Aosta-Courmayeur road.

All year

2.5HEC H R + lau

SAN ANTONIO DI MAVIGNOLA

Trento

Faé ✆(0465) 81229 & 57178

Situated in famous winter skiing region of Madonna di Campiglio. Good base for climbing in Brenta mountain range. On four gravel terraces, and alpine meadow in hollow next to SS239.

15 Jun-Sep & Dec-Apr

2.1HEC H G R H + lau LR

Prices A5200 pitch7100

SAN FELICE DEL BENACO

Brescia

Europa-Silvella ✆(0365) 651095

Two sites under same management separated only by the joint approach road. The beach is situated about 80m below.

Signposted.

All year

7HEC H G H LP + lau

Prices A4700-6000 pitch11500-13000

Fornella ✆(0365) 62294

May-20 Sep

5.4HEC H G LP + lau

Prices A5200-6000 pitch11200-13000

Ideal Molino ✆(0365) 62023

Situated right beside Lake Garda amid beautiful scenery. Charming and quiet site 1km from S. Felice. Tennis courts, windsurf school. On the beach there is a pier and boat moorings. Pedal boats can be hired for lake trips.

1km from S Felice.

15 Mar-24 Sep

1.7HEC H H L + lau

Prices A4400-6900 pitch9100-14500

Weekend via dei Lauri 10, Cisano ✆(0365) 43712

Etr-Sep

5HEC H G R H P + L

Prices A6500 pitch14000

SAN LORENZEN

Bolzano

Wildberg ✆(0474) 44080

All year

1HEC H R PR lau G

Prices A3500-5000 pitch5000-6000

SAN PIETRO DI CORTENO

Brescia

Aprica via Nazionale 44, strada Statale 39 ✆(0342) 746784

All year ➔

2.1HEC G R R lau L +
Prices A5800 pitch11000

SAN SIGMUND
Bolzano
Gisser (0474) 55305
May-10 Oct
2HEC H PR + lau G R L
Prices A3900-4900 V2700-3400 3900-4900 3000-4100

SARRE
Aosta
International Touring (0165) 257061 & 35187
4km W of Aosta on SS26.
15 May-15 Sep
6HEC H G H P + lau
Prices A4500-4800 V2700-2900 4000-4300 2850-4300

Monte Bianco (0165) 57523
Apr-Sep
0.5HEC H G R P + lau

SORICO
Como
Grande Quiete via Boschetto 52 (0344) 84041
Well-maintained quiet site by the side of the lake.
Near the 'Ristorante Mera' and the bridge across the Mera. Access via the SS340d at Km27 near the road fork Splugen/Sondrio/Como. Turn towards the lake and continue along an uneven lane for 2.2km.
Apr-Sep
1.5HEC H G R R P lau L

Lac de Como (0344) 84035
The well-kept site lies on the right of the River Mera as it flows into Lake Como.
Turn off the SS340d at Km25 near TOTAL petrol station and drive 200m towards the lake.
All year
1.7HEC H G R H LR + lau
Prices A4700 pitch9800

See advertisement on page 189

TORRE DANIELE
Torino
Mombarone (0125) 757907
13km N of Ivrea on SS26. Very close to River.
All year
1.2HEC H G R + lau
Prices A4000 V2000 3500 3000

TOSCOLANO MADERNO
Brescia
Chiaro di Luna via Statale 218 (0365) 641179
Etr-Sep
8HEC H G R H L P +
Prices A4400-5000 pitch10000-12000

VIVERONE
Vercelli
Rocca via Lungo Lago 35 (0161) 98416
Apr-Sep
1HEC H H LP + lau
Prices A4300-4700 pitch7500-8000

VOLS
Bolzano
Seiseralm (0471) 706459
All year
2.5HEC H G R lau L +

VENICE/NORTH

Venice dominates this region. It is an ancient centre of arts and trade and is unique in having waterways as roads and many architectural splendours, as well as producing fine glass and lace and, due to the revival of the carnival, masks.
Venetian influence is apparent in towns like Udine with its Piazza della Libertà surrounded by Renaissance buildings or at Treviso, with its own canal system, and where concerts and theatre performances are held in the main square. Echoes of Rome can be found in Palladio's architecture in Vicenza or in Verona where the amphitheatre is the setting for the July-September opera season.
Art lovers can enjoy Giotto's frescoes and Donatello's sculptures in the university town of Padua, and at Rovigo are paintings by Bellini and Tiepolo.
Trieste, on the Yugoslav border is the major port and contains handsome 19th-century architecture and there are attractive villages like Bellini on the southern edge of the Dolomites built overlooking two rivers. Vineyards and wineries (Soave and Valpolicella) welcome tourists.

ARSIE
Belluno
Gajole Loc Soravigo (0439) 58505
Access from SS50 bis.
Apr-Sep
1.1HEC H lau L
Prices A2500-3000 V2000-2500 2500-3000 2500-3000

ASIAGO
Vicenza
Ekar (0424) 63752
All year
3.5HEC H G R + lau
Prices A6000 pitch9000

AURISINA
Trieste
Imperial Aurisina Cave 55 (040) 200459
Access via SS14 in Sistiana-Aurisina direction.
25 May-Sep
1.5HEC H G R H P + S
Prices A3500-5000 V2500-3500 3000-4000 3000-3500

BARDOLINO
Verona
Rocca (045) 7211111
Subdivided site in slightly sloping grassland broken up by rows of trees. Separated from the lake by a public path (no cars). Part of site on the other side of the main road is terraced amongst vines and olives with lovely view of lake.
Below the SS249 at Km40/IV
May-Sep
5HEC H G H LP + lau

Serenella (045) 7211333
Apr-Sep
6HEC H G H LP + lau
Prices A4800-5600 pitch8500-13000

BIBIONE
Venezia
Villagio Turistico Internazionale via Colonie (0431) 43231 & 43232
Mostly sandy terrain under pine trees. Some meadowland with a few deciduous trees. Wide sandy beach. Tennis court.
Access is well signed along approach.
May-27 Sep
13HEC H G R PS + lau
Prices A3500-6500 pitch6000-16000

BRENZONE
Verona
Primavera via Benaco 5 ✆(045) 7420421
Etr-Oct
0.8HEC ● H ⊖ R lau G P
Prices A4000-5000 V4000-4500 3500-4500 3500-4500

CA'NOGHERA
Venezia
Alba d'Oro via Triestina 214/B ✆(041) 5415102
Camping Carnet Compulsory.
Access from SS14.
Apr-Sep
6HEC ● H ⊖ G R PR + lau
Prices A5500 V2500 8500 4500-8000

CAORLE
Venezia
Falconera ✆(0421) 84282
Level site partially on sandy meadowland under tall poplars on the Porto di Falconera.
E on riverside road to Pizzeria Capri, then turn seawards.
May-15 Sep
2.9HEC ● H ⊖ G R lau S +
Prices A3100-6000 pitch5200-9000

Jolly via dei Cacciatori 5 ✆(0421) 81586
15 May-15 Sep
7.5HEC S ● H ⊖ G R S +
Prices A3200-6000 pitch5000-9000

San Francesco ✆(0421) 89333
This generously laid-out site, on level lawns with shady poplars, lies in the midst of a holiday village. ➔

Follow signs from Caorle for access.
Closed May
30HEC ● H G
R PS + lau

CASTELLETTO DI BRENZONE
Verona
San Zeno (045) 7430231
May-Sep
1.3HEC H H L
\+ G R
Prices A3300-5000 pitch6500-9800

CAVALLINO
Venezia
Europa via Fausta 332 (041) 968069
On grassland reaching to the sea, with some poplars. Lunchtime siesta 13.00-15.00 hrs.
Well signposted on Punta Sabbioni road.
25 Apr-Sep
11HEC ● H G
R H S + lau
Prices A3000-6000 pitch8000-15000

Garden Paradiso (041) 968075
An attractive, pleasantly laid-out holiday site. Lunchtime siesta 13.00-15.30 hrs.
On road to Cavallino.
5 May-Sep
13HEC ● H G
R H S + lau
Prices A3500-6500 pitch8100-17850

Germania via Radaelli 10 (041) 968068
25 Apr-Sep
3.3HEC S ● H G
R S + lau
Prices A2200-5300 pitch4000-10500

Holiday (041) 968178
A site with poplars next to the sea.
15 May-20 Sep
1.3HEC S ● H
H S + lau
Prices A1800-5000 pitch3500-11000

Italy via Fausta 272 (041) 968090
May-Sep
39HEC S ● H G
R H PS +
Prices A3500-6000 pitch5000-15500

Joker via Fausta 318 (041) 968019 & 968216
Between coastal road and the sandy beach with tall poplars. Partially subdivided.
May-Sep
4.4HEC ● H G
R H PS + lau

Residence (041) 968027
Well laid out site on level grassland, by a sandy beach. Lunchtime siesta 13.00-15.00 hrs.
Signposted.
Apr-22 Sep
8HEC ● H G
S P + lau
Prices A4200-6800 pitch9000-16000

Sant' Angelo via F-Boracca 63 (041) 968882
May-Sep
17HEC H G
H S + lau

Silva via F-Boracca 53 (041) 968087
The site lies on sand and grassland and is located between road and beach, divided by a vineyard. The section of site near the beach is quiet.
10 May-15 Sep
3HEC S ● H G
S + lau
Prices A3500-5000 pitch7000-13000

Union-Lido (041) 968080
This site lies on a long stretch of land next to a 1km-long beach. Separate section for tents and caravans.
Minimum stay during peak period is one week.
May-Sep
60HEC ● H G
R H PS + lau
Prices A6000-8000 pitch7500-19500

See advertisement in colour section

Villa al Mare (041) 968066
Level site divided into plots behind the lighthouse.
12 Apr-Sep
2HEC ● H G
H S + lau
Prices A3000-5500 pitch8000-15000

CHIOGGIA
Venezia
Continental via A-Barbarigo (041) 490990
May-15 Sep
2.2HEC ● H R
PRS +
Prices A3000-6000 pitch5000-12000

Miramare via A-Barbarigo (041) 490610
Longish site reaching as far as the beach, clean and well-maintained.
Access from Strada Romeo (SS309) in direction of Chiòggia Sottomarina, turn right on reaching beach and continue 500m.
May-20 Sep
4HEC ● H G R
PS + lau
Prices A3500-6000 pitch3500-12000

Villaggio Turistico Isamar
Isolaverde (041) 498100
The site lies on level grassland at the mouth of the River Etsch. Shade is provided by high poplars. Good beach.
Access via the SS309. Caravans are advised to approach via Km84/VII near the Brenta village.
15 May-15 Sep
20HEC S ● H G
R H PRS + lau
Prices A3800-8100 9900-18800 5500-14000

See advertisement on page 191

CISANO
Verona
Cisano (045) 7210107
Partly terraced site beside Lake Garda.
AFFI exit on Brenner-Verona motorway, access 4km further.
Etr-Sep
14HEC ● H G
H LP + lau

See advertisement on page 191

CORTINA D'AMPEZZO
Belluno
Cortina via Campo 2 (0436) 2483
This site lies amongst pine trees, several hundred metres away from the edge of town, off the Dolomite road towards Belluno.
Turn off road and drive 1km to the campsite which is situated by a small river.
All year
4.5HEC S ● H
G R P + lau

Dolomiti (0436) 2485
The site is beautifully situated on grassland with pine trees in a hollow, not far from the Olympic ski-jump.
For access, follow the directions for Camping Cortina. The camp is then 500m further on 2.7km S of Cortina.
15 May-Sep
5.4HEC H G
R P +
Prices A5600-6400 pitch7800-11500

Olympia (0436) 5057
A very beautiful site set in the centre of the centre of the magnificent Dolomite landscape.
It lies N of town off the SS51 towards Toblach at Km107.2
All year
4HEC H G R
H + lau PR
Prices A5600-6400 pitch7800-11500

Rocchetta (0436) 5063
In beautiful wooded surroundings.
Access S from Cortina via SS51.
Jun-20 Sep
2.3HEC H G
R lau PR +

DUINO-AURISINA
Trieste
At **SISTIANA**
Marepinetá (040) 299264
May-Sep
10.8HEC H
H P + lau G S
Prices A6000-7000 pitch11000-13500

GEMONA DEL FRIÚLI
Udine
Ai Poppi (0432) 980358
15 Mar-15 Nov
1HEC ● H R H
G R +
Prices A3500-4500 V7500-9000 5000-7000

International Camping
DOLOMITI

I-32043 Cortina d'Ampezzo, Tel. (0436) 2485

Access: From the north pass Cortina and Rocchetta campsites. From south turn left at Sprungschanze. Please ask for our colour brochure and price list.

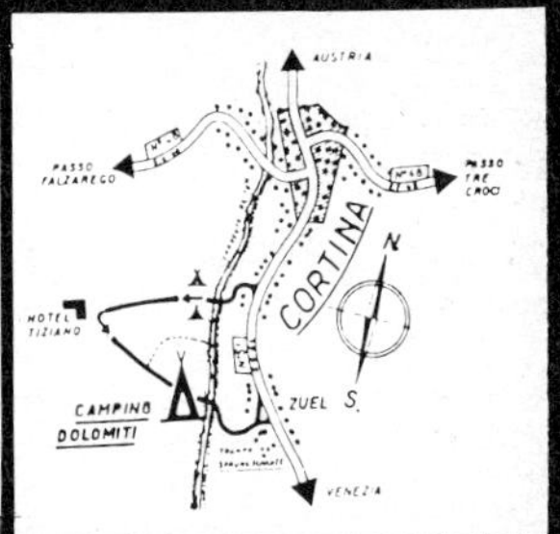

Camping Rocchetta

Campo 1 I-32043 CORTINA D'AMPEZZO – Tel. (0436) 5063

Sunny and quiet location, easy access whatever your means of transport. You can enjoy the following facilities: bar, food store, hot water (showers are free), electricity supplied, launderette, children's playground, table tennis, mini golf. We can offer you a pleasant stay in friendly surroundings.

Located by the SS14 road of NW of Trieste, near the sea and Sistiana harbour in an enchanting bay. From autostrada take Duino/ Sistiana exit. Beaches, swimming pool, modern sanitary and other installations. Bus service to the beach – free of charge. Its situation makes it suitable for both long and short stays. Caravans and maxi-caravans for hire!

I 34019 SISTIANA (TRIESTE) ITALY
Tel. 040/299264-299265 - Fax 0365/520690

INTERNATIONAL
CAMPING IDEAL

INTERNATIONAL CAMPING IDEAL, LAZISE, ITALY
I-37017 LAZISE SUL GARDA – TEL 045/758 00 77

On the shore of Lake Garda. Flat beach makes it suitable for children and non swimmers as well. Well stocked self service shop. Telephone, post office, First Aid, modern washing facilities with hot water. Showers etc. in several buildings spread throughout the site. Asphalt roads. Adequate shade. Staff speak German.

GRADO
Gorizia

Europa ✆(0431) 80877
In level terrain under half grown poplars. Partially in shade in pine forest.
On road to Monfalcone.
23 Mar-Sep
220HEC ~ ◑ ⛆H ♜ 🍷 ✕ ⊖ ⊡ [G] ⌂ [H] ≋PS ◘ + lau
Prices A4400-7800 pitch7400-12900

Tenuta Primero ✆(0431) 81371
The site lies in extensive level grassland between the road and the dam, which is 2m high along the narrow and level beach. Tennis court.
Access from Monfalcone road. Signposted.
16 May-20 Sep
18HEC ~ ● ⛆H ♜ 🍷 ✕ ⊖ ⊡ [G] ⌂ ≋PS ◘ P + 🐎 lau
Prices A6300-8800 pitch10600-13500

IÉSOLO
See **JÉSOLO, LIDO DI**

JÉSOLO, LIDO DI
Venezia

At **JÉSOLO PINETA** (6km E)
Malibu Beach ✆(0421) 362212
From Venezia via Cavallino on coast road to Cortellazzo.
15 May-15 Sep
10HEC ~ **S** ◑ ● ⛆H ♜ 🍷 ✕ ⊖ ⊡ [G] [R] ⌂ ≋PS ◘ 🐎 lau ☞ ≋R +
Prices A5000-8000 ⊡11000-18000 ▲6500-15000

Waikiki viale Oriente 124 ✆(0421) 980186
Jun-Aug
5.2HEC ~ ◑ ⛆H ♜ 🍷 ✕ ⊖ ⊡ [G] [R] [H] ≋PRS ◘ lau ☞ +
Prices A4000-6500 ⊡8000-13500 ▲5000-11000

At **PORTO DI PIAVE VECCHIA**(8km S)
Internazional ✆(0421) 971826
Site on sandy beach and also on far side of coast road.
W opposite ESSO filling station.
May-Sep
5.2HEC ~ **S** ⛆H ♜ 🍷 ✕ ⊖ ⊡ [G] [R] ≋S + 🐎 lau
Prices A3500-5500 V2500-4500 ⊡5000-8500 ▲4000-6500

JÉSOLO PINETA
See **JÉSOLO, LIDO DI**

LAZISE
Verona

Ideal ✆(045) 7580077
Etr-Sep
10HEC ~ ◑ ⛆H ♜ ✕ ⊖ ⊡ [G] ≋PS ◘ 🐎 lau

See advertisement on page 193

Parc via Sentieri ✆(045) 7580127
Well-kept, lakeside site off main road.
If approaching from Garda, the site is on S side of Lazise just after turning for Verona.
15 Mar-Oct
4.5HEC ~ ● ⛆H ♜ 🍷 ✕ ⊖ ⊡ ⌂ ≋L ◘ + lau
Prices A4200-5700 pitch9500-13200

Quercia ✆(045) 7580051
The site is divided into many large sections by tarred drives and lies on terraced ground that slopes gently down to the lake. There is a large private beach.
For access, turn off the main road SS49 at Km31/8 and drive for 400m.
Apr-Sep
4.5HEC ~ ◑ ⛆H ♜ 🍷 ✕ ⊖ ⊡ [G] ⌂ ≋LP ◘ + lau
Prices A6300-8800 pitch12600-21500

LIDO DI JÉSOLO
See **JÉSOLO, LIDO DI**

LIGNANO PINETA
Udine

Pino Mare ✆(0431) 428512
On mouth of River Tagliamento on undulating terrain in a natural pine forest.
10 May-20 Sep
16HEC **S** ● ⛆H ♜ 🍷 ✕ ⊖ [G] ⌂ ≋S ◘ 🐎

MALCESINE
Verona

Claudia via Molini 2 ✆(045) 7400786
Apr-20 Oct
1HEC ~ ◑ ⛆H ♜ 🍷 ✕ ⊖ ⊡ [G] [R] ⌂ ◘ ☞ ≋L
Prices A5000 V3500 ⊡6300 ▲6000

MARGHERA
Venezia

Jolly delle Querce ✆(041) 920312
The site lies on meadowland scattered with poplars.
For access, turn off into the Autostrada in Venezia in the direction of Chioggia on the SS309 and continue for 10m.
Mar-Oct
3.6HEC ~ ● ⛆H ♜ 🍷 ✕ ⊖ ⊡ [G] ⌂ [H] ◘ ☞ ≋P +
Prices A5800 pitch14000

MASARÈ
Belluno

Alleghe ✆(0437) 723737 &
Several terraces on a wooded incline below a road.
Jun-15 Sep & Dec-15 Apr
2HEC **S** ◑ ⛆H 🍷 ✕ ⊖ ⊡ [G] [R] ◘ lau ☞ ♜ ≋LR +
Prices A5500-6000 ⊡5500-6000 ▲3500-4000

MONFALCONE
Gorizia

Albatros ✆(0481) 40562
Level site by the sea with young poplars.
Access from Monfalcone in direction of Marine Julia for 5km. Adjoining bungalow village.
10 May-25 Sep
15HEC ~ ● ⛆H ♜ 🍷 ✕ ⊖ ⊡ [G] ⌂ [H] ≋PS ◘ +
Prices A3000-6500 pitch6000-17000

Isola Panzano Lido via Bagni 171 ✆(0481) 411202
15 May-15 Sep
13HEC ~ ● ⛆H ♜ 🍷 ✕ ⊖ ⊡ [G] [R] ⌂ [H] ≋S ◘ + lau
Prices A5500-6500 pitch9000-10000

MONTEGROTTO TERME
Padova

Sporting Center ✆(049) 793400
Mar-Oct
6.5HEC ~ ● ⛆H 🍷 ✕ ⊖ ⊡ ⌂ ≋P ◘ + lau ☞ ♜
Prices A5760-7200 ⊡11200-14000 ▲8000-10000

ORIAGO
Venezia

Serenissima ✆(041) 920286
Etr-Oct
2HEC ~ ● ⛆H ♜ 🍷 ✕ ⊖ ⊡ [G] ⌂ [H] ◘ + lau ☞ ≋L
Prices A5000 pitch10000

PACENGO
Verona

Lido via Peschiera 2 ✆(045) 7590611
Apr-Sep
10HEC ~ ● ⛆H ♜ 🍷 ✕ ⊖ ⊡ [G] ⌂ ≋LP ◘ +

PESCHIERA DEL GARDA
Verona

Bella Italia ✆(045) 6400688
Extensive lakeside site.
Turn off Brescia road between Km276.2 and Km275.8 and head towards lake.
Apr-Sep
15HEC ~ ◑ ⛆H ♜ 🍷 ✕ ⊖ ⊡ [G] ⌂ ≋P ◘ + lau ☞ ≋L
Prices A4300-6500 pitch7500-14000

Bergamini via Bergamini 51 ✆(045) 7550283
Apr-Sep
1.5HEC ~ ● ⛆H ♜ 🍷 ✕ ⊖ ⊡ ⌂ ≋L ◘ 🐎 lau ☞ [G] +

Garda ✆(045) 7550540 & 7551899
Apr-Sep
20.4HEC ~ ◑ ⛆H ♜ 🍷 ✕ ⊖ ⊡ [G] ⌂ ≋P ◘ 🐎 lau ☞ [R] ≋L +
Prices A4000-6500 pitch9500-14000

Gasparina ✆(045) 7550775
The site lies at Hotel Gasparina and is very clean and well kept. There is a lawn for sunbathing and a concrete quay.
Turn off main road at Km59.9 and drive towards lake for a further 1.4km.
Apr-20 Sep
5HEC ~ ● ⛆H ♜ ⊖ ⊡ [G] [R] ⌂ ≋L +

San Benedetto via Bergamini 14 ✆(045) 7550544
Apr-Sep

CAMPING MIRAMARE, PUNTA SABBIONI, ITALY
Right next door to Venice.
A shady grassy park set in a magnificent location with a view of the lagoon, pleasant beach and unattended moorings. Bungalows made of wood and brick which can sleep 4 to 5 persons. TV room. Motor boats leave for Venice from quay only 500m away. **Open 1.4 to 30.9**

Camping "ROMEO e GUILETTA"

Via Besciana 54, 37139 Verona Telephone: (045) 8510243 open throughout the year

Motorway exit "VERONA NORTH" from the Brenner motorway.

Swimming pool. Bar. Market. Play Area. Thickly wooded. Camper service. Cooling systems. Public bus to the town centre. Comfortable campsite. Ideal for visitors attending the Opera and Ballet festivals in the Arena.

CAMPING DEL GARDA

I-37019 PESCHIERA, ITALY
TELEPHONE: 045/755 18 99 AND 755 05 40
On the shore of Lake Garda, quiet and shady with a beautiful sandy beach, only 100m from the centre of town, 2 kilometres from the motorway exit Milan/Venice. Good washing facilities, showers with hot water, post, telephone, bar, self-service shop, pizzeria, market, car wash area, swimming pool, tennis, minigolf, children's playing area, table tennis.
Free entertainment. Our motto: to be cheerful and polite!

CAMPING LA QUERCIA

I-37017 LAZISE SUL GARDA – (Verona) Italia
Tel. (045) 7580051-7580328

The camp site LA QUERCIA is situated directly on the lakeshore. Enjoy the splendid view over the Lake Garda. The many trees on the site will give you shade and it lies on a slight slope towards the sandy beach. Lazise is approx. 2 kms away.
Sports facilities include: 2 swimming pools, basketball and volleyball courts, a tennis court, table tennis facilities, boules court, crazy golf, a roller skates rink, a football pitch, playground, body building room and an assault course.
The following courses are on offer: swimming, canoeing, tennis and windsurfing, archery, judo, yoga, contemporary dance, climbing without ropes, circus school (trapeze act and juggling), karate, synchronised swimming and many more.
All activities are supported by 30 congenial games organisers. Enjoy your holiday with games, music, dance, parties and excursions.

The following is on offer outside the main seasons:
- *All guests over 60 receive a 'silver card' which allows for discounts.*
- *All children under the age of 7 are free.*
- *At special times, we provide a babysitter for children between 3 and 7. The amount of children accepted is limited.*
- *One day will be free of charge if it rains longer than two consecutive days.*

220HEC H L + lau G R R
Prices 10000

PORTO DI PIAVE VECCHIA
See **JÉSOLO, LIDO DI**

PORTO SANTA MARGHERITA
Venezia
Pra'delle Torri (0421) 299063
Extensive site on flat ground.
3km W at edge of beach.
27 Apr-Sep
53HEC H G PS + lau
Prices 3900-7000 pitch6300-13300

PUNTA SABBIONI
Venezia
Marina di Venezia via Montello 6 (041) 966146
Extensive, well-organised and well maintained holiday centre, extremely well appointed, with ample shade by trees. A section of the site is designated for dog owners, caravans and tents.
Access from the coastal road, turn seawards about 500m before the end then continue along narrow asphalt road. Well signposted approach.
All year
80HEC H G R H PS + lau
Prices 3500-6500 pitch8500-18000

Miramare Lungomare D-Alighieri 29 (041) 966150
Site next to the sea.
Apr-Sep
1.8HEC H G + lau S
Prices 3800-4900 6800-9000 5600-7600

See advertisement on page 195

ROSOLINA MARE
Rovigo
Margherita via Foci Adige 10 (0426) 68181
25 Apr-Sep
6HEC S H G R H PS +
Prices 3800-7000 pitch10500-13000

Rosapineta (0426) 68033
The site lies in the grounds of an extensive holiday camp. Pitches for caravans and tents are separate.
Take Strada Romea towards Ravenna and drive to the bridge over the River Adige. Continue for 800m, then turn off, cross bridge and head towards Rosolina Mare and Rosapineta (approx 8km).
19 May-16 Sep
22HEC S H G R H PS + lau R
Prices 3900-5500 7300-9450 4950-7000

SISTIANA
See **DUINO-AURISINA**

TREPORTI
Venezia
Cá Pasquali via Poerio 33 (041) 966110
Sandy, meadowland site with poplar and pine trees.
Access from Cavallino-Punta Sabbioni coast road, along an asphalt road for 400m.
May-Sep
9HEC H G R H S + lau
Prices 3200-5600 pitch8000-17000

Cá Savio via Cá Savio (041) 966017
A level site along the edge of the sea with private, sandy beach. Separate pitches for caravans and tents.
From Cá Savio, at traffic lights, turn towards the sea and continue for 500m to the beach.
May-Sep
26HEC H G H S + lau
Prices 3200-5500 pitch6000-16000

Fiori (041) 966448
The site stretches over a wide area of sand dunes and pine trees with separate sections for caravans and tents.
5 May-8 Oct
11HEC S H G H PS + lau

Mediterráneo (041) 966721
Slightly hilly grassland site with trees and sunshade roofs. Lunchtime siesta 13.00-15.00 hrs.
Camping Carnet Compulsory.
Well signposted.
2 May-Sep
17HEC H G R H PS + lau

Scarpiland via A-Poerio 14 (041) 966488
15 May-15 Sep
3HEC H G R S
Prices 3000-5000 pitch5000-9000

VERONA
Verona
Romeo & Giulietta (045) 8510243
All year
3.5HEC H G P lau

See advertisement on page 195

ZOLDO ALTO
Belluno
Camping Pala Favera (0437) 788506 & 789161
Site with some woodland, at the foot of Monte Pelmo.
9 Jun-20 Sep & Dec-Apr
5HEC H G R + lau PR
Prices 5000-6000 5000-6000 3000-4000

NORTH WEST/MED COAST

Liguria is known as the Italian Riviera, having many small harbours and a large and prosperous port, Genoa. Inland, the slopes of the Alps and Apennines, covered in lavender and herbs, provide the sheltering warmth in which carnations and chrysanthemums are grown as a major industry.
Tuscany stretches down the north western coast with medieval hill towns, towers and cultural centres such as Florence and Sienna, a medieval town famous for its fan shaped square Piazza del Campo and the Palio horse races run twice a year. Landscapes vary from oak and chestnut woods near the Apennines, tall cypresses and farmhouses, vineyards (red Chianti is produced here), olive groves, and the rugged hills of the Carrara marble. Jousting and archery competitions take place between rival towns and festivals are occasions for pageantry.
Elba, off the Tuscan coast, is a thriving holiday island with resorts around the coast, and inland you can find some attractive old villages with narrow alleyways or take the cable car from the village of Marciano to the top of Monte Capanne.

ALASSIO
Savona
Monti e Mare (0182) 43036
In an attractive situation among olive trees.
Turn off SS1 at Km619.5.
Apr-Sep
7HEC S H G R + lau RS
Prices pitch17000-48500 (incl 2 persons)

ALBENGA
Savona
Bella Vista Campo Chiesa (0182) 540213
1km from Km613.5 on SS1.
All year

0.8HEC ◑ H ! ✕ ⊖ H + lau S
Prices A3000-5000 V2500-4500 3000-5000 A2000-5000

Green Village ✆(0182) 52286
Signposted
Apr-Sep
2HEC ● H ! ✕ ⊖ G R PRS lau +

Roma Regione Foce ✆(0182) 52317
The site is divided into pitches and laid out with many flower beds.
N of bridge over Centa, turn left.
Apr-Sep
0.8HEC ● H ! ✕ ⊖ G R + lau PRS
Prices A4300-6000 pitch4300-6000

ALBINIA
Grosseto
Acapulco ✆(0564) 870165
Set on hilly terrain in pine woodland.
Take coast road from via Aurelia at Km155.
15 May-15 Sep
2HEC S ● H ! ✕ ⊖ G R P + S
Prices A3900-6100 pitch6500-10700

Gabbiano ✆(0564) 870202
Site in pine woodland and open meadowland with sunshade roofing.
Turn off SS at Km155.
Apr-Sep
3HEC S ● H ! ✕ ⊖ G R H S P + lau

Hawaii ✆(0564) 870164
The site lies in a pine forest on rather hilly ground.
Turn off via Aurelia at Km154/V and drive towards the sea.
15 May-Sep
4HEC ● H ! ✕ ⊖ G R S +
Prices A3900-6100 pitch6500-10700

International Argentario ✆(0564) 870302
Set in a pine forest on the shores of the Bay of Porto S Stefano. Mooring facilities.
Etr Sep

10HEC S ● H ! ✕ ⊖ G P P + lau

Strand ✆(0564) 870304
Site lies in pine wood and grassland, equipped with roof matting to provide shade. One section of the site has wooden bungalows. Private beach.
Access from via Aurelia, at Km153/III turn seawards.
May-Sep
6.5HEC S ● H ! ✕ ⊖ G R P + lau S

Voltoncino ✆(0564) 870158
Undulating terrain in pine woodland and on grass.
Turn seawards at Km153/VII of the via Aurelia and continue to site in 100m.
15 May-15 Sep
7HEC ○ ◑ H ! ✕ ⊖ G R P + lau S

BIBBONA, MARINA DI
Livorno
See also FORTE DI BIBBONA

Capannino ✆(0586) 600252
Well tended park site in pine woodland with private beach.
On via Aurelia by Km272/VII turn towards sea.
May-Sep
3HEC S ● H ! ✕ ⊖ R P + lau S
Prices A4500-7100 pitch5500-8400

Free Beach via Cavalleggeri Nord ✆(0586) 600388
Etr-Sep
10HEC ● H ! ✕ ⊖ R H P lau S
Prices A7100 V2900 pitch8400

BOTTAI
Firenze
Internationale Firenze via S Cristoforo 1 ✆(055) 2034704
Apr-15 Oct
6HEC ◑ H ! ✕ ⊖ G R H PR +
Prices A5000 pitch9700

CAPÁLBIO
Grosseto
Villagio Turistico Capálbio via Pedemontand Snc ✆(0564) 898462
All year
3.3HEC ● H ! ✕ H PS P G R +
Prices A4500-7000 V2600 4000-9700 A4000-9650

CARBONIFERA
Livorno
Pappasole ✆(0565) 20414
Landscaped area inland off the coastal road.
All year
13HEC ◑ H ! ✕ ⊖ G H P + lau P

CASALE MARITTIMO
Pisa
Valle Gaia ✆(0586) 681236
Site amongst pines and olive trees in a quiet rural location.
In Southern Cecina turn off the SS1 inland. Site about 9km from the coast.
23 Mar-19 Oct
4HEC ● H ! ✕ ⊖ G R P + lau
Prices A4800-6600 pitch7500-11000

CASCIANO DI MURLO
Siena
Soline ✆(0577) 817410
All year
16HEC ◑ H ! ✕ ⊖ R P + lau R
Prices A6000 V1500 7500 A5000-6500

CASTEL DEL PIANO
Grosseto
Amiata ✆(0564) 955107
A grassland site with a separate section for dog owners.
Off the Arcidossa SS323, on the outskirts of the town at Km25.
All year
4HEC ● H ! ✕ ⊖ G R P + lau

CASTIGLIONE DELLA PESCAIA
Grosseto
Santa Pomata via della Rocchette ➔

(0564) 941037
Site in hilly woodland terrain with some pitches amongst bushes. Flat clean sandy beach.
Turn off the SS322 at Km20, then in direction of Le Rocchette 4.5km NW and continue towards the sea for 1km to site on left.
Apr-20 Oct
6HEC ● H G R S P + lau

CAVO
See **ELBA, ISOLA D'**

CECINA
Livorno
Mareblu via dei Campilunghi (0586) 620983
May-Sep
10HEC ● H H S + lau
Prices A4000-7800 V2300-3300 4500-9500 4500-9500

CÉCINA, MARINA DI
Livorno
Tamerici (0586) 620629
All year
8HEC ● H G R H S + lau P
Prices A4600-6800 V2000-2900 5500-7700 5500-7700

CERIALE
Savona
Baciccia via Torino 19 (0182) 90743
An orderly site, lying inland off the via Aurelia.
Entrance 100m W of Km613/V.
All year
1.2HEC ● H G R H P + lau S
Prices pitch21500-36000 (incl 3 persons)

CERVO
Imperia
Lino (183) 400087
A seaside site shaded by grape vines, which is clean and well managed. There is a knee-deep lagoon suitable for children.
Turn off via Aurelia at Km637/V near the railway underpass and follow via Nazionale Sauro towards sea.
16 Mar-14 Oct
1.1HEC S ● H G R S + lau P

DIANO MARINA
Imperia
Diana (0183) 495302
400m NW of road to Imperia.
All year
3.3HEC ● H G R H P + lau S
Prices pitch15000-30000

ELBA, ISOLA D'
Livorno
CAVO
Paguro's (0565) 949966 & 915176
Very quiet extensive site in a natural valley partially terraced 0.6km from the sea.
Camping Carnet Compulsory.
1km S in Velle di Baccetti.
Jun-Sep
3.5HEC ● H G R H P + lau S
Prices A6000-9600 V1500-2000 7000-10300 6000-10300

LACONA
Lacona Pineta (0565) 964149
Apr-Oct
3.4HEC ● H G R S P + lau P
Prices A7500-9000 V2000-2550 8000-9550 8000-9550

Stella Mare (0565) 964007 & 964051
Terraced site with level pitches on a hillside peninsula overlooking the Gulf of Lacona. Plenty of shade provided by pines and deciduous trees. Lovely views. Steep steps and paths to the beach.
Turn left 100m beyond the turn off for Camping Lacona and past this site to the Stella Mare.
Apr-10 Oct
8HEC ● H G S + lau R
Prices A9000 V2550 9550 9550

MORCONE
Croce del Sud de Vago Giovanna (0565) 968640
Apr-14 Oct
1HEC H G R H + lau S
Prices A6000-8000 V1900-2500 6000-9000 6000-9000

NISPORTO
Sole e Mare (0565) 934907
All year
1.5HEC ● H G R H S P + lau
Prices A6300-9000 V1800-2550 6700-9550 6700-9550

ORTANO
Canapai (0565) 939165
Camping Carnet Compulsory.
May-14 Oct
3.5HEC ● H G H P + S
Prices A5800-8300 V1800-2500 6300-9000 6300-9000

OTTONE
Rosselba le Palme (0565) 933101
Apr-Sep
30HEC ● H G H P + lau S
Prices A7100-9100 V2600 7650-9650 7650-9650

PORTO AZZURRO
Reale (0565) 95678
Apr-Oct
2.5HEC ● H G R S + lau L
Prices A6500-8350 V2000-2500 6500-9000 6500-9000

PORTOFERRAIO
Enfola Enfola (0565) 939001
Apr-15 Oct
1HEC S ● H G R H S +
Prices A7200-9000 V2000-2550 7600-9550 7600-9550

Scagleiri via Biodola 1 (0565) 969940
Apr-15 Oct

1HEC ● H ⊖ [G] S + lau
Prices A7800-9000 V2200-2550 8300-9550 A8300-9550

FIÉSOLE
Firenze
Panoramico via Peramonda 1 ✆(055) 599069
All year
5HEC ● H ⊖ [G] [H] lau +
Prices A6500 V2200 9950 A9950

FIGLINE VALDARNO
Firenze
Norcenni Girasole ✆(055) 959666
Terraced site on partial slope. Separate section for young people.
3km W of village. Take Valdarno motorway exit and drive N for 15km.
All year
11HEC ◑ H ⊖ [G] [H] P + lau
Prices A68000 V3800 6400 A5800

FIRENZE (FLORENCE)
Firenze
At **MARCIALLA**
Toscana Colliverdi St. Provinciala Tavernelle, Certaldo ✆(0571) 669334
10 Mar-Sep
2.2HEC ◑ H ⊖ [G] P + lau

FLORENCE
See **FIRENZE**

FORTE DI BIBBONA
Livorno
See also BIBBONA, MARINA DI
Capanne ✆(0586) 600064
Site is situated on level tidy grassland amongst peach and olive trees.
Access from Km273 via Aurelia travelling inland.
Apr-15 Sep
6HEC ● H ⊖ [G] [R] P + lau S
Prices A4200-6900 pitch6900-8200

Esperidi ✆(0586) 600196
Site stretching to the sea with pines and other coniferous trees.
Turn off via Aurelia, at Km727.7.
Apr-Sep
11HEC ● H ⊖ [G] S + lau
Prices A6600-6900 V2400-2600 6500-6900 A6500-6900

Forte ✆(0586) 600155
Level site, grassy, sandy terrain.
Apr-Sep
8HEC ● H ⊖ [G] [R] P + lau S

GROSSETO, MARINA DI
Grosseto
Rosmarina via delle Colonie 37 ✆(0564) 36319
A modern site situated in a pine wood and close to the sea.
Apr-Sep
1.4HEC ● H ⊖ [G] [R] + lau S
Prices A4500-7800 pitch6600-12000

IMPERIA
Imperia
Wijnstok via Poggi 2 ✆(0183) 64986
W of village, at Km650.95 turn off via Aurelia inland towards Poggi, then right to site.
All year
10HEC ● H ⊖ [G] [R] [H] + lau S

LACONA
See **ELBA, ISOLA D'**

LERICI
La Spezia
Maralunga via Carpanini 61, Maralunga ✆(0187) 966589
Jun-Sep
1HEC ● H ⊖ [G] [R] S P +
Prices A8000 V5000 12000 A7000-11000

MARCIALLA
See **FIRENZE (FLORENCE)**

MASSA, MARINA DI
Massa Carrara
Citta di Massa via delle Pinete ✆(0585) 241225
Sandy meadowland.
On the land side of coastal road.
May-Sep
4HEC ● H ⊖ [G] + PS
Prices A3000-4500 V3000 12000-16000 A12000-16000

Giardino ✆(0585) 241605
Site in pine woodland and on two meadows, shade provided by roof matting.
On the island side of the SS328 to Pisa.
May-Sep
3HEC ● H ⊖ [R] [H] + lau PS
Prices A3000-4500 V3000 12000-16000 A12000-16000

MONTECATINI TERME
Pistoia
Belsito via delle Vigne ✆(0572) 67185
Apr-Oct
6.4HEC ◑ H ⊖ [G] [R] [H] P + LR
Prices A6000-7000 pitch7000-16000

MONTE DI FO
Firenze
Sergente ✆(055) 8423018
All year
1HEC ● H ⊖ [G] [R] + lau
Prices A5000 pitch9500

MONTERIGGIONI
Siena
Camping Piscina Luxor Quies Castellina Scala Stazion ✆(0577) 743047
Lies on a flat-topped hill, partly in an oak wood, partly in meadowland.
Turn off via Cassia (SS2) at Km239/II or Km238/IX and continue for further 2.5km, crossing railway line. Approach to site via very steep and winding road.
Jun-Aug
1.4HEC ● H ⊖ [G] [H] P +
Prices A6500 V3000 3500 A3000

MONTESCUDÁIO
Livorno
Montescudáio ✆(0586) 683477
This modern site is situated on a hill and is completely divided into individual pitches, some of which are naturally screened. Children under 2 years are not accepted.
From Cecinia (on SS1, via Aurelia) follow road to Guardistallo for 2.5km.
15 May-15 Sep
25HEC ● H ⊖ [G] [R] [H] P + lau S
Prices A5500-7000 pitch11000-15000

MONTICELLO AMIATA
Grosseto
Lucherino ✆(0564) 992975
15 Jun-15 Sep
1.6HEC ● H ⊖ [G] [H] P P + lau [R]
Prices A6500 pitch5000-7000

MORCONE
See **ELBA, ISOLA D'**

NISPORTO
See **ELBA, ISOLA D'**

ORTANO
See **ELBA, ISOLA D'**

OTTONE
See **ELBA, ISOLA D'**

PEGLI
Genova
Villa Doria ✆(010) 680613
All year
1HEC ● H ⊖ [G] [R] PS +
Prices A5000 V3000 5500 A4500

PISA
Pisa
Torre Pendente viale della Cascine 86 ✆(050) 561704 & 560665
Etr-15 Oct
2.5HEC ◑ H ⊖ [G] + lau [R] P
Prices A6500 V4500 5000 A4500

POPULÓNIA
Livorno
Sant'Albínia ✆(0565) 29389
10 May-15 Sep →

3HEC ◑ H R H S P + lau P

Prices A5400-6000 V2160-2400 6390-7100 Å4680-5200

PORTO AZZURRO

See **ELBA, ISOLA D'**

PORTOFERRAIO

See **ELBA, ISOLA D'**

PUNTA ALA

Grosseto

Báia Verde ✆(0564) 922298

The site lies partly in a pine forest and partly in open meadowland. It is divided into pitches. There is a wide range of amenities. Strict observance of the resting periods.

Apr-Oct

20HEC S ● H ⊖ G H S P + lau

SAN BARONTO

Firenze

Barco Reale via Nardini 11-13 ✆(0573) 88332

23 Mar-15 Oct

5HEC ● H ⊖ R H P P + lau

Prices A6100 V2700 7500 Å5500

SAN GIMIGNANO

Siena

Boschetto di Piemma ✆(0577) 940352

Apr-Oct

1.5HEC S ● H ⊖ G P +

Prices A4500 V1600 3500 Å2500

SAN PIERO A SIEVE

Firenze

Mugello Verde via Masso Rondinaio 2 ✆(055) 848511

Terraced site in wooded surroundings. Lunchtime siesta 14.00-16.00 hrs.

Leave motorway at exit 18 and follow signs.

All year

12HEC ● H ⊖ G R P + lau R

Prices A6200 V2200 7100-10200

SAN REMO

Imperia

San Remo ✆(0184) 60635

All year

2.3HEC ● H ⊖ G R H S + lau

SANTA VITTORIA

Genova

Santa Vittoria ✆(0185) 409204

The site lies on meadowland in a wide valley at the foot of a pine-covered mountain. A very clean site.

2km inland from via Aurelia. North of Sestri Levante and the motorway.

All year

1.5HEC ● H ⊖ G R H + lau

Prices pitch22000-33000

SAN VINCENZO

Livorno

Park Albatros ✆(0565) 702414 & 701018

The site lies amongst beautiful, tall pine trees. 1km from sea.

Turn off SP23 beyond Piombino at Km7/III and drive 600m inland.

25 May-9 Sep

11.4HEC ● H ⊖ G R + lau S

SARZANA

La Spezia

Iron Gate via xxv Aprile 54 ✆(0187) 673391

All year

5.5HEC H ⊖ G PR

SESTRI LEVANTE

Genova

Fossa Lupara via Costa 31 ✆(0185) 43992

All year

1.3HEC ● H ⊖ G R H + lau

Prices A5500-6500 V1500-2000 9000 Å4500-9000

SIENA

Siena

Siena Colleverde strada di Scacciafensien 47 ✆(0577) 280044

16 Mar-15 Nov

4HEC ● H ⊖ G P + lau

Prices pp7000-8600

STELLA SAN GIOVANNI

Savona

Stella Riobasco 62 ✆(019) 703269

15 May-10 Oct

1HEC ● H ⊖ G R H P + lau

Prices A5500-6500 V3000-4000 6000-7000 Å5500-7000

TORRE DEL LAGO PUCCINI

Lucca

Burlamacco via le Marconi Int ✆(0584) 340797

Apr-Sep

4HEC ● H ⊖ G R H P P + LS

Prices A3400-5900 V2800 6500-10000 Å6500-10000

Europa ✆(0584) 341524

Site in pine amd poplar woodland.

On the land side of the viale dei Tigli, coming from Viareggio.

Apr-Sep

6HEC ● H ⊖ G R H + lau S

Prices A3500-5900 pitch6000-10000

Italia ✆(0584) 341504

This site is divided into pitches and lies in meadowland planted with poplar trees.

Inland from the Viareggio road (viale dei Tigli).

Apr-15 Sep

9HEC ● H ⊖ G R H P + lau LPS

Prices A4000-65000 pitch6800-10700

Tigli ✆(0584) 341278

Camping Carnet Compulsory.

Apr-Sep

9HEC ● H ⊖ G R + lau LPS

Prices A4000-5000 V2500 6000-8000 Å6000-8000

VADA

Livorno

Flori ✆(0586) 770096

Level grassland surrounded by fields. Shade provided by roof matting.

Access from the SS1 S of Vada, after 1.5km turn right and continue for 500m.

May-Sep

15HEC ● H ⊖ G R H P + lau S

Prices A6000-7700 pitch10000-13000

Pineta via di Pietrabianca ✆(0586) 788524

The site lies on grassy and sandy terrain with some reed mat roofs and lies inland from the access road in a pine grove. Private beach.

Camping Carnet Compulsory.

15 Apr-Oct

1.5HEC S ● H ⊖ G R + PS

Prices A4700-6600 pitch5500-10800

Rada Etrusca via Cavalleggeri 77 ✆(0586) 788344

May-Sep
4.5HEC H G R S P +
Prices A4500-5800 V2500 5500-7050 5500-7050

VIAREGGIO
Lucca
Paradiso via dei Tigli (0584) 392005
Site with tall pine trees and firm terrain.
2.5km S off via Aurelia at Km354/V onto via Comparini towards the sea to site in 600m.
May-Sep
5HEC H G R P + PS
Prices A3300-5400 pitch8500-12700

Pineta via dei Lecci (0584) 383397
May-20 Sep
3.2HEC H G R S P + P
Prices A4600-6500 pitch7700-11000

Viareggio via Comparinivale dei Tigli (0584) 391012
The site lies in a poplar wood.
1.5km S of town. At Km354/V head towards coast.
15 Apr-15 Sep
2HEC H G R + lau S
Prices A4600-6400 pitch11600-14800

VILLANOVA D'ALBENGA
Savona
C'era una Volta (0182) 580461
Holiday centre set on a hill overlooking the surrounding area. Disco, tennis court.
Apr-Oct
150HEC H G P P lau

VOLTERRA
Pisa
Balze via di Mandringa (0588) 87880
Apr-Sep
30HEC H G R P +
Prices A5500 V1000 6500 5500

ZINOLA
Savona
Buggi International via N S del Monteis (0191) 860120
All year
3HEC H H + G R PS
Prices A5000 V4000 5000 4500

NORTH EAST/ADRIATIC

This area covers some very dissimilar regions east of the Apennine mountains on whose slopes the glaciers glint for much of the year. Fish from the Adriatic make specialities like the fish soup "brodetto" worth trying. Inland you may like to try Bologna's Mortadella sausage and the Lambrusco Frizzante wine. Emilia Romagna's varied geography – mountains, the river Po and the sea – allows winter skiing, and walking in pine forests in summer. Art lovers can see the mosaics in Ravenna, or Corrigio's paintings in Parma, a town which is famous for its dried ham and cheese. In the rugged Marches you can find the splendid Renaissance palace of Urbino or perhaps visit the hill town of Maceratas which has a Roman arena where concerts and dramas are held, or go to Ascoli Piceno, enclosed by two rivers and with a delightful town centre.
The Abruzzo in the centre of Italy is dramatic with high mountains, and a National Park where bears, chamois and wolves live. Attractive towns like L'Aquila dominated by its castle, contrast with the flourishing seaside resorts such as Pescara.

ADRIANO, LIDO
See **PUNTA MARINA**

ALBA ADRIATICA
Teramo
At **TORTORETO, LIDO** (4km S)
Salinello (0861) 786306
Well-tended meadowland site with numerous rows of poplars. Private beach, siesta 14.00-16.00 hrs.
On southern outskirts, signposted from Km405 of the SS16.
May-Sep
12HEC H G R + lau S

AQUILA, L'
L'Aquila
Funivia del Gran Sasso (0862) 606163
Closed Oct & May
0.7HEC H R P + lau
Prices A4500-5500 V2000 7000-8000 7000-8000

ASSISI
Perugia
Fontemaggio Eremo Carceri 8 (075) 813636 – Summer
This terraced site is scattered with olive trees and has a beautiful view of surrounding countryside.
It lies just off the road that climbs up to the hermitage of St Francis of Assisi. Short steep approach.
All year
10HEC H G H + lau P

BELLARIA
Forlì
Happy via Panzini 228 (0541) 346102
May-Sep
1.8HEC H G P + lau S
Prices A4700-6800 pitch10500

BORGHETTO
Perugia
Badiaccia strada Umbro Casentinese, Bivio Borghetto (075) 954147
Apr-Sep
5HEC S H G H LP +
Prices A5000 V1800 6000 5000

BRUCIATA
Modena
Modena via Cave Ramo 111 (059) 332252
Apr-Sep
0.7HEC H G P +
Prices A4800 V2600 4800 4000

CASALBORDINO, MARINA DI
Chieti
S. Stefano (0873) 918118
Level terrain, below road, within agricultural area, adjoining railway line. Open air disco. Lunchtime siesta 14.00-16.00 hrs.
Camping Carnet Compulsory.
Exit off Vastro-Nord of A14 (Percara-Bari) and continue north via SS16 to Km498.
All year
2.5HEC H P S

CASAL BORSETTI
Ravenna
Adria (0544) 445217
The site lies in a field behind the Ristorante Lugo.
Turn off the motorway at the Ravenna exit or take the SS309 (Romea) Km13 N of Ravenna.
5 May-20 Sep
4.4HEC H G P + lau PS

Florida ✆(0544) 445105
On level meadow, separated from the sea by dunes and pines, subdivided by various bushes and trees. Private beach with guarded area where boats may be left.
4km on via Romeo at Km14.
Jun-Aug
2.7HEC H G S + lau
Prices A4100-5900 pitch10000

Reno ✆(0544) 445213
Meadowland in sparse pine woodland and separated from the sea by dunes.
Turn off SS309 at Km8 or 14.
May-Sep
3.3HEC H G R + S

CERVIA
Ravenna
Adriatico via Pinarella 30 ✆(0544) 71537 & 72346
Level meadowland site with plenty of shade, pleasantly landscaped with olives, willows, elms and pine trees.
Located shortly before Pinarella di Cervia. Access by via Cadulti per le Liberta (SS16) 600m from sea.
15 May-15 Sep
3.4HEC H G R P + lau S
Prices A3600-5400 pitch7500-9500

CESENATICO
Forli
Camping Motel via Cavour 1 ✆(0547) 82748
400m from sea, a subdivided park-like terrain in between local housing, partially surrounded by bushes and grape vines.
N of town off SS16 at Km178.
15 May-Sep
2.8HEC S H G R H + lau S

Cesenatico via Mazzini 182 ✆(0547) 81344
The site stretches over an area of land belonging to the Azienda di Soggiomo e Turismo.
Camping Carnet Compulsory.
1.5km N at Km178 turn off the SS16 towards the sea.
Apr-Sep
16HEC H G R + lau S
Prices A3300-4700 pitch6000-11500

Zadina ✆(0547) 82310
Very pleasant terrain in dunes on two sides of a canal.
6 May-10 Sep
9.8HEC S H G S +
Prices A3250-4600 10000 8500

CIVITANOVA MARCHE
Macerata
Nuove Giare via Castelletta 34 ✆(0733) 70440
15 May-15 Sep
6HEC H G R H PS + lau
Prices A2000-5600 V2700-3800 6000-12800 6000-12800

CLASSE, LIDO DI
See **MILANO MARITTIMA**

DANTE, LIDO DI
Ravenna
Classe ✆(0544) 494021 & 494481
Level meadowland in grounds of former farm.
Camping Carnet Compulsory.
Access from the SS16 turning towards the sea at Km154/V and continue 9km to site.
May-Sep
7HEC H G R H PS + lau

ESTENSI, LIDO DEGLI
Ferrara
Mare e Pineta ✆(0533) 330194 & 330110
Extensive site on slightly hilly ground under pines and decidous trees, providing shade. Near the beach and has numerous mobile homes.
2km SE of Port Garibaldi.
15 May-15 Sep
16HEC H G R H P + S
Prices A4200-7400 pitch5200-10400

FANO
Pesaro & Urbino
Fano ✆(0721) 802652
Mar-9 Sep
3HEC H G R PRS P + lau
Prices A3200-5100 7700-10300

Stella Maris via A-Cappellini 5 ✆(0721) 884231
24 Apr-Sep
3HEC S H G PS + lau R
Prices A4350-6000 pitch8250-10150

FIORENZUOLA DI FOCARA
Pesaro & Urbino
Panorama Strada Panoramica ✆(0721) 208145
May-Sep
2HEC H G R H S +
Prices A3850-5300 V2300-2500 5200-7000 5200-7000

GATTEO MARE
Forli
Rose ✆(0547) 86213
Turn off SS16, at Km186.
15 May-20 Sep
5HEC S H G R H P + lau S
Prices A40900-6300 pitch6000-9700

GIULIANOVA LIDO
Teramo
Holiday Village ✆(085) 864425
15 Apr-20 Oct
4.5HEC S H G R H PS R +

MADONNA DEL PONTE
Pesaro & Urbino
Madonna Ponte ✆(0721) 804520
Jun-Aug
2.5HEC H G R H S + lau
Prices A3500-5500 pitch7500-9500

MARCELLI DI NUMANA
Ancona
Conero Azzurro via Litoranea ✆(071) 7390507
May-15 Sep
5HEC H G R P + lau R
Prices A5000-7000 V3000-4000 10000-14000 10000-14000

MARMORE
Terni
Cascata delle Marmore via C-Battisti 38 ✆(0744) 67198
Jun-Sep
32HEC S H + R
Prices A5000 V2000 6500 5000

MAROTTA
Pesaro & Urbino
Gabbiano via Faa' di Bruno 95 ✆(0721) 960033
May-Sep
2.1HEC H G R H P + lau S
Prices A4000-5500 pitch6500-9000

MARTINISCURO
Teramo
Duca Amedeo Lungomare Europa 158 ✆(0861) 797376
May-23 Sep
1.2HEC H R S + lau G
Prices A3000-5000 pitch9000-15000

MASERNO DI MONTESE
Modena
Chiocciola via Maserno Testa 271 ✆(059) 981503
All year
2HEC H R H +
Prices A4000-6000 8000-10000 6000-8000

MILANO MARITTIMA
Ravenna
Villaggio Turistico Romagna viale Matteoti 190 ✆(0544) 949326
Level and flat site with young trees.
Access via the SS16 (Strada Adriatica) turn off beyond Milano Marittima and follow signs.
May-10 Sep

3.5HEC H G S lau R +
Prices A3850-5400 pitch7500

At **CLASSE, LIDO DI** (8km N)
Pineta Ramazzotti ✆(0544) 494207
In uneven grassy and sandy terrain with wild olive trees separated from the sea by dunes and a narrow strip of pines.
Turn off towards the sea at Km154/V SS16 and continue for 9km to site.
May-Sep
3.3HEC H G R H S +

MONTENERO, MARINA DI
Campobasso
Costa Verde ✆(0873) 52144
This seaside site lies E of San Salvo Marino.
Camping Carnet Compulsory.
Leave the coast road, SS16, at Km525/VII and continue by a farm road for 300m to the site.
15 May-15 Sep
1.1HEC H G R H S + lau PR
Prices A4000-5000 pitch7000-8000

NAZIONI, LIDO DELLE
Ferrara
Tahiti ✆(0533) 39500
Pleasantly laid out site 650m from sea. Has own private beach accessible via a miniature railway. Lunchtime siesta 13.30-15.30 hrs.
Turn off SS309 near Km32.5 then 2km to site. Signposted.
15 May-20 Sep
8HEC H G R P + lau LS
Prices A4300-6900 pitch7400-12500

OLMO
Perugia
Rocolo strada Trinita Fontana 1-N ✆(075) 798550
15 Jun-15 Sep
2.4HEC H R + LP
Prices A5000 V1800 5000 4000

ORVIETO
Terni
Orvieto Lago di Corbara ✆(0744) 950240
Turn off SS448 at Km3.770.
Etr-Sep
1.6HEC H G H LP + lau
Prices A6000 V2000 7500 5000

PALMENSE, MARINA
Ascoli Piceno
Villaggio Verde Mare ✆(0734) 53167
Extensive level grassy terrain with poplars of medium height, divided into two by a stream.
At Km363 on N16.
May-Sep

12HEC H G R PS P + lau

PARMA
Parma
Cittadella ✆(0521) 581546
Camping Carnet Compulsory.
Apr-Oct
0.4HEC H PR
Prices A4600 V5250 5250 5250

PASSIGNANO
Perugia
Kursaal ✆(075) 827765 & 828085
The site is situated between the road and the lake, near the villa of the same name.
Access from SS75, Arezzo to Perugia road, from Km35.2.
Apr-10 Oct
3HEC H G LP + lau
Prices A5500-6000 V1800-2000 6000-7000 4000-5000

PASSIGNANO SUL TRASIMENO
Perugia
Europa ✆(075) 827405 & 827403
Apr-Oct
2.2HEC H G H L lau +
Prices A5000 V1800 6000 4000

PESARO
Pesaro & Urbino
Marinella via Adriatica 244 ✆(0721) 55795
Access is through railway underpass from Km244 of SS16.
Apr-Sep
1.5HEC H G R H S P + lau

PINARELLA
Ravenna
Pinarella viale Abruzzi 52 ✆(0544) 987408
Subdivided terrain surrounded by houses. Partially shaded, some young poplars. Private beach.
May-15 Sep
1.8HEC H G R + lau LS
Prices A3500-5300 8000-9000 7000-8000

Safari viale Titano 130 ✆(0544) 987356
The site is divided into several sections. Only families are accepted.
6 May-17 Sep
2.5HEC H G R + lau S
Prices A3800-5500 8000-10000

PINETO
Teramo
International ✆(085) 930639 & 8279676
Site on level terrain with young poplars. Sunshade roofing on the beach.
Camping Carnet Compulsory.

Turn off SS16 at Km431.2 and continue under railway underpass. Adjoining railway line.
May-Sep
18HEC H G S P + lau
Prices A4000-5500 pitch9000-14500

POMPOSA
Ferrara
International Tre Moschettieri ✆(0533) 380376
Camp site set beneath pine trees next to sea.
Signposted from SS309.
Apr-Sep
11HEC H G R S +

Vigna sul Mar via Capanno Garibaldi 20 ✆(0533) 380216
Well tended meadowland under poplars. Well signposted from entrance to Lido.
Private beach of 1km beyond the dunes.
May-15 Sep
12HEC H G R H PS + lau L
Prices A3700-5300 pitch7300-9500

PORTO RECANATI
Macerata
Bellamare ✆(071) 976628
On the S side of the mouth of the Musone.
Access from the Autostrada exit Ancona Sud via the SS16 turn to S bank at Km324.
May-Sep
5HEC H G H PS + lau
Prices A4000-6000 8300-12000 7000-8600

PORTO SANT'ELPÍDIO
Ascoli Piceno
Holidays International via Trieste ✆(0734) 993393
The site lies in beautiful meadowland.
Turn off SS16 at Km347.3 and drive 0.4km towards the sea.
May-14 Oct
10HEC H G R H PS + lau
Prices A3150-6500 pitch7900-14000

Risacca ✆(0734) 991423
Clean, well-kept site on level meadowland, with some trees surrounded by fields.
Turn off main SS16 N of village, follow road seawards under railway (narrow underpass maximum height 3m), then 1.2km along field paths to site. Caravan access is 400m further S along SS16, then under railway and along field paths to site.
18 May-20 Sep
8HEC H G R H PS P + lau
Prices A3300-6000 pitch8400-14700

PUNTA MARINA
Ravenna
At **ADRIANO, LIDO** (4.5km S)
Adriano via dei Campeggi 7 ✆(0544) 437230
300m from the sea. A pleasantly landscaped site amidst the dunes of the Punta Marina.
On SS309 via Lido Adriano to Punta Marina.
28 May-22 Sep
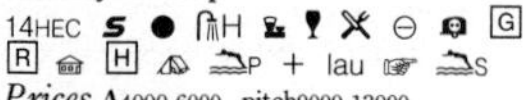
14HEC ● H G R H P + lau S
Prices A4000-6000 pitch9000-13000

Coop 3 via dei Campeggi 8 ✆(0544) 437353
300m to the sea. Level site under isolated high pines and poplars. Across flat dunes to the beach.
Signposted.
21 Apr-17 Sep
7HEC ● H ⊖ G R H + PS
Prices A3300-5600 V2000-3000 5700-6800 2600-4800

RAVENNA, MARINA DI
Ravenna
International Piomboni via Lungomare 421 ✆(0544) 530230
Site on slightly undulating mainly sandy terrain with pines and poplars. Separate section for tents. Lunchtime siesta 14.00-16.00 hrs. No reservations.
Access is 1km S from town centre off coast road.
May-20 Sep
5HEC ● H ⊖ G R H + lau PS
Prices A3600-5200 pitch6000-8500

RICCIONE
Forli
Alberello via Torino 80 ✆(0541) 615402
28 Apr-25 Sep
3.8HEC ● H ⊖ G R S + lau
Prices A3900-5600 pitch7800-9600

Fontanelle ✆(0541) 615449
On southern outskirts separated from beach by coast road. Underpass to public beach.
Camping Carnet Compulsory.
Turn off SS16 between Km216 and 217.
Etr-20 Sep
6HEC ● H ⊖ G R H PS + lau

Riccione via Marsala ✆(0541) 690160
About 300m from sea. Extensive flat meadowland, with poplars of medium height.
From SS16 turn seawards on the S outskirts of the town and continue for 200m. Alternative access from coast road, turn inland on S outskirts at sign and continue for 700m.
May-Sep
6.5HEC ● H ⊖ G H PS + lau
Prices A3900-5600 pitch8900-16300

ROSETO DEGLI ABRUZZI
Teramo
Eurcamping-Roseto ✆(085) 8993179
A meadow site at the S end of the beach road.
Leave the SS16 within the town, then continue for 500m to the site.
All year
5HEC ● H ⊖ G R PS + lau
Prices A4700-6500 V3300-4700 4600-7100 4200-6800

Gilda viale Makarska ✆(085) 8941023
Jun-Sep
1.5HEC ● H ⊖ G R H S + lau
Prices A3700-5800 pitch3100-15300

SALSOMAGGIORE TERME
Parma
Arizona ✆(0524) 66141
Apr-15 Oct
10HEC H ⊖ P P lau

SAN MÁURO MARE
Forli
Green ✆(0541) 346929
Site lies in well-kept grassland with poplars and plane trees by the railway.
Camping Carnet Compulsory.
About 300m from the sea.
Apr-Oct
1.2HEC ● H ⊖ G + lau S
Prices A3000-4000 pitch5000-6000

At **SAVIGNANO SUL RUBICONE**
Rubicone via M-Destra 1 ✆(0541) 346377
An extensive, level site divided into two sections by a narrow canal. It extends to the beach.
Situated about 0.8km from the road fork at Km187/0 off SS16 (Strada Adriatica).
15 May-Sep
12HEC ● H ⊖ G R H PS + lau
Prices A3950-5800 pitch6000-12900

SAN PIERO IN BAGNO
Forli
Altosavio strada Provinciale per Alfero ✆(0543) 917670
25 Apr-Sep
1.2HEC ● H ⊖ lau
Prices A3200-4600 pitch7000

SASSO MARCONI
Bologna
Piccolo Paradiso ✆(051) 842680
Pleasant site with plenty of trees.
Leave A1 autostrada (Milano-Roma) at town exit and continue towards Vado for 2km. Signposted.
All year
6.8HEC ● H ⊖ G R P + lau LPR
Prices A3850-5500 pitch8350-10700

SAVIGNANO SUL RUBICONE
See **SAN MÁURO MARE**

SÁVIO, LIDO DEL
Ravenna
Nuovo International ✆(0544) 949014
Well tended meadowland with high poplars.

Turn E off the main road in the village at Km168/IV then drive 4.5km towards sea.
15 May-10 Sep
6HEC H G P + lau S

SCACCHI, LIDO DEGLI
Ferrara
Florenz (0533) 380193
Site with sand dunes extending to the sea.
Turn off the Strada Romea in the direction of Lido Degli Scacchi, and continue along an asphalt road to the sandy beach.
15 May-15 Sep
60HEC H G R H S + lau P
Prices A3300-4800 pitch8400

SCHIANCETO
Macerata
Monte Prata (0737) 98124
On large, level terrace with some trees on an incline. Fine mountain views. Signposted from Castel Sant' Angelo.
15 Jun-15 Sep
5.5HEC H G R H + lau

SENIGALLIA
Ancona
Summerland via Podesti 236 (071) 7926816
On SS16.
Jun-15 Sep
2.4HEC H G + S
Prices A3200-5000 V2500-2800 A5500-6500

SESTOLA
Modena
Sestola via Palazzvola (0536) 61208
All year
2.5HEC H G R + lau PR
Prices A4000-8000 V8000-11000 8000-11000 A6000-8000

SIROLO
Ancona
Green Garden via Peschiera 3 (0471) 936887
May-Sep
22HEC H PS G R +
Prices A4000-6500 V2000-2700 7000-12500 A6000-11500

SPINA, LIDO DI
Ferrara
Spina (0533) 330179
Widespread site on level meadowland and on slightly hilly sand dune terrain. Separate section for dog owners.
Off SS309. Signposted.
May-24 Sep
28HEC H R PS + lau G
Prices A4500-5200 pitch8200

STACCIOLA DI SAN COSTANZO
Pesaro & Urbino
Green & Blue via delle Grazie 22 (0721) 957289
All year
4HEC H R H P +
Prices A4000-5500 pitch6000-9500

TORINO DI SANGRO MARINA
Chieti
Belvedere (0873) 911381
Jun-Sep
1.5HEC H G R + PS
Prices A3000-3500 pitch6000-8000

TORTORETO, LIDO
See **ALBA ADRIATICA**

VASTO
Chieti
Europa (0873) 801988
Site on level terrain by the road with poplars.
At Km522 of road SS16.
May-Sep
2.3HEC H G R P + lau S

Grotta del Saraceno (0873) 310295
Site in olive grove on steep coastal cliffs with lovely views. Steep path to beach. Siesta 14.00-16.00 hrs.
Camping Carnet Compulsory.
Turn off SS16 at Km512.200.
Jun-15 Sep
14HEC H G H S P + lau R
Prices A3000-6500 pitch6000-12500

Pioppeto (0873) 801466
Camping Carnet Compulsory.
May-Sep
1.5HEC H G R S +
Prices A5000-5500 V3000-3500 7000-7500 A7000-7500

VILLALAGO
L'Aquila
I Lupi (0864) 740100
All year
7HEC H G R lau L

ROME

Rome has affected western culture and attitudes for more than 2,000 years. The city is uniquely beautiful; from the famous Colosseum (a third of which is still intact) to the elegantly proportioned piazzas and churches, there are historic buildings which provide dramatic examples of changing architectural ideals. Of the 22 bridges which span the Tiber, some date from the first century BC. Situated on the famous seven hills, the city is the focus of the province of Latium, which has been described as 'the cradle of Roman civilization'. Stretching from the Apennines to the Tyrrhenian sea, it is characterised by magnificent and beautiful scenery, especially in the volcanic regions, where long extinct volcanoes form the lakes of Albano, Bracciano, Bolsena and Vico. Viterbo, in the northern hills, is a large town with many fine examples of religious architecture, including the 13th-century Papal Palace. Rieti's Civic Museum houses an extensive collection of Roman artifacts, while Frosinone commands breathtaking views of surrounding countryside. The Latin Lido features sheltered harbours and sandy beaches.

ANGUILLARA-SABAZIA
Roma
Parco del Lago (06) 3046602
Alongside Lake Bracciano, off the Trevignano road.
May-15 Oct
3HEC H G R H L lau
Prices A5100-5600 pitch6500-7100

BOLSENA
Viterbo
Amalasunta via del Lago 77 (0761) 825294
Apr-Sep
3HEC H R L +
Prices A4000-5000 V2000-3500 3000-5500 A2000-4500

Lido via Cassia (0761) 799258
15 Mar-Sep

CONTI CAMP/FE

ROMA CAMPING
VIA AURELIA Nr. 831 (Km. 8,2)
TEL. 06/6223018
I-00165 ROMA (ITALIA)

The campsite is located near the Grande Raccordo Anulare (GRA) – the city ring road Exit No. 1 on the Aurelia Road to the Centre of Rome. Well shaded, grassy, terraced site. Central location, 4km from Vatican and 8km from Town Centre. Bus Stop at entrance to campsite. Regular connection every 15 minutes. Rome excursions organised from campsite. The Roma Campsite is particularly suitable for groups. **NEW** Camper service – Laundry – Ironing Room.

Via Salaria, 2141
00138 Rome
Tel and Fax: 06/6917642

Snackbar – TV – Video – Discotheque – Festive occasions – Minimarket – Playground – Volleyball court – Football pitch – Camping gas – Caravan hire. Hot water and electricity free.

Ideal location for excursions into the city. 10 kilometres to the City Centre by bus every 15 minutes.

Motorway A1 Firenze-Rome, Exit Rome-Settebagni. From other directions take the G.R.A. towards Firenze, Settebagni exit

MasterCard E VISA

HAPPY CAMPING

ROMA

Favourable location in the north of the city. Near exit 5 of the "Grade Raccordo Anulare" (motorway round Rome). Direct underground connection to the city centre every ten minutes. Modern facilities. Electricity and hot water free. Washing machines, bar, supermarket, restaurant, swimming pools.

I-00123 Roma. Tel.: 0039/6/3002401-6913800
S.S. Cassia bis Veientana – Exit 5 of the G.R.A.

Discount on presentation of this guide if you stay longer than 5 days + discount for young people under 30 during April, May, June, September and October.

ROME
CAMPING
BUS SERVICE
PRIMA PORTA STATION
VITERBO SIENA FIRENZE
OTTAVIANO STATION
S PIETRO
COLOSSEO STATION
EUR STATION
ANAGNINA STATION
G.R.A.

10HEC ● H G H L P lau
Prices A5500-6500 pitch7500-9000

BRACCIANO
Roma

Roma Flash Sporting via Settevene Palo ✆(06) 9023669 & 9017038
Apr-Sep
5.5HEC ● H G H L P lau

FORMIA
Latina

Gianola ✆(0771) 270223
Situated in a narrow grassland area near a little stream and trees amidst agricultural land. Pleasantly sandy beach edged by rocks.
Access via Roma-Napoli road, from S Croce 800m.
Apr-Oct
4HEC ● H G R H RS P +
Prices pitch18300-25200 (incl 2 persons)

MINTURNO, MARINA DI
Latina

Golden Garden via Dunale 74 ✆(0771) 680167
Secluded quiet site within agricultural area by the sea.
Camping Carnet compulsory.
Access from the SS7 across river bridge (Garigliano) and continue 4.6km changing direction. Last km sandy field track.
Etr-Sep
18HEC ● H G R S P + lau PR
Prices pitch18000-29800 (incl 2 persons)

MONTALTO DI CASTRO, MARINA DI
Viterbo

Internazionale Pionier Etrusco via Vulsinia ✆(0766) 820012
Camping Carnet Compulsory.
15 Apr-15 Sep
3HEC S ● H G R H lau PRS +

PESCIA ROMANA, MARINA DI
Viterbo

Amici del Camping ✆(0766) 830250
A quiet, pleasantly situated site behind dunes. Clean wide beach.
Turn off via Aurelia seawards at Km118.5. After 4.3km turn right and continue on sandy tracks 900m.
All year
2.6HEC ● H R H P lau PS
Prices pitch22000 (incl 2 persons)

RIVA DEI TARQUINI
See **TARQUINIA**

ROMA (ROME)
Roma

Fabulous via C-Colombo ✆(06) 5259354
All year
30HEC ● H G R H P + lau
Prices A6500 V3800 6000 Å3800

Flaminio via Flaminia Nuova 821 ✆(06) 3279006
An exstensive site, which lies in a quiet valley on narrow terraces on a hill.
From ring road follow via Flaminia, S33, for 2.5km towards city centre.
All year
8HEC ● H G P + lau

Happy via Prato della Corte 1915 ✆(06) 3002401
Conveniently placed in northern area of town. Modern installations, electricity and hot water free throughout.
Exit No.5 "Grande Raccordo Anulare" (ring road).
15 Mar-Oct
3.6HEC ● H G H P + lau
Prices A6900 V3900 5900 Å3900

Roma via Aurelia 831 ✆(06) 6223018
The site lies on terraces on a hill near the AGIP Motel. All kinds of excursions can be arranged. ➤

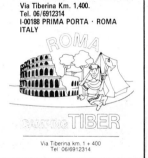

From ring road follow SS1 (via Aurelia) for 1.5km towards town centre turn off to site at Km8/11.
All year
3HEC ● H ❗ ✕ ⊖ G H
P lau
Prices A6500-7200 V3000-3300 6000-6600 Λ3000-3300

Salaria via Salaria 2141 ✆(06) 6917642
May-Oct
17HEC ● H ❗ ✕ ⊖ G
R H P + ☞ R
Prices A6000 V3300 5000 Λ3500

See advertisement on page 206

Seven Hills via Cassia 1216 ✆(06) 3765571
Partly terraced, set in a small valley. 2.5km NE of outer ring road.
15 Mar-Oct
5HEC ● H ❗ ✕ ⊖ G R
P P + lau

See advertisement on page 207

Tiber via Tiberina ✆(06) 6912314
On level grassland, shaded by poplars beside the Tiber.
N of city. Signposted from ringroad.
Mar-10 Nov
5HEC ● H ❗ ✕ ⊖ G
H PR P + lau
Prices A6700-7400 V3500 5500-6000 Λ3500-3800

See advertisement on page 207

SALTO DI FONDI
Latina
Fondi Holiday Camp ✆(0771) 555009
Apr-Sep
4HEC S ◑ H ❗ ✕ ⊖ R
PS P lau
Prices pitch26200-43000 (incl 2 persons).

SAN LORENZO NUOVO
Viterbo
Patrizia ✆(0763) 77483
The site is situated in meadowland, on terraces above lake.
At Km118/VIII turn off via Cassia and drive 0.3km towards lake.
15 May-15 Sep
2HEC S ◑ ● ❗ ✕ ⊖ G
R L P + lau

SPERLONGA
Latina
Nord-Sud via Flacca ✆(0771) 54255
1km from town towards Gaera.
May-13 Oct
4.5HEC ◑ ● H ❗ ✕ ⊖ G
P lau ☞ S
Prices pitch18900-29400 (incl 2 persons)

TARQUINIA
Viterbo
At **RIVA DEI TARQUINI**(9km NW)
Riva dei Tarquini ✆(0766) 814027
Site in tall pine woodland by the sea.
Turn seawards at Km102/II via Aurelia to site in 3km.
Jun-Sep
4HEC S ● H ❗ ✕ ⊖
PS P ☞ G R
Prices A5000-7000 pitch7500-9500

TERRACINA
Latina
Badino Porto Badino ✆(0773) 71130
Apr-Sep
2HEC S ◑ H ❗ ✕ ⊖ S P
☞ G R
Prices pitch19300-27100 (incl 2 persons)

Blue via Badino KM 4,350 ✆(0773) 730727
The site is divided into plots on even grassland, with roof matting providing shade on mouth of River Badino. The tenting section is located in pine woodland. Berthing facilities for boats in river mouth. Football pitch.
May-Sep
4.5HEC S ● H ❗ ✕ ⊖
G R H RS P
Prices pitch17000-27000 (incl 2 persons)

SOUTH

The area known as the Mezzogiorno, takes in Campania and the 'toe and heel' provinces of Calabria (the toe), Basilicata, and Apulia(the heel).
From Naples, a port set in a beautiful bay with volcanic Vesuvius behind it, you travel south to an area in which you look back in time and where the language is different from northern Italian. Apulia is mountainous but has fertile plains producing olives, wines and tobacco. In the university town of Lecce you can see the exuberant 'Lecce Baroque' ornate stone carving while in Alberobella you find the circular 'trulli' houses made of drystone with cone shaped roofs. Equally intriguing is the abandoned city at Matera where semi-cave dwellings made of tufa used to house hundreds of families.
Baby octopus and other fish are part of a healthy diet of seafood, vegetables and pulses. Travel though the poorest region of Italy, Basilicata, before arriving in Calabria – also mountainous, with skiing in winter, but with 372 miles of coastline. Reggio di Calabria, right on the toe, has a mild climate in which exotic plants like the bergamot orange flourish.

ACCIAROLI
Salerno
Ondina ✆(0974) 904040
Delightful seaside site, full of flowers. Lunchtime siesta 14.00-16.00 hrs.
Turn off towards the sea at Km35/VII.
Apr-Sep
2HEC ● H ❗ ✕ ⊖ G
R H P + lau ☞ S

ASCEA, MARINA DI
Salerno
Alba Piana di Velia ✆(089) 233307
Jun-15 Sep
3HEC S ● H ❗ ✕ ⊖ P
+ ☞ R RS
Prices A3186-5310 pitch8629-20835

BAIA DOMIZIA
Caserta
Báia Domizia ✆(0823) 930164
Part of this extensive seaside site is laid out with flower beds. No children under 3 and no radios allowed.
Turn off the SS7 (qtr) at Km6/V, then 3km seawards.
24 Apr-Sep
30HEC ◑ ● H ❗ ✕ ⊖ G
H LPRS P + lau
Prices A4400-8900 V1900-3700 6100-12400 Λ6100-12400

BAIA SAN FELICE
Foggia
Báia San Felice ✆(0884) 708604
Mar-Oct
16HEC ◑ H ❗ ✕ ⊖ G R
H S P +
Prices A5000-9000 V2000-4000 4500-12000 Λ4500-12000

BRANCALEONE
Reggio di Calabria
Villaggio Africa via S Giorgio ✆(0964) 933164
All year
1.7HEC ◑ H ❗ ✕ ⊖ R
S P ☞ +
Prices A1650-4650 V1650-2200 2200-5300 pitch2200-5300

BRIATICO
Catanzaro
Dolomiti ✆(0963) 391355
The site is in a delightful setting on two terraces planted with olive trees. It lies by the road and 150m from railway.
Turn off road 522 between Km17 and Km18 and head towards the sea.
May-10 Oct
5HEC ● H ❗ ✕ ⊖ G R
H S P + lau

CAMEROTA, MARINA DI

Salerno

Happy ✆(0974) 932405

The site lies on a park-like hill sloping down to the sea and is scattered with olive trees.

1km N of village just off the coast road.
Jun-Sep

100HEC ● H R P + S

Prices A9000-14000 8000-13000

Isola ✆(0974) 932230

Lies on several terraces in an olive grove. Pleasant bathing area with sandy beach.

Entrance is just off Palinuro-Marina coast road (SS562) 1km N of village near ESSO petrol station.
Jun-20 Sep

2.5HEC ● H G R H S +

Prices A3600-5950 pitch9500-15600

Pineta ✆(0974) 931771

The site is divided into pitches amongst shrubs and pines. Wide beach stretching for several kilometres.

Jun-Aug

3HEC ● H R RS P + lau

Risacca via delle Barche 31 ✆(0974) 932415

20 May-15 Sep

2HEC S ● H G R S P +

Prices A3300-5300 pitch8300-14300

CAMPORA SAN GIOVANNI

Cosenza

Principessa ✆(0982) 46047

Modern motel with camp site annexed to it, lying 150m from the sea and a fine sandy beach.

2km S and inland from Campora on SS18.
All year

10HEC S ● H G R + lau S

Prices A4000-4600 V2600-3600 4500-5500 Å4000-4600

CAPOIALE

Foggia

Rancho ✆(0884) 97269

All year

20HEC S ● H G R H LS +

Prices A4500-6500 V2500-3000 4500-6000 Å4500-6000

CAPO VATICANO

Catanzaro

Quattro Scoglí San Nicolo di Ricadi ✆(0963) 663126 & 663115

The site is in a quiet sandy bay surrounded by rocks.

Camping Carnet Compulsory.

Drive from San Nicolo di Ricardi to Capo Vaticano.
Apr-Oct

1.2HEC S ● H G R H S P

Prices A6500-9000 V2500-3500 7000-9000 Å6000-8000 pitch8

CAROVIGNO

Brindisi

At **SPECCHIOLLA, LIDO**

Pineta al Mare ✆(0831) 968057

Site in pine woodland with sandy beach and some rocks.

Camping Carnet Compulsory.

E of Bari-Brindisi road at Km31.5.
All year

55HEC ● H G R P + S

Prices A5000-5550 V2000-2500 7150-7750 Å7150-7750

CIRÒ MARINA

Catanzaro

Punta Alice ✆(0962) 31160

The site lies on meadowland amidst lush Mediterranean vegetation and borders a fine gravel beach, some 50m wide.

2km from town. From SS106 (Strada Ionica) turn off at Km290 seaward to Cirò Marina. Pass through village and follow beach road for 1.5m towards the lighthouse.
Apr-Sep

5.5HEC ● H G R S + lau

Prices A3400-6200 V2300-3300 4600-6900 Å4200-6300

Villaggio Torrenova ✆(0962) 01039

May-Sep

1.2HEC S ● H G R H S + lau L

Prices pitch18000-32000

CORIGLIANO CÁLABRO

Cosenza

Thurium ✆(0983) 851092

Jun-Sep

16HEC ◑ H G R H S P + R

Prices A4300-7300 V2100-3600 4900-8200 Å3900-6500

DAVOLI MARINA

Catanzaro

Rodano ✆(0967) 70602

10 Jun-Sep

3HEC ● H H lau S

Prices A4600 V1200 4800 Å3800-4600

EBOLI

Salerno

Paestum ✆(0828) 691003

Sandy, meadowland site in tall poplar wood by river mouth. Steps and bus service to private beach, 600m from site.

Access from the Litoranea at Km20 from the road fork to Santa Cecilia and continue for 0.3km. Signposted.
2 Apr-11 Sep

80HEC ● H G R H P + lau RS

Prices A2400-4600 pitch8000-14600

FUSCALDO

Cosenza

Lago ✆(081) 681949

Site lies below road in olive grove.

Turn off SS18, at Km307.
Jun-Sep

2HEC S ● H R + lau S

Prices A5300 V2500 6000 Å6000

GAGLIANO DEL CAPO

Lecce

Village St Maria di Leuca ✆(0833) 548157

All year

3HEC ● H G R P +

Prices A4000-6500 V2700 4000-5000 Å4000-4800

GALLICO

See **REGGIO DI CALABRIA**

GALLIPOLI

Lecce

Baia di Gallipoli ✆(0833) 476906

Camping Carnet Compulsory.

All year

11HEC ● H G R P P + S

Prices A5500-7800 V2000-2500 4000-5600 Å4000-5600

Vecchia Torre ✆(0833) 209083 & 209009

This well-kept and clean site lies amidst sand dunes in a pine wood. Small size pitches.

5km N of Gallipoli and 200m S of Hotel Rivabella at seaward side of coast road.
May-Sep

8HEC S ● H R P + lau S

Prices A4500-6500 6500-10500 Å5500-10000

GIOVINAZZO

Bari

Freddo ✆(080) 8942112

Site in level terrain by the sea, mainly under sunshade roofing. Siesta 14.00-16.00 hrs.

Turn off the SS16, 20km N of Bari at Km784,300.
May-Sep

34HEC ◑ H G R + lau S

Prices A7000 5000

GUARDAVALLE, MARINA DI

Catanzaro

Dello Ionio via Nazionale ✆(0967) 86002

Jun-15 Sep

5HEC ● H G R S + lau

Prices A5000-6500 V2500-3300 7900-10000 Å4500-6000

ISOLA DI CAPO RIZZUTO
Catanzaro
Oasi (0962) 791628
The site lies in an isolated situation, above a wide red sand beach which can be reached by a winding road.
Turn off coast road (N106) and drive 5km towards sea.
10 Jun-20 Sep
1HEC H H P S

LÁURA
Salerno
Hera Argiva (0828) 851193
Site in sandy terrain in eucalyptus grove by the sea.
Signposted from Km88/VII SS18.
Apr-Oct
10HEC H G R H S + lau
Prices A3000-5000 pitch7000-10000

LEPORANO, MARINA DI
Taranto
Porto Pirrone Litoranea Salentina Km 12 (099) 632316
All year
4HEC H G R S +
Prices A5200-6500 V2200-2700 6000-7000 2500-7000

MÁCCHIA
Foggia
11 Monaco (0884) 23489
Jun-Sep
5.3HEC H G R H PS P lau
Prices A3000-7000 V1000-3000 4000-8000 4000-8000

MANFREDÓNIA
Foggia
Gargano (0884) 371063
May-Sep
5HEC H G LRS +

MASSA LUBRENSE
Napoli
Villa Lubrense via Partenope 31 (081) 8771255
All year
3HEC H G H S + lau

MATTINATA
Foggia
Degli Ulivi (0884) 4000
This well-kept grassland site lies in an old olive grove.
Camping Carnet Compulsory.
Off SS89, 0.6km N of turning to Mattinata.
Jun-Sep
2.1HEC H G R H P + lau S
Prices pp6000-10500

Europa (0884) 4452
Gently sloping meadowland in sparse olive grove near the sea. Siesta 13.00-16.00 hrs.
Access from coast road.
May-15 Sep
1.3HEC H G R H P lau S
Prices pitch6500-9500

Villaggio Turistico San Lorenzo (0884) 4152
The site is situated above the coast road in direction of Viesta. Bungalows for hire.
Camping Carnet Compulsory.
All year
5HEC H G R H P + lau S
Prices A3500-8500 V3000 5000-9000 1750-42500

METAPONTO, LIDO DI
Matera
Camel Camping Club viale Magna Grecia (0835) 741926
All year
3.2HEC H G R H P P RS +
Prices A4500-8000 V2000-3500 4500-8500 4500-8500

Magna Grecia via Lido 1 (0835) 741855
All year
7HEC H G R P +
Prices A4500-6500 V1500-2000 4500-6500 4500-6500

MOLA DI BARI
Bari
Caloria (080) 644897
Site in meadowland enclosed by wall.
In southern outskirts below the busy SS16 at Km824/VII
20 May-10 Sep
4HEC H G H lau PS

NAPOLI (NAPLES)
Napoli
Complesso Turistico Averno via Domitiana (081) 8661202
Camping carnet compulsory.
Access via Tangenziale 16km W of Napoli to site 4km W of Pozzuoli.
All year
3HEC H G P + lau

NICÓTERA MARINA
Catanzaro
Sabbia d'Oro (0963) 81545
Lies on level ground amidst farmland 100m from a beautiful lonely beach.
Turn off SS18 at Km453/VII and continue 15km.
May-Sep
2.7HEC H R H lau S
Prices A6000 V3000 6500 6200

NOCERA TERINESE, MARINA DI
Catanzaro
Torre Casale (0968) 93179
Jun-Oct
15HEC H + G R S
Prices A2000-5900 V2500 2000-5500

OTRANTO
Lecce
Mulino d'Acqua via S Stefano (0836) 81196
15 Jun-15 Sep
10HEC H G R PS P +
Prices A5000-7500 pitch5000-7000

PAESTUM
Salerno
Vilaggio del Pini (0828) 811030 & 811323
The site lies on hilly ground in a pine forest beside clean and sandy beach.
Camping Carnet Compulsory.
Turnoff via Tirrenia at Km95/1X and continue 1km.
All year
3HEC H G R H PRS + lau
Prices A5000-6000 V2000-3000 4000-10000 4000-10000

PALINURO
Salerno
Arco Naturale Club via Molpa 1 (0974) 931157
Jun-15 Sep
10HEC H R PRS P
Prices A7000-12500 pitch7700-13500

PALMI
Reggio di Calabria
San Fantino via S-Fantino (0966) 479430
Site on several terraces with lovely views of the bay of Lido di Palmi. 200m to the beach. Siesta 13.00-16.00 hrs.
Camping Carnet Compulsory.
Turn off road SS18 seawards N of Palmi.
All year
4HEC H G R H + lau S
Prices A5000-5500 V2000-2500 5000-5500 4500-5000

PESCHICI
Foggia
Centro Turistico San Nicola (0884) 94024
Terraced site in lovely situation by the sea, in a bay enclosed by rocks. Can become overcrowded.
Turn off coast road Peschici-Vieste, follow signs along winding road to site in 1km.
Apr-15 Oct

12HEC H G + lau S
Prices A5000-9000 V3500-5000 6500-11000 3500-10000

Manacore (0884) 964050
Meadowland with a few terraces in attractive bay, surrounded by wooded hills.
Turn off the coastal road (Peschici-Vieste) towards ths sea in a wide U bend.
Apr-20 Oct
20HEC S H G R S +

Parco degli Ulivi (0884) 962099
Jun-20 Sep
12HEC H G R P + S
Prices A4500-8500 V2000-4000 6000-9000 5000-3000

PIZZO, MARINA DI
Catanzaro
Pinetamare (0963) 264071
N of town.
2 Jun-29 Sep
11HEC S H G R PS + lau

POLICORO, MARINA DI
Matera
Heraclea via Lido 37 (0835) 910191
All year
3.5HEC H G R S P +
Prices pitch9000-15000 (incl 2 persons)

POMPEI
Napoli
Spartacus via Plinio (081) 8614901
Site is on a level meadow with orange trees.
Lies near the motorway exit, Scafati-Pompei and access is from the main Nápoli road, opposite Scari di Pompei near an IP petrol station.
All year
1HEC H G R H S + lau P
Prices A4500-6500 V3000 5000 4000

POZZUOLI
Napoli
Vulcano Solfatara (081) 8673413
Clean and orderly site situated in a deciduous forest near the crater of the extinct Solfatara volcano.
Leave Nuova via Domiziana (SS7 qtr) at Km60/1 (at about 6km short of Napoli) and turn inland through stone gate.
Etr-15 Oct
HEC H G P + S
Prices A6600-7700 V4400-5500 7400-8000 4000-000

At **VARCATURO, MARINA DI** (12km N)
Partenope (081) 5091076
Partially undulating terrain in woodland of medium height.

Turn seawards for 300m at Km45/II of the SS7 (via Domiziana).
May-15 Sep
5.6HEC S H G R R + lau PS
Prices A5900-7200 V3300-3900 5500-7200

REGGIO DI CALABRIA
Reggio di Calabria
At **GALLICO** (10.7km N)
Paradiso (0965) 302482
Level, totally subdivided site with view of Straits of Messina. All pitches provided with sunshade roofing. Extensive sandy beach.
At Km527.300 of SS18 turn seawards 1km.
15 Jun-20 Sep
3HEC H G R P P + lau S

ROCCELLETTA
Catanzaro
Calabrisella (0961) 391207
15 Jun-15 Sep
6HEC S H G R S lau +
Prices A4500-8500 10000-14000 7000-11000

RODI GARGANICO
Foggia
Ripa via Ripa (0884) 965133
Jun-Sep
6HEC H G R LPS P lau +

SAN MENÁIO
Foggia
Calanella (0884) 98105
2 Jun-16 Sep
9HEC H P lau S

Valle d'Oro via Degli Ulivi (0884) 991580
Site in olive grove surrounded by wooded hills with some terraces.
Turn off the SS89 onto SS528 and to site at Km1.800. 2km from the sea.
All year
3HEC H G R H + lau
Prices pp6000-8000

SAN NICOLO DI RICADI
Catanzaro
Agrumento (0963) 663175
The access road leads over a dusty field track, then on to a steep ramp with large, wide bends. Because the trees are very close together, the pitches are rather narrow. Lying in a lemon grove beside the sea, this site looks more like a garden. Beautiful beach. Excursions by boat can be arranged.
15 May-Sep
370HEC H R S + lau

SANTA CESÁREA TERME
Lecce
Scogliera (0836) 944216

1km S on SS173.
All year
8HEC S H G H PS P + lau R
Prices A4900-6500 V2700-3500 4900-7000 4500-5800

SANTA MARIA DI CASTELLABATE
Salerno
Trezene (0974) 965027
The site is partly divided into pitches and consists of two sections lying either side of the access road. Pitches between road and fine sandy beach are reserved for touring campers.
Apr-Oct
2.7HEC H R + lau G S
Prices A3500-5000 pitch11000-17000

SOLE, LIDO DEL
Foggia
Lido del Mare (0884) 97039
Jun-15 Sep
2HEC S H R H lau G LPS
Prices A4000-8000 V1500-3500 4800-9000 4800-9000

SORRENTO
Napoli
Campogaio via Capo 39 (081) 8781444
Lies on terraces scattered with olive trees.
2km from town centre and 400m beyond the turning from the SS145 on road towards Massa Lubrense and 50m from sea.
Apr-Sep
10HEC H G R H PS + lau

International Camping Nube d'Argento Via Capo 21 (081) 8781344
The site lies on narrow terraces just off a steep concrete road between the beach and the outskirts of the town.
Access is rather difficult for caravans.
All year
1.5HEC S H G H P lau S +
Prices A7600-8800 V3500-4100 7600-8800 4100-8800

Santa Fortunata via Capo (081) 8782405
Extensive site lying on terraces in a shady olive grove with many small secluded pitches.
1km from town and 50m from sea.
Apr-Sep
12HEC H G R H PS + lau

SPECCHIOLLA, LIDO
See **CAROVIGNO**

TORRE RINALDA
Lecce

Torre Rinalda ✆(0832) 652161
On an extensive level meadow, separated from the sea by dunes. Discotheque. Lunchtime siesta 13.30-16.00 hrs.
Camping Carnet Compulsory.
Access via SS613 (Brindisi-Lecce) exit Trepuzzi then coastal road for 1.5km.
Jun-Sep
23HEC 〰 ◑ ⋔H ⛟ ! ✕ ⊖ ⊕ [G] ⌂ [H] ≈PS ▣ + lau

UGENTO
Lecce

Riva di Ugento Fontanelle ✆(0833) 931040
May-Sep
32HEC **S** ● ⋔H ⛟ ! ✕ ⊖ ⊕ [G] ≈PS ▣ + ✶
Prices A4500-7000 V6000 ⛟4500-9000 ▲4500-9000

VARCATURO, MARINA DI
See **POZZUOLI**

VICO EQUENSE
Napoli

Sant' Antonio via Marina d'Equa ✆(081) 8799261
Camping Carnet Compulsory.
15 Mar-15 Oct
1.5HEC 〰 ● ⋔H ⛟ ! ✕ ⊖ ⊕ [G] [R] ⌂ ≈S ▣ + ✶ lau
Prices A5800-7500 V3200 ⛟5800-7500 ▲4500-6000

Seiano Spiaggia via Marina d'Equa ✆(081) 8798165
About 200m from the sea.
15 Mar-15 Oct
2.2HEC 〰 ● ⋔H ⛟ ! ✕ ⊖ ⊕ [G] [R] ⌂ ▣ + lau ☞ ≈PS
Prices A6500-7000 V3300-3600 ⛟6500-6900 ▲5500-6000

VIESTE
Foggia

Baia dei Lambardi Santa Maria di Merino ✆(0884) 706480
Apr-Sep
2.5HEC 〰 **S** ● ⋔H ⛟ ! ✕ ⊖ ⊕ [G] [R] ⌂ ≈S P
Prices A4500-7800 V2000-2500 ⛟6500-10000 ▲6500-10000

Baia Turchese ✆(0884) 708587
1km N of Vieste on Strada Panoramica towards Peschici.
15 May-Sep
3.3HEC 〰 ● ⋔H ⛟ ! ✕ ⊖ ⊕ [G] [R] ⌂ ≈S ▣ + ✶ lau
Prices A4000-7000 V2500 ⛟4000-10000 ▲4000-10000

Capo Vieste ✆(0884) 76326
The site lies on a large area of unspoilt land, planted with a few rows of poplar and pine trees. It is by the sea and has a large bathing area.
Off coastal road to Peschici about 7km beyond Vieste.
Etr-Oct
6HEC 〰 **S** ◑ ⋔H ⛟ ! ✕ ⊖ ⊕ [G] ⌂ [H] ⛺ ≈S P lau

Castello ✆(0884) 707415
Apr-Sep
2.5HEC 〰 ● ⋔H ⛟ ! ✕ ⊖ ⊕ [G] [R] ⌂ [H] ≈S P + ✶

Centro Vacanze Crovatico ✆(0884) 706487
Site with poplars in a bay with lovely sandy beach surrounded by wooded hills. Siesta 14.00-16.00 hrs.
At Km9 on coast road Vieste-Peschici.
May-Sep
6HEC 〰 ● ⋔H ⛟ ! ✕ ⊖ ⊕ [G] [R] ⌂ ≈S ▣ + ✶ lau

Diomedee ✆(0884) 76472
Level meadowland site with poplars, by the sea.
5km on coast road.
3.5HEC 〰 ⊟ ◑ ⋔H ⛟ ✕ ⊖ ⊕ ⌂ ≈S + ✶

Eden Garden ✆(0884) 78696
A fairly level site, in an olive grove, situated about 200m from the sea.
From town, follow the well-signposted road to Lido di Portonuovo.
Jun-Sep
2.5HEC ⋔H ! ✕ ⊖ ⊕ [G] [R] [H] ⛺ P + ✶ ☞ ≈S

Porticello ✆(0884) 76125
The site lies in a long, sandy bay which is bordered on one side by rocks.
Camping Carnet Compulsory.
5km on coast road to Peschici and then turn right.
May-Sep
2.7HEC 〰 **S** ◑ ⋔H ⛟ ! ✕ ⊖ ⊕ [G] [R] ⌂ P lau

Umbramare Santa Maria di Merino ✆(0884) 706174
18 Mar-15 Oct
1.3HEC 〰 ● ⋔H ! ✕ ⊖ ⊕ ⌂ [H] ≈S ▣ + ☞ ⛟ [G] [R]
Prices A3500-7500 pitch7000-14000

Vieste Marina ✆(0884) 706471
Level site adjacent to the coast road.
Camping Carnet Compulsory.
5km N of Vieste, signposted.
Jun-15 Sep
5HEC 〰 **S** ● ⋔H ⛟ ! ✕ ⊖ ⊕ [G] [R] ⌂ ≈PS ▣ +
Prices A3200-7600 V1800-3200 ⛟4800-10000 ▲4800-10000

Village Punta Lunga ✆(0884) 706031
A terraced site including two sandy bathing bays, a rocky peninsula and the village of Vieste.
2km N of Vieste, signposted from coast road.
14 Apr-7 Oct
6HEC 〰 ● ⋔H ⛟ ! ✕ ⊖ ⊕ [G] ⌂ ≈S P + ✶ lau
Prices A3000-9500 V2500 ⛟7000-12000 ▲4000-7000

ZAPPONETA
Foggia

Ippocampo ✆(0884) 371121
In grounds of a holiday village.
Jun-15 Sep
5HEC ⊟ ◑ ⋔H ⊖ ⊕ ▣ lau ☞ ⛟ ! ✕ ≈S
Prices A3850-4400 V3300-3850 ⛟3300-4400 ▲3300-4400

THE ISLANDS

Sardinia and Sicily are virtually the same size but Sardinia's population is 1.5 million compared with Sicily's 5 million. Sardinia's mountains are less dramatic, much of the coast is deserted and the people with their distinctive dialect, clothes and folklore, seem far removed from the 20th century. The Costa Smeralda on the north-east coast is luxuriously developed but elsewhere on the coast tourism is increasing only slowly, and inland, the old town of Nuoro set high on a 1500ft granite hill, remains mysterious. Cagliari is the capital, a modern city, whilst Oristano is the provincial capital with old streets and lively atmosphere. Where Sardinia is an island on which to relax, in Sicily there is much to see: classical sites at Taormina, Syracuse or Agrigento; busy cities like Palermo and Catánia and the dramatic, erupting volcano Etna in whose foothills oranges and lemons grow profusely. There is also poverty and the occasional outburst from the Mafia. The best beaches and clearest waters are around the Aolian islands to the north, but Sicily is not primarily a seaside resort island. Seafood, vegetables and fresh fruit are in abundance, not forgetting of course, the inimitable ice-cream.

SARDEGNA (SARDINIA)

AGLIENTU
Sassari
Tortuga Pineta di Vignola Mare
(079) 602060
May-Sep
1.7HEC H G H S + lau
Prices pp11200
See advertisement on page 214

ALGHERO
Sassari
Mariposa (079) 950360
The site lies among sand dunes and is scattered with pine and eucalyptus trees.
From harbour 1km towards Lido S Giovanni turn left and cross first bridge.
15 Mar-Oct
4HEC H G H S + lau
Apr-Oct
15HEC H G R S P +
Prices A4200-8000 V3000-5100 5800-12900 3400-11300

ARBATAX
Nuoro
Telis (0782) 667140
All year
3HEC H G R H S lau +
Prices A6000-7000 V2000 6000-7000 4000-7000

BARI SARDO
Nuoro
Domus de Janas Torri di Bari
(0782) 29361
All year
2.5HEC H G R H S + lau
Prices A5000-5700 V3100-3200 6700-7800 6700-7800

CAGLIARI
Cagliari
At **SANT'ANTIOCO**
Tonnara (0781) 83803
Jun-Sep
?HEC H G R S P
Prices A6800-7000 V1000-1200 10700-11300 10700-11300

CANNIGIONE DI ARZACHENA
Sassari
Isuledda (0789) 86003

PLATAMONA LIDO
Sassari
Cristina (079) 310230
15 May-Sep
10HEC H G R H PS P lau +
Prices pp8700-10800

SANTA LUCIA
Nuoro
Calapinta (0784) 819184
Jun-Sep
5HEC H H S
Selema (0784) 819068
Jun-Sep
7HEC H G H RS P R +
Prices pp9500-10000

SAN TEODORO
Nuoro
San Teodoro la Cinta via Tirreno
(0784) 865777
15 May-15 Oct
3HEC H G R S + lau
Prices A6000-7000 pitch6000-7000

TEULADA
Cagliari
Porto Tramatzu (070) 9870518
All year
3.5HEC H S P +
Prices A4500-4900 4100-4600 6600-7600

VALLEDORIA
Sassari
Foce via Ampurias (079) 582103
15 May-15 Oct
20HEC H G R H PRS lau +
Prices A10500 V2500

Valledoria Maragnani (079) 584070
Jun-Sep
10HEC H G R H S P lau R +
Prices A9500-10500 V2000-2500

SICILIA (SICILY)

ACIREALE
Catania
At **CARRUBA** (10.2km N)
Praiola (095) 964321 & 964366
In idyllic location, very quiet.
5km S of Riposto by the sea between orchards. 6km from A18 exit Giarre.
Apr-Sep
20HEC H G R + lau S
Prices A4500-5500 V3000-3500 7500-9500 4500-6000

BRUCOLI
Siracusa
Baia del Silenzio (0931) 981211
Jun-Sep
1.4HEC H R S
Prices A4500-5800 V2500-3000 7400-9800 4500-9800

CASTEL DI TUSA
Messina
Scoglio (0921) 34345
A terraced site. No shade on the gravel beach.
Camping Carnet Compulsory.
Turn off SS113 st Km164, 2km W of Castel di Tusa.
May-Sep
1.5HEC H G S lau
Prices A6000 V3000 8000 7000

CATANIA
Catania
Ionio via Villini a Mare 2 (095) 491139
On a clifftop plateau. Access to beach via steps. Lunchtime siesta 14.00-17.00 hrs.
Turn off SS14 N of town towards sea.
All year ➔

1.2HEC G R H S P + lau
Prices A4400-5900 V2700-3600 7400-9800 7400-9800

CEFALÚ
Palermo

Rais Gerbi (0921) 26570
Take the SS113 Messina-Palermo road to Km172.9.
All year
5HEC H R H PS +
Prices A4500-5300 V2500-3000 6000-7000 4000-7000

Sanfilippo Contrada Ogliastrillo (0921) 20184
Slightly terraced site in olive grove, surrounded by vineyards. View of the sea.
Camping Carnet Compulsory.
3km W signposted from coastal road.
Mar-Oct
1.1HEC S H G H P + lau S
Prices A4500-4600 V2600 5800-6000 4000-6000

FONDACHELLO
Catania

Mokambo (095) 938731
Level terrain, thickly wooded in parts not directly next to the sea.
Camping Carnet Compulsory.
For access leave A18 (Messina-Catania) at Giarre exit, through Giarre and via Máscali to Fondachello on coast.
Apr-Sep
1.4HEC H G R H + lau S
Prices A5000-5500 V2700-3500 6500-8000 4900-5500

FÚRNARI MARINA
Messina

Village Bazia (0941) 81235
Jun-28 Sep
5HEC S H R PS P + G R
Prices A6000 V2500 7000 5000-7000

GIARRE
Catania

At **MILO** (11km E)
Mareneve ETNA (095) 7082163
Site in hilly terrain with lovely view of the sea.
Camping Carnet Compulsory.
Approach from the A18 exit Giarre direction Venerina and Milo about 10km.
All year
2HEC H G R H P + lau

ÍSOLA DELLE FÉMMINE
Palermo

La Playa viale Marino 55 (091) 8677001
Apr-Oct
2.2HEC S H G R H S + lau
Prices A4500 V2500 6000 4000-6000

MILAZZO
Messina

Savonara Pineta via Riviera di Ponente, Contrada Grunda (090) 9283647
All year
25HEC S H G H S +
Prices A4400 V2700 6200 6200

OLIVERI
Messina

Marinello (0941) 33000
Apr-15 Oct
5HEC S H G R H P + lau LS

PACHINO
Siracusa

At **PORTOPALO** (6.6km SE)
Capo Palssero (0931) 842333
Site slightly sloping towards the sea with view of fishing harbour of Portopalo. Discotheque.
Turn S on 115 in Noto or Iolspica in direction of Pachino.
All year

3.5HEC H P + lau S
Prices A5000-5500 V2000-2500 7500-8000 5000-7000

PALAZZOLO ACREIDE
Siracusa

Torre Torre Tudica (0931) 883322
All year
10HEC H R P G +
Prices A2000-5000 V2000-3000 5000-7000 2000-5000

PALERMO
Palermo

Internazionale Trinacria via Barcarello (091) 530590
Lying on level ground near a large rock, the site is separated from a rocky beach by an asphalt road.
12km NW of Palermo. Turn off SS113 at Km273/1 and drive 1km towards the sea.
All year
4.5HEC H G + lau S

PUNTA BRACCETTO
Ragusa

Eurocamping (0932) 918126
Jun-Sep
1.4HEC S H S +
Prices A3500 V2500 7500 7500

Rocca dei Tramonti (0932) 918054
The site lies in a quiet setting on rather barren land near a beautiful sandy bay surrounded by cliffs.
Camping Carnet Compulsory.
From Marina di Ragusa 10km W on coast road to Punta Braccetto.
Etr-Oct
3HEC H G H S + lau
Prices A3000-4000 V2500-3000 6500-7500 6500-7500

RAGUSA, MARINA DI
Ragusa

Baia del Sole Lungomare A-Doria (0932) 39844

Well tended level site. Pitches provided with roofs of straw matting.
All year
5HEC G R H PRS lau
Prices A4000-4500 V3000-5000 5000-8000 4000-10000

SAN GIORGIO
Messina
Cicero via Cicero ✆(941) 39551
15 May-Sep
2.5HEC G R S P + lau
Prices A4600 V2700 6700 3300

SAN LEONE
Agrigento
Nettuno International ✆(0922) 416268
All year
1.4HEC G H S +

SANT' ANTONIO DI BARCELLONA
Messina
Centro Vacenze Cantoni ✆(090) 9710165
May-Sep
1HEC R PS P + lau

SCOPELLO
Trapani
Baia di Guidaloca via Modena ✆(0924) 596022
May-Sep
3HEC G R S +
Prices A5500-6000 V3500-4000 7500-8000 4500-8000

TAORMINA
Messina
At **CALATABIANO**(5.2km SW)
Castello San Marco ✆(095) 641181
In lemon grove by an old castle, 9km S of Taormina.
Turn off SS114 between Calatabiano and Fiumefreddo in direction of the sea and continue for 1km.
All year
3.5HEC G R + lau S
-

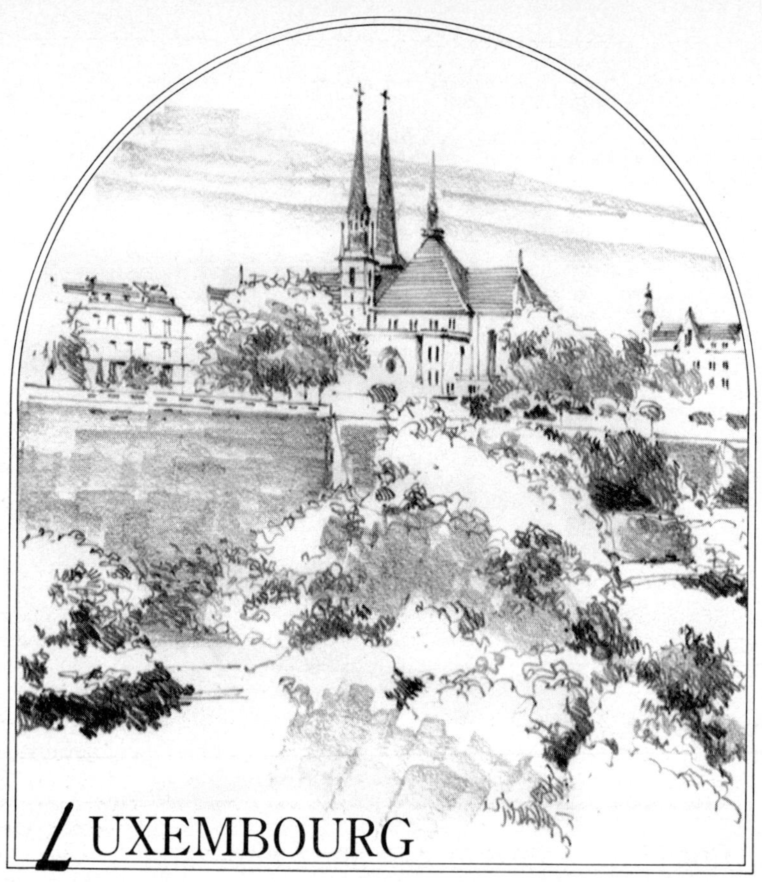

LUXEMBOURG

Luxembourg, the tiny Grand Duchy only 999 square miles in size, offers a wide range of facilities to the visitor. Entirely landlocked, it is bordered by three countries: Belgium, France and Germany. One third of the country is occupied by the hills and forests of the Ardennes, while the rest is taken up by the wooded farmland and, in the south-east, the rich wine-growing valley of the Moselle. The Grand Duchy enjoys a temperate climate, the summer often extending from May to late October. The official languages are French and German, but most of the people speak Luxembourgeois as an everyday language. Tourists will find, however, that English is also widely spoken and understood.

There are over 100 officially recognised campsites throughout the country. Most of them are open from April to October, but some function throughout the year. A booklet containing details of campsites is obtainable from the National Tourist Office (B.P.1001, L-1010 Luxembourg). All campsites open to the public must be authorised by the Minister of Tourism.

International camping carnet is not compulsory but recommended. Very few campsites will allow a reduction to the advertised charge to the holders of a camping carnet. See page **47** for further information.

Off-site camping is permitted but permission must always be obtained from the authorities in the case of public land and the owner in respect of private land before camping or parking a caravan. It is prohibited to camp on the shores of the lake (dam) of Esch/Sûre.

HOW TO GET THERE

The usual Continental Channel ports for this journey

are Boulogne, Calais or Dunkerque (Dunkirk) in France, and Oostende (Ostende) or Zeebrugge in Belgium.

Distance
Luxembourg City is just over 320km (200 miles) from the Belgian ports, or about 420km (260 miles) from the French ports, and is, therefore, within a day's drive of the Channel coast.

See Belgium for location map

GENERAL INFORMATION

The information given here is specific to Luxembourg. It **must** be read in conjunction with the European ABC at the front of the book, which covers those regulations which are common to many countries.

British Embassy/Consulate*

The British Embassy together with its consular Section is located at Luxembourg Ville, 14 Boulevard Roosevelt ✆29864/66.

Currency, including banking hours*

The unit of currency is the *Luxembourg franc (LFr)* divided into 100 *centimes*. At the time of going to press £1 = *LFr*61. Denominations of bank notes are *LFr* 50, 100, 1,000; standard coins are *LFr* 1, 5, 10, 20 and 25 and 50 *centimes*. Belgian currency is also used in Luxembourg (*BFr1 = LFr1*). There are no restrictions on the amount of foreign or local currency which can be taken into or out of the country, but because of the limited market for Luxembourg notes in other countries, it is advisable to change them into Belgian or other foreign notes before leaving.

Banks are open Monday to Friday from 08.30/09.00–12.00hrs and 13.30/14.00–16.30/17.00hrs.

Emergency telephone numbers

Fire, police, ambulance ✆012-Civil Defence emergency service (*Secours d'urgence*).

Foodstuffs*

Visitors entering from an EC country may import duty-free, 1,000g of coffee or 400g of coffee extract and 200g of tea or 80g of tea extract; a reduced allowance applies if entering from a non-EC country. Visitors under 15 years of age do not qualify for the duty-free concession on coffee.

Shopping hours

While some shops are closed on Monday mornings, the usual hours of opening for *food shops* are: from Monday to Saturday 08.00–12.00hrs, 14.00–18.00hrs. *Supermarkets* open from 09.00–20.00hrs but close at 18.00hrs on Saturdays.

Tourist information*

The National Tourist Office has an office at 36–37 Piccadilly (entrance Swallow Street), London W1V 9PA ✆071-434 2800 (recorded message service out of office hours). In Luxembourg the Office National du Tourisme (National Tourist Office), local authorities, and tourist information societies (*Syndicts d'Initiative*) organise information services and will be pleased to assist you with queries regarding tourism.

MOTORING

Children in cars

Children under 10 are not permitted to travel in a vehicle as front-seat passengers when rear seating is available.

Dimensions and weight restrictions

Private **cars** and towed **trailers** or **caravans** are restricted to the following dimensions – height, 4 metres; width, 2.50 metres; length, 12 metres. The maximum permitted overall length of vehicle/trailer or caravan combination is 18 metres.

The weight of a caravan must not exceed 75% of the weight of the towing vehicle.

Driving licence*

A valid UK or Republic of Ireland licence is acceptable in Luxembourg. The minimum age at which a visitor may use a temporarily imported car or motorcycle is 17 years.

Motoring club*

The **Automobile Club du Grand-Duché de Luxembourg** (ACL) has its head office at 8007 Bertrange, 13 route de Longwy ✆450045. ACL office hours are 08.30–12.00hrs and 13.30–18.00hrs from Monday to Friday; closed Saturday and Sunday.

Roads

There is a comprehensive system of good main and secondary roads.

***Additional information will be found in the European ABC at the front of the book.**

Speed limits*

Car

Built-up areas	60kph	(37mph)
Other roads	90kph	(56mph)
Motorways	120kph	(74mph)

Car/caravan/trailer

Built-up areas	60kph	(37mph)
Other roads	75kph	(45mph)
Motorways	90kph	(56mph)

All lower signposted speed limits must be adhered to.

Warning triangle

The use of a warning triangle is compulsory in the event of accident or breakdown. The triangle must be placed on the road about 100 metres (110yds) behind the vehicle to warn following traffic of any obstruction. See also *Warning triangle/Hazard warning lights* in the European ABC.

***Additional information will be found in the European ABC at the front of the book.**

Prices are in Belgian Francs
Abbreviations:
r rue
rte route

BERDORF

Belle Vue 2000 r de Consdorf 15A ✆79635
Jun-11 Sep
4.5HEC H G R lau

Parc Martbusch 3 Baim Maartbesch ✆79545
All year
3HEC H G R P lau
Prices A120 pitch120

BOURSCHEID-PLAGE

Bel-Air ✆90019
A clean, well-kept site, partly on meadowland and partly on terraces.
The entrance lies to the N of CR308.
Apr-Sep
10HEC H G R H LR + lau
Prices A100 pitch160

Bourscheid r du Château ✆90377
The site is partly on meadowland and partly on terraces and surrounded by rows of shrubs.
Entrance off N side of CR308 at Km21.
Apr-Oct
1.2HEC H R

BOUS/REMICH

Source rte de Luxembourg 47 ✆698332
Mar-Oct
0.5HEC H G +

CLERVAUX

Official de Clervaux Klatzewe 33 ✆92042
Situated next to the sports stadium, between the La Clervé stream and the railway in a forested area. Trains only run during the day and there is little noise. Separate field for tents.
0.5km SW from the village.
Apr-15 Nov
3HEC H G R P + lau

Reilerweier ✆92160
Apr-Nov
1.5HEC H G lau

COLPACH

Colpecher Dall r Haupstr 1 ✆61227
Mar-Oct
1.8HEC H G R P + lau L

CONSDORF

Bel Air Burgkapp ✆79353
The site is divided into pitches and lies on level meadowland in the forest area of 'Petite Suisse Luxembourgeoise'.
Camping Carnet Compulsory.
On W outskirsts of village. Turn right off E42. 6km S of Echternach.
Apr-15 Sep
2HEC H G R P + lau
Prices A120 pitch130

DIEKIRCH

Op der Sauer rte de Gilsdorf ✆808590
500m from town centre on Larochette road near the sports stadium.
All year
5HEC H G H + lau R
Prices A100 pitch100

DILLINGEN

Benelux chemin de la Forêt 1 ✆86267
A terraced, grassland site partially in an orchard and divided into pitches.
Off N10, turn right before reaching the church.
Apr-Nov
1.7HEC H G R R + lau

ECHTERNACH

Alferwelher Alferweiher 1 ✆72271
N
May-15 Sep
4HEC H G P + lau R L
Prices A110 pitch140

Official rte de Diekirch 5 ✆72272
25 March-15 Oct
2.5HEC H H P + lau G R LPR
Prices A90 90 A100

ENSCHERANGE

Val d'Or ✆352 92691
All year
2.2HEC H R H R + lau

ESCH-SUR-ALZETTE

Gaalgebierg ✆541069
A level park-like site with lovely trees on a hillock.
SE along N6 from the town centre in the direction of Dudelange as far as the motorway underpass. Then turn right and follow the steep climb uphill.
All year
2.5HEC H G R H + lau P
Prices A90 pitch100

GREVENKNAPP

Loos ✆63141
An extensive, slightly sloping grassy site on the edge of a large woodland area on the Helperknapp-Berg.
Approach from Mersch via N8 to Grevenknapp turn-off. Continue to site via CR115.
Apr-Sep
5HEC S H G R P + lau

HALLER

Relax r Henerecht 6 ✆86748
All year
2HEC H G P + lau
Prices A95 pitch90

HEIDERSCHEID

Fuussekaul rte de Bastogne 2 ✆89659
A level grassland site with a large subdivision of pitches on a plateau adjoining a woodland area.
Turn off the N15 (Ettelbruck-Wiltz/Bastogne) S of Heiderscheid in a westerly direction.
All year
30HEC H G P + lau
Prices A130 V90 90 A90

INGLEDORF
Gritt r du Pont ✆802018
On southern bank of River Sûre between Ettelbruck and Diekirch. In beautiful country setting ideal for fishing.
21 Mar-28 Oct
5HEC ◑ ⊖ G R R P + lau

KOCKELSCHEUER
Kockelscheuer 22 rte de Bettembourg ✆471815
Etr-Oct
4HEC ○ ⊖ G P + lau ☞ ✕
Prices A90 pitch100

LAROCHETTE
Kengert ✆87186
On gently sloping meadow.
Take the N8 towards Mersch, then the CR119 towards Nommern and turn right after approx 2km.
Mar-7 Nov
2HEC ● ✕ ⊖ G R P P + lau
Prices pitch400-440 (incl 2 persons)

LINTGEN
Waldesruh ✆328484
May-15 Oct
3HEC ○ ✕ P

MERSCH
Um Krounebierg r des Quatre Vents ✆328578
A clean, well-kept site on five terraces, split into sections by hedges.
Approx 0.5km W of village church.
25 March-25 Sep
5HEC ◑ ✕ ⊖ G P P + lau ☞ R
Prices A110-125 pitch110-125

MERTERT
Mertert r du Parc ✆7481745
15 Apr-15 Oct
2HEC ◑ ⊖ P P ☞ R

MONDORF-LES-BAINS
Mondorf-les-Bains rte de Burmerange ✆660746
Set on a hill, divided into pitches with plenty of trees.
SE of town to the N of the CR152 (Schengen road) at Km15.
All year
11HEC ◑ ✕ ⊖ G P lau ☞ P
Prices A90 pitch110

NOMMERN
Belle Vue r Principale 3 ✆87868
15 Mar-30 Oct
2HEC ◑ ✕ ⊖ G H P P + lau
Prices pitch320-410

Europe Nommerlayen ✆87878
A terraced site in wooded surroundings.
All year
15HEC ○ ✕ ⊖ G P P + lau

REISDORF
Rivière rte de la Sûre ✆86398
The entire site is divided into pitches and lies on a field near the church.
Between the River Sûre/Sauer and Km9.5 off the N19, 10km E of Diekirch.
Apr-Oct
1.1HEC ○ ✕ ⊖ G R P +

Sûre r de la Sûre 23 ✆86509
Apr-Oct
2.1HEC ◑ ✕ ⊖ G H R P +

REMICH
CM Europe ✆698018
A level grassland site on the edge of town with a separate section for young campers.
Access 200m S of the E42 between the banks of the Mosel to the W and Remich.
22 Apr-17 Sep
1HEC ◑ ⊖ P + lau ☞ ✕ PR

ROSPORT
Luxembourg
Barrage rte d'Echternach ✆73160
Mar-Oct
3HEC ◑ ⊖ LP P + lau ☞ ✕ G R
Prices A80 pitch120

SCHWEBSANGE
Port ✆60460
Apr-15 Oct
2.3HEC ◑ ✕ ⊖ G R P + lau ☞ L
Prices A80 pitch90

SEPTFONTAINES
Simmerschmeiz ✆307072
All year
2.5HEC ◑ ✕ ⊖ G R P P lau ☞ R

STEINFORT
Steinfort 72 rte de Luxembourg ✆(09) 398827
All year
3.5HEC ◑ ✕ ⊖ G R H P P + lau
Prices A80 V70 70 70

TROISVIERGES
Walensbongert Grand r 33 ✆97141
In a gently sloping grassy area with tarred drives and some terraced pitches. Next to a sports field and a swimming pool.
On S outskirts of the village by the CR337.
Mar-Oct
3HEC ◑ ⊖ P P lau

VIANDEN
Deich ✆84375
23 Mar-Sep
3HEC ○ ⊖ R P lau
Prices A100 pitch100

Moulin rte de Bettel ✆84501
On Bettel-Vianden road beside the river.
15 May-Aug

3HEC ⁓ ◑ ⋔H ⊖ ⊖ ⊠ ⩯R ◼ + lau ☞ ⩯P
Prices A100 pitch100

At **WALSDORF** (2km SW)
Romantique ✆84464
A terraced grassland site.
W of Diekirch-Vianden road, access from the N17 and CR354.

Mar-Oct
6HEC ⁓ ◑ ⋔H ⊠ ▼ ✕ ⊖ ⊠ G ◼
+ lau
Prices pitch500 (incl 2 persons)

WALSDORF
See **VIANDEN**

WILTZ
Kaul r Jos Simon ✆95359
In a valley, surrounded by trees.
2km NW of Clervaux road. Turn left at Grummelscheid 6 sign, then right.
May-Sep
6.5HEC ⁓ ◑ ⋔H ▼ ✕ ⊖ ⊠ ⩯P ◼
+ lau ☞ ⊠ G
Prices A100 pitch100

Selection of useful numbers for help and advice on Motoring in Europe

Hints & Advice	
Austria	0836 401 866
Belgium	0836 401 867
Denmark	0836 401 868
France	0836 401 869
Germany	0836 401 870
Gibraltar	0836 401 871
Greece	0836 401 872
Ireland (Republic of)	0836 401 873
Italy	0836 401 874
Luxembourg	0836 401 875
Netherlands	0836 401 876
Norway	0836 401 877
Portugal	0836 401 878
Spain	0836 401 879
Sweden	0836 401 880
Switzerland	0836 401 881
Yugoslavia	0836 401 882

European Weather Forecasts	
Germany & Benelux	0836 401 105
France	0836 401 106
Switzerland & Austria	0836 401 107
Iberia & Italy	0836 401 108

Other Useful Information	
French Motorway Tolls	0836 401 884
European Fuel Prices	0836 401 883

Port Information	
Hampshire/Dorset Ports	0836 401 891
Kent Ports	0836 401 890

Messages last from about 1 minute up to 7 minutes and are charged at 25p per minute cheap rate, 38p per minute at all other times. Callers pay only for the time they use. Prices are correct at time of going to press.

NETHERLANDS

The Netherlands is bordered by two countries, Belgium and Germany. A fifth of this flat, level country criss-crossed by rivers and canals lies below sea-level. The areas reclaimed from the sea, known as *polders*, are extremely fertile. The landscape is broken up by the forests of Arnhem, the bulbfields in the west, the lakes in the central and northern areas, and the coastal dunes which are the most impressive in Europe.

The climate is generally mild and tends to be damp. The summers are moderate with changeable weather and are seldom excessively hot. The language, Netherlandish or Dutch, is fairly guttural and closely allied to the low German dialect. Other dialect forms exist throughout the Netherlands.

There are some 900 officially recognised and classified campsites throughout the Netherlands. It is not generally possible to book sites in advance. Coastal sites tend to be crowded in June, July and August when many of the Dutch take their holidays. Local tourist information offices (VVV) can provide detailed information about sites in their area. The camping season is generally from April to September, but some sites are open all year.

International camping carnet is not compulsory but may be requested on certain campsites; generally it is recommended when camping in the Netherlands. Few campsites will allow a reduction to the advertised charge to the holders of a camping carnet. See the European ABC for further information.

Off-site camping is not possible outside organised sites. Overnight stops are not permitted.

HOW TO GET THERE

There are direct ferry services to the Netherlands: Harwich to the Hoek van (Hook of) Holland ($6^3/_4$hrs day, 8hrs night); Hull to Rotterdam-Europoort (14hrs); Sheerness to Vlissingen/Flushing (7hrs day, 8½hrs night). Alternatively, take one of the short Channel crossings and drive through France and Belgium.

Distance
From Calais to Den Haag (The Hague) is just over 320 km (200 miles) (within a day's drive).

GENERAL INFORMATION

The information given here is specific to The Netherlands. It **must** be read in conjunction with the European ABC at the front of the book, which covers those regulations which are common to many countries.

British Embassy/Consulate*

The British Embassy is located at 2514 ED Den Haag, Lange Voorhout 10 ✆(070)3645800, but the Embassy has no consular section. The British Consulate is located at 1074 AE Amsterdam, Koninglaan 44 ✆(020) 764343.

Currency, including banking hours*

The unit of currency is the *Dutch guilder* or *Florin (Fls)* divided into 100 *cents*. At the time of going to press £1 = *Fls*3.34. Denominations of bank notes are *Fls* 5, 10, 25, 50, 100, 250, 1,000; standard coins are 5, 10, 25 *cents* and *Fls* 1, 2.50 and 5. There are no restrictions limiting the import of currency. All imported currency may be freely exported, as well as any currency exchanged in, or drawn on, an account established in the Netherlands.

Banks are open 09.00–15.00hrs Monday to Friday and closed on Saturday. At all ANWB offices, money can be exchanged from 08.45–16.45hrs Monday to Friday and 08.45–12.00hrs on Saturday. There are exchange offices at the principal railway stations, *eg* Amsterdam, Arnhem, Eindhoven, Den Haag (The Hague), Hoek van Holland (Hook of Holland), Maastricht, Rosendaal, Rotterdam, Utrecht and Venlo.

Emergency telephone numbers

Fire Amsterdam ✆212121, Den Haag ✆3222333, and Rotterdam ✆4292929; **Police** Amsterdam ✆222222, Den Haag ✆3222222, and Rotterdam ✆4141414; **Ambulance** Amsterdam ✆5555555, Den Haag ✆3222111, and Rotterdam ✆4333300. Numbers for other towns are in the front of the local telephone directories. If necessary, contact the Police Emergency Centre ✆0611.

Firearms

Dutch laws concerning the possession of firearms are the most stringent in Europe. Any person crossing the frontier with any type of firearm will be arrested. The law applies also to any object which, on superficial inspection, shows any resemblance to real firearms (*eg* plastic imitations). If you wish to carry firearms, real or imitation, of any description into the Netherlands, seek the advice of the Netherlands Consulate.

Foodstuffs*

Visitors from EC countries may import duty-free, 1,000g of coffee or 400g of coffee extract and 200g of tea or 80g of tea extract bought duty and tax-paid; a reduced allowance applies if bought duty-free. Visitors under 15 years of age do not qualify for the duty-free concessions on coffee. The importation of unpreserved meat products is forbidden.

Shopping hours

Generally food shops are open 08.00–18.00hrs Monday to Saturday. Most food shops close for one half-day per week, but this varies according to location. Most other shops, including department stores are open from 13.00–17.30hrs on Monday, from 09.00–17.30hrs Tuesday to Friday, and from 09.00–16.00hrs Saturday.

Tourist information*

The Netherlands Board of Tourism, 25–28 Buckingham Gate, London SW1E 6LD ✆071-630 0451 will be pleased to assist you with any queries regarding tourism; it has branch offices (VVV) in all towns and large villages in the Netherlands. They can be recognised by the blue sign with white lettering.

There are three types of these branches: *Travel Offices* giving detailed information about the whole of the Netherlands; *Information Offices* giving general information about the Netherlands and detailed information about their own region; and *Local Information Offices* giving detailed information about that locality.

MOTORING

Children in cars

Children under 12 are not permitted to travel in front seats, with the exception of children under 4 in a special baby seat and children over 4 using a safety belt which does not cross their chest.

***Additional information will be found in the European ABC at the front of the book.**

Dimensions and weight restrictions

Private **cars** and towed **trailers** or **caravans** are restricted to the following dimensions – height, 4 metres; width, on 'A' roads† 2.55 metres, on 'B' roads† 2.20 metres; length‡, with 2 axles, 12 metres. The maximum permitted overall length of vehicle/trailer or caravan combination is 18 metres. The maximum weight of caravan/luggage trailers will be determined by the instructions of the manufacturer of the towing vehicle and/or the manufacturer of the caravan/luggage trailer.

†'A' roads are main roads, 'B' roads are secondary roads. 'B' roads are indicated by signs bearing the capital letter 'B', roads which do not have these signs may be considered 'A' roads.
‡Trailers with single axle and manufactured before 1967: 10 metres, after 1967: 8 metres.

Driving licence*

A valid UK or Republic of Ireland licence is acceptable in the Netherlands. The minimum age at which a visitor may use a temporarily imported car or motorcycle is 18 years.

Motoring club*

The **Koninklijke Nederlandse Toeristenbond** (ANWB) has its headquarters at 2596 EC Den Haag, Wassenaarseweg 220, and offices in numerous provincial towns. They will assist motoring tourists generally, and supply road and touring information. Offices are usually open between 08.45 and 16.45hrs Monday to Friday 08.45 and 12.00hrs on Saturday. Traffic information can be obtained from the ANWB on ✆(070) 3313131 (24 hour service).

Roads

Main roads usually have only two lanes, but are well-surfaced. The best way to see the countryside is to tour along minor roads, often alongside canals.

Speed limits*

Car

Built-up areas	50kph (31mph)
Other roads	80kph (49mph)
Motorways	120kph (74mph)

Car/caravan/trailer

Built-up areas	50kph (31mph)
Other roads	80kph (49mph)
Motorways	80kph (49mph)

On motorways there is a *minimum* speed limit of 70kph (43mph) for cars and 60kph (37mph) for vehicles with trailers.

Warning triangle

In the event of accident or breakdown a motorist may use either a warning triangle or hazard warning lights. However, it is compulsory to carry a warning triangle outside built-up areas as hazard warning lights may be damaged or inoperative. See also *Warning triangle/Hazard warning lights* in the European ABC.

***Additional information will be found in the European ABC at the front of the book.**

Prices are in Dutch Florins (Guiden or Guilder)

Abbreviations:
Str Straat

Each name preceded by 'Den' is listed under the name that follows it.

NORTH

The Dutch have been doing battle with the sea for centuries. It is part of their history, an essential element in the country's security and prosperity, and a large influence on the people's make-up. It is a battle the people have, for the most part, won. Where there once was nothing but water, we now find one of the most fertile countries in Europe; vast polders with peacefully grazing Frisian cattle, drainage mills along the canals, and drawbridges leading to farmhouses.
The West Frisian islands extend along the coast like a string of pearls, sheltering the mainland from the unpredictable and stormy North Sea, offering visitors long white beaches and many nature parks.
On the mainland, visit Dokkum, the small walled town where St Boniface was murdered in 754; Noordbergum, where clogmakers demonstrate their skills; Hindeloopen, famed for painted furniture; and Leeuwarden, the home of Mata Hari – whose statue stands on the Korfmakerspijp – and of the Princesshof, which houses a unique ceramic museum.

AMELAND (ISLAND OF)
See**NES**

AMEN
Drenthe
Reservaat Diana Heide ✆(05920) 89297
An ideal site for relaxation, which lies away from the traffic amongst forest and heathland.
If approaching from Assen along the E35, drive through Ekehaar and Amen and on towards Hooghalen.
15 Mar-Oct
27HEC ◑ H ✕ ⊖ G R H LP + lau
Prices A4 9 9

ANNEN
Drenthe
Hondsrug Annerweg 3 ✆(05922) 1292
Apr-21 Oct
18HEC ◑ H ✕ ⊖ G R P + lau
Prices pitch30

ASSEN
Drenthe
Witterzomer Witterzomer 7 ✆(05920) 55688
A large site with asphalt internal roads, lying in mixed woodland near nature reserve. Separate sections for dog owners. Individual washing facilities for the disabled.
Turn off the E35 at Assen W exit into Europaweg Zuid and continue for 100m, then turn right. Continue through Witten and follow signs.
All year
75HEC ● H ✕ ⊖ G R H LP P + lau
Prices A5 V5 5 5

BORGER
Drenthe
Hunzedal De Drift 3 ✆(05998) 34698
The site is clean, well-kept and lies NE of the village.
Camping Carnet Compulsory.
For access, turn off the road towards Buinen, drive 200m E of the bridge over the Buinen-Schoondoord canal, then head S for a further 1km.
Apr-15 Oct
22.5HEC ◑ H ✕ ⊖ G R + lau LP
Prices pitch20 (incl 2 persons)

Lunsbergen Rolderstr 3 ✆(05998) 36565
On main road between Emmen and Groningen.
Apr-24 Oct
23HEC ● H ✕ ⊖ G H P P + lau
Prices pitch13-26 (incl 4 persons)

DELFZIJL
Groningen
Delfzijl Kustweg 13 ✆(05960) 12870
On coast.
Apr-Sep
1.5HEC ● H ⊖ P ✕
Prices A3 V3 3 3

DIEVER
Drenthe
Hoeve aan de Weg Bosweg 12 ✆(05212) 7269
Camping Carnet Compulsory.
Apr-Oct
9HEC ○ H ✕ ⊖ G R H P + lau L
Prices A4 V3 4 2

At **DIEVERBRUG** (2km SE)
Ellert en Brammert Groningerweg 13 ✆(05219) 1207
On hilly ground in a forest of conifers and deciduous trees.
0.2km W of Km22.4 off the E35.
Apr-Oct
28HEC S ◑ ● H ✕ ⊖ G R H + lau

DIEVERBRUG
See **DIEVER**

DWINGELOO
Drenthe
Noordster Noordster 105 ✆(05219) 7238
3km S on E35.
All year
40HEC ● H ✕ ⊖ G R P + lau
Prices pitch24-30

Torentjeshoek Leeuweriksveldweg 1 ✆(05219) 1706
Camping Carnet Compulsory.
Apr-Sep
7.5HEC ● H ✕ ⊖ G R H + lau P
Prices A4 V1 4 4

EES
Drenthe
Land van Bartje Buinerweg 8 ✆(05998) 36162
Apr-23 Oct
40HEC ◑ H ✕ ⊖ G R H P P + lau

EMMEN
Drenthe
Emmen Angelsloerdijk 31 ✆(05910) 12018
On several pitches of well-kept meadowland, near an indoor swimming pool.
From village drive towards Angelso for 1.5km, then follow signposts.
May-Aug
8HEC ◑ H ⊖ G P

EXLOO
Drenthe
Hunzebergen Valtherweg 36 ✆(05776) 49116
2.5km SE.
Apr-Oct
4HEC ◑ H ✕ ⊖ G P + lau

FORMERUM (ISLAND OF TERSCHELLING)
Friesland
Nieuw Formerum ✆(05620) 8977

Apr-Sep
7HEC ◑ ⊖ G R S
Prices A6 V6

GASSELTE
Drenthe
Berken Borgerweg 23 ✆(05999) 64255.
Part of this site lies in wooded surroundings.
0.5km SW.
Apr-Oct
5.5HEC ● H ⊖ G R + lau
Prices A4 pitch26

Hoefslag Achter de Brinken 14 ✆(05999) 64343
Camping Carnet Compulsory.
E of town.
Apr-23 Oct
8HEC ◑ H ⊖ G R H P P + lau

GROLLOO
Drenthe
Berenkull De Pol 15 ✆(05925) 242
Partly in a forest and partly on heathland.
On the western outskirts of the village towards Hooghalen. Drive a further 0.8km along a road which narrows at the end.
18 Mar-23 Oct
30HEC S ◑ H ⊖ G R + lau

GRONINGEN
Groningen
Stadspark Campinglaan 6 ✆(050) 251624
A well-kept site on patches of grass between rows of bushes and groups of pine and deciduous trees. Some of its pitches are naturally screened.
Camping Carnet Compulsory.
For access from the SW outskirts of the town, take the road towards Peize and Roden.
15 Mar-15 Oct
7.2HEC ◑ H ⊖ G R + P
Prices A4 V4 4 4

HARKSTEDE
Groningen
Grunostrand ✆(050) 416371
Apr-23 Oct
45HEC ◑ H ⊖ G R H + lau L

HARLINGEN
Friesland
Zeehoeve ✆(05178) 13465
A well-kept meadow site which is divided into large sections by rows of bushes.
Camping Carnet Compulsory.
It lies 1km S of Harlingen near a dyke.
Apr-Sep
7.5HEC ◑ H ⊖ G R PS + lau

HEE (ISLAND OF TERSCHELLING)
Friesland
Kooi ✆(05620) 2743
Mar-Oct
7HEC ◑ H ⊖ R P + lau G L
Prices A5 V3 6 2-6

HOORN, DEN (ISLAND OF TEXEL)
Texel
Loodsmansduin Rommelpot 19 ✆(02220) 19203
Extensive site, numerous large and small hollows between some quite high dunes, connected by paved paths. Several sanitary blocks. At the highest part there is a bungalow village in amongst a shopping and administrative complex.
From the ferry drive N towards Den Burg, then turn left at crossroads towards Den Hoorn.
Apr-20 Oct
38HEC ◑ H ⊖ G R P + lau S
Prices A5 V2 8 8

KOUDUM
Friesland
Kuilart Kuilart 1 ✆(05142) 1606
Apr-Oct
37HEC ◑ H ⊖ G R H L + lau
Prices 8 pitch21-25 (incl 2 persons)

LEEUWARDEN
Friesland
At **TIETJERK** (7km E)
Kleine Wielen de Groene Ster 14 ✆(05118) 1660
This municipal site is the best in Friesland. It is completely divided into pitches and lies on grassland beside a lake.
Camping Carnet Compulsory.
Off the E10 and 4km E of Leeuwarden, towards Groningen.
Apr-Nov
15HEC H ⊖ G R H L + lau

NES (ISLAND OF AMELAND)
Ameland
Duinoord J-van Eijckweg 4 ✆(05191) 2070
Take ferry at Holward, site left off road towards beach.
Apr-Nov
17HEC S ○ H ⊖ G P + lau PS

ONNEN
Groningen
Fruitberg Dorpsweg 67 ✆(05906) 1282
S of the village, and right of the Haren-Zuidlaren road.
Apr-Sep
4.7HEC ◑ H ⊖ G R + lau LP
Prices A3 V3 4 4

OPENDE
Friesland
'T Strandheem Parkweg 2 ✆(05946) 59555
Apr-Oct
16HEC ◑ H ⊖ G R H LP + lau
Prices A4 V4 8 8

RODEN
Drenthe
Leekstermeer Meenweg 13 ✆(05945) 12073
On the S shores of the Leekstemeer.
For access, turn off the N13 about 1.6km SE of Leek (towards Roden) and drive NE. Then take a narrow paved road, and continue for a further 2.7km.
Apr-Nov
2.5HEC ○ H ⊖ G + lau L
Prices A4 V4 4 4

RUINEN
Drenthe
ENNIA-Wiltzangh Witteveen 2 ✆(05221) 1227
N of the village in the middle of a coniferous and deciduous forest, and within the grounds of a big holiday village. Advance booking is necessary for the peak season.
For access, drive from Ruinen towards Ansen for 3km, then turn and head N.
Apr-Oct
13HEC ◑ H ⊖ G R P P + lau

SNEEK
Friesland
Potten Paviljoenweg 3 ✆(05150) 15205
Apr-Oct
40HEC ● H ⊖ G R L P + lau
Prices pitch27-36

SONDEL
Friesland
Sondel Beuckeswijkstr 26 ✆(05140) 2300
In a dense wood.
Just off the Sondel-Rijs road.
29 Mar-Oct
6HEC ◑ H ⊖ G P lau
Prices A5 V3 4 4

TERHORNE
Friesland
Oan'e Poel Buorren 1 ✆(05668) 373
11 Apr-27 Sep
1.8HEC ◑ H ⊖ P lau

TERSCHELLING (ISLAND OF)
See **FORMERUM, HEE & WEST TERSCHELLING**

TEXEL (ISLAND OF)
See **COCKSDORP, DE, HOORN, DEN & KOOG, DE**

TIETJERK
See **LEEUWARDEN**

WEDDE
Groningen
Wedderbergen Molenweg 2 ✆(05976) 1673
On meadowland divided by deciduous trees and bush hedges.
On the E outskirts of the village take a narrow asphalt road, and drive N for 3.2km. Then take Spanjaardsweg and Molenweg to the camp.
Closed Jan-13 Feb
125HEC H G R H LPR + lau
Prices pitch28 (incl 4 persons)

WEST TERSCHELLING (ISLAND OF TERSCHELLING)
Friesland
Cnossen Hoofdweg 8 ✆(05620) 2321
Several patches of meadowland, left of the road towards Formerum, and right of the forest.
For access, take the ferry from Harlingen.
Mar-Oct
2.5HEC H G R H P + P
Prices A5 V3 6 A4-6

WINSCHOTEN
Groningen
Burcht Bovenburen 46 ✆(05970) 13290
All year
3.5HEC H G + lau

WORKUM
Friesland
It Soal Süderseleane 27 ✆(05151) 1443
In front of a dyke, beside the sea (Ijsselmeer). It is a good bathing area for children.
SW towards lake.
Mar-Oct
21HEC H G L + lau

ZUIDWOLDE
Drenthe
Ekelenberg Slagendijk 2 ✆(05287) 1356
SE of town.
All year
14HEC H G R H P P + lau

CENTRAL

In the heart of the Netherlands lies the country's largest nature reserve – the Hogwe Veluwe National Park. In addition to its many rare species, there are numerous museums and galleries, including the National Kröller-Müller Museum which houses a wonderful Van Gogh collection.
The Noord-Holland is *the* flower province of the Netherlands, with fields of daffodils, tulips, hyacinths and crocuses. Beautiful canals run through its capital, Amsterdam, with richly ornamental mansions on their banks. The most attractive and compact shopping centre in Holland, it is said you can buy anything in Amsterdam!
In winter, the region of Overijsell is a paradise for those who enjoy long-distance skiing "anglauf" Alternatively, a visit in July to Dedomsvaart during its week-long festival will show you the largest open-air dinner and the largest shovel-board in the world.
Utrecht is truly unique; it combines a rich past and a dynamic present. It is the home of the tallest and finest church tower in Holland – the 'Dom'. Breathtaking views will reward those who climb its 465 steps.

AALSMEER
Noord-Holland
Amsterdamse Bos Kleine Noorddijk 1 ✆(020) 6416868
The site is in a park-like setting in the Amsterdam wood. The camp is near the Airport flight path and is subject to noise depending on the wind direction.
If approaching from The Hague along the motorway, turn at the northern edge of the airport, and head towards Amstelveen. Then follow directions for Aalsmeer. Alternatively, if approaching from Utrecht, leave the motorway at the Amstelveen exit, and drive towards Aalsmeer, passing through Bovenkerk.
Apr-Oct
6.8HEC H G + R LP
Prices pp7

ALKMAAR
Noord-Holland
Alkmaar Bergerweg 201 ✆(072) 116924
The site is well-kept and divided into many sections by rows of trees and bushes.
Camping Carnet Compulsory.
Lies on the NW outskirts of the town, off the Bergen road.
Apr-15 Sep
3HEC H G H + lau LPRS
Prices A4 V4 5 A5

AMERONGEN
Utrecht
Ossenberg Dwarsweg 1 ✆(03431) 354
4km NE.
All year
16HEC H G P + lau

AMSTERDAM
Noord-Holland

See also AALSMEER& GAASPERPLAS

Vliegenbos Meeuwenlaan 138 ✆(0031) 20 368855
This is a tent site for young people.
From main railway station through tunnel, then right and right again at traffic lights, then follow signposts.
Apr-Sep
3HEC H G P + lau P
Prices A5-6 V8 14

ANDIJK
Noord-Holland
Vakantiedorp Het Grootslag
Praelpolder 4 ✆(050) 143434
Jul-Oct
5HEC ⩋ ○ ⌂ P lau ☞ ≈L
Prices ⛟28-48 ⛺28-48

APPELTERN
Gelderland
Het Groene Eiland Lutenkampshaat 2 ✆(08876) 2130
15 Mar-Oct
16HEC ⩋ ◑ ⫛H ⊾ ♀ ✕ ⊖ ⊕ G R H ≈LR P + lau
Prices V3 ⛟9-12 ⛺5-9

ARNHEM
Gelderland
Arnhem Kemperbegerweg 771 ✆(085) 431600
The site lies on grassland and is surrounded by trees.
NW of town and S of E36.
Mar-Oct
36HEC ⩋ ◑ ⫛H ⊾ ♀ ✕ ⊖ ⊕ G R ⌂ P + lau ☞ ≈P
Prices A5-6 pitch16-18

Hooge Veluwe Koningsweg 14 ✆(085) 432272
Camping Carnet Compulsory.
From Apeldoorn exit on E36 drive NW towards Hooge Veluwe.
28 Mar-20 Oct
18HEC ⩋ ◑ ⫛H ⊾ ♀ ✕ ⊖ ⊕ G R ⌂ H ≈P P + lau
Prices pitch24-28 (incl 2 persons)

Warnsborn Bakenbergseweg 257 ✆(085) 423469
The site is surrounded by woodland and lies on slightly sloping meadowland. Near zoo and open-air museum.
Near the E36 motorway NW of town in the direction of Utrecht. 200m S of SHELL filling station, continue in W direction for 0.7km.
Apr-15 Sep
3.5HEC ⩋ ◑ ⫛H ⊾ ⊖ ⊕ G R ⌂ ≈P P + lau ☞ ♀ ✕

BABBERICH
Gelderland
Rivo Torto Beekseweg 8 ✆(08364) 7332
3km W on E36.
Apr-15 Oct
8HEC ⩋ ◑ ⫛H ⊾ ✕ ⊖ ⊕ R + lau ☞ ≈L
Prices A3 V4 ⛟6 ⛺4

BEEKBERGEN
Gelderland
Bosgraaf Kanaal Zuid 444 ✆(05765) 1359
Situated on hilly grassland and woodland, but the woodland pitches are mainly used by residential caravans.
For access from the N50, Arnhem-Apeldoorn road, turn N in West Hoeve onto the Loenen road, then follow signs for 2km.
Apr-Oct
20HEC ⩋ ◑ ⫛H ⊾ ♀ ✕ ⊖ ⊕ G R ⌂ H ≈P + ⚘ lau
Prices pitch27 (incl 4 persons)

Groot Panorama Groot Panorama 36 ✆(05766) 2707
Apr-Sep
3HEC ⩋ ◑ ⫛H ⊾ ✕ ⊖ ⊕ G ≈P P + lau

Lange Bosk Hoge Bergweg 16 ✆(05765) 1252
On level ground in a spruce forest. Divided into pitches.
Turn off the Beekbergen-Loenen road at Km4.3 and drive N. Site about 3.5km from town.
23 Feb-26 Oct
37.5HEC ⩋ ◑ ⫛H ⊾ ✕ ⊖ ⊕ G ⌂ ≈P P + lau
Prices A3 V5 ⛟5 ⛺5

Pietersberg ✆(05766) 1953
Apr-15 Oct
2HEC S ● ⫛H ⊾ ✕ ⊖ ⊕ G H ≈P P + lau

BERKHOUT
Noord-Holland
Westerkogge ✆(02295) 1208

Apr-1 Oct
11HEC G R H P P + lau
Prices A3 V2 10 7-10

BERKUM
See **ZWOLLE**

BIDDINGHUIZEN
See **DRONTEN**

BLOEMENDAAL
Noord-Holland
Het Helmgat Zeeweg 97 (023) 260820
On sandy ground in a deep valley among the sand dunes with tarred drives.
Apr-Sep
4HEC G lau

BLOKZIJL
Overijssel
Tussen de Diepen Duinigermeerweg 1A (05272) 1565
15 Mar-Oct
5HEC G R H LP P + lau
Prices A4 V2 4 4

BUSSUM
Noord-Holland
Goois Natuurreservaat Franse Kampweg 3 (02159) 17751
SW towards Hilverson.
Apr-1 Oct
8HEC G R + lau P
Prices A4 V4 5 5

BUURSE
Overijssel
't Hazenbos Oude Buurserdyk 1 (05426) 338
On several meadows, partially surrounded by trees.
All year
7.5HEC G R H + lau LPR
Prices A3 V3 3 3

COCKSDORP, DE (ISLAND OF TEXEL)
Noord-Holland
Krim Roggeslootweg 6 (022220) 16275
All year
30HEC G R H S + lau
Prices A5 11 11

SlufterVallei Krimweg 102 (02220) 16214
On sand-dunes. It is advisable to book in advance during the peak season.
From the ferry landing stage, drive to the N tip of the island. Just before entering the village, turn left and head towards Vuurtoren (lighthouse). Turn left again after several hundred metres. The road leads directly to the site.

15 Mar-Oct
36HEC G P + lau R S
Prices pitch17-27 (incl 5 persons)

CULEMBORG
Gelderland
Welborn Rietveldseweg 21 (03450) 13050
On SW edge of village.
23 Feb-26 Oct
10HEC G H PR + lau
Prices A3 V5 5 5

DALFSEN
Overijssel
Gerner Haersolteweg 17 (05293) 1224
Camping Carnet Compulsory.
All year
14HEC G R LP P + lau
Prices A5-6 pitch9-11

DELDEN
Overijssel
International De Mors 6 (05407) 61922
On two grassy terraces at the edge of a wood, to the SE of town.
For access, turn S off the E8, Hengelo to Deventer road, in the E outskirts of town, then take two left turns to Zwemmbad.
15 Mar-Sep
5HEC G P + lau
Prices A4 V4 4 4

DENEKAMP
Overijssel
Papillon Kanaalweg 30 (05413) 1670
Predominantly a chalet site on meadowland in a tall coniferous and deciduous forest, about 2km N of Denekamp. It has a few naturally screened pitches.
For access, turn off the E72 towards Nordhorn (Germany), about 0.3km N of the signposts for Almelo-Nordhorn canal, and drive NE for 1.5km.
23 Feb-26 Oct
11HEC G H P + lau
Prices A3 V5 5 5

DIEPENHEIM
Overijssel
Molnhofte Nyhofweg 5 (05475) 1514
E of town.
All year
5HEC G R H P + lau
Prices A4 V3 4 4

DOESBURG
Gelderland
Ijsselstrand Eekstr 18 (08334) 72727
On level meadow with trees and hedges beside the River Ijssel. Separate field for young people. Water sports.
NE across river. Signposted.
All year
40HEC G R H LR P + lau

DOETINCHEM
Gelderland
Wrange Rekhemseweg 144 (08340) 24852
On the eastern outskirts of the town. It is set in meadowland and surrounded by bushes and deciduous trees.
200m E of link road between roads to Varsseveld and Terborg.
Apr-Sep
10HEC G R H P P + lau
Prices A4 V3 4 4

DOORN
Utrecht
Bonte Vlucht Leersumsestraatweg 23 (03430) 12476
3km E.
Apr-Sep
10HEC G R P + lau
Prices pitch27

Het Grote Bos Hydeparkin 24 (03430) 13644
Well layed out site on wooded grassland. Varied leisure activities for children and adults.
About 1km NW of Doorn.
All year
80HEC G R P + lau

DRONTEN
Gelderland

At **BIDDINGHUIZEN**(9km S)
Flevostrand Strandweg 1 (03202) 480
Plots of grassland separated by close belts of shrubs. Own marina.
On the Polder, 5km S of Biddinghuizen turn right near the Veluwemeer.
Apr-Oct
25HEC G R H LP P + lau
Prices A4 V4 10 10

Riviera Spijkweg 15 (03211) 344
Situated on grassland near a forest of deciduous trees and surrounded by shrubs.
On the Polder beside the Veluwemeer, 5km S of Biddinghuizen turn left.
28 Mar-15 Sep
30HEC G H P + lau

EDAM
Noord-Holland
Strandbad Zeevangszeedijk 7a (02993) 71994
Apr-Sep
4HEC G R H L + lau
Prices A3 V3 4 3

EERBEEK
Gelderland
Coldenhove Boshoffweg 6 (08338) 59101
In woodland.
From Apeldoorn-Dieren road, drive 2km SW, then NW for 1km.
29 Mar-19 Oct
74HEC H G P + lau

Robertsoord Doonweg 4 (08338) 51346
1km SE.
All year
2.5HEC H G H + lau

EMST
Gelderland
Wildhoeve Hanendorperweg 102 (05787) 1324
3.5km W. Signposted.
All year
11HEC H G R H P P + lau

ENSCHEDE
Overijssel
Klein-Zandvoort Keppelerdijk 200 (053) 611392
E towards Glanerbrug.
All year
9HEC H G R P + lau
Prices pitch16-23

EPE
Gelderland
Schaapskool Centrumweg 5 (05780) 16204
SW of village.
23 Feb-26 Oct
15HEC H G H P + lau
Prices A3 V5 5 5

ERMELO
Gelderland
Haeghehorst Fazantlaan 4 (03417) 53185
All year
9.8HEC H G R H P + lau
Prices pitch28 (incl 2 persons)

GAASPERPLAS
Noord-Holland
Gaasper Loosdrechtdreef 7 (020) 967326
Camping Carnet Compulsory.
All year
5.5HEC H G R H + lau LP
Prices A5 V3 6 4-6

See advertisement under AMSTERDAM

GARDEREN
Gelderland
Hertshoorn Putterweg 68 (05776) 1529
W on road to Putten.
Apr-20 Oct
10HEC H G R P + lau

GROENLO
Gelderland
Kunne Lichtenvoordsweg 68 (05440) 61260
Wooded with sandy lanes. There is a pleasant bar and a café situated in an old farm.
2km from old road to Lichtenvoorde.
Apr-Sep
1.5HEC H G P + lau

GROET
See **SCHOORL**

HAAKSBERGEN
Overijssel
't Stien'nboer Scholtenhagenweg 42 (05427) 12610
All year
11HEC H G R H + lau
Prices A4 V4 4 4

Scholtenhagen Scholtenhagenweg 30 (05427) 12384
The internal site roads are asphalt and there are pony-rides for children.
Turn off by-pass W of town and drive towards Eilbergen for 0.7km, then turn right and follow Zwemmbad signposts.
Apr-Oct
8HEC H G

HALFWEG
Noord-Holland
Houtrak (023) 382424
Grassy site on several levels subdivided by trees, hedges and shrubs. Separate section for young campers.
Camping Carnet Compulsory.
Signposted from Spaarwonde exit on A5.
May-Sep
5HEC H + LP
Prices A7 pitch5

HATTEM
Gelderland
Leemkule Leemkuilen 6 (05206) 41945
2.5km SW.
Apr-Oct
24HEC H G R P P + lau
Prices pitch17-30

HEERDE
Gelderland
Buitencentrum de Koerberg (05782) 2066
Apr-Oct
23HEC S H G R P P + lau L

HEILOO
Noord-Holland
Heiloo De Omloop 24 (072) 331950
One of the best sites in the area. It is divided into many large squares by hedges.
Apr-Sep
5HEC H G R P + lau S
Prices A1 16-22 15

Klein Varnebroek De Omloop 22 (072) 331627
Apr-15 Sep
4.2HEC H G lau

HELDER, DEN
Noord-Holland
Donkere Dulnen Jan Verlailleweg 616 (02230) 14731
3km SW.
Etr-15 Sep
7HEC H G R P + lau S

Noorder Sandt Noorder Sandt 2 (02230) 41266
A flat, well-maintained site on meadowland, with good sanitary blocks.
Access from the Den Helder to Callantsoog coastal road.
All year
10HEC H R H P + lau G S
Prices A4 14

HENGELO
Gelderland
Kom-Es-An Handwijzersdijk 4 (05753) 7242
NE of village in wooded area in the direction of Ruurlo.
Apr-Sep
6.5HEC H G R H P P + lau

HENGELO
Overijssel
Kristalbad-Hengelo Kettingbrugweg 60 (074) 916560
SE towards Enschede between canal and road.
15 Apr-15 Sep
4HEC H G R P P +

HEUMEN
Gelderland
Heumens Bos Vosseneindseweg 46 (080) 581481
NW of village, 100m N of the Wijchen road.
Apr-Sep
15HEC H G R H PR + lau L
Prices pitch21 (incl 2 persons)

HOENDERLOO
Gelderland
't Veluws Hof Krimweg 154 (05768) 1777
W of N93.
All year
16HEC H G R H P + lau
Prices A4 V3 5 A5

Miggelenberg Migglenbergweg 65 (05768) 1251
Site situated in sparse, mixed woodland.
For access, turn off the Arnhem to Apeldoorn road at Woesterhoeve and drive W to Hoenderloo and continue for 2.5km on the Beekbergen road.
27 Mar-23 Oct
33HEC H G P P lau

Pampel (05768) 1760
All year
14.5HEC H P + lau G R
Prices A6 V4 6 A6

HOLTEN
Overijssel
Prins Wildweg 2 (05480) 12272
A holiday complex operated by the Dutch ENNIA Company, in an area of attraction to the rambler. Swimming pool on edge of site.
Access from the E8 Deventer-Almelo road. Take the Holten/Rijssen exit then turn off.
Apr-Sep
11HEC H G P + lau
Prices A3 V5 5 A5

KESTEREN
Gelderland
Lede en Oudewaard Hogedijkseweg 40 (08886) 1477
On level meadowland surrounded by bushy hedges and divided into individual pitches. 100m from private beach and pool.
2km N of village, turn W off main Rhenen-Kesteren road, and continue for 2.7km.
All year
15HEC H G R H L + lau
Prices A4 V3 6 A4-6

KOOG, DE (ISLAND OF TEXEL)
Noord-Holland
Kogerstrand Badweg 33 (02220) 17208
Apr-Sep
50HEC H G S P + lau R P
Prices A4 8 A8

Shelter (02220) 17475
15 Mar-25 Oct
1.1HEC H lau G R PS +
Prices A5 V2 8 A8

LAAG-SOEREN
Gelderland
Jutberg De Jutberg 78 (08337) 220
1km S.
All year
20HEC H G P lau

LATHUM
Gelderland
Honingraat Marsweg 2 (08336) 32211
Site with modern facilities on an arm of the Ijssel with good boating facilities and its own marina.
For access, turn off Arnhem-Doesburg road and pass through the village to the site in 1.5km.
17 Mar-Sep
17HEC H G R LPR P + lau

Mars Marsweg 6 (08336) 31131
Divided into pitches on level meadowland beside a dammed tributary of River Ijssel.
Turn off Arnhem-Doesberg road N of village and continue W for 1.7km.
Apr-Sep
10HEC H R + lau L
Prices A5 V2 4 A4

LOCHEM
Gelderland
Ruighenrode Vordenseweg 6 (05730) 53151
Site among mixed woodland with tall spruce.
2km SW of town. For access, turn off the road to Zutphen at Km10.4 in S direction on the Vorden road for the site in 4.5km.
All year
60HEC H G P + lau
Prices A4 13 A25-26

LUTTENBERG
Overijssel
Luttenberg Heuvelweg 9 (05724) 1405
23 Feb-26 Oct
11.9HEC H G P + lau
Prices A3 V5 5 A5

MAARN
Utrecht
Laag-Kanje Laan van Laag-Kanje 1 (03432) 1348
Situated 500m from the lake.
2km NE.
16 Mar-14 Oct
29HEC H G R P + lau L

MARKELO
Overijssel
Hessenheem Potdijk 8 (05476) 1200
Situated near a swimming pool.
3km NE.
All year
32HEC H G R P + lau
Prices A4 V4 7

NEEDE
Gelderland
Eversman Bliksteeg 1 (05450) 1906
Situated in a quiet position, surrounded by trees.
W of town.
Apr-Oct
1.5HEC H G H P + lau

't Klumpe Diepenheimseweg 38 (05450) 1780
N of town.
Apr-Oct
9.7HEC H G lau

NIEUW-MILLIGEN
Gelderland
AEGON-Rabbit Hill Grevenhout 21 (05775) 6431
On hilly ground in a forest of coniferous and deciduous trees. Advance booking required for peak season.
From E8 drive 0.3km S towards Kootwijk then turn E and continue 400m.
22 Mar-18 Oct
48.6HEC H G R P + lau
Prices pitch15-28 (incl 5 persons)

NIJMEGEN
Gelderland
Kwakkenberg Luciaweg 10 (080) 232443
On gently sloping meadowland between rows of deciduous trees and groups of bushes.
Situated on E outskirts of town and reached by turning off N53 (Nijmegen-Klef/Kleve) and drive S.
Apr-Sep
5HEC H G P
Prices A3 V3 3 A3

NOORD SCHARWOUDE
Noord-Holland
Molengroet Molengroet 1 (02269) 3444
All year

10HEC fH G R H L + lau PS
Prices A4 V3 9 6

NUNSPEET
Gelderland
Het Plashuis Randmeerweg 8
(03412) 52406
Apr-Sep
12HEC fH G H LP P + lau
Prices pitch17-31

Vossenberg Groenlaantje 25
(03412) 52458
Apr-15 Oct
1HEC S fH G H + lau
Prices A5 V2 4 3

OMMEN
Overijssel
Calluna Stouweweg 3 (05297) 1234
NW on left off road to Zwolle.
Apr-Sep
25HEC S fH G R H LP +

OTTERLO
Gelderland
Beek en Hei Heldeweg 4 (08382) 1483
Camping Carnet Compulsory.
All year
3HEC fH P + lau G R L
Prices A4 V3 4 4

PETTEN
Noord-Holland
Corfwater Korfwaterweg 1a
(02268) 1981
15 Apr-15 Sep
5.5HEC S fH S P + lau G R P
Prices A4 V4 4 4

Watersnip Pettemerweg 4 (02268) 1432
SW towards N9.
22 Mar-Sep
14HEC fH G H P P + lau

RENSWOUDE
Utrecht
Batterljen Dijkje 1 (08387) 1130
S before railway.
Apr-Sep
5HEC fH G H P + lau

RHENEN
Utrecht
Thymse Berg Nieuwe Veenendaalseweg 229 (08376) 12384
N of town.
Apr-Oct
10HEC fH G H P P + lau
Prices A6 pitch7

RUURLO
Gelderland
't Sikkeler Sikkelerweg 8 (05736) 1221
4km SW.
All year
7HEC fH G + lau P
Prices A4 V2 4 4

ST MAARTENSZEE
Noord-Holland
St Maartenszee Westerduinweg 30
(02246) 1401
Completely surrounded and divided into pitches by hedges, lying on meadowland on the edge of a wide belt of sand dunes.
Camping Carnet Compulsory.
For access, turn off the Alkmaar to Den Helder road at St Maartensvlotburg and drive towards the sea. Take the road over the dunes and follow it for about 1.5km, then turn right and continue for a further 300m.
Apr-Oct
5HEC fH G R + lau PS
Prices A5 pitch11-14

SCHOORL
Noord-Holland
Elba Omloop 35 (02209) 1936
On meadowland and divided into pitches by hedges, which provide some shelter from the wind.
For access follow the Bergen road and turn left at the 'Aagtdorp' bus stop.
Apr-Oct
2.5HEC fH G R + lau LS
Prices A4 8 4

At **GROET**(4km NW)
Groede Hargerweg 8 (02209) 1555
The site consists of a meadow enclosed by hedges.
15 Apr-15 Sep
3HEC fH G R P + S
Prices A5 7 7

SOEST
Utrecht
King's Home Birkstr 136 (033) 619118
15 Mar-Oct

5HEC H G R P + lau P
Prices A4 V4 7 7

STEENWIJK
Overijssel
Kom Bultweg 25 (05210) 13736
Split into two sections, lying near a country house, and is surrounded by a beautiful oak forest.
The access road off the Steenwijk-Frederiksoord road is easy to miss.
Apr-Sep
10HEC H G R H + lau P
Prices A4 V3 5 5

UITDAM
Noord-Holland
Uitdam Zeedijk 2 (02903) 1433
Camping Carnet Compulsory.
Apr-Oct
23HEC H G R H L + lau
Prices A5 V5 5 4-5

URK
Flevoland
Vormt Vormtweg 9 (05277) 1785
Camping Carnet Compulsory.
Apr-Oct
10HEC H G P + lau R L
Prices A5 V3 5 5

UTRECHT
Utrecht
Berekuil Arienslaan 5 (030) 713870
On N outskirts near motorway to Hilversum.
Apr-Oct
4.5HEC H G R + lau P
Prices A4 V4 4 3-4

VAASSEN
Gelderland
Bosrand Elspeterweg 45 (05788) 1343
In castle grounds.
All year
2.5HEC H G R H P + lau
Prices A6 9 4

VELSEN-ZUID
Noord-Holland
Weltevreden (023) 383726
Camping Carnet Compulsory.
Apr-Oct
10HEC H + lau G LP
Prices A8 pitch5

VIERHOUTEN
Gelderland
Saxenhelm Plaggeweg 90 (05771) 283
1.5km N.
All year
40HEC H G P + lau

VOGELENZANG
Noord-Holland
Vogelenzang 2e Doodweg 17 (02502) 7014
1km W.
Apr-15 Sep
25HEC H G R P + lau
Prices A3 9 9

VOORTHUIZEN
Gelderland
Ponderosa Kieftveen 30 (06429) 1945
23 Feb-26 Oct
27HEC H G P + lau
Prices A3 V5 5 5

Zanderij Hoge Boeschoterweg 96 (03429) 1343
Apr-Oct
13HEC H G R H P + lau
Prices A5 7 7

WAPENVELD
Gelderland
Ennerveld Molenweg 2 (05206) 78552
On partly hilly ground in a dense forest of coniferous and deciduous trees, left off the Wapenveld-Wezep road.
For access turn off the N93 (Zwolle-Apeldoorn) in Wapenveld and drive W for 0.7km.
All year
12HEC H G P + lau

WEZEP
Gelderland
Heidehoek Heidehoeksweg 7 (05207) 1382
0.5km W of railway station.
Apr-Oct
15HEC H G R L + lau P

ZEEWOLDE
Flevoland
RCN Zeewolde Dasselaarweg 1 (03424) 1246
Apr-Oct
42HEC H G L P + lau
Prices pitch30-37

ZELHEM
Gelderland
Het Zonnetje Ruurloseweg 30 (08342) 1455
3km NE.
Apr-Oct
6.5HEC H G R P P + lau

ZWOLLE
Overijssel
At **BERKUM**(1km E)
Agnietenberg Haersterveerweg 27 (038) 531530
1km W.
Apr-Sep
14HEC H G R lau

SOUTH

The south of the Netherlands is the home of the traditional Delft china and Gouda cheese, and is also the location of a project which is the first of its kind in the world: the building of a moveable marine floodgate across the outlet of the Oostenschelde River.
One of the oldest cities in Holland, and the provincial capital of Limburg, is Naastricht. Shaped through the ages by art and culture, the city has a rich heritage and a wealth of historic monuments.
The region also includes two prominent and very different cities. The Hague, with its favourable reputation as the City of Arts, has parliamentary buildings and stately palaces, wide streets and spacious squares, giving an impression of distinction and elegance.
The world's premier harbour has expanded to become the dynamic metropolis of Rotterdam; a city full of vitality and conviviality with a variety of architecture ranging from snug Delfshaven to the futuristic pencil flats and cube houses.

AFFERDEN
Limburg
Hengeland Hengeland 10 ✆(08853) 1355
On slightly hilly heathland, near a farm.
To the N of the town, about 1km E of the N95.
All year
10HEC ≈ ◑ H ✗ ⊖ G P P +

Klein Canada Dorpstr 1 ✆(08853) 1223
All year
10HEC ≈ ◑ H ✗ ⊖ G R P P + lau
Prices 35

ARCEN
Limburg
Maasvallei Dorperheideweg 34 ✆(4703) 1564
Off the N271
All year
12HEC ≈ ◑ H ✗ ⊖ G R H LP P P + lau
Prices pitch18-34 (incl 2 persons)

Schans ✆(4703) 1957
All year
15HEC ≈ ○ H ✗ ⊖ G R LP P + lau

ARNEMUIDEN
Zeeland
Witte Raaf Muidenweg 3 ✆(01182) 1212
A modern well-maintained site in meadowland, divided into sections by rows of shrubs, ideal for sailing and motor boat enthusiasts with yacht marina.
Situated on the Veersmeer, N of the Goes-Vlissingen motorway, from Arnemuiden exit follow signs for about 5km.
Apr-Oct
20HEC ≈ ◑ H ✗ ⊖ G R LP + lau

ASSELT
Limburg
Maasterras Eind 4 ✆(4740) 1287
Well-kept site on terrace. Private beach.
W of Swalmen-2.3km W of the SHELL petrol station on the N273.
All year
3HEC ≈ ◑ H ✗ ⊖ G P +

BAARLAND
Zeeland
Scheideoord Landingsweg 1 ✆(01193) 226
S of town on the coast.
All year
10HEC ≈ ◑ H ✗ ⊖ G R H P P lau

BAARLE NASSAU
Noord-Brabant
Heimolen Heimolen 6 ✆(04257) 8001
1.5km SW.
All year
15HEC ≈ ◑ H ✗ ⊖ G P + lau

BAARSCHOT
See **DIESSEN**

BELFELD
Limburg
Eekhoorn ✆(04705) 1326
On a flat-topped hill covered with trees.
Camping Carnet Compulsory.
3km E of village and N95.
Apr-Oct
12HEC ≈ ◑ H ✗ ⊖ G R H P P P + lau

BERG EN TERBLIJT
Limburg
Oriëntal Rijksweg 6 ✆(04406) 40075
On Maastrict-Valkenburg road 3km from Maastrict.
May-25 Oct
5HEC ≈ ◑ H ✗ ⊖ G R H P + lau ☞ R
Prices A3 pitch12

BERGIJK
Noord-Brabant
Paal De Paaldreef 14 ✆(04975) 1977
Signposted.
Apr-25 Oct
17HEC ≈ ◑ ● H ✗ ⊖ G R P P + lau
Prices A4-5 pitch18-21

BLADEL
Noord-Brabant
Achterste Hoef Tropríjt 10 ✆(04977) 81579
S of town.
All year
15HEC ≈ ◑ H ✗ ⊖ G R P + lau
Prices pitch42 (incl 4 persons)

BORSSELE
Zeeland
Estancia Catalijneweg 47 ✆(01105) 1568
Clean well-kept site surrounded by trees and hedges.
W of town of N shore of Westerschelde.
All year
1.9HEC ≈ ◑ H ✗ ⊖ G P

BOXTEL
Noord-Brabant
Dennenoord Dennendreef 5 ✆(04110) 1280
Level, grassy site with hedging and groups of trees. Leisure activities organised for adults and young people. Soundproof disco.
Turn off the N2 at Esch in direction of Osterwijk. Follow signs.
Mar-Oct
7HEC ≈ ● H ✗ ⊖ G R H P P + lau

BRESKENS
Zeeland
Schoneveld ✆(01172) 3220
Camping Carnet Compulsory.
All year
14HEC ≈ ◑ H ✗ ⊖ G R PS + lau
Prices pitch20-42

Zeebad Nieuwesluisweg 5 ✆(01172) 1815
The site lies NW of Breskens below the dyke road to Nieuwesluis and the lighthouse.
15 Mar-Oct
16HEC ≈ ◑ H ✗ ⊖ G P lau

BRIELLE
Zuid-Holland
Krabbeplaat Oude Veerdam 4 (01810) 12363
On level ground scattered with trees and groups of bushes. It has asphalt drives. Nearest campsite to the coast and ferries.
Apr-Sep
26HEC H G R L + lau
Prices pitch16-18 (incl 2 persons)

BROEKHUIZENVORST
Limburg
Kasteel Ooyen Blitterswijkseweg 2 (04763) 1307
All year
16HEC H G H P P + lau

BROUWERSHAVEN
Zeeland
Osse Blankersweg 4 (01119) 1513
Apr-Oct
8.5HEC H G R H LPS + lau
Prices pitch27-38 (incl 2 persons)

BURGH-HAAMSTEDE
Zeeland
Ginsterveld J-J-Boeyesweg 45 (01115) 1590
Apr-Sep
14HEC H G H + lau S

Nordzeecamping Duinoord Sveenweg 16 (01115) 1964
All year
4.2HEC G H S +
Prices pitch21-35 (incl 2 persons)

CROMVOIRT
Noord-Brabant
Vondst Pepereind 13 (04118) 1431
1km SE.
All year
8HEC H G R lau L
Prices A4 V3 3 3

DIESSEN
Noord-Brabant
At **BAARSCHOT** (2km S)
Kempenbos Westelbeersedijk 6 (04254) 1567
All year
16HEC H G R P P + lau

DOMBURG
Zeeland
Domburg Schelpweg 7 (01188) 1679
On meadowland divided into several sections, with asphalt drives. It is on the inland side of the road, along the dyke, with a belt of shrubs dividing it from the road. 2 tennis courts, small golf course, a children's swimming pool and play garden.
500m on main road to Westkapelle.
Apr-Oct
13.5HEC H G P + lau

DORDRECHT
Zuid-Holland
Bruggehof Rijksstraatweg 186 (078) 183241
Near Moerdijkbrug.
Apr-15 Oct
21HEC H G P + lau
Prices A5 V4 5 4

ECHT
Limburg
Marisheem Brugweg 89 (04754) 81458
The site is well-kept and lies E of the village.
From town drive approx 2.2km towards Echterbosch and the border, then turn left.
15 Mar-15 Oct
10HEC H G R P + lau

FLUSHING
See **VLISSINGEN**

's-GRAVENZANDE
Zuid-Holland
Jagtveld Nieuwlandsedijk 35 (01748) 13479
Apr-Sep
3.3HEC H G R + lau LS
Prices A4 V2 8 8

HAAG, DEN (THE HAGUE)
Zuid-Holland
Ockenburg Wijndaelerweg 25 (070) 3252364
Site lies on the W of town and 500m from beach. Advance booking not accepted.
For access follow signs towards Kijkduin.
24 Mar-20 Oct
46HEC S H G R + lau PS
Prices A6 V3 11 11

HEEL
Limburg
Heelderpeel De Peel 13 (04748) 1596
This well-maintained site lies in mixed woodland, next to a lake surrounded by forest.
For access, drive 6km W from Roermond, then turn SW on to the Maaseyk road for 3.5km to site approach road with sign 'Hotel de Peel'.
15 Mar-Oct
21HEC H G R L + lau

HEEZE
Noord-Brabant
Heezerenbosch Heezerenbsoch 6 (04907) 63811
All year
25HEC H G R H LP + lau
Prices pitch17-30

HELDEN-DORP
Limburg
Heldense Bossen (04760) 72476
Access via Maastricht via A67/E3 (Venio-Eindhoven). Signposted.
All year
18HEC H G R H P lau

HELLEVOETSLUIS
Zuid-Holland
'T Weergors Zuiddyk 2 (01883) 12430
15 Mar-Nov
5.5HEC H G R P + lau R
Prices A4 V2 5 5

HENGSTDIJK
Zeeland
Vogel Vogelweg 4 (01148) 1625
All year
30HEC H G R H L P + lau
Prices 21-29 13-21

HERKENBOSCH
Limburg
Elfenmeer Meinweg 1 (04752) 1689
Hilly, well-maintained site in pine forest beside a small lake.
NE off Roermond road.
All year
35HEC H G R P P + lau
Prices A3-4 pitch6-10

HERPEN
Noord-Brabant

Herperduin Schaijkesweg 12 ✆(08867) 1383

Situated in extensive woodland.

Access from the 'S-Hertogenbosch-Nijmegen motorway. Take the Ravenstein exit and continue towards Herpen, then in direction Bergheim/Oss.

27 Mar-23 Oct

26HEC ◑ H ⊖ G + lau LP

Prices A3 V4 10-15

HILVARENBEEK
Noord-Brabant

Beekse Bergen Beekse Bergen 1 ✆(013) 360032

Situated in a holiday centre in the Brabant afforestation on the edge of a safari park. Lake suitable for swimming. Various other facilities.

10km S of Tilburg.

23 Mar-22 Oct

27HEC ◑ H ⊖ G H + lau L

HOEK
Zeeland

Braakman Middenweg 1 ✆(01152) 1730

On meadowland between a wood and shrubs.

About 4km W of town and 40m N of expressway to Breskens.

All year

56HEC ◑ H ⊖ G H + lau

HOEK VAN HOLLAND
Zuid-Holland

Hoek van Holland Wierstr 101 ✆(01747) 2801

On grass, surrounded by rows of poplar trees, bushes and paved drives.

If approaching from the N, turn off the E36, take the Riipstraat and drive to the end of the road.

28 Mar-27 Sep

7.8HEC ◑ H ⊖ G H P + lau S

Prices 26 23

HOEVEN
Noord-Brabant

Hoeven Oude Antwerpse Postbaan 81b ✆(01659) 2570

Between Breda and Rosendaal W of Etten-Leur.

7 Apr-23 Sep

34HEC ◑ H ⊖ G R H P + lau

Prices A5 7 7

KAATSHEUVEL
Noord-Brabant

't Hoekske van Haestrechtstr 22 ✆(04167) 72794

A flat site divided into plots.

For access turn E off the Tilburg to Waalwijk road at the windmill and drive for 600m.

Apr-Oct

16HEC ◑ H ⊖ G R P + lau

Duinlust Duinlaan 1 ✆(04167) 72775

In a meadow surrounded by hedges.

Turn off main road 200m N of village and drive 1.1km E.

All year

5.5HEC ◑ H ⊖ G R + lau

Prices A4 V2 2 2

KAMPERLAND
Zeeland

Molenhoek Molenweg 69 ✆(01107) 1202

On meadowland and is surrounded by tall bushy hedges.

NW outskirts of village.

15 Mar-Oct

8HEC ◑ H ⊖ G lau

Roompot Mariapolderseweg 1 ✆(01107) 4000

A level, well-maintained site with a private beach.

Turn off Kamperland-Wissenkerke road and drive N for 0.5km.

All year

33HEC ◑ H ⊖ G R H PS P + lau

Schotsman Schotsmanweg 1 ✆(01107) 1751

On a large, level meadow beside the Veerse Meer, next to a Nature Reserve. Water sports.

Signposted.

28 Mar-21 Oct

30HEC ◑ H ⊖ G R H P + lau LS

KATWIJK AAN ZEE
Zuid-Holland

Noordduinen Campingweg 1 ✆(01718) 25295

Apr-Sep

11HEC H ⊖ + G S

Prices pitch24-31

KORTGENE
Zeeland

Paardekreek Havenweg 1 ✆(01108) 2051

A municipal site next to a canal that flows into the Veerse Meer.

Camping Carnet Compulsory.

For access, turn off the Zierikzee-Goes trunk road at the CHEVRON petrol station and drive towards Kortgene, continue through the village and drive SW.

Apr-Oct

10HEC ◑ H ⊖ G R H LP + lau

Prices pitch18-35 (incl 2 persons)

KOUDEKERKE
Zeeland

Dishoek Dishoek 2 ✆(01185) 1348

W on Vlissingen-Westkapelle road.

29 Mar-24 Oct

2.3HEC ◑ H ⊖ G R H + lau S

Prices pitch20-28

Duinzicht Strandweg 7 ✆(01185) 1397

3km SW of Koudekerke.

15 Apr-1 Oct

5HEC G H + lau S
Prices A4 V3 3 3

LAGE MIERDE
Noord-Brabant
Vakantlecentrum de Hertenwei Wellenseind 7-9 (04259) 1295
Camping Carnet Compulsory.
2km N.
All year
20HEC G R P + lau
Prices pitch26-42 (incl 4 persons)

See advertisement on page 236

LUYKSGESTEL
Noord-Brabant
Zwarte Bergen Zwarte Bergen 1 (04974) 1373
The site is isolated and very quiet, and lies on undulating dune-like ground in a pine forest.
From Eindhoven through Valkenswaard and Bergiejkl. Signposted.
All year
25HEC G R P + lau
Prices A4 V4 4 4

MAASBREE
Limburg
Ruige Hoek De Ruige Hoek 2 (04765) 2360
On the E3 just before Venlo, on the border with Germany.
Apr-Sep
10.5HEC G P + lau
Prices A4 pitch8

MAASTRIGHT
Limburg
Dousberg Dousbergweg 102 (043) 432171
Mar-Oct
10HEC G R H P + lau
Prices A6 V3 6 6

MIDDELBURG
Zeeland
Middelburg Koninginnelaan 55 (01180) 25395
On meadowlands surrounded by trees and bushes.
On W outskirts of town.
Etr-Oct
2.4HEC G R + P
Prices A3 V2 4 4

MIERLO
Noord-Brabant
Wolfsven Patrijslaan 4 (04927) 61661
All year
75HEC S G LP + lau
Prices pitch18-20 (incl 2 persons)

MILHEEZE
Noord-Brabant
Peel Hutten 5 (04924) 1225
N on road to Boxmeer.
Apr-15 Sep
11HEC G P lau

NIEUWVLIET
Zeeland
International St-Bavodk 2 (01171) 1233
On N outskirts, near a windmill on the road leading to the dyke.
Apr-Oct
3.3HEC G H + lau S
Prices pitch17 (incl 2 persons)

Pannenschuur Zeedijk 19 (01171) 1391
NW of town. Signposted.
All year
14HEC G R H PS + lau
Prices A4 pitch15

NOORDWIJK AAN ZEE
Zuid-Holland
Carlton Kraaierslaan 13 (02523) 72783
Camping Carnet Compulsory.
Apr-Nov
2HEC R H LP P lau G S
Prices A6 10 6

Jan de Wit Kapelleboslaan 10 (02523) 72485
15 Mar-Oct
4.5HEC G R + lau LS
Prices A5 7 7

At **NOORDWIJKERHOUT** (5km NE)
Club Soleil Kraaierslaan 7 (02523) 74225
Camping Carnet Compulsory.
Signposted.
Apr-Oct
5.5HEC G R H P P + lau S
Prices A7 pitch7

NOORDWIJKERHOUT
See **NOORDWIJK AAN ZEE**

NULAND
Noord-Brabant
Vinkeloord Vinkeloord 1 (04102) 2966
S of village.
All year
45HEC G R H P + lau P

OISTERWIJK
Noord-Brabant
Reebok Burg Vd Oeverweg 19 (04242) 82309
Situated in a large pine forest, hardly fenced off and impossible to overlook. In attractive surroundings with numerous small lakes.
SE of town.
Apr-Oct
10HEC S G R P + lau L

OOSTERHOUT
Noord-Brabant
Katjeskelder (01620) 53539
Apr-Nov
28HEC G R H P + lau
Prices pitch33 (incl 4 persons)

OOSTKAPELLE
Zeeland
Dekelinge Landmetersweg 1 ✆(01188) 2820
The on-site facilities have seasonal opening.
Apr-Oct
10HEC ~ ○ ⋔H 🏪 ♀ ✕ ⊖ ⚲ 𝐆 ≈P P + lau ☞ ≈S
Prices A4 ⚲12 ⅄12

Dennenbos Duinweg 64 ✆(01188) 1310
Mar-Oct
1.6HEC ~ ☾ ⋔H 🏪 ♀ ✕ ⊖ ⚲ 𝐆 𝐑 ⌂ 𝐇 ≈PS ◼ + ✱ lau
Prices V5 ⚲5 ⅄5

In de Bongerd Brouwerijstr 13 ✆(01188) 1510
Well-kept in a meadow with hedges and apple trees.
500m S.
20 Mar-Oct
3.8HEC ~ ☾ ⋔H ✕ ⊖ ⚲ 𝐆 𝐑 ⌂ 𝐇 ≈P + lau ☞ 🏪 ♀ ≈S
Prices A4 V3-5 ⚲4 ⅄4

Ons Buiten Aagtekerkeseweg 2 ✆(01188) 1813
From church drive S towards Gapinge, turn W and continue 400m.
15 Mar-Oct
8HEC ~ ☾ ⋔H 🏪 ♀ ✕ ⊖ ⚲ 𝐆 𝐑 𝐇 ≈P P + ✱ lau ☞ ≈LS
Prices A5 V5 ⚲5 ⅄5

OUDDORP
Zuid-Holland
Groene Welde Oude Nieuwlandseweg 11 ✆(01878) 1747
A municipal site on flat grassland.
On outskirts. Signposted.
Apr-Sep
12HEC ~ ☾ ⋔H 🏪 ⊖ ⚲ 𝐆 𝐑 𝐇 ◼ + lau

Klepperstee Klepperstee ✆(01878) 1511
On level meadow divided by hedges and trees. Soundproof disco.
Access via A29 (Rotterdam-Willemstad) exit Middelharnis.
Apr-Nov
38HEC S ○ H ⊖ G R H P P + lau S

PLASMOLEN
Limburg
Eldorado Witteweg 18 ✆(08896) 1914
Camping Carnet compulsory.
S of N271.
Apr-Sep
6HEC ○ H ⊖ G R L P + lau
Prices A4 V3 5 5

RENESSE
Zeeland
Bremhoeve Hoogenboomlaan 11 ✆(01116) 1403
Well-kept site belonging to a trade union, but also accepting tourists. The last camping site in Hoogenboomlaan with numbered sections. It is advisable to reserve pitches between 21 Jun and 9 Aug.
Apr-25 Oct
12HEC ◑ H ⊖ G R H P P + lau
Prices pitch14-28 (incl 4 persons)

International Scharendijkseweg 8 ✆(01116) 1391
On grassland, between rows of tall shrubs and trees. Between dyke road and main road to Scharendijk on E outskirts of village.
Mar-Oct
3HEC ◑ H ⊖ G R P P + S

Oase Roelandsweg 8 ✆(01116) 1358
Well-kept park like site.
S of village, turn off Haamstede-Scharendijke trunk road at petrol station, take road to Hogezoom, then turn left.
Apr-Sep
7.5HEC ○ H ⊖ G R H P + lau S
Prices A6 V5 5 5

Vakentiepark 'Schouwen' Hoogenboomlaan 28 ✆(01116) 1231
Mar-Oct
9HEC ◑ H ⊖ G H P + lau

RIJEN
Noord-Brabant
D'n Mastendol Oosterhoutseweg 7-13 ✆(01612) 22664
SW of town.
15 Mar-15 Oct
10.5HEC ◑ H ⊖ G R P + lau
Prices A4 V3 3 3

RIJNSBURG
Zuid-Holland
Koningshof Elsgeesterweg 8 ✆(01718) 26051
Modern site on level meadow.
1km N.
All year
7HEC ◑ H ⊖ G R P P + lau
Prices A3 V3 13 13

See advertisement on page 238

ROCKANJE
Zuid-Holland
Rondeweibons Schapengorsedijk 19 ✆(01814) 1944
15 Mar-Oct
32HEC ◑ H ⊖ G R P + lau PRS
Prices A5 V3 4 4

See advertisement on page 238

ROELOFARENDSVEEN
Zuid-Holland
Braassem Galgekade 2A ✆(01713) 12091
Off highway A4/E10. (Amsterdam-Leiden). Follow signs for Braassemer Meer from Roelofarendsveen exit.
Apr-Sep
2HEC ◑ H ⊖ G R H + lau LP
Prices A4 V4 7 7

ROOSENDAAL
Noord-Brabant
Zonneland Tufvaartsestr 6 ✆(01656) 429
S of town towards the Belgian border.
Mar-22 Oct
14HEC ● H ⊖ R P P + lau
Prices A3 V3 3 3

ROTTERDAM
Zuid-Holland
Kanaalweg Kanaalweg 84 ✆(010) 159772
Leave motorway by-pass (roads E10/E36) at exit Rotterdam-Centrum, then follow signs.
Apr-Sep
4HEC ◑ H ⊖ G P + lau

ST ANTHONIS
Noord-Brabant
Ullingse Bergen Bosweg 36 ✆(08858) 1700
W of town.
Apr-20 Oct
11HEC ◑ H ⊖ G R P P + lau
Prices pitch16-21 (incl 2 persons)

ST OEDENRODE
Noord-Brabant
Kienehoef Zwembadweg 35 ✆(04138) 72877
NW towards Boxtel.
All year
10.5HEC ◑ H ⊖ G R H P P + lau R
Prices A4 pitch13-14

See advertisement on page 238

SCHAESBERG
Limburg
Bousberg Parklaan 8 ✆(045) 311213
NW towards Kakert.
Apr-Oct
7HEC ◑ H ⊖ G R H P P + lau
Prices pitch21-29 (incl 4 persons)

SCHIN OP GEUL
Limburg
Schoonbron Valkenburgerweg 128 ✆(04459) 1209
SE towards Wijlre.
Mar-Oct
9HEC ◑ H ⊖ G P P + lau

SCHINVELD
Limburg
Brenkberg Bouwbergstr 126 ✆(045) 255096
S towards Brunssum.
All year
2.5HEC ◑ ● H ⊖ G P lau

SEVENUM
Limburg
Schatberg Midden Peelweg 5 ✆(04767) 1756
SW towards Eindhoven.
All year
76HEC ◑ H ⊖ G R H LP + lau
Prices A5 V2 2 2

SLUIS
Zeeland
Meldoorn Hoogstr 68 ✆(01178) 1662
In a meadow surrounded by rows of deciduous trees.
Camping Carnet Compulsory.
N on the road to Zuidzande.
Mar-Oct
5HEC ◯ H G R P + lau S

STRAMPROY
Limburg
't Vosseven Lochstr 26 ✆(04956) 1560
Turn right at the church and continue for 5km.
Apr-Oct
10.6HEC ◑ H P + lau

VALKENBURG
Limburg
Europa Couberg 29 ✆(04406) 13097
Camping Carnet Compulsory.
SW of town.
Apr-Oct
13.5HEC ◑ H G R H P + lau

VENRAY
Limburg
Oude Barrier Maasheseweg 93 ✆(04780) 82305
NE of town.
Apr-Sep
9.8HEC ◑ H G P + lau
Prices A4 pitch4

VIJLEN
Limburg
Cottesserhoeve Cottessen 6 ✆(04455) 1352
All year
5.5HEC ◑ H G R H P lau
Prices A4 V2 4 4

VLISSINGEN (FLUSHING)
Zeeland
Lange Pacht Boksweg 1 ✆(01184) 60447
Apr-Sep
1HEC ◑ H P S

Nolle Woelderenlaan 1 ✆(01184) 14371
The site consists of five sections near two tennis courts.
15 Mar-2 Jan
1.2HEC ◑ H G H P + lau S
Prices A6 V3 7 4-7

VROUWENPOLDER
Zeeland
Oranjezon Koningin Emmaweg 16 ✆(01189) 1549
Well-kept between tall, thick hedges and bushes. SW of the village.
Camping Carnet Compulsory.
For access drive towards Oostkapelle for approx 1.5km, then turn N and continue for 300m.
Apr-Oct
5.3HEC ◑ H G R H P + lau RS
Prices pitch22-38 (incl 2 persons)

Zandput Vroondijk 9 ✆(01189) 2810
On level ground behind sand dunes. Separate area for young people.
2km N.
Apr-Oct
13HEC ◑ H G R H + lau LS

WASSENAAR
Zuid-Holland
Duinrell Duinrell 5 ✆(01751) 19314
Very well maintained site with additional recreation centre which is free for campers. NW in area of same name. Some noise from aircraft. Toilets for invalids. Area restricted to cars. Naturist beach nearby.
Turn off A44 (Den Haag-Leiden) at traffic lights in Wassenaar dorp' and camping signs.
All year
27HEC ● H G R H P + lau S
Prices A10 V4 4 5

See advertisement under AMSTERDAM

WEERT
Limburg
Ijzeren Man Herenvennenweg 60 ✆(04950) 33202
Well-kept with asphalt drives, in a big nature reserve with zoo, heath and forest.
Off E9.
Apr-Oct
10.5HEC ◑ H G R H LP + lau
Prices A5 V4 5 5

WEMELDINGE
Zeeland
Linda Oostkanaalweg 4 ✆(01192) 1259
On meadowland surrounded by rows of tall shrubs.
Turn opposite bridge in town and continue 100m, over bridge to camp.
All year
5HEC ◯ H G R H + lau S
Prices A5 V4 4 4

WESTKAPELLE
Zeeland
Boomgaard Domineeshofweg 1 ✆(01187) 1377
A flat grassy site.
For access turn off the Middleburg road on the S outskirts of the town, then follow signs.
Apr-Oct
8HEC ◑ H G R H + S
Prices A5 V5 5 5

ZEVENHUIZEN
Zuid-Holland
Zevenhuizen Tweemanspolder 8 ✆(01802) 1654
Situated NW of the village, this site is surrounded by a wide belt of bushes.
Camping Carnet Compulsory.
On NW outskirts follow signs for Roerdamp. Site on right of the road beyond a car park.
Apr-Sep
6HEC ◑ H G R H P + lau P
Prices A5 V3 4 4

ZOUTELANDE
Zeeland
Meerpaal Duinweg 133 ✆(01186) 1300
On meadowland hidden behind bushy hedges at the end of a cul-de-sac.
1km SE.
Apr-Oct
1.8HEC ◑ H G R H S + lau
Prices A5 V4 5 4-5

PORTUGAL

A relatively small country lying in the south western corner of the Iberian peninsula, Portugal's only land frontier is the Spanish border in the east. The country is, perhaps, best known for its five hundred miles of coastline. The Algarve in the extreme south is one of the finest stretches of coastline in Europe, with unique caves and a remoteness which has been conserved despite the development of the area. Inland, the cool valleys and pastures of the Tagus contrast sharply with the wooded mountain slopes of the Minho area in the north.

Generally the country enjoys a mild climate with the Algarve being very hot in the summer. The language is Portugese, which was developed from Latin and closely resembles Spanish, although English is often spoken in the Algarve.

Portugal has about 154 campsites most of which are on the coast. There are about 16 *Orbitur* parks in the country which are privately owned and of a high standard, as indeed are the municipal sites. Orbitur sites are open throughout the year and most of them offer fully-equipped bungalows which accommodate four people. A booklet containing details of officially classified sites is produced by the Direccão Geral de Turismo, Palácio Fox, Praça Fox, Praça dos Restauradores, Lisboa ✆(01) 363314. The Oporto office is at Praça D João 125 ✆(02) 27556 and the Coimbra office is at Largo da Portagem. Otherwise ask for Comissão Municipal de Turismo, Junta de Turismo or Câmara Municipal.

International camping carnet is compulsory on campsites belonging to the Federaçaö Portuguesa de Campismo and for camping clubs offering special prices. Elsewhere the camping carnet is recommended, but no reduction in the advertised charge can be expected. See European ABC for further information.

Off-site camping is permitted but not advisable. However, overnight stops in parking and rest areas are not permitted.

HOW TO GET THERE

You can ship your vehicle to Spain, using the Plymouth to Santander car ferry (24hrs), and then travel onwards by road.

Distance
From Santander to Lisboa is about 1,050km (550 miles), normally requiring one or two overnight stops. Using the Channel ports, driving through France and Spain (enter Spain on the Biarritz to San Sebastian road at the western end of the Pyrenees).

Distance
From the Channel ports to Lisboa (Lisbon) is about 2,100km (1,300 miles). This will require 3 or 4 overnight stops

Car sleeper trains
Services are available from Boulogne or Paris to Biarritz, or Paris to Madrid.

Freight trains
Cars may be sent from Paris to Lisboa (50 hours). Passengers travel by **'Sud Express'** Paris–Lisboa.

See Spain for location map

GENERAL INFORMATION

The information given here is specific to Portugal. It **must** be read in conjunction with the European ABC at the front of the book, which covers those regulations which are common to many countries.

British Embassy/Consulates*

The British Embassy together with its consular section is located at 1296 Lisboa Cedex, 35–37 Rua de São Domingos à Lapa ✆9361122. There is a British Consulate in Porto (Oporto) and one with an Honorary Consul in Portimão.

Currency, including banking hours*

The unit of currency is the *escudo (ESc)* divided into 100 *centavos.* It is sometimes written with the dollar sign *eg* 1$50 (one *escudo,* fifty *centavos*). One thousand escudos are known as 1 *conto.* At the time of going to press £1 = *ESc*258.60. Denominations of banks notes are *ESc* 100, 500, 1,000, 5,000; standard coins are *ESc* 1, 2½, 5, 20, 25, 50 and 50 *centavos.* Visitors may import up to *ESc*100,000 in Portugese currency and unlimited amounts of foreign currency, but amounts of foreign currency in excess of *ESc*500,000 must be declared on arrival. However, visitors entering Portugal must be in possession of a minimum amount in Portugese or foreign currency equivalent to *ESc*10,000 plus *ESc*2,000 for each day of their stay. Any amount of foreign currency may be exported provided it was declared on entry, but no more than *ESc*100,000 in Portugese currency may be exported.

Banks are open Monday to Friday from 08.30–15.00hrs. During the summer, currency exchange facilities are usually provided throughout the day in main tourist resorts, at frontier posts, airports and in some hotels.

Emergency telephone numbers

Fire, police and **ambulance** – Public emergency service ✆115

Foodstuffs*

Visitors from EC countries may import into Portugal duty-free 1,000g of coffee or 400g of coffee extract and 200g of tea or 80g of tea extract bought duty and tax-paid; a reduced allowance applies if bought duty-free.

Shopping hours

Shops are usually open Monday to Friday 09.00–13.00hrs and 15.00–19.00hrs, and Saturdays 09.00–13.00hrs.

Tourist information*

The Portugese National Tourist Office, New Bond Street House, 1/5 New Bond Street (above National Westminster Bank, entrance in Burlington Gardens opposite Burlington Arcade), London W1Y 0NP ✆071 493 3873, will be pleased to assist you with information regarding tourism. There is an office of the *Direccão Geral de Turismo* in Lisboa, and local information offices will be found in most provincial towns under this name or one of the following: *Comissào Municipal de Turismo, Junta de Turismo* or *Càmara Municipal.*

MOTORING

Children in cars

Children under 12 are not permitted to travel in front seats unless that seat is fitted with a child restraint system.

Dimensions and weight restrictions

Private **cars** and towed **trailers** or **caravans** are restricted to the following dimensions – height, 4 metres; width, 2.50 metres; length, 12 metres. The

***Additional information will be found in the European ABC at the front of the book.**

maximum permitted overall length of vehicle/trailer or caravan combination is 18 metres.

There are no weight restrictions governing the temporary importation of trailers into Portugal. However, it is recommended that the following be adhered to – weight (unladen), up to 750kg if the towing vehicle's engine is 2,500cc or less; up to 1,500kg if the towing vehicle's engine is between 2,500cc and 3,500cc; up to 2,500kg if the towing vehicle's engine is more than 3,500cc.

Driving licence*

A valid UK or Republic of Ireland licence is acceptable in Portugal. The minimum age at which a visitor may use a temporarily imported motorcycle (over 50cc) or car is 17 years†. See also page **44** and *Speed limits* below.
†Visiting UK or Republic of Ireland driving licence holders under 18 may encounter local difficulties in some areas as the official minimum age to hold a driving licence in Portugal is 18 years.

Motoring club*

The **Autómovel Club de Portugal** (ACP) which has its headquarters at Lisboa 1200, rua Rosa Araújo 24 ✆563931 has offices in a number of provincial towns. ACP offices are normally open 09.00–16.45hrs Monday to Friday; English and French are spoken. Offices are closed on Saturday and Sunday.

Roads

Main roads and most of the important secondary roads are good, as are the mountain roads to the north-east.

Speed limits*

Car

Built-up areas	60kph (37mph)
Other roads	90kph (56mph)
Motorways	min† 40kph (24mph)
	max 120kph (74mph)

Car/caravan/trailer

Built-up areas	50kph (31mph)
Other roads	70kph (43mph)
Motorways	min† 40kph (24mph)
	max 90kph (56mph)

†Minimum speeds on motorways apply, except where otherwise signposted.

Visiting motorists to Portugal who have held a full driving licence for less than one year are restricted to driving at a top speed of 90kph (56mph). They must also display a yellow disc bearing the figure '90' at the rear of their vehicle (obtainable from any vehicle accessory shop in Portugal). Leaflets giving details in English are handed to visitors at entry point.

Warning triangle

The use of a warning triangle is compulsory in the event of accident or breakdown. The triangle must be placed on the road 30 metres (33yds) behind the vehicle and must be clearly visible from 100 metres (110yds). See also *Warning triangle/Hazard warning lights* in the European ABC.

***Additional information will be found in the European ABC at the front of the book.**

Prices are in Portuguese Escudos
Abbreviation: r rua

SOUTH

Bordered by the Atlantic coast on two sides, by mountains in the north and by Spain in the east, the Algarve enjoys one of the most settled climates in the world. Though poorer than the rest of Portugal in art and architecture, the region is rich in subtropical vegetation; almond and orange groves, cotton plantations, and fields of rice and sugar cane. Beyond the mountains in the north, the land is predominantly agricultural, with low rolling hills stretching beyond the horizon. Cork oaks are grown to provide much-needed shade, making an important contribution to the region's economy. Water is also a major source of income in the south; inland, the salt-pans of the Sado river maintain the pretty towns of narrow twisting lanes and whitewashed houses. On the coast, towns such as Faro, Lagos, and Cape St. Vincent, glory in a history of trade, shipbuilding, sea battles and exploration.

ALBUFEIRA
Algarve
Albufeira ✆(089) 53851 & 53848
Signposted from N125
All year
15HEC H G R H P + lau S

ALCANTARILHA
Algarve
Turismovel – Parque Campismo de Canelas ✆(082) 312612
All year
6.5HEC H G R H P + lau S
Prices A140-280 V115-230 150-300 140-280

BEJA
Baixo Alentejo
CM de Beja av Vasco da Giadia ✆(084) 24328
All year
1.7HEC S H lau G R P +
Prices A100-200 V60-120 100-320 60-240

PRAIA DA LUZ
Algarve
At **VALVERDE**
Parque de Turismo Valverde ✆(082) 789211
Well-equipped site with children's playground and tennis courts.
Off N125 Lagos-Cape St Vincent road. 4km from Lagos.
All year
12HEC H G R H P + lau S

PRAIA DE SALEMA
See **VILA DO BISPO**

QUARTEIRA
Algarve
Orbitur Barros da Fonte Santa ✆(089) 315238
A terraced site at the top of a hill.
Off M125 in Almoncil and follow signs to Quarteira. About 500m before reaching the sea turn left into the camp.
All year
11HEC H G R + PS

SAGRES
Algarve
Parque de Campismo de Sagres Cerro das Moitac ✆(082) 64351
Closed Dec-1 Jan
6HEC S H G S + R
Prices A250 V200 300 250

SINES
Baixo Alentejo
CM ✆(069) 634011
In a pine wood on the Cabo de Sines peninsula, to the N of the town.
Camping Carnet Compulsory.
Follow signs from the rua de Marinquez Pompal and past the water tower.
Closed 16 Dec-14 Jan
3.3HEC H G R + lau S

S Torpes ✆(069) 632105
Jun-Sep
7HEC S H G H P lau RS
Prices A250 V200 350 300

VALVERDE
See **PRAIA DA LUZ**

VILA DO BISPO
Algarve
At **PRAIA DE SALEMA**(7.5km SE)
Quinta dos Caricos ✆(082) 65201
All year
10HEC S H G H + lau S
Prices A40-420 V400-420 570-600 400-420

VILA NOVA DE MILFONTES
Baixo Alentejo
Parque de Campismo de Milfontes ✆(083) 96140
All year
6HEC S H G R RS +
Prices A275 V200 290 240

NORTH

Northern Portugal offers medieval castles perched on mountain crags, grey stone villages, and purple vineyards whose grapes produce the popular Vinho Verde, Mateus Rosé and Portugal's most famous product – port wine. There are magnificent forests, spectacular lakes, long sandy beaches sheltered by pinewoods, and villages hidden by the springtime blossom of almond and chestnut trees.

A region of ancient human settlement, even the smallest towns are rich in architectural treasures, from palaces of the Renaissance period to prehistoric rock engravings. The region also boasts a wealth of traditional crafts of a variety and colour to match the splendid local costumes worn for the many religious festivals and "romaries" celebrated with enormous enthusiasm and energy throughout the year.

The capital of the region, Oporto, is Portugal's second largest city and also its most untypical – a lively port, a university town and a hub of industry and commerce in one.

ANGEIRAS
See **MATOSINHOS**

CAMINHA
Minho
Orbitur Mata do Camarido ✆(058) 921295
On undulating sandy ground with trees.
Turn off N13 at Km89.7 and drive W, along the Rio Minho for about 800m, then turn left.
All year
3HEC S ● H ⊖ G R + ☞ RS

MATOSINHOS
Douro Litoral
At **ANGEIRAS**(12km N)

Angeiras ✆(02) 9270571
A modern, well-kept site in a pine wood on a hill overlooking the sea.
W of the N13 at the X-roads at Km12.1, E of Vila do Pinheiro and towards the sea for 5km.
All year
7.7HEC ● H ✕ ⊖ G R + lau ☞ S
Prices A81-216 V62-148 96-525 47-525

VILA FLOR
Tras-Os-Montes Alto Douro
CM ✆(078) 52350
Woodland area next to the municipal swimming pool and a small lake.
20km S of Mirandela.
All year
5HEC ● H ✕ ⊖ G R P + lau

VILA REAL
Tras-Os-Montes Alto Douro
Parque Campismo ✆(059) 24724
In the E part of town off N2 by GALP petrol station. Site in 300m near new school.
2 Feb-12 Dec
3HEC ◑ H ✕ ⊖ G R PR + lau ☞

CENTRAL

This is a vast and wonderful region of infinite variety; to the west, the popular Costa da Prata; the beautiful park-like landscape in the south; the dramatic mountains in the north and east; and the cattle-herding country in the centre, where the fighting bulls graze along the River Tejo, watched by mounted cattle herders in colourful local costume.

The highest town in Portugal is Guarda, the ideal base from which to explore the magnificent Serra da Estrala. Further west is the romantic town of Coimbra, whose university is amongst the oldest in the world and until 1911, was the only one in the country.

Portugal's capital, Lisbon, has the attraction of combining the charm of the past with the excitement of a progressive capital city. It is also the heart of the production of the famous Azulejos – the glazed ornamental tiles which are Portugal's favourite form of architectural decoration.

ALCOBAÇA
Estremadura
CM ✆(062) 42265
Terraced hill site with tall eucalyptus trees overlooking the town. Divided into pitches and partly bordered by hedges and flower beds.
Turn off by-pass (N8) in NE outskirts at large roundabout and turn towards hills at covered market.
All year
11HEC S ◑ H ⊖ + lau ☞ ✕ S
Prices A190 V115 205-255 105-256

ALMORNOS
Estremadura
CM de Almornos CCL ✆9273960
Camping Carnet Compulsory.
All year
6HEC ○ H ✕ ⊖ G P P + lau

ARGANIL
Beira Litoral
CM de Arganil ✆(035) 22706
All year
3HEC ● H ✕ ⊖ G R + lau

CALDAS DA RAINHA
Estremadura
Orbitur Parque D Leonor ✆(062) 832367
Long narrow site on wooded hill.
300m from N8 on S outskirts.
16 Jan-15 Nov
4HEC ● H ✕ ⊖ G + lau ☞ L

COIMBRA
Beira Litoral
CM de Coimbra Praça 25 de Abril ✆(039) 712997
Camping Carnet Compulsory.
All year
1.1HEC ● H ✕ ⊖ G + lau ☞ R PR
Prices A150 V170 140-200 90-200

COSTA DE CAPARICA
Estremadura
Obitur ✆(01) 2900661
1km N turn right at Km9.9.
All year
7.2HEC S ◑ H ✕ ⊖ G R + ☞ PS

ÉVORA
Alto Alentejo
Orbitur ✆(066) 25190
2km S right of road near Km94.5.
All year
4HEC ● H ⊖ G R P
\+ lau

FIGUEIRA DA FOZ
Beira Litoral
Orbitur Gala ✆(033) 31492
In an enclosed area within a municipal park on top of Guarda Hill.
At Km177, on the NW outskirts of the town, turn left off the N16 Porto road and drive uphill for about 500m.
16 Jan-15 Nov
6HEC ● H ⊖ G R
\+ ☞ PS

GUINCHO
Estremadura
Orbitur Crismina ✆(01) 2851014
On hilly ground amidst a pine wood in the Parque du Guincho, near the Boca do Inferno.
4km W of Cascais at Km98, turn right and follow road no 247-6 for 1km.
All year
7HEC ● H ⊖ G R
\+ ☞ PS

LISBOA (LISBON)
Estremadura
CM Monsanto Estrada da Circunvalação ✆(01) 704413
Park like site on flat hill. Metalled interior roads and pitches.
Turn off motorway at KmV2/111 towards Estoril and follow signs.
All year
38HEC ● H ⊖ G
P P + lau
Prices A82-242 V63-161 82-242 82-242

NAZARÉ
Estremadura
Orbitur Valado ✆(062) 51137
300m E of village, S of road 8-4 Nazaré-Alcobaca.
16 Jan-15 Nov
7HEC ◑ H ⊖ G R
\+ ☞ PS

Vale Paraiso ✆(062) 51546
All year
7.8HEC S ● H ⊖
G P P + lau ☞ S
Prices A425 V350 450-540 390-440

PALHEIROS DE MIRA
Beira Litoral
Orbitur ✆(031) 47234
Site lies in a dense forest.
N off the N334 at KM2, towards Videira, opposite a road fork.
16 Jan-15 Nov
4HEC ◑ H ⊖ G R
\+ ☞ PRS

PENICHE
Estremadura
CM ✆(062) 72025
On a sandy hillock, partly wooded 0.5km from sea.
2km E.
All year
12.6HEC S ◑ H ⊖ G
R P + lau ☞ S
Prices A110 V110 230 180

SALVATERRA DE MAGOS
Ribatejo
Parque de Campismo de Escaropim Mota Florestal Escaroupim ✆(063) 55484
Closed Dec-2 Jan
4HEC S ● H ⊖ G
P P + lau

SAN MARTINHO DO PORTO
Estremadura
Colina do Sol ✆(062) 989763
Closed 16 Dec-14 Jan
8.5HEC ○ H ⊖ G
P + lau ☞ R S
Prices A300 V250

SÃO JACINTO
Beira Litoral
Orbitur ✆(034) 48284
In a dense pine wood seawards from the uneven, paved road from Ovar which runs alongside the lagoon.
1.5km away from the sea.
N
16 Jan-15 Nov
3HEC ● H ⊖ G R
\+ lau ☞ L

SÃO PEDRO DE MUEL
Estremadura
Orbitur ✆(044) 59168
On a hill amidst pine trees.
Off road No 242-2 from Marinha Grande at the roundabout near the SHELL petrol station on the E outskirts of the village and drive N for 100m.
All year
7HEC ● H ⊖ G R
\+ ☞ PS

SETÚBAL
Estremadura
Toca do Pai Lopes ✆(065) 22475
Divided into pitches, on level land between steep hills and the mouth of the Rio Sado.
Camping Carnet compulsory.
Turn SW off N10 in town centre, on outskirts turn left and continue for 200m.
All year
2.5HEC S ● H ⊖ G R
R P + lau ☞

VAGOS
Beira Litoral
Orbitur Vagueira ✆(034) 791618
All year
14HEC ● H ⊖ +
☞ G R PS

ZAMBUJEIRA
Alto Alentejo
Zambujeira ✆(083) 95193
All year
3HEC S ● ⊖ G R
P + ☞ P
\-

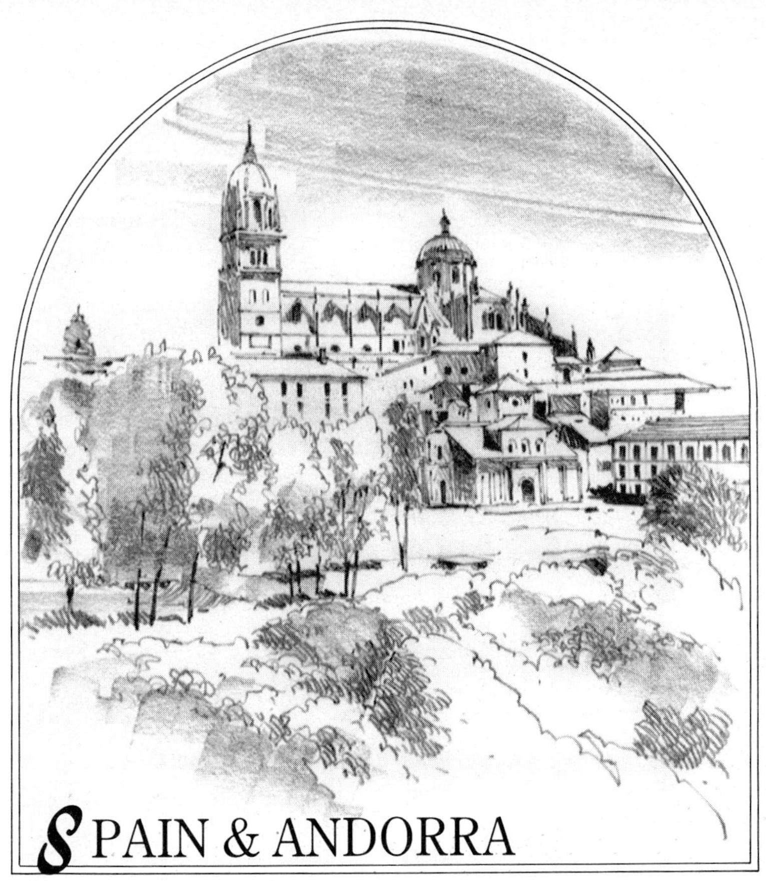

SPAIN & ANDORRA

Rich in history and natural beauty, Spain is bordered by two countries, France in the north and Portugal in the west. Central Spain is mountainous and barren while the coastline is mostly extremely rocky. Some of the most popular holiday areas in Europe are in Spain, the best known being the Costa Brava, the Costa Blanca, the Costa Dorada and the Costa del Sol. All these regions offer fine, sandy and safe beaches. Spain has a varied climate; temperate in the north, dry and hot in the south and in the Balearic Islands. The language is Spanish and has developed from the Castilian dialect. Certain words are of Arabic origin and there are many local dialects spoken throughout the provinces.

Sites are numerous on the Costa Brava and elsewhere along the coast, but there are not many inland. they are officially classified according to the facilities and services provided and their classification should be displayed at the site entrance and on any literature. If you intend visiting sites at popular resorts along the coast between late spring and mid-October, it is best to book in advance. Late spring is recommended, as the intense heat of mid-summer is avoided and sites and roads are less congested. Opening dates vary considerably and some sites are open all year. Information about campsites and a detailed guide book are available from the Spanish National Tourist Office (see *Tourist Information*) and local tourist information offices.

Hire of equipment is not generally possible, but some campsites have bungalow accommodation.

International camping carnet is not compulsory but recommended. Generally campsites will allow a reduction in the advertised charge to the holders of a camping carnet. See European ABC for further information.

Off-site camping is permitted, except in mountain areas, provided there are no more than three tents or caravans and ten campers at any one place and they do not remain for more than three days. However, permission must be obtained before camping on private property. Camps may not be set up within a radius of 150 metres of a main road, or within 100 metres of a national monument. Camp fires within 200 metres of a main road are forbidden. Free camping near to beaches, rivers, towns or established campsites is forbidden.

HOW TO GET THERE

You can ship your vehicle direct to Spain on the Plymouth to Santander car ferry (taking about 24 hours). Using the Channel ports, approach Spain through France; pass either end of the Pyrénéan mountains: ***For central and southern Spain*** take the Biarritz to San Sebastián–Donostia road at the western end; ***For the Costa Brava and beyond*** take the Perpignon to Barcelona road, or motorway, at the eastern end of the mountains. ***For Andorra*** from France via the Pas de la Casa (6851ft) then over the Envalira Pass (7897ft). Between November and April the roads may sometimes be closed. From Spain, the approach via La Seu d'Urgell is always open. Weather information on the Envalira Pass is available on ✆21166 or 21055. Wheel chains must be used on the Pass whenever conditions require them.

Distance

From Calais to Madrid is about 1,900km (990 miles), usually requiring two or three overnight stops.

Car sleeper trains

Boulogne, Calais or Paris to Narbonne; Boulogne or Paris to Biarritz; Paris to Madrid.

GENERAL INFORMATION

The information given here is specific to Spain and/or Andorra. It **must** be read in conjunction with the European ABC at the front of the book, which covers those regulations which are common to many countries.

British Embassy/Consulates*

The British Embassy is located at Madrid 4, Calle de Fernando el Santo 16 ✆(91) 4190200 (12 lines), but the Embassy has no consular section. However, there is a Consulate-General in Madrid at Centro Colón, Marqués de la Ensenada 16–20 ✆(91) 3085201. There are British Consulates in Alicante, Barcelona, Bilbao, Malaga, Seville and Palma (Majorca); there are British Consulates with Honorary Consuls in Santander, Tarragona and Vigo. There is a British Vice-Consulate in Algeciras and Ibiza and a British Vice-Consulate with Honorary Consul in Menorca.

Currency, including banking hours*

The unit of currency is the *Spanish peseta (Ptas)* divided into 100 *centimos*. At the time of going to press £1 = *Ptas*181.45. Denominations of bank notes are *Ptas* 500, 1,000, 2,000, 5,000 and 10,000; standard coins are *Ptas* 1, 5, 25, 50, 100, 200 and 500. Visitors may import unlimited amounts of Spanish and foreign currency, but amounts over *Ptas*100,000 of Spanish currency and *Ptas*500,000 equivalent of a foreign currency must be declared on arrival. No more than *Ptas*100,000 in Spanish currency and *Ptas*500,000 in foreign currency may be exported.

Banks In the summer, banks are usually open 08.30–13.30hrs Monday to Friday, and 08.30–12.30hrs on Saturday. There are also exchange offices at travel agents which are open 09.00–13.00hrs and 16.00–19.00hrs from Monday to Friday, and 09.00–13.00hrs on Saturday.

Customs regulations

A television set, radio, pocket calculator, tape recorder, video camera or video recorder may be temporarily imported, but only against a deposit of duty and a permit valid for three months issued by the Spanish Customs. See also *Customs regulations for European countries* in the European ABC for further information.

Emergency telephone numbers

Fire, police, ambulance. In all places ✆091 for **police**, and ✆080 for **fire** service in Madrid and Barcelona; in other towns call the operator.

Foodstuffs*

Visitors from EC countries may import duty-free 1,000g of coffee or 400g coffee extract and 200g of tea or 80g of tea extract bought duty and tax-paid; a reduced allowance applies if bought duty-free.

Shopping hours

Generally, shops are open Monday to Saturday from 09.00–14.00hrs and 15.00–20.00hrs, with a two-hour break for lunch; department stores may open at 10.00hrs and close at 20.00hrs.

Tourist information*

The Spanish National Tourist Office, Metro House,

***Additional information will be found in the European ABC at the front of the book.**

57–58 St James's Street, London SW1A 1LD ✆071 499 0901, will be pleased to assist you with information regarding tourism. There are branch offices in most of the leading Spanish cities, towns and resorts. Local offices are normally closed at lunchtime.

MOTORING

Accidents – Bail Bond

An accident in Spain can have very serious consequences, including the impounding of the car, and property, and the detention of the driver, pending bail. A Bail Bond can often facilitate release of person and property, and you are advised to obtain one of these from your insurer, for a nominal premium, together with your *Green Card*.

A Bail Bond is a written guarantee that a cash deposit of usually up to £1,500 will be paid to the Spanish Court as surety for bail, and as security for any fine which may be imposed, although in such an event you will have to reimburse any amount paid on your behalf.

In very serious cases, the Court will not allow bail, and it has been known for a minor Spanish Court to refuse to accept Bail Bonds, and to insist on cash being paid by the driver. Nevertheless, motorists are strongly advised to obtain a Bail Bond and to ensure that documentary evidence of this (in Spanish) is attached to the Green Card.

Children in cars

It is recommended that children do not travel in the front seats.

Dimensions and weight restrictions

Private **cars** and towed **trailers** or **caravans** are restricted to the following dimensions – height, 4 metres; width, 2.50 metres; length, 12 metres. The maximum permitted overall length of vehicle/trailer or caravan combination is 18 metres.

Trailers with an unladen weight exceeding 750kg must have an independent braking system.

Driving licence

The minimum age at which a visitor may use a temporarily imported motorcycle (over 75cc) or car is 18 years. An *International Driving Permit (IDP)* is compulsory for the holder of a red three-year Republic of Ireland† or green UK† driving licence, unless the licence is accompanied by an official Spanish translation stamped by a Spanish Consulate. The IDP is not compulsory for the holder of a pink EC type UK (all pink or part pink) or Republic of Ireland driving licence but, as local difficulties may arise over its acceptance, an IDP is recommended. See under *Driving licence and International Driving Permit* in the European ABC for further information.

†The respective licensing authorities cannot exchange a licence purely to facilitate continental travel.

Motoring club*

The **Real Autómovil Club de España** (RACE), which has its headquarters at 28003 Madrid, Calle José Abascal 10 ✆(01) 4473200, is associated with local clubs in a number of provincial towns. Motoring club offices are normally open from 09.00–14.00hrs Monday to Friday and are closed on Sundays and Public holidays. Some, including Madrid, are closed on Saturdays.

Roads, including holiday traffic

The surfaces of the main roads vary, but on the whole are good. The roads are winding in many places, and at times it is not advisable to exceed 30–35mph. Secondary roads are often rough, winding, and encumbered by slow, horse-drawn traffic. Holiday traffic, particularly on the coast road to Barcelona and Tarragona and in the San Sebastián–Donostia area, causes congestion which may be severe at weekends.

In the Basque area, local versions of some placenames appear on signposts together with the national version used in current AA guides and maps. Some local names differ considerably from the national spelling – *eg* San Sabastián = Donostia. In the Catalonia area, some local spellings are used exclusively on signposts but most of these are recognisable against the national version – *eg* Gerona = Girona, Lérida = Lleida.

Speed limits*

Car

Built-up areas	60kph (37mph)
Other roads	†90kph (56mph) or ‡100kph (62mph)
Motorways	120kph (74mph)

Car/caravan/trailer

Built-up areas	60kph (37mph)
Other roads	†70kph (43mph) or ‡80kph (49mph)
Motorways	80kph (49mph)

†On ordinary roads
‡On roads with more than one lane in each direction, a special lane for slow-moving vehicles or wide lanes.

***Additional information will be found in the European ABC at the front of the book.**

Warning triangles

In the event of accident or breakdown, the use of two warning triangles is compulsory for vehicles weighing more than 3,500kg (3 tons, 8cwt, 100lbs) and passenger vehicles with more than nine seats (including the driver's). The triangles must be placed on the road in front of and behind the vehicle at a distance of 30 metres (33yds) and be visible from at least 100 metres (110yds). It is recommended that all other vehicles carry a warning triangle for use in an emergency. See also *Warning triangle/Hazard warning lights* in the European ABC.

ANDORRA

Andorra is an independent Principality covering 190 sq miles, with a population of 32,700. It is situated high in the Pyrénées, between France and Spain, and jointly administered by the two co-princes (the President of France, the Bishop of La Seu d'Urgeil) and the Andorrans. French and Spanish are both spoken, and the currency of either country is accepted. General regulations for France and Spain apply to Andorra with the following exceptions.

Accidents

There are no firm rules of procedure after an accident; however in most cases the recommendations under *Accidents* in the European ABC are advisable.

British Consulate*

Andorra comes within the consular district of the British Consul-General at Barcelona.

Emergency telephone numbers

Fire and **ambulance** ✆18 **police** ✆17.

Motoring club*

The **Automobil Club d'Andorra** has its head office at Andorra la Vella, Carrer Babot Camp 4 ✆(078) 20890.

Roads

Andorra can be approached from France via the Pas de la Casa (6,851ft), then from the frontier over the Envalira Pass (7,897ft). Roads may occasionally be closed for short periods between November and April. The approach from Spain via La Seu d'Urgell is always open. The three main roads radiating from the town are prefixed 'N' and numbered; side roads are prefixed 'V'.

Speed limits*

Car, car/caravan combinations

Built-up areas	40kph (25mph)
Other roads	70kph (43mph)

Some villages have a speed limit of 20kph (12mph). The maximum height for vehicles where tunnels are involved is 3.5m.

Warning triangle

The use of a warning triangle is compulsory in the event of accident or breakdown. See also *Warning triangle/Hazard warning lights* in the European ABC.

Weather information*

The condition of the Envalira pass is available on ✆21166 or 21055.

***Additional information will be found in the European ABC at the front of the book.**

Prices are in Spanish Pesetas
Abbreviations:
ctra carretera
Gl Generalissimo
Each name preceded by 'El' 'La' or 'Las' is listed under the name that follows it.

NORTH EAST COAST

The brava, or 'wild' coast, and resorts such as Tossa and Lloret de Mar, have long been a favourite with sun-seekers. Low season can be a perfect time to visit the beautiful coastline, and art lovers are drawn year-long to Figueres' Salvador Dali Museum and historic Girona's impressive cathedral, interesting monuments and medieval Jewish quarter.

On the Mediterranean to the south lies Barcelona, capital of Catalonia. Catalonians are proud of their heritage and language. Host of the 1992 Olympics, this bustling, vital seaport has many faces: literary capital of Spain, shopper's paradise and beach town. Walk along its famous boulevards, the Ramblas, or visit Gaudi's monumental Church of the Holy Family – symbol of the city and its region. The site of the Olympic stadium at Montjuic also boasts several museums and shares spectacular views with its neighbouring hilltop, Tibidabo. The fiesta in September is a colourful carnival famed for its enormous papier-maché figures, its street celebrations and bullfights, and the local sardana dancing.

ARENYS DE MAR
Barcelona
Carlitos ctra NII (93) 7921355
All year
5.5HEC H G lau S

BAGUR
See **BEGUR**

BANYOLES
Girona
El Lago de Banyoles (972) 570305
2km NW, 800m W of lake.
All year
0.2HEC H G H P + lau LR
Prices A334-387 V334-387 334-387 334-387

BEGUR
Girona
Bagur (972) 623201
A terraced site in a dip.
1.4km SE of town and right of the road to Palafrugell, 400m after the turn towards Fornells and Aiguablava.
May-3 Sep
4HEC H G P + lau S
Prices A460 V460 460 415-460

Maset Playa de sa Riera (972) 623023
A well-kept terraced site, divided into pitches in a beautiful valley.
3km N of Begur. If entering from the W, turn left just before reaching the town.
25 May-27 Sep
1.2HEC H G P + lau S
Prices A375-465 V375-465 465-565 375-465

BERGA
Barcelona
Berga ctra C1411 (93) 8211250
All year
5.5HEC H G R P + lau
Prices A300 pitch1100

BLANES
Girona
Bella Terra (972) 331955
May-Sep
10HEC H G PS + lau

Blanes (972) 331591
In a pine forest bordering the beach beyond Camping El Roca.
On left of the Paseo Villa de Madrid coast road towards town.
May-Sep
2HEC H G R S + lau
Prices A205-410 pitch610-1220

Masia (972) 331013
50m inland from Paseo Villa de Madrid coast road.
Apr-Sep
6HEC H G P + lau S
Prices A300-410 pitch1000-1220

Pinar (972) 331083
Divided into two by the coastal road. Partially meadow under poplars.
1km on Paseo Villa de Madrid coast road.
May-Sep
73HEC H G S + lau
Prices A334-445 pitch1113-1335

Sabanell (972) 331809
Within a pine wood, a section of which is inland and open to the public.
On either side of the Paseo Villa de Madrid road. Off coast road S of Blanes.
Apr-30 Oct
3.5HEC H G R S + lau

Vora Mar av de Madrid (972) 330349
Level site with pine trees on sandy beach.
1.5km from Blanes on seaward side of the Paseo Villa de Madrid coast road.
May-Sep
2.4HEC H G + lau LS

CABRERA DE MAR
Barcelona
Costa de Oro (93) 7591234
The beach is reached via a railway underpass.
Lies at Km650 of the N11, on the seaward side, between the road and the railway embankment.
15 May-15 Sep
1.5HEC H G H S + lau
Prices A410 V410 425 410

CALELLA DE LA COSTA
Barcelona
Botanic Bona Vista (93) 7692488
Totally subdivided and well tended terraced site on a hillside, beautifully landscaped. Internal roads steep. Access to beach via pedestrian underpass.
Camping Carnet Compulsory.
Turn off the N11 at Km672 beyond road bridge.
All year
3HEC H G + lau S
Prices A375 V375 375 375

Faro (93) 7690967
Terraced site on a hillock under deciduous trees with lovely view of Calella and out to sea. Steep internal roads.
For access, travel S before reaching a major left hand bend at Km673.7 to the right of the N11.
May-Sep
2.5HEC H G + lau S

CALELLA DE PALAFRUGELL
Girona
Siesta (972) 304807
Partly terraced, on hillside with some trees.
From Palafrugell site lies just before ➔

Calella, approx 200m to right of the wide asphalt road.
May-Sep
2.8HEC S ● H G
P lau S

See advertisement in colour section

CALONGE
See **PALAMÓS**

CASTELL D'ARO
Girona
Castell d'Aro (972) 819699
May-Sep
6HEC S ● H G
H P P + lau R RS
Prices A360-403 V360-403 360-403 360-403

CASTELLÓ D'EMPURIES
Girona
Castell-Mar Platja de la Rubina (972) 450822
May-22 Sep
4HEC ○ ◑ H G
H PS P + lau
Prices A185-460 V185-460 185-460 185-460

Laguna (972) 208667
Flat grassland site by the sea.
Turn right at Km11 Figueres-Roses road in direction of Sant Pere Pescador and continue, last 4km poorly surfaced lane.
20 Mar-15 Oct
12.5HEC ◑ H G
H S P + lau R
Prices A434-540 V434-540 434-540 434-540

Mas-Nou (972) 250575
Etr-1 Oct
6HEC ● H G
H P P + lau
Prices A371-445 V371-445 371-445 371-445

Nautic Almanta (972) 250447
Level meadowland, no shade, good facilities, reaching as far as the sea. Alongside the Rio Fluvia which has been made into a canal. Boating is possible in the canal which flows into the sea.
Turn S at Km11 on C260, approx, halfway along the road and turn E along the track and continue 2.2km.
15 May-Sep
14HEC ◑ H G
R PRS P + lau

See advertisement in colour section

CUBELLES
Barcelona
Rueda (343) 8950207
Level terrain between road and railway. Access to beach by means of an underpass.
The site lies about 1km N of Cunit near Km52.1 of the C146.
Jun-Sep
6HEC ◑ H G
P P + lau S
Prices A280-460 pitch840-1380

ESCALA, L'
Girona
Escala (972) 770084
Level site, partially under pines.
Within village on the left of the road towards Riells.
Etr-Sep
1.8HEC ● H
G P S
Prices A225 pitch1100-1650

Maite Playa Riells (972) 770084
An extensive site, lying inland, but near the sea, at a small lake. Partly on a hillock under pine trees.
The access is well signed from the outskirts of L'Escala on the road towards Cala Montgo.
Jun-15 Sep
6HEC ● H G
L + lau

ESTARTIT, L'
Girona
Castell Montgri (972) 758630
On a large terraced meadow in pine woodlands.
100m N of GE road from Torroella de Montgri and about 0.5km before L'Estartit on a hillock.

May-Oct
25HEC ● H ⊖ G H P + lau S
Prices A130-325 pitch900-2250
See advertisement in colour section

Estartit ✆(972) 758909
In a valley on sloping ground which is rather steep in places. Some terraces, shaded by pine trees.
It is located about 200m from the church and the road from Torroella de Montgri.
Apr-Sep
1.5HEC ● H ⊖ G + lau RS
Prices A400 V400 400 A350-400

Medes ✆(972) 758405
Turn right off GE641 from Torroella di Montgri by Km5 and continue for 1.5km.
Apr-Sep
2.6HEC ● H ⊖ G + lau PS
Prices A403 V870

Molino ✆(72) 758629
Divided into several sections of open meadowland near the beach on grassland with young poplars. The reconstructed mill is a landmark.
Approaching from Torroella de Montgri turn right on entering L'Estartit and follow signs.
May-Sep
10HEC ◑ H ⊖ G S + lau
Prices A350 V350 350 A350

GAVÁ
Barcelona
Albatros ✆(93) 6622031
In a shady pine wood divided into pitches on partly level, partly uneven terrain by the sea.
For access, turn off the C246, dual carriageway at Km15 and drive towards the sea.
27 Mar-27 Sep
15HEC S ● H ⊖ G R PS +

Tortuga Ligera ✆(93) 6621229
All year
9HEC S ● H ⊖ G R PS + lau

LLAFRANC
See **PALAFRUGELL**

LLORET DE MAR
Girona
Santa Elena Ciudad ✆(972) 364009
Brick terraces on a hill with some poplars and pines.
500m from the sea. For access turn right off the GE682 to Blanes about 1.3km S of town, between Km10 and 11 and continue for 200m.
Apr-Sep
8HEC S ● H ⊖ G P + lau S

MALGRAT DE MAR
Barcelona
Naciones ✆(93) 7611153
Level site divided by a small stream. Partially dusty, another part in meadow under high poplars.
Approach road passes through Camping Malgrat de Mar.
Apr-Sep
9.6HEC ◑ ● H ⊖ G S + lau R
Prices A329-371 329-371 A329-371

MASNOU, EL
Barcelona
Masnou Camillo Fabra 33-35 ✆(93) 5551503
Inland from the N11 at Km639.8.
All year
2HEC ● H ⊖ G R H PS + lau

MONTGAT
Barcelona
Don Quijote ✆(93) 3891016
On a hill, inland from the main road, on the N outskirts of Montgat. Very few trees, but many sunshade roofs.
Access to the sea leads over N11, then through a railway underpass. On N11 at Km638.8.
Jun-Sep
2.5HEC ◑ H ⊖ G PS lau
Prices A350 V350 350 A350

MONTRÁS
See **PALAFRUGELL**

PALAFRUGELL
Girona
At **LLAFRANC**
Kim's ✆(972) 301156
Terraced site with winding drives, lying on the wooded slopes of a narrow valley leading to the sea.
For access, turn right off the Palafrugell-Tamariu road, follow a wide tarred road for 1km, past the El Paranso Hotel and head towards Llafranc. 0.4km from sea.
May-Sep
5.5HEC ◑ H ⊖ G H P + lau S
Prices A375-450 V375-450 400-525 A400-500

At **MONTRÁS**(3km SW)
Relax-Ge ✆(972) 301549
Level meadow under poplars and olive trees.
Turn off the C255 at Km38.7. 4km to

the sea.
10 Jun-Aug
2HEC ● H ⊖ P
P
Prices A345 pitch850

Relax-Nat ✆(0472) 300818
Etr-Sep
5HEC ● H ⊖ P + lau
Prices A415 pitch300-1065

At **PLAYA DE ENSUEÑOS**
Tamariu ✆(972) 300422
Terraced site with mixture of high young pines.
Turn towards site at beach parking area and continue 300m.
May-Sep
2HEC ● H ⊖ G R PS + lau
Prices A350-435 V350-430 390-480 A350-435

PALAMÓS
Girona
Benelux Playa Castell ✆(972) 315575
On hilly ground, stretching over an area planted with pine trees and a field planted with poplars.
Camping Carnet Compulsory.
If approaching from Girona take the C255 and turn east near Km40.5. Take rather narrow asphalted road and follow it for a further 1.3km.
Apr-Sep
4.6HEC ● H ⊖ G P + lau S
Prices A425-455 V425-455 595-640 A540-580

Coma Cami Vell de la Fosca 2 ✆(972) 314638
Sloping terraced terrain with young deciduous trees and isolated pines. 0.8km from the sea.
In N outskirts turn seawards off the C255 near the RENAULT garage.
All year
5.2HEC ● H ⊖ G PS + lau

Internacional Palamos Apartado 100 ✆(972) 314736
Signposted.
Apr-15 Oct
5.5HEC ● H ⊖ H P + lau G S
Prices A325 pitch1050-1475

International Kings La Fosca ✆(972) 317511
15 Apr-4 Oct
18HEC ● H ⊖ G H P lau S
Prices A470-520 V475-525 575-640 A440-640

Palamós Cala Margarida ✆(972) 314296
Etr-15 Oct
5.5HEC ● H ⊖ PS + lau
Prices A375 pitch700-1200

Vilarromá ✆(0972) 314375
Clean and tidy site, almost completely divided into pitches.
Turn off on the eastern outskirts of Palamós near big petrol station.
Apr-Sep
1.8HEC S ● H ⊖ G R H + lau S
Prices A380-450 V380-490 420-550 A420-550

At **CALONGE** (5km W)
Internacional ✆(972) 651233
All year
10.3HEC S ◑ ● H ⊖ G P + lau S
Prices A330-495 V355-540 460-570 A425-570
See advertisement on page 256

PALS
Girona
Cypsela ✆(972) 636211 & 636234
Well-kept grassy site in a pine wood.
For access, turn towards the sea N of Pals and follow road towards Playa de Pals, then turn left after Km3.
15 May-Sep
20HEC S ● H ⊖ G P + lau S
Inter Pals ✆(972) 636179
Terraced site on gently sloping ground in pine wood.
4.8km E of Pals between Km4 and Km5 of the GE road to Playa de Pals. 1km past Cypsela.
Apr-Sep
4HEC S ● H ⊖ G P + lau S
Prices A392-490 V392-490 392-490 A392-490

Mas Patoxas ✆(972) 636928
Apr-Sep
7.5HEC ● H ⊖ G H P + lau
Prices A320-400 pitch1100-1400

At **PLAYA DE PALS**
Playa Brava ✆(972) 636894
Recently opened site on level terrain adjoining pine woodlands, golf course, rivers and sea.
From N end of village of Pals turn towards sea and Playa de Pals.
15 May-15 Sep
11HEC ● H ⊖ G PRS + lau
Prices A155-220 pitch1645-2350
See advertisement on page 256

PINEDA DE MAR
Barcelona
Caballo de Mar ✆(93) 7625566
On sandy terrain on both sides of the railway line and scattered with poplars and sunshade roofs.
Access from southern outskirts turning seawards and to the right at beach to site.
Apr-Sep
3HEC S ◑ H ⊖ G P + lau S
Prices A300-420 V300-420 300-420 A300-420

Camell ✆(93) 7671520
Surrounded by deciduous trees next to a small wood owned by the Taurus Hotel.
Camping Carnet Compulsory.
Turn off the N11 at Km677 and drive along av de los Naranjos in direction of sea.
May-Sep
2.2HEC S ● H ⊖ G PS + lau
Prices A375 pitch950

Enmar ✆(93) 7625918
Leave autopista at exit 9 (Lloret and Malgrat) and continue towards Pineda de Mar.
All year
2.5HEC S ○ H ⊖ G H PS + lau

PLATJA D'ARO, LA
Girona
Riembau ✆(972) 817123
Level grassland site under poplar trees, in quiet rural area.
Turn off the C253 inland on southern outskirts after the Rio Riudau bridge and continue 0.9km to site, signposted, and 1km from sea.
May-Sep
18HEC ● H ⊖ G P + lau S
Prices A276-339 pitch1511-1829

Valldaro ✆(972) 817515
Extensive level meadowland under poplars, pines and eucalyptus trees. Some large pitches without shade.
Site lies on the left of the GE662 towards Castell and Santa Cristinia d'Aro at Km4.
Oct-Mar
15HEC ● H ⊖ G H P + lau S

PLAYA DE ENSUEÑOS
See **PALAFRUGELL**

PLAYA DE PALS
See **PALS**

PUERTO DE LA SELVA
Girona
Port de la Selva ✆(972) 387287
Level, grassland site with young poplar trees.
1.5km from the village, in a valley off the Puerto de la Selva to Cadaques road.
Jun-15 Sep
3HEC ● H ⊖ G P + lau LRS
Prices A450 V450 450 A450

PUIGCERDÀ
Girona
Stel ctra Puigcerda-Llivia ✆(972) 882361
Modern campsite in the Pyrenees on level land. First class sanitary installations.
All year
7.5HEC ◑ H ⊖ G R P lau

SANT ANTONI DE CALONGE
Girona
Euro ✆(972) 650879 ➔

May-Sep
10.3HEC ● H G
P + lau S
Prices A395-485 V445-560 445-560 A445-560

Treumal (972) 651095
Entrance on Sant Feliú-Platja d'Aro-Palamós road.
23 Mar-Oct
6HEC ● H G
PS + lau
Prices A336-560 V360-600 492-820 A432-720

SANTA SUSANA
Barcelona
Bon Répos (93) 7634075
In pine woodland between railway and the beach with some sunshade roofing.
Turn off the N11 at Km681 and approach via the underpass (height 2.5m) just before reaching the beach.
All year
4HEC ◑ ● H G
PS + lau

SANT CEBRIÁ DE VALLALTA
Barcelona
Verneda (93) 7630087
Inland and among tall trees.
Leave the N11 Girona-Barcelona road at the far end of Sant Pol de Mar, turn inland at Km670. Continue for 2km to edge of the village and short of the bridge over the River Vallala turn right.
May-Sep
1.6HEC S ● H G
lau

SANT PERE PESCADOR
Girona
Amfora Mas Sopas (72) 520540
Apr-Sep
7HEC ○ H G
PS + lau R
Prices A250 pitch1975

Aquarius ✆(972) 520003
Level meadowland. Partially in shade, quiet well organised site by the lovely sandy beach of Bahia de Rosas.
Travel in direction of L'Escala and turn towards the beach following signs.
10 May-Sep
5.6HEC ∿ ◑ ♨H ⚑ ▼ ✕ ⊖ ◙ G
⛴S P lau ☞ ⛴R
Prices A413-540 V500 ◙413-540 Ⓐ413-540

Ballena Alegre 2 ✆(972) 520506
Extensive site near wide sandy beach with dunes. Large shopping complex.
Access from L'Escala to San Martin de Ampurias, then onward to site in 2km.
All year
2.1HEC ∿ ● ♨H ⚑ ▼ ✕ ⊖ ◙ G
⌂ H P lau ☞ ⛴RS

See advertisement in colour section

Dunas ✆(972) 520400
Level extensive grassland site with young poplars, some of medium height on the beach, totally subdivided.
It lies 5km SE of village. If approaching from L'Escala follow an asphalt road to San Martin, then follow a dusty earth track for 2.5km.
15 May-15 Sep
29HEC ∿ ◑ ♨H ⚑ ▼ ✕ ⊖ ◙ G
H ⛴PRS P + lau
Prices A225 pitch1100-2250

See advertisement in colour section

Palmeras ✆(972) 520506
On level grassland with, as yet, little shade.
Off the road from Sant Pere Pescador to the beach about 300m from the sea.
All year
2.1HEC ∿ ● ♨H ⚑ ▼ ✕ ⊖ ◙ G
⌂ H P + lau ☞ ⛴RS
Prices A430 pitch430

SANT POL DE MAR
Barcelona

Kanguro ✆(93) 7600205
On the terraced slopes of a hill overlooking the sea. Large sandy beach is accessible via rather low pedestrian tunnels under the road and railway line.
Off the N11 at Km668.5.
Apr-15 Sep
2HEC S ◑ ♨H ⚑ ▼ ✕ ⊖ ◙ G
⛴PS P + lau

SITGES
Barcelona

Roca ✆(93) 8940043
On three terraces with a view of Sitges. Shade is provided by pines and deciduous trees. Separate section for young people. 1km from the sea.
Camping Carnet Compulsory.
Turn off the C246 (Barcelona-Tarragona) in the direction of Sant Pere de Ribes/San Pedro de Ribas. In 15m turn right to site.
15 Mar-Oct
2HEC S ● ♨H ⚑ ▼ ✕ ⊖ ◙ G P
+ lau ☞ ⛴PS
Prices A360-400 V360-400 ◙360-400 Ⓐ360-400

TORROELLA DE MONTGRI
Girona

Delfin Verde ✆(72) 758450
On undulating ground with some pine trees, and an open meadow beside the long sandy beach.
Turn left off the road to Begur approx 2km S of Torroella de Montgri, and head towards Maspinell following a wide asphalt road 4.8km towards the sea.
11 May-24 Sep
35HEC ∿ ◑ ♨H ⚑ ▼ ✕ ⊖ ◙ G
R ⌂ ⛴PRS P + lau
Prices A238 pitch1166-2380

See advertisement in colour section

Sirena ✆(972) 758542
Level site with some grass near the sea.
Approaching from Toroella de Montgri turn right about 400m from 'Estartit' sign at Km1 and continue 300m.
May-Oct
2HEC ∿ ◑ ♨H ⚑ ▼ ✕ ⊖ ◙ G R
⌂ H ⛴PS P + lau
Prices A390-450 V390-450 ◙390-450 Ⓐ390-450

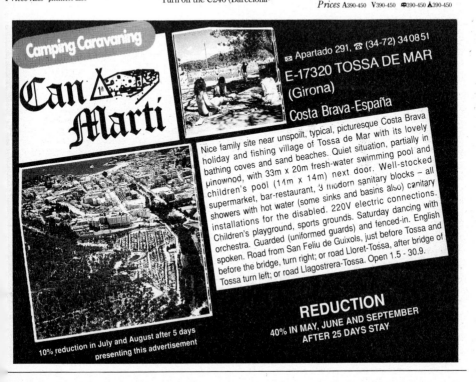

TOSSA DE MAR
Girona

Cala Llevadó ✆(972) 340314
Magnificent terraced site with hairpin roads overlooking three bays, all suitable for bathing. Narrow, winding drives which are quite steep in parts. Separate section for caravans.
Take the coast road for about 4km towards Lloret de Mar and turn towards the sea.
May-Sep
13HEC S ● H + lau PS
Prices A370-515 V370-515 430-580 A370-515

Can Marti ✆(72) 340851
1km from the sea.
May-Sep
9.5HEC ● H R LPRS + lau
Prices A425-545 V425-475 490-595 A425-545

Pola ✆(972) 341050
Partly on flat ground and partly on terraces, in a valley which opens out into a rocky bay with a sandy beach. Advance booking necessary for July and August. In height of the season cars are accommodated in separate car parks.
From Tossa take the winding coast road, GE684 and drive N for for 5km towards Sant Feliú. The camp lies between Km27 and Km28.
All year
23HEC ● H G R S + lau
Prices A500-570 V400-550 650-750 A450-530

Tossa ✆(972) 340547
On a meadow in a quiet, isolated valley, in a deciduous forest. 3km from the sea.
3km SW near the GE681 (Tossa de Mar-Llagostera), in 600m to site along an unmade road.
15 Apr-Sep
5.6HEC S ● H G R + lau P
Prices A450 500 A450

Turismar ✆(972) 341105
Partly terraced on a slope. Shade is provided by plane, olive and poplar trees.
On both sides of the GE681 to Llagostera between Km14 and 15, 1.7km NW of Tossa de Mar.
May-Sep
8HEC ● H G P P + lau
Prices —

VALL-LLOBREGA
Girona

Castell Park ✆(72) 315263
Level and gently sloping meadow with poplars and pine woodland on a hill.
At Km40 about 100m to the right of the C255 to Palamós and 3km S of Montras.
Jun-15 Sep
4.5HEC ● H G P + lau S
Prices A325-370 V325-370 335-380 A275-310

VILADECANS
Barcelona

Ballena Alegre I ✆(93) 6580504
15 May-Sep
22HEC S ● H G R PS + lau
Prices A350-400

See advertisement in colour section

Toro Bravo Autovia de Castelldefels, Km11 ✆(343) 6373462
Level site in extensive pine woodland area by the sea. To the left of the access road on the banks of a stagnant canal about 1km long is a leisure and sports complex with many facilities including evening entertainment in the season.
Leave the C246 (Barcelona-Castelldefels), at Km11 and continue towards the sea for 1km.
All year
30HEC ● H G H PS + lau
Prices A400-440 V400-440 400-440 A400-440

VILANOVA I LA GELTRÚ
Barcelona

Vilanova Park ✆(93) 8933402
All year
50HEC ● H G H P + lau S
Prices A475-700 V475-700 475-700 A475-700

CENTRAL

The La Mancha plains and Don Quixote's windmills, massive mountain ranges, pastures, wheatfields, vineyards, and ancient forests are some of the regions's contrasts.
Here are St Teresa's walled city of Avila, Cáceres' exceptional old quarter, Guadajara's outstanding Renaissance palace, Salamanca, with its university and beautiful square and Segovia's dramatic Roman aqueduct and 14th-century palace.
Architectural and artistic riches continue with Cuenca's hanging houses and Teruel, part of which, like Toledo, belongs to the Heritage of Mankind. The framed walled city of Toledo, with its mosque, synagogue and medieval cathedral, has its associations with El Cid and contains El Greco's house and museum.
Spain's vital capital, Madrid, is home to the Prado and numerous other museums, a colourful old town, lovely parks, squares and palaces, while a short drive away lie the Sierra of Guadarrama with its forests, wild animals and birds of prey and the Pedriza del Manzaneres' geological wonderland.

ALDEA DEL FRESNO
Madrid

Fresno ✆(91) 8637191
A well-maintained site totally enclosed by chain link fencing near the Rio Alberche.
1.3km towards Méntrida.
All year
6HEC S ● H G PR +

ALDEANUEVA DE LA VERA
Cáceres

Yuste ✆(927) 560910
Meadowland with dense woodland on a hill above two valleys.
300m S of C501 at Km49.1.
Apr-Sep
3HEC ● H G P + lau R
Prices A265 V265 265 A265

ARANJUEZ
Madrid

Soto del Castillo ctra de Andalucia 1 ✆(91) 8911395
Site developed into two parts with trees and lawns in large castle park.
Turn off NIV at Km46. In the village 200m beyond FIRESTONE petrol station turn sharp NE and continue for 1km.
Mar-Oct
1.5HEC ● H G PR +

BURGO DE OSMA, EL
Soria

Pedriza ✆(975) 340806
In an orchard on rising ground.
Turn off N122 (Soria-Aranda de Duero), turn left in town and follow signs.
Jun-Oct
3HEC H G lau PR +
Prices A300 V300 350 A300

CABRERA, LA
Madrid
Cabrera ✆(91) 8688082 & 8688541
All year
30HEC lau

FUENTE DE SAN ESTEBAN, LA
Salamanca
Cruce ✆(923) 440130
Useful transit site.
Camping Carnet Compulsory.
On N620 at Km288.
May-Sep
0.5HEC lau
Prices A250 V250 250 250

GARGANTILLA DE LOZOYA
Madrid
Monte Holiday ✆(91) 8693076
Turn off N1 (Burgos-Madrid) at Km69 towards Cotos and continue for 10km.
All year
40HEC lau

GETAFE
Madrid
Alpha ctra de Andalucia ✆(91) 6958069
All year
4.2HEC lau
Prices A405 425 395-425

JARANDILLA DE LA VERA
Cáceres
Jaranda ✆(927) 560454
18 Mar-Sep
3HEC lau

MADRID
Madrid
Arco Iris ✆(091) 6160387
All year
4HEC P lau
Prices A400 V400 400 400

Osuna ✆(91) 7410510
On long stretch of land, shade being provided by pines, acacias and maple. Some noise from airfield, road and railway.
If approaching from the town centre take N11 road and drive towards Barajas for about 7.5km. At Km1 in 300m and after railway underpass turn right.
All year
2.3HEC lau

MÉRIDA
Badajoz
Lago de Proserpina ✆(924) 313236
May-15 Sep
5HEC lau
Prices A245 245 245

OLMEDILLA DE ALARCÓN
Cuenca
Don Pepe ctra N111 Madrid-Valencia ✆(966) 332294
Apr-Oct
8.5HEC lau
Prices A400 V300 375 350

SANTA MARTA DE TORMES
Salamanca
Regio ✆(923) 200250
Divided into several fields.
100m from the N501 (Salamanca-Avila) behind Hotel Jardin-Regio.
All year
3HEC lau

SEGOVIA
Segovia
Acueducto ✆(911) 42500
SE next to N601 at Km85.
Jun-Sep
20HEC lau

TOLEDO
Toledo
Circo Romano ✆(925) 220442
All year
4HEC lau

Greco ✆(925) 220090
Few shady terraces on slope leading down to the River Tajo. On SW outskirts of town.
Approaching from the town centre take the C401, Carretera Comarcal and drive SW for about 2km. Turn right at Km28 and drive 300m towards Puebla de Montalban.
All year
2.5HEC lau
Prices A350 400 350

VALDEMORILLO
Madrid
Valdemorillo ✆(91) 8990002
On sandy meadowland under trees surrounded by hills.
1km E at Km10.4 on the C600 road between Madrid and El Escorial.
All year
2.7HEC lau

SOUTH EAST COAST

The Costa Blanca is a household name; Benidorm a tourist mecca. South of Alicante, tourism is less developed and, inland, there are lemon and orange groves and picturesque mountain towns.
A busy port and relatively unspoiled, Alicante has a cathedral and museum of 20th-century art, and there are tremendous views from its fascinating castle. Roman remains surround Tarragona, whose medieval walled city has a gothic cathedral, interesting palace and architectural museum. Journey out to the Monastery of Poblet inside its three perimeter walls and the Abbey of Santa Creus, burial place of the kings of Aragon.
Valencia, home of paella, is Spain's third largest city with a countryside criss-crossed by ancient irrigation channels. Numerous historic buildings include a cathedral with legendary Holy Grail, beautiful bridges and gardens and many museums. The Fallas – a fortnight of celebrations – take place in mid-March. Inland, Requena has a moorish castle, medieval walls and the house of El Cid.

ALCANAR
Tarragona
Casas ✆(977) 737165
A pleasant subdivided garden-like site in an orange grove on the beach.
Turn seawards off the N340 at Km58.3.
All year
2.1HEC lau

Mare Nostrum ✆(977) 737179
Gently sloping towards the sea with pines, olive and deciduous trees.
Turn towards the sea off the N340 at Km58.3.
All year
1.4HEC lau
Prices A275-295 V275-295 275-295 275-295

ALCOCEBER
Castellón
Playa Tropicana ✆(964) 410885
On a 500m long sandy beach 3km from the village.

For access, leave motorway at exit 44, then drive 3km N on the CN340 and turn towards the sea at Km109.
Mar-Oct
3.1HEC H G
S P + lau

ALTEA
Alicante
Cap Blanch Playa del Albir (96) 5845946
A new site on Albir beach.
All year
3.5HEC H
+ lau G S
Prices A200-500 V200-500 200-500 200-500

BENICARLÓ
Castellón
Alegria del Mar ctra Valencia/ Barcelona 340 (964) 470871
Apr-Sep
4.5HEC H G
H PS + lau
Prices A325 325 325

BENICASIM
Castellón
Azahar (964) 303196
All year
4HEC H G
PS + lau
Prices A425-450 V425-450 425-450 425-450

Bonterra (964) 300007
Between the railway line and avenida de Barcelona with a number of deciduous trees.
300m N towards Las Villas de Benicasim.
15 May-Sep
5HEC S H G
R + lau PS

BENIDORM
Alicante
Arena Blanca av Rincon de Loix Sin (96) 586889
All year
2.5HEC S H G
H P + lau R S
Prices A300-360 V300-360 345-400 300-380

Armanello (96) 5853190
Divided by bushes with large pitches on terraces under olive and palm trees next to a small orange grove.
For access turn off the N332 at Km123.1 N of the town.
All year
1.9HEC H G
R H P + lau S
Prices A330 V300 350 300

Benisol ctra General de Valencia (96) 5851673
All year
1.9HEC H G
H P + lau
Prices A380 pitch1000

BENISA
Alicante
Fanadix (96) 5747307
Terraced site completely divided into pitches.
10km E & 400m from the sea. Access off AV-1445.
15 Mar-Sep
1.5HEC S H G
P + lau S
Prices A350 V350 425 350

CALPE
Alicante
Viñã de Calpe (96) 5831551
Level site with sunshade roofing.
1.5km towards Benisa and turn inland towards Cometa.
All year
2HEC H P P
+ lau S

CAMBRILS
Tarragona
Don Camilo (977) 361490
Divided into pitches, lying on both sides of the coast road.
Drive 2km N of the town towards Salou and W of the bridge over the river.
16 Mar-15 Oct
11HEC S H G
PS + lau
Prices A260-400 V26-400 260-400 260-400

Llosa (977) 362615
Camping Carnet Compulsory.
Turn left off N340 from Tarragona just after Km231 SW of town. Cross railway and continue for 500m towards sea.
All year
4HEC H G R
S + lau P

CAMPELLO
Alicante
Costa Blanca (965) 630670
On most level ground scattered with old olive and eucalyptus trees. The Alicante-Denia railway line runs behind the camp.
For access turn ooff the N332 at Km94.2 next to the big petrol station, and drive along a narrow gravel track towards the sea for 0.5km.
All year
1.1HEC S H G
H P lau S

CREIXELL
Tarragona
Sirena Dorada (957) 801303
Level site shaded by medium poplars. Beach lies across the railway.
Turn off N340 at Km268 and follow signposts.
All year
7HEC H G
P + lau S
Prices A160-250 pitch800-1350

DENIA
Alicante
Marinas Les Bovetes, Nord-A / 1 Los Angeles (96) 5781446
For access turn off the N332 in Vergel and drive E on the Denia road for 4km. Turn N, cross the P1324, turn right near the beach and continue for 200m.
Etr-Sep
1.3HEC S H G
+ lau PS
Prices A265-398 V265-398 318-477 265-398

ELCHE
Alicante
Palmeral ctra F-Garcia Sanchiz 14 (96) 5422766
Long narrow site in a palm forest. It has

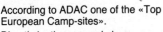

many pitches in recesses between groups of trees.
Camping Carnet Compulsory.
Off the N340 and continue for 200m. Signposted.
All year
1.8HEC S ● ⋔H ⛟ ! ✕ ⊖ ⊜ G
⩦P ▣ + lau ☞ ⩦S
Prices pitch2250 (incl 2 persons)

GUARDAMAR DEL SEGURA
Alicante
Mare Nostrum ✆(96) 5728073
Partially terraced meadow with some shade from roofing.
Turn towards the sea off the N332 Alicante-Cartagena road at about Km38.5.
All year
20HEC ◑ ⋔H ⛟ ! ✕ ⊖ ⊜ G ▣
lau ☞ ⩦PS

Palm Mar ✆(96) 5728856
Jun-Sep
1.8HEC S ● ⋔H ⛟ ! ✕ ⊖ ⊜ G
⩦S ▣ + lau
Prices A400 V400 ⊕475 ⅄400

HOSPITALET DE L'INFANT, L'
Tarragona
Masia Playa de la Almadraba ✆(977) 823102
All year
2.6HEC S ◑ ⋔H ⛟ ! ✕ ⊖ ⊜ G
⌂ H ⩦S ▣ + lau
Prices A275-400 pitch550-800

JARACO
Valencia
San Vincente ✆(96) 2890188
Level subdivided site with some trees.
On leaving Jaraco at Km332 turn off at Km304 (Valencia-Alicante) in the direction of Playa to the site in 3.5km.
All year
4.3HEC S ● ⋔H ⛟ ! ✕ ⊖ ⊜ R
⌂ ▣ + lau ☞ ⩦S

MARINA, LA
Alicante
Internacional ✆(96) 5419051
At Km29 on Alicante-Cartagena road.
All year
5.1HEC ⁓ ● ⋔H ⛟ ! ✕ ⊖ ⊜ G
H ⩦P ▣ + lau ☞ ⩦S
Prices A375 pitch1200

See advertisement on page 260

MIRAMAR PLAYA
Valencia
Coelius av del Mar ✆(96) 2819574
May-Sep
1.8HEC S ◑ ● ⋔H ⛟ ! ✕ ⊖ ⊜ G
R ⌂ H ⩦PS ▣ + lau
Prices A250-350 V250-350 ⊕350-500 ⅄250-350

MONT-ROIG DEL CAMP
Tarragona
Marius ✆(977) 810684
Pitches are planted with flowers and shrubs. Separate section for dog owners.
For access, leave the N340, Tarragona to Valencia road, at Km224.8 and drive through a 4.9m-wide railway underpass with a clearance of 3.65m, then head towards the beach.
Apr-15 Oct
4HEC ⁓ ● ⋔H ⛟ ! ✕ ⊖ ⊜ G ▣
+ lau ☞ ⩦S
Prices A220-400 pitch900-1700

Miami Playa ✆(977) 810920
Partially terraced in pine woodland between the main road and the sea.
To the left of the N340 (Tarragona-Valencia) at Km219.6.
May-Sep
0.8HEC ⁓ S ● ⋔H ⛟ ! ✕ ⊖ ⊜
G ▣ + lau ☞ ⩦S

Oasis Mar ✆(977) 837395
Completely divided into pitches, about 5km S of Cambrils. Shade is provided by trees.
For access, leave N340 at Km226.7 and turn seawards, then continue on an unsurfaced road for 500m.
All year
2.5HEC ⁓ ● ⋔H ⛟ ! ✕ ⊖ ⊜ G
H ⩦S ▣ + lau
Prices A200-400 V200-400 ⊕300-600 ⅄300-600

Playa Montroig ✆(977) 811203
Extensive totally subdivided meadowland site, well shaded by trees. Unfortunately the railway passes right through the site: there is an underpass. TV's are prohibited.
Turn left off the N340 at Km223.5. Use motorway exit 37 or 38.
All year
30HEC ⁓ ○ ⋔H ⛟ ! ✕ ⊖ ⊜ G ⌂
⩦S P ✱ lau

MORAIRA
Alicante
Buena Vista ✆(96) 5744839
Terraced site with pines and eucalyptus trees. 0.4km from the sea. It is more suitable for tents than caravans.
Camping Carnet compulsory.
Turn seawards for 100m at Km2.4, coast road to Calpe E of N332.
All year
1HEC ⁓ ● ⋔H ⊖ ⊜ G ▣ P lau ☞
⛟ ! ✕ ⩦S

Moraira
0.5km from the sea in a pine forest. On several terraces and divided into pitches.
1km S on AP1347, turn W and continue up a hill for 500m.
15 Jun-10 Sep
11HEC ⁓ ● ⋔H ⛟ ! ✕ ⊖ ⊜ G ▣
P + lau ☞ ⩦S

NULES
Castellón
Huertas ✆(34) 64-670817
Clean, well-kept site, completely divided into pitches. Few trees but equipped with straw mat roofs. Dancing every Saturday and Sunday.
Turn off N340 at Km47.1 and drive towards sea for 5.3km. Site about 20m from the sea.
All year
45HEC ⁓ S ● ⋔H ⛟ ! ✕ ⊖ ⊜ G
⌂ H ⩦PS ▣ + ✱ lau

OLIVA
Valencia
Azul Partida Rabdells ✆(96) 2854106
Apr-Nov
1.5HEC S ◑ ⋔H ⛟ ! ✕ ⊖ ⊜ G
R H ⚠ ⩦RS ▣ + lau
Prices A371 V371 ⊕477 ⅄398

camping Sangulí

SALOU TARRAGO

1ª ***

Tel. (003477) 381641 & 381698 Fax: 384616

CAMPING SANGULI Salou tel.381641

CAMPING CARAVANNING SANGULI is because of its situation, its climate and installations, one of the best sites in Spain and one of the most appreciated in Europe.

It is situated only 50 m from the beach and the town of SALOU, in the very heart of the COSTA DORADA, and one of the most beautiful tourism centres of the Mediterranean coast. Well known for its golden beaches, crystal-clear water and extraordinary mild climate throughout the year.

On the site, 3000 trees – typical of the Mediterranean region, such as pine, palm, mulberry, eucalyptus, olive and carobean trees, as well as poplars, provide abundant shade.

In the shopping area you will find a supermarket, boutique, souvenirs, bar, restaurant, pub-discotheque, laundry service, nursery, children's playground, ice-cream shop, etc.

SPECIAL OFFER
(except 16/6-31/8)

STAY	TO PAY
7 days	5 days
10 "	7 "
14 "	10 "
21 "	14 "
1 month	21 "

Open: 1/3-30/11

The sports and leisure complex gives you the opportunity to practise all kinds of sports, such as tennis, squash, mini-golf, frontón, boules, swimming, football, basketball, handball, and table-tennis. You will also find a games room, cinema, satellite TV, etc.

Four marvellous swimming pools, surrounded by grass, invite you to free swimming fun.

The site is fenced-in, guarded day and night and well illuminated. Daily doctor's visit. Large, modern and well kept ablution blocks provide free hot water 24 hours a day. Abundant water of excellent quality in all taps.

Euro Camping ✆(96) 2851753
On a wide sandy beach between orange groves and well shaded with poplar and eucalyptus trees.
For access turn off the N332 at Km184.9, 600m from Oliva. Following signs for camp drive towards the sea for 3.3km. The access road has narrow stretches and some blind corners so beware of oncoming traffic.
Mar-Oct
5.7HEC S ● H ! ✕ ⊖ [G] [R] S [P] + lau

Ferienplatz Olé ✆(96) 2851180
An extensive site with some pitches amongst dunes.
Turn off the N332 at Km182.4 about 5km S of Oliva. In about 3km continue to site on access road partially asphalt, through an orchard.
May-Oct
5HEC S ● H ! ✕ ⊖ [G] [R] RS + lau

Kiko Playa de Oliva ✆(96) 2850905
Family holiday camp, divided into pitches, lying between marshland and vineyard. The sea can be reached by crossing a dyke and there are sunshade roofs.
2.2km on W1065, turn along camino Pont de Bolo, turn left along camino Azagadar de Carro.
All year
1.5HEC ● H ! ✕ ⊖ [G] [R] S [P] + lau ☞ P
Prices A330 V330 500 350

Pepe Partida Aigua Morta ✆(96) 2853170
All year
2.4HEC S ◑ H ! ✕ ⊖ [G] [H] S [P] + lau
Prices A260-371 V260-371 371-530 278-398

OROPESA DEL MAR
Castellón

Blavamar ✆(964) 310347
Sloping site with shade provided by roofing. Individual pitches which are relatively close together.
Turn left off the N340 (Tarragona-Valencia) at Km90.6, a few kms before Oropesa and continue on a stony lane. In 1km turn right to site along an asphalt access road.
All year
15HEC ● H ! ✕ ⊖ [G] PS [P] + lau
Prices A350 V350 350 350

Didota ✆(964) 311166
15 May-Sep
1.5HEC ● H ! ✕ ⊖ [R] S [P] + lau

PLAYA DE NULES
Castellón

Las Huertas Camino Serratelles ✆(964) 670817
All year
2.5HEC S ◑ H ! ✕ ⊖ [G] [R] [H] PS [P] + lau
Prices A350 V350 350 350

PLAYA DÉ SAN JUAN
Alicante

Playa Muchavista ✆(96) 5654526
Within high walls, under a few palms and sunshade roofing. Inland from coast road A190 (Campello-Alicante). Narrow beach can be reached by crossing the coastal road.
For access turn off near Km9.2, cross single track railway line, drive on for 400m then turn right. For better route turn off near Km8.6.
All year
1.8HEC ● H ! ✕ ⊖ [G] S [P] + lau
Prices A250-390 V250-390 270-450 270-425

PUEBLA DE FARNALS
Valencia

Brasa ✆(96) 1460388
Level meadowland site with poplars near village centre.
For access leave motorway Barcelona-València at exit 3, towards Playa Puebla de Farnals.
All year
0.5HEC ● H ! ✕ ⊖ [G] [H] PS [P] + lau ☞
Prices A345-350 V325-350 425-460 350-390

RODA DE BERÁ
Tarragona

Arco ✆(977) 800902
About 200m SW of the Arco de Berá (Triumphant arch), on the seaward side of the N340 at Km269.9.
All year
3HEC ● H ! ✕ ⊖ [G] [P] lau ☞ S
Prices A400-420 V400-420 400-420 400-420

Stel ✆(977) 802002
Via motorway (A7) exit 31.
Apr-Sep
10.5HEC ● H ! ✕ ⊖ [G] [P] + lau ☞ PS
Prices A550 pitch1100-1400

SAGUNTO
Valencia

Malvarrosa de Corinto ✆(96) 2608975
All year
10HEC S ◑ ● H ! ✕ ⊖ [H] S [P] + lau
Prices A300 V300 420 300

SALOU
Tarragona

Sanguli ✆(977) 381641
In two parts on two levels separated from the sea by the road, a row of houses and a railway. Front section is landscaped with good facilities and a pool, rear part consists of sparse and stony grassland with poplars.
SW outskirts, 200m inland from coast road to Cambrils
All year
17HEC S ● H ! ✕ ⊖ [G] PS [P] + lau

See advertisement on page 263
Siesta ✆(977) 380852
Divided into pitches and planted with young deciduous trees and old olive trees. Sunshade roofs.
Camping Carnet Compulsory.
If approaching from Tarragona, turn right off the main road on outskirts of Salou and drive a further 150m to the camp. The site is between the railway and road 0.4km from the sea.
Mar-Nov
6HEC S ● H ! ✕ ⊖ [G] P [P] + lau ☞ S

Union ctra Pompeu Fabra 31 ✆(977) 384816
Apr-Oct
4HEC ● H ⊖ P [P] + lau ☞ ! ✕ [G] S
Prices A345-505 V345-505 475-635 345-505

SAN MIGUEL DE SALINAS
Alicante

Florantilles
All year
5.6 ○ H ✕ P[P] lau

SANTA OLIVA
Tarragona

Santa Oliva Jaume Balmes, 122 ✆(977) 661252
At Km3 on calle Vendrell-Santa Oliva road.
All year
1.9HEC S ◑ H ! ✕ ⊖ [G] P [P] + lau
Prices A275-350 275-350 275-350

TAMARIT
Tarragona

Trillas ✆(977) 650249

terraces planted with olive trees next to a farm.
For access, turn off the N340 at Km259.3, about 8km N of Tarragona. Follow road and cross a narrow railway bridge. (Beware of oncoming traffic).
23 Mar-Sep
4.5HEC
Prices A366-477 V366-477 366-477 366-477

TARRAGONA
Tarragona
Gaya El Catllar (977) 653070
On level grassland with single poplars on the River Gaya.
Turn N inland at Km259.7 off the N340 (Barcelona-Tarragona). Continue on metalled road in 7.5km via T202 and T203 to just before the Gaia river bridge at El Cattlar. To site via unmade road to right in 0.2km.
15 May-Sep
1.5HEC
Prices A325 pitch325

Palmeras (977) 236722
Divided into three parts under trees between railway and sea.
From Barcelona on N340 before reaching town turn seawards at Km255.6 and continue 200m via guarded level crossing.
15 Apr-Sep
15HEC

Tamarit Platja Tamarit (977) 650128
Well-kept site at the sea beneath ruins of Tamarit Castle. One section lies under tall shady trees, and a new section lies in a meadow with some trees.
Turn off N340 and Km259.3 about 8km N of Tarragona and drive 800m seaward along a narrow track.
All year
10HEC

TORREBLANCA
Castellón
Mon Rossi (964) 420296
Apr-Sep
0.7HEC
Prices A350 pitch350

TORREDEMBARRA
Tarragona
Valle de Oro (977) 640902
On level, rather barren meadow with some trees on the outskirts of village, between the road and railway.
Turn seawards at Km264.7 of the N340.
20 Mar-Oct
2HEC

VALENCIA
Valencia
Saler (96) 3670411
Amongst pines providing shade with its own entrance to sandy beach in 300m.
Access from Valencia via coastal road towards Cullera as far as El Saler, then turn left at SE end of village and turn right.
All year
9HEC

VENDRELL, EL
Tarragona
Franca's (77) 680725
Slopes gently towards the sea, between the beach and the railway line which separates the two sections. These are connected by a pedestrian underpass.
Lies about 100m away from the N340 on the seaward side at Km273.
Apr-Sep
3.5HEC

San Salvador (77) 680804
On two large grassy terraces and has some sunshade roofs. Near the sea and next to some tall buildings.
Easiest route is to turn off the N340 at

➔

Km275 and drive towards the sea and Comal-Ruga.
Etr-Sep
3HEC lau S
Prices A233-466 V233-466 233-466 A233-440

Vendrell (77) 694106
Camping Carnet Compulsory.
Etr-Sep
7HEC PS lau
Prices A318-466 V318-466 318-466 A318-466

VERGEL
Alicante
Llanos (96) 5750272
In a field next to an orange grove and shaded by tall trees.
Turn off N332 between Km176.3 and Km176.4 and continue on gravel road for 200m.
All year
2.2HEC lau PS

Patos (96) 5784325
15 Jun-15 Sep
3.2HEC S lau
Prices A450 V550-600 550-600 A500

VILLAJOYOSA
Alicante
Garoa Camping la Cala (6) 5851461
On level ground on the seaward side of the N332. Large pitches, asphalt interior roads. Different types of trees provide shade.
On N332 at Km17.2.
All year
4HEC P lau S
Prices A350 pitch1050-1330

Hércules (96) 5891343
Section near sea is well shaded. Asphalt interior road, separate section for caravans with numbered pitches.
Turn E off N332 near Km114.4 then turn S.
All year
10HEC PS lau
Prices A375 V375 450 A375

Sertorium (96) 5891599
On level ground on the seaward side of the N332. Small stony beach, suitable for non-swimmers.
On N332 at Km117.2.
All year
2HEC PS lau
Prices A330 330 A330 pitch990

VINAROZ
Castellón
Garoa-Sol de Riu Playa (964) 454917
All year
5HEC P lau S
Prices A300 pitch665-1105

NORTH COAST

The region varies from the beaches of the Cantabrian coast to mountain gorges, and attracts sun-lovers as well as hikers, fishermen and outdoor enthusiasts. Of the two coastal provinces, Cantabria has dairy farms and a huge hunting reserve; its capital, Santander, has a cathedral and specatacular beaches, with superb views from the Magdalene peninsular. The Altamira caves, with wall-paintings, are nearby. Asturias has a more rugged countryside. Its capital, Oviendo, is a cathedral city with fine buildings in the old quarter. On the Pilgrim Way to Compostela lies Lugo, with its cathedral and picturesque old quarter of ancient streets and wrought-iron balconies. Walk around the city's perimeter on top of encircling walls dating from Roman times. Famous in both Spanish and British history is Corunna. Now a bustling seaside resort and good touring centre, this old town saw the departure of the ill-fated Spanish Armada and has the tomb of Sir John Moore, killed in the Napoleonic Wars. There is also a Roman lighthouse. North east of Corunna is Ferrol, Franco's birthplace.

BAÑUGUES
Asturias
Molino (985) 880785
Meadow with rows of trees by canal-like stream.
SE, near Avilés-Podes-Luanco road.
15 May-15 Sep
4.4HEC S lau

BARRO
Asturias
Sorraos (985) 401161
Level meadowland on a rocky bay.
Well signposted.
Apr-Oct
1.5HEC S lau

BERGONDO
La Coruña
Santa Marta (981) 795428
5HEC P lau S
Prices A400-450 400-450 A400-450

CADAVEDO
Asturias
Regalina (985) 645056
The site has mountain and sea views.
Camping Carnet Compulsory.
All year
1HEC lau RS

CÓBRECES
Cantabria
Cóbreces Playa de Luana (942) 725120
15 Jun-15 Sep
1.5HEC lau S
Prices A250-270 250-275 A225-275

COMILLAS
Cantabria
Comillas (42) 720074
Level grassland site to the right of the road to the beach.
E on C6316 at Km23.
Jun-Sep
3HEC lau S
Prices A290 V290 315 A290

CUDILLERO
Asturias
Amuravela (985) 590995
Apr-Sep
2.5HEC lau RS
Prices A328 V318 345 A291

FRANCA, LA
Asturias
Las Hortensais Playa de la Franca, ctra CN 634 (985) 412442
20 Jun-5 Sep
2.8HEC lau S
Prices A318 V318 371 A318

IGUELDO
See **SAN SEBASTIAN (DONOSTIA)**

ISLARES
Cantabria
Playa Arenillas (942) 863152

In meadowland with some pine trees.
Camping Carnet Compulsory.
On N634 at Km155.8 turn N and continue 100m. The entrance is rather steep.
May-Sep
3HEC H [G] S + lau [R]
Prices A315 pitch700

LAREDO
Cantabria
Carlos V plaza de Carlos V (942) 605593
Camp surrounded by walls and buildings on W outskirts of Laredo.
Turn off N634 at Km171.6 into an avenue and drive towards the sea. Turn left before reaching the beach and drive around the roundabout on the plaza Carlos V.
Jun-Sep
0.5HEC H [G] + lau S
Prices A400 350 A350

Laredo (942) 605035
In meadowland, part of which is provided with shade by poplars.
Turn off old N634 (Bilbao-Santander) at Km71.6 and drive N towards the sea and beach. Turn left between the tall buildings and a wood and follow a field track for a further 350m.
Jun-15 Sep
35HEC H [G] [R] lau S +

LLANES
Asturias
Barcenas Antigua C N 634 (985) 401570
Jun-Sep
2.5HEC H [G] S + lau
Prices A275-350 V225-275 400-500 A300-400

Brao (985) 400014
Humpy hillside side on three terraces totally enclosed by 2m-high wall.
0.5km from the sea. At Km96.2 on N634 turn N for 1.8km and turn towards Cue for 200m.
Jun-Sep
27HEC H [G] [R] + lau S

Palacio de Garaña (985) 407487
15 Jun-15 Sep
1.8HEC H [G] P + lau S
Prices A371 V371 450 A371

Rio Purón (985) 401699
15 Jun-10 Sep
2HEC H [G] PRS + lau
Prices A300 V250 325 A300

LUARCA
Asturias
Cantiles (985) 640938
Meadowland beautifully situated high above the cliffs with little shade form bushes. Footpath to bay 70m below.
At Km308.5 turn off the N634 from Oviedo, turn towards Faro de Luarca beyond the Firestone filling station. In Villar de Luarca turn right and onwards 1km to site.
All year
2HEC H [G] S + lau
Prices A235 V225 315 A210-235

MOTRICO (MUTRIKU)
Guipúzcoa
Aitzeta (943) 603356
On two sloping meadows, partially terraced. Lovely view of the sea 1km away.
Camping Carnet Compulsory.
0.5km NE on C6212 turn at KmSS56.1.
All year
1.5HEC H [G] + lau PS

ORIO
Guipúzcoa
CM Playa de Orio (943) 834801
On two flat terraces along cliffs and surrounded by hedges.
Turn off the N634 San Sebastian-Bilbao road at about Km12.5 in Orio. Shortly before the bridge over the Rio Orio turn towards the sea and continue for 1.5km.
All year
5.5HEC H [G] P + lau S
Prices A350 pitch915-1100

PECHÓN
Cantabria
Arenas (942) 717188
On numerous terraces between rocks, reaching down to the sea.
Turn off N634 E of Unquera at Km74 towards sea and take road towards S. Difficult for caravans.
Jun-Sep
10HEC H [G] LRS lau

PERLORA-CANDAS
Asturias
Perlora (985) 870048
On top of a large hill on a peninsula with a few terraced pitches.
Access 7km W of Gijon, turn off N632 in direction Luanco and continue for 5km.
All year
1.6HEC [G] [R] S + lau

REINANTE
Lugo
Reinante (982) 130180
Longish site beyond a range of dunes on lovely sandy beach.
On N634 at Km391.7.
15 Jun-15 Sep
2.5HEC S H [G] S + lau

RENTERIA
Guipúzcoa
Oliden (943) 490728
All year
160HEC H [G] [H] PR + lau [R]
Prices A275-300 V275-300 275-300 A275-300

SAN SEBASTIAN (DONOSTIA)
Guipúzcoa
At **IGUELDO**
Garoa Camping Igueldo (943) 214502
Terraced site on Monte Igualdo divided by hedges.
Follow signs Monte Igualdo from town, and beach road, about 4.5km.
All year
3HEC H [G] +
Prices A375 pitch1050-1350

SANTANDER
Cantabria
Bella Vista avenida del Faro (942) 271016
Municipal site on edge of pine woodland. Many steps leading to beach.
About 10km N along coastal road to Cabo Maior. Turn left shortly before lighthouse.
All year
4.2HEC H [G] + lau S
Prices A275 pitch850

SANTILLANA DEL MAR
Cantabria
Santillana (942) 818250
Slightly sloping meadow with bushes on a hillock within the area of a restaurant adjoining a swimming pool.
Camping Carnet Compulsory.
Access from Santander via C6316 turn off shortly after the Santillana sign and continue up the hill.
All year
2.4HEC H [G] [R] [H] P + lau
Prices A375 V375 400 A375

VALDOVIÑO
La Coruña
Valdoviño (981) 487076
Six gently sloping fields partly in shade. Located behind Cafeteria Andy and block of flats with several villas beyond.
Turn off the C646 towards Cedeira seawards and continue 700m to site.
Jun-Sep
2HEC H [G] [R] + lau

VEGA DE LIÉBANA
Cantabria
Molino (942) 730489
In an orchard by river about 300 m outside town.

Jan-Sep
1HEC H G
PR + lau
Prices A300 V300 350 300

VIDIAGO
Asturias
Paz (985) 411012
Camping Carnet Compulsory.
15 Jun-15 Sep
1HEC H G
S + lau R
Prices A315 V315 370 315

VIVEIRO
Lugo
Vivero (982) 560004
In tall woodland near beach road and sea.
Turn off the C642 Barreois-Ortueire road at Km443.1 and follow signs.
Jun-Sep
1.6HEC H G
lau S

ZARAUZ (ZARAUTZ)
Guipúzcoa
Talai Mendi (943) 830042
In meadowland on hillside divided by interior roads without shade. 0.5km from the sea.
On outskirts of town at FIRESTONE filling station at Km16.9 on N634 turn towards the sea and continue for 350m along narrow asphalt road.
Jun-15 Sep
3HEC H G
+ lau S

Zarauz (943) 831238
Site with terraces separated by hedges.
1.8km from the N634 San Sebastian-Bilbao road. Asphalt access road from Km15.5.
All year
4HEC H G
+ lau S
Prices A325 pitch325

NORTH EAST

Medieval villages, green valleys, forests, and arid gorges are some of this region's varied attractions.
Tranquil Burgos, with its pleasant river setting and old centre, was Franco's capital during the Civil War. The principal city of Castille has a magnificent Gothic cathedral which reflects its importance on the Pilgrim Way to Compostela and contains the tomb of the legendary El Cid.
The city of Saragossa lies in a fertile pocket. Its basilica contains a national shrine to the Virgin of the Pillar. The province of the same name contains Spain's largest natural inland lake and is a great attraction for ornithologists.
Beautiful scenery surrounds the pleasant cathedral city of Huesca. Nearby Loarre Castle is a wonderful medieval fortress; superb views can be had from its rocky heights and the amazing grotto site of the Monastery of San Juan de la Peña.
Lush valleys and Pyrennean crags are just two faces of Navarre. Its ancient capital, Pamplona, is notorious for the Running of the Bulls each morning during its week-long fiesta celebrations in July. Wine lovers will be attracted to La Rioja – an area renowned for its fine wines.
At the French border, in the heart of the Pyrenees, is the tiny principality of Andorra, rich in natural beauty, and with a wonderful historic and artistic heritage.

ARANDA DE DUERO
Burgos
Costajàn (947) 502070
Turn off N1 (Burgos-Madrid) at Km162.1 N of town.
Mar-Oct
20HEC S H G
R LPR + lau

BELLVER DE CERDANYA
Lleida
Solana del Segre (973) 510310
On the River Segre, known for its trout fishing.
15 Sep-11 Oct
6.5HEC H G
R PR + lau
Prices A415 V415 415 415

BIESCAS
Huesca
Edelweiss (974) 485084
In meadow with deciduous trees on a hill in a pleasant situation.
Turn right off C138 at Km97.
15 Jun-15 Sep
40HEC H G
PR + lau
Prices A390 V390 390 390

BONANSA
Huesca
Baliera Cruce crta Castejon Desos (974) 554016
15 Jun-15 Sep
5HEC H G R
PR

BORDETA, LA
Lleida
Bedurá-Park ctra N280 (973) 648293
5HEC H G
H LPR + lau
Prices A360 pitch1000

Prado Verde (973) 640241
Level meadowland on River Garona with sparse trees and sheltered by high hedges from traffic noise.
On the N230, Puente de Rey (French border)-Lleida road, at Km199 behind PIRELLI GENERAL filling station.
All year
1.4HEC H G
PR + lau
Prices A300-360 V300-360 300-360 300-360

BURGOS
Burgos
CM Fuentes Blancas (947) 221016
Apr-Sep
3.5HEC H G
R + lau
Prices A350 V350 350 350

CALATAYUD
Zaragoza
Calatayud ctra Madrid-Barcelona (976) 880592
Apr-15 Oct
1.7HEC H G PR
+ lau R
Prices A315 V315 315 300

CASTAÑARES DE RIOJA
La Rioja
Rioja ctra Haro a Sto Domingo de la, Calzada (941) 324184
Closed 10-30 Dec
9HEC H G
PR + lau

ESPOT
Lleida
Sol y Neu (973) 635001
15 Jun-15 Sep

1.3HEC H G PR
+ lau
Prices A360 360 360

GUASA
See **JACA**

GUINGUETA, LA
Lleida
Vall d'Aneu (973) 626083
In meadowland on rising ground on both sides of the road, partially in shade. No shade on terrace between road and lake.
On outskirts of town near the by-pass, C147.
Mar-Sep

0.5HEC H G P
+ lau R L
Prices A300 V300 300 300

HECHO
Huesca
Selva de Oza (974) 375168
On meadowland, partly covered with pines and deciduous trees and between a dirt track and a mountain stream.
12.5km NE towards Espata.
15 Jun-15 Sep
2HEC H G
R lau

HUESCA
Huesca
San Jorge (974) 221560
Site with sports field surrounded by high walls. Subdivided by hedges, sparse woodland.
From town centre, about 1.5km along M123 in Zaragoza direction and follow signs.
May-Sep
0.7HEC H +
lau P

JACA
Huesca
Victoria (974) 360323
On level meadow subdivided by rows of tall poplars.
N of C134 at Km18.6.
All year
1.7HEC H G
R + lau PR

At **GUASA**
Peña Oroel (974) 360215
Grassland site with rows of high poplars.
At Km13.8 of the C134 Jaca-Sabiñanigo road.
Jul-14 Sep
50HEC H G
R + lau P
Prices A390 V390 390 390

LABUERDA
Huesca
Pena Montanesa (974) 500032
All year
10HEC H G
H PR + lau L
Prices A365-420 V365-420 385-440 365-420

MENDIGORRÍA
Navarra
El Molino ctra N111 (943) 340604
15HEC H G
H PR + lau R
Prices A325 pitch1000

NÁJERA
La Rioja
Ruedo (941) 360102
Amongst poplars and the area of the bullring, almost no shade.
Turn off the N120 Logroño-Burgos road in Nájera and then continue along the river banks just before the stone bridge across the River Majerilla, then turn left.
Apr-Oct
1HEC S H G +
lau PR

NUEVALOS
Zaragoza
Laga Park (976) 849038
NE towards Alhama de Aragon.
Apr-Sep
3HEC H G + lau
LR

ORICAIN
Navarra
Ezcaba (948) 330315
Gently sloping meadowland and a few terraces on a flat topped hill.
N of Pamplona. Turn off N121 at Km7.3 and drive towards Berriosuso. Turn right and drive uphill after crossing the bridge over the River Ulzama.
June-Sep
2HEC H G P
+ R
Prices A325 V325 415 325

PANCORBO
Burgos
Desfiladero (947) 354027
Off N1 at Km305.2.
All year
13HEC H G
H PR + lau

PUEBLA DE CASTRO, LA
Huesca
Lago de Barasona ctra de Barbastra-Graus (974) 545148
Apr-Sep
20HEC H G
LPR + lau
Prices A400-420 pitch400-420

RIBERA DE CARDÓS
Lleida
Cardós (973) 633012
Long stretch of meadowland divided by four rows of poplars.
Camping Carnet Compulsory.
Near the electricity plant in Llavorsi turn NE onto the Ribera road and follow it for 9km. Entrance near hostel Soly
Neu.
Apr-Sep
2.2HEC S H
G H PR + lau
Prices A360 V360 360 360

SOLSONA
Lleida
Solsonès (973) 482861
Camping Carnet Compulsory.
All year
3HEC S H G R
H P + lau
Prices A390-430 V390-430 390-430 390-430

TALARN
Lleida
Gaset (973) 650737 & 650102
Meadowland with trees providing shade below the main road and by the Embalse San Antonio reservoir.
Turn off at Km71 on C147 and continue for 400m.
All year
3.5HEC S H G R
LP + lau

TIERMAS
Zaragoza
Mar del Pirineo (948) 887009
On broad terraces sloping down to the banks of the Embalse de Yese. Roofing provides shade for tents and cars.
Situated on the N240 Huesca-Pamplona road at Km317.7.
May-Sep
3.2HEC H G
P + lau

ZARAGOZA
Zaragoza
Casablanca (976) 330322
Totally enclosed on flat terraces, subdivided by paths.
Turn off N11 in Madrid direction between Km316 and 317, at traffic lights turn towards Valdifiero and follow signs.
Apr-Oct
20HEC H G
P + lau
Prices A350-420 V350-420 350-420 350-420

ANDORRA

Prices are in French Francs or Spanish Pesetas.

SANT JULIÀ DE LÒRIA
Huguet 41019
On level strip of meadowland with rows of fruit and deciduous trees.
Off La Seu d'Urgell road N1, S of village and drive W across river.
All year
20HEC H G
PR

NORTH WEST

In this region of contrasts are beautiful green valleys, rugged mountains still roamed by bears and wolves, a wealth of historic monuments, fine resorts such as Bayona, and quiet fishing villages. This is Galicia, a land of mild climate mostly bordered by the Atlantic – a celtic land with strong traditions, local costume, bagpipes and drums. The regional capital, Santiago de Compostela, was once the most visited city in Europe, ranking alongside Rome and Jerusalem. The pilgrimage tradition lives on in its cathedral – one of the finest in the world – and the architecture it inspired on the Pilgrim Way. This legacy has left a wealth of historic monuments, such as the magnificent cathedral at Léon, with its wonderful stained glass. Mountains form the backdrop to Orense, with its fine cahedral and interesting museums, while a green valley is the setting for Pontevedra. Here, in the old town, lie a fascinating museum and cathedral, and houses bearing armorial badges and narrow streets, just as they were hundreds of years ago.

BAIONA
Pontevedra

Baiona Playa ctra Vigo-Baionna (986) 350035
Jun-Sep
16HEC ● H G R H RS + lau
Prices A286-440 V293-451 293-451 A293-451

CUBILLAS DE SANTA MARTA
Valladolid

Cubillas (983) 585002
Meadowland with young trees, subdivided by hedges.
Entrance on the right of the N620 from Burgos between Km100 & 101.
All year
3HEC H G R P + lau R
Prices A265 V265 265 A225-265

LEIRO
Orense

Leiro (988) 488036
On level meadow in a pine forest in a valley by a stream, behind the football ground.
Camping Carnet Compulsory.
All year
1HEC ● H G R R + lau
Prices A325 V350 350 A325-340

MOUGAS
Pontevedra

Pedra Rubia (986) 355133
In meadowland enclosed by a wall in sterile terrain with views of the mountains. Seawater swimming pool.
Access from Vigo on coastal road C550 to La Guardia at Km67.2 turn off in southerly direction.
Jun-Sep
2.2HEC ○ H G PS + lau

NIGRÁN
Pontevedra

Playa America (986) 365404
Apr-Sep
4HEC ● H G P + lau R RS
Prices A360 V360 370 A370

PANXÓN
Pontevedra

Playa de Patos (986) 366110
Gently sloping towards the sea in deciduous woodland on edge of built up area.
Camping Carnet Compulsory.
Turn off the C550 Vigo la Guardia road at Km48.6 in direction of Panjón. Continue on coastal road PO333 to within 3km of the bay then turn sharp right.
Jun-Sep
12.2HEC ● H G S + lau
Prices A300-360 300-360 A300-360

PORTONOVO
Pontevedra

Paxariñas (986) 723055
Slightly sloping towards a bay, in amongst dunes, with high pines and young deciduous trees. Lovely beach.
Camping Carnet Compulsory.
All year
2HEC ● H G + lau S
Prices A360 V350 390 A390

SANTA MARINA DE VALDEON
Léon

El Cares (987) 270476
N off N621 from Portilla de la Reina.
Jun-Sep
1.2HEC ● H G R R + lau
Prices A290 V290 350 A340

SANTO DOMINGO DE LA CALZADA
Logrono

Bañares (941) 342804
All year
7.5HEC ● H G R H P + lau
Prices A390 V390 390 A390

SIMANCAS
Valladolid

Plantió (983) 590082
In a poplar wood, on the river bank.
On outskirts turn off N620 at Km132.2 and continue 500m on narrow asphalt road and a long single track stone bridge over the River Pisverga.
15 Apr-15 Oct
1.5HEC ● H G PR +

TORDESILLAS
Valladolid

Astral (983) 770953
Apr-Sep
3HEC S ● H G H P + lau R
Prices A250-275 V225-250 240-265 A190-210

VALENCIA DE DON JUAN
Léon

Pico Verde C/Santas Martas 18 (987) 750525
Turn E off the N630 (Léon-Madrid) at Km32.2 and continue for 4km.
15 Apr-13 Sep
2.7HEC ● H G PR + lau
Prices A310 310 A310

SOUTH

Forbidding crags, dry river beds, spectacular snow-capped mountains, terraced olive groves, flamenco and some of Spain's finest historic cities, draw the visitor to the Andalusian south, a region with attractions as varied as itself.
The amazing backdrop of the Sierra Nevada towers over lovely Granada and its palace-fortress, the Alhambra. The Moorish heritage of ancient Córdoba is proclaimed by its astonishing mosque-cathedral – one of the glories of Spain. Inside the dazzlingly beautiful mosque's forest of archways and columns, sits a Gothic cathedral. The wonderful gardens of a 14th-century castle are nearby. Bullfights and carnival are part of the excitement of Cadiz. In Seville, Easter week sees the procession of penitents while, in May, colourful celebrations drawing vast numbers from throughout Spain, mark the El Rocío pilgrimage.
The isolation of much of Andalusia contrasts with the better-known hectic charms of the coast, which draws sun-seekers and pleasure-lovers to the resorts of Marbella, Malaga and many more.

ADRA
Almeria

Habana
2km W at Km58.3 on N340 (Almeria-Málaga).
All year
1.5HEC S ● H ⊖ G S + lau
Prices A280 V280 280 280

Las Gaviotas (951) 400660
2km W on N340 (Almeria-Málagar)
Jun-Sep
2HEC ● H ⊖ G R H PS + lau
Prices A275 275 275

AGUILAS
Murcia

Calarreona ctra de Aguilas a Vera (968) 413704
All year
3.6HEC S ◑ H ⊖ G S + lau
Prices A260 V260 300 260

ALJARAQUE
Huelva

Las Vegas (955) 318141
From Huelva cross the bridge over the River Odiel and continue for 8km towards Punta Umbria. Signposted
All year
30HEC ● H ⊖ G P + lau
Prices A300 300 300

BAÑOS DE FORTUNA
Murcia

Fuente (968) 685454
Jun-Aug
0.9HEC S ○ H ⊖ R P lau R
Prices A175 V175 175

Las Palmeras (968) 685123
Camping Carnet Compulsory.
All year
0.9HEC S ○ ◑ H ⊖ G R P + lau
Prices A200 V200 200 200

BOLNUEVO
Murcia

Garoa Camping Playa de Mazarrón (968) 594535
On level ground divided by a footpath and partly bordered by palm trees.
Turn W off N332 in Puerto de Mazarrón at approx Km111 and head towards Bolnuevo. Then take the MU road and drive 4.6km to site entrance which is 1km E of Punta Bela.
8HEC ● H ⊖ G + S

CARTAGENA
Murcia

Los Madriles Isla-Plana (968) 152151
All year
5HEC ● H ⊖ G + PS

CASTELL DE FERRO
Granada

Palmeras (958) 646130
SW on N340.
Jun-Aug
3.5HEC ● H S + lau

CHICLANA DE LA FRONTERA
Cádiz

Barrosa (965) 403605
Jun-Sep
6HEC ● H ⊖ G H PS + lau
Prices A385 V330 420 330-385

CONIL
Cádiz

Conil (965) 440009
On a flat hillock 700m from the sea. Shade is provided by eucalyptus trees.
Well singposted from the N340.
June-15 Sep
1.3HEC ● H lau S

EJIDO, EL
Almeria

Mar Azul Playa de San Miguel (951) 481535
Sports and recreational facilities available.
6km from village.
Etr-Sep
20HEC S ● H ⊖ G PS + lau
Prices A375 375 375

FUENGIROLA
Málaga

Calazul Mijas Costa (952) 493219
All year
6HEC ● H ⊖ G R H PS + lau
Prices A295-350 V295-350 295-350 295-350

GRANADA
Granada

Sierra Nevada ctra de Jaen 107 (958) 150062
Almost level grassy site, in numerous sections, within motel complex.
N of N323, W of road at Km428.8.
Mar-Oct
➔

4HEC H G P + lau
Prices A375 V375 400 375

GUIJAROSSA, LA
Cordoba
Campiña (957) 313348
In a quiet location.
Access via N4 turn off at Km24 onto C3312 25km to site.
All year
0.7HEC H ⊖ G H P + lau
Prices A270-300 V270-300 270-325 200-300

ISLA PLANA
Murcia
Madrilles ctra de la Azohia 45 (68) 152151
All year
5HEC S H ⊖ G R P + lau S
Prices A275-325 275-325 275-325

MARBELLA
Málaga
Buganvilla (952) 831973
Camping Carnet Compulsory.
All year
4.5HEC S H ⊖ G H + lau S

MAZAGÓN
Huelva
Playa de Mazagón (955) 376208
Undulating terrain amongst dunes in sparse pine forest. Long sandy beach.
Turn off the N431 Sevilla-Huelva road just before San Juan del Puerto in direction of Moguer and continue S via Palso de la Frontera.
All year
8HEC S H ⊖ G R + lau PS

PUERTO DE SANTA MARÍA, EL
Cádiz
Guadalete (956) 861749
Undulating in parts, very sandy terrain, 0.9km to the sea.
Camping Carnet Compulsory.
Access from Km65.8 off NIV-25 Sevilla-Cádiz road. Signposted.
All year
5.5HEC S H ⊖ G + lau PS

Playa Las Dunas de San Anton paseo Maritimo de la Puntilla (956) 870112
All year
13.2HEC S H ⊖ G + lau S
Prices A340 V276 339 339

PUERTO LUMBRERAS
Murcia
Los Angeles (968) 402782
All year
13.2HEC S H ⊖ G + lau P
Prices A200 V250 250 250

SANTA ELENA
Jaén
El Estanque (953) 623093
May-15 Sep
1.5HEC S H ⊖ + lau LPR
Prices A275 V275 275 275

SANTA FÉ
Granada
Alamos
Level site in dense poplar woodland.
7km W of Granada.
All year
1.5HEC H ⊖ G P + lau

SEVILLA (SEVILLE)
Sevilla
Sevilla (954) 514379
Level site near airfield, road and railway.
About 2km from airfield, 100m from the NIV (Madrid-Sevilla) at Km533.8.
All year
7.5HEC S H ⊖ G P + lau

TARAMAY
Granada
Paraiso (958) 632370
All year
0.7HEC S H ⊖ G S + lau
Prices A395 V395 550 395

TARIFA
Cádiz
Paloma (956) 684203
All year
2.6HEC H ⊖ G H + lau RS
Prices A350 pitch275

Rió Jara (956) 643570
Extensive site on meadowland with good tree coverage. Long sandy beach.
On the N340 Málaga-Cádiz road at Km79.7 turn towards the sea.
All year
2.5HEC H ⊖ G lau RS +
Prices A350 275 275

At **TORRE DE LA PEÑA** (7km NW)
Torre de la Peña (956) 684903
Terraced, on both sides of through road. Upper terraces are considerably more quiet. Roofing provides shade. View of the sea, Tarifa and on clear days N Africa (Tangier).
Entrance on the N340 Cádiz-Málaga, at Km76.5 turn inland by the old square tower.
All year
3HEC H ⊖ G PS + lau
Prices A350 V275 275 275

TORRE DE LA PEÑA
See **TARIFA**

TORRE DEL ORO
Huelva
Doñana Playa (955) 376281
All year
2.7HEC S H ⊖ G H P + lau S

VEJER DE LA FRONTERA
Cádiz
Vejer ctra National (N340) (956) 450098
Jun-Sep
0.8HEC S H ⊖ P lau
Prices pp 700-800

SWITZERLAND

Bordered by France in the west, Germany in the north, Austria in the east, and Italy in the south, Switzerland is one of the most beautiful countries in Europe. It has the highest mountains in Europe and some of the most awe-inspiring waterfalls and lakes, features that are offset by picturesque villages set amid green pastures and an abundance of Alpine flowers covering the valleys and lower mountain slopes during the spring. The highest peaks are Monte Rosa (15,217ft) on the Italian border, the Matterhorn (14,782ft), and the Jungfrau (13,669ft). Some of the most beautiful areas are the Via Mala Gorge, the Falls of the Rhine near Schaffhausen, the Rhône Glacier, and the lakes of Luzern and Thun.

The Alps cause many climatic variations throughout Switzerland, but generally the climate is said to be the healthiest in the world. In the higher Alpine regions temperatures tend to be low, whereas the lower land of the northern area has higher temperatures and hot summers. French is spoken in the western cantons (regions), German in the central and northern cantons and Italian in Ticino. Romansch is spoken in Grisons and there are numerous regional dialects throughout the country notably the Swiss-German dialects.

Switzerland has over 450 campsites, about 80 of them are run by the Touring Club Suisse (TCS) who publish details of classified sites annually. Information can also be obtained from tourist offices, which are to be found in most provincial towns and resorts.

The season extends from April or May to September or October, although some sites are open all year, particularly at winter sports resorts.

International camping carnet is not compulsory but

recommended. Some non-TCS campsites will allow a reduction in the advertised charge to the holders of a camping carnet. See European ABC for further information.

Off-site camping regulations differ from canton (region) to canton. However, overnight parking may be tolerated in rest areas of some motorways, but at all times the high standard of hygiene regulations must be observed. Make sure you do not contravene local laws. It is recommended that an official site should be used for this purpose.

HOW TO GET THERE

From Britain, Switzerland is usually approached via France.

Distance

From the Channel ports to Bern is approximately 1000km (530 miles), a distance which will normally require only one overnight stop.

If you intend to use Swiss motorways, you will be liable for a tax of SFr30 – see 'Motorways' below for full details.

GENERAL INFORMATION

The information given here is specific to Switzerland. It **must** be read in conjunction with the European ABC at the front of the book, which covers those regulations which are common to many countries.

British Embassy/Consulates*

The British Embassy together with its consular section is located at 3000 Berne 15, Thunstrasse 50 ✆(031) 445021/6. There are British Consulates in Genève (Geneva) and Zürich, a British Consulate with Honorary Consul in Lugano and a British Vice-Consulate with Honorary Vice-Consul in Montreux.

Currency, including banking hours*

The unit of currency is the *Swiss franc (SFr)* divided into 100 *centimes* or *rappen*. At the time of going to press £1 = *SFr*2.52. Denominations of bank notes are *SFr* 10, 20, 50, 100, 1,000; standard coins are *SFr* 1, 2, 5 and 5, 10, 20, 50 *centimes* or *rappen*. There are no restrictions on the import or export of foreign or Swiss currency.

Banks are open Monday to Friday and closed on Saturday. The opening hours in Basel are 08.15–17.00hrs (Wednesday or Friday 18.30hrs); Bern 08.00–16.30hrs (Thursday 18.00hrs); Genève 08.30–16.30/17.30hrs; Lausanne 08.30–12.00hrs and 13.30–16.30hrs (Friday 17.00hrs); Lugano 09.00–12.00/12.30hrs and 13.00/13.30–16.00hrs; Zürich 08.15/09.00–16.30/17.00hrs (Thursday 18.00hrs).

There are exchange offices in nearly all Touring Club Suisse offices, open during office hours. At railway stations in large towns and at airports, exchange offices are open 08.00–20.00hrs although these hours may vary slightly from place to place.

Foodstuffs*

Each traveller over 15 may import a total of 2.5kg of provisions made up of 125gm of butter, 500gm of meat, 1kg of meat products or 2.5kg of one of the following: cooked poultry, poultry products, rabbit, game, fish and shell fish. The importation of meat and pork products from Spain, Portugal and Sardinia is forbidden, as is the importation of game (fresh and frozen) and many types of meat from countries in Africa, Asia, Turkey and the USSR.

Shopping hours

Generally, shops are open from 08.00/09.00–18.30/18.45hrs Monday to Friday and 08.00/09.00–16.00/17.00hrs on Saturday. In large towns, some shops close on Monday morning; in suburban areas and small towns, shops normally close on Wednesday or Thursday afternoons.

Tourist information*

The Swiss Government maintains an excellent information service at the Swiss National Tourist Office, 1 New Coventry Street, London W1V 8EE ✆071-734 1921. In all the provincial towns and resorts throughout the country, there are tourist information offices able to help tourists with local information and advice.

MOTORING

Children in cars

Children under 7 are not permitted to travel in a vehicle as front-seat passengers, with the exception of children using a suitable restraint system or if there are not rear seats available. Children over 7 occupying a front seat must wear a seat belt.

Dimensions and weight restrictions

Private cars and towed trailers or caravans are restricted to the following dimensions – **car** height, 4 metres; width, 2.30 metres; length, up to 3,500kg (8 metres), over 3,500kg (12 metres).
Trailer/caravan height, 4 metres; width†, 2.10 metres; length†, 6 metres (including tow bar). The maximum permitted overall length of vehicle/trailer or caravan combination is 18 metres.

***Additional information will be found in the European ABC at the front of the book.**

Note It is dangerous to use a vehicle towing a trailer or caravan on some mountain roads; motorists should ensure that roads on which they are about to travel are suitable for the conveyance of vehicle/trailer or caravan combinations.

The fully-laden weight of trailers which do not have an independent braking system should not exceed 50% of the unladen weight of the towing vehicle, but trailers which have an independent braking system can weigh up to 100% of the unladen weight of the towing vehicle.

†The Swiss Customs authorities can authorise slightly larger limits for foreign caravans for direct journeys to their destination and back, *ie* caravans up to 2.20 metres (7ft 2in) in width and up to either 6.50 metres (21ft 4in) or 7 metres (23ft) in length, depending on whether Alpine passes are used. A charge is made for these special authorisations. Caravans up to 2.50 metres (8ft 2in) in width may enter Switzerland if towed by a four-wheel-drive vehicle or one exceeding 3.5 tonnes; then no special authorisation is required.

Driving licence*

A valid UK or Republic of Ireland licence is acceptable in Switzerland. The minimum age at which a visitor may use a temporarily imported car is 18 years and a temporarily imported motorcycle of between 50–125cc 16 years, exceeding 125cc 20 years.

Emergency telephone numbers

Fire ✆118 **police** and **ambulance** ✆117 (144 for ambulance if the area code of the number on the telephone from which you are making the call is 01, 022, 030, 031, 032, 033, 034, 035, 036, 042, 043, 052, 056, 057, 061, 062, 063 or 064).

Lights*

Driving on sidelights only is prohibited. Spotlights are forbidden. Fog lamps can be used only in pairs of identical shape, brilliance and colour; dipped headlights must be used in cities and towns. Dipped headlights must be used at all times in tunnels, whether they are lit or not, and failure to observe this regulation can lead to a fine. Switzerland has a '*tunnel*' road sign (a red triangle showing a tunnel entrance in the centre), which serves to remind drivers to turn on their dipped headlights. In open country, headlights must be dipped as follows: at least 200 metres (220yds) in front of any pedestrian or oncoming vehicle (including trains parallel to the road); when requested to do so by the driver of an oncoming vehicle flashing lights; or when reversing, travelling in lines of traffic or stopping. Dipped headlights must be used when waiting at level crossings, or near roadworks. They must also be used in badly-lit areas when visibility is poor. It is recommended that *motorcyclists* used dipped headlights during the day.

Motoring club*

The **Touring Club Suisse** (TCS) has branch offices in all important towns, and has its head office at 1211 Genève 3, rue Pierre-Fatio 9 ✆(022) 7371212. The TCS will extend a courtesy service to all motorists but their major services will have to be paid for. TCS offices are usually open from 08.30–12.00hrs and 13.30–17.00hrs Monday to Friday and between 08.00–11.30hrs on Saturday mornings (summer only). They are not open on Sunday.

Motorway tax

The Swiss authorities levy an annual motorway tax. A vehicle sticker, costing *SFr*30 for vehicles up to 3.5 tonnes maximum total weight and known locally as a *vignette*, must be displayed by vehicles using Swiss motorways including motorcycles, trailers and caravans. Motorists may purchase the stickers from the AA or at the Swiss frontier. Vehicles over 3.5 tonnes maximum total weight are taxed on all roads in Switzerland; a licence for one day, 10 days, one month and one year periods can be obtained. There are no stickers, and the tax must be paid at the Swiss frontier.

Roads

The road surfaces are generally good, but some main roads are narrow in places. Traffic congestion may be severe at the beginning and end of the German school holidays.

On any stretch of mountain road, the driver of a private car may be asked by the driver of a postal bus which is painted yellow, to reverse, or otherwise manoeuvre to allow the postal bus to pass. Postal bus drivers often sound a distinctive three note horn; no other vehicles may use this type of horn in Switzerland.

Speed limits*

Car	
Built-up areas	50kph (31mph)
Other roads	80kph (49mph)
Motorways	120kph (74mph)
Car/caravan/trailer	
Built-up areas	50kph (31mph)
Other roads	80kph (49mph)†
Motorways	80kph (49mph)

***Additional information will be found in the European ABC at the front of the book.**

These limits do not apply if another limit is indicated by signs, or if the vehicle is subject to a lower general speed limit.
†If the weight of the caravan or luggage trailer exceeds 1,000kg, a speed limit of 60kph (37mph) applies on roads outside-built-up areas, but 80kph (49mph) is still permissible on motorways.

Warning triangle/Hazard warning lights

The use of a warning triangle is compulsory in the event of accident or breakdown. The triangle must be placed on the road at least 50 metres (55yds) behind the vehicle on ordinary roads, and at least 150 metres (164yds) on motorways. If the vehicle is in an emergency lane, the triangle must be placed on the right of the emergency lane. Hazard warning lights may be used in conjunction with the triangle on ordinary roads, but on motorways and semi-motorways they must be switched off as soon as the warning triangle is erected. If this is not done, the police may impose an on-the-spot fine (see *Police Fines* and *Warning triangle/Hazard warnings lights* in the European ABC.

***Additional information will be found in the European ABC at the front of the book.**

Prices are in Swiss Francs
Abbreviations
str strasse
TCS Touring Club Suisse
Each name preceded by 'Bad', 'La', 'Le' or 'Les' is listed under the name that follows it.

NORTH

Basle owes its prosperity to its key geographical position – at the junction of the borders of France, Germany and Switzerland, and at the point on the Rhine where it becomes navigable. It has evolved into an important business and industrial centre. The old town has a great Gothic cathedral – with a fine view from the top of the towers, and a remarkable collection of art in the Fine Arts Museum, "Kunstmuseum" The town also has an extensive Zoological Garden, with an emphasis on breeding threatened species. The countryside of this area is one of medieval castles, quaint vilages, thermal spas, dense forests, lush meadows and sparkling lakes. But above the charming Baroque town of Solothurn is the last ridge of the Jura – the giddy crests of the Weissenstein, from where, at over 4,000ft, there is an outstanding view over Berne and the lakes of Neuchâtel, Murten and Biel.

FRICK
Aargau
Sportzentrum (TCS) ✆(064) 613700
12 Apr-Sep
1HEC H G P + lau

GRENCHEN
Solothurn
At **STAAD**
Strausak (TCS) ✆(065) 521133
12 Apr-Sep
1HEC H L P + P

LÄUFELFINGEN
Basel
Läufelfingen ✆(062) 691189
On road from Basel to Olten.
Apr-Oct
0.5HEC H +
Prices A3 V2 2 A2

MÖHLIN
Aargau
Bachtalen (TCS) ✆(061) 882863
2km N.
12 Apr-Sep
1HEC H H P + P

REINACH
Basel
Waldhort Heideweg 16 ✆(061) 7116429
2 Mar-12 Oct
23HEC H G R P + R
Prices A6 V3 6 A4

STAAD
See **GRENCHEN**

ZURZACH
Aargau
Oberfeld ✆(56) 492575
Apr-Oct
2HEC H G R H + lau PR
Prices A4 V2 4-8 A2-4

NORTH EAST

At the northern gateway to Switzerland, the town of Schaffhausen falls in terraces from the 16th-century Munot Castle, and is the traditional starting point for a visit to the Rhine Falls, "Rheinfall". The most powerfall waterfall in Europe, the Rhine makes a spectacular 70ft drop – one of the most famous sights in Europe. St Gallen is popular with visitors; the twin domed towers of the cathedral overlook the attractive old town. The cathedral's plain exterior belies a wonderfully rich Baroque interior, with mural paintings covering the central dome and nave, and there is a remarkable chancel with a huge high altar.
The largest city in Switzerland, cosmopolitan Zurich hums around the Bahnhofstrasse – a fine, wide, tree-lined boulevard of glittering shops and modern offices and banks. For more sedate pursuits visit the quays along the banks of Lake Zurich – lined with immaculate gardens and lawns, visit the old quarters with their cobbled streets, or take a boat trip on the lake. The Swiss National Museum, "Schweizerisches Landesmuseum" is a treasure-house of Swiss civilisation from prehistoric times to the present.
The countryside of the region provides good walking, and the mountains and hills are dotted with attractive farms. Picturesque villages contain traditional colourful houses, and sparkling lakes adorn the valleys. Between the borders of Switzerland and Austria is the principality of Leichtenstein, with its extensive tourist attractions, but retaining its own individual charm and appeal. The capital and main centre is Vaduz, overlooked by its 14th-century castle.

ALT ST JOHANN
St-Gallen
3 Eidgenossen (TCS) ✆(074) 51274
All year
0.5HEC ○ H G S P + lau P

ANDELFINGEN
Zürich
Rässenwies (TCS) ✆(052) 412408
15 Apr-14 Oct
0.3HEC ○ H G P + lau

ARBON
Thurgau
Arbon Strandbad ✆(071) 466545
By Lake Bodensee.
1km W
14 Apr-15 Oct
1.2HEC H G P

ESCHENZ
Thurgau
Hüttenberg ✆(054) 412337
Terraced site lying above village.
1km SW.
All year
5HEC H G R P + lau

FLAACH
Zürich
TCS ✆(052) 421413
In village turn off at Ziegelhaus Restaurant continue for 600m.
12 Apr-7 Oct
8HEC

KREUZLINGEN
Thurgau
Fischerhaus ✆(072) 754903
Near Fischerhaus Restaurant, separated from lake by a road and car park.
From Romanshornstr turn into Bleicherstr and continue 1km.
Apr-Oct
2HEC H G + lau L

KRUMMENAU
St-Gallen
Adler ✆(074) 41030
On edge of village.
All year
0.8HEC ○ H G R P + lau P

LANGWIESEN
Zürich
Rheinwiesen (TCS) ✆(053) 293300
In grounds of Langweisen municipal beach.
From Constance turn sharp right at the large left-hand bend in Langweisen.
May-23 Sep
1.3HEC H ✕ ⊖ G PR P
+ lau

LEUTSWIL BEI BISCHOFFZELL
Thurgau
Sitterbrücke ✆(071) 811014
Signposted from Bischoffzell on the Konstanz-St Gallen road.
Apr-Oct
1HEC ○ H ⊖ G R R P
+ lau ☞ ✕
Prices A4 V2 2 Å2

MAUR
Zürich
Maurholz (TCS) ✆(01) 9800266
15 Apr-14 Oct
1HEC S ● H ✕ ⊖ G
PS P +

OTTENBACH
Zürich
Reussbrücke (TCS) ✆(01) 7612022
By river of same name.
Access from Zürich via road 126 in SW direction, via Affeltern to Ottenbach.
15 Apr-15 Oct
1.5HEC ◑ H ✕ ⊖ G R
lau

ST GALLEN
St-Gallen
Leebrücke (TCS) ✆(071) 384969
May-14 Oct
1.5HEC ○ H ✕ ⊖ G
LP P lau

ST MARGRETHEN
St-Gallen
Bruggerhorn ✆(071) 712201
Apr-Oct
5HEC ◑ H ✕ ⊖ G LP
P + lau
Prices A4 V1 3 Å1-2

SCHÖNENGRUND
Appenzell
Schönengrund ✆(071) 571166
All year
0.5HEC ◑ H ✕ ⊖ P + lau
☞ G R
Prices A4 V3 3 Å3

STÄFA
Zürich
Kehlhof (TCS) ✆(01) 9264334
Small meadow between noisy road and lake with separate patch of grass near the shore.
Site lies opposite GULF petrol station, on edge of village towards Rapperswill.
May-Sep
0.5HEC ◑ H ✕ ⊖ L P
+ ☞ G

STEIN AM RHEIN
Schaffhausen
Grenzstein ✆(054) 412379
1.8km E.
All year
1.5HEC ◑ H ✕ ⊖ G
R H P P + lau

WILDBERG
Zürich
Weid ✆(052) 453388
In a terraced meadow surrounded by woods and is very peaceful.
In Winterthur, follow Tösstal signs, then turn right after spinning-mill in Turbenthal.
All year
5HEC ◑ H ✕ ⊖ G H P
+ lau ☞ P
Prices A5 V2 3 Å2

WILDHAUS
St-Gallen
Dusi ✆(074) 52202
All year
1HEC ○ H ⊖ R L P +
lau ☞ ✕

WINTERTHUR
Zürich
Schützenhaus Rosenberg
Schaffhauserstr ✆(052) 225260
To the left of the Schaffhausen road, near the Schützenhaus restaurant.
All year
0.8HEC ● H ✕ ⊖ G P lau
Prices A6 V2 3 Å3

ZÜRICH
Zürich
Seebucht Seestr 557 ✆(01) 4821612
Beautiful park-like site between the shore road and the lake.
1km S.
May-Sep
2.5HEC ● H ✕ ⊖ G
R H L P + lau
Prices A4 V6-8 6-8 Å6-8
See advertisement on page 277

NORTH WEST/CENTRAL

This region extends from the French border in the northwest, to Adermatt in the canton of Uri, in the heart of the St Gothard Massif at the crossroads of the Alps. The Province of Jura makes a lovely transition from the Saône plain to the Germanic 'middle country' – it is a gentle land of peaceful pastures and low houses, and is a favourite with cross-country skiers in winter. Neuchâtel, capital of its own canton, stands in a delightful position between the lake of Neuchâtel and the mountains, and has a picturesque old town. The lake offers good facilities for watersports and cruising, and a nearby funicular railway serves Chaumont, from where there is a vast panorama of the Bernese Alps and the Mont Blanc Massif.
Bern is a delight, with pretty arcaded buildings lining the streets of the old town, and a lovely setting facing the Alps. Lucerne has a superb site at the northwestern end of Lake Lucerne, and cruises on the lake offer breathtaking changing panoramas. The Transport Museum in Lucerne contains a fascinating story of the development of Swiss transport.
But the highlight of the central region must be the Alps, with the Jungfrau Massif reaching heights of over 13,600ft. Of course during the winter this is a paradise for winter sports, but during the summer there is good access to the most well-known peaks by road, rail or cable-car, with dizzy heights and spectacular views.

AESCHI
Bern
Panorama ✆(033) 544377
400m SE of Camping Club Bern.
Jun-Oct
1HEC ◑ H ⊖ G P +
lau ☞ ✕ P
Prices A4 V2 4 Å3-5

BERN (BERNE)
Bern
At **HINTERKAPPELEN** (6km NW)
Kappelenbrücke (TCS) ✆(031) 361007
On grassy terrain.
S of the River Aare and E of Bern-Aarberg-Wohlen road.
All year

3.3HEC ~ ○ ◑ ⋔H ▙ ✕ ⊖ ⊜ [G]
[R] P + lau ☞ ≋P

At **WABERN**

SC Eichholz ✆(031) 542602
In municipal parkland. Separate section for caravans.
Approach via Grossetstr and track beside lake.
May-Sep
3.5HEC ~ ◑ ⋔H ✕ ⊖ ⊜ [G] ⌂ ≋R
P + lau ☞ ▙ ≋P
Prices A3-4 V1-2 ⊜5 Å2

BLUMENSTEIN
Bern
Restaurant Bad (TCS) ✆(033) 562159
May-Sep
1HEC ~ ◑ ● ⋔H ▙ ⚲ ✕ ⊖ ⊜ [G]
P + lau

BÖNIGEN
Bern
See Terasse (TCS) ✆(036) 222041
In a quiet beautiful setting near a lake.
May-Oct
0.4HEC ~ ◑ ⋔H ⚲ ✕ ⊖ ⊜ ▣ +
lau ☞ ≋LP

BRENZIKOFEN
Bern
Wydeli (TCS) ✆(031) 971141
8km N of Thun.
May-Sep
1.5HEC ~ ○ ◑ ⋔H ▙ ⊜ [R] ≋P +

BRUNNEN
Schwyz
Hopfreben ✆(043) 311873
On the right bank of the Muotta stream 100m before it flows into the lake.
1km W.
26 Apr-29 Sep
1.5HEC ~ ◑ ⋔H ▙ ✕ ⊖ ⊜ [G] ▣
+ lau

Urmiberg ✆(043) 313327
16km N of Altdorf.
Apr-Oct
1.5HEC ~ ◑ ⋔H ✕ ⊖ ⊜ [G] ▣ +
☞ ▙ ≋L

BUOCHS
Nidwalden
Sportzentrum (TCS) ✆(041) 643474
Near local football field and tennis courts.
Signposted.
12 Apr-Sep
2.2HEC ~ ○ ⋔H ▙ ⚲ ⊜ [R] ▣ +
lau ☞ ✕ ≋PS

BURGDORF
Bern
Waldegg (TCS) ✆(034) 227943
On Oberburg road, turn left at petrol station.
Etr-15 Oct
0.8HEC ~ S ○ ⋔H ⊖ ⊜ ≋PR ▣ +
☞ ▙ ⚲ ✕

CHÂTELET, LE
See **GSTEIG**

CHAUX-DE-FONDS, LA
Neuchâtel
Bois du Couvent ✆(039) 232555
Partly on uneven ground.
Take turning off Neuchâtel road near the Zappella and Moeschier factory an drive for 200m.
All year
2.5HEC ~ ◑ ⋔H ▙ ⚲ ✕ ⊖ ⊜ [G]
⌂ [H] ≋P ▣ + lau

COLOMBIER
Neuchâtel
Paradis-Plage ✆(038) 412446
Mar-Oct
10HEC ~ ◑ ⋔H ▙ ✕ ⊖ ⊜ [G] [R]
≋LP ▣ + lau
Prices A4 V1-2 ⊜5-7 Å5-7

COURGENAY
Jura
Moulin de la Terre (TCS) ✆(066) 711716
16 Jun-16 Sep
1HEC ~ ⋔H ⚲ ✕ ⊖ ⊜ ≋P ▣ +
lau ☞ ▙

DELÉMONT
Jura
Grand Écluse ✆(066) 227598
In a meadow beside the River Sorne, surrounded by trees and bushes.
7 Apr-Sep
1HEC ~ ○ ⋔H ⚲ ✕ ⊖ ⊜ [G] [R] ▣
+ lau ☞ ▙ ≋P

ENGELBERG
Obwalden
Eienwäldli ✆(041) 941949
1.5km SW behind restaurant Einwäldi.
All year
4HEC ~ ◑ ⋔H ▙ ⚲ ✕ ⊖ ⊜ [G] [R]
⌂ ≋P ▣ + lau
Prices A5 V2 ⊜4 Å4

FRUTIGEN
Bern
Grassi ✆(033) 711149
Scattered with fruit trees beside a farm on the right bank of the River Engstilgern.
From the Haupstr, turn right at the Simplon Hotel.
All year
1.5HEC ~ ◑ ⋔H ▙ ⊖ ⊜ [G] [R] [H]
▣ + lau ☞ ⚲ ✕ ≋P
Prices A4 pitch4-10

GADMEN
Bern
Alpenrose ✆(036) 751155
About 150m above the Alpenrose Hotel Restaurant.
May-Sep
0.7HEC ~ ◑ ⋔H ▙ ✕ ⊖ ⊜ ≋P ▣
☞ ≋R
Prices A3-4 V1 ⊜6 Å3

GAMPELEN
Bern
Fanel (TCS) ✆(032) 832333
On the shore of Lake Neuchâtel.
7 Apr-Sep
11.5HEC ~ ◑ ⋔H ▙ ⚲ ✕ ⊖ ⊜ [G]
[R] ≋L ▣ + lau

GOLDAU
Schwyz
Bernerhöhe ✆(041) 821887
On the edge of a forest with a beautiful view of Lake Lauerz. Separate field for tents.
1.5km SE and turn left.
All year
2.5HEC ~ ○ ⋔H ▙ ⊖ ⊜ [G] ▣ +
✱ lau ☞ ⚲ ✕ ≋L
Prices A4 V1 ⊜1 Å1

Buosingen ✆(041) 822519
All year
1.5HEC ~ ○ ⋔H ▙ ✕ ⊖ ⊜ [G] ⌂
[H] ≋LP ▣ + lau
Prices A3 V2 ⊜2 Å2

GSTAAD
Bern
Bellerive ✆(030) 46330
All year
1HEC ○ ⋔H ✕ ⊖ ⊜ [G] ⌂ P + lau
☞ ▙ ≋P
Prices A5-6 V2 ⊜8-10 Å4

GSTEIG (LE CHÂTELET)
Bern
Heiti ✆(030) 51029
16 Jun-16 Sep
0.6HEC ~ ⋔H ⊖ ⊜ ▣ + lau ☞ ✕

GWATT
Bern
Bettlereiche (TCS) ✆(033) 364067
12 Apr-14 Oct
1.5HEC 〰 ○ ⋒H ▙ ▼ ✕ ⊖ ◘ [G] ⛱L P + lau ☞ ⛱P

HINTERKAPPELEN
See **BERN (BERNE)**

HORW
See **LUZERN (LUCERNE)**

INNERTKIRCHEN
Bern
Grund ✆(036) 714409
Next to a farm on southern outskirts of village.
Turn S off main road in centre of village at BP petrol station. Drive for 0.3km, turn right.
All year
0.5HEC 〰 ◑ ⋒H ▙ ⊖ ◘ ⌂ [H] ▣ lau ☞ ▼ ✕
Prices A3 pitch3-8

Innertkirchen ✆(036) 711348
S bank of River Aare.
Apr-Oct
0.5HEC 〰 ◑ ⋒H ⊖ ◘ [G] [R] ▣ + ☞ ▙ ▼ ✕ ⛱P

INTERLAKEN
Bern
Alpenblick Seestr 135, Neuhaus ✆(036) 227757
On the left bank of the River Lombach upstream from the bridge in a meadow bordering a forest opposite the Neuhaus Motel and the Strandbad Restaurant.
8km N of Interlaken.
All year
2HEC 〰 ◑ ⋒H ▙ ⊖ ◘ [G] [R] ⌂ ▣ + lau ☞ ▼ ✕ ⛱LR

Jungfrau Steindlerstr 60 ✆(036) 227107
Has a beautiful view of the Eiger, the Monch and the Jungfrau.
Turn right at Unterseen, drive through the Schulhaus and Steinler Str to site.
Mar-Oct
2HEC 〰 ● ⋒H ▙ ▼ ✕ ⊖ ◘ [G] ⌂ ⛱P ▣ + lau ☞ ⛱LR
Prices A4-6 pitch6-18

Jungfraublick Gsteigstr 80 ✆(036) 224414
Take Autobahn N8 through tunnel, leave at Lauterbrunnen-Grindelwald exit, site on left, 300m from N8 sliproad.
15 Mar-Sep
1.3HEC 〰 ○ ⋒H ▙ ⊖ ◘ [G] [R] ⛱P ▣ + lau ☞ ▼ ✕
Prices A4-5 pitch5-15

Lazy Rancho ✆(036) 228716
Motorway N8: exit Unterseen, turn toward Gunten. After 2km turn right, then at Motel Golf turn left.
Apr-Oct
1.6HEC 〰 ◑ ⋒H ▙ ⊖ ◘ [G] [R] ⛱P ▣ + lau ☞ ▼ ✕ ⛱LR
Prices A4-5 pitch5-16

Manor Farm 1 ✆(036) 222264
From motorway N8 (Bern-Speiz-Interlaken-Brienz), exit Gunten/Beatenberg; follow signposts.
All year
7HEC 〰 ◑ ⋒H ▙ ▼ ✕ ⊖ ◘ [G] [R] ⌂ [H] ⛺ ⛱LR ▣ + lau
Prices A4-6 pitch4-23

Sackgut (TCS) ✆(036) 224434
Between a hill and the River Aare.
From Brienz turn left before Interlaken opposite the Ost railway station.
May-Oct
1.2HEC 〰 ◑ ⋒H ▙ ▼ ✕ ⊖ ◘ [G] ▣ + lau ☞ ⛱P

ISELTWALD
Bern
Lac ✆(036) 451148
Beside an inn of the same name.
Turn off the road along the lake shore E of village just before Gasthof.
May-Sep
0.6HEC 〰 ◑ ● ⋒H ▙ ✕ ⊖ ◘ [G] ▣ lau ☞ ⛱L

KANDERSTEG
Bern
Rendez-Vous ✆(033) 751354
750m E of town.
All year
1HEC 〰 ◑ ⋒H ▼ ✕ ⊖ ◘ [G] [R] lau ☞ ▙ ⛱P
Prices A4 V2 ⛟7 ⛺3-7

KRATTIGEN
Bern
Stuhlegg ✆(033) 542723
Closed 15 Oct-Nov
2HEC 〰 ◑ ⋒H ▙ ⊖ ◘ [G] ▣ + lau
Prices A4 V1 ⛟4-6 ⛺4-6

LANDERON, LE
Neuchâtel
Peches ✆(038) 512900
Apr-Sep
10HEC 〰 ◑ ⋒H ▙ ⊖ ◘ [G] [R] [H] ▣ lau ☞ ▼ ✕ ⛱LPR
Prices A4 V3 ⛟6 ⛺4-6

LAUTERBRUNNEN
Bern
Jungfrau ✆(036) 552010
Widespread site in meadowland crossed by a stream. Partly divided into pitches.
100m before the church turn right, drive a further 400m.
All year
5HEC 〰 ◑ ⋒H ▙ ✕ ⊖ ◘ [G] [R] ⌂ [H] ⛺ ▣ + lau ☞ ▼ ⛱P

Schützenbach (TCS) ✆(036) 551268
About 300m from the lake.
S of village to the left of road leading to Stechelberg opposite B50. 0.8km SE towards Stechelberg.
All year
2.5HEC 〰 ◑ ⋒H ▙ ▼ ✕ ⊖ ◘ [G] [R] ⌂ [H] ⛺ ▣ + lau

LENK
Bern
Seegarten ✆(030) 31616
Only winter camping. 700m S.
Dec-Apr
1HEC 〰 ○ ⋒H ⊖ ◘ [G] ▣ ✱ lau ☞ ▙ ▼ ✕ ⛱P

LOCLE, LE
Neuchâtel
Communal (TCS) ✆(039) 317493
May-14 Oct
1.2HEC 〰 ⋒H ▼ ✕ ⊖ ◘ [G] [R] ⛱P ▣ + lau

LUCERNE
See **LUZERN**

LUNGERN
Obwalden
Obsee ✆(041) 691463
Beside lake.
1km W.
All year
1.5HEC 〰 ◑ ⋒H ▼ ✕ ⊖ ◘ [G] [R] ⛱LR ▣ + lau ☞ ▙
Prices A4 V2 ⛟4

LÜTSCHENTAL
Bern
Dany's Camp ✆(036) 531824
May-Oct
0.4HEC 〰 ◑ ⋒H ▙ ⊖ ◘ [G] ▣ + lau
Prices A3-4 V1 ⛟4-8 ⛺4-8

LUZERN (LUCERNE)
Luzern
Lido Lidostr ✆(041) 312146
Park-like site lying behind the beach. No admittance for vehicles or new arrivals 22.00-07.00 hrs.
Camping Carnet Compulsory.
Signposted.
15 Mar-Oct
2.7HEC 〰 ◑ ⋒H ▙ ▼ ✕ ⊖ ◘ [G] [R] [H] ▣ lau ☞ ⛱L

At **HORW**
Steinibachried (TCS) ✆(041) 473558
In gently sloping meadow next to the football ground and the beach, separated from the lake by a wide belt of reeds.
3.2km S of Luzern.
Apr-Sep
2HEC 〰 ◑ ⋒H ✕ ⊖ ◘ [G] [R] P + lau ☞ ▙ ⛱L

MAUENSEE
Luzern
Sursee ✆(045) 211161
Next to Waldheim Country Estate.
0.8km W of Sursee, 100m from Sursee-Basel road.
Apr-Oct
1.5HEC 〰 ◑ ⋒H ▙ ⊖ ◘ [G] ▣ lau ☞ ▼ ✕ ⛱P
Prices A4 V2 ⛟2 ⛺2

MERLISCHACHEN
Schwyz
Unterbergiswil am See ✆(041) 371804
Beside lake. Own beach.
Apr-Sep
1.4HEC ⩋ ◑ ⋒H ⊕ ▼ ✕ ⊖ ⊙ G R H ⩳L P + lau

MOSEN
Luzern
Seeblick ✆(041) 851666
In two strips of land on edge of lake, divided by paths into several squares.
N on the N26.
Apr-Oct
3HEC ⩋ ◑ ⋒H ⊕ ⊖ ⊙ G ⩳L P + lau ☞ ✕

NOTTWIL
Luzern
St Margrethen ✆(045) 541404
Natural meadowland under fruit trees, with own access to lakeside.
Turn off road to Sursee 400m NW of Nottwil and drive towards lake for 100m.
Apr-Oct
1HEC ⩋ ◑ ⋒H ⊕ ⊖ ⊙ G P + ☞ ▼ ✕ ⩳L
Prices A4 V2 ⊙2 Å2

PRÊLES
Bern
Prêles ✆(032) 951716
Camping Carnet Compulsory.
Turn off the main Biel-Neuchâtel road at Twann and follow signs for Prêles. Pass through village, site on left.
May-Sep
3HEC ⩋ ○ ⋒H ▼ ✕ ⊖ ⊙ G R + lau ☞ ⊕ ⩳P
Prices A4 V2 ⊙3 Å3

RINGGENBERG
Bern
Lac ✆(036) 222616 ➔

Between the slopes of a slate quarry and the shore of Lake Brienz.
NW on lakeside.
All year
0.8HEC ◑ H ⊖ [G] [H] L
P + lau ✕

Talacker ✆(038) 221128
Camping Carnet Compulsory.
All year
0.8HEC ◑ H ⊖ [G] [R] P
+ lau LP
Prices A5 V3 7

SAANEN
Bern
Beim Kappeli (TCS) ✆(030) 46191
In a long meadow between railway and River Saane.
1km SE.
Closed Nov
0.8HEC ◑ H ⊖ [G] [R] P +
lau ✕ P

SACHSELN
Obwalden
Ewil ✆(041) 664454
On Lake Sarnersee.
All year
1.3HEC ◑ H ⊖ [G] [H] P
+ lau ✕
Prices A3-4 V2 4 A2-3

SARNER SEE
See **GROSSTEIL & SACHSELN**

SCHÜPFHEIM
Luzern
Bad ✆(041) 761163
Between railway and road, close by an inn of the same name.
Turn off N10 Luzern-Bern about 2km S in the direction of Sorenberg.
All year
0.6HEC ◑ H ✕ ⊖ [G] P
+ lau PR

SEMPACH
Luzern
Seeland (TCS) ✆(041) 991466
Rectangular, level site on SW shore of lake.
700m S on Luzern road by lake.
12 Apr-14 Oct
5.2HEC ◑ ● H ✕ ⊖ [G] P +
lau

STECHELBERG
Bern
Breithorn ✆(036) 551225
3km S of Lauterbrunnen.
All year
2.5HEC ◑ H ⊖ [G] [H]
P + lau ✕
Prices A4-5 pitch4-8

THÖRISHAUS
Bern
Freizeitzentrum ✆(031) 880296
Clean site with well-kept grass.
9km SW of Bern, Motorway 12; exit Flamatt, 1km N, on River Sense.
Apr-Oct
5.5HEC ◑ H ✕ ⊖ [G] [R]
R + lau

UNTERAEGERI
Zug
ZKZS Unteraegeri Wilbrunnenstr 81
✆(042) 723928
All year
6HEC ◑ H ⊖ [G] L P
+ lau P
Prices A5 7 A5

VITZNAU
Luzern
Vitznau ✆(041) 831280
Well tended terraced site about the resort in lovely countryside with fine views of lake.
Approaching from N, turn towards mountain at church and follow signs.
Apr-15 Oct
2HEC ◑ H ⊖ [G] [R] P +
lau ✕ LP

VORDERTHAL
Schwyz
Wägital Wei 1 ✆(055) 691259
In a beautiful circular valley high up in mountains.
12km SW of Lachen.
Mar-Oct
0.8HEC ◑ H ⊖ [G] R P +
lau ✕ LP
Prices A4 V2 4 A2-4

WABERN
See **BERN (BERNE)**

WILDERSWIL
Bern
Oberei ✆(036) 221335
15 Mar-15 Oct
5.5HEC ◑ H ⊖ [G] [R]
P + lau ✕ P
Prices A4 pitch6-10

WILLERZELL
Schwyz
Grüene Aff ✆(055) 534131
Quiet, terraced site, separated from lake by the road.
1km N of village beside lake.
All year
3HEC ○ H ✕ ⊖ [G] [R]
P + lau L

ZUG
Zug
Innere Lorzenallmend (TCS)
✆(042) 418422
Pleasantly situated with beautiful view of Lake Zug and surrounding mountains. Much traffic on railway which passes the site.
1km NW by lake.
12 Apr-Sep
1.1HEC ◑ H ✕ ⊖ [G] L
P + lau

ZWEISIMMEN
Bern
Camping Vermeille ✆(030) 21940
Well laid-out site along the River Simme.
1km N towards Lake Thun.
All year
0.9HEC ◑ H ⊖ [G] [R] P
lau ✕ P +
Prices A4-5 V3 5-8 A3-5

EAST

The cantons of Glarus and Grisona make up this region of eastern Switzerland. The town of Glarus still maintains the practice of direct democracy, when every spring all active citizens fill the great Zaunplatz, and in a highly ceremonial meeting decide all issues affecting the community by a show of hands. Grisons, astride the Alps, is truly Switzerland's holiday corner. Superb road, railway and cable-car networks, run with usual Swiss efficiency, access the wonderful winter sports regions and well-equipped resorts – the elegant Arosa, Davos, Chur, Flims, the famous royal retreat of Klosters and glittering St Moritz. This efficient transport makes the area a summer paradise for walkers and hikers – there are over 3,000 miles of unsignposted cross-country footpaths. Many areas of superb natural beauty are protected by law – the largest is the 65-square-mile Swiss National Park, reached from Zernez, where authorised roads and paths (and guided walks in season), give glimpses of a flora and fauna completely protected from man.

ANDEER
Graubünden
Sut Baselgia (TCS) ✆(081) 611453
N towards Chur.
All year
1.2HEC ○ ◑ H [R] P + lau

AROSA
Graubünden
Arosa ✆(081) 311745
All year
0.6HEC ◑ H ⊖ [G] LP
Prices A5-6 V1 4 Å3

CHUR (COIRE)
Graubünden
Camp Au (TCS) Felsenaustr 61 ✆(081) 242283
Take exit Chur-Süd from N13. 2km NW of town centre on bank of Rhein. Access is via outskirts of town.
All year
2.6HEC ◑ H ⊖ [G] [R] [H] P + P

DAVOS
Graubünden
Färich (TCS) ✆(0833) 51043
19 May-Sep
1.3HEC ● H ⊖ [G] P + lau P

DISENTIS-MUSTER
Graubünden
Fontanivas (TCS) ✆(086) 74422
Next to a swimming pool in a pine forest.
Take N61 for 1.5km towards Lukmanier Pass then turn left and drive on for 100m.
19 May-7 Oct
1.5HEC ◑ H ⊖ [G] [R] PR + lau

FLIMS-WALDHAUS
Graubünden
Prau ✆(081) 391575
500m N of village, about 30m below the Ilanz road.
All year
1HEC ◑ H ⊖ [R] lau

LANDQUART
Graubünden
Neue Ganda (TCS) ✆(081) 513955
Undulating grassy site in a wood, separated from the trunk road by a narrow stream lined with bushes.
Access from N28 towards Davos between Km2 and Km2.5 N of CHEVRON petrol station.
All year
4.5HEC ◑ ● H ⊖ +

LENZERHEIDE
Graubünden
Gravas (TCS) ✆(081) 342335
All year
1HEC ● H ⊖ [R] P + lau LP

MALOJA
Graubünden
Plan Curtinac (TCS) ✆(082) 43181
2 Jun-16 Sep
1.5HEC ○ H [G] PS + lau

MÜSTAIR
Graubünden
Clenga ✆(082) 85410
Next to small river near the Italian frontier.
15 May-20 Oct
1HEC ◑ H ⊖ [G] [H] + lau P

PONTRESINA
Graubünden
Plauns (TCS) ✆(082) 66285
Beautiful situation at foot of Pit Palü.
Access from road towards Bernina pass about 4.5km beyond Pontresina. Turn off main road 29 towards Hotel Morteratsch then 0.5km to site.
7 Jun-12 Oct
4HEC ◑ H ⊖ [G] [R] + lau LR

POSCHIAVO
Graubünden
Boomerang ✆(082) 50713
In a quiet setting.
2km SE.
All year
5HEC ● H ⊖ + lau

ST MORITZ
Graubünden
Olympiaschanze (TCS) ✆(082) 34090
Above the River En.
1km E of Champfèr.
Jun-17 Sep
1.5HEC H ⊖ [G] + lau L

SAMEDAN
Graubünden
Punt Muragl (TCS) ✆(082) 34497
Near Bernina railway halt, to the right of the fork of the two roads Samedan and Celerina/Schlarigna to Pontresina.
All year
2HEC ◑ H ⊖ [G] + lau P

SCHULS
See **SCUOL**

SCUOL (SCHULS)
Graubünden
Gurlaina (TCS) ✆(084) 91501
Camping Carnet Compulsory.
Turn SE off N27 at OPEL garage in village and cross narrow bridge leading to the site.
Jun-Sep
1.5HEC ◑ ⊖ [G] [R] + lau

SILVAPLANA
Graubünden
Silvaplana ✆(082) 48492
Lies S of village, to left of the road leading to Maloja mountain pass.
25 May-15 Oct
4HEC ● H ⊖ [G] + lau P

SPLÜGEN
Graubünden
Sand ✆(081) 621476
On left bank of River Hinterrhein.
Turn off the main trunk road in the village and follow signposts.
All year ➔

0.8HEC H G R + lau
Prices A5 V2 5 A3

STRADA IM ENGADIN
Graubünden
Arina (084) 93212
At the foot of a mountain, SW of village.
15 May-Sep
0.6HEC H P + lau R

SUR EN
Graubünden
Lischana (TCS) (084) 93544
15 Jun-Oct
3HEC H G H PS + lau

SUSCH
Graubünden
Muglinas (082) 81244
200m W.
Jun-Sep

1HEC H G R
Prices A4 V1 2 A1

THUSIS
Graubünden
Rheinau (TCS) (081) 812472
May-Sep
4.5HEC H G + PR
Prices A4 pitch5-10

TRUN
Graubünden
Trun (TCS) (086) 81666
0.5km from village centre. Take road 7166.
May-14 Oct
3HEC H G + lau

TSCHIERV
Graubünden
Sternen (TCS) (082) 85551
In village behind the Sternen Hotel.
Camping Carnet Compulsory.
Between Ofen Pass and Santa Maria.
All year
2HEC H G R + lau P

VICOSOPRANO
Graubünden
Albigna (082) 41316
May-15 Oct
1.5HEC S H P G

ZERNEZ
Graubünden
Cul (082) 81462
Camping Carnet Compulsory.
Off road 27 W of Zernez.
15 May-Sep
3.6HEC H G R + lau PR
Prices A4-5 V3 4 A2-3

SOUTH

Here, in the canton of Ticino, the German and Italian cultures mingle in a land where Alpine mountains and valleys fall towards the great lakes and the plain of Lombardy. The province is a climatic oasis: the Alpine chain protects it from strong winds, and even in winter there is a comparatively high number of sunny days. Alpine and Mediterranean plant species flourish side by side, giving Ticino a unique flora.
In this area of outstanding beauty, Lugano remains a favourite with visitors. The town has a traditional atmosphere, with attractive lanes and shopping arcades, spacious parks and lakeside promenades. Excursions from Lugano lead to high mountains and some of the best views in the country – Mount San Salvatore, Mount Bré and Mount Generoso.
Locarno, a lovely town on the shores of Lake Maggiore, is also popular, and the exceptionally mild southern climate produces lush vegetation and a wonderfully colourful display of flowers in early spring.

ACQUAROSSA
Ticino
Acquarossa (092) 781603
Beautifully situated on large, unspoilt area of land.
1km above Acquarossa and road to Lukmanier Pass.
All year
3HEC H G P lau

AGNO
Ticino
Eurocampo (091) 592114
Part of site is near its own sandy beach and is divided by groups of trees.
600m E on road from Lugano to Ponte Tresa. Entrance opposite Aeroport sign and Alfa Romeo building.
Apr-Oct
4.5HEC H G R LP + lau
Prices A6 V2 5-7 A5

Golfo del Sole (091) 594802
By lake. Separate play area for children.
Apr-Oct
0.6HEC H G L P + lau
Prices A5 V2 6-9 A5-7

Piodella (TCS) (091) 547788
Enclosed on a beautiful, flat sandy beach, and partly level grassland with trees.
1km E on shore of Lake Lugano.
Apr-Oct
3.2HEC H G R LR P + lau

AVEGNO
Ticino
Piccolo Paradiso (093) 811581
In the Maggia Valley between the main road and River Maggia.
6km NW from Locarno on the Maggia Valley road.
20 Mar-Oct
4HEC H G R R P + lau P

BELLINZONA
Ticino
Molinazzo (TCS) (092) 291118
2km N of city.
May-Sep
1HEC H G R PR + lau

CADENAZZO
Ticino
Cadenazzo (TCS) (092) 622653
Divided into two parts by a stream, and by rows of trees and a gravel path.
Turn off at GULF filling station in direction of Mignos and continue 100m.
20 May-11 Sep
0.8HEC S H G L + lau P

CHIGGIOGNA
Ticino
Gottardo (094) 381562
Open meadowland on mountain slope partly on natural terraces.
1km S of Faido, 20m above N2.
Jan-Oct
0.8HEC H G PR + lau

CLARO
Ticino
Censo (092) 661753

Below a woodland slope.
Off the N2 (E9).
Apr-Sep
2HEC ～ ● ⋔H ⛺ ♀ ✕ ⊖ ⊕ G R
⛵PR P + lau
Prices A5 V2 ⊕7-12 ▲7-12

CUGNASCO
Ticino
Park-Camping Riarena ✆(092) 641688
Beautiful park-like site.
1.5km NW. Turn off road 13 at BP filling station 9km NE of Locarno and continue 0.5km.
Apr-22 Oct
3.2HEC ～ S ◑ ⋔H ⛺ ♀ ✕ ⊖ ⊕
G R H ⛵PR P + lau
Prices A5 V2 ⊕6-8 ▲6-8

CUREGLIA
Ticino
Moretto (TCS) ✆(091) 567662
Open meadowland, wide strips which gently slope towards the Vedeggio Valley.
On outskirts, on road to Lugano.
7 Apr-28 Oct
3HEC ⊟ ○ ⋔H ♀ ✕ ⊖ ⊕ G R
⛵P P + lau

GORDEVIO
Ticino
Bellariva ✆(093) 871444
In quiet location between the road and the left bank of the River Maggia.
Apr-Oct
15HEC ～ ◑ ⋔H ⛺ ♀ ✕ ⊖ ⊕ G
⛵PR P + lau
Prices A5-6 V3 ⊕12-15 ▲10-12

Renato ✆(093) 871364
Gently sloping meadowland.
Site lies off main road running through the Maggia Valley.
6 Apr-20 Oct
2.5HEC ～ ◑ ⋔H ♀ ✕ ⊖ G ⛵P P
+ lau

GUDO
Ticino
Gudo Hauptstr ✆(092) 641642
In deciduous woodland surrounded by meadows.
Off the main road (via Cantonale) running from Bellinzona to Locarno, about 0.6km S of village.
27 Mar-12 Oct
3HEC ～ ◑ ⋔H ⛺ ⊖ G ⛵P P +
lau ☞ ⛵R

LOCARNO
Ticino
Delta via G-Respini ✆(093) 316081
A beautiful, well-equipped and well-organised site.
1.6km S of Lake Maggiore.
15 Mar-23 Oct
6.5HEC ～ ◑ ⋔H ⛺ ♀ ✕ ⊖ ⊕ G
R ⌂ H ⛵LPR P + ⚕ lau

□At **LOSONE**(4km W)
Zandone ✆(093) 356563
A level site amidst deciduous forest behind an extensive military area.
Situated between the Losone-Golino road and the River Melezza.
Apr-Oct
2.1HEC ～ ◑ ⋔H ⛺ ⊖ ⊕ G ⌂ ⛵R
P + ☞ ♀ ✕ ⛵P

LOSONE
See **LOCARNO**

MAROGGIA
Ticino
Piazzale Mare (TCS) ✆(091) 687245
2km S on lake.
May-21 Oct
0.6HEC ～ ○ ⋔H ⛺ ♀ ✕ ⊖ ⊕ G
R P + lau ☞ ⛵L

MELANO
Ticino
Paradiso ✆(091) 482863
Leave motorway N2/E9 at Bissone exit. Turn off road no.2 on northern outskirts of village towards lake. After motorway underpass, continue 200m to site.
May-Sep
2HEC ～ ◑ ⋔H ⛺ ♀ ✕ ⊖ ⊕ G R
⛵L P + lau

Pedemonte ✆(091) 688333
Between railway and lake with own private beach.
Turn off road no.2 in S outskirts of Maroggia towards lake.
Apr-10 Oct
2HEC ～ ◑ ⋔H ⛺ ♀ ✕ ⊖ ⊕ G R
H ⛵L P + lau

MÉRIDE
Ticino
Parco al Sole (TCS) ✆(091) 464330
On gently sloping ground surrounded by a bushy wood, next to a small lake suitable for bathing.
Turn off motorway N2/E9 at Mendrisio and follow signs for Serpiano. Turn left past the railway station, then right via underpass, continuing through Rancate, Besázio, and Arzo to site.
19 May-Sep
1.4HEC ～ ● ⋔H ⛺ ♀ ✕ ⊖ ⊕ G
P + lau ☞ ⛵L

MEZZOVICO
Ticino
Palazzina ✆(091) 951467
On Bellinzona-Lugano road 100m after restaurant.
Apr-Oct
2HEC ～ ◑ ⋔H ♀ ✕ ⊖ ⊕ G ⌂ P
+ lau ☞ ⛺ ⛵R

MOLINAZZO DI MONTÉGGIO
Ticino
Tresiana ✆(091) 732342
Meadowland with trees on riverbank.
Turn right after bridge in Ponte Tresa, then 5km to site.
May-20 Oct
1.5HEC ～ ◑ ⋔H ⛺ ⊖ ⊕ G ⌂ H
⛵P P + lau ☞ ♀ ✕
Prices A6 V2 ⊕8-10 ▲4-10

MUZZANO
Ticino
Piodella (TCS) ✆(091) 547788
7 Apr-Oct
3.2HEC ～ S ○ ◑ ⋔H ⛺ ♀ ✕ ⊖ ⊕
G R ⛵L P + lau

ROVEREDO
Ticino
Vera ✆(092) 821857
10km N of Bellinzona.
May-Oct
1.6HEC ～ ◑ ⋔H ♀ ✕ ⊖ ⊕ G ⛵PR
P + lau ☞ ⛺
Prices A4-8 V3 ⊕6-12 ▲6-10

TENERO
Ticino
Campofelice ✆(093) 671417
Beautifully situated and extensive site completely divided into pitches, and crossed by asphalt drives.
1.9km S. Signposted.
20 Mar-25 Oct
15HEC ～ ○ ⋔H ⛺ ♀ ✕ ⊖ ⊕ G
R ⌂ H ⛵LR P + ⚕ lau ☞ ⛵P
Prices pitch31-46 (incl 3 persons)

Lago Maggiore ✆(093) 671848
Extensive site by the lake, well laid out and completley sub-divided.
Signposted.
11 Apr-17 Oct
3.2HEC ～ ◑ ● ⋔H ⛺ ✕ ⊖ ⊕ G
H ⛵L P + ⚕ lau

Lido Mappo ✆(093) 671437
Beautifully situated, well appointed site on lakeside. Teenagers not accepted on their own. Minimum stay, 1 week in Jul-Aug.
700m SW. Signposted.
15 Mar-20 Oct
6.5HEC ∿ ● H ⊖ R LP P + lau
Prices pitch24-30 (incl 2 persons)

Miralago ✆(093) 671255
Situated in pleasant position by the lake. Caravans only.
Access 1km S from via Gottardo to via Mappo and via Ronaccio.
All year
2HEC ∿ ◑ ● H ⊖ G H P + lau ☞ ✕ LP

Rivabella ✆(093) 672213
Beautiful lakeside site.
1km S of village. Signposted.
All year
1HEC ∿ ◑ H ✕ ⊖ G R H P P + lau

Tamaro ✆(093) 672161
Partly on sandy shore.
Signposted.
18 Mar-22 Oct
6HEC ∿ ◑ H ✕ ⊖ G R H L P + lau

Verbano ✆(093) 671020
Site in two sections, of which one is on the lakeside. The larger section has access to the lake about 150m distance.
Signposted.
Apr-Oct
2.6HEC ∿ ◑ H ⊖ H LR + lau ☞ ✕
Prices A5-6 V3-5 2 A2

VIRA GAMBAROGNO
Ticino
Vira Bellavista (TCS) ✆(093) 611477
2km W on lake.
19 May-23 Sep
0.3HEC ∿ S ○ H ⊖ L P + lau ☞ ✕

SOUTH WEST

Vaud, Fribourg, Valais and Geneva are the cantons in this south-west region. All these provinces have resorts at every altitude to welcome both summer and winter visitors – the mountains and glaciers are easily accessed in winter for skiers, and in summer mountain huts, chalets, and hotels provide facilities for walkers and hikers.
Valais has been a trading crossroads since Roman times, with its passes at St Bernard and Simplon. The Rhône, with its tributaries, cuts a lovely swathe through Valais on its way to the jewel of the south west – Lake Geneva. Resorts dot the lake shores – small towns like Crans, Nyon and Vevey, popular Montreux, cosmopolitan lausanne, and, of course, the country's capital and great international centre, Geneva.
Art, culture and education are great traditions here, and there is a wealth of attractions for tourists – excellent shopping centres, renowned restaurants, an attractive old town, fascinating museums, and miles of attractive promenades along the shores of the lake with wonderful views of the mountains.

AGARN
Valais
Gemmi ✆(4127) 631154
Signposted
Apr-20 Oct
1HEC ∿ ◑ H ✕ ⊖ G R H P lau ☞ P +
Prices A5 7-9 A4-8

AIGLE
Vaud
Glariers (TCS) ✆(025) 262660
Near railway line and the avenue des Glariers.
800m NE off the N9 near SHELL/ MIGROL petrol station.
15 Apr-Sep
1HEC S ○ H ⊖ G R P lau ☞ ✕ P

AVENCHES
Vaud
Plage ✆(037) 751750
Apr-Sep
8HEC S ◑ H ✕ ⊖ G L P + lau

BALLENS
Vaud
Bois Gentil ✆(021) 8095120
200m S of station.
Apr-Oct
3HEC ∿ ◑ H ⊖ G R P P + lau
Prices A5 V2 3 A3

BOUVERET, LE
Valais
Rive Bleue ✆(025) 812161
Beside lake.
Turn off the N37 to Monthey in the SW district of Bouveret and drive NE for about 0.8km.
Apr-Sep
3HEC ∿ ◑ H ✕ ⊖ G R H P + lau ☞ LP

BRAMOIS
Valais
Valcentre ✆(027) 311642
1km NE of Bramois to the right of the road towards Gröne.
All year
1HEC ∿ ◑ H ✕ ⊖ G H P P + lau
Prices A4 V4 4 A4

BRIG (BRIGUE)
Valais
Geschina (TCS) ✆(028) 232698
1km S of town on the banks of the River Saltina.
May-14 Oct
1.8HEC ∿ ◑ ● H ✕ ⊖ G R P + lau ☞ P

BULLET
Vaud
Cluds ✆(024) 611440
In beautiful mountain setting.
1.5km NE.
All year
1.2HEC ∿ ◑ H ✕ ⊖ G R P + lau ☞
Prices A4 V2 4-6 A3-4

CHAMPEX
Valais
Rocailles ✆(026) 831216
All year
10HEC ∿ ○ H ⊖ G P + lau ☞ ✕ LP
Prices A5 V2 8 A6-8

CHÂTEAU-D'OEX
Vaud
Berceau (TCS) ✆(029) 46234
On level strip of grass between the mountain and the river bank.
1km SE at junction of roads 77 and 76.
May-Sep
1HEC ∿ ◑ H ✕ ⊖ G R P P + lau

CORCELETTES
Vaud
Belle Rive ✆(024) 243800
SW of Neuchâtel and 500m SE of town.
Apr-Sep

3HEC ◑ H G L P + lau
Prices A4 V2 3 A3

Pins ✆(024) 244740
In a quiet lakeside setting interspersed with trees.
1km E.
3 Apr-27 Sep
2.5HEC ◑ H ⊖ G L
P + lau

CULLY
Vaud
Moratel ✆(021) 7991914
On main Lausanne-Vevey road E of Cully.
Mar-Sep
3HEC ◑ H ⊖ G P +
lau L
Prices A5 pitch6

ENNEY
Fribourg
Haute Gruyère (TCS) ✆(029) 62260
8km S of Bulle on road 77
All year
1.5HEC ◑ H ⊖ G
R P + lau

EPAGNY-GRUYÈRES
Fribourg
Sapins ✆(029) 29575
1km N on the edge of a forest.
30 May-Sep
1.6HEC ◑ H ⊖ G
R P + lau LPR
Prices A5 V2 5 A4-5

ESTAVAYER-LE-LAC
Fribourg
Nouvelle-Plage (TCS) ✆(037) 631693
Situated beside the lake.
7 Apr-Sep
1.5HEC S ◑ H ⊖
G R L P + lau

EVOLÈNE
Valais
Evolène ✆(027) 831144
200m from town
All year
8HEC ○ H ⊖ G P + lau
R
Prices A4 V2 3 A2

FOULY, LA
Valais
Glaciers ✆(026) 832498
At end of village.
Jun-Sep

5HEC ◑ H ⊖ G R P +
lau
Prices A5 pitch6-9

GAMPEL
Valais
Rhône ✆(028) 422041
By the railway station towards the bridge over the Rhône.
31 Mar-Oct
3.3HEC ◑ H ⊖ G
H P P + lau

GENÈVE (GENEVA)
Genève
At **VÉSENAZ** (6km NE)
Pointe á la Bise (TCS) ✆(022) 521296
Small pool for children. On shores of lake.
NE between Vésenaz and Bellerive.
7 Apr-Sep
3.2HEC ○ H ⊖ G
R L P + lau

GRANDSON
Vaud
Pécos ✆(024) 244969
400m SW of railway station between railway and lake.
All year
2HEC ○ H ⊖ G R
L P + lau P
Prices A5 V2 4-6 A3-4

GUMEFENS
Fribourg
Lac ✆(029) 52162
On the borders of the lake.
15 May-15 Sep
1.6HEC ◑ H ⊖ L
P lau G P
Prices A6 V2 8 A6

HAUDÈRES, LES
Valais
Molignon ✆(027) 831296
Terraced site beside the river in a beautiful setting.
All year
1.2HEC ◑ H ⊖ G
H P lau

LAUSANNE
Vaud
At **OUCHY**
Vidy ✆(021) 242031
All year
4.5HEC ◑ H ⊖ G
R H L P + lau P
Prices A7 8-10 A4-8

LEUK
See **SUSTEN**

LEUKERBAD
Valais
Leukerbad ✆(027) 612062
On road N of Leuk.
May-Oct
1.6HEC ○ H ⊖ G R
P + lau

LEYSIN
Vaud
Semiramis ✆(025) 341148
After entering the village turn left at SHELL filling station and continue for 400m.
All year
1.7HEC ◑ H ⊖ G
R H P + lau P
Prices A5-6 V5-6 5-6 A3

MARÉCOTTES, LES
Valais
Médettaz (TCS) ✆(026) 61830
10km NW of Martigny.
All year
0.6HEC ○ ◑ H ⊖ G
R P + P

MARTIGNY
Valais
Neuvilles (TCS) ✆(026) 24544
All year
1.2HEC ◑ H ⊖ G
R P + lau P

MISSION
Valais
Pont de Mission ✆(027) 651391
In a meadow partly divided into pitches.
15 Jun-20 Aug
0.7HEC ○ H ⊖ R P
P

MORGES
Vaud
Petit Bois (TCS) ✆(021) 8011270
Follow Geneva road from town. Site by lakeside.
Apr-Sep
3.2HEC ○ H ⊖ G
H P + lau LP

MORGINS
Valais
Morgins (TCS) ✆(025) 772361
A terraced site below pine forest.
Turn left at end of village towards Pas de Morgins near Swiss Customs. ➔

All year
1.3HEC ○ fH ⊖ P + lau ☞ [G] [R] PR

NAX
Valais
Grand-Paradis (027) 311730
Apr-Oct
2HEC ◑ fH ⊖ [G] P + lau
Prices A4 V1 6 4

Grand Paradis (027) 311730
6 May-Oct
3HEC ◑ fH ⊖ [G] [R] P P + lau
Prices A4 6 4

NYON
Vaud
Colline (TCS) (022) 612630
Terraced site in a beautiful setting between the shore road and lakeside.
1.4km S.
Etr-Sep
1HEC ○ fH ⊖ [G] [R] L P + lau ☞ PR

ORBE
Vaud
Signal (TCS) (024) 413857
800m from Orbe, off the road towards Yverdon.
12 Apr-Sep
2HEC ◑ ● fH ⊖ [G] [R] + lau ☞ P

OUCHY
See **LAUSANNE**

PACCOTS, LES
Fribourg
Bivouac (TCS) (021) 9487849
Turn E in Châtel-St Denis and continue for 2km.
15 Apr-15 Sep
2HEC ◑ fH ⊖ [G] [R] P + lau

PAYERNE
Vaud
Piscine de Payerne (037) 614322
Apr-Sep
2HEC ◑ fH ⊖ [G] [R] P + lau ☞
Prices A4 V2 3-4 2-3

RARON
Valais
Santa Monica (028) 442424
All year
4HEC ◑ fH ⊖ [G] PR lau ☞
Prices A5 pitch8

Simplonblick (028) 441274
300m W of Turtig.
All year
6HEC ◑ fH ⊖ [G] [R] PR ☞ +
Prices A5 pitch8

RECKINGEN
Valais
Ellbogen (TCS) (028) 731355
400m S on bank of Rhône.
13 May-13 Oct
1.3HEC ○ fH ⊖ [G] [R] + lau ☞ P

RIED-BRIG
Valais
Tropic (028) 232537
To the left of Simplon road near entrance to village. 3km above Brig.
Apr-Nov
0.5HEC ◑ fH ⊖ [G] [R] [H] + lau
Prices A4 V3 4-5 3-4

RÖCHE
Vaud
Clos de la George (TCS) Les Ecots (025) 265828
4.5km from Aigle.
All year
2.6HEC ◑ fH ⊖ [G] [R] P + lau

ROLLE
Vaud
Vernes (TCS) (021) 8251239
Off the Chemin de la Plage and on the outskirts of the village towards Lausanne, between shore road and the lake.
1km NE.
7 Apr-2 Oct
1.5HEC ○ fH ⊖ [G] [R] L + lau

SAAS-GRUND
Valais
Kapellenweg (028) 572989
Turn right over bridge towards Saas-Almagell.
All year
2HEC fH ⊖ [G] [R] [H] lau ☞ P

Schönblick (028) 572267
Lies next to the Schönblick Restaurant.
2km from village, off road towards Saas-Almagell.
All year
0.5HEC ○ fH ⊖ [G] [R] + lau ☞ PR
Prices A3 V5-6 5-6

ST CERGUE
Vaud
Cheseaux (022) 601267
1km W.
All year
0.6HEC ○ fH ⊖ [R] ☞

ST MAURICE
Valais
Bois Noir (TCS) (026) 671176
From Martigny, turn right at Bois Noir Motel, then turn left uphill. Take next turning on right after underpass and continue for 200m.
12 Apr-Sep
3HEC ◑ fH ⊖ [G] + lau ☞ PR

SALAVAUX
Vaud
Chablais (TCS) (037) 771476
Beautifully situated in a deciduous wood.
800m SE near Lake.
Apr-Oct
6HEC ○ fH ⊖ [G] [R] L + lau

SALGESCH
Valais
Swiss Plage (027) 556608
Etr-Oct
10HEC ◑ fH ⊖ [G] LR
Prices A5 pitch10

SEMBRANCHER
Valais
Moulin d'Allèves (026) 85254
12km from Martigny at first Alpine road tunnel on road to Grand-St-Bernard.
All year
10HEC ◑ fH ⊖ [G] [H] lau ☞ P

Prairie (TCS) (026) 852206
12km from Martigny and 500m from town.
All year
12HEC ○ fH ⊖ [G] lau
Prices A3-4 V5-6 8-9 5-6

SENTIER, LE
Vaud
Rocheray (021) 8455174
All year
2.8HEC ○ fH ⊖ [G] L lau ☞ +
Prices A5 7 3-7

SIERRE (SIDERS)
Valais
Bois de Finges (TCS) (027) 550284
Very beautiful site.
Access difficult for caravans.
Apr-Sep
2HEC ● fH ⊖ [G] P + lau ☞

SION (SITTEN)
Valais
Iles (TCS) (027) 364347
Site with leisure centre.
4km SW of Sion on the road to Aproz.
All year
5HEC ○ fH ⊖ [G] [R] P lau ☞ L
Prices A4-5 pitch8-12

Sedunum (027) 364268
On right of road just before bridge over the River Rhône. Turn S off Simplon road W of Pont de la Margue and follow

signposts to Aproz.
15 Apr-15 Oct

SITTEN
See **SION**

SORENS
Fribourg
Forêt (029) 51882
Turn right off the N12 in Gumefens and drive on to the village.
All year
4HEC G R P +

SUSTEN
Valais
Bella Tola (TCS) (027) 631491
In a quiet position. Easy access for caravans.
2km from village.
17 May-29 Sep
3.6HEC G R P + lau

At **LEUK**
Monument (027) 631827
Large site divided into small individual pitches. Set in forest, protected from traffic noise.
15 May-15 Sep
5.5HEC G P lau

ULRICHEN
Valais
Nufenen (028) 731437
1km SE to right of road to Nufenen Pass.
Jun-Sep
8HEC G +
lau PR
Prices A3 V1 2 2

VALLORBE
Vaud
Pré sous Ville (TCS) (021) 843309
On left bank of River Orbe.
May-Sep
0.5HEC G R P
+ lau R

VERS-l'ÉGLISE
Vaud
Murée (TCS) (021) 299604 & 8011908
All year
1.1HEC G R P
+ lau

VÉSENAZ
See **GENÈVE (GENEVA)**

VETROZ
Valais
Botza (TCS) (027) 361940
All year
3HEC G R
H P + lau
Prices A5-6 pitch8-12

VEX
Valais
Val d'Hérens (027) 271985
Near main road, about 500m from village.
All year
1HEC G R P
+ lau
Prices A4 V1 3 1-3

VILLENEUVE
Vaud
Horizons Bleus (021) 5601547
Near the noisy shore road and 800m from the Lake.
From Montreux SW on road 9.
Apr-Sep
0.6HEC
L

VISSOIE
Valais
Anniviers (027) 651409
9km S of Sion road to Ayer.
All year
5HEC G R
H P + lau P
Prices A5 pitch7

YVERDON-LES-BAINS
Vaud
Iris (024) 211089
Apr-Sep
25HEC G
R P + lau LP
Prices A4 V2 5 3

YVONAND
Vaud
Pointe d'Yvonand (024) 311655
6km NE of Yverdon bordering Lake Neuchâtel with private beach 1km away, boat moorings, private jetty and boat hire.
3km W of Yvonand. Signposted.
Apr-Sep
5HEC G R
L P + lau
Prices A4 V2 4-6 3-4

AUSTRIA

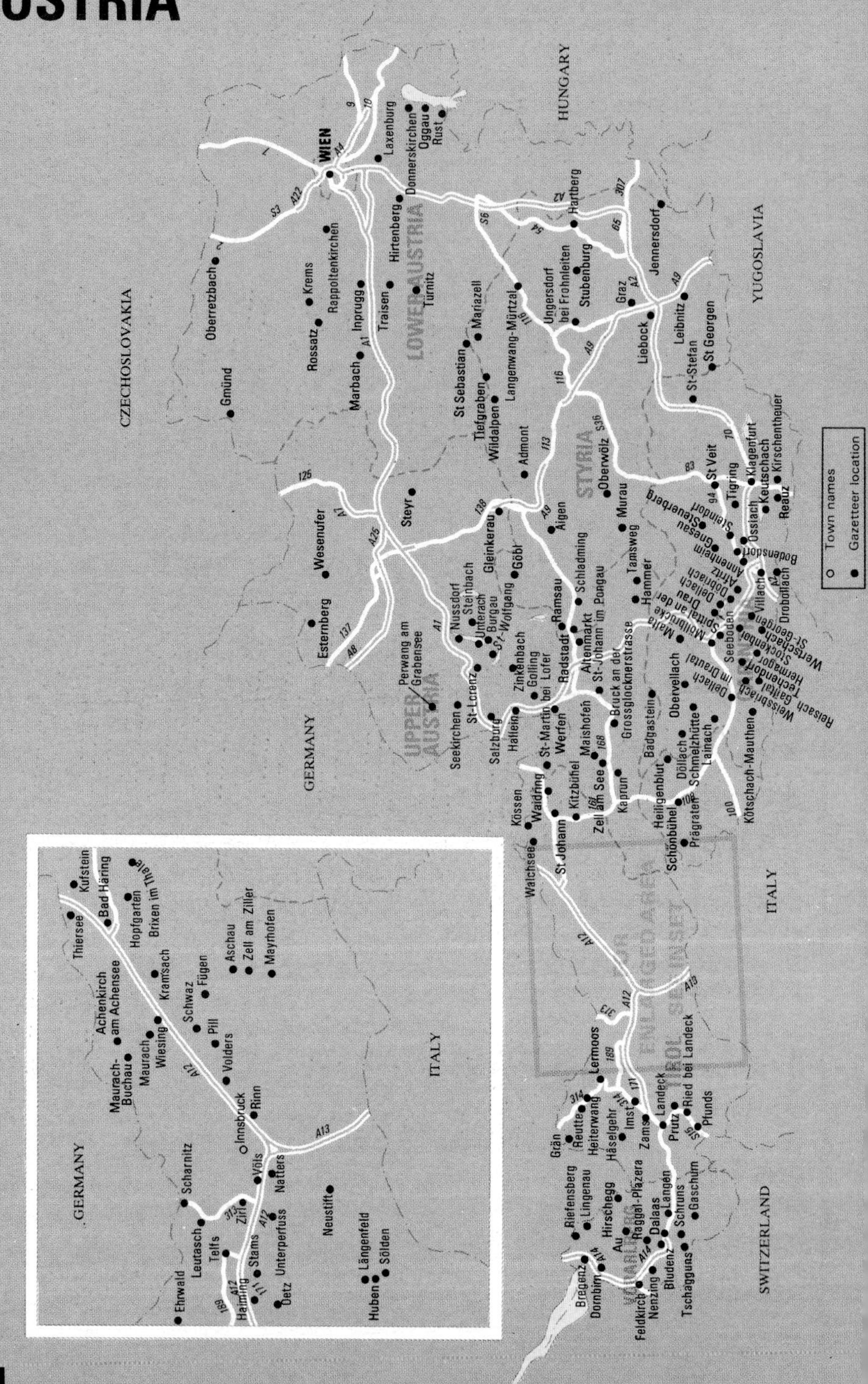
CZECHOSLOVAKIA
GERMANY
HUNGARY
YUGOSLAVIA
ITALY
SWITZERLAND
LOWER AUSTRIA
UPPER AUSTRIA
STYRIA
WIEN
Laxenburg
Donnerskirchen
Oggau
Rust
Hirtenberg
Rappoltenkirchen
Oberretzbach
Gmünd
Krems
Rossatz
Marbach
Inprugg
Traisen
Türnitz
Mariazell
St Sebastian
Tiefgraben
Wildalpen
Langenwang-Mürztal
Ungersdorf bei Frohnleiten
Stubenburg
Hartberg
Jennersdorf
Graz
Leibnitz
St Georgen
Liebock
St-Stefan
Admont
Steyr
Wesenufer
Esternberg
Perwang am Grabensee
Nussdorf
Steinbach
Unterach
Burgau
St-Wolfgang
Gleinkerau
Göbl
Aigen
Oberwölz
Murau
Tamsweg
Schladming
Ramsau
Radstadt
Altenmarkt
St-Johann im Pongau
Hammer
Zinkenbach
Golling
St-Martin bei Lofer
Seekirchen
St-Lorenz
Salzburg
Hallein
Werfen
Maishofen
Bruck an der Grossglocknerstrasse
Badgastein
Obervellach
Malta
Möllbrücke
Spittal an der Drau
Seeboden
Dellach
Döbriach
Afritz
Annenheim
Gnesau
Steuerberg
Steindorf
Ossiach
Bodensdorf
Villach
Drobollach
St Veit
Klagenfurt
Tigring
Keutschach
Kirschentheuer
Reauz
Wertschach
St-Georgen
Stockenboi
Hermagor
Techendorf
Weissbriach
Reisach Gailtal
Dellach im Drautal
Kötschach-Mauthen
Lainach
Schmelzhütte
Döllach
Heiligenblut
Kaprun
Zell am See
Kitzbühel
Waidring
Kössen
St Johann
Walchsee
Schönbühel
Prägraten
FOR ENLARGED AREA TIROL SEE INSET
Lermoos
Landeck
Ried bei Landeck
Pfunds
Prutz
Zams
Imst
Häselgehr
Heiterwang
Reutte
Grän
Riefensberg
Lingenau
Hirschegg
Au
Bregenz
Dornbirn
Feldkirch
Nenzing
Bludenz
Dalaas
Langen
Raggal-Plazera
Schruns
Gaschurn
Tschagguns
Town names
Gazetteer location
GERMANY
ITALY
Kufstein
Bad Häring
Thiersee
Hopfgarten
Brixen im Thale
Achenkirch am Achensee
Kramsach
Schwaz
Fügen
Aschau
Zell am Ziller
Mayrhofen
Maurach-Buchau
Maurach
Wiesing
Pill
Volders
Innsbruck
Rinn
Scharnitz
Völs
Natters
Zirl
Unterperfuss
Leutasch
Telfs
Stams
Neustift
Längenfeld
Sölden
Huben
Ehrwald
Haiming
Oetz

1

ELGIUM

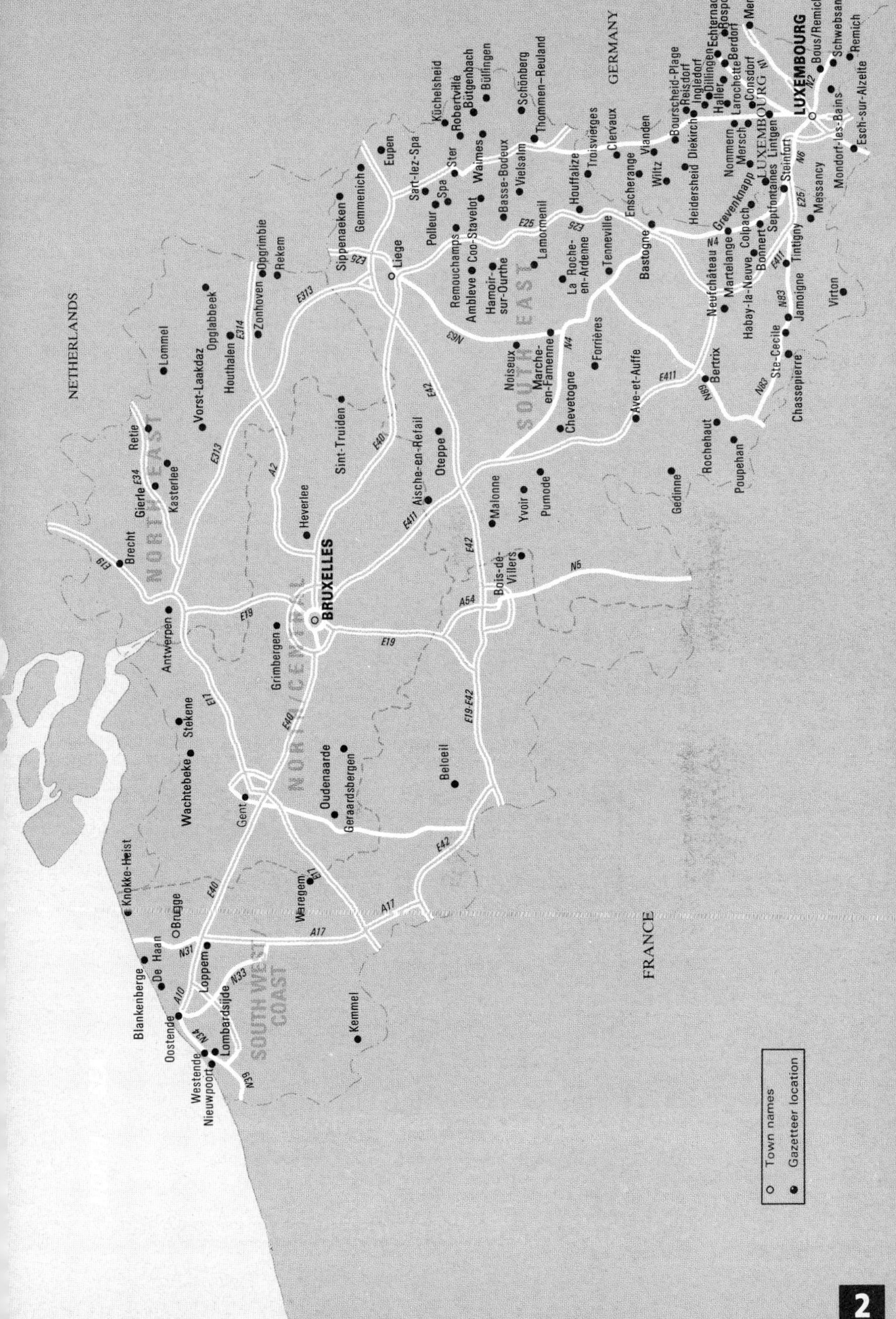

NETHERLANDS

GERMANY

FRANCE

LUXEMBOURG

NORTH EAST

NORTH/CENTRAL

SOUTH EAST

SOUTH WEST COAST

Knokke-Heist
Brugge
Blankenberge
De Haan
Oostende
Westende
Nieuwpoort
Lombardsijde
Loppem
Kemmel
Waregem
Gent
Wachtebeke
Stekene
Antwerpen
Oudenaarde
Geraardsbergen
Beloeil
Grimbergen
BRUXELLES
Heverlee
Brecht
Gierle
Kasterlee
Retie
Vorst-Laakdaz
Lommel
Houthalen
Opglabbeek
Zonhoven
Opgrimbie
Rekem
Sint-Truiden
Aische-en-Refail
Oteppe
Malonne
Bois-de-Villers
Yvoir
Pumode
Gedinne
Sippenaeken
Gemmenich
Eupen
Liege
Sart-lez-Spa
Polleur
Spa
Ster
Küchelsheid
Robertville
Bütgenbach
Büllingen
Waimes
Remouchamps
Coo-Stavelot
Amblève
Hamoir-sur-Ourthe
Basse-Bodeux
Vielsalm
Schönberg
Thommen-Reuland
Lamormenil
La Roche-en-Ardenne
Houffalize
Troisvierges
Tenneville
Noiseux
Marche-en-Famenne
Forrières
Chevetogne
Ave-et-Auffe
Bastogne
Enscherange
Clervaux
Wiltz
Vianden
Bourscheid-Plage
Heidersheid
Diekirch
Reisdorf
Ingledorf
Dillingen
Echternach
Bosport
Haller
Berdorf
Larochette
Consdorf
Nommern
Mersch
Lintgen
Mertert
Neufchâteau
Martelange
Grevenknapp
Colpach
Bonnert
Septfontaines
Steinfort
Habay-la-Neuve
Bertrix
Rochehaut
Poupehan
Ste-Cecile
Chassepierre
Jamoigne
Tintigny
Virton
Messancy
Mondorf-les-Bains
Esch-sur-Alzette
LUXEMBOURG
Bous/Remich
Schwebsange
Remich

E19 E34 E313 E314 A2 E40 E411 E42 E25 N63 N4 N5 A54 E19-E42 E17 A17 N31 A10 N33 N34 N39 N89 N83 N6 N1 N2

○ Town names
● Gazetteer location

FRANCE

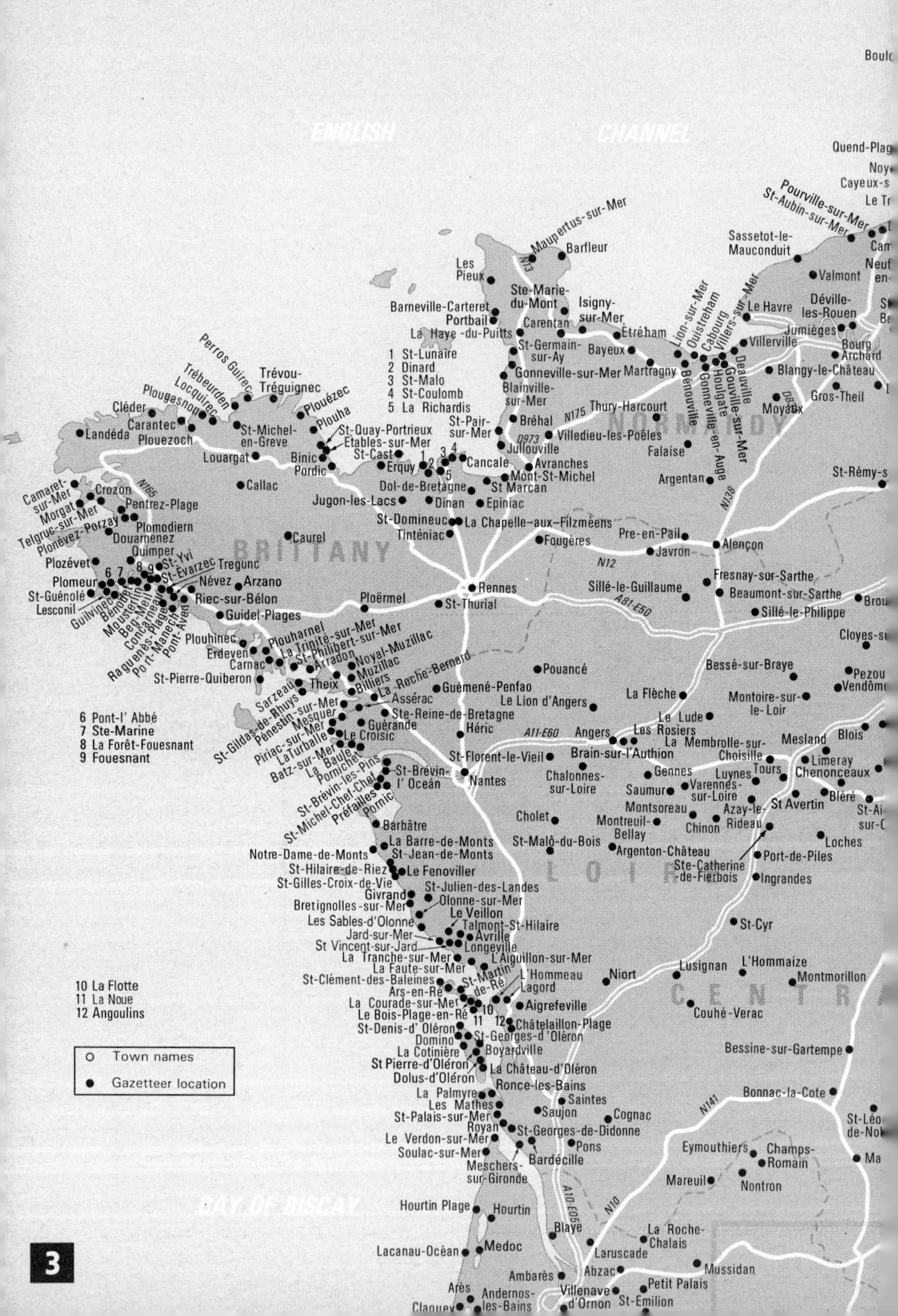

ENGLISH CHANNEL

Quend-Plag
Noy
Cayeux-s
Le Tr
Pourville-sur-Mer
St-Aubin-sur-Mer
Sassetot-le-Mauconduit
Valmont
Déville-les-Rouen
Le Havre
Jumièges
Villerville
Bourg Archard
Blangy-le-Château
Gros-Theil
Moyaux
Deauville
Villers-sur-Mer
Gouville-sur-Mer
Houlgate
Cabourg
Gonneville-en-Auge
Ouistreham
Lion-sur-Mer
Bénouville
Maupertus-sur-Mer
Barfleur
Les Pieux
Ste-Marie-du-Mont
Barneville-Carteret
Portbail
Carentan
Isigny-sur-Mer
Étréham
La Haye-du-Puitts
St-Germain-sur-Ay
Bayeux
Martragny
Gonneville-sur-Mer
Blainville-sur-Mer
Thury-Harcourt
Bréhal
St-Pair-sur-Mer
Villedieu-les-Poêles
Jullouville
Falaise
Argentan
NORMANDY
Avranches
Mont-St-Michel
St Marcan
Cancale
St-Rémy-s

1 St-Lunaire
2 Dinard
3 St-Malo
4 St-Coulomb
5 La Richardis

Perros Guirec
Trébeurden
Trévou-Tréguignec
Locquirec
Plougasnou
Plouézec
Cléder
Carantec
Plouha
Landéda
Plouezoch
St-Michel-en-Greve
St-Quay-Portrieux
Etables-sur-Mer
Binic
Pordic
St-Cast
Erquy
Louargat
Callac
Camaret-sur-Mer
Crozon
Morgat
Telgruc-sur-Mer
Pentrez-Plage
Plonévez-Porzay
Plomodiern
Douarnenez
Dol-de-Bretagne
Jugon-les-Lacs
Dinan
Epiniac
St-Domineuc
La Chapelle-aux-Filzmeens
Tinténiac
Caurel
BRITTANY
Fougères
Pre-en-Pail
Alençon
Javron
N12
Fresnay-sur-Sarthe
Sillé-le-Guillaume
Beaumont-sur-Sarthe
Brou
Sillé-le-Philippe
Quimper
Plozévet
St-Yvi
Tregunc
St-Évarzec
Plomeur
Névez
Arzano
St-Guénolé
Lesconil
Guilvinec
Bénodet
Mousterlin
Beg-Meil
Concarneau
Raguenès-Plage
Port-Manech
Pont-Aven
Riec-sur-Bélon
Guidel-Plages
Rennes
Ploërmel
St-Thurial
A81-E50
Cloyes-s
Plouhinec
Plouharnel
La Trinité-sur-Mer
St-Philibert-sur-Mer
Noyal-Muzillac
Erdeven
Carnac
Arradon
Muzillac
St-Pierre-Quiberon
Sarzeau
Theix
Billiers
La Roche-Bernard
Guémené-Penfao
Pouancé
Bessé-sur-Braye
Pezou
Vendôme
St-Gildas-de-Rhuys
Pénestin-sur-Mer
Mesquer
Assérac
Ste-Reine-de-Bretagne
Le Lion d'Angers
La Flèche
Montoire-sur-le-Loir
Piriac-sur-Mer
La Turballe
Guérande
Le Croisic
Héric
Le Lude
Les Rosiers
Angers
A11-E60
La Membrolle-sur-Choisille
Mesland
Blois
Batz-sur-Mer
La Baule
Pornichet
St-Brévin-les-Pins
St-Brévin-l'Océan
St-Florent-le-Vieil
Brain-sur-l'Authion
Limeray
Nantes
Chalonnes-sur-Loire
Gennes
Luynes
Tours
Chenonceaux
Saumur
Varennes-sur-Loire
Bléré
St-Michel-Chef-Chef
Préfailles
Pomic
Montsoreau
Azay-le-Rideau
St Avertin
St-Ai
sur-C
Cholet
Montreuil-Bellay
Chinon
Barbâtre
La Barre-de-Monts
Notre-Dame-de-Monts
St-Jean-de-Monts
St-Malô-du-Bois
Argenton-Château
Loches
Port-de-Piles
St-Hilaire-de-Riez
Le Fenoviller
St-Gilles-Croix-de-Vie
Ste-Catherine-de-Fierbois
Ingrandes
LOIR
St-Julien-des-Landes
Givrand
Bretignolles-sur-Mer
Olonne-sur-Mer
Les Sables-d'Olonne
Le Veillon
Talmont-St-Hilaire
Jard-sur-Mer
Avrille
St Vincent-sur-Jard
Longeville
St-Cyr
La Tranche-sur-Mer
L'Aiguillon-sur-Mer
La Faute-sur-Mer
St-Clément-des-Baleines
St-Martin-de-Ré
L'Hommeau
Lagord
Niort
Lusignan
L'Hommaize
Montmorillon
Ars-en-Ré
Aigrefeville
CENTR
La Courade-sur-Mer
Le Bois-Plage-en-Ré
10
11
12
Châtelaillon-Plage
Couhé-Verac

10 La Flotte
11 La Noue
12 Angoulins

St-Denis-d'Oléron
St-Georges-d'Oléron
Domino
La Cotinière
Boyardville
Bessine-sur-Gartempe
St Pierre-d'Oléron
La Château-d'Oléron
Dolus-d'Oléron
Ronce-les-Bains
La Palmyre
Saintes
Bonnac-la-Cote
Les Mathes
Saujon
Cognac
St-Palais-sur-Mer
N141
St-Léo
de-No
Royan
St-Georges-de-Didonne
Le Verdon-sur-Mer
Pons
Soulac-sur-Mer
Bardécille
Eymouthiers
Champs-Romain
Meschers-sur-Gironde
Ma
Mareuil
Nontron
BAY OF BISCAY
Hourtin Plage
Hourtin
A10-E05
N10
Blaye
La Roche-Chalais
Lacanau-Océan
Medoc
Laruscade
Mussidan
Ambarès
Abzac
Petit Palais
Arès
Andernos-les-Bains
Villenave-d'Ornon
St-Emilion
Claouey

6 Pont-l'Abbé
7 Ste-Marine
8 La Forêt-Fouesnant
9 Fouesnant

○ Town names
● Gazetteer location

Calais
Bray-Dunes
Dunkerque
Hondschoote
N1
Ardres
Serques
St-Omer
Thiembronne
A25
A22
Nielles-les-Bléquin
BELGIUM
A1
E17
La Neuville
St-Amand-les-Eaux
St-Georges
Frévent
A2
Tollent
sur-Somme
Brunémont
E19
Potelle
A26
Bertangles
GERMANY
E17
A26
Guise
N43
Montherme
A26
E17
Charleville-Mezières
LUXEMBOURG
PARIS/NORTH
Orvillers-Sorel
A203
Laon
Beauvais
N1
Berny-Rivière
N43
Thionville
Villers-Helon
Grandpré
St Leu-d'Esserent
Reims
A32
E50
A4
A4-E50
Verdun
A4
Varreddes
Ste Menehould
Metz
E25
Hanau-Plage
Épernay
A4-E50
Baerenthal
Torcy
ALSACE/LORRAINE
Oberbronn
PARIS
N44
Phalsbourg
La Ferté-Gaucher
Sézanne
A31
E21
Mandres Aux
Quatre Tours
Nancy
Henridorff
Saverne
N4
Villers-les-Nancy
Wasselonne
Eclaron-Braucourt
Melun
Romilly-sur-Seine
N67
Molsheim
Samois-sur-Seine
N19
Chatonrupt
Tonnoy
Schirmeck
Obernai
A31
E21
Le Hohwald
Bernardswiller
Grez-sur-Loing
N59
Rhinau
Mesnil-St-Père
Nemours
Corcieux
Kayserberg
Bruyères
Sélestat
Bar-sur-Aube
A35
Granges-sur-Vologne
Riquewihr
Nibelle
BURGUNDY
Le Tholy
Turckheim
Wihr-au-Val
Gérardmer
Colmar
Montargis
N19
Xonrupt-Longemer
Eguisheim
Ruaux
La Bresse
Luttenbach
Munster
Metzeral
Châtillon-s-Seine
Sully-sur-Loire
Auxerre
St-Maurice-sur-Moselle
Ranspach-sur-Wesserling
Urbès
A31
Moosch
Gien
Cernay
Gien
A36
Heimsbrunn
Bonny-sur-Loire
Vermenton
N19
Port-sur-Saône
Montbard
CHAMPAGNE
Avallon
D67
L' Isle-sur-le-Doubs
Rougemont
Cosne-sur-Loire
Gray
Darios
Saulieu
Dijon
Vandenesse-en-Auxois
Ornans
Pougues-les-Eaux
N7
Montsauche
Arnay-de-Duc
A36
Premeaux
Auxonne
A6
St-Péreuse
ALPS/EAST
Beaune
Dole
Nevers
Ounans
St-Honoré
Meursault
Seurre
Parcey
Mouchard
Chagny
Charnay-
lès-Chalon
Decize
Arbois
Tazilly
SWITZERLAND
St-Amand-Montrond
Torcy
Champagnole
Malbuisson
St Marcel
Bourbon-Lancy
Lons-le-Saunier
Marigny
Gigny-sur-Saône
Bourbon-l' Archambault
Patornay
Digoin
Uchizy
Clairvaux-les-Lacs
A6-E15
St
Charolles
Disdille
Évian-les-Bains
Paray-le-Monial
Montrevel-en-Bresse
St Claude
Lugrin
A40-E21
Varennes-sur-Allier
St Etienne-du-Bois
Thonon-les-Bains
Mâcon
Anthy
Bourg-en-Bresse
Sciez
Messery
A71
N9
Fleurie
Vichy
N7
Thoissey
Nantua
Ebreuil
Thizy
Bellegarde-sur-Valserine
St-Rémy-
Ars-sur-
Villars-
Châtelguyon
sur-Durolle
Formans
les-Dombes
Seyssel
Argentière
A72
E70
Annecy
Servoz
Chamonix-Mont-Blanc
St-Ours
La Balme-
les-Grottes
Dallet
E70
A72
Les Houches
Sallanches
Dardilly
St-Jorioz
Bout-du-
St-Gervais-les-Bains
Cournon-
Olliergues
Lac
Megève
Ceyrat
d'Auvergne
L'Arbresle
Lyon
Trept
Albens
N89
St-Innocent-Brison
Talloires
Doussard
Séez
Murol
St-Symphorien-
Aix-les-Bains
sur-Coise
Pollionnay
A43
Albertville
Bourg-st-Maurice
St-Pierre-Colamine
Bourget-du-Lac
Les Pradeaux
Les Abrets
Challes-Les-Eaux
Plagne-Montchavin
Condrieu
A47
Novalaise
Vernioz
St-Jean-de-Couz
Allevard
Tignes-
Anglards-de-
Salers
Voiron
les-Brévières
Monistrol-sur-Loire
St-Sorlin-
Rives
Entre-deux-Guiers
Massiac
en-Valloire
Renage
Miribel-
St-Pierre-
N9
AUVERGNE
Vorey
Albon
les-Echelles
de-Chartreuse
Murat
Langeac
Yssingeaux
St Paul-
Tain-l'Hermitage
les-Romans
Le Puy
Autrans
Le Bourg-d'Oisans
Tournon-sur-Rhône
Neuvèglise
ITALY
3

FRANCE

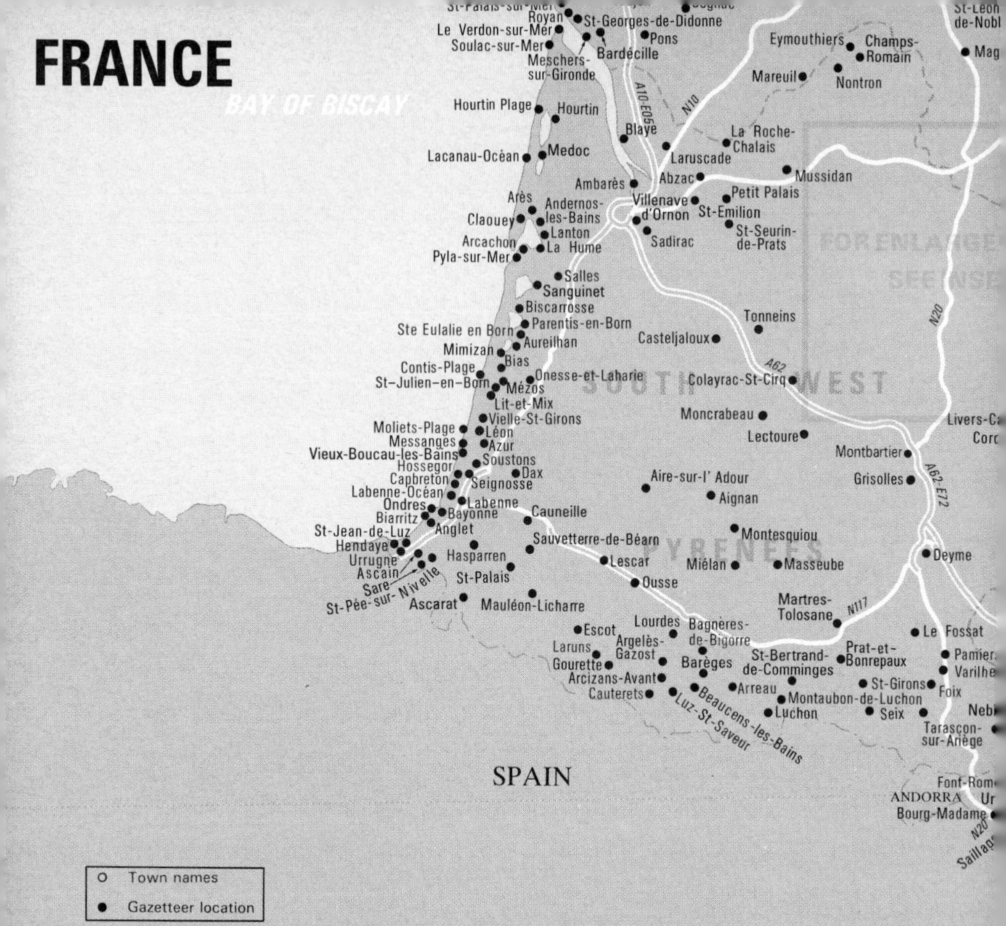

BAY OF BISCAY

St-Palais-sur-Mer
Royan
St-Georges-de-Didonne
Le Verdon-sur-Mer
Pons
Soulac-sur-Mer
Bardécille
Meschers-sur-Gironde
Eymoutiers
Champs-Romain
Mareuil
Nontron
St-Léon
de-Nobl
Mag
Hourtin Plage
Hourtin
A10-E05
N10
Blaye
La Roche-Chalais
Laruscade
Lacanau-Océan
Medoc
Ambarès
Abzac
Mussidan
Arès
Andernos-les-Bains
Villenave d'Ornon
Petit Palais
St-Emilion
Claouey
Lanton
Sadirac
St-Seurin-de-Prats
Arcachon
La Hume
Pyla-sur-Mer
Salles
Sanguinet
Biscarrosse
Tonneins
N20
Ste Eulalie en Born
Parentis-en-Born
Casteljaloux
Mimizan
Aureilhan
Bias
Contis-Plage
A62
Onesse-et-Laharie
St-Julien-en-Born
Mézos
Colayrac-St-Cirq
Lit-et-Mix
SOUTH WEST
Vielle-St-Girons
Moncrabeau
Moliets-Plage
Léon
Messanges
Azur
Lectoure
Livers-Ca
Corc
Vieux-Boucau-les-Bains
Soustons
Montbartier
Hossegor
Dax
Capbreton
Seignosse
Grisolles
A62-E72
Aire-sur-l' Adour
Labenne-Océan
Aignan
Ondres
Labenne
Biarritz
Bayonne
Cauneille
Anglet
Montesquiou
St-Jean-de-Luz
Sauvetterre-de-Béarn
PYRENEES
Hendaye
Hasparren
Deyme
Urrugne
Lescar
Miélan
Masseube
Ascain
Sare
St-Palais
Ousse
St-Pée-sur-Nivelle
Ascarat
Mauléon-Licharre
Martres-Tolosane
N117
Lourdes
Bagnères-de-Bigorre
Escot
Le Fossat
Laruns
Argelès-Gazost
Prat-et-Bonrepaux
Gourette
Barèges
St-Bertrand-de-Comminges
Pamier
Varilhe
Arcizans-Avant
Arreau
St-Girons
Foix
Cauterets
Montauban-de-Luchon
Beaucens-les-Bains
Luz-St-Saveur
Luchon
Seix
Nebi
Tarascon-sur-Ariège

SPAIN

Font-Rome
ANDORRA
Ur
Bourg-Madame
N20
Saillag

○	Town names
●	Gazetteer location

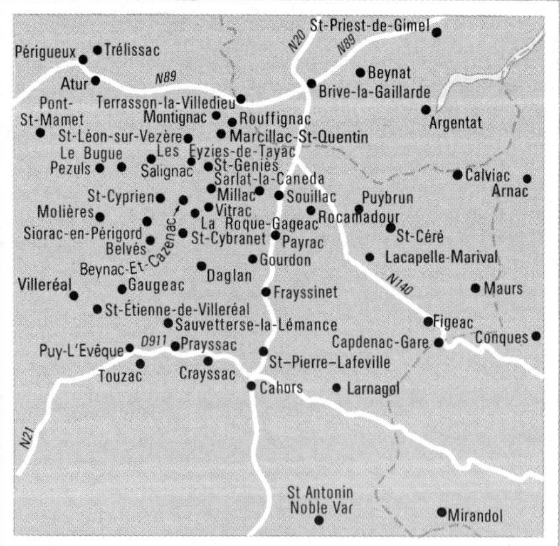

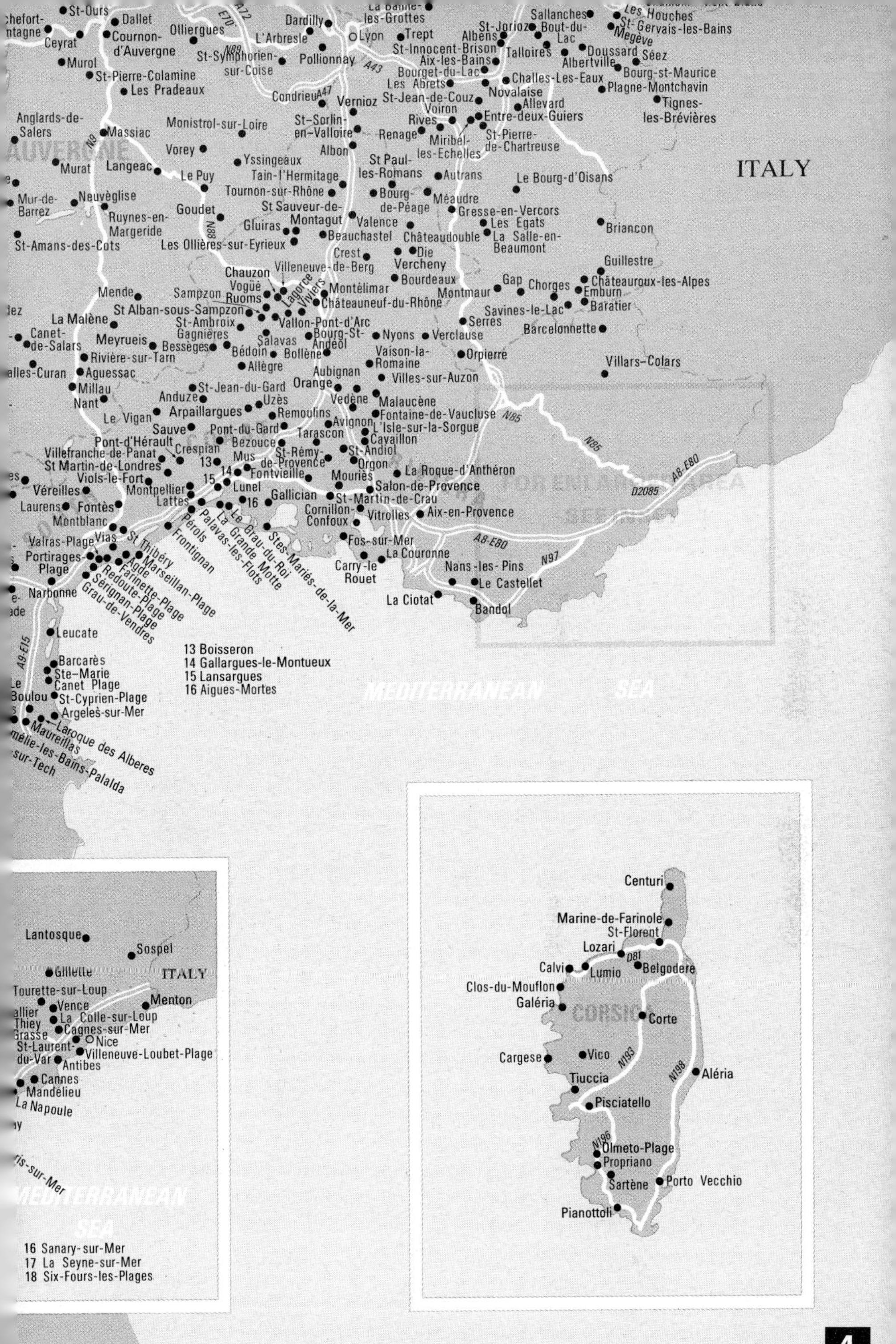

ITALY

13 Boisseron
14 Gallargues-le-Montueux
15 Lansargues
16 Aigues-Mortes

MEDITERRANEAN SEA

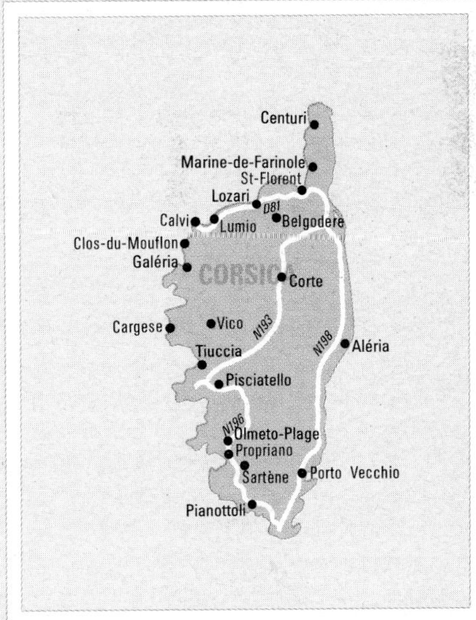

ITALY

SWITZERLAND
AUSTRIA
FRANCE
YUGOSLAVIA
Corsica
Sardinia
ADRIATIC SEA
MEDITERRANEAN SEA
San Sigmund
Merano
Naturno
San Lorenzen
Brunico
Dobbiaco-Toblach
Bolzano
Chiusa
Kaltern
Láives
Pera di Fassa
Peio
Dimaro
Cortina d'Ampezzo
Zoldo Alto
Canazei
Campitello di Fasso
Vols
Ora-Aver
Pozza di Fassa
Masarè
Arsie
Gemona del Friúli
Courmayeur
La Salle
Gignod
Maen
Arvier
Sarre
Buisson
Rhêmes-St-Georges
Lillaz
Monfalcone
Aurisina
Duino-Aurisina
Grado
Lignano Pineta
Bibione
Cáorle
Lido di Jesolo
Ca' Noghera
Venezia
Oriago
Fusina
Montegrotto Terme
Chioggia
Marghera
Punta Sabbioni
Treporti
Cavallino
Porto Santa Margherita
Asti
Salsomaggiore Terme
Parma
Bruciata
Rosolina Mare
Pomposa
Lido delle Nazioni
Lido degli Scacchi
Lido di Spina
Lido degli Estensi
Sasso Marconi
Marina di Ravenna
Casal Borsetti
Punta Marina
Sestola
Maserno di Montese
Lido di Dante
Lido del Sávio
Milano Marittima
Cérvia
Monte di Fo
Pinarella
Cesenático
Fiésole
Gatteo Mare
Bellária
Torre del Lago Puccini
San Pieroa Sieve
San Máuro Mare
Riccioni
Fiorenzuola di Focara
Pisa
San Baronto
Firenze
Bottai
San Piero in Bagno
Pésaro
Fano
Marotta
Senigállia
Montescudáio
San Gimignano
Figline Valdarno
Vada
Volterra
Monteriggioni
Sirolo
Cécina
Marcelli di Numana
Marina di Bibbona
Marina di Cécina
Siena
Stacciola di San Costenzo
Porto Recanati
Forte di Bibbona
Casaciano di Murlo
San Vincenzo
Civitanova Marche
Populónia
Carbonifera
Borghetto
Passignano
Nisporto
Punta Alla
Casale Marittimo
Olmo
Porto Sant' Elpidio
Portoferraio
Cavo
Castel del Piano
Assisi
Morcone
Ortano
Castiglione della Pescaia
Lacona
Porto Azzorro
Monticello Amiata
Marina Palmense
Marina di Grosseto
San Lorenzo Nuovo
Martinsicuro
Orvieto
Alba Adriatica
Albinia
Bolsena
Schianceto
Giulianova Lido
Capálbio
Roseto degli Abruzzi
Marina di Montalto Castro
Marmore
Pineto
Marina di Pescia Romana
Tarquinia
Anguillara-Sabazia
l'Aquila
Marina di Casalbordino
Bracciano
Torino di Sangro Marina
Vasto
ROMA
Marina di Montenero
Villalago
Rodi Garganico
Lido del Sole
Capoiale
Mattina
Aglientu
Valledoria
Cannigione di Arzachena
Platamona Lido
San Teodoro
Alghero
Santa Lucia
Arbatax
Bari Sardo
Cagliari
Teulada
VENICE
NORTH WEST, ALPS & LAKES
FOR ENLARGED AREA SEE INSET
A4
A5
A8
A9
A21
A22
A23
A26
A6
A10
A12
A15
A1
A14
A24
A25
A16
A30
A3
A29
A19
A20
SS24
SS33
SS309
SS113
N197
D81
N193
N198
N196
SS125
SS131
SS199
SS597
SS131 dir
SS130
SS126
SS195
Town names
Gazetteer location

NETHERLANDS

○ Town names

● Gazetteer location

SPAIN/PORTUGAL

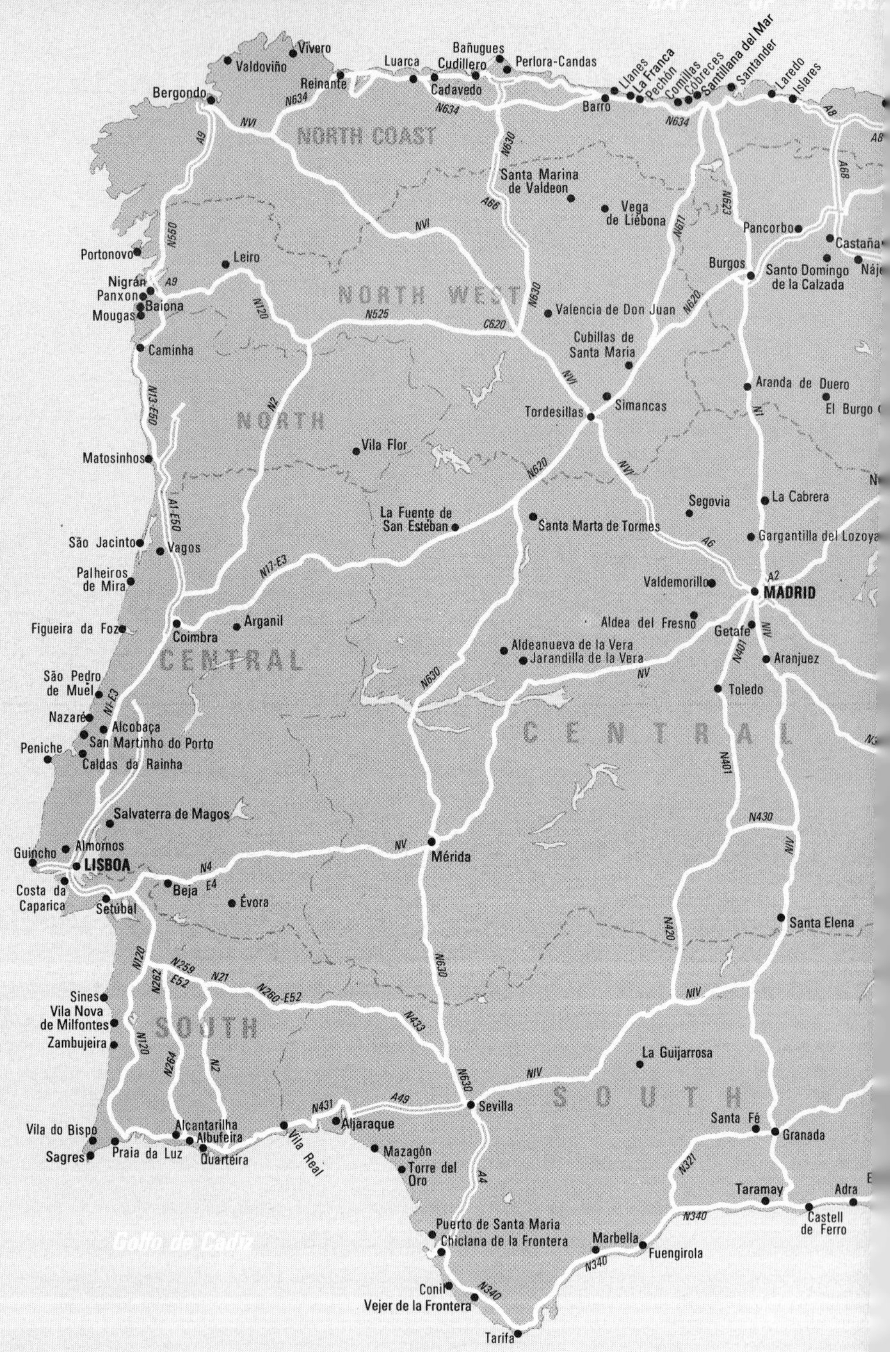

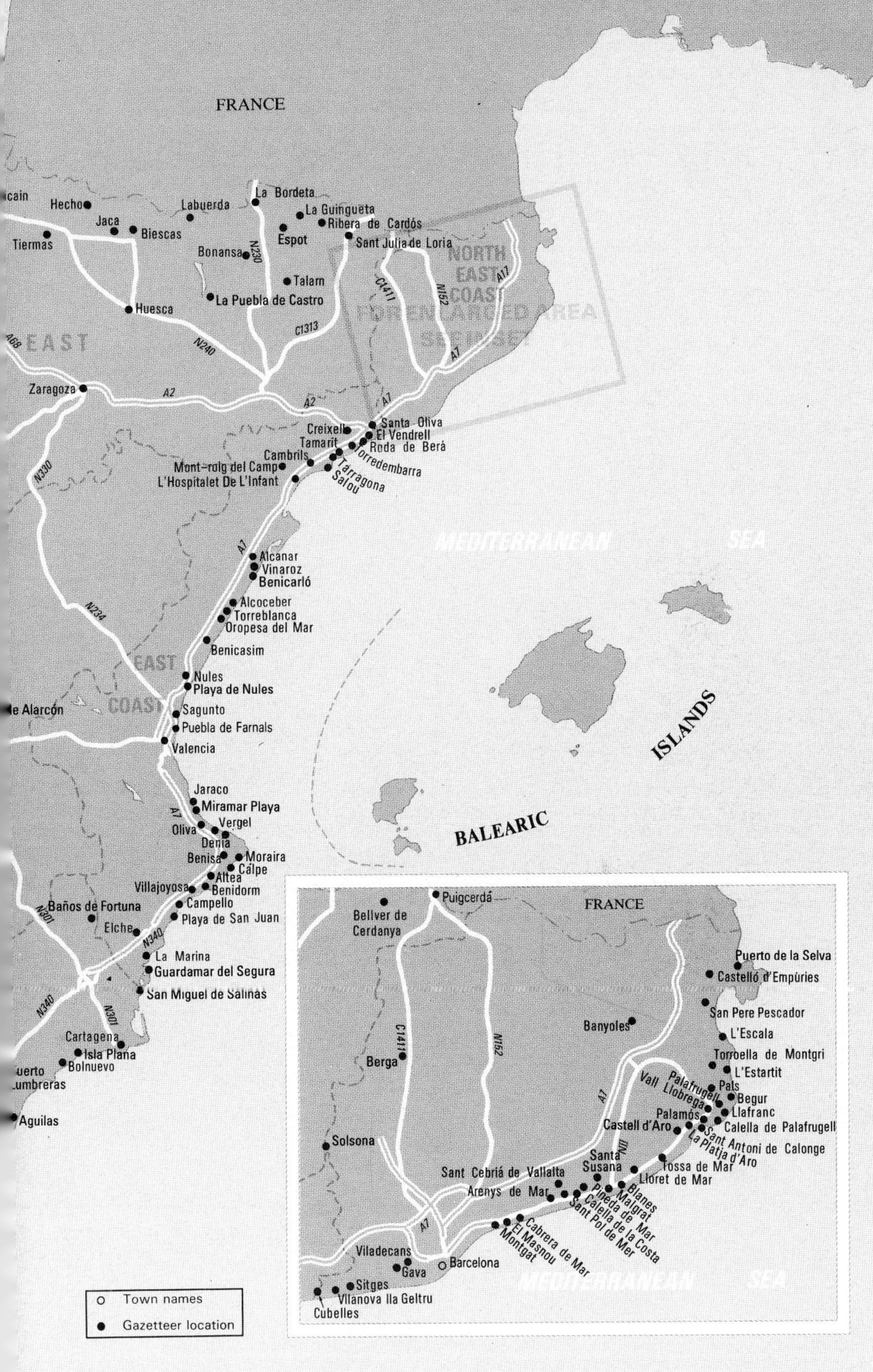
FRANCE
Hecho
Jaca
Biescas
Labuerda
La Bordeta
La Guingueta
Ribera de Cardós
Espot
Sant Julia de Loria
Tiermas
Bonansa
Talarn
La Puebla de Castro
Huesca
NORTH EAST COAST
EAST
Zaragoza
Creixell
Santa Oliva
El Vendrell
Tamarit
Roda de Berá
Cambrils
Torredembarra
Mont-roig del Camp
Tarragona
L'Hospitalet De L'Infant
Salou
MEDITERRANEAN SEA
Alcanar
Vinaroz
Benicarló
Alcoceber
Torreblanca
Oropesa del Mar
Benicasim
EAST COAST
Nules
Playa de Nules
Sagunto
Puebla de Farnals
Valencia
ISLANDS
BALEARIC
Jaraco
Miramar Playa
Vergel
Oliva
Denia
Benisa
Moraira
Calpe
Altea
Villajoyosa
Benidorm
Baños de Fortuna
Campello
Playa de San Juan
Elche
La Marina
Guardamar del Segura
San Miguel de Salinas
Cartagena
Isla Plana
Bolnuevo
Aguilas
Puigcerdá
Bellver de Cerdanya
FRANCE
Puerto de la Selva
Castelló d'Empúries
San Pere Pescador
Banyoles
L'Escala
Berga
Torroella de Montgri
L'Estartit
Palafrugell
Vall Llobrega
Pals
Begur
Llafranc
Palamós
Castell d'Aro
Calella de Palafrugell
Sant Antoni de Calonge
La Platja d'Aro
Solsona
Santa Susana
Tossa de Mar
Sant Cebriá de Vallalta
Lloret de Mar
Arenys de Mar
Blanes
Malgrat
Pineda de Mar
Calella de la Costa
Sant Pol de Mer
Cabrera de Mar
El Masnou
Montgat
Viladecans
Barcelona
Gava
Sitges
Vilanova Ila Geltru
Cubelles
MEDITERRANEAN SEA
Town names
Gazetteer location

SWITZERLAND

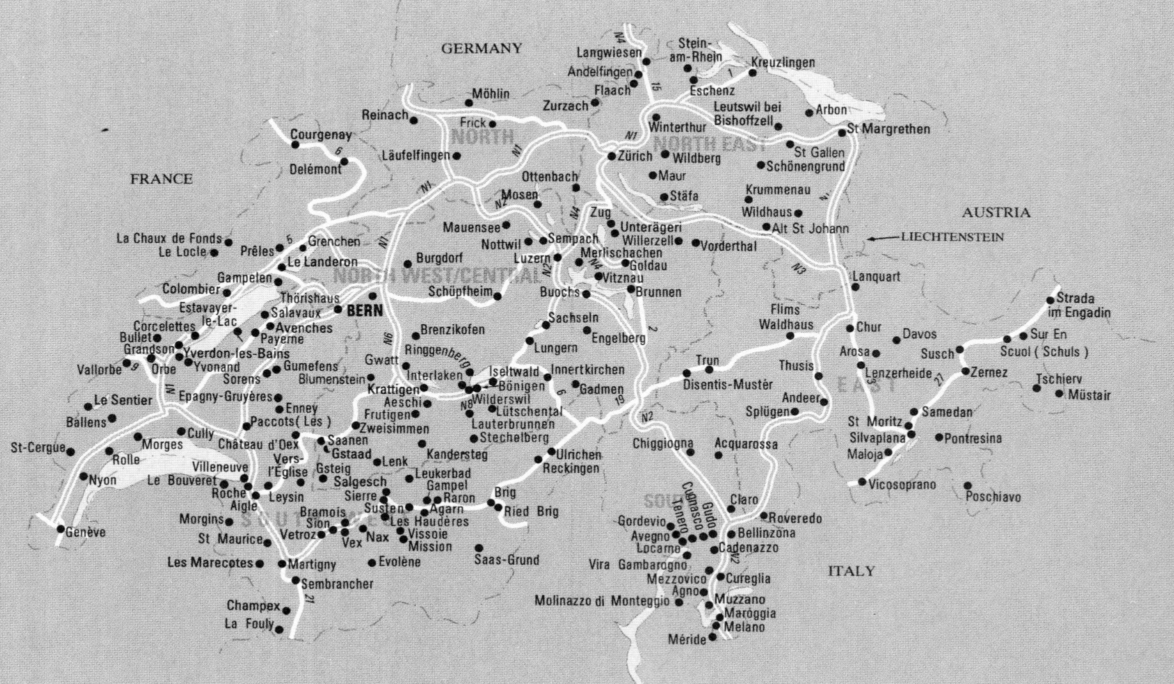

PLACE INDEX

Selection of useful numbers for help and advice on Motoring in Europe

Hints & Advice	
Austria	0836 401 866
Belgium	0836 401 867
Denmark	0836 401 868
France	0836 401 869
Germany	0836 401 870
Gibralter	0836 401 871
Greece	0836 401 872
Ireland (Republic of)	0836 401 873
Italy	0836 401 874
Luxembourg	0836 401 875
Netherlands	0836 401 876
Norway	0836 401 877
Portugal	0836 401 878
Spain	0836 401 879
Sweden	0836 401 880
Switzerland	0836 401 881
Yugoslavia	0836 401 882

European Weather Forecasts	
Germany & Benelux	0836 401 105
France	0836 401 106
Switzerland & Austria	0836 401 107
Iberia & Italy	0836 401 108

Other Useful Information	
French Motorway Tolls	0836 401 884
European Fuel Prices	0836 401 883

Port Information	
Hampshire/Dorset Ports	0836 401 891
Kent Ports	0836 401 890

Messages last from about 1 minute up to 7 minutes and are charged at 25p per minute cheap rate, 38p per minute at all other times. Callers pay only for the time they use. Prices are correct at time of going to press.

USING THE TELEPHONE ABROAD

LOCAL AND INTERNATIONAL CALLS

It is no more difficult to use the telephone abroad than it is at home. It only appears to be so because of unfamiliarity within the language and equipment. The following chart may be helpful with elementary principles when making local calls from public callboxes but try to get assistance in case you encounter language difficulties

International Direct Dial (IDD) calls can be made from many public callboxes abroad, thus avoiding the addition of surcharges imposed by most hotels. Types of callboxes from which IDD calls can be made are identified in the chart. You will need to dial the international code, international country code (for the UK it is 44), the telephone dialling code (omitting the initial 'O'), followed by the number. For example to call the AA, Basingstoke (0256) 20123 from Italy dial 00 44 256 20123. Use higher-denomination coins for IDD calls to ensure reasonably lengthy periods of conversation before coin expiry warning. The equivalent of £1 should allow a reasonable period of uninterrupted conversation.

Cardphones are in use in Austria, Belgium, France, Italy, Netherlands, Portugal and Switzerland; the cards to operate them are available from a post office or shop in the vicinity. ➔

USING THE TELEPHONE ABROAD

Country	Insert coin before or after lifting receiver	Dialling tone	Making local and national calls	Coins needed to operate callbox (local calls)
AUSTRIA	After (instructions in English in many callboxes)			3 coin slot *ASch* 1, 5, or 10 4 coin slot *ASch* 1, 5, 10 or 20
BELGIUM	After	Same as UK	Precede number with relevant area code when necessary	*BFr*5
FRANCE	After	Continuous tone	Always dial 8 digit number except for calls to and from Paris area: – from province add prefix '161' – to province add prefix '16'	*Fr*1 (2 × 50 centimes in some callboxes) or, in some areas, phonecard (available from railway stations, phoneshops and post offices)
ITALY	Before	Short & long tones	Precede number with relevant area code when necessary	*Lit* 200 *gettoni* (tokens available from bars, tobacconists and slot machines) or coins in payphones
LUXEMBOURG	After	Same as UK	There are no area codes	*Fr*5 (Lux. or Belg.)
NETHERLANDS	After (instructions in English in all callboxes)			25 cents × 2
PORTUGAL	After	Same as UK	Precede number with relevant area code when necessary	*ESc*5, 10 or 20
SPAIN	Before Do **not** press button to left of the dial or you may lose your money	Short and long tones	Precede number with relevant area code when necessary	*Ptas* 5, 25 or 100
SWITZERLAND	After	Continuous tone	Precede number with relevant area code when necessary	40 centimes

Higher value coins accepted	International callbox identification	What to dial for the UK	What to dial for the Irish Republic
*ASch*10 or 20	Payphones with 3/4 coin slots. Cardphones	00 44	00 353
BFr 5 (20 in some boxes)	Payphones identified with European flags. Cardphones	00 *44	00 *353
*Fr*1, 5 or 10	Metallic grey payphones. Cardphones	19 *44	19 *353
tokens or *Lit*100, 200 or 500	Yellow or red sign showing telephone dial and receiver. Cardphones	00 44	00 353
*Fr*5 or 20	Roadside callboxes	00 44	00 353
2½ guilders	All payphones. Cardphones	09 *44	09 *353
*ESc*50	Payphones with notice in English. Cardphones	00 44	00 353
*Ptas*100	Any payphone with the sign 'Telefono Internacional' or special 'Locutorios Telefonos'	07 *44	07 *353
*SFr*1 or 5	All phones including Cardphones	00 44	00 353

*Where asterisk is shown wait for second dialling tone

MEASUREMENT CONVERSIONS

CAPACITY

litres	*gallons or litres*	*gallons*
4.546	**1**	0.22
9.092	**2**	0.44
13.64	**3**	0.66
18.18	**4**	0.88
22.73	**5**	1.10
27.28	**6**	1.32
31.82	**7**	1.54
36.37	**8**	1.76
40.91	**9**	1.98
45.46	**10**	2.2
90.92	**20**	4.4
136.38	**30**	6.6
181.84	**40**	8.8
227.30	**50**	11.0
272.76	**60**	13.2
318.22	**70**	15.4
363.68	**80**	17.6
409.14	**90**	19.8
454.60	**100**	22.0
909.20	**200**	44.0

TEMPERATURE

Centigrade	*Fahrenheit*
−20	−4
−10	+14
− 5	+23
0	+32
+ 5	+41
+10	+50
+15	+59
+20	+68
+25	+77
+30	+86
+35	+95
+36.9*	+98.4*
+40	+104
+45	+113
+50	+122
+60	+140
+80	+176
+100**	+212**

* *Normal body temperature*
** *Boiling point (of water)*

PRESSURE

lb per sq in	*kg per sq cm (bar)*
18	1.266
20	1.406
22	1.547
24	1.687
26	1.828
28	1.969
30	2.109
32	2.250
34	2.390
36	2.531
38	2.672
40	2.812
42	2.953
44	3.093
46	3.234
48	3.375
50	3.515

WEIGHT

kg	*lb or kg*	*lb*
0.454	**1**	2.205
0.907	**2**	4.409
1.361	**3**	6.614
1.814	**4**	8.818
2.268	**5**	11.02
2.722	**6**	13.23
3.175	**7**	15.43
3.629	**8**	17.64
4.082	**9**	19.84
4.536	**10**	22.05
9.072	**20**	44.09
13.61	**30**	66.14
18.14	**40**	88.18
22.68	**50**	110.23
27.22	**60**	132.88
36.29	**80**	176.37
45.36	**100**	220.46

MEASUREMENT CONVERSIONS

FUEL: miles/kilometres/gallons/litres

miles per gallon	*miles per litre*	*km per litre*
10	2.2	3.5
15	3.3	5.3
20	4.4	7.1
25	5.5	8.8
30	6.6	10.6
35	7.7	12.4
40	8.8	14.2
45	9.9	15.9
50	11.0	17.7
55	12.1	19.5
60	13.2	21.3
65	14.3	23.0
70	15.4	24.8

FUEL: pence/gallons/litres

pence per gallon	*pence per litre*
160	35.2
165	36.3
170	37.4
175	38.5
180	39.6
190	41.8
200	44.0
210	46.2
220	48.4
230	50.6
240	52.8
250	55.0
260	57.2

LENGTH: miles/kilometres

km	*miles or km*	*miles*
1.609	**1**	0.621
3.219	**2**	1.243
4.828	**3**	1.864
6.437	**4**	2.485
8.047	**5**	3.107
9.656	**6**	3.728
11.27	**7**	4.350
12.87	**8**	4.971
14.48	**9**	5.592
16.09	**10**	6.214
32.19	**20**	12.43
48.28	**30**	18.64
64.37	**40**	24.85
80.47	**50**	31.07
96.56	**60**	37.28
112.65	**70**	43.50
128.75	**80**	49.71
144.84	**90**	55.92
160.93	**100**	62.14
402.34	**250**	155.34
804.67	**500**	310.68
1,609.34	**1,000**	621.37

SYMBOLS AND ABBREVIATIONS

For a more detailed explanation refer to About the Book (see contents page).

Pour plus amples informations venillez vous référer à About the Book (voir la table de matières).

Für weitere Angaben beziehen Sie sich auf About the Book (siehe inhaltsverzeichnis).

ENGLISH

A	adult (charge per night)
V	car (charge per night)
pp	per person (charge per night)
🚐	caravan or motor caravan (charge per night)
⛺	tent (charge per night)
✆	telephone
HEC	1 hectare (equals approx 2 acres)
ᴧᴧᴧ	grass
S	sand
⊟	stone
○	little shade
◑	partly shaded
●	mainly shaded
🚿	shower
🛒	shop
✕	cafe/restaurant
🍷	bar
🐕	no dogs
⊖	electric points for razors
🔌	electric points for caravans
[G]	Camping Gaz International
[R]	gas other than Camping Gaz
🏠	bungalows for hire
[H]	caravans for hire
⛺	tents for hire
🏊	swimming: L Lake, P Pool, R River, s sea
P (boxed)	parking by tents permitted
P	compulsory separate car park
☞	facilities not on site, but within 2km
+	first-aid facilities
♖	site belongs to *'Castle & Camping'* chain (France only)
CM	*camping municipal, parque municipal de campismo, or parque de la cämara municipal* (local authority site)
KC	*Kommunens Campingplads* (local authority site)
lau	laundry
pitch	pitch charge per night for car with tent or caravan (there is usually a charge per adult in addition to this)
➔	Entry continued overleaf

Entries in italics indicate that particulars have not been confirmed by management.

FRANÇAIS

A	Adulte (tarif pour une nuit)
V	Voiture (tarif pour une nuit)
pp	par personne (tarif pour une nuit)
🚐	Caravane ou camping car (tarif pour une nuit)
⛺	Tente (tarif pour une nuit)
✆	Téléphone
HEC	1 hectare (correspond à environ 2 acres (mesures impériales))
ᴧᴧᴧ	Gazon
S	Sable
⊟	Pierres
○	Peu ombragé
◑	En partie ombragé
●	Surtout ombragé
🚿	Douches
🛒	Magasin
✕	Café/Restaurant
🍷	Bar
🐕	Chiens non admis
⊖	Prises de courant pour rasoirs électriques
🔌	Branchements électriques pour caravanes
[G]	Camping Gaz International
[R]	Gaz autre que Camping Gaz
🏠	Bungalows à louer
[H]	Caravanes à louer
⛺	Tentes à louer
🏊	Natation: L Lac, P Piscine, R Rivère, s Mer
P (boxed)	Stationnement voiture près des tentes autorisé
P	Utilisation des parkings voitures obligatoire
☞	Aménitiès par sur le terrain, mais au plus, à 2km
+	Poste de premiers-secours
♖	Terrain fait partie de la chaîne *'Castle & Camping'* (en France seulement)
CM	Camping municipal
KC	*Kommunens Campingplads* (camping municipal)
lau	Blanchisserie
pitch	Tarif d'un emplacement pour une nuit pour voiture avec tente ou caravane (en général s'ajoute un tarif par adulte)
➔	Suite au verso

Une insertion imprimèe en italiques indique que la direction de l'établissement n'a pas confirmé les précisions.

DEUTSCH

A	Erwachsene (r) (Preis pro nacht)
V	Auto (Preis pro nacht)
pp	Pro person (Preis pro nacht)
🚐	Caravan bzw. Campingbus (Preis pro nacht)
⛺	Zeit (Preis pro nacht)
✆	Telefon
HEC	1 Hektar (ca 2 acres)
ᴧᴧᴧ	Grasboden
S	Sandgelände
⊟	Steiniges Gelände
○	Wenig Schatten
◑	Teilsschattig
●	Grösstenteilsschattig
🚿	Dusche
🛒	Laden
✕	Imbiss/Restaurant
🍷	Bar
🐕	Hundeverbot
⊖	Stromanschlüsse für Rasierapparate
🔌	Stromanschlüsse für Caravans
[G]	Camping Gaz International
[R]	Gas ausser Camping Gaz International
🏠	Mietbungalows
[H]	Mietcaravans
⛺	Mietzelte
🏊	Schwimmen: L See, P Schwimmbad, R Fluss, s Meer
P (boxed)	Abstellen des PKWs neben dem Zeit gestattet
P	Separates Abstellen des PKWs obligatorisch
☞	Einrichtungen nicht an Ort und Stelle aber nicht weiter als 2 Kilometer entfernt
+	Unfallstation
♖	Platz gehört der Schloss und
CM	Stadischer Campingplatz
KC	*Kommunens Campingplads* (städtischer Campingplatz)
lau	Wäscherei
pitch	Stellplatzpreis pro Nacht für Auto mit Zelt bzw. Caravan (normalerweise eine zusätzliche Berechnung pro Erwachsener)
➔	siehe umseitig

Eine kursiv gedruckte Eintragung zeigt an, dass die entsprechenden Angaben nicht von der Direktion bestätigt worden sind..

SYMBOLS AND ABBREVIATIONS

Per una spiegazione piú dettagliata, consultare la sezione 'About the Book' (vedi indice).

ITALIANO

Prezzo per notte:

- **A** Adulto
- **V** Vettura
- **pp** a persona
- Roulotte o camper
- Tenda

- Telefono
- HEC 1 ettaro (pari a 2 acri circa)
- Erba
- **S** Sabbia
- Pietra
- ○ Poca ombra
- ◑ Ombreggiato in parte
- ● Ombreggiato in gran parte
- Doccia
- Negozio
- Caffé ristornate
- Bar
- Proibito ai cani
- Prese elettriche rasoi
- Prese elettriche roulotte
- [G] Camping Gaz International
- [R] Altri tipi di gas che non siano il Camping Gaz
- Affittansi bungalows
- [H] Affittansi roulotte
- Affittansi tende
- Nuoto
  - L Lago
  - P Piscina
  - R Fiume
  - s Mare
- **P** É permesso parcheggiare vicino alle tende
- P É obbligatorio parcheggiare nel posteggio apposito
- ☞ Le attrezzature non sono nel campeggio, bensi in un raggio di 2km
- \+ Proto soccorso
- Il campeggio appartienne alla catena *'Castle & Camping'* (per la Francia solamente)
- CM *Camping municipal* (campeggio municipale)
- KC *Kommunens Campingplads* (Campeggio municipale)
- lau Lavanderia
- pitch Prezzo per notte di un posto macchina e tenda o roulotte (di solito ciascun adulto paga un extra oltre al posto macchina)
- ➔ La lista delle voci continua a tergo

Le voci in corsivo stanno a indicare che i particolari non sono stati confermati dalla Direzione.

Para una explicación más detallada, consúltese la sectión 'About Gazetteer' (véase el indice de materias).

ESPAÑOL

Precio por noche:

- **A** Adulto
- **V** Automóvil
- **pp** Por persona
- Rulota o coche-rulota
- Tienda

- Téléfono
- HEC 1 hectárea (igual a 2 acres aproximadamente)
- Hierba
- **S** Arena
- Piedra
- ○ Poca sombra
- ◑ Sombreado en parte
- ● Sombreado en su mayor parte
- Ducha
- Almacén
- Café/restaurante
- Bar
- Se prohiben los perros
- Tomas de corriente para máquinillas eléctricas
- Tomas de corriente para rulotas
- [G] Camping Gaz International
- [R] Otros tipos de gas que no sean el Gaz International
- Se alquilan bungalows
- [H] Se alquiln rulotas
- Se alquin tiendas
- Natación:
  - L Lago
  - P Piscina
  - R Rio
  - s Mar
- **P** Se permite estacionar el coche junto a las tiendas
- P Prohibido estacionarse fuera del aparcamiento
- ☞ Los servicios no están en el camping, sino en un radio de 2km
- \+ Puesto de socorro
- Este camping pertenece al grupo *'Castle & Camping'* (para Francia solamente)
- CM Camping municipal
- KC *Kommunens Campingplads* (camping municipal)
- lau Lavanderia
- pitch Precio por noche de un puesto para coche y tienda o rulota (cada adulto pagará un suplemento además del precio susodicho)
- ➔ La lista de simbolos continua a la vuelta

Los articulos en bastardilla indican que los detalles no han sido confirmados por la Dirección.